D1402652

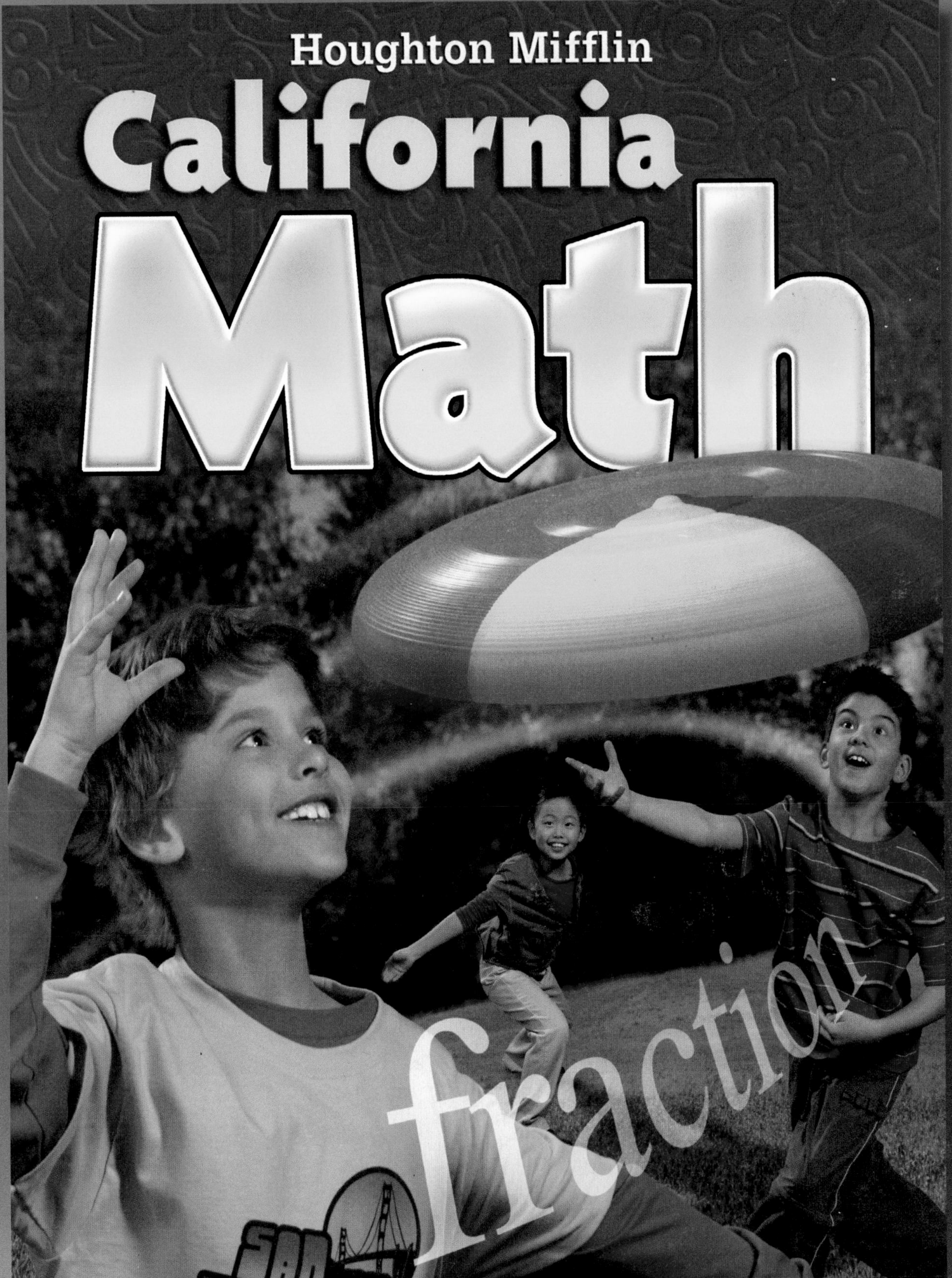

Houghton Mifflin

California Math

fraction

HOUGHTON MIFFLIN BOSTON

Printed in the U.S.A.

ISBN-13: 978-0-618-82740-4

ISBN-10: 0-618-82740-4

1 2 3 4 5 6 7 8 9 - DOW - 15 14 13 12 11 10 09 08 07

Houghton Mifflin

California Math

Authors & Consultants

Authors

Renee Hill
Mathematics Specialist
Riverside Unified School District
Riverside, CA

Matt Larson
Curriculum Specialist for Mathematics
Lincoln Public Schools
Lincoln, NE

Miriam A. Leiva
Bonnie E. Cone Distinguished Professor Emerita
Professor of Mathematics Emerita
University of North Carolina
Charlotte, NC

Jean M. Shaw
Professor Emerita of Curriculum and Instruction
University of Mississippi
Oxford, MS

Dr. Lee Stiff
Professor of Mathematics Education
North Carolina State University
Raleigh, NC

Dr. Bruce Vogeli
Clifford Brewster Upton Professor of Mathematics
Teachers College, Columbia University
New York, NY

Consultants

Mental Math Strategies

Greg Tang
Author and Mathematics Consultant
Belmont, MA

English Learners

Dr. Russell M. Gersten
Executive Director, Institutional Research Group & Professor Emeritus
College of Education, University of Oregon
Long Beach, CA

Lisette Estrella-Henderson
Director of District and School Support
Solano County Office of Education
Fairfield, CA

Language and Vocabulary

Dr. Shane Templeton
Foundation Professor, Department of Educational Specialties
University of Nevada at Reno
Reno, NV

Strategic Consultant

Dr. Liping Ma
Senior Scholar
Carnegie Foundation for the Advancement of Technology
Palo Alto, CA

Special Projects

Catherine Valentino
Author-in-Residence
Houghton Mifflin
West Kingston, RI

Content Reviewers

Dr. W. Stephen Wilson
(Grades K–2)
Professor of Mathematics
Johns Hopkins University
Baltimore, MD

Dr. Kurt Kreith
(Grades 3–4)
Emeritus Professor of Mathematics
University of California at Davis
Davis, CA

Dr. Solomon Friedberg
(Grade 5)
Professor of Mathematics
Boston College
Chestnut Hill, MA

Dr. Bert Fristedt
(Grade 6)
Professor of Mathematics
University of Minnesota
Minneapolis, MN

California Reviewers

Grade K

Cynthia Dominguez
Highlands Elementary School
Saugus, CA

Dana Hight
Royal Oaks Elementary School
Visalia, CA

Patricia Mahoney
John Adams Elementary School
Madera, CA

Teresa Rogers
Skyline North Elementary School
Barstow, CA

Schelly Solko
Roy W. Loudon Elementary School
Bakersfield, CA

Julie Towne
Jurupa Vista Elementary School
Fontana, CA

Grade 1

Kirsten Marsh
Edgemont Elementary School
Moreno Valley, CA

Jill McCarthy
Edgemont Elementary School
Moreno Valley, CA

Brandee Ramirez
Myford Elementary School
Tustin, CA

Rebecca Solares
Cerritos Elementary School
Glendale, CA

Leanne Thomas
Scott Lane Elementary School
Santa Clara, CA

Sheila Vann
Folsom Hills Elementary School
Folsom, CA

Grade 2

Deborah Nelson
North Park Elementary School
Valencia, CA

Kathryn Smith
Quail Run Elementary School
San Ramon, CA

Angelica Yates
Allen at Steinbeck Elementary School
San José, CA

Grade 3

Pamela Aurangzeb
Grapeland Elementary School
Etiwanda, CA

Veronica Fowler
Challenger School of Sports & Fitness
Victorville, CA

Nancy Hayes
Toro Park School
Salinas, CA

Megan Heavens
North Park Elementary School
Valencia, CA

Caryl Lyons
Manuel L. Real Elementary School
Perris, CA

Stacey McKay
Glenn E. Murdock Elementary School
La Mesa, CA

Peggy Morrill
Grapeland Elementary School
Etiwanda, CA

Kristine Salomonson
Freedom Elementary School
Clovis, CA

Susan Steubing
Folsom Hills Elementary School
Folsom, CA

The reviewers work with the authors, consultants, and publisher to be sure that problems are correct, instructions work, and this book is the best it can be.

California Reviewers

Grade 4

Cheryl Robertson
McPherson Magnet School
Orange, CA

JoAnna Trafecanty
North Park Elementary School
Valencia, CA

Grade 5

Karen Clarke
Manuel L. Real Elementary School
Perris, CA

Bonita DeAmicis
Highlands Elementary School
Saugus, CA

Gretchen Oberg
Ralph Dailard Elementary School
San Diego, CA

Grade 6

Judy Denenny
McPherson Magnet School
Orange, CA

Terri Parker
Leo B. Hart Elementary School
Bakersfield, CA

George Ratcliff
Joseph Casillas Elementary School
Chula Vista, CA

Patricia Wenzel
Cloverly Elementary School
Temple City, CA

Across Grade

Gina Chavez
California State University, Los Angeles
Los Angeles, CA

Catherine De Leon
Washington Elementary School
Madera, CA

Cindy Ellis
Madera Unified School District
Madera, CA

Jenny Maguire
Orinda Union School District
Orinda, CA

Ernest Minelli
Selby Lane School
Redwood City, CA

Barbara Page
Modesto City Schools
Modesto, CA

Ian Tablit
Delano Union Elementary School District
Delano, CA

Jeannie Tavolazzi
Grapeland Elementary School
Etiwanda, CA

Dina Tews
John J. Pershing Elementary School
Madera, CA

These reviewers are math teachers, principals, and other people who are really committed to helping kids learn math.

California Mathematics

Content Standards

What are Key Standards?

- The California math standards are goals for what you will learn in math this year.
- The standards have five strands: Number Sense; Algebra and Functions; Measurement and Geometry; Statistics, Data Analysis, and Probability; Mathematical Reasoning.
- The symbol ⬬ means a standard is a KEY to success this year.
- Knowing and understanding the content standards means you can do well on tests.

How will this book help you succeed?

It's as easy as one, two, three.

1. Look for **Key Standards** in this book.
2. Do your best work. Ask questions.
3. Use the Key Standards Handbook on KSH1–KSH34.

Doing well feels terrific!

Number Sense

	Standards You Will Learn	Some Places to Look
1.0	Students understand the place value of whole numbers and decimals to two decimal places and how whole numbers and decimals relate to simple fractions. Students use the concepts of negative numbers:	Lessons 1.1, 1.2, 1.3, 1.4, 1.5, 2.1, 2.2, 2.3, 2.4, 3.3, 16.1, 16.2, 16.3, 17.1, 17.2, 19.1, 19.2, 19.3, 19.4, 19.5 Challenge pp. 31, 77
KEY 1.1	Read and write whole numbers in the millions.	Lessons 1.1, 1.3, 1.4, 1.5, 2.2, 2.4, 8.4, 11.4, 20.2, 20.3 Key Standards Handbook, pp. KSH 2–3; Chapter 1 Vocabulary; Chapter 1 Math Works!; Chapter 26 Key Standards Review
KEY 1.2	Order and compare whole numbers and decimals to two decimal places.	Lessons 2.1, 2.2, 2.5, 12.3, 19.4, 19.5, 22.5 Key Standards Handbook, pp. KSH4–KSH5; Units 1, 2, 5, 9 Get Ready Game; Chapters 3, 4, 20, 26 Key Standards Review
KEY 1.3	Round whole numbers through the millions to the nearest ten, hundred, thousand, ten thousand, or hundred thousand.	Lessons 2.3, 2.4, 2.5, 3.3, 4.2, 10.2 Key Standards Handbook, p. KSH6; Chapters 3, 5 Key Standards Review
KEY 1.4	Decide when a rounded solution is called for and explain why such a solution may be appropriate.	Lessons 2.3, 3.3, 4.2, 10.2, 15.6, 20.3, 20.4 Key Standards Handbook, p. KSH7 Chapters 9, 11 Key Standards Review
1.5	Explain different interpretations of fractions, for example, parts of a whole, parts of a set, and division of whole numbers by whole numbers; explain equivalence of fractions (see Standard 4.0).	Lessons 17.1, 17.2, 17.6, 18.2, 18.4, 18.5, 28.5 Unit 8 Get Ready Game; Challenge p. 403
1.6	Write tenths and hundredths in decimal and fraction notations and know the fraction and decimal equivalents for halves and fourths (e.g., $\frac{1}{2} = 0.5$ or 0.50; $\frac{7}{4} = 1\frac{3}{4} = 1.75$).	Lessons 19.1, 19.2, 19.3, 19.5, 19.6, 25.6
1.7	Write the fraction represented by a drawing of parts of a figure; represent a given fraction by using drawings; and relate a fraction to a simple decimal on a number line.	Lessons 17.1, 17.2, 17.3, 18.3, 19.1, 19.2, 19.3
KEY 1.8	Use concepts of negative numbers (e.g., on a number line, in counting, in temperature, in "owing").	Lessons 16.1, 16.2, 16.3, 16.4, 22.1, 22.2, 22.4, 24.5 Key Standards Handbook, p. KSH8; Chapters 17, 20 Key Standards Review
KEY 1.9	Identify on a number line the relative position of positive fractions, positive mixed numbers, and positive decimals to two decimal places.	Lessons 17.3,17.4, 18.1, 18.2, 18.3, 18.4, 18.5, 19.3, 19.4, 19.5 Key Standards Handbook, p. KSH9-KSH10; Challenge p. 355; Chapters 19, 21, 24, 28 Key Standards Review

Number Sense (continued)

	Standards You Will Learn	Some Places to Look
2.0	Students extend their use and understanding of whole numbers to the addition and subtraction of simple decimals:	Lessons 20.1, 20.3, 20.4, 20.5 Challenge p. 445
2.1	Estimate and compute the sum or difference of whole numbers and positive decimals to two places.	Lessons 20.1, 20.3, 20.4, 20.5
2.2	Round two-place decimals to one decimal or the nearest whole number and judge the reasonableness of the rounded answer.	Lessons 20.2, 20.3, 20.4, 20.5
KEY **3.0**	Students solve problems involving addition, subtraction, multiplication, and division of whole numbers and understand the relationships among the operations:	Lessons 3.1, 3.2, 3.3, 3.4, 4.1, 4.4, 4.5, 5.4, 6.1, 6.2, 6.3, 6.6, 7.1, 7.2, 9.4, 10.1, 10.2, 10.3, 10.4, 10.5, 11.1, 11.3, 11.4, 11.5, 12.1, 12.2, 12.3, 12.4, 12.5, 13.1, 13.2, 13.5, 15.6, 16.4, 20.5 Key Standards Handbook pp. KSH 11–12; Units 3, 6 Get Ready Game; Chapter 6 Practice Game Chapters 6, 7, 8, 12, 13 Key Standards Review; Challenge p. 219, 241, 265
KEY **3.1**	Demonstrate an understanding of, and the ability to use, standard algorithms for the addition and subtraction of multidigit numbers.	Lessons 3.2, 3.4, 4.1, 4.3, 4.4, 4.5, 6.6, 9.4, 14.5, 15.6 Key Standards Handbook, pp. KSH13–KSH14; Chapters 5, 8 Key Standards Review; Unit 2 Get Ready Game
KEY **3.2**	Demonstrate an understanding of, and the ability to use, standard algorithms for multiplying a multidigit number by a two-digit number and for dividing a multidigit number by a one-digit number; use relationships between them to simplify computations and to check results.	Lessons 6.5, 11.3, 11.4, 11.5, 12.2, 12.3, 13.3, 13.4, 15.6 Key Standards Handbook, pp. KSH15–KSH16; Chapters 12, 13, 15, 16 Key Standards Review
KEY **3.3**	Solve problems involving multiplication of multidigit numbers by two-digit numbers.	Lessons 11.1, 11.2, 11.3, 11.4, 11.5 Key Standards Handbook, pp. KSH17-KSH18; Chapter 12 Key Standards Review
KEY **3.4**	Solve problems involving division of multidigit numbers by one-digit numbers.	Lessons 12.1, 12.2, 12.3, 12.4, 12.5, 13.1, 13.2, 13.5, 15.6, 16.4 Key Standards Handbook; pp. KSH19–KSH20 Chapters 14, 18, 21 Key Standards Review
4.0	Students know how to factor small whole numbers:	Lessons 14.1, 14.2, 14.3, 14.4, 14.5
4.1	Understand that many whole numbers break down in different ways (e.g., $12 = 4 \times 3 = 2 \times 6 = 2 \times 2 \times 3$).	Lessons 14.1, 14.2, 14.3, 14.4, 14.5
KEY **4.2**	Know that numbers such as 2, 3, 5, 7, and 11 do not have any factors except 1 and themselves and that such numbers are called prime numbers.	Lessons 14.1, 14.3, 14.4, 14.5, 20.5 Key Standards Handbook, pp. KSH21–KSH22; Challenge p. 311; Chapter 16 Key Standards Review

Algebra and Functions

	Standards You Will Learn	Some Places to Look
1.0	Students use and interpret variables, mathematical symbols, and properties to write and simplify expressions and sentences:	Lessons 3.2, 5.1, 5.2, 5.3, 6.3, 7.2, 7.3, 7.5, 8.1, 8.2, 8.3, 9.1, 9.2, 9.3, 10.4, 11.2, 11.3, 13.4, 14.2, 16.2 Units 4, 5, 6 Get Ready Game; Practice Game p. 179
1.1	Use letters, boxes, or other symbols to stand for any number in simple expressions or equations (e.g., demonstrate an understanding and the use of the concept of a variable).	Lessons 8.1, 8.2, 8.3, 8.4, 8.5, 9.1, 9.2, 9.3, 9.4, 10.5, 13.4, 14.2, 19.5, 27.2, 27.3 Unit 4 Get Ready Game; Challenge p. 195
KEY **1.2**	Interpret and evaluate mathematical expressions that now use parentheses.	Lessons 3.2, 5.1, 5.2, 5.3, 5.4, 5.5, 6.6, 7.1, 7.2, 7.3, 7.4, 7.5, 8.1, 8.4, 13.4, 27.2 Key Standards Handbook p. KSH23; Challenge pp. 101, 147; Chapter 6 Key Standards Review
KEY **1.3**	Use parentheses to indicate which operation to perform first when writing expressions containing more than two terms and different operations.	Lessons 5.1, 5.2, 5.3, 5.4, 5.5, 6.6, 7.1, 7.2, 7.3, 7.5 Key Standards Handbook, p. KSH24; Challenge pp. 97, 147; Chapters 7, 8 Key Standards Review
1.4	Use and interpret formulas (e.g., area = length × width or $A = lw$) to answer questions about quantities and their relationships.	Lessons 27.2, 27.3, 27.4, 27.5, 28.4 Challenge p. 631
KEY **1.5**	Understand that an equation such as $y = 3x + 5$ is a prescription for determining a second number when a first number is given.	Lessons 9.2, 9.3, 10.5, 11.4, 13.3, 15.2, 15.4, 21.3, 21.4 Key Standards Handbook, pp. KSH25–KSH26; Challenge pp. 195, 475; Chapters 10, 15 Key Standards Review
KEY **2.0**	Students know how to manipulate equations:	Lessons 5.4, 7.4, 8.3, 8.4, 8.5, 9.4, 10.5, 11.4, 13.2, 17.5, 19.5, 20.4 Key Standards Handbook, p. KSH27; Chapters 9, 10 Key Standards Review
KEY **2.1**	Know and understand that equals added to equals are equal.	Lessons 5.4, 8.3, 8.5, 9.4, 10.5, 11.4, 19.5, 20.4 Key Standards Handbook p. KSH28; Chapter 10 Key Standards Review
KEY **2.2**	Know and understand that equals multiplied by equals are equal.	Lessons 7.4, 8.4, 8.5, 10.5, 11.4, 13.2 Key Standards Handbook, p. KSH29; Chapter 9 Key Standards Review

Measurement and Geometry

Standards You Will Learn		Some Places to Look
1.0	Students understand perimeter and area:	Lessons 27.1, 27.2, 27.3, 27.4, 27.5, 28.3, 28.5 Chapter 27 Game; Unit 7 Get Ready Game
1.1	Measure the area of rectangular shapes by using appropriate units, such as square centimeter (cm^2), square meter (m^2), square kilometer (km^2), square inch ($in.^2$), square yard ($yd.^2$), or square mile ($mi.^2$).	Lessons 27.1, 27.3, 27.4, 28.3, 28.5
1.2	Recognize that rectangles that have the same area can have different perimeters.	Lessons 27.1, 27.3, 27.5, Chapter 26 Math Works!
1.3	Understand that rectangles that have the same perimeter can have different areas.	Lessons 27.1, 27.3, 27.5, Chapter 26 Math Works!
1.4	Understand and use formulas to solve problems involving perimeters and areas of rectangles and squares. Use those formulas to find the areas of more complex figures by dividing the figures into basic shapes.	Lessons 27.2, 27.3, 27.4, 27.5, 28.3, 28.5 Challenge p. 607, Chapter 27 Game
KEY **2.0**	Students use two-dimensional coordinate grids to represent points and graph lines and simple figures:	Lessons 21.1, 21.2, 21.3, 21.4, 22.1, 22.2, 22.4, 22.5, 25.3, 26.5 Key Standards Handbook, pp. KSH30–KSH31; Unit 10 Get Ready Game; Chapters 21, 22, 27 Key Standards Review
KEY **2.1**	Draw the points corresponding to linear relationships on graph paper (e.g., draw 10 points on the graph of the equation $y = 3x$ and connect them by using a straight line).	Lessons 21.3, 21.4, 21.5, 22.5 Key Standards Handbook, p. KSH32; Chapter 27 Key Standards Review
KEY **2.2**	Understand that the length of a horizontal line segment equals the difference of the x-coordinates.	Lessons 21.1, 21.4, 22.3, 22.4, 24.5, 25.3 Key Standards Handbook, p. KSH33
KEY **2.3**	Understand that the length of a vertical line segment equals the difference of the y-coordinates.	Lessons 21.1, 21.4, 22.3, 22.4, 25.3 Key Standards Handbook, p. KSH34
3.0	Students demonstrate an understanding of plane and solid geometric objects and use this knowledge to show relationships and solve problems:	Lessons 25.1, 25.2, 25.3, 25.4, 25.5, 25.6, 26.1, 26.2, 26.3, 26.4, 26.5, 27.5, 28.1, 28.2, 28.3, 28.4, 28.5 Chapter 25 Game; Challenge p. 625
3.1	Identify lines that are parallel and perpendicular.	Lessons 25.1, 25.2, 25.3
3.2	Identify the radius and diameter of a circle.	Lessons 25.5, 25.6 Chapter 25 Game

Measurement and Geometry (continued)

	Standards You Will Learn	Some Places to Look
3.3	Identify congruent figures.	Lessons 26.4, 26.5, 27.4, 28.3 Chapter 26 Vocabulary; Chapter 26 Math Works!
3.4	Identify figures that have bilateral and rotational symmetry.	Lessons 26.1, 26.2, 26.3 Chapter 26 Vocabulary; Challenge p. 587
3.5	Know the definitions of a right angle, an acute angle, and an obtuse angle. Understand that 90°, 180°, 270°, and 360° are associated, respectively, with $\frac{1}{4}$, $\frac{1}{2}$, $\frac{3}{4}$, and full turns.	Lessons 25.2, 25.5, 26.3 Unit 12 Get Ready Game; Challenge p. 563
3.6	Visualize, describe, and make models of geometric solids (e.g., prisms, pyramids) in terms of the number and shape of faces, edges, and vertices; interpret two-dimensional representations of three-dimensional objects; and draw patterns (of faces) for a solid that, when cut and folded, will make a model of the solid.	Lessons 28.1, 28.2, 28.3, 28.4, 28.5 Challenge p. 625
3.7	Know the definitions of different triangles (e.g., equilateral, isosceles, scalene) and identify their attributes.	Lessons 25.4, 25.6, 26.3, 27.2 Chapter 25 Vocabulary; Chapter 25 Wrap Up
3.8	Know the definition of different quadrilaterals (e.g., rhombus, square, rectangle, parallelogram, trapezoid).	Lessons 25.3, 25.6, 26.3, 26.4, 27.3, 27.4, 27.5 Chapter 25 Vocabulary, Chapter 25 Wrap Up

Statistics, Data Analysis, and Probability

	Standards You Will Learn	Some Places to Look
1.0	Students organize, represent, and interpret numerical and categorical data and clearly communicate their findings:	Lessons 23.1, 23.2, 23.3, 23.4, 23.5, 24.3
1.1	Formulate survey questions; systematically collect and represent data on a number line; and coordinate graphs, tables, and charts.	Lessons 23.1, 23.2, 23.3, 23.5, 24.3
1.2	Identify the mode(s) for sets of categorical data and the mode(s), median, and any apparent outliers for numerical data sets.	Lessons 23.2, 23.5, 24.2 Chapter 23 Vocabulary; Chapter 23 Practice Game
1.3	Interpret one- and two-variable data graphs to answer questions about a situation.	Lessons 21.5, 23.2, 23.3, 23.4, 23.5, 24.3, 24.5

Statistics, Data Analysis, and Probability (continued)

	Standards You Will Learn	Some Places to Look
2.0	Students make predictions for simple probability situations:	Lessons 24.1, 24.2, 24.3, 24.4 Chapter 24 Wrap Up
2.1	Represent all possible outcomes for a simple probability situation in an organized way (e.g., tables, grids, tree diagrams).	Lessons 2.5, 24.3, 24.4 Chapter 24 Vocabulary; Challenge p. 543; Chapter 24 Wrap Up
2.2	Express outcomes of experimental probability situations verbally and numerically (e.g., 3 out of 4; $\frac{3}{4}$).	Lessons 24.1, 24.2, 24.3, 24.4, 24.5 Unit 11 Get Ready Game; Chapter 24 Wrap Up

Mathematical Reasoning

	Standards You Will Learn	Some Places to Look
1.0	Students make decisions about how to approach problems:	Lessons 1.5, 3.5, 4.5, 5.5, 7.5, 8.5, 9.4, 10.5, 11.5, 12.5, 14.3, 14.5, 15.6, 16.4, 17.6, 18.5, 19.5, 20.5, 22.5, 23.1, 23.5, 24.5, 27.5, 28.5
1.1	Analyze problems by identifying relationships, distinguishing relevant from irrelevant information, sequencing and prioritizing information, and observing patterns.	Lessons 2.5, 4.5, 5.2, 5.5, 7.1, 7.2, 7.3, 7.5, 8.2, 8.5, 9.1, 9.2, 9.3, 9.4, 10.5, 11.5, 12.5, 13.5, 14.5, 15.5, 16.1, 16.4, 17.6, 18.5, 20.5, 21.5, 22.5, 23.5, 24.5, 26.5, 27.5, 28.5
1.2	Determine when and how to break a problem into simpler parts.	Lessons 5.5, 7.2, 7.5, 8.5, 10.3, 10.4, 10.5, 12.4, 15.6, 26.5, 27.5, 28.5
2.0	Students use strategies, skills, and concepts in finding solutions:	Lessons 1.5, 2.5, 3.5, 4.5, 5.5, 6.6, 7.5, 8.5, 9.2, 9.4, 10.2, 10.5, 11.5, 12.5, 13.5, 14.5, 16.4, 17.6, 18.5, 19.5, 20.5, 21.5, 22.5, 23.2, 23.4, 24.5, 26.5, 27.5, 28.5
2.1	Use estimation to verify the reasonableness of calculated results.	Lessons 4.3, 4.4, 4.5, 6.6, 10.3, 10.4, 20.4, 27.5
2.2	Apply strategies and results from simpler problems to more complex problems.	Lessons 10.3, 14.1, 17.6, 20.4
2.3	Use a variety of methods, such as words, numbers, symbols, charts, graphs, tables, diagrams, and models, to explain mathematical reasoning.	Every lesson in every chapter, for example lessons 2.1, 2.5, 4.5, 8.5, 11.5, 13.1, 15.6, 16.1, 21.5, 23.4, 23.5, 26.1, 26.5, 27.1, 27.5
2.4	Express the solution clearly and logically by using the appropriate mathematical notation and terms and clear language; support solutions with evidence in both verbal and symbolic work.	Every lesson in every chapter, for example lessons 2.5, 5.5, 8.5, 9.4, 10.5, 11.5, 12.5, 13.4, 13.5, 15.6, 16.4, 17.6, 20.5, 21.5, 23.5, 26.5, 27.5

Mathematical Reasoning (continued)

Standards You Will Learn		Some Places to Look
2.5	Indicate the relative advantages of exact and approximate solutions to problems and give answers to a specified degree of accuracy.	Lessons 3.3, 4.2, 10.2, 15.6, 20.2, 20.3, 20.4
2.6	Make precise calculations and check the validity of the results from the context of the problem.	Lessons 10.3, 11.4, 12.2, 12.3, 13.2, 13.3, 13.5, 17.6, 20.5, 27.4, 27.5
3.0	Students move beyond a particular problem by generalizing to other situations:	Lessons 2.5, 4.5, 5.5, 7.5, 8.1, 8.4, 8.5, 9.2, 10.1, 10.2, 11.4, 11.5, 12.2, 12.4, 12.5, 13.2, 13.5, 14.1, 14.2, 14.5, 15.6, 17.6, 18.1, 20.1, 20.5, 21.5, 23.2, 23.3 23.4, 26.5, 27.4, 27.5, 28.5
3.1	Evaluate the reasonableness of the solution in the context of the original situation.	Lessons 2.5, 4.5, 5.5, 7.5, 8.5, 9.2, 10.2, 10.3, 11.4, 11.5, 12.5, 13.2, 13.5, 15.6, 17.6, 20.5, 21.5, 23.5, 27.5, 28.5
3.2	Note the method of deriving the solution and demonstrate a conceptual understanding of the derivation by solving similar problems.	Lessons 2.5, 4.5, 5.5, 7.5, 8.5, 10.2, 11.4, 11.5, 13.5, 14.2, 15.6, 17.6, 18.4, 20.5, 23.2, 23.5, 26.5, 27.5, 28.5
3.3	Develop generalizations of the results obtained and apply them in other circumstances.	Lessons 2.5, 4.5, 5.5, 7.5, 8.4, 9.2, 10.1, 10.2, 11.1, 11.4, 11.5, 12.5, 13.2, 13.5, 14.2, 14.5, 16.3, 20.5, 21.5, 23.2, 23.4, 23.5, 26.5, 28.5

Key Standards Handbook

Understanding the key standards will help me meet my goals in math.

These are my goals in math this year.

I use the correct operations when solving a problem.

I share mathematical ideas with others.

I know that different strands of math are related.

I can think logically about a problem and analyze ideas.

I always find math in everyday life.

Math is important to me and everyone around me!

NS 1.1 How do you read and write whole numbers?

Read More
See Unit 1, Chapter 1, Lessons 1–4, pages 6–17 on place value through millions.

Connect It

Numbers are read from left to right, or from greatest place value to least place value. Each group of digits that is separated by a comma represents a **period**. The place-value chart below shows the periods *millions*, *thousands*, and *ones*. You can write numbers in different ways, such as: short word form and word form.

Millions		Thousands				Ones		
millions		hundred thousands	ten thousands	thousands		hundreds	tens	ones
5	,	3	1	9	,	6	0	4

Short word form: 5 million, 319 thousand, 604.

Word form: five million, three hundred nineteen thousand, six hundred four

USE YOUR SKILLS

Write each number in short word form and word form.

1. 7,208,033
2. 690,751
3. 4,024,910
4. 302,509
5. **Apply** What form of a number is easier to read—the short word form or the word form?

KEY NS 1.1 Read and write whole numbers in the millions.

NS 1.1 What other ways can you write whole numbers?

Read More
See Unit 1, Chapter 1, Lessons 1–4, pages 6-17 on place value through millions

Connect It

You can write a number such as 9,625,403 in short word form or word form. You can also write it two other ways: standard form and **expanded notation**. Expanded notation shows the value of each digit.

Standard form: 9,625,403

Expanded notation: 9,000,000 + 600,000 + 20,000 + 5,000 + 400 + 3

USE YOUR SKILLS

Write each number in standard form and expanded notation.

1. one million, seven hundred fifty thousand, eight hundred nine
2. five hundred thousand, two hundred sixty-eight

Write each number in standard and word form.

3. 10,000 + 3,000 + 400 + 90
4. 6,000,000 + 50,000 + 6,000 + 700 + 1
5. **Analyze** When adding two numbers, which form of the numbers is easiest to use?

KEY NS 1.1 Read and write whole numbers in the millions.

NS 1.2 How do you compare and order whole numbers?

Read More
See Unit 1, Chapter 2, Lessons 1–2, pages 26–30, on comparing and ordering whole numbers.

Connect It

Use a Number Line

You can use a number line to **compare** numbers and **order** them from greatest to least.

Example Suppose you wanted to order these numbers from greatest to least.

26,345 26,184 26,010 26,357 26,969

Decide where each number belongs on the number line.

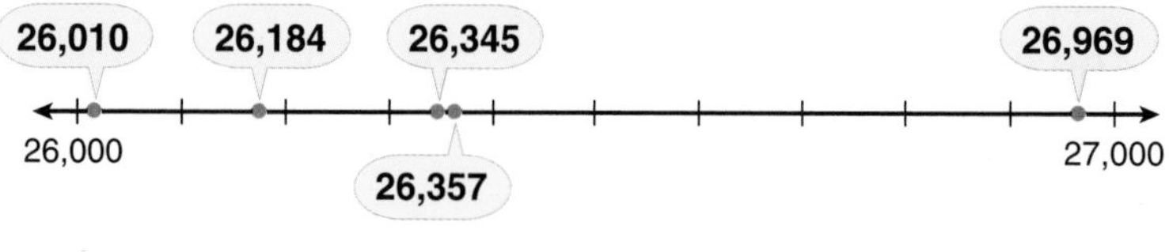

26,010 < 26,184 < 26,345 < 26,357 < 26,969

So the numbers in order from greatest to least are:

26,969 26,357 26,345 26,184 26,010

Hint

is less than (<)
is greater than (>)

Use Place Value

You can also use place value to compare and order numbers.

Example Suppose you wanted to order these numbers from least to greatest.

305,748,075 398,195,673 348,249,405

1. Line up the digits. Find the greatest place where the digits are different.
2. Compare the digits.

3 0 5 , 7 4 8 , 0 7 5
3 9 8 , 1 9 5 , 6 7 3
3 4 8 , 2 4 9 , 4 0 5

Same **Different**

The numbers in order from least to greatest are:

305,748,075 348,249,405 398,195,673

USE YOUR SKILLS

1. Order from least to greatest.
   213,808 214,981 214,962
   7,936,404 692,976 7,372,958
2. Order from greatest to least.
   355,598 354,902 355,801
   1,952,743 192,565 1,021,724
3. **Synthesize** Which method would you use to compare and order the numbers? Why? 259,825 87,934 258,296 399,872 6,567

KEY NS 1.2 Order and compare whole numbers and decimals to two decimal places.

NS 1.2 How do you compare and order decimals?

> **Read More**
> See Unit 9, Chapter 19, Lessons 4, pages 426–427, on ordering and comparing decimals to two decimal places.

Connect It

You can use a place-value chart to compare and order decimals.

Example Here's how to order these decimal numbers from least to greatest.

2.4 2.45 2.34 2.1 1.96

Place the numbers in the place-value chart, lining up the decimal points. Add zeros as place holders if you need to.

Ones		Tenths	Hundredths
2	.	4	0
2	.	4	5
2	.	3	4
2	.	1	0
1	.	9	6

1. Start comparing digits in the ones place. Since 2 > 1, 1.96 is the least number.
2. Compare the digits in the tenths place. 2.34 is greater than 2.10 because 3 > 1.
3. There are two numbers with 4 in the tenths place. Compare the digits in the hundredths place. 5 > 0, so 2.45 > 2.40.

Ordered from least to greatest, the numbers are:

1.96 2.1 2.34 2.4 2.45

USE YOUR SKILLS

1. Order the numbers from least to greatest.

   4.3, 5.12, 4.75, 5.2

2. Order the numbers from greatest to least.

   6.79, 5.97, 6.34, 6.3

3. **Synthesize** Students measured three objects in their classroom. The measurements are 0.64 m, 0.72 m, and 0.46 m. Which is the shortest measurement? How do you know?

KEY NS 1.2 Order and compare whole numbers and decimals to two decimal places.

NS 1.3 How do you round whole numbers?

Connect It

When you round a number, you find a number that is close to the actual number. You can use place value to round to the nearest ten, hundred, thousand, ten thousand, or hundred thousand. Look for the clue word *about* in questions to know when to **round** to **estimate.**

Read More
See Unit 1, Chapter 2, pages 32–36, on rounding whole numbers through the millions to the nearest ten, hundred, thousand, ten thousand, or hundred thousand.

Example Here's how to round 358,726 to the nearest thousand.

1. Find the place you want to round to. Underline the digit in that place.
   35<u>8</u>,726
   thousands place

2. Circle the digit to its right.
   358,726
   digit to the right

3. If the circled digit is 5 or greater, round up. If the circled digit is less than 5, round down.

7 is greater than 5, so, rounded to the nearest thousand, 358,726 rounds to 359,000.

USE YOUR SKILLS

Round each number to the nearest thousand.

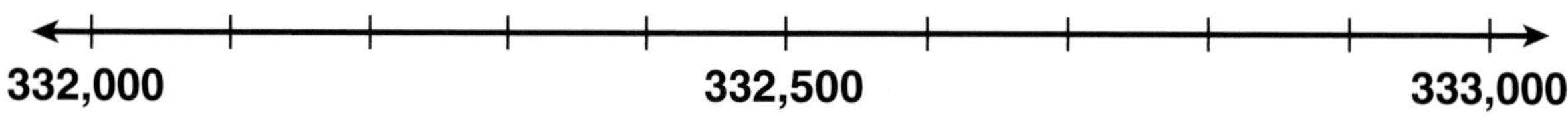

332,000 **332,500** **333,000**

1. 332,900 **2.** 332,210 **3.** 332,499

Round each number to the place of the underlined digit.

4. 812,7<u>6</u>2,434 **5.** 60<u>1</u>,971 **6.** 369,<u>2</u>05,496

7. Apply How would you round 6,325,249 to the nearest hundred thousand?

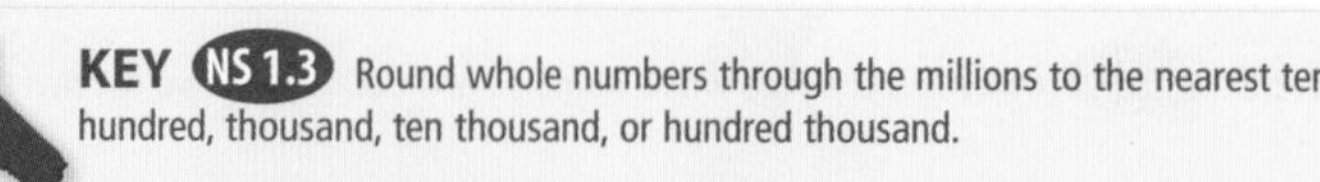

KEY NS 1.3 Round whole numbers through the millions to the nearest ten, hundred, thousand, ten thousand, or hundred thousand.

NS 1.4 How do you decide when to round?

Connect It

You should not always use estimation. Sometimes, an exact answer is called for. However, estimation is an excellent way to check your work to see if your answer is close to what it should be.

Read More
See Unit 1, Chapter 2, Lessons 3 and 4, pages 32–36, on rounding.

USE YOUR SKILLS

Choose whether to estimate or give an exact answer. Then solve each problem.

1. A train leaves at 3:47 P.M. You need to arrive at the station at least 5 minutes before the train leaves. What time do you need to be at the station? Can you use an estimated time?

2. Three suitcases each weigh about 45 pounds. How much do they weigh altogether? Will your answer be exact or an estimate? Why?

3. Four friends will equally share the cost of lunch. The total cost for lunch is $19.40. How much will each friend pay? Do you need an exact answer or an estimate?

4. **Apply** You want to buy 4 DVDs for $9.29 each. You have $37. Can you estimate to see if you have enough money, or do you need an exact answer?

KEY NS 1.4 Decide when a rounded solution is called for and explain why such a solution may be appropriate.

NS 1.8 How do you use a number line to solve problems with negative numbers?

Read More

See Unit 7, Chapter 16, Lessons 1–3, pages 348–354, on using concepts of negative numbers.

Connect It

Numbers can be positive, such as +5, or negative, such as $^{-}8$. Zero is neither positive nor negative. You can use a number line to solve problems containing positive and negative numbers. As you move right on a number line, the numbers increase. As you move left, the numbers decrease.

Example Mark plays a game. He scores 2 points. He plays another round and loses 6 points. What is Mark's final score?

Since Mark started with a score of 2 points, start at 2. Move 6 numbers to the left to show the points he lost. Now you are at $^{-}4$.

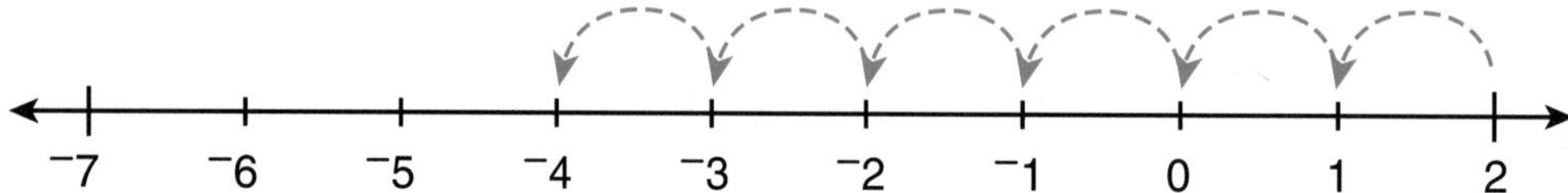

Mark's final score is -4 points.

USE YOUR SKILLS

Use the number line to solve.

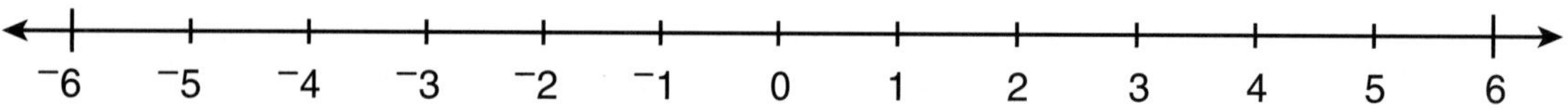

1. 3 more than $^{-}4$
2. 4 fewer than 2
3. 5 fewer than 5
4. 4 more than $^{-}2$
5. 6 more than $^{-}1$
6. 7 fewer than 3
7. **Know** Will 5 fewer than $^{-}1$ be $^{-}6$ or 4? Explain.

KEY NS 1.8 Use concepts of negative numbers (e.g., on a number line, in counting, in temperature, in "owing").

NS 1.9 How do you use a number line to compare fractions?

Read More
See Unit 8, Chapter 18, Lessons 1 and 4, pages 392–396 and 400–402; and Unit 9, Chapter 19, Lesson 4, pages 426–430, on identifying the relative position of numbers on a number line.

Connect It

You can use a number line to **compare** and order fractions with different denominators, or **unlike denominators.** Here's how.

Example Michelle has $\frac{3}{8}$ yard of felt and Lindsay has $\frac{1}{4}$ yard of felt. Who has more felt?

Locate the fractions on two number lines. Make sure the number lines are aligned.

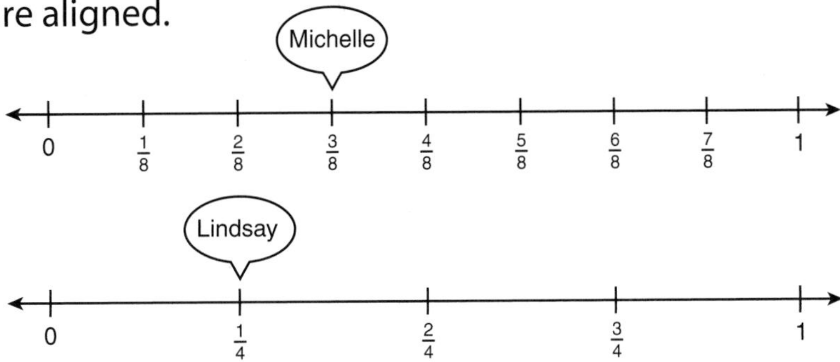

$\frac{3}{8}$ is farther to the right, so $\frac{3}{8} > \frac{1}{4}$. Michelle has more felt.

USE YOUR SKILLS

Use the number lines to compare the fractions. Write >, <, or = for each ⬭.

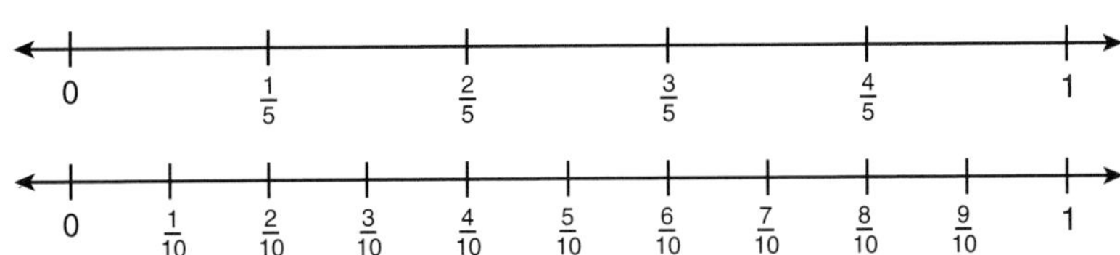

1. $\frac{3}{10}$ ⬭ $\frac{2}{5}$
2. $\frac{4}{5}$ ⬭ $\frac{8}{10}$
3. $\frac{5}{10}$ ⬭ $\frac{2}{5}$
4. **Explain** How can you use number lines to find the greater of two fractions with unlike denominators?

KEY NS 1.9 Identify on a number line the relative position of positive fractions, positive mixed numbers, and positive decimals to two decimal places.

NS 1.9 How do you compare mixed numbers and decimals?

Connect It

When you need to compare mixed numbers and decimals, you can use a place-value chart or a number line. Here's how:

Read More
See Unit 8, Chapter 17, Lesson 4, pages 376–378; Unit 8 Chapter 18, Lessons 1, 2, and 4, pages 392–396, 400–402; and Unit 9, Chapter 19, Lessons 4 and 5, pages 426–430, on identifying on a number line the relative position of positive fractions, positive mixed numbers, and positive decimals to two decimal places.

Example Samantha drove $1\frac{2}{5}$ miles to the library. Then she drove 1.85 miles to her yoga class. She then drove $\frac{5}{4}$ miles to the store. Her ride home was $\frac{7}{10}$ mile. What is the order of all the distances from least to greatest?

Use a place-value chart.

1 Change the fractions to decimals.

	Ones		Tenths	Hundredths
$1\frac{2}{5}$ →	1	.	4	0
1.85 →	1	.	8	5
$\frac{5}{4}$ →	1	.	2	5
$\frac{7}{10}$ →	0	.	7	5

2 Write the decimals in the chart.

3 Compare.

Use a number line.

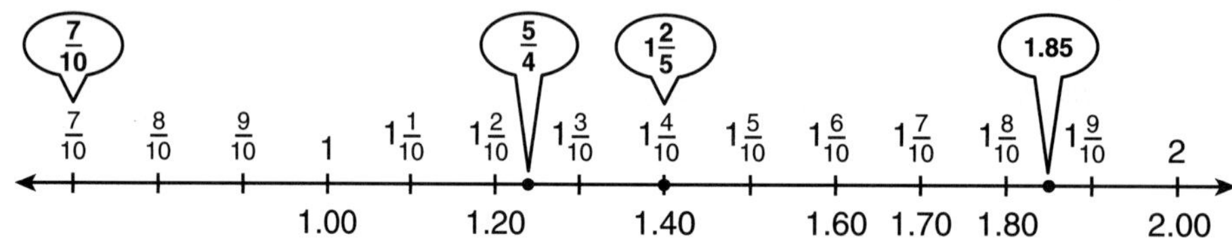

The order of the distances from least to greatest is:

$\frac{7}{10}$ mile $\quad \frac{5}{4}$ mile $\quad 1\frac{2}{5}$ mile $\quad$ 1.85 mile

USE YOUR SKILLS

Write >, <, or = for each ⬭.

1. $\frac{3}{2}$ ⬭ 1.9
2. $5\frac{3}{4}$ ⬭ 5.75
3. 7.45 ⬭ $7\frac{1}{2}$
4. **Compare** How is comparing fractions like comparing decimals?

KEY NS 1.9 Identify on a number line the relative position of positive fractions, positive mixed numbers, and positive decimals to two decimal places.

NS 3.0 How does addition help you subtract?

Read More
See Unit 2, Chapter 4, Lessons 2 and 3, pages 76–78 and 80–81, on understanding the relationship among addition and subtraction.

Connect It

Addition and subtraction are inverse operations. Subtraction "undoes" addition. Addition "undoes" subtraction. A fact family shows this relationship.

Example The equations using the numbers 5, 7, and 12 form a **fact family.**

Addition	**Subtraction**
$5 + 7 = 12$	$12 - 5 = 7$
$7 + 5 = 12$	$12 - 7 = 5$

You can use addition to check subtraction, and you can use subtraction to check addition.

$$\begin{array}{r} 56 \\ -\,45 \\ \hline 11 \end{array} \qquad \begin{array}{r} 11 \\ +\,45 \\ \hline 56 \end{array}$$

USE YOUR SKILLS

Complete the fact family.

1. $4 + 6 = \square$ $\qquad$ $10 - 4 = \square$

   $6 + 4 = \square$ $\qquad$ $10 - 6 = \square$

2. **Write the fact family for each set of numbers.**

   8, 0, 8

   3, 6, 9

   5, 6, 11

3. **Subtract. Use addition to check your answer.**

   $28 - 15$

   $95 - 79$

   $84 - 55$

4. **Analyze** Why does the fact family with the numbers 9, 9, 18 have only two facts? Explain.

KEY NS 1.2 Students solve problems involving addition, subtraction, multiplication, and division of whole numbers and understand the relationships among the operations.

NS 3.0 How does multiplication help you divide?

Connect It

Multiplication and division are inverse operations. Division "undoes" multiplication. Multiplication "undoes" division. A fact family shows this relationship.

Read More
See Unit 3, Chapter 6, Lessons 2–5, pages 122–130, on understanding the relationship among multiplication and division.

Example The equations using the numbers 4, 3, and 12 form a fact family.

Multiplication	Division
$4 \times 3 = 12$	$12 \div 4 = 3$
$3 \times 4 = 12$	$12 \div 3 = 4$

You can use multiplication to check division and you can use division to check multiplication.

$15 \times 3 = 45$ $\quad\quad$ $45 \div 3 = 15$

USE YOUR SKILLS

1. **Complete the fact family.**

   $4 \times 8 = \square$ $\quad\quad$ $32 \div 4 = \square$

   $8 \times 4 = \square$ $\quad\quad$ $32 \div 8 = \square$

2. **Write the fact family for each set of numbers.**

   5, 5, 25

   3, 9, 27

   4, 6, 24

3. **Analyze** Why does the fact family with the numbers 6, 6, 36 have only two facts? Explain.

KEY NS 3.0 Students solve problems involving addition, subtraction, multiplication, and division of whole numbers and understand the relationships among the operations.

NS 3.1 How do you add numbers with more than one digit?

Read More
See Unit 2, Chapter 3, Lessons 1–4, pages 51–60 and 62–63, for addition of multidigit numbers.

Connect It

Addition properties can help you add multidigit numbers.

Zero Property of Addition When you add zero to a number, the sum is that number. $12 + 0 = 12$

Commutative Property of Addition When you change the order of the addends, the sum stays the same.

$8 + 7 = 15$

$7 + 8 = 15$

Associative Property of Addition When you change the way the addends are grouped, the sum stays the same.

Example Here's how to add 3,749 + 1,096.

1 Add the ones. $9 + 6 = 15$

```
    1
  3,749
+ 1,096
      5
```

Regroup 15 ones as 1 ten and 5 ones.

2 Add the tens. $1 + 4 + 9 = 14$

```
   1
  3,749
+ 1,096
     45
```

Regroup 14 tens as 1 hundred and 4 tens.

3 Add the hundreds. $1 + 7 + 0 = 8$

```
   11
  3,749
+ 1,096
    845
```

4 Add the thousands. $3 + 1 = 4$

```
   11
  3,749
+ 1,096
  4,845
```

Remember, you can use subtraction to check addition because subtraction and addition are inverse operations.

USE YOUR SKILLS

Add. Use subtraction to check your answer

1. 7,593 + 8,541

2. 25,195 + 93,261

3. 36,595 + 29,805

4. 175,682 + 469,937

5. 71,724 + 234,192 805,9

6. 395,890 + 472,125 868,015

7. **Synthesize** When adding 109,832 + 623,782, how many times do you need to regroup?

KEY NS 3.1 Demonstrate an understanding of, and the ability to use, standard algorithms for the addition and subtraction of multidigit numbers.

NS 3.1 How do you subtract numbers with more than one digit?

> **Read More**
> See Unit 2, Chapter 4, Lessons 1–4, pages 72–83, for subtraction of multidigit numbers.

Connect It

The Rules of Subtraction can help you subtract multidigit numbers.

Zeros in Subtraction

- When you subtract zero from a number, the difference is that number.
  12 − 0 = 12
- When you subtract a number from itself, the difference is zero.
  47 − 47 = 0

Example Here's how to subtract 8,645 − 647.

1 Subtract the ones.	**2** Subtract the tens.	**3** Subtract the hundreds.	**4** Subtract the thousands.
3 15 8,645 − 647 8	13 5 3 8,645 − 647 98	15 13 7 5 3 8,645 − 647 998	15 13 7 5 3 8,645 − 647 7,998
Regroup 1 ten as 10 ones.	**Regroup 1 hundred as 10 tens.**	**Regroup 1 thousand as 10 hundreds.**	

Remember, you can use addition to check subtraction because addition and subtraction are inverse operations.

USE YOUR SKILLS

1. 4,537 − 629

2. 7,325 − 6,781

3. 24,574 − 13,937

4. 244,684 − 115,932

Subtract. Use addition to check your answer.

5. 6,243 − 4,185

6. 62,839 − 3,145

7. **Analyze** What if the tens digit in the minuend was 9 in Question 1. How would your answer change?

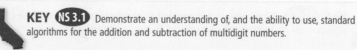

> **KEY NS 3.1** Demonstrate an understanding of, and the ability to use, standard algorithms for the addition and subtraction of multidigit numbers.

NS 3.2 How do you multiply multidigit numbers by two-digit numbers?

Connect It

Multiplication Properties can help you multiply.

Commutative Property

When you change the order of the factors, the product stays the same.

$12 \times 3 = 36$
$3 \times 12 = 36$

Property of One

When you multiply a number by 1, the product is the number.

$76 \times 1 = 76$

Zero Property

When you multiply a number by 0, the product is 0.

$55 \times 0 = 0$

Read More
See Unit 5, Chapter 11, Lesson 3, pages 238–239, on solving problems involving multiplication of multidigit numbers by two-digit numbers.

Example Here's how to multiply 18×12.

1. Multiply 18 by 2 ones.

$$\begin{array}{r} {}^{1} \\ 18 \\ \times 12 \\ \hline 36 \end{array}$$

2. Multiply 18 by 1 ten.

$$\begin{array}{r} {}^{1} \\ 18 \\ \times 12 \\ \hline 36 \\ 180 \end{array}$$

3. Add the partial products.

$$\begin{array}{rl} {}^{1} & \\ 18 & \\ \times 12 & \\ \hline 36 & \leftarrow 2 \times 18 \\ +180 & \leftarrow 10 \times 18 \\ \hline 216 & \leftarrow (2 \times 18) + (10 \times 18) \end{array}$$

The **Distributive Property** shows why this works.

$12 \times 18 = (2 + 10) \times 18$ $\quad$ $(2 + 10) \times 18 = (2 \times 18) + (10 \times 18)$

216 students can sit in the gymnasium.

USE YOUR SKILLS

Multiply.

1. $\begin{array}{r} 75 \\ \times 24 \\ \hline \end{array}$
2. $\begin{array}{r} 39 \\ \times 66 \\ \hline \end{array}$
3. $\begin{array}{r} 44 \\ \times 58 \\ \hline \end{array}$
4. 15×14
5. 63×19
6. 52×25
7. **Analyze** Why is it helpful to estimate a product before multiplying multidigit numbers?

KEY NS 3.2 Demonstrate an understanding of, and the ability to use, standard algorithms for multiplying a multidigit number by a two-digit number and for dividing a multidigit number by a one-digit number; use relationships between them to simplify computations and to check results.

NS 3.2 How do you divide two-digit numbers by one-digit divisors?

Connect It

Read More

See Unit 3, Chapter 6, Lessons 1–5, pages 120–132; Unit 6, Chapter 12, Lessons 1–5, pages 260–273; and Chapter 13, Lessons 1–4, pages 280–291, on solving problems involving division of multidigit numbers by one-digit numbers.

Division Rules can help you divide.

- When you divide any number (except 0) by itself, the quotient is 1. $17 \div 17 = 1$
- When you divide a number by 1, the quotient is the number. $8 \div 1 = 8$
- When you divide 0 by any number except for 0, the quotient is 0. $0 \div 43 = 0$

Remember, the number that is left over is the *remainder*. The remainder is always less than the divisor.

Example Here's how to divide 86 ÷ 9.

1 Think of a 9 fact whose product is close to 86.

9 × ? is close to 86
$9 \times 8 = 72$
$9 \times 9 = 81$
8 is too little.
Try 9 as the quotient.

2 Divide.

$$\begin{array}{r} 9 \\ 9\overline{)86} \\ -81 \\ \hline 5 \end{array}$$

−81 ← 9 × 9
5 ← 86 − 81

3 Show the remainder.

$$\begin{array}{r} 9 \text{ R5} \\ 9\overline{)86} \\ -81 \\ \hline 5 \end{array}$$

5 ← remainder

Remember, you can use multiplication to check division.

Multiply the quotient by the divisor. Then add the remainder.

$(9 \times 9) + 5 = 86$

The sum equals the dividend so the answer is correct.

USE YOUR SKILLS

Divide. Then multiply to check your answer.

1. $3\overline{)14}$ **2.** $7\overline{)24}$ **3.** $25 \div 4$ **4.** $52 \div 6$

5. **Analyze** Carter divided 33 by 6. His answer showed a quotient of 4 and a remainder of 9. How do you know his answer is incorrect?

KEY NS 3.2 Demonstrate an understanding of, and the ability to use, standard algorithms for multiplying a multidigit number by a two-digit number and for dividing a multidigit number by a one-digit number; use relationships between them to simplify computations and to check results.

NS 3.3 How do you multiply multidigit numbers by two-digit numbers?

Read More

See Unit 3, Chapter 6, Lessons 1–4, pages 119–129; Unit 5, Chapter 10, Lessons 1–4, pages 213–225; and Chapter 11, Lessons 1–4, pages 232–244, on multiplying a multidigit number by a two-digit number

Connect It

The Multiplication Properties help you multiply all numbers, including numbers with more than two digits. When you multiply multidigit numbers, ask yourself three questions: What numbers do I multiply first? What numbers do I multiply next? What do I add to find the product? Estimate to check your answer.

Example There are 24 sections of 516 seats each in a stadium. How many total seats are there? Multiply 516 × 24.

1 What numbers do I multiply first? Multiply 516 by 4 ones.

$$\begin{array}{r} {}^{2}\\ 516 \\ \times\ 24 \\ \hline 2064 \end{array}$$

2 What numbers do I multiply next? Multiply 516 by 2 tens.

$$\begin{array}{r} {}^{1}\\ 516 \\ \times\ 24 \\ \hline 2064 \\ 10320 \end{array}$$

3 What do I add to find the product? Add the partial products.

$$\begin{array}{rl} 516 & \\ \times\ 24 & \\ \hline 2064 & \leftarrow 516 \times 4 \\ +\ 10320 & \leftarrow 516 \times 20 \\ \hline 12{,}384 & \leftarrow \end{array}$$

(516 × 4) + (516 × 20)

So, there is a total of 12,384 seats.

USE YOUR SKILLS

Multiply. Estimate to make sure your answer is reasonable.

1. $\begin{array}{r} 412 \\ \times 41 \\ \hline \end{array}$

2. $\begin{array}{r} 706 \\ \times 23 \\ \hline \end{array}$

3. $\begin{array}{r} 947 \\ \times 84 \\ \hline \end{array}$

4. 52 × 517

5. 46 × 586

6. **Apply** Why would it be helpful to estimate a product before multiplying?

KEY NS 3.3 Solve problems involving multiplication of multidigit numbers by two-digit numbers.

NS 3.3 How do you multiply a number when there is a zero in a factor?

Read More

See Unit 5, Chapter 11, Lessons 1–4, pages 234–244, on multiplying a multidigit number by a two-digit number.

Connect It

When multiplying any number by zero, use the Zero Property of Multiplication. The product of any number multiplied by 0 is 0.

Examples

Zero in the Tens Place

Multiply. 304 × 38

```
    1
    3
  304
×  38
 2432
+9120
11,552
```

Zero in the Ones Place

Multiply. 540 × 64

```
     2
     1
   540
 ×  64
  2160
+32400
34,560
```

Multiple of 10

Multiply. 146 × 50

```
   23
  146
×  50
    0
+7300
7,300
```

USE YOUR SKILLS

Multiply. Estimate to make sure your answer is reasonable.

1. 430 × 26

2. 988 × 20

3. 609 × 48

4. 73 × 709

5. 90 × 274

6. **Explain** When multiplying by a multiple of 10, why is the first partial product zero?

KEY NS 3.3 Solve problems involving multiplication of multidigit numbers by two-digit numbers.

NS 3.4 How do you divide multidigit numbers by one-digit divisors?

Read More
See Unit 6, Chapter 13, Lessons 1–4, pages 280–291, on solving problems involving division of multidigit numbers by one-digit numbers.

Connect It

The Division Rules help you divide all numbers, including numbers with more than two digits. When you divide multidigit numbers, ask yourself three questions: Can I divide the hundreds? Can I divide the tens? Can I divide the ones? Multiply to check your answer.

Example A book warehouse ships 736 notebooks to 2 schools. If each school gets the same number of notebooks, how many notebooks does each school get?
Divide. 736 ÷ 2 = ▢ or 2)736

1 Can I divide the hundreds? Divide the hundreds.
? hundreds

Think: 2)7 hundreds

```
   3
2 )736
 - 6    Multiply. 3 × 2
   1    Subtract. 7 − 6
        Compare. 1 < 2
```

2 Bring down the tens. Can I divide the tens? Divide the tens.
? tens

Think: 3)13 tens

```
   36
2 )736
 - 6↓
   13    Bring down the tens.
 - 12    Multiply. 6 × 2
    1    Subtract. 13 − 12
         Compare. 1 < 2
```

3 Bring down the ones. Can I divide the ones? Divide the ones.
? ones

Think: 2)16 ones

```
   368
2 )736
 - 6
   13
 - 12↓
    16
 -  16    Multiply. 8 × 2
     0    Subtract. 16 − 16
          Compare. 0 < 2
```

Check.
Multiply.
2 × 368 = 736
The product equals the dividend. So the quotient is correct.

USE YOUR SKILLS

1. 6)786 **2.** 7)917 **3.** 4)508

4. 849 ÷ 3 **5.** 630 ÷ 5 **6.** 916 ÷ 2

7. **Synthesize** While dividing a 3-digit number by a 1-digit number, you find that the quotient has a 1 in the hundreds place. How many digits will the final quotient have? Explain.

KEY NS 3.4 Solve problems involving division of multidigit numbers by one-digit numbers.

NS 3.4

How do you solve division problems with one-digit divisors?

Read More

See Unit 3, Chapter 6, Lessons 1–5, pages 120–132; Unit 6, Chapter 12, Lessons 1–5, pages 260–273; and Chapter 13, Lessons 1–4, pages 280–291, on solving problems involving division of multidigit numbers by one-digit numbers.

Connect It

When dividing by a one-digit divisor, you must decide where to place the first digit in the quotient.

Example

Sara has 381 boxes to place on 8 shelves. If each shelf gets the same number of boxes, how many boxes will be on each shelf? Divide. 381 ÷ 8 = ▢ or $8\overline{)381}$

1 Decide where to place the first digit.

$8\overline{)381}$

Decide: Since **3** < **8**, there will be no hundreds in the quotient. The first digit will be in the tens place.

2 Regroup the hundreds as tens. Divide the tens. ? tens

Think: $8\overline{)38}$ tens

```
   4
8 )381
 - 32    Multiply. 4 × 8
    6    Subtract. 38 − 32
         Compare. 6 < 8
```

3 Bring down the ones. Divide the ones. ? ones

Think: $8\overline{)61}$ ones

```
   47 R5
8 )381
 - 32
    61   Bring down the ones.
 -  56   Multiply. 7 × 8
     5   Subtract. 61 − 56
         Compare. 5 < 8
```

USE YOUR SKILLS

Divide. Use multiplication to check.

Check.
Multiply. Then add. (8 × 47) + 5 = 381 The sum equals the dividend, so the quotient is correct.

1. $5\overline{)462}$

2. $8\overline{)623}$

3. $6\overline{)591}$

4. **Apply** Devon wants to share 249 dimes among 7 of his friends. How many dimes will each friend get?

KEY NS 3.4 Solve problems involving division of multidigit numbers by one-digit numbers.

NS 4.2 How do you use the division to find out whether a number is a prime number?

Read More

See Unit 6, Chapter 14, Lessons 3–4, pages 306–310 on prime numbers.

Connect It

The factors of a number can help you tell whether the number is *prime* or *composite*.

A **prime number** is a number that has exactly two factors, 1 and itself.

A **composite number** is a number that has more than two factors.

Since the number 1 has only 1 factor, it is neither prime nor composite.

You can use division to find factors.

You already know that 1 and 11 are factors of 11. Use division to find any other factors of 11. If there is a remainder, the divisor is not a factor.

$11 \div 2 \longrightarrow$ 5 R1, so 2 is not a factor.

$11 \div 3 \longrightarrow$ 3 R2, so 3 is not a factor.

$11 \div 4 \longrightarrow$ 2 R3, so 4 is not a factor.

$11 \div 5 \longrightarrow$ 2 R1, so 5 is not a factor.

$11 \div 6 \longrightarrow$ 1 R5, so 6 is not a factor.

Since 11 has only two factors, 1 and itself, 11 is a prime number.

USE YOUR SKILLS

List the factors of each number. Then tell if the number is prime or composite.

1. 37 **2.** 26 **3.** 9

4. 41 **5.** 17

6. **Comprehend** What numbers between 30 and 40 are prime?

KEY NS 4.2 Know that numbers such as 2, 3, 5, 7, and 11 do not have any factors except 1 and themselves and that such numbers are called prime numbers.

NS 4.2

How do you make a factor tree to show a number as the product of its prime factors?

Read More
See Unit 6, Chapter 14, Lessons 3–4, pages 306–310, on prime numbers.

Connect It

A composite number can be written as the product of its **prime factors**. To find the prime factors of a composite number, you can make a **factor tree**.

Example Here is how to make a factor tree for 32.

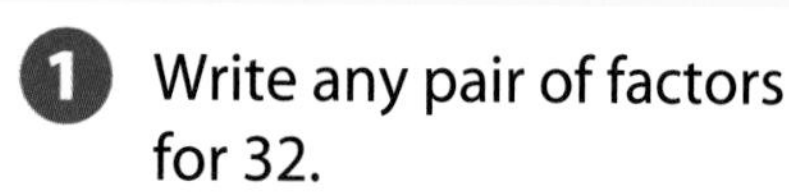

1 Write any pair of factors for 32.

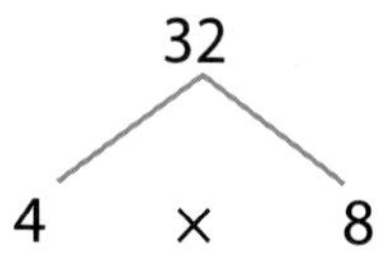

2 Write a pair of factors for each factor until all the factors are prime numbers.

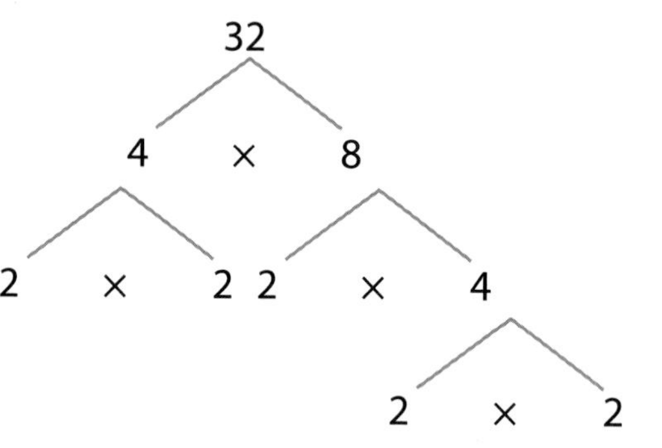

$2 \times 2 \times 2 \times 2 \times 2 = 32$, so the prime factors of 32 are 2, 2, 2, 2, and 2.

A factor tree is complete when each branch ends with a prime number.

USE YOUR SKILLS

Make a factor tree for each number.

7. 18 **8.** 48 **9.** 64 **10.** 80

11. **Analyze** Can the same number have more than one factor tree?

KEY NS 4.2 Know that numbers such as 2, 3, 5, 7, and 11 do not have any factors except 1 and themselves and that such numbers are called prime numbers.

AF 1.2 How do you interpret and evaluate expressions with parentheses?

Read More

See Unit 2, Chapter 5, Lessons 1–2, pages 92–96, on interpreting and evaluating mathematical expressions that use parentheses.

Connect It

An **expression** is a number or group of numbers and operation symbols. When you **evaluate**, or find the value of, an expression, you do all of the operations and write the result.

Sometimes an expression contains **parentheses**. Parentheses show the operations that should be done first.

Example Here's how to simplify the expression
(98 − 38) + (75 − 45) − 12.

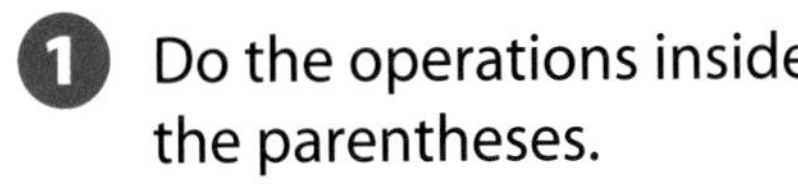

1 Do the operations inside the parentheses.

(98 − 38) + (75 − 45) − 12.
60 + 30 − 12

2 Do the rest of the operations from left to right.

60 + 30 − 12
90 − 12
78

USE YOUR SKILLS

Write an expression for the situation.

1. 29 more than 35

2. 125 minus the sum of 76 and 19

Evaluate the expression.

3. (63 – 22) + 9

4. (86 – 37) + (99 – 34)

5. **Describe** How would you simplify the expression 15 + (75 + 70) − 10?

KEY AF 1.2 Interpret and evaluate mathematical expressions that now use parentheses.

AF 1.3 How do you write and evaluate expressions?

Read More
See Unit 3, Chapter 7, Lessons 1–3, pages 142–149, on writing expressions containing more than two terms and different operations.

Connect It

To evaluate, or **simplify**, an expression, follow the **order of operations**.

Example Nikki buys 4 picture frames. Each picture frame costs \$4. If Nikki pays with a \$20 bill, how much change will she get back? Evaluate $20 - (4 \times 4)$.

Order of Operations

- Do the operations inside the parentheses ( ).
- Multiply and divide in order from left to right.
- Add and subtract in order from left to right.

1. Multiply. $20 - (4 \times 4)$

3. Subtract. $20 - 16$

   4

Nikki gets \$4 in change.

USE YOUR SKILLS

Write an expression for the situation. Use parentheses to show what to do first.

1. 34 fewer than 8 times 12

2. 53 more than $42 \div 6$

Simplify the expression.

3. $68 - 6 \times (7 + 2)$

4. $(44 - 24) \div 2$

5. $72 \div 12 + 9 \times 3$

6. **Evaluate** Look at Exercise 4. Will the answer change if the parentheses are around $24 \div 2$ instead of $44 - 24$?

KEY AF 1.3 Use parentheses to indicate which operation to perform first when writing expressions containing more than two terms and different operations.

AF 1.5 How can you use variables to write function rules?

Read More
See Unit 4, Chapter 9, Lessons 2–3, pages 192–197, on solving with equations.

Connect It

A **function table** is a table of **ordered pairs** that follow a rule. A **variable** represents a number in the rule. You can use the rule to find the value of an unknown number in an ordered pair if you know the value of the other number.

Example

The Sports Club buys tennis balls in packages of 3. How many balls will they have if they buy 4 packages?

Write a rule and use it to solve.

Input: Number of packages	Output: Number of tennis balls
1	3
2	6
3	9
4	*n*

1 Let *n* stand for the number of packages. The number of tennis balls is always 3 times the number of packages.

The rule is: Output = $3n$.

There are 12 tennis balls in 4 packages.

2 Use the rule to find the number of tennis balls in 4 packages.

number of tennis balls = $3n$

3×4 → Substitute 4 for *n*.

12

USE YOUR SKILLS

Copy and complete.

Rule: Output = $5a - 3$

	Input (*a*)	Output
1.	2	
2.	4	
3.	6	

4. Rule: ?

Input (*c*)	Output
20	120
12	72
6	36

5. Verify How can you check your output numbers when using a function rule?

KEY AF 1.5 Understand that an equation such as $y = 3x + 5$ is a prescription for determining a second number when a first number is given.

AF 1.5 How do you write function rules using two variables?

Read More
See Unit 4, Chapter 9, Lessons 2–3, pages 192–198, on solving equations.

Connect It

You can write a rule for a function table using two variables. One represents the Input and one represents the Output.
Check your rule: Does my rule work for every pair of numbers in the table?

Example

Mike is having a party at a sports center. Each guest's ticket costs \$6. The function table at the right shows the relationship between the number of tickets and the cost of the tickets.

Input: Number of tickets	Output: Cost of tickets
1	\$6
2	\$12
3	\$18

Write a rule for the function table. Use variables to represent numbers in the rule.

Use one variable.

- Let m stand for the number of guests.
- $6m$ stands for the cost of tickets, the output.
  The rule for the function table can be written as Output $= 6m$.

Rule: Output $= 6m$

Use two variables.

- Let m stand for the number of guests.
- Let p stand for the cost of tickets.
  The rule for the function table can be written as the equation $p = 6m$.

Rule: $p = 6m$

USE YOUR SKILLS

Copy and complete.

Rule: $s = 6r - 8$

	Input (r)	Output (s)
1.	4	
2.	8	

3. Rule: ______________

Input (t)	Output (u)
32	8
72	18
80	20

4. Verify How can you make sure your rule is correct?

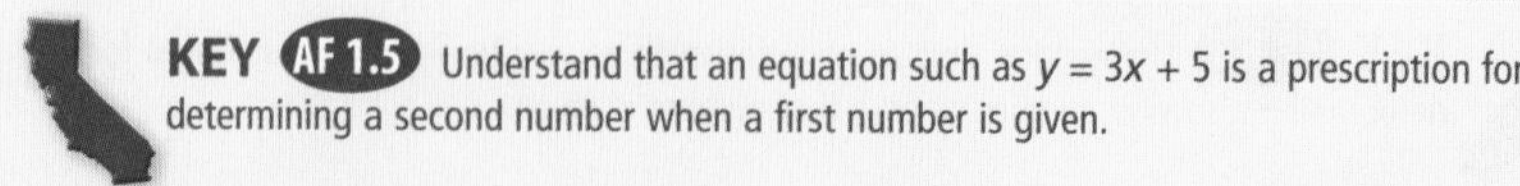

KEY AF 1.5 Understand that an equation such as $y = 3x + 5$ is a prescription for determining a second number when a first number is given.

AF 2.0 How do you tell the difference between an equation and an inequality?

Connect It

Read More
See Unit 3, Chapter 7, Lessons 2–3, pages 144–150, on manipulating equations.

An **equation** relates two expressions that have the same value. Every equation contains an equals sign to show that both expressions are equal.

An **inequality** involves two expressions that are not equal. The symbols $>$, $<$, and $\neq$ show an inequality.

Example Sandy has 9 quarters. Alex has 4 times as many quarters as Sandy. Max has 27 more quarters than Sandy.

Write an equation to compare Alex's quarters and Max's quarters.

	Alex		Max
1 Write expressions to show how many quarters Alex and Max have.	9×4		$27 + 9$
2 Evaluate each expression and compare.	9×4 36	 =	$27 + 9$ 36

Write an inequality to compare Sandy's quarters and Max's quarters.

	Sandy		Max
1 Write expressions to show how many quarters Sandy and Max have.	9		$27 + 9$
2 Evaluate each expression and compare.	9 9	 <	$27 + 9$ 36

USE YOUR SKILLS

Hint
Use $=, >, <,$ or $\neq$ to compare.

Copy and complete. Use $=, <, >,$ or $\neq$ for  **.**

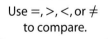

1. $42 \div 7 + 6$ ⬭ 2×9
2. $11 + (5 \times 3) - 12$ ⬭ $(9 \times 9) \div 9$
3. $3 + 6 \times 5$ ⬭ $99 \div 9$
4. $(2 \times 8) \div (0 + 4)$ ⬭ $2 \times (8 + 4)$
5. **Explain** Do these expressions form an equation or an inequality? Explain.
   $42 - (12 \div 4)$ and $(39 \div 3) + (11 + 15)$

KEY AF 2.0 Students know how to manipulate equations.

AF 2.1 What happens when you add the same number to both sides of an equation?

Read More
See Unit 2, Chapter 5, Lesson 4, pages 102–103, on knowing and understanding that equals added to equals are equal.

Connect It

The expressions in an equation are equal. When you add the same number to both expressions, they remain equal.

Example If $27 + 13 = 40$ is true, is $(27 + 13) + 36 = 40 + 36$ true?

When 36 is added to both sides of the equation, the equation is still true.

Rule: Equals added to equals are equal.

1. Simplify both sides of the original equation to check that they are equal.
$$27 + 13 = 40$$
$$40 = 40$$

2. Now rewrite the equation, adding 36 to each side.
$$(27 + 13) + 36 = 40 + 36$$

3. Now simplify the equation.
$$(27 + 13) + 36 = 40 + 36$$
$$40 + 36 = 40 + 36$$
$$76 = 76$$

USE YOUR SKILLS

Copy and complete.

1. $(47 - 21) + 12 = 26 + 12$
$\square + 12 = \square$
$\square = \square$

2. $(47 - 21) + 53 = 26 + 53$
$\square + 53 = \square$
$\square = \square$

3. $(72 + 67) + 24 = 139 + 24$
$\square + 24 = \square$
$\square = \square$

4. $16 + (78 - 32) = 16 + 46$
$16 + \square = \square$
$\square = \square$

5. **Synthesize** If you add a number to one side of an equation and not to the other side, what happens? Explain.

KEY AF 2.1 Know and understand that equals added to equals are equal.

AF 2.2 What happens when you multiply both sides of an equation by the same number?

Read More

See Unit 3, Chapter 7, Lesson 4, pages 152–153, on knowing and understanding that equals multiplied by equals are equal.

Connect It

The expressions in an equation are equal. When you multiply both expressions by the same number, they remain equal.

Example Will the equation $6 \times 5 = 30$ still be true if both sides are multiplied by 7?

1. Simplify both sides of the original equation to check that they are equal.

$$6 \times 5 = 30$$
$$30 = 30$$

2. Now rewrite the equation, multiplying each side by 7.

$$(6 \times 5) \times 7 = 30 \times 7$$

3. Simplify both sides of the new equation.

$$(6 \times 5) \times 7 = 30 \times 7$$
$$30 \times 7 = 30 \times 7$$
$$210 = 210$$

The expressions on both sides of the equation still have the same value.
When both sides of the equation are multiplied by 7, the equation is still true.

Rule: Equals multiplied by equals are equal.

USE YOUR SKILLS

Copy and complete.

1. $3 \times (4 + 3) = 3 \times \square$

2. $6 \times (10 \times 7) = 6 \times \square$

3. $(6 + 17) \times \square = 23 \times 12$

4. $(9 - 4) \times \square = (8 - 3) \times 9$

5. **Synthesize** If you multiply one side of an equation by 6 and the other side of the equation by 5, what happens? Explain.

KEY AF 2.2 Know and understand that equals multiplied by equals are equal.

MG 2.0 How do you locate a point on a grid?

Connect It

You can plot, or place, points on a grid using the two numbers in an ordered pair. The coordinates, or numbers, in an ordered pair represent a location on the grid.

Read More

See Unit 10, Chapter 21, Lessons 1–2, pages 466–470, on using two-dimensional coordinate grids to represent points.

Example Use the ordered pair (2, 3) to plot point *A*.

1. Start at 0 on the grid. The first coordinate, or number, tells how far to move to the right. Move 2 units to the right.
2. The second coordinate, or number, tells how far to move up. Move 3 units up.
3. Label the point *A* (2, 3).

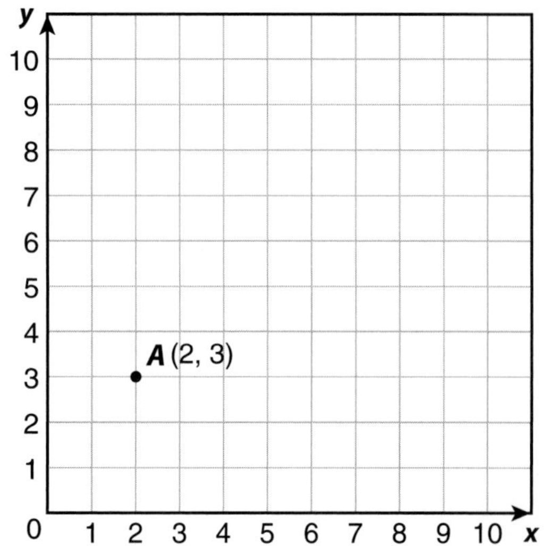

USE YOUR SKILLS

Copy the coordinate grid. Plot the point and label it with the correct letter.

1. *B* (3, 7)
2. *D* (0, 5)
3. *C* (5, 0)
4. *F* (8, 8)
5. *E* (4, 3)

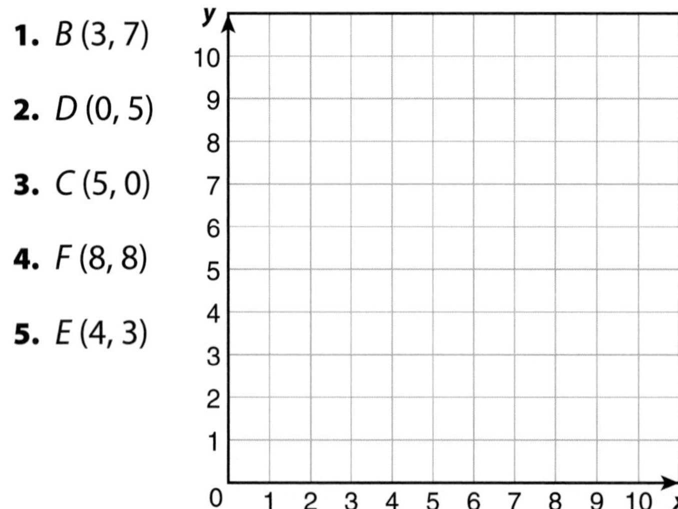

6. **Synthesize** Explain why (9, 4) and (4, 9) are not the same point.

KEY MG 2.0 Students use two-dimensional coordinate grids to represent points and graph lines and simple figures.

MG 2.0 How do you use two ordered pairs to draw a line segment on a grid?

Read More
See Unit 10, Chapter 21, Lessons 3–4, pages 472–477, on using two-dimensional coordinate grids to represent points and graph lines.

Connect It

You can use two ordered pairs to draw a line segment on a grid by plotting each point on the grid and then connecting the points.

A vertical line segment lies straight up and down, perpendicular to the horizon. A horizontal line segment lies straight across, parallel to the horizon.

Example Use points *C* and *D* to draw a line segment. Then tell if the line segment is horizontal, vertical, or neither. Point *C* (10, 7) Point *D* (2, 7)

1 Use the ordered pair (10, 7) to plot point *C*.

- Start at 0 on the grid.
- The first coordinate, or number, tells how far to move to the right. Move 10 units to the right.
- The second coordinate, or number, tells how far to move up. Move 7 units up.
- Label the point *C*.

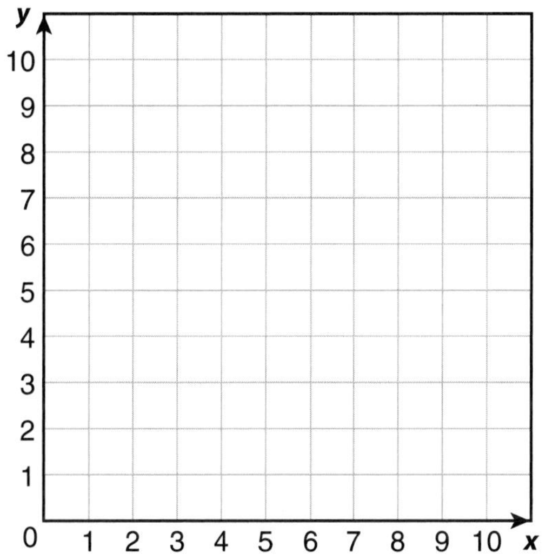

2 Now use the ordered pair (2, 7) to plot point *D*.

- Start at 0 on the grid.
- Move 2 units to the right.
- Next, move 7 units up.
- Label the point *D*.

3 Use a ruler to connect point *C* and point *D*.

USE YOUR SKILLS

Use Workmat 6. Plot and connect the points. Is the line segment horizontal, vertical, or neither?

1. C (5, 4) D (5, 2) **2.** C (6, 8) D (3, 8) **3.** C (3, 7) D (9, 9) **4.** C (0, 9) D (4, 1)

5. Comprehend How can you tell whether the line segment formed by two ordered pairs is vertical?

KEY MG 2.0 Students use two-dimensional coordinate grids to represent points and graph lines and simple figures.

MG 2.1 How do you draw a graph to represent an equation?

Read More
See Unit 10, Chapter 21, Lessons 3 and 4, pages 472–474 and 476–477, on drawing the points corresponding to linear relationships on graph paper.

Connect It

Think of an equation as a rule for a function. Equations can be used to make function tables of input and output values. You can then plot the ordered pairs on a graph.

Example Draw a graph to represent the equation $y = 2x + 2$.

1 Use the equation to make a function table. Choose x-values that make the values of y easy to find, such as 1, 2, 3, and 4.

Use the rule to find the values for y.

For $x = 1 \longrightarrow y = 2 \times 1 + 2$
$= 2 + 2 = 4$

Rule: $y = 2x + 2$

Input: (x)	Output: (y)
1	4
2	6
3	8
4	10

2 Use the function table to write ordered pairs:
(1, 4), (2, 6), (3, 8), and (4, 10).

3 Plot the ordered pairs on a coordinate grid like the one shown. Draw a line through the points.

The graph is a straight line that represents all the values of x and y for the equation $y = 2x + 2$.

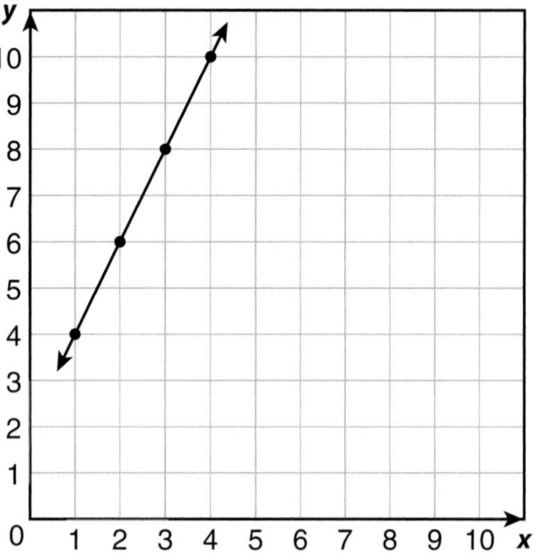

USE YOUR SKILLS

Use the equation to make a function table with 10 values. Then graph the equation on a coordinate grid.

1. $y = 3x + 2$

2. **Comprehend** What axis do you use for the x values? What axis do you use for the y values?

KEY MG 2.1 Draw the points corresponding to linear relationships on graph paper (e.g., draw 10 points on the graph of the equation $y = 3x$ and connect them by using a straight line).

MG 2.2 How do you find the length of horizontal line segments using coordinates?

Read More
See Unit 10, Chapter 22, Lessons 3–4, pages 492–496, on lengths of horizontal and vertical line segments.

Connect It

A horizontal line segment is parallel to the *x*-axis.
All the points on a horizontal line have the same *y*-coordinate.

Example 1 What is the length of the horizontal line segment that connects points *G* (2, 5) and *H* (8, 5)?

Find the difference between the *x*-coordinates. Subtract the smaller from the larger.

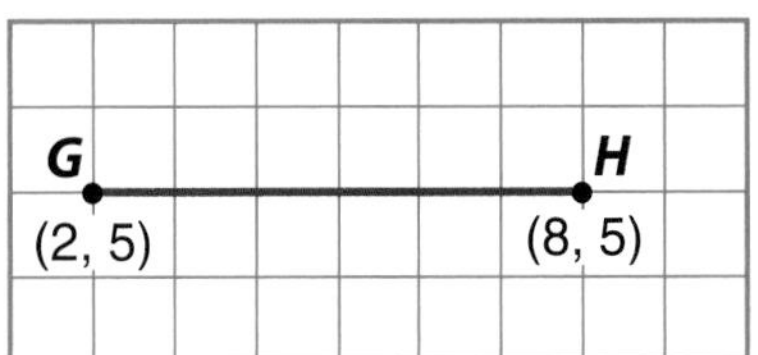

$8 - 2 = 6$

The horizontal line segment connecting *G* to *H* is 6 units long.

Example 2 What is the length of the horizontal line segment that connects points *M* (3, $^-6$) and *P*(5, $^-6$)?

Find the difference between the *x*-coordinates. Subtract the smaller from the larger.

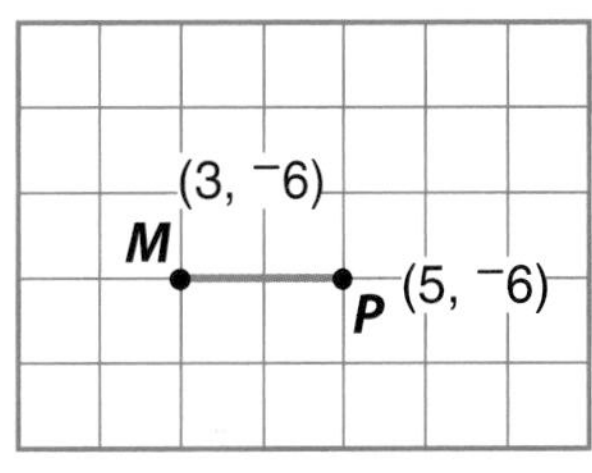

$5 - 3 = 2$

The horizontal line segment connecting *M* to *P* is 2 units long.

Check by counting the units on the grid.

USE YOUR SKILLS

Graph each pair of points. Then count units to find the length of the line segment.

1. (3, 9) (8, 9) **2.** (7, $^-4$) (9, $^-4$) **3.** (6, 5) (7, 5)

Subtract to find the length of the line segment that connects each pair of points.

4. (10, 2) (7, 2) **5.** (9, $^-7$) (5, $^-7$) **6.** (3, $^-8$) (5, $^-8$)

7. Investigate Do you need to use the *y*-coordinates to find the length of horizontal line segments? Explain.

KEY MG 2.2 Understand that the length of a horizontal line segment equals the difference of the *x*-coordinates.

MG 2.3 How do you find the length of vertical line segments using coordinates?

Read More
See Unit 10, Chapter 22, Lessons 3–4, pages 492–496, on lengths of horizontal and vertical line segments.

Connect It

A vertical line segment is parallel to the y-axis.
All the points on a vertical line have the same x-coordinate.

Example 1 What is the length of the vertical line segment that connects points $K(8, 7)$ and $L(8, 3)$?

Find the difference between the y-coordinates. Subtract the smaller from the larger.

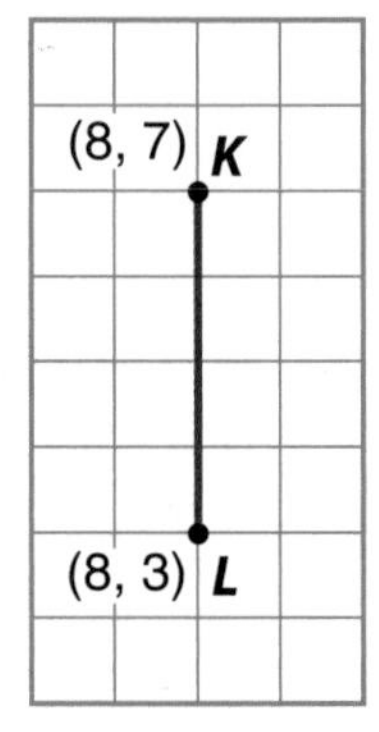

$7 - 3 = 4$

The vertical line segment connecting K to L is 4 units long.

Example 2 What is the length of the vertical line segment that connects points $R(^-9, 6)$ and $S(^-9, 4)$?

Find the difference between the y-coordinates. Subtract the smaller from the larger.

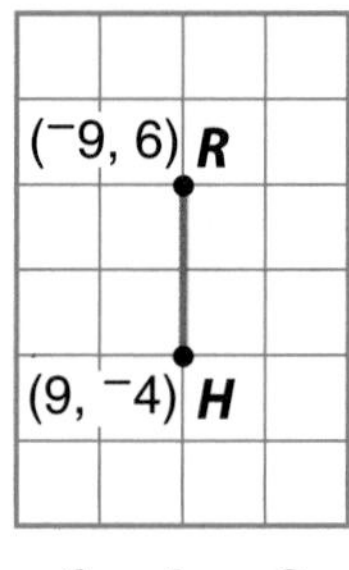

$6 - 4 = 2$

The vertical line segment connecting R to S is 2 units long.

Check by counting the units on the grid.

USE YOUR SKILLS

Graph each pair of points. Then count units to find the length of the line segment.

1. (3, 10) (3, 5) **2.** ($^-9$, 6) ($^-9$, 2) **3.** (6, 7) (6, 4)

Subtract to find the length of the line segment that connects each pair of points.

4. (2, 7) (2, 1) **5.** ($^-8$, 9) ($^-8$, 7) **6.** ($^-3$, 8) ($^-3$, 6)

7. Investigate Do you need to use the x-coordinates to find the length of vertical line segments? Explain.

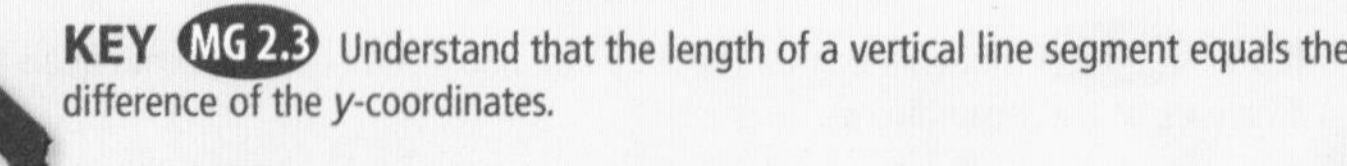
KEY MG 2.3 Understand that the length of a vertical line segment equals the difference of the y-coordinates.

Using the Table of Contents

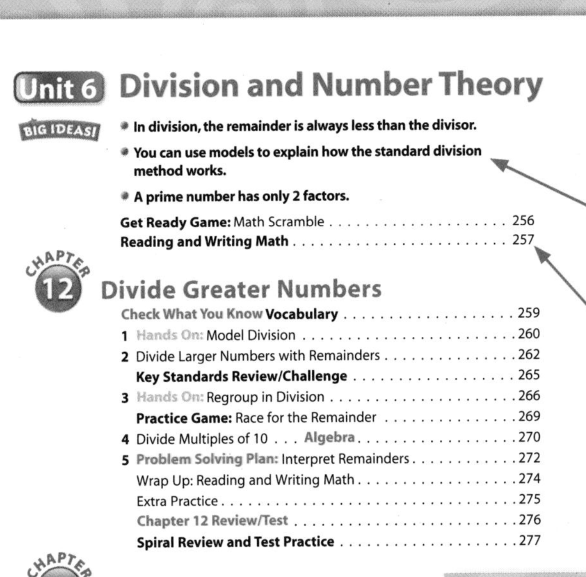

Unit 6 Division and Number Theory

BIG IDEAS!

- In division, the remainder is always less than the divisor.
- You can use models to explain how the standard division method works.
- A prime number has only 2 factors.

CHAPTER 13 Divide 3-Digit Numbers

TOC 12 Table of Contents

A table of contents helps you find special features in your math book.

Each unit teaches big ideas in math in 2–4 chapters. You get ready for the unit with a game!

Reading and writing can help you learn math.

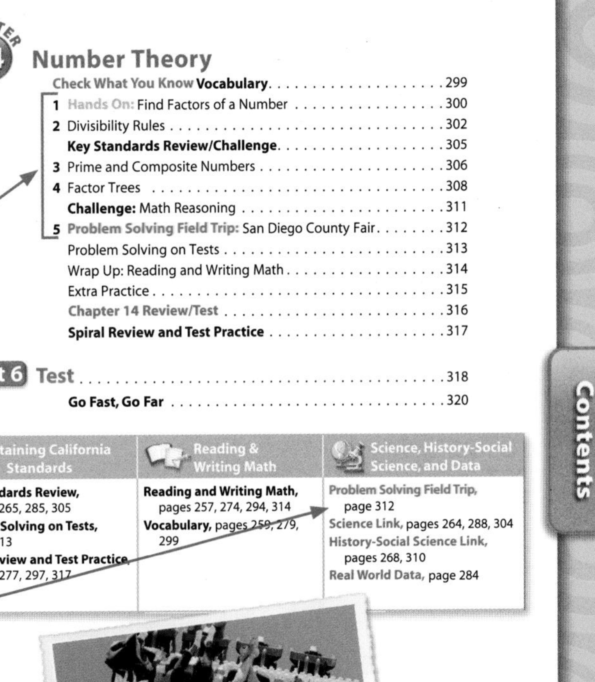

CHAPTER 14 Number Theory

Maintaining California Standards	Reading & Writing Math	Science, History-Social Science, and Data
Key Standards Review, pages 265, 285, 305 **Problem Solving on Tests,** page 313 **Spiral Review and Test Practice,** pages 277, 297, 317	**Reading and Writing Math,** pages 257, 274, 294, 314 **Vocabulary,** pages 259, 279, 299	**Problem Solving Field Trip,** page 312 **Science Link,** pages 264, 288, 304 **History-Social Science Link,** pages 268, 310 **Real World Data,** page 284

San Diego County Fair

Table of Contents TOC 13

All chapters have hands on and problem solving lessons.

Field Trips let you do math in special places in California.

Table of Contents

Unit 1 Numbers Through Millions

BIG IDEAS!

- **In large numbers, each group of three digits is separated by a comma, which makes the number easier to read.**
- **You can compare whole numbers using a number line and place value.**
- **Rounding can help you understand real world situations involving large numbers.**

Chapter 1 Place Value Through Millions

CHAPTER 2 Order and Round Numbers

Unit 1 Test

Contents

Maintaining California Standards	  Reading & Writing Math	 Science, History-Social Science, and Data
Key Standards Review, pages 11, 31 **Problem Solving on Tests,** page 19 **Spiral Review and Test Practice,** pages 23, 43	**Reading and Writing Math,** pages 3, 20, 40 **Vocabulary,** pages 5, 25	**Problem Solving Field Trip,** page 18 **Science Link,** pages 10, 36 **History-Social Science Link,** page 14 **Real World Data,** page 30

Unit 2 Addition and Subtraction

BIG IDEAS!

- **Addition and subtraction are related operations.**
- **Parentheses in expressions show which operation to perform first.**
- **Equals added to equals are equal.**

Chapter 3 Addition

Chapter 4 Subtraction

CHAPTER 5 Expressions and Equations

Contents

Unit 3 Multiplication and Division

- **Multiplication and division are related operations.**
- **The order of operations tells how to simplify an expression.**
- **Equals multiplied by equals are equals.**

Chapter 6 Relate Multiplication and Division

Contents

More Expressions and Equations

Unit 3 Test

Contents

Maintaining California Standards	Reading & Writing Math	Science, History-Social Science, and Data
Key Standards Review, pages 127, 147 **Problem Solving on Tests,** page 135 **Spiral Review and Test Practice,** pages 139, 159	**Reading and Writing Math,** pages 117, 136, 156 **Vocabulary,** pages 119, 141	**Problem Solving Field Trip,** page 134 **Science Link,** pages 126, 146 **History-Social Science Link,** page 132 **Real World Data,** page 150

Unit 4 Algebra and Functions

- **A letter or symbol used to stand for a number is called a variable.**
- **An equation with two variables can describe the rule for a function table.**

CHAPTER 8 Variables

Contents

Equations with Two Variables

Maintaining California Standards	 Reading & Writing Math	 Science, History-Social Science, and Data
Key Standards Review, pages 173, 195 **Problem Solving on Tests,** page 201 **Spiral Review and Test Practice,** pages 187, 205	**Reading and Writing Math,** pages 165, 182, 202 **Vocabulary,** pages 167, 189	**Problem Solving Field Trip,** page 200 **Science Link,** pages 172, 198 **History-Social Science Link,** page 178 **Real World Data,** page 194

Contents

Unit 5 Multiplication

- You can estimate to decide if your multiplication answer is reasonable.
- Basic facts, patterns, and the mulitplication properties help you multiply large numbers.

Multiply by 1-Digit Numbers

Contents

Multiply by 2-Digit Numbers

Maintaining California Standards	 Reading & Writing Math	 Science, History-Social Science, and Data
Key Standards Review, pages 219, 241 **Problem Solving on Tests,** page 227 **Spiral Review and Test Practice,** pages 231, 251	**Reading and Writing Math,** pages 211, 228, 248 **Vocabulary,** pages 213, 233	**Problem Solving Field Trip,** page 226 **Science Link,** pages 218, 240 **History-Social Science Link,** page 244 **Real World Data,** page 222

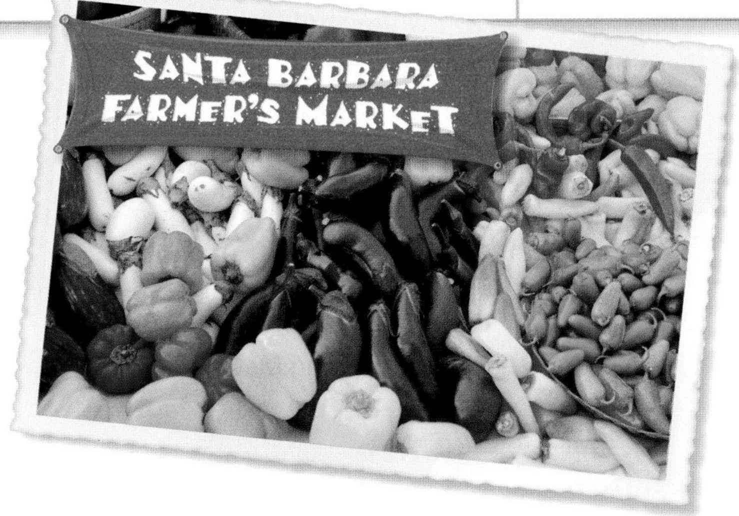

Contents

Unit 6 Division and Number Theory

BIG IDEAS!

- **In division, the remainder is always less than the divisor.**
- **You can use models to explain how the standard division method works.**
- **A prime number has only 2 factors.**

Chapter 12 Divide Greater Numbers

Chapter 13 Divide 3-Digit Numbers

Number Theory

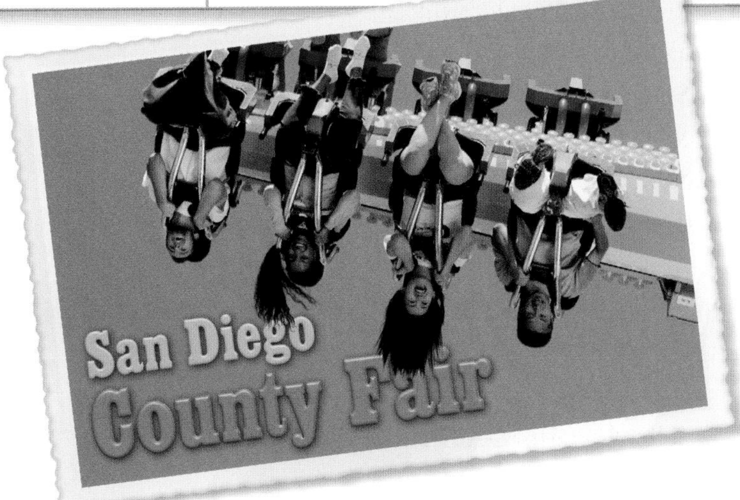

Contents

Unit 7 Measurement and Negative Numbers

- **When you convert larger units to smaller units, you multiply. When you convert smaller units to larger units, you divide.**
- **For every positive number, there is an opposite negative number.**

Units of Measurement

Contents

Temperature and Negative Numbers

Maintaining California Standards	 Reading & Writing Math	Science, History-Social Science, and Data
Key Standards Review, pages 331, 355 **Problem Solving on Tests,** page 357 **Spiral Review and Test Practice,** pages 345, 361	**Reading and Writing Math,** pages 323, 342, 358 **Vocabulary,** pages 325, 347	**Problem Solving Field Trip,** page 356 **Science Link,** pages 330, 351 **History-Social Science Link,** page 354 **Real World Data,** page 338

Contents

Unit 8 Fractions and Mixed Numbers

- **Fractions can show parts of a whole, parts of a set, or the division of whole numbers by whole numbers.**
- **Equivalent fractions have the same value.**
- **You can compare and order fractions and mixed numbers on a number line.**

Fractions

Contents

Compare and Order Fractions

Maintaining California Standards	 Reading & Writing Math	 Science, History-Social Science, and Data
Key Standards Review, pages 383, 403 **Problem Solving on Tests,** page 405 **Spiral Review and Test Practice,** pages 389, 409	**Reading and Writing Math,** pages 367, 386, 406 **Vocabulary,** pages 369, 391	**Problem Solving Field Trip,** page 404 **Science Link,** pages 382, 402 **History-Social Science Link,** page 396 **Real World Data,** page 378

Contents

Unit 9 Decimals

- **Decimal place values get smaller as you read farther to the right of a decimal point.**
- **You can use a number line to compare decimals to whole numbers, fractions, and mixed numbers.**
- **You can add and subtract decimals like whole numbers if the decimal points are lined up.**

Understand Decimals

Add and Subtract Decimals

Contents

Maintaining California Standards	 Reading & Writing Math	 Science, History-Social Science, and Data
Key Standards Review, pages 423, 445 **Problem Solving on Tests,** page 433 **Spiral Review and Test Practice,** pages 437, 457	**Reading and Writing Math,** pages 415, 434, 454 **Vocabulary,** pages 417, 439	**Problem Solving Field Trip,** page 432 **Science Link,** pages 422, 450 **History-Social Science Link,** pages 430, 444

Unit 10 Graphs and Algebra

BIG IDEAS!

- The location of every point on a coordinate grid can be shown by an ordered pair.
- You can graph ordered pairs and connect the points to draw lines or line segments.
- The coordinate plane is formed by two intersecting perpendicular lines called axes.

Chapter 21 Graphs and Ordered Pairs

Contents

Integers on a Coordinate Grid

Maintaining California Standards	 Reading & Writing Math	 Science, History-Social Science, and Data
Key Standards Review, pages 475, 491 **Problem Solving on Tests,** page 499 **Spiral Review and Test Practice,** pages 483, 503	**Reading and Writing Math,** pages 463, 480, 500 **Vocabulary,** pages 465, 485	**Problem Solving Field Trip,** page 498 **Science Link,** pages 474, 496 **History-Social Science Link,** page 490 **Real World Data,** page 470

Contents

Unit 11 Statistics and Probability

BIG IDEAS!

- **You can use line plots, coordinate graphs, tables, and charts to display and organize data.**
- ***Mode* and *median* are two ways to describe what is typical in a set of data.**
- **You can describe the probability of each outcome of a situation.**

Chapter 23 Data

Contents

Probability

Maintaining California Standards	 Reading & Writing Math	 Science, History-Social Science, and Data
Key Standards Review, pages 523, 543 **Problem Solving on Tests,** page 545 **Spiral Review and Test Practice,** pages 529, 549	**Reading and Writing Math,** pages 509, 526, 546 **Vocabulary,** pages 511, 531	**Problem Solving Field Trip,** page 544 **Science Link,** pages 522, 542 **Real World Data,** pages 516, 536

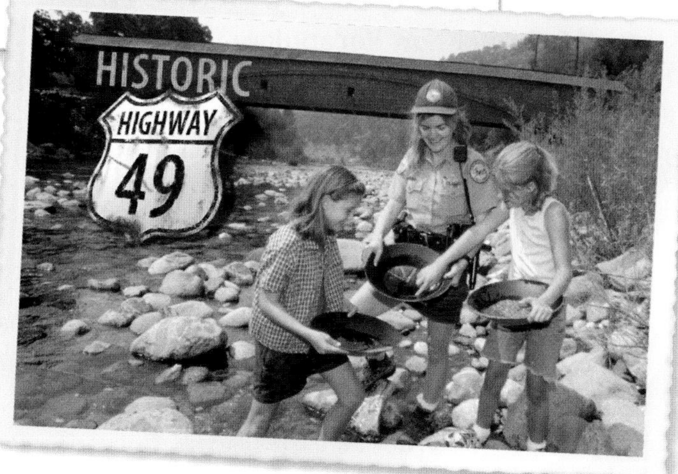

Contents

Unit 12 Geometry and Measurement

BIG IDEAS!

- **You can define and classify plane figures. You can describe and model solid figures by relating them to plane figures.**
- **You can make drawings, measure, and use formulas to show how perimeter and area relate.**

Chapter 25 Plane Figures

Chapter 26 Congruence and Symmetry

CHAPTER 27 Perimeter and Area

CHAPTER 28 Solid Figures

Maintaining California Standards	Reading & Writing Math	Science, History-Social Science, and Data
Key Standards Review, pages 563, 587, 607, 631 **Problem Solving on Tests,** page 573 **Spiral Review and Test Practice,** pages 577, 597, 617, 637	**Reading and Writing Math,** pages 555, 574, 594, 614, 634 **Vocabulary,** pages 557, 579, 599, 619	**Problem Solving Field Trip,** page 572 **Science Link,** pages 570, 586, 610, 630 **History-Social Science Link,** page 624 **Real World Data,** pages 562, 590, 606

Contents

Back to School

Welcome!

Scientists, athletes, artists, and health-care workers all use math every day—and you will too. This year in math you'll learn about numbers, patterns, shapes, and different ways to measure. You'll use the mathematics you know to solve problems and describe objects and patterns you see. You can get started by finding out about yourself as a mathematician and about the other students in your class.

Real Life Connection

Collecting Data

About Me

Write your math autobiography by answering these questions. You can draw a picture to go with your autobiography, if you want.

- Tell about a time you first remember doing math, even if you were very young.
- What are you good at in math?
- What would you like to improve or know more about?
- How do you (or someone in your family) use math outside of math class?

About My Class

Your classmates may be just like you in some ways and different in other ways. You can collect data to find out something about the whole class.

- Think of one topic you'd like to know about all your classmates.
- Write a survey question for your topic.
- Take a survey among your classmates. Use tally marks to collect the data.
- Make a bar graph or picture graph to show your results.
- Use your graph and data to write what you learned about your class.

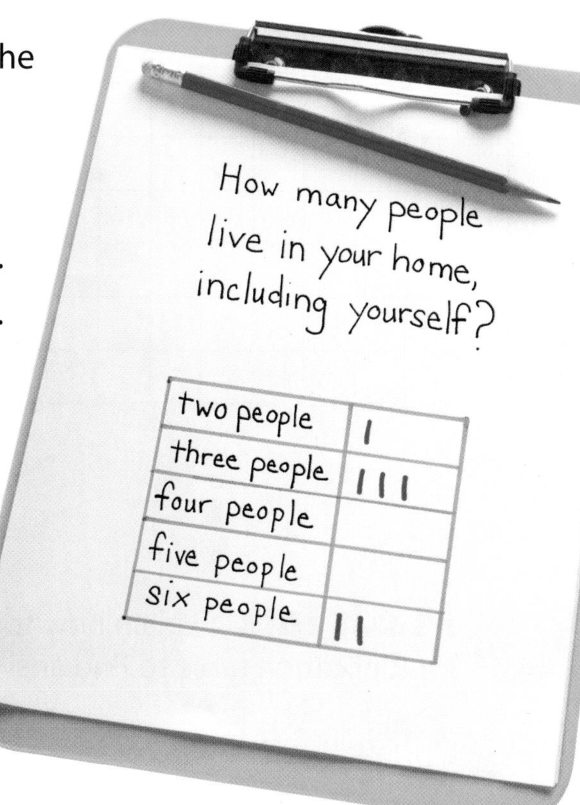

How many people live in your home, including yourself?
two people | I
three people | III
four people
five people
six people | II

Problem Solving and Numbers

Objective Review basic number and problem-solving skills

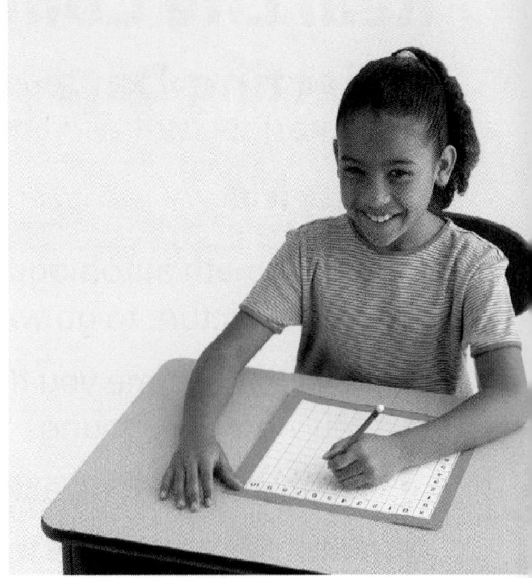

Review and Remember

In this lesson, you will review the basic multiplication and division facts. You will also use basic facts to solve problems.

Guided Practice

1. Copy and complete a multiplication table like this one.

2. Highlight any facts that gave you trouble. These are facts to practice and learn.

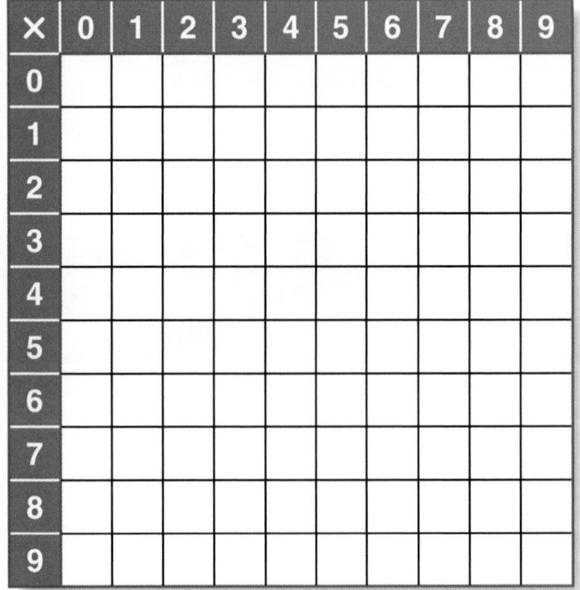

×	0	1	2	3	4	5	6	7	8	9
0										
1										
2										
3										
4										
5										
6										
7										
8										
9										

Ask Yourself

What strategies and patterns can I use to complete the table?

Divide.

1. 45 ÷ 5
2. 42 ÷ 7
3. 2 ÷ 2
4. 56 ÷ 8
5. 36 ÷ 6

Math Talk Explain how to use your completed multiplication table to find answers to division facts.

Practice and Problem Solving

Multiply or divide.

6. 6×4 **7.** $54 \div 9$ **8.** 7×7 **9.** $35 \div 5$ **10.** 6×8

Solve each problem. Choose the strategy and computation method that works best for the problem.

11. How many students and teachers are in your classroom right now?

12. How many human elbows and knees are in your classroom right now? Explain how you found your answer.

13. An after-school group found that there were 28 elbows and knees. How many people were in that group?

14. **Multistep** Suppose that 15 students in your class are 10 years old and the rest are 9 years old. How many years have all the students in your class been living?

15. In one class, students built a pyramid. They put 9 cans on the bottom row, 8 cans on the next row up, and 7 cans on the third row. They continued building until they put 1 can on the top row. How many cans did they use in the entire pyramid?

Spiral Review and Test Practice

Write each number in word form. (Grade 3)

16. 7 hundreds, 6 tens, 5 ones **17.** 120 **18.** $300 + 90 + 2$

Write the letter of the correct answer.

19. Paula bought 8 beads for 7¢ each and 2 bracelets for $3 each. How much did she spend? (Grade 3)

A 56¢ **B** 62¢ **C** $3.62 **D** $6.56

Back to School

Measurement

Objective Review basic measurement skills.

Explore

You can use math to describe objects in your classroom. First, review how to measure length with a ruler.

Work with a partner. Estimate the length of the pencil below to the nearest inch. Record your estimate; then measure.

Vocabulary

centimeter (cm)

foot (ft)

inch (in.)

meter (m)

yard (yd)

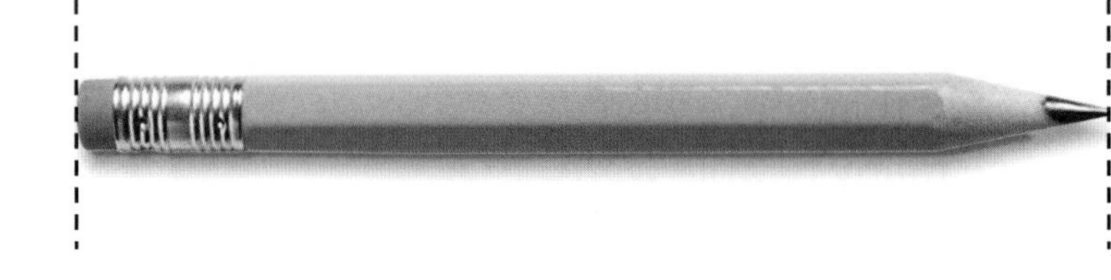

1 Line up the left end of the pencil with the zero mark of the inch ruler. If there is no zero mark, line up the pencil with the end of the ruler.

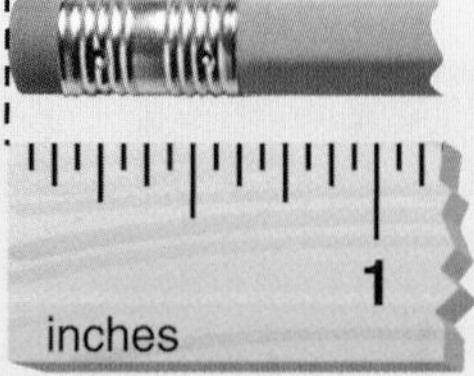

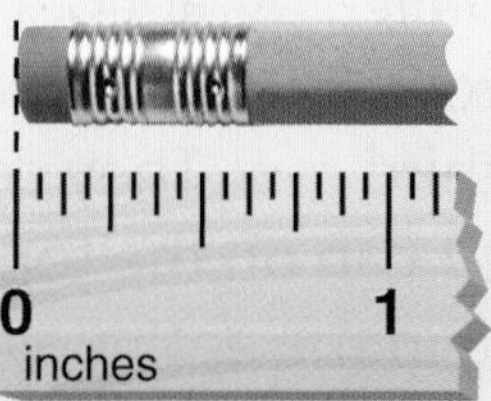

2 Find the inch mark closest to the right end of the pencil.

- What is the length of the pencil to the nearest inch?
- How close is your measurement to your estimate?

Repeat the steps above to estimate and measure the length of the pencil to the nearest centimeter.

Extend

Find 3 classroom objects to measure. Copy each table. Then follow the directions.

- Estimate the length of each object to the nearest inch. Record your estimate.
- Measure the object. Record your measurement.

	Object	My Estimate	Length to the Nearest Inch
1.			
2.			
3.			

- Estimate the length of each object to the nearest centimeter. Record your estimate.
- Measure the object. Record your measurement.

	Object	My Estimate	Length to the Nearest Centimeter
4.			
5.			
6.			

12 inches = 1 foot
3 feet = 1 yard
100 centimeters = 1 meter

Use an inch ruler, a centimeter ruler, a yardstick, or a meterstick to solve each problem.

7. Find three objects that you estimate are each about 1 foot long. Measure each object to check your estimate.

8. Find 3 objects that you estimate are about 20 centimeters long. Measure each object to check your estimate.

9. Find an object about 1 yard long or wide. Measure to check your estimate.

10. Find an object about 1 meter long or wide. Measure to check your estimate.

Writing Math

11. Describe how to find the length of the pencil.

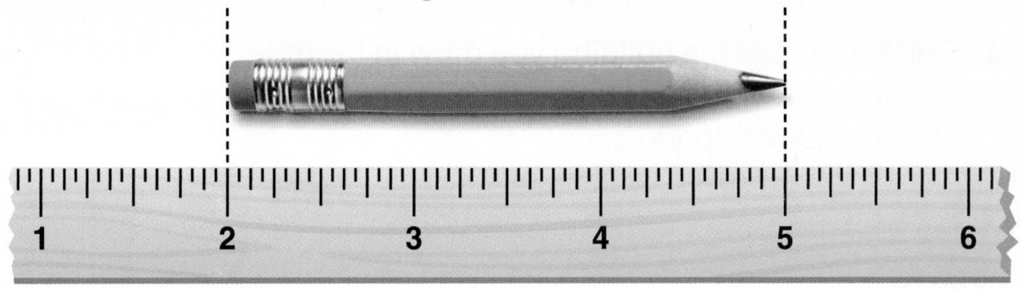

Back to School

Math Connection

Geometric Pieces

Vocabulary

area

perimeter

Materials
grid paper

The figure below was made by tracing around two rectangles on grid paper.

Can you find each rectangle?

Compare your answer with a classmate.

The distance around any figure is called the **perimeter**.

Find the perimeter of this figure.

Can you find the perimeter in more than one way?

How do you label your answer?

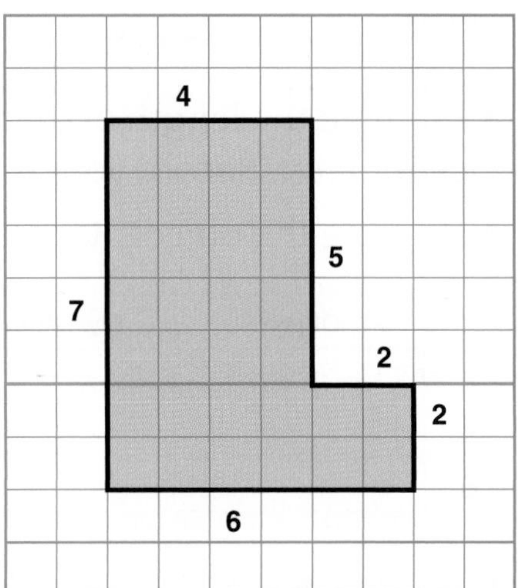

The **area** of a figure is the number of square units needed to cover the figure without overlapping.

Find the area of the figure at the right.

Can you find the area in more than one way?

How do you label your answer?

Use grid paper. Follow the directions.

1. Draw a rectangle. Find its perimeter and area.
2. Draw a figure that combines two rectangles or squares. Find the perimeter and area of the entire figure.
3. Draw the front of a rectangular apartment building. Put in doors and windows. Use other geometric shapes to finish your picture.
4. Find the area of the building you drew in Exercise 3. The area of the building should NOT include the area of the windows or doors.

Unit

1

Numbers Through Millions

BIG IDEAS!

- In very large numbers, each group of three digits is separated by a comma, which makes the numbers easier to read.
- You can compare whole numbers using a number line and place value.
- Rounding can help you understand real world situations involving very large numbers.

Chapter 1
Place Value Through Millions

Chapter 2
Order and Round Numbers

Songs and Games

Math Music Track 1: *Counting the Days*
eGames at
www.eduplace.com/camap/

Math Readers

Make It Greater

Object of the Game Use place value to make a greater number than the other player.

Materials
- 2 number cubes labeled 1–6
- 2 number cubes labeled 4–9
- recording sheet

Set Up
Make two recording sheets. Draw four boxes for Round 1. Repeat for ten or more rounds of play.

Number of Players 2

How to Play

1. Player 1 tosses the four number cubes and writes the digits in the blanks on the recording sheet, trying to make the greatest number possible.

Round 1	6,	4	3	1
Round 2	,			
Round 3	,			
Round 4	,			

2. Player 2 repeats Step 1.

3. Players read their 4-digit numbers aloud and compare them. The player with the greater number wins the round and circles the winning number on the recording sheet. If players make the same number, the round is a tie.

4. Players follow Steps 1-3 for each round of play. The first player to win five rounds is the winner.

CA Standards
KEY NS 1.2 Order and compare whole numbers and decimals to two decimal places.

Education Place
Visit www.eduplace.com/camap/ for **Brain Teasers** and **eGames** to play.

Reading Before reading a story or article, you can preview it to get an idea of what it is about and how it's organized. You can also preview a math lesson.

Michaela previewed Lesson 1 on pages 6–7. This is what she found.

Lesson 1 Preview

- ✓ Lesson title: How Big Is 1 Million?
- ✓ Special kind of lesson: Hands On
- ✓ Objective (what you will learn): Relate one million to hundreds and thousands.
- ✓ Vocabulary (highlighted words): million
- ✓ Main headings: Explore, Extend
- ✓ Special sections: Writing Math
- ✓ Special features: Numbered steps, tables

This is a hands-on lesson. I'll be exploring the size of 1 million. I'll follow the numbered steps.

Writing Use the checklist to preview another lesson. See if the lesson includes the items listed in **red type**. Then write a sentence or two telling what you think the lesson is about or what you expect to do or learn.

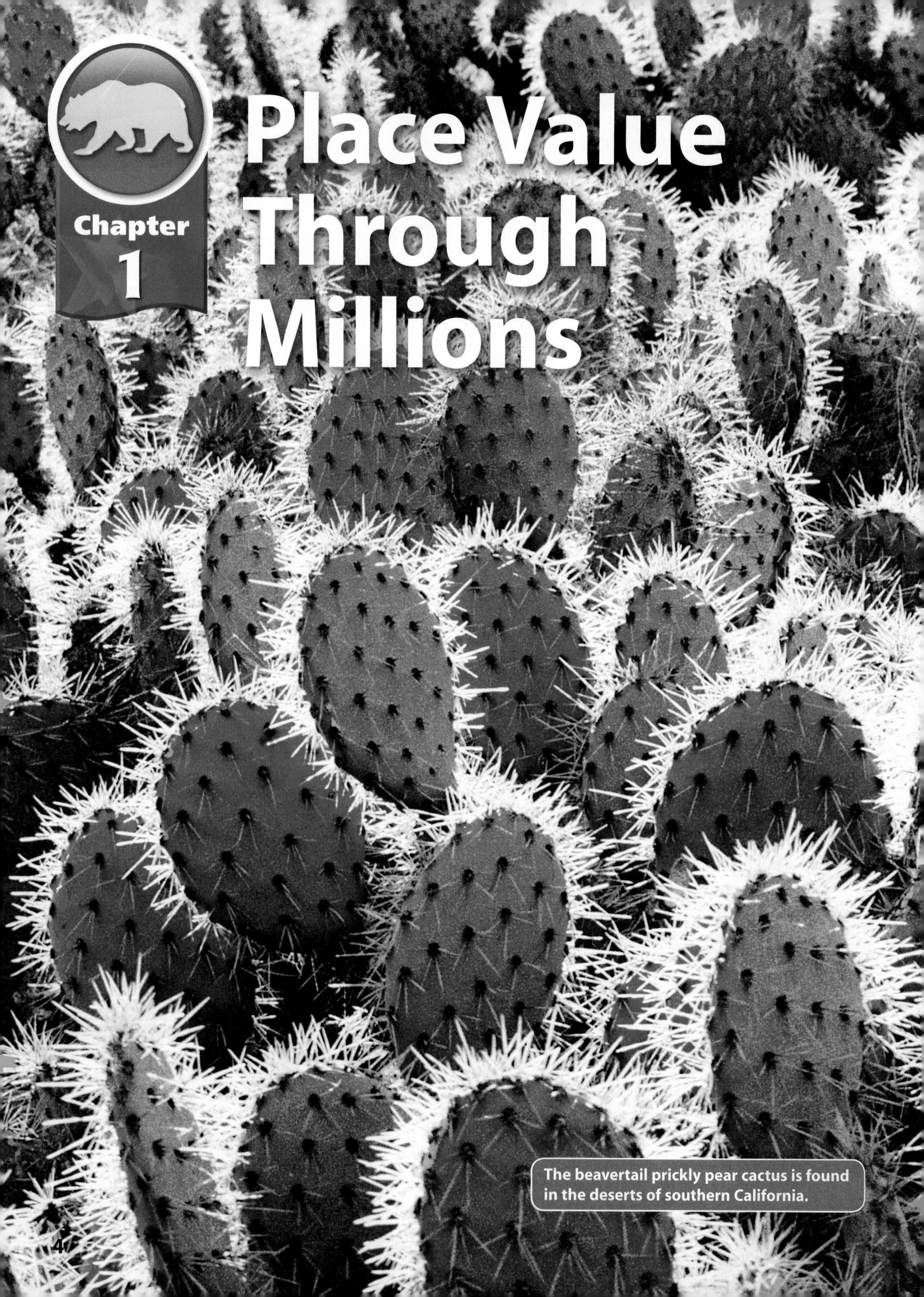

Chapter 1

Place Value Through Millions

The beavertail prickly pear cactus is found in the deserts of southern California.

Check What You Know

Vocabulary and Concepts GRADE 3 KEY NS 1.3, NS 1.0, MR 2.3

Choose the best word to complete the sentence.

Word Bank
- digits
- hundreds
- place value
- thousands

1. In the number 3,245, the 2 is in the ____ place.
2. Numbers are written with the ____ 0, 1, 2, 3, 4, 5, 6, 7, 8, and 9.

Skills GRADE 3 KEY NS 1.5

Write the number in two other ways.

3. 7,206
4. eight hundred twenty-five
5. 9,000 + 100 + 90 + 8

Write the value of the underlined digit in word form.

6. 30<u>1</u>
7. 5,<u>4</u>12
8. <u>6</u>,002
9. 3,8<u>3</u>0

Problem Solving and Reasoning GRADE 3 NS 1.0

10. What is the greatest number that can be made using the digits 2, 5, 1, and 3?

Vocabulary

Visualize It!

word form
uses words only
six thousand, three hundred twenty-eight

Different Ways to Write a Number

standard form
uses digits only
6,328

expanded notation
shows the value of each digit
6,000 + 300 + 20 + 8

Language Tips

The word *standard* has many meanings. In mathematics, when you write a number in *standard form*, you write the number using only digits.

Words that look alike in English and Spanish often have the same meaning.

English	Spanish
form	forma
digit	dígito
value	valor
comma	coma

See **English-Spanish Glossary** pages 644–666.

Education Place Visit www.eduplace.com/camap/ for the **eGlossary** and **eGames**.

CA Standards MR 2.3 Use a variety of methods, such as words, numbers, symbols, charts, graphs, tables, diagrams, and models, to explain mathematical reasoning. **Also NS 1.0**

LESSON 1

CA Standards
KEY NS 1.1 Read and write whole numbers in the millions.

Also MR1.1, MR 2.0, MR 2.3

Vocabulary

million

Materials
10 pages of a newspaper (for each team)

Hands On
How Big Is 1 Million?

Objective Relate one million to hundreds and thousands.

Explore

Question Could you read 1,000,000 words in a day? How big is 1 **million**?

Divide your class into 10 teams to find out.

1 Count and circle 100 words in a newspaper article. Write "100 words" on the circle. Use estimation to circle 9 more groups of 100 words until you have 1,000 words circled.

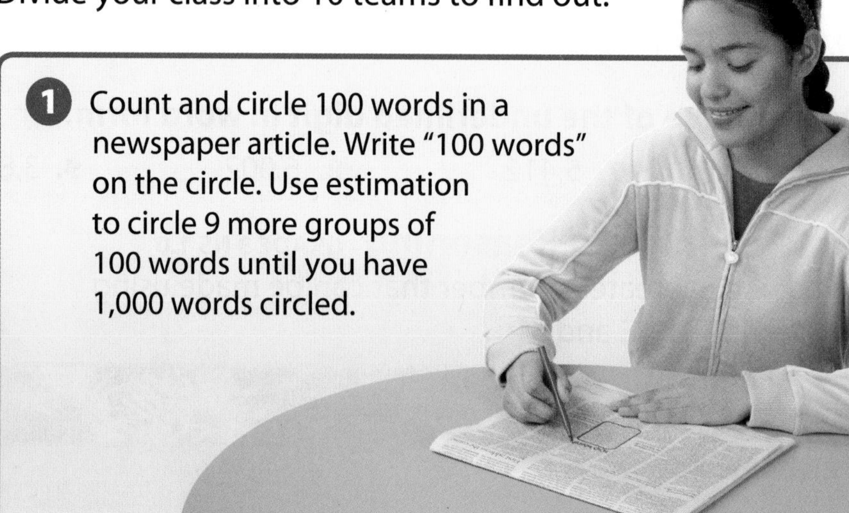

2 Use estimation to circle 1,000 words on each of nine more pages. Make a table like the one shown. Fill in the first row.

One Class		
Number of Teams	Pages Altogether	Words Altogether
1	10	10,000
2		
10		

3 Put your 10 pages together with 10 pages from another team. Fill in the second row of your table. Then combine all the pages from the whole class. Complete your table.

Spread out the pages from all teams. Look at the number of circled words. One million words is 10 times the number of words you see!

4 Suppose 10 classes combined pages. Use a table to record how many pages and how many words there are altogether.

Ten Classes		
Number of Classes	Pages Altogether	Words Altogether
1	100	100,000
2	200	200,000
3		
10		

Extend

Use your completed tables to answer the questions.

1. How many pages did your class use altogether?
2. How many pages would 6 classes use altogether?
3. About how many words would 4 classes circle altogether?

Use your tables to find the number of hundreds in the number.

4. 1,000
5. 10,000
6. 100,000
7. 1,000,000

Use your tables to find the number of thousands in the number.

8. 10,000
9. 100,000
10. 1,000,000
11. 1,000

12. Describe the patterns you see in your tables.

Writing Math

Write About It Do you think you could read 1,000,000 words in one day? About how many newspaper pages would you have to read?

LESSON 2

CA Standards
KEY NS 1.0 Students understand the place value of whole numbers and decimals to two decimal places and how whole numbers and decimals relate to simple fractions. Students use the concepts of negative numbers.

Also MR 1.0, MR 1.1, MR 2.0, MR 2.3, MR 2.4

Vocabulary

digit
period
standard form
word form

Materials
Workmat 2

Place Value Through Hundred Thousands

Objective Read and write numbers through 999,999.

Learn by Example

A **digit** is any one of the ten number symbols—0, 1, 2, 3, 4, 5, 6, 7, 8, 9. The value of a digit depends on its place in a number.

In the year 2000, the population of Bakersfield, California, was 271,035. What does the number 271,035 mean?

The number 271,035 has six digits. You can use a place-value chart to understand the value of the digits in 271,035.

Using a Place-Value Chart

Start at the right of the place-value chart. The value of each place, or column, is 10 times the value of the place to its right. So, the value of the digit 7 is 7 ten thousands, or 70,000.

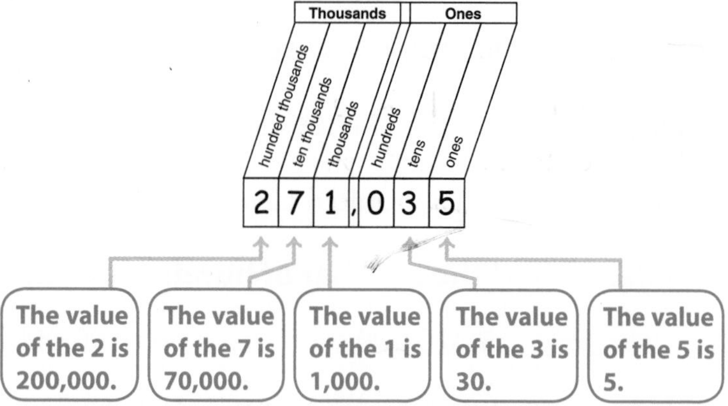
Thousands
Ones
hundred thousands
ten thousands
thousands
hundreds
tens
ones
2 7 1 , 0 3 5
The value of the 2 is 200,000.
The value of the 7 is 70,000.
The value of the 1 is 1,000.
The value of the 3 is 30.
The value of the 5 is 5.

Each group of 3 digits, separated by a comma, is called a **period**. The periods help you read 271,035.

Read the number in the thousands period and then say *thousand*. Then read the number in the ones period, but do not say the word *one*.

Say: two hundred seventy-one *thousand*, thirty-five.

You can express this number in two ways.

standard form	271,035
word form	two hundred seventy-one thousand, thirty-five

Guided Practice

Write the number in word form. Use Workmat 2 to help you.

1. 124,662 **2.** 950,127 **3.** 608,509

Write the number in standard form.

4. one hundred forty thousand, six hundred eighteen

5. five hundred thirty thousand, twelve

Write the value of the underlined digit.

6. <u>7</u>02,209 **7.** 4<u>1</u>0,494 **8.** 436,<u>0</u>80

Ask Yourself

- How can the thousands and ones periods help me write a number in word form?
- When do I use a zero?

Guided Problem Solving

Use the questions to solve this problem.

9. Robert has four number cards. He needs to choose a number card using these clues:

- 8 in the hundred thousands place
- 5 in the ten thousands place
- 9 in the thousands place

Which number should Robert choose?

598,230

895,023

855,932

859,023

a. Understand What is Robert's task?

b. Plan What information does Robert have? How should he use that information?

c. Solve Check each of the numbers against each clue. Which number matches all the clues?

d. Look Back Did Robert need to check every number against every clue? Why?

Math Talk Do both 4s in the number 468,452 have the same value? Explain your answer.

Practice and Problem Solving

Write the number in word form. Use Workmat 2 to help you.

10. 561,328 **11.** 290,615 **12.** 994,720 **13.** 708,780

Write the number in standard form.

14. three hundred four thousand

15. three hundred thousand, four

16. six hundred thirteen thousand, one hundred ninety-nine

Write the value of the underlined digit.

17. 6$\underline{3}$9,572 **18.** $\underline{9}$56,112 **19.** 2$\underline{1}$2,048 **20.** 89$\underline{0}$,973

Science Link

Use the Fun Facts to solve Problems 21–24.

21. Mount St. Helens erupted in 1980. Before the eruption, its height was 9,677 feet. How many feet shorter is the mountain now?

22. The height of which volcano has a 0 in the thousands place?

23. The height of which volcano has a 0 in the ones place?

24. **Explain** The digit 4 occurs two times in the altitude of Mount Rainier. What is the value of each 4? Explain your answer.

Cascade Range Volcanoes

- A volcano is a hill or mountain that surrounds an opening in Earth's surface through which ash, molten rock, and gases erupt.
- Volcanoes are mountains, but not all mountains are volcanoes.
- The height of a volcano changes after each eruption. The table shows the current heights of the volcanoes.

Name	State	Height (ft)
Lassen Peak	CA	10,457
Mt. Rainier	WA	14,410
Mt. Shasta	CA	14,161
Mt. St. Helens	WA	8,364

Science ES 5.a

Spiral Review and Test Practice

Divide. Use multiplication to check. GRADE 3 KEY NS 2.3, NS 2.5

25. $465 \div 5$ **26.** $369 \div 3$ **27.** $168 \div 8$ **28.** $420 \div 6$

Write the letter of the correct answer. NS 1.0

29. A new building will cost about seven hundred twenty-five thousand dollars. What is this number in standard form?

A \$702,500 **B** \$700,025 **C** \$725,000 **D** \$700,250

Extra Practice See page 21, Set A.

Key Standards Review

Identify the value of the underlined digit. GRADE 3 KEY NS 1.3

1. $5,\underline{6}32$ **2.** $\underline{9},854$ **3.** $10,0\underline{0}0$

4. $3,20\underline{1}$ **5.** $\underline{2}7$ **6.** $\underline{9}99$

> **Hint**
> The **perimeter** is the distance around a figure.

Find the perimeter of the polygon. GRADE 3 KEY MG 1.3

7.

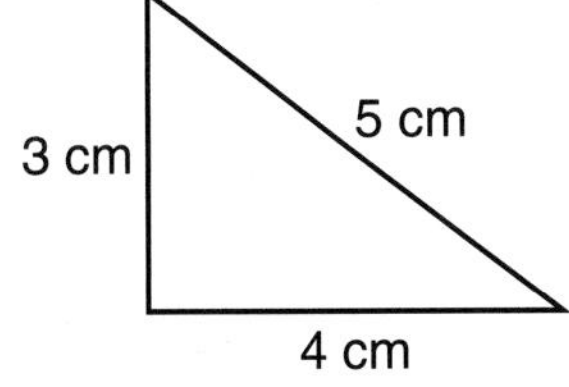

8.

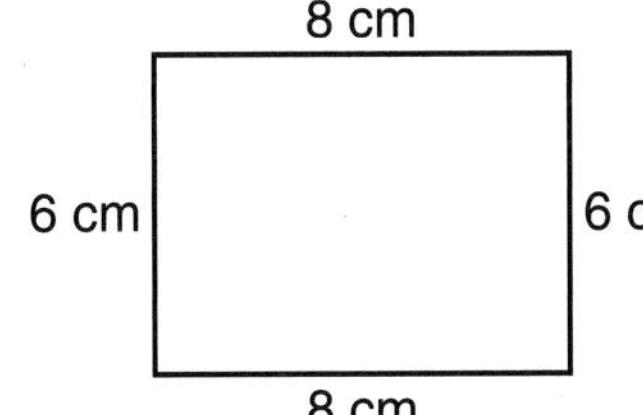

9.

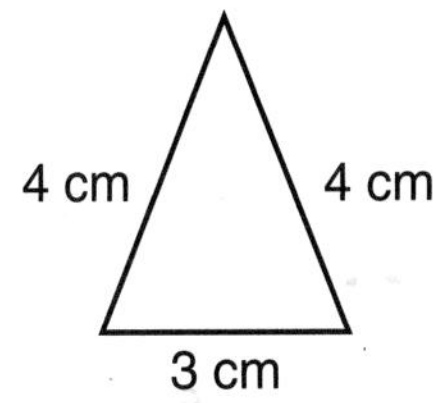

Challenge — Math Reasoning

Mystery Number NS 1.0

Use the clues to find the mystery number.

1. Clues:

- Its hundreds digit is 0.
- Its hundred thousands digit is two times its ten thousands digit.
- The sum of its ones and tens digit is 9.
- Its thousands digit is 1.
- Its tens digit is 5 less than its ones digit.
- Its hundred thousands digit is one more than its ones digit.

2. Clues:

- Its hundred thousands digit is 3 less than its ten thousands digit.
- Its thousands digit is 3 more than its ten thousands digit.
- Its hundreds digit is 1.
- Its ones digit is the same as its hundred thousands digit.
- Its tens digit is one more than its hundreds digit.
- Its ten thousands digit is 6.

LESSON 3

CA Standards
KEY NS 1.1 Read and write whole numbers in the millions.
Also NS 1.0, MR 2.0, MR 2.2, MR 2.3, MR 2.4

Materials
Workmat 2

Place Value Through Hundred Millions

Objective Read and write numbers through 999,999,999.

Learn by Example

The table shows the estimated populations of the three West Coast states in 2005.

State	Population
California	36,132,147
Oregon	3,641,056
Washington	6,287,759

In the year 2005, the population of Oregon was 3,641,056. What do the digits in this number mean?

Think
Remember, each group of 3 digits separated by a comma is called a **period**.

The patterns in the place-value chart for whole numbers continues for larger and larger numbers. The value of each place is 10 times the value of the place to its right.

Millions			Thousands			Ones		
hundred millions	ten millions	millions	hundred thousands	ten thousands	thousands	hundreds	tens	ones
		3,	6	4	1,	0	5	6

The value of the 3 is 3,000,000.
The value of the 6 is 600,000.
The value of the 4 is 40,000.
The value of the 1 is 1,000.
The value of the 5 is 50.
The value of the 6 is 6.

The periods help you read 3,641,056. Read the number in the millions period first, and then say *million*. Next, read the number in the thousands period, and say *thousand*. Then read the number in the ones period, but do not say the word *one*.

Say: three *million*, six hundred forty-one *thousand*, fifty-six.

You can express this number in two ways.

standard form 3,641,056

word form three million, six hundred forty-one thousand, fifty-six

Another Example

Use the periods to read the numbers.

Millions			Thousands			Ones		
hundred millions	ten millions	millions	hundred thousands	ten thousands	thousands	hundreds	tens	ones
	8	6,	1	3	2,	1	4	7
5	1	0,	6	0	4,	2	2	9

Say: eighty-six *million*, one hundred thirty-two *thousand*, one hundred forty-seven.

Say: five hundred ten *million*, six hundred four *thousand*, two hundred twenty-nine.

Guided Practice

Write the number in word form. Use Workmat 2 to help you.

1. 5,316,517 **2.** 803,059,275 **3.** 28,000,001

Write the number in standard form.

4. four million, two hundred thirty-five thousand, three

5. eight hundred seventy million, thirty

Write the value of the underlined digit.

6. 53,435,910 **7.** 940,749,908 **8.** 829,475,292

Ask Yourself

- How can the periods help me write a number in word form?
- When do I use a zero in a number?

Math Talk Which digit in 376,459,218 has the greatest value? Write its value. Which digit has the least value? Write its value. Explain how you know.

Practice and Problem Solving

Write the number in word form. Use Workmat 2 to help you.

9. 6,007,002 **10.** 911,394,116 **11.** 36,707,242

Write the number in standard form.

12. seven hundred eight million, nine hundred ninety-three thousand, one hundred forty

13. twelve million, seven thousand, eight hundred forty-five

Write the value of the underlined digit.

14. <u>7</u>,990,841 **15.** 2<u>5</u>3,895,227 **16.** 608,068,08<u>6</u>

17. 8,0<u>3</u>2,563 **18.** <u>3</u>65,223,389 **19.** 532,8<u>2</u>1,075

History–Social Science Link

Use the table to solve.

20. What is the value of the 6 in the quantity of Kansas quarters released?

21. Write the total number of California quarters released in 2005 in word form.

22. For which state were seven hundred twenty million, two hundred thousand quarters released?

23. For which state were the least number of quarters released?

24. For which state were the greatest number of quarters released?

25. Choose one number from the table. Change one digit of that number. Explain how the value of the number changed.

State Quarters

The 50 State Quarters Program began in 1999. The back of each state quarter shows an important image in the state's history.

John Muir came to California in 1868. He was one of the founders of the Sierra Club and helped create some of California's National Parks.

State	Quantity	Released
California	520,400,000	January 2005
Kansas	563,400,000	August 2005
Minnesota	488,000,000	April 2005
Oregon	720,200,000	June 2005
West Virginia	721,600,000	October 2005

History-Social Science 4.4.3

Spiral Review and Test Practice

Divide. GRADE 3 NS 2.0

26. 10 ÷ 10 **27.** 6 ÷ 3 **28.** 8 ÷ 2 **29.** 7 ÷ 1

Write the letter of the correct answer. KEY NS 1.1

30. Which of these is the number 567,890,000?

A five hundred sixty-seven million, eight hundred thousand, ninety
B five hundred sixty-seven million, eight hundred ninety thousand
C five hundred million, six hundred seventy thousand, eight hundred ninety
D five hundred sixty-seven million, eight hundred thousand, nine hundred

Extra Practice See page 21, Set B.

Math Works! Webmaster

Manage a Website

Ted is a webmaster. He collects data on the number of hits to different websites.

The table at the right shows the number of hits to a website for the last six months.

Month	Number of Hits
March	865,000
April	412,500
May	679,800
June	349,200
July	1,209,500
August	759,999

Use the table to answer Problems 1–8.

1. Which month had more than a million hits?
2. Which month had the least number of hits?
3. Which month had four hundred twelve thousand, five hundred hits?
4. Look at the number for June. What is the value of the digit 9?
5. Which number in the table has a 7 in the ten thousands place?
6. Which number in the table has an 8 in the hundred thousands place?
7. Which number in the table does not have a 0 in the ones place?
8. In which number does the digit 5 have the greatest value? Explain.

CA Standards
NS 1.0, KEY NS 1.1, MR 1.1, MR 3.2

LESSON 4

CA Standards
KEY NS 1.1 Read and write whole numbers in the millions.
Also NS 1.0, MR 1.1, MR 2.0, MR 2.3, MR 2.4

Vocabulary

expanded notation

Materials
- Workmat 2
- Workmat 5

Expanded Notation

Objective Write numbers in expanded notation and understand the value of zero in numbers.

Learn by Example

Expanded notation is an expression that shows a number as the sum of the values of each digit except 0 in a number.

10,950 fans came to the basketball stadium to watch the Los Angeles Lakers play.

Different Ways to Write a Number in Expanded Notation

Way 1 Use a place-value chart.

Use the chart to find the value of each digit except 0. Write an expression to show the sum.

10,000 + 900 + 50

Thousands			Ones		
hundred thousands	ten thousands	thousands	hundreds	tens	ones
	1	0,	9	5	0

The value of the 1 is 10,000.
The value of the 0 is 0.
The value of the 9 is 900.
The value of the 5 is 50.
The value of the 0 is 0.

Way 2 Use grid paper.

Write the value of each **non-zero** digit in a chart. Write an expression to show the sum.

10,000 + 900 + 50

	1	0,	9	5	0
	1	0,	0	0	0
			9	0	0
				5	0
					–

Vocabulary Tip
1, 2, 3, 4, 5, 6, 7, 8, and 9 are **non-zero** digits.

Guided Practice

Write the number in expanded notation.

1. 40,950
2. 601,005,327
3. 50,340,007

Write the number in standard form.

4. 3,000,000 + 800,000 + 60,000, + 400 + 20 + 5
5. 200,000,000 + 70,000 + 400,000 + 7 + 30,000,000 + 5,000 + 100

Ask Yourself

- What is the value of each digit?
- Did I write an addend for each non-zero digit?

Math Talk How can you tell how many addends the **expanded form** for a number will have?

Vocabulary Tip

Expanded form is another way to say expanded notation.

Practice and Problem Solving

Write the number in expanded notation.

6. 59,000,710
7. 310,540,027
8. 5,000,000
9. 405,405

Write the number in standard form.

10. 5,000 + 700 + 30
11. 40,000 + 10 + 2,000
12. 70,000,000 + 600,000,000 + 9,000 + 80,000

Solve.

13. **Right or Wrong?** When Jena wrote 19,070 in expanded notation, she wrote 10,000 + 9,000 + 000 + 70 + 0. Is this correct? Explain.
14. **Analyze** Which digits in the number 204,397,068 have the same value? Explain.

Spiral Review and Test Practice

Use <, >, or = to complete the number sentence. GRADE 3 KEY AF 1.1, AF 1.0

15. 75 ⬭ 50
16. 12 + 3 ⬭ 10 + 5
17. 3 × 4 ⬭ 2 × 7

Write the letter of the correct answer. KEY NS 1.1

18. Which is 90,000,000 + 2,000 + 5 + 500,000,000 + 60,000 + 300?

A 590,062,305 **B** 92,556,300 **C** 590,623,500 **D** 500,962,305

Extra Practice See page 21, Set C.

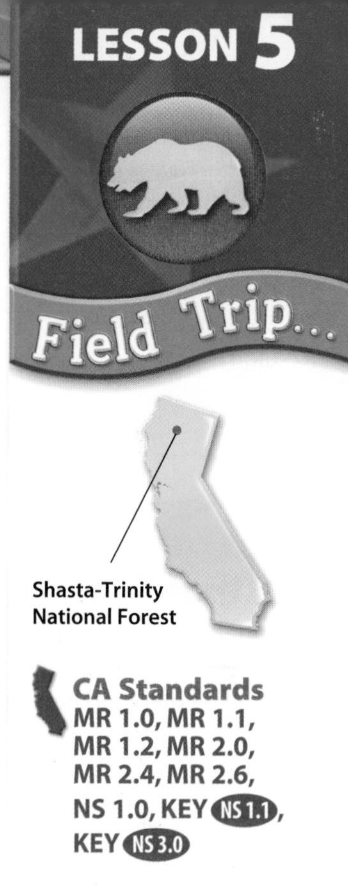

LESSON 5
Field Trip...
Shasta-Trinity
National Forest
CA Standards
MR 1.0, MR 1.1,
MR 1.2, MR 2.0,
MR 2.4, MR 2.6,
NS 1.0, KEY NS 1.1,
KEY NS 3.0

Problem Solving

Objective Use skills and strategies to solve word problems.

The bald eagle is the symbol of our nation.

From 1967 to 1995, bald eagles were endangered, but now they are making a comeback. You can view nesting eagles at the Shasta-Trinity National Forest from January through July.

Solve. Tell which strategy or method you used.

1. The 2,100,000-acre Shasta-Trinity National Forest is the largest national forest in California. Write this number in word form: 2,100,000.

2. **Multistep** Use the map. How many weeks did it take the young eagle to fly from Lake Shasta to central British Columbia? Show your work.

3. The table shows the number of pairs of eagles that lived in the Shasta-Trinity area one year. How many more eagles lived near Shasta Lake than Lewiston Lake? Show your work. Is your answer reasonable?

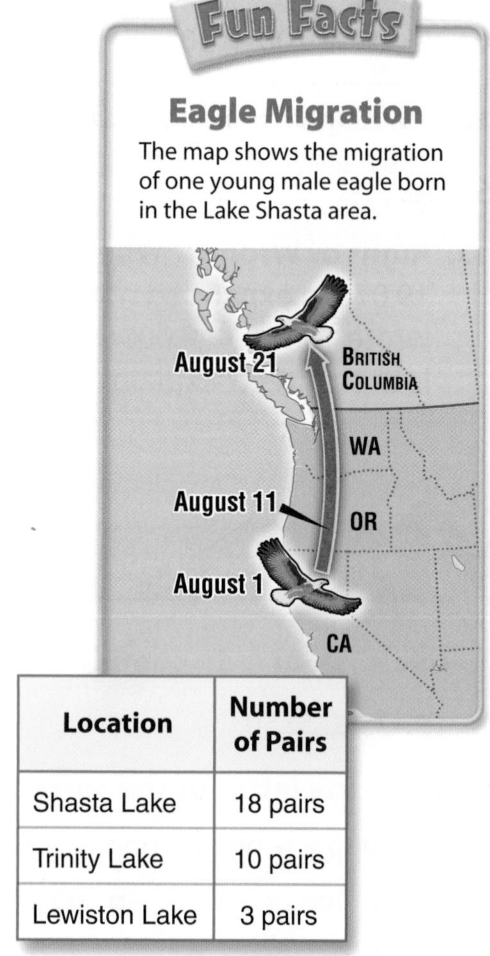

Eagle Migration
The map shows the migration of one young male eagle born in the Lake Shasta area.
August 21

August 11

Location	Number of Pairs
Shasta Lake	18 pairs
Trinity Lake	10 pairs
Lewiston Lake	3 pairs

Problem Solving on Tests

Select a Strategy

- Estimate
- Choose the Operation
- Draw a Picture
- Make a Table
- Make an Organized List

1. Malia says her house number has a 7 in the tens place and 7 in the thousands place. Which number could be Malia's house number?

A 7704 **B** 4077 **C** 4707 **D** 7470

GRADE 3 KEY NS 1.3

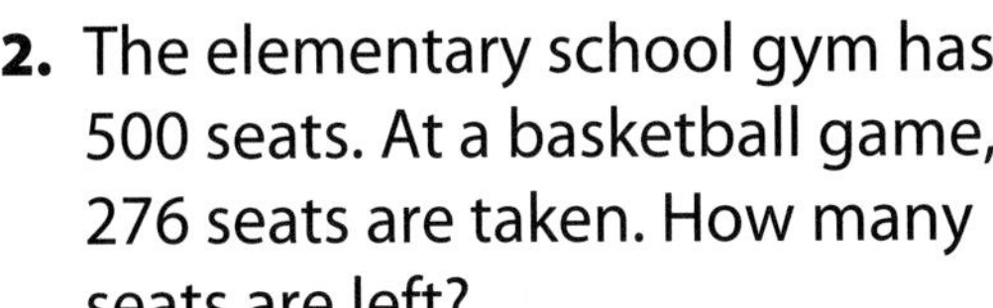

2. The elementary school gym has 500 seats. At a basketball game, 276 seats are taken. How many seats are left?

A 124
B 224
C 376
D 776

Test Tip
Is your answer reasonable? Try estimating to find out.

GRADE 3 KEY NS 2.1

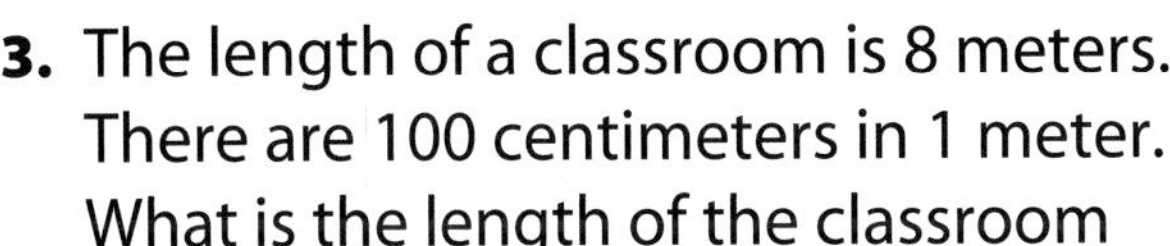

3. The length of a classroom is 8 meters. There are 100 centimeters in 1 meter. What is the length of the classroom in centimeters?

A 80 centimeters
B 92 centimeters
C 800 centimeters
D 8,000 centimeters

GRADE 3 MG 1.4

4. The line plot shows the results of spinning a spinner 12 times. Which color did the spinner land on 6 times?

Number of Spins

Blue	Red	Yellow	Green
	X		
	X		
	X		
X	X		
X	X	X	
X	X	X	X

A blue **C** yellow
B red **D** green

GRADE 3 KEY SDAP 1.3

5. A person who is 77 years old has lived about 40,498,560 minutes. Which of these is the number 40,498,560?

A four hundred million, four hundred ninety-eight thousand, five hundred sixty
B forty million, four hundred ninety-eight thousand, fifty-six
C four thousand, four hundred ninety-eight
D forty million, four hundred ninety-eight thousand, five hundred sixty

KEY NS 1.1 page 12

Education Place
Visit www.eduplace.com/camap/ for **Test-Taking Tips** and **Extra Practice**.

Vocabulary

We write and name numbers in different ways, depending on the situation. The chart below shows different ways to name numbers. Look at the number in the place-value chart. Use this number to complete the table.

Millions				Thousands				Ones		
hundreds	tens	ones		hundreds	tens	ones		hundreds	tens	ones
4	5	6	,	9	8	2	,	3	7	1

Ways to Write a Number		
standard form		
		four hundred fifty-six million, nine hundred eighty-two thousand, three hundred seventy-one
	Shows the value of each digit	

Writing Find the population of California. Write the number in word form, in standard form, and in expanded form.

Reading Check out this book in your library. *How Much Is a Million?*, by David M. Schwartz.

CA Standards
MR 2.3 Use a variety of methods, such as words, numbers, symbols, charts, graphs, tables, diagrams, and models, to explain mathematical reasoning.

Also KEY NS 1.1, NS 1.0

Standards-Based Extra Practice

Set A

KEY NS 1.1 page 8

Write the number in word form or standard form.

1. 324,063
2. 199,254
3. 678,332
4. 111,491
5. Two hundred twenty-three thousand, forty-five
6. Nine hundred ninety-eight thousand, seven hundred sixty-five
7. **Analyze** Greg saw these numbers on a license plate while driving: 2, 4, 5, 3 and 9. Write one possible number that could be on the license plate.

Set B

KEY NS 1.1 page 12

Write the number in word form or standard form.

1. 6,225,427
2. 39,531,022
3. 914,160,385
4. 4,246,385
5. Eighty-six million, three hundred ninety-six thousand, two hundred thirty-five
6. Three million, four hundred sixty-three thousand, seventy-two
7. **Challenge** Write a 6-digit number that has a 5 in the ten thousands place, a 3 in the thousands place, a 4 in the tens place, and one digit that is 0. Underline the 5, 3, 4, and the 0 in your number. Is this the only number you could have written? Explain your answer and provide an example, if possible.

Set C

KEY NS 1.1 page 16

Write the number in expanded notation or standard form.

1. 33,865
2. 792,106,438
3. 48,026,103
4. 60,000 + 8,000 + 30 + 3
5. 900,000,000 + 80,000,000 + 300 + 2
6. **Compare** Jack and Ben were looking at their zip codes. Jack thinks his zip code has a value greater than Ben's zip code. Which zip code has a greater value? How do you know?

   Jack's Zip Code: 93601   Ben's Zip Code: 93510

Education Place
Visit www.eduplace.com/camap/ for more **Extra Practice**.

Chapter Review/Test

Vocabulary and Concepts — KEY NS 1.1, MR 2.3

Write the best term to complete the sentence.

1. The value of a digit is determined by its ______.
2. When 653 is written as 600 + 50 + 3, it is said to be written in ______.
3. In a number, a group of 3 digits, separated by a comma, is called a ______.

Skills — KEY NS 1.1, NS 1.0

Write the number in word form.

4. 6,224,483
5. 83,000,001

Write the number in standard form.

6. Three million, four hundred fifty-six thousand, five
7. Seven hundred twenty-six thousand, five hundred twelve

Write the value of the underlined digit.

8. $\underline{7}$13,219
9. 4$\underline{2}$9,282,000
10. 8$\underline{7}$8,000
11. 91$\underline{9}$,345,769

Write the number in standard form.

12. 30 + 200,000,000 + 600,000 + 80,000,000
13. 40,000 + 500 + 70 + 9,000 + 1 + 100,000

Problem Solving and Reasoning — KEY NS 1.1, MR 1.1, MR 2.3

Solve.

14. The population of the United States in 2005 was 296,410,404. Write the value of the digit 9 in that number.
15. Mt. Shasta is a 14,000-foot mountain. Jack needs to write the number in word form for a report. What should he write?

Writing Math How does the period of a number help you read a number?

Spiral Review and Test Practice

1. Which number, rounded to the nearest hundred, is zero?

   A 94

   B 68

   C 52

   D 31

GRADE 3 NS 1.4

2. Sue put her photos in an album. She put in 105 photos of her family, 56 photos of friends, 12 photos of pets, and 21 nature photos. How many photos did Sue put in her album?

   A 294 photos

   B 194 photos

   C 184 photos

   D 183 photos

Test Tip

Before you choose an answer choice, check your work.

GRADE 3 KEY NS 2.1

3. 592 − 365 =

   A 127

   B 237

   C 227

   D 957

GRADE 3 KEY NS 2.1

4. Last year, three hundred twenty-three thousand people visited the museum. What is this number in standard form?

   A 323,000

   B 323,300

   C 232,300

   D 232,000

Test Tip

Look at the greatest place first to rule out some answer choices.

NS 1.0 page 8

5. Which of these is the number 892,560,000?

   A eight hundred twenty-nine million, five hundred sixty thousand

   B eight hundred ninety-two million, six hundred fifty thousand

   C eight hundred ninety-two million, five hundred thousand, sixty

   D eight hundred ninety-two million, five hundred sixty thousand

KEY NS 1.1 page 12

6. Which is 60,000,000 + 3,000 + 7 + 400,000,000 + 20,000 + 800 in standard form?

   A 460,230,807

   B 460,023,807

   C 460,023,870

   D 406,023,807

KEY NS 1.1 page 16

Education Place
Visit www.eduplace.com/camap/ for **Test-Taking Tips** and **Extra Practice.**

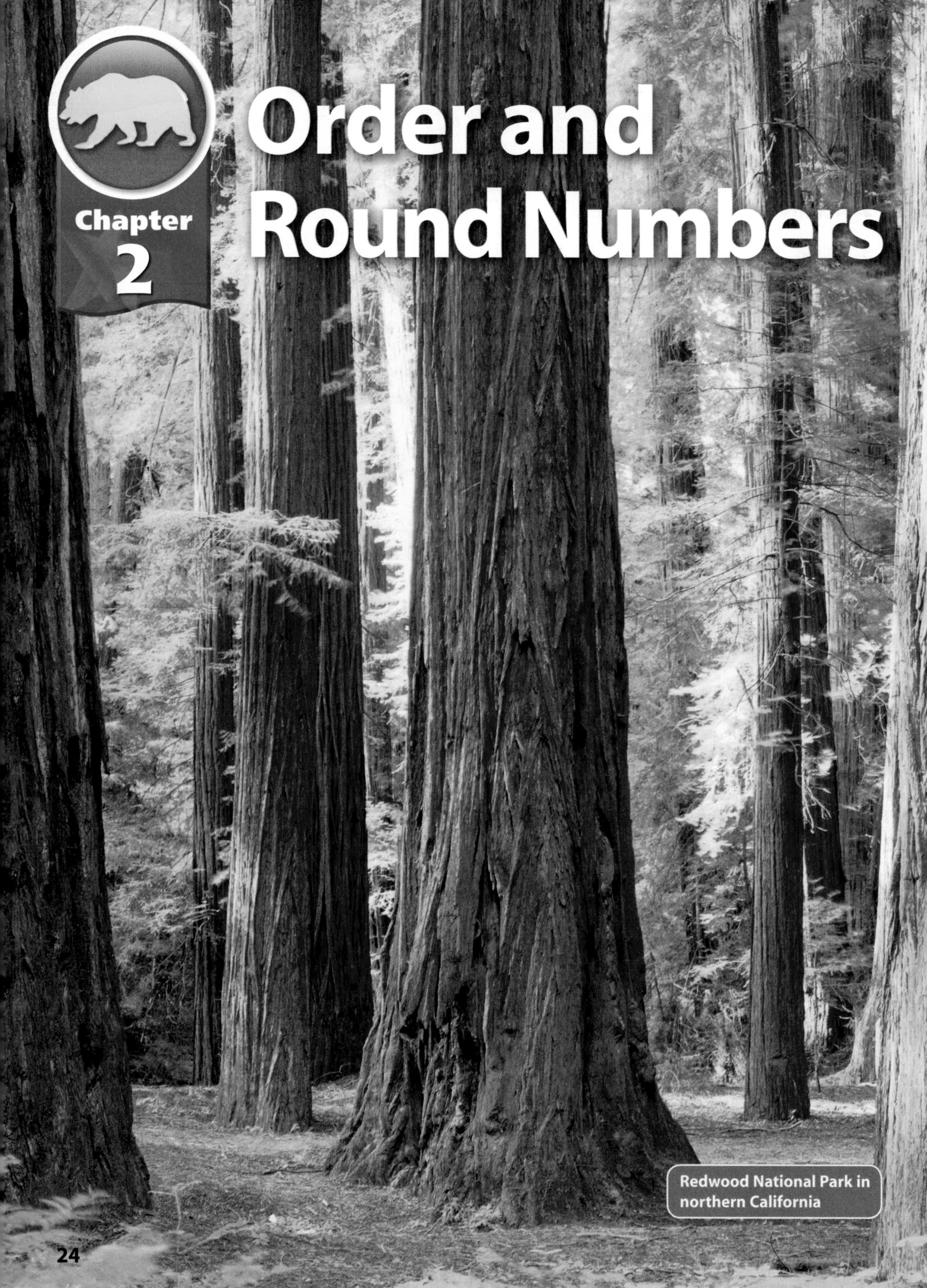

Chapter 2

Order and Round Numbers

Redwood National Park in northern California

Check What You Know

Vocabulary and Concepts GRADE 3 NS 1.2, MR 2.3

Match each word with a symbol.

1. greater than — a. =
2. less than — b. <
3. equal to — c. >

Skills GRADE 3 NS 1.2

Write the numbers in order from least to greatest.

4. 65 73 45
5. 175 204 192
6. 973 745 945

Problem Solving and Reasoning GRADE 3 NS 1.4

7. Rounded to the nearest hundred, about 300 people visited a park on Sunday. What could the actual number of people be who visited the park?

Vocabulary

Visualize It!

estimate

a number close to the actual number; to find about how many

round

to find out about how many or how much by expressing a number to the nearest ten, hundred, thousand, and so on

You can **round** numbers to any place. Round 3,845 to the nearest thousand, hundred, and ten.

Rounding Place	Digit to look at	Decide whether to round up or down	Rounded Number
Thousand	3,845	8 > 5, so round up.	4,000
Hundred	3,845	4 < 5, so round down.	3,800
Ten	3,845	5 = 5, so round up.	3,850

Language Tips

You can *order* food in a restaurant. When you *order* numbers, you list them from least to greatest or greatest to least.

Words that look alike in English and Spanish often have the same meaning.

English	Spanish
compare	**comparar**
order	**ordenar**
equal	**igual**
estimate	**estimación**

See **English-Spanish Glossary** pages 644–666.

Education Place Visit www.eduplace.com/camap/ for the **eGlossary** and **eGames**.

CA Standards MR 2.3 Use a variety of methods, such as words, numbers, symbols, charts, graphs, tables, diagrams, and models, to explain mathematical reasoning. Also **KEY** NS 1.3

Hands On
Compare and Order Whole Numbers

Objective Compare and order numbers on a number line.

CA Standards
KEY NS 1.2 Order and compare whole numbers and decimals to two decimal places.
Also NS 1.0, MR 1.1, MR 2.0, MR 2.3, MR 2.4, MR 3.0, MR 3.3

Vocabulary

compare
is greater than (>)
is less than (<)
order

Materials
- Workmat 4
- eManipulatives (optional) www.eduplace.com/camap/

Explore

Question How can you compare and order numbers?

When you **compare** numbers, you find which of the numbers is greater or lesser.

You can use a number line. Compare 6,450 and 6,045.

1. Label Number Line 2 on Workmat 4 from 6,000 to 7,000.

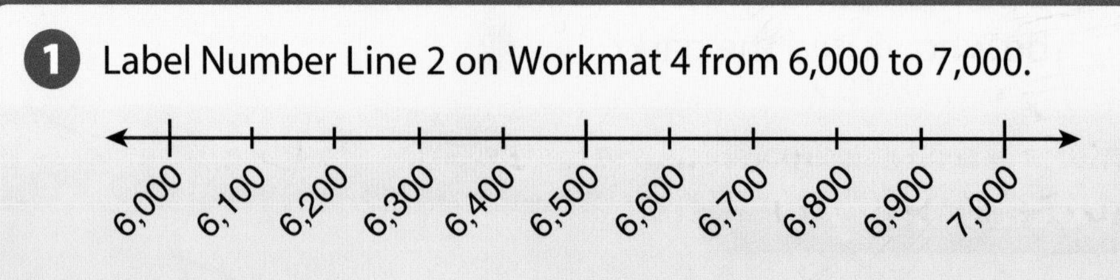

2. Decide where the numbers 6,045 and 6,450 belong, and label the points.

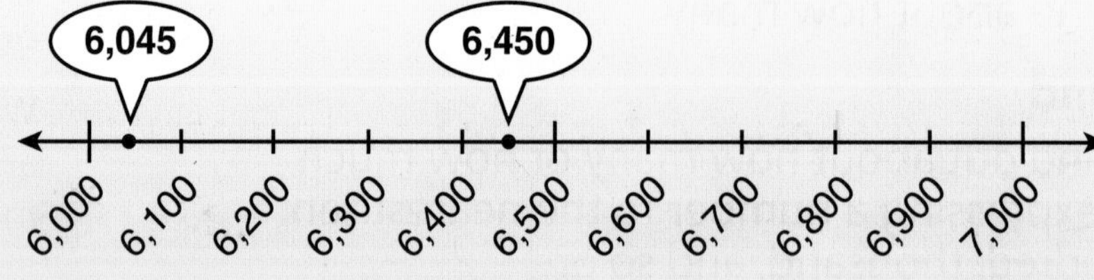

3. Compare.

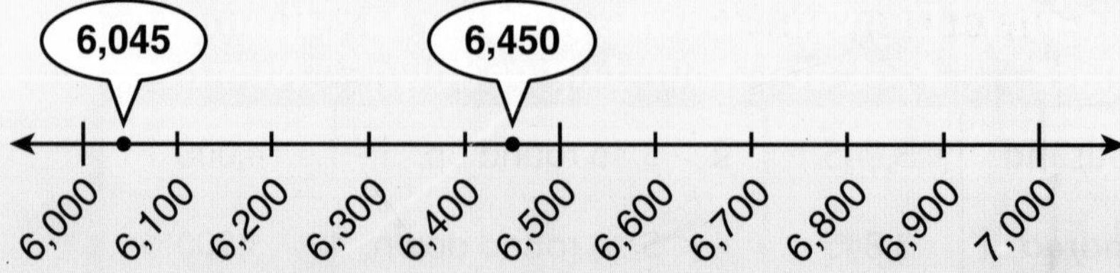

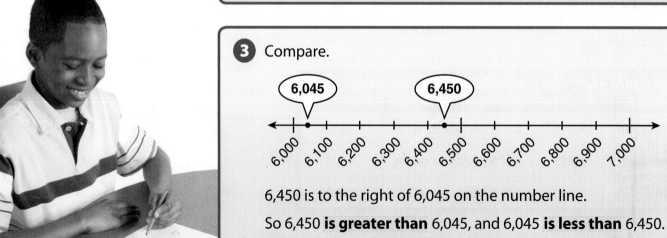

6,450 is to the right of 6,045 on the number line.

So 6,450 **is greater than** 6,045, and 6,045 **is less than** 6,450.

6,450 > 6,045 6,045 < 6,450

You can also use a number line to order numbers. When you **order** numbers, you list the numbers from greatest to least or from least to greatest.

Order 6,450, 6,045, and 6,540 from greatest to least.

1. Find and label each number on a number line.

2. 6,540 is farthest to the right on the number line.

   6,540 is the greatest number.

3. 6,045 is farthest to the left.

   6,045 is the least number.

4. 6,450 is between 6,540 and 6,045.

   $6{,}540 > 6{,}450 > 6{,}045$

Extend

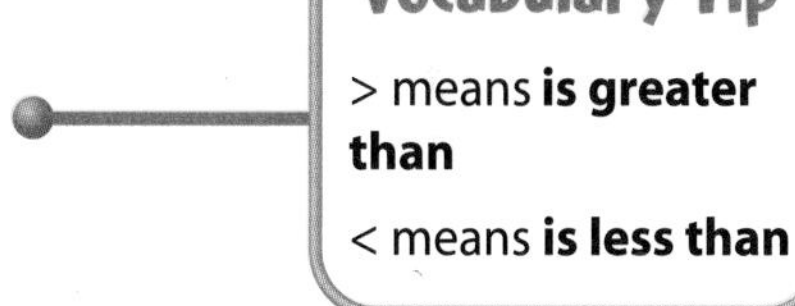
Vocabulary Tip
$>$ means **is greater than**
$<$ means **is less than**

Make a number line like the one below. Use $>$ or $<$ to compare the numbers.

11,000 11,500 12,000

1. 11,250 ⬭ 11,520
2. 11,670 ⬭ 11,760
3. 12,000 ⬭ 11,000
4. 11,999 ⬭ 11,111
5. 11,340 ⬭ 11,403
6. 11,542 ⬭ 11,424

Write the numbers in order from least to greatest.

7. 11,682 11,862 11,286
8. 11,973 11,937 11,933
9. 11,250 10,999 10,750
10. 10,390 10,903 9,999
11. **Reasoning** Do you need to use a number line to tell whether 9,254 or 10,000 is the greater number? Why or why not?

Math Journal

Writing Math

Generalize Look at the number lines that you made. Write a sentence that tells how the values on a number line change as you move from left to right.

LESSON 2

CA Standards

KEY NS 1.2 Order and compare whole numbers and decimals to two decimal places.

KEY NS 1.1 Read and write whole numbers in the millions.

Also NS 1.0, MR 1.0, MR 1.1, MR 1.2, MR 2.0, MR 2.2, MR 2.3

Vocabulary

compare

order

Compare and Order Whole Numbers Through Millions

Objective Compare and order numbers up to nine digits.

Learn by Example

You can use place value to **compare** or **order** numbers.

Our country has several national parks that cover over 1 million acres. Grand Canyon National Park covers 1,217,403 acres. Joshua Tree National Park covers 1,022,703 acres. Compare to find out which park has the greater number of acres.

Compare Numbers

1 Line up the digits. Find the greatest place where the digits are different.

1,022,703
1,217,403

same — different

2 Compare the digits.

1,022,703
1,217,403

2 > 0

So, 1,217,403 > 1,022,703

Solution: The Grand Canyon National Park has the greater number of acres.

Order 150,031,426 and 83,445,128 and 83,901,339 from greatest to least.

Order Numbers

1 Line up the digits. Find the greatest place where the digits differ.

150,031,426
83,445,128
83,901,339

150,031,426 is the greatest number. It is the only number with hundred millions.

2 Compare the other numbers. Find the first place where the digits are different. Write > or <.

150,031,426
83,445,128
83,901,339

9 > 4 so 83,901,339 > 83,445,128

Solution: 150,031,426 > 83,901,339 > 83,445,128

Joshua Tree National Park, CA

Guided Practice

Compare. Write > or < for the ○.

1. 505 ○ 550
2. 42,021 ○ 4,220
3. 72,066 ○ 72,600
4. 135,734 ○ 55,724
5. 34,291,146 ○ 34,302,146
6. 98,760,032 ○ 98,790,032

Ask Yourself

- Which digits do I compare first?
- What do I do when digits in the same place have the same value?

Write the numbers in order from least to greatest. Be sure to compare digits with the same place value.

7. 1,209 9,120 9,102
8. 69,541 689,541 68,541
9. 11,152,348 1,115,248 11,532,348

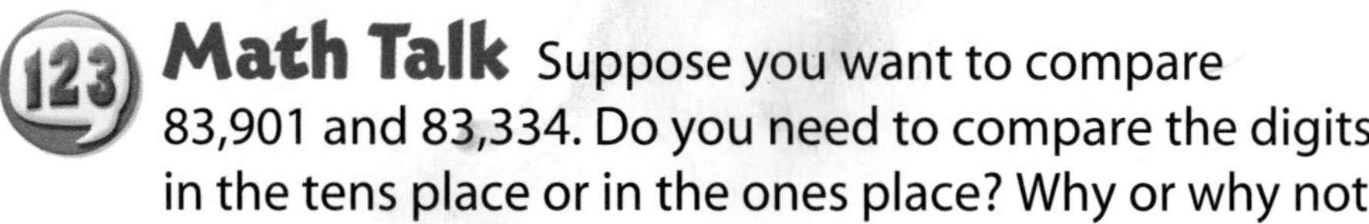

Math Talk Suppose you want to compare 83,901 and 83,334. Do you need to compare the digits in the tens place or in the ones place? Why or why not?

Practice and Problem Solving

Compare. Write =, >, or < for the ○.

10. 1,207 ○ 1,207
11. 1,009 ○ 999
12. 4,901 ○ 14,901
13. 75,704 ○ 75,074
14. 92,876 ○ 101,001
15. 54,932 ○ 54,932
16. 75,344 ○ 55,724
17. 879,566 ○ 869,566
18. 101,902 ○ 671,110
19. 99,902,234 ○ 112,311,011
20. 98,760,032 ○ 987,600,032
21. 404,004,004 ○ 444,440,004
22. 190,098,181 ○ 99,090,870

Write the numbers in order from least to greatest.

23. 1,209 12,909 9,999
24. 79,541 689,541 78,541
25. 999 1,009 199 19,009
26. 441,876 421,876 42,876

Write the numbers in order from greatest to least.

27. 170,909 180,909 190,909
28. 102,000 12,000 100,200
29. 85,407,363 8,407,363 85,073,630
30. 225,522,145 25,522,145 252,522,145

Solve.

31. **Multistep** Mr. Kane drove 1,038 miles. Ms. Lok drove 987 miles, and Mrs. Alba drove 100 miles more than Ms. Lok. Order the distances they drove from greatest to least.

32. A seven-digit number has a 7 in the millions place, a 3 in the tens thousands place, and a 5 in the hundreds place. All other places have ones. Write the number in word form.

33. Use these digits to make the least number possible.
9 6 3 4 1 1 8

34. Use these digits to make the greatest number possible.
2 6 1 0 0 8 9 2

Real World Data

Use the table to solve.

35. Which park is larger—Acadia or Mammoth Cave?

36. Which park is smaller—the Badlands or Capitol Reef?

37. Which park's size has a 5 in the ten thousands place? Write its size in word form.

38. Could you compare the sizes of Hot Springs and Yellowstone by looking only at the number of digits? Explain your thinking.

39. **Challenge** Write the names of the parks in order from greatest to least number of acres.

Size of National Parks

Park	Size (acres)
Acadia	48,419
Badlands	242,756
Capitol Reef	241,904
Hot Springs	5,549
Mammoth Cave	52,830
Yellowstone	2,219,791

Spiral Review and Test Practice

Write each number in expanded form. KEY NS 1.1 page 16

40. 1,453,924
41. 9,403,292
42. 12,003,201
43. 3,127,191

Write the letter of the correct answer. KEY NS 1.2

44. Which of the following has the greatest value?

A 1,704,702 **B** 1,780,282 **C** 1,497,207 **D** 1,408,200

Extra Practice See page 41, Sets A and B.

Key Standards Review

Need Help?
See Key Standards Handbook.

Write the number in standard form. KEY NS 1.1

1. fifty-two million
2. seventy-six million, three
3. six hundred thirty-two thousand, sixteen
4. twenty-four million, eight hundred thousand
5. three million, eight hundred thousand, fifty-two
6. fifteen million, three hundred twenty thousand, six hundred

Write the number in word form. KEY NS 1.1

7. 6,021,372
8. 300,031
9. 50,000,800
10. 10,462,311
11. 216,007
12. 27,302,913

Math Reasoning

What Are the Numbers?

What could the number be? List all possible answers in order from least to greatest. NS 1.0, KEY NS 1.1

1. A number is between 100 and 1,000.
   - The sum of its digits is 11.
   - The tens digit is less than the hundreds digit.
   - There are no zeros.
2. A number is between 100,000 and 1,000,000.
   - The sum of its digits is 14.
   - The ten thousands digit is greater than the hundreds digit.
   - The hundred thousands digit is 8.
   - There are exactly three zeros.
3. You include the words "two thousand" and the word "fifteen" when you read this 4-digit number.

CA Standards
KEY NS 1.3 Round whole numbers through the millions to the nearest ten, hundred, thousand, ten thousand, or hundred thousand.

Also NS 1.0, KEY NS 1.4, MR 1.1, MR 2.0, MR 2.3, MR 2.5, MR 3.0, MR 3.2

Vocabulary

round

estimate

Round Whole Numbers

Objective Round whole numbers through the thousands.

Learn by Example

When you **round** to **estimate** a number, you find a number that is close to the actual number.

Boris and Marta hiked a nature trail that is 5,843 feet long. About how long is the trail?

Since the question asks *about* how long the trail is, you do not need an exact number. So you can round to estimate the length of the trail.

You can use place value to round 5,843 to the nearest thousand.

Round to the Nearest Thousand

1 Find the place you want to round to. Underline the digit in that place.

5,843 (5 underlined) — thousands place

2 Look at the digit to its right. Circle that digit.

5,843 (5 underlined, 8 circled) — digit to the right

3 Round.

- If the circled digit is 5 or greater, round up.
- If the circled digit is less than 5, round down.

5,843 (5 underlined, 8 circled) — $8 > 5$ So, round 5 up to 6. Write zeros to the right.

5,843 **rounds to** 6,000

Solution: To the nearest thousand, the trail is about 6,000 feet long.

Yosemite National Park, CA

Guided Practice

Round each number to the nearest thousand.

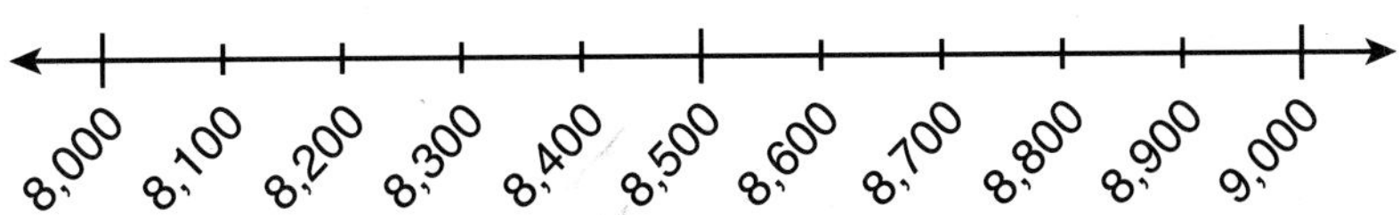

1. 8,900 **2.** 8,210 **3.** 8,499 **4.** 8,600

> **Ask Yourself**
> - What is the digit to the right of the rounding place?
> - Is this digit 5 or greater, or is it less than 5?

Round each number to the place of the underlined digit.

5. $\underline{3}$,812 **6.** 12$\underline{5}$,601 **7.** 792,3$\underline{6}$9 **8.** 8$\underline{2}$5,102

Math Talk Can a 4-digit number round to 10,000? Give an example to support your answer.

Practice and Problem Solving

Round each number to the place of the underlined digit.

9. 2$\underline{6}$,754 **10.** 19,8$\underline{8}$7 **11.** 3$\underline{3}$,501 **12.** 1$\underline{1}$3,772

13. 42$\underline{8}$,674 **14.** $\underline{2}$49,352 **15.** 90$\underline{1}$,223 **16.** 6$\underline{2}$5,348

Use the picture to solve.

17a. Boris wants to buy a trail guide and a compass. About how much will he spend?

b. **Challenge** Boris has exactly $40. Is it a good idea for him to use his estimate to decide if he has enough money?

Spiral Review and Test Practice

Compare. Write > or < for the 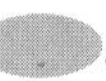. KEY NS 1.2 page 28

18. 543,266 ◯ 534,622 **19.** 2,453,975 ◯ 2,453,675

Write the letter of the correct answer. KEY NS 1.3

20. What is 430,428 rounded to the nearest hundred?

A 430,500 **B** 430,400 **C** 430,000 **D** 430,430

More on Rounding Whole Numbers

Objective Round whole numbers through the millions.

CA Standards
KEY NS 1.3 Round whole numbers through the millions to the nearest ten, hundred, thousand, ten thousand, or hundred thousand.

Also NS 1.0, MR 1.0, MR 1.1, MR 2.0, MR 2.2, MR 2.3

Learn by Example

In 2005, 13,602,629 people visited the Golden Gate National Recreation Area. To the nearest million, about how many people is that?

You can use place value to round 13,602,629 to the nearest million.

Round to the Nearest Million

1 Find the place you want to round to. Underline the digit in that place.

13,602,629 — millions place

2 Look at the digit to its right. Circle that digit.

13,602,629 — digit to the right

3 Round.

13,602,629 **rounds to** 14,000,000

13,602,629 — $6 > 5$ So, round 3 up to 4. Write zeros to the right.

Solution: About 14,000,000 people visited the Golden Gate National Recreation Area in 2005.

Golden Gate National Recreation Area, CA

Other Examples

A. Round to the nearest ten million.

238,427,592 **rounds to** 240,000,000.

238,427,592

ten millions place

$8 > 5$ Change 3 to 4. Write zeros.

B. Round to the nearest hundred million.

238,427,592 **rounds to** 200,000,000.

238,427,592

hundred millions place

$3 < 5$ Don't change 2. Write zeros.

Guided Practice

Round each number to the place of the underlined digit.

1. 965,113 **2.** 9,547,211 **3.** 7,449,716

4. 524,387,210 **5.** 524,387,210 **6.** 750,329,846

7. 476,004,350 **8.** 539,117,956 **9.** 387,246,905

Ask Yourself

- What digit is underlined?
- What is the digit to its right?
- Do I change the underlined digit?

Guided Problem Solving

Use the questions to solve this problem.

10. Jonah says that each of the parks except the Great Smoky Mountains had about 3 million visitors. Is Jonah correct? Explain your answer.

- **a. Understand** Look at the table. Which parks should you consider when solving this problem?
- **b. Plan** What place should you round the number of visitors to?
- **c. Solve** Round. Then write the answer to the problem.
- **d. Look Back** Did you round all the numbers correctly? Did you answer the question that was asked?

National Park Visitors (2005)

Park	Visitors
Great Smoky Mountains	9,192,477
Grand Canyon	4,401,522
Yosemite	3,304,144
Olympic	3,142,774
Yellowstone	2,835,651

Visitor at Grand Prismatic Spring, Yellowstone National Park

Math Talk How would you change one digit in 7,856,041 so that it rounds to 7,800,000?

Practice and Problem Solving

Round each number to the place of the underlined digit.

11. 57,304,600 **12.** 9,527,201 **13.** 7,435,333 **14.** 482,001,674

15. 1,020,890 **16.** 78,901,223 **17.** 7,425,333 **18.** 670,827,023

Which place was each number rounded to?
Write *hundred thousands* or *millions*.

19. 36,768,401 → 37,000,000

20. 879,463 → 900,000

21. 9,345,099 → 9,300,000

22. 135,877,980 → 136,000,000

Solve.

23. Tara's number is the greatest number that when rounded to the nearest ten thousand, is 510,000. What is Tara's number?

24. Richie says that his number, rounded to the nearest hundred, is 0. What could his number be?

Science Link

Solve.

25. A basalt sample is 1,790 years old. What is its age rounded to the nearest hundred?

26. A scientist estimates that 3,520,000 separate bits made one limestone sample. What is this number rounded to the nearest hundred thousand?

27. The mass of a marble sample, rounded to the nearest ten, is 5,480 grams. What is the least possible mass of the sample? The greatest possible mass?

Fun Facts
Earth's Rocks
Earth's rocks are constantly forming, breaking apart, and reforming again. These changes usually take place very gradually. Some rocks are billions of years old!
• Limestone forms from bits of calcium that are pressed together.
• Marble forms when limestone is changed by heat and pressure.
• Basalt may form when a volcano erupts and the lava cools.
basalt

Science ES 4.a

Spiral Review and Test Practice

Write each number in word form. KEY NS 1.1 pages 8, 12

28. 506,840 **29.** 650,009 **30.** 523,010,000 **31.** 606,025,709

Write the letter of the correct answer. KEY NS 1.3

32. What is 68,478,996 rounded to the nearest ten million?

A 60,000,000 **B** 68,479,000 **C** 70,000,000 **D** 68,480,000

Extra Practice See page 41, Set C.

Practice **Game**

Round and Match

Object of the Game To match an exact number with the number rounded to the nearest ten thousand.

Materials
Learning Tool 9 (*Round and Match* Game Cards)

Set Up
Each player is dealt 5 cards and the rest are placed in a pile face down.

Number of Players 2

How to Play

1. Player 1 asks Player 2 for a match. For example, if Player 1 has the 100,000,000 card, he or she might ask for a number that rounds to 100 million. Or if Player 1 has the 99,999,999 card, he or she would round to the nearest ten thousand and ask, "Do you have 100 million?"
2. If Player 2 has the match, he or she gives that card to Player 1 who then keeps that pair of cards and puts them aside. Player 1 continues to ask for matches until Player 2 cannot make a match.
3. When Player 2 cannot make a match he or she responds, "Go fish," and Player 1 draws a card from the pile.
4. Player 2 then repeats Steps 1–3.
5. Players alternate turns until one player runs out of cards. The player with more matched pairs is the winner.

CA Standards

KEY NS 1.3 Round whole numbers through the millions to the nearest ten, hundred, thousand, ten thousand, or hundred thousand.

KEY NS 1.1 Read and write whole numbers in the millions.

Education Place
Visit www.eduplace.com/camap/ for **Brain Teasers** and **eGames** to play.

LESSON 5

Problem Solving Strategy
Make an Organized List

Objective Use an organized list to solve a problem.

CA Standards
MR 2.3 Use a variety of methods, such as words, numbers, symbols, charts, tables, graphs, diagrams, and models, to explain mathematical reasoning.

KEY NS 1.3 Round whole numbers through the millions to the nearest ten, hundred, thousand, ten thousand, or hundred thousand.

Also KEY NS 1.2, SDAP 2.1, MR 1.1, MR 2.0, MR 2.4, MR 3.0, MR 3.1, MR 3.2, MR 3.3

Think
What large groups of numbers can you omit?

Learn by Example

Janise wants to make a list of all the numbers between 41,000 and 43,000 that have 0 in the tens and ones places and that round to 42,000. How many numbers are there?

She can make an organized list.

UNDERSTAND

You want to find how many numbers between 41,000 and 43,000 that have a 0 in the tens and ones places round to 42,000.

PLAN

Decide what digits must be in the thousands place and what digits must be in the hundreds place for a number to round to 42,000.

SOLVE

1 Identify the digits.

4 1, _ 0 0 — 5 or >5

Thousands place: 1
Hundreds place: 5 or greater

4 2, _ 0 0 — <5

Thousands place: 2
Hundreds place: less than 5

2 List the numbers that fit under each heading.

41,_00	42,_00
41,500	42,000
41,600	42,100
41,700	42,200
41,800	42,300
41,900	42,400

There are 10 numbers in the list.

LOOK BACK

Did you round the numbers correctly?

Guided Problem Solving

Solve using the Ask Yourself questions.

1. Hadi is making sandwiches. He has wheat bread, pita bread, cheese, tuna fish, and hummus. If Hadi uses one kind of bread and one kind of filling, list the types of sandwiches he can make.

Ask Yourself

- How many columns do I need in my list?
- What does each column represent?

Math Talk Look at the organized list in the Example on page 38 and the one you made for Problem 1. How did using an organized list help you find the correct solution?

Independent Problem Solving

Use an organized list to solve. Explain why your answer makes sense.

2. Colin is thinking of a group of numbers between 40,000 and 60,000 that round to 54,450. Use an organized list to find Colin's numbers.

3. Paula is buying a new shirt. The sign shows her choices of styles and colors. How many possible combinations of style and color does Paula have?

4. Cameron has a number cube labeled 1–6 and a number cube labeled 7–12. What are the number combinations he can roll with these cubes?

5. A game includes two spinners. One has the letters A, B, C, and D. The other has the numbers 1, 2, 3, 4, 5, and 6. How many different combinations of letters and numbers can the players spin?

6. **Challenge** Ji Sun has these number cards: 2, 4, 5, 6. How many 4-digit numbers can she make that will round to 5 in the thousands place?

7. **Create and Solve** Write and solve a problem in which an organized list will help you find the solution.

Styles	Colors
• long sleeve	• black
• short sleeve	• blue
• sleeveless	• red
	• white

Hint
What digits can be in the thousands place? In the hundreds place?

Reading & Writing 

Vocabulary

When you **compare** and **order** numbers, you find which of the numbers is lesser and greater. When you **round** to **estimate** a number, you find a number that is close to the exact number.

Zoe is doing a report on the three largest cities in California. She finds the populations on the Internet.

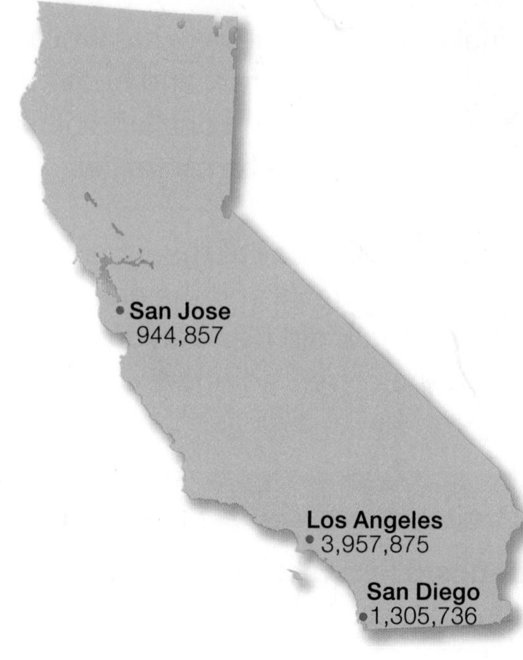

Use the city populations. Follow the directions.

1. **Compare.** Use < or >. 3,957,875 ◯ 1,305,736 944,857 ◯ 3,957,875	2. **Order** the three numbers from greatest to least.
3. **Order** the three cities from least to greatest population.	4. **Round** the population of Los Angeles to the nearest 10,000.

Writing Zoe decides to round the numbers to the nearest million before ordering them. Is this a good idea? Tell why or why not.

Reading Look for this book in your library. *Knots on a Counting Rope*, by John Archambault and Bill Martin

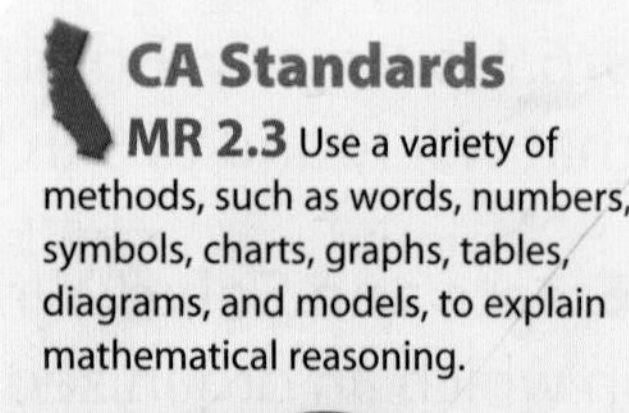
CA Standards
MR 2.3 Use a variety of methods, such as words, numbers, symbols, charts, graphs, tables, diagrams, and models, to explain mathematical reasoning.
Also KEY NS 1.3

Standards-Based Extra Practice

Set A

KEY NS 1.2 page 28

Compare. Write > or < for the ◯.

1. 660 ◯ 606
2. 43,021 ◯ 4331
3. 58,033 ◯ 58,300
4. 142,845 ◯ 42,815
5. 76,890,041 ◯ 76,860,041
6. 83,127,221 ◯ 83,137,221
7. 158,000 ◯ 159,000
8. 287,546,909 ◯ 287,546,009
9. **Compare** A zip code in California is 92274. A zip code in Arizona is 72274. Compare the zip codes using > or <. Explain how you know.

Set B

KEY NS 1.2 page 28

Write the numbers in order from least to greatest.

1. 48,221,987 48,001,980 47,598,243
2. 23,532,001 23,432,001 23,433,001
3. 6,235,503 6,235,987 5,995,985
4. 4,023 44,023 40,023
5. 58,033 58,300 58,999
6. 87,468 8,746 87,746
7. 99,234,456 98,987,334 99,345,678
8. 21,021,342 20,020,341 21,022,345
9. **Order** Cassidy's family is taking a road trip. Order the distances from least to greatest. Palm Springs, CA to Houston, TX: 1,272 miles; Houston, TX to Washington, D.C.: 1,220 miles; Washington, D.C. to Lincoln, NE: 1,048 miles

Set C

KEY NS 1.3 page 34

Round each number to the place of the underlined digit.

1. $\underline{9}54{,}113$
2. $8{,}\underline{3}47{,}673$
3. $5\underline{8}{,}245{,}333$
4. $96{,}\underline{5}67{,}021$
5. $239{,}\underline{6}74{,}000$
6. $\underline{7}7{,}942{,}004$
7. $625{,}794{,}\underline{8}91$
8. $25{,}961{,}\underline{2}54$
9. **Explain** In Problem 9 of Set B, round the distances to the nearest thousand to estimate how far Cassidy's family will drive in all. Is this a good estimate? Why or why not?

Education Place
Visit www.eduplace.com/camap/ for more **Extra Practice**.

Chapter Review/Test

Vocabulary and Concepts

KEY NS 1.2, KEY NS 1.3, MR 2.3

Write the best word to complete the sentence.

1. When you ______ numbers, you write them from greatest to least or least to greatest.
2. You can ______ a number up or down to help make an estimate.

Skills

KEY NS 1.2, KEY NS 1.3

Compare. Write $>$ or $<$ for the ⬭.

3. 1,543 ⬭ 1,453
4. 148,021 ⬭ 14,821
5. 162,845 ⬭ 166,854
6. 891,345,890 ⬭ 892,345,890
7. 546,304,321 ⬭ 546,340,321
8. 1,396,421 ⬭ 1,936,241

Write the numbers in order from greatest to least.

9. 357,218 373,018 375,218
10. 5,207,812 25,107,812 25,171,812

Round the number to the place of the underlined digit.

11. 4<u>8</u>,362
12. 85<u>5</u>,851
13. <u>9</u>70,999
14. 253,<u>9</u>43,236
15. <u>4</u>95,500,744
16. 2<u>3</u>,580,811
17. 1<u>7</u>,638
18. 1<u>1</u>2,386

Problem Solving and Reasoning

MR 2.3, KEY NS 1.3, KEY NS 1.2

Solve.

19. Hope wants to make a list of all the numbers between 23,400 and 23,500 that round to 23,450. What are her numbers?
20. One week 30,568 people attended a football game. The next week 30,865 people attended a football game. In which week did more people attend the football game?

Math Journal

Writing Math Explain how you round 98,736 to the nearest ten thousand.

Spiral Review and Test Practice

1. A bottle factory produced six hundred seventy-five thousand, three hundred bottles. What is this number in standard form?

A 765,300 **C** 675,300

B 675,330 **D** 675,003

NS 1.0 page 8

2. Which of these is the number 456,702,000?

A four hundred sixty-five million, seven hundred two thousand

B four hundred fifty-six million, seven hundred twenty thousand

C four hundred fifty-six million, seven hundred two thousand

D four hundred fifty-six million, seven hundred two

KEY NS 1.1 page 12

3. Which is 40,000,000 + 2,000 + 500,000 + 900,000,000 + 300 + 8,000,000 in standard form?

A 984,502,300

B 948,052,300

C 948,520,300

D 948,502,300

Test Tip
Remember to use a zero when a place in a number has no value.

KEY NS 1.1 page 16

4. Which of the following has the greatest value?

A 2,395,213

B 2,356,342

C 2,562,409

D 2,542,789

Test Tip
Compare each digit in the answer choices, starting at the greatest place.

KEY NS 1.2 page 28

5. What is 238,615 rounded to the nearest hundred?

A 238,700

B 238,620

C 238,610

D 238,600

KEY NS 1.3 page 32

6. What is 32,657,873 rounded to the nearest ten million?

A 30,000,000

B 32,660,000

C 32,700,000

D 40,000,000

KEY NS 1.3 page 34

Education Place
Visit www.eduplace.com/camap/ for **Test-Taking Tips** and **Extra Practice**.

Unit 1 Test

Vocabulary and Concepts — KEY NS 1.1, MR 2.3 Chapter 1, Lessons 2 and 4

Complete each sentence with a vocabulary word from this unit.

1. We can use groups of three digits, called ______, to help us read large numbers.

2. 600 + 50 + 7 is an example of ______.

Computation — KEY NS 1.1, KEY NS 1.2, KEY NS 1.3 Chapter 1, Lessons 2–3

Write the number in word form or standard form.

3. 568,421

4. 1,298,438

5. three hundred twenty-nine thousand, five hundred ninety-nine.

Write the value of the underlined digit.

6. 4$\underline{8}$,362

7. 8$\underline{5}$6,151

8. $\underline{9}$70,999

9. 2$\underline{5}$0,943,236

Compare. Use $>$ or $<$. Chapter 2, Lessons 1–2

10. 601,004,327 ⬭ 61,004,327

11. 50,340,007 ⬭ 500,340,007

Order from least to greatest.

12. 945,628,291 3,860,425 95,632,100 3,864 96,340,824

Round each number to the place of the underlined digit. Chapter 2, Lesson 3

13. 2$\underline{4}$6,783

14. $\underline{1}$,830,203

15. $\underline{2}$48,204,111

16. 284,501,$\underline{9}$30

Problem Solving and Reasoning — KEY NS 1.1, KEY NS 1.2, MR 1.1 Chapters 1 and 2

Solve.

17. Alfred found a rock estimated to be 21,800 years old. What is the age of the rock rounded to the nearest thousand?

18. Mrs. Talbert drove 1,221 miles. Mr. Green drove 868 miles. Mr. Thomas drove 200 miles more than Mr. Green. Order the distances from greatest to least.

19. Steven has a six-digit number on his bike. A 2 is in the hundred thousands place, a 6 in the ones place, and a 1 in the hundreds place. Write two different numbers that could be on his bike.

20. My mystery number has 0 in the tens and thousands places, 3 in the ten thousands and ones places, 4 in the hundred thousands places, and 6 in hundreds place. Write my number in three ways.

Writing Math Explain how the periods help us understand and read big numbers.

Performance Assessment

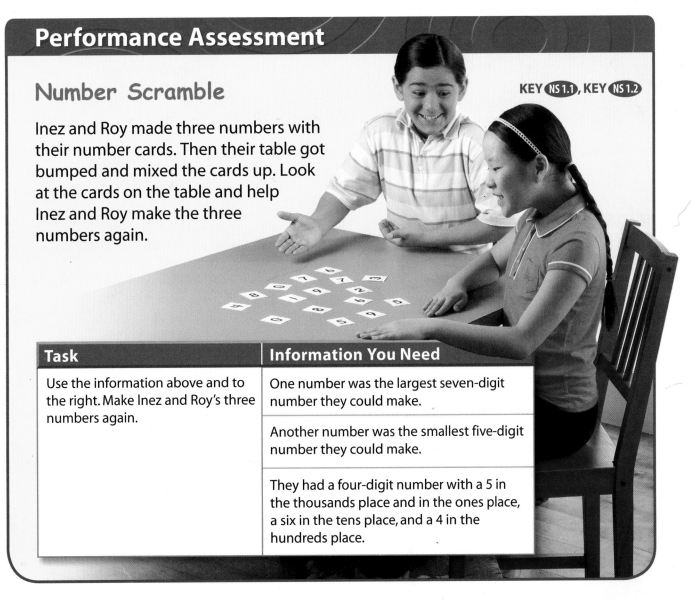

Number Scramble

KEY NS 1.1, KEY NS 1.2

Inez and Roy made three numbers with their number cards. Then their table got bumped and mixed the cards up. Look at the cards on the table and help Inez and Roy make the three numbers again.

Task	Information You Need
Use the information above and to the right. Make Inez and Roy's three numbers again.	One number was the largest seven-digit number they could make.
	Another number was the smallest five-digit number they could make.
	They had a four-digit number with a 5 in the thousands place and in the ones place, a six in the tens place, and a 4 in the hundreds place.

Greg Tang's Go Fast, Go Far

Unit 1 Mental Math Strategies

Add Up to Subtract

When take away is feeling slow, adding up's the way to go!

I have a fast way to do 45 – 36. Instead of doing 45 take away 36, I start with 36 and add up to 45. First I add 4 to get to 40, then I add 5 more to get to 45. The answer is 4 + 5 = 9!

1. 45 – 36 = 9 → 4 (Make 40.) + 5 (Add the rest.)

2. 74 – 48 = ☐ → 2 (Make 50.) + ☐ (Add the rest.)

3. 32 – 25 = ☐ → 5 (Make 30.) + ☐ (Add the rest.)

4. 91 – 33 = ☐ → ☐ (Make 40.) + 51 (Add the rest.)

Good work! Keep it up!

Doing Great!

5. 35 – 19 = ☐ → ☐ + ☐

6. 54 – 35 = ☐ → ☐ + ☐

7. 65 – 27 = ☐ → ☐ + ☐

8. 84 – 49 = ☐ → ☐ + ☐

Take It Further!

Now try doing all the steps in your head!

9. 43 – 28

10. 62 – 56

11. 31 – 18

12. 73 – 45

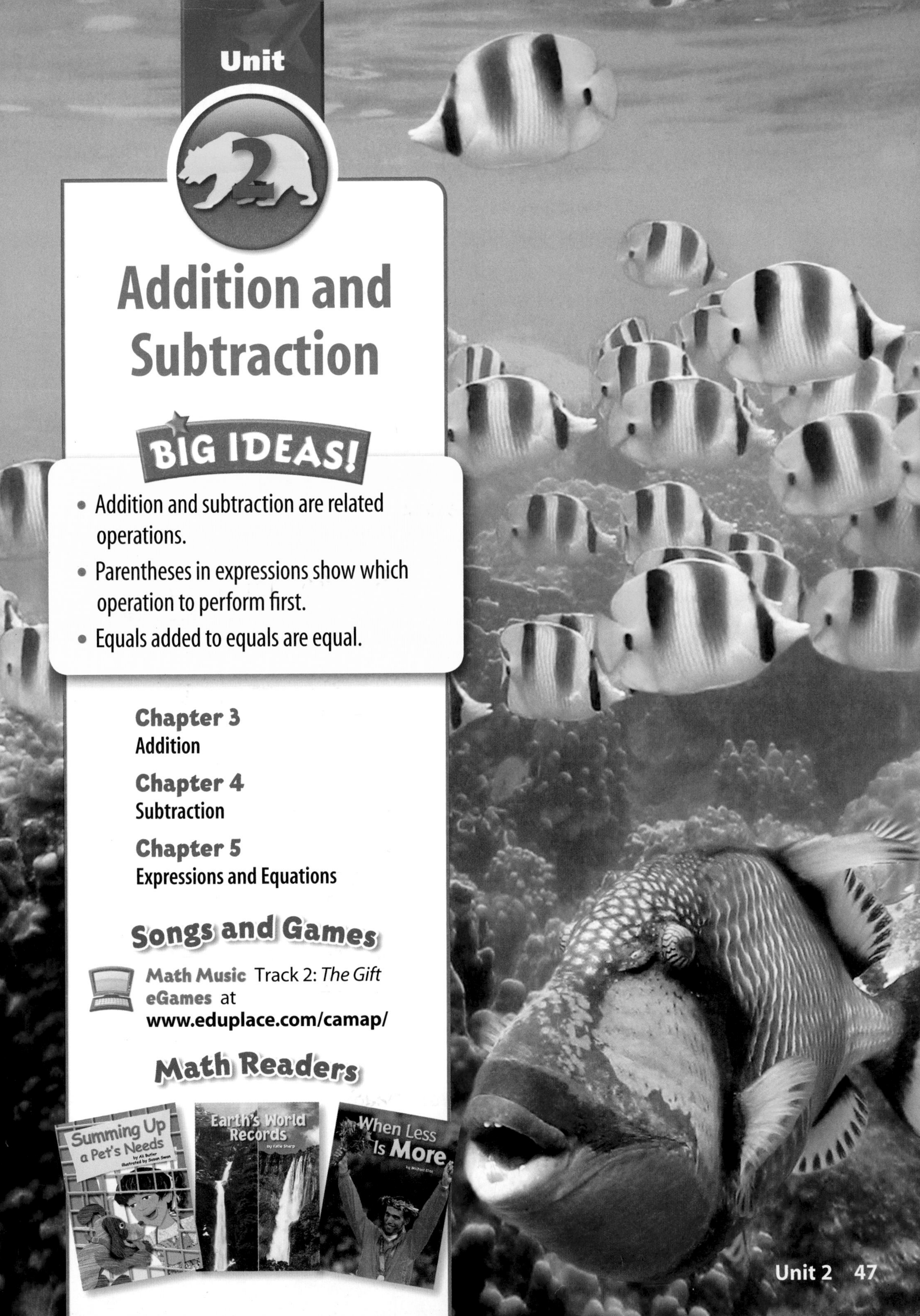

Unit 2

Addition and Subtraction

BIG IDEAS!

- Addition and subtraction are related operations.
- Parentheses in expressions show which operation to perform first.
- Equals added to equals are equal.

Songs and Games

Math Music Track 2: *The Gift*
eGames at
www.eduplace.com/camap/

Math Readers

Get Ready **Game**

Add Them Up!

Object of the Game Create 3-digit and 2-digit addends to make the greatest sum.

Materials
- Learning Tool 12 (Digit and Symbol Cards) (3 sets of digits only)

Number of Players 2–3

Set Up
Shuffle the digit cards. Place them in a stack face down.

How to Play

1. Each player takes five cards from the stack and makes a 3-digit addend and a 2-digit addend.
2. Each player finds the sum of the addends. The player with the greatest sum earns 1 point.
3. Players return the cards to the stack, shuffle them, and repeat Steps 1–2.
4. After a third round, players add their totals from all three rounds. The player with the greatest total earns 1 more point.
5. The player with the greatest number of points is the winner.

CA Standards
KEY NS 1.2 Order and compare whole numbers and decimals to two decimal places.

KEY NS 3.1 Demonstrate an understanding of, and an ability to use, standard algorithms for the addition and subtraction of multidigit numbers.

Education Place
Visit www.eduplace.com/camap/ for **Brain Teasers** and **eGames** to play.

Reading It can be helpful to show the information and numbers in a word problem in a different way. You can make a list, write a number sentence, make notes, or draw a picture or diagram.

Read the word problem. Study the drawing.

Problem 1

Nikki has 96 coins in her collection. Jenny has 25 more coins than Nikki. Elana has 75 more coins than Jenny. How many coins does Elana have?

Nikki	96		
Jenny	96	25	
Elana	96	25	75

You need to add the three numbers to find the number of coins in Elana's collection.

Here is how I showed the information in the problem.

Writing Read Problem 2. Then show the information in a different way.

Problem 2

Arlene has 84 coins in her collection. 18 of Arlene's coins are from other countries. How many of the coins are from the United States?

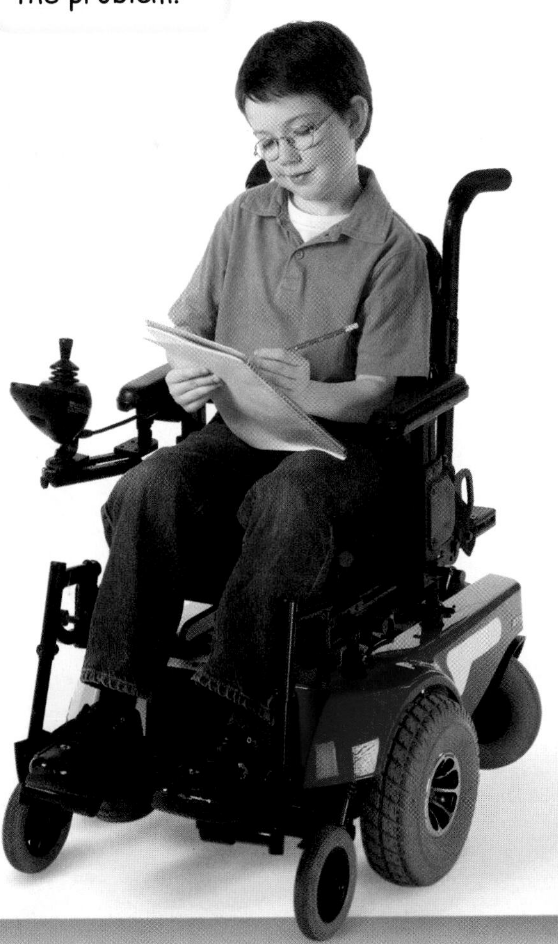

Addition

Check What You Know

Vocabulary and Concepts GRADE 3 KEY NS 2.1, MR 2.3

Choose the best word to complete the sentence.

Word Bank
addend
estimate
round
sum

1. When you add 2 and 4, the ____ is 6.
2. The numbers 5, 6, 7, 8, and 9 all ____ to 10.

Skills KEY NS 1.3

Round each number to the place of the underlined digit. pages 32 and 34

3. 425 (underlined: 4)
4. 1,756 (underlined: 7)
5. 25,496 (underlined: 5)

Find the sum. GRADE 3 KEY NS 2.1

6. 246 + 142
7. 314 + 252
8. 310 + 87
9. 725 + 214

Problem Solving and Reasoning GRADE 3 KEY NS 2.1

10. Kenesha has 54 dolls in her collection. Then she bought 18 more. How many dolls does she have now?

Vocabulary

Visualize It!

Properties of Addition

Commutative Property of Addition
23 + 47 = 47 + 23

Associative Property of Addition
(39 + 21) + 62 = 39 + (21 + 62)

Zero Property of Addition
34,789 + 0 = 34,789

Language Tips

The word *round* has many meanings. A ball can be described as *round*. In mathematics, when we *round* a number, we write the number to the nearest ten, hundred, or thousand.

Words that look alike in English and Spanish often have the same meaning.

English	Spanish
exact	exacto/exacta
problem	problema
sum	suma

See **English-Spanish Glossary** pages 644–666.

Education Place Visit www.eduplace.com/camap/ for the **eGlossary** and **eGames**.

CA Standards MR 2.3 Use a variety of methods, such as words, numbers, symbols, charts, graphs, tables, diagrams, and models, to explain mathematical reasoning. **Also AF 1.0**

CA Standards
KEY NS 3.0 Students solve problems involving addition, subtraction, multiplication, and division of whole numbers and understand the relationships among the operations.

Also KEY NS 1.3, MR 2.0, MR 2.1, MR 2.3, MR 2.4

Vocabulary

estimate

Materials
- Workmat 1
- base-ten blocks
- eManipulatives (optional) www.eduplace.com/camap/

Hands On
Estimate and Check

Objective Estimate a quantity and estimate sums.

Explore

In Chapter 2, you rounded numbers on a number line.
In this lesson, you will use rounding to **estimate** sums.

Question How can you use base-ten blocks to estimate sums?

Todd collected 37 pounds of newspaper to recycle. Jack collected 22 pounds. About how many pounds of paper did they recycle?

1 Use base-ten blocks to show 37 and 22.

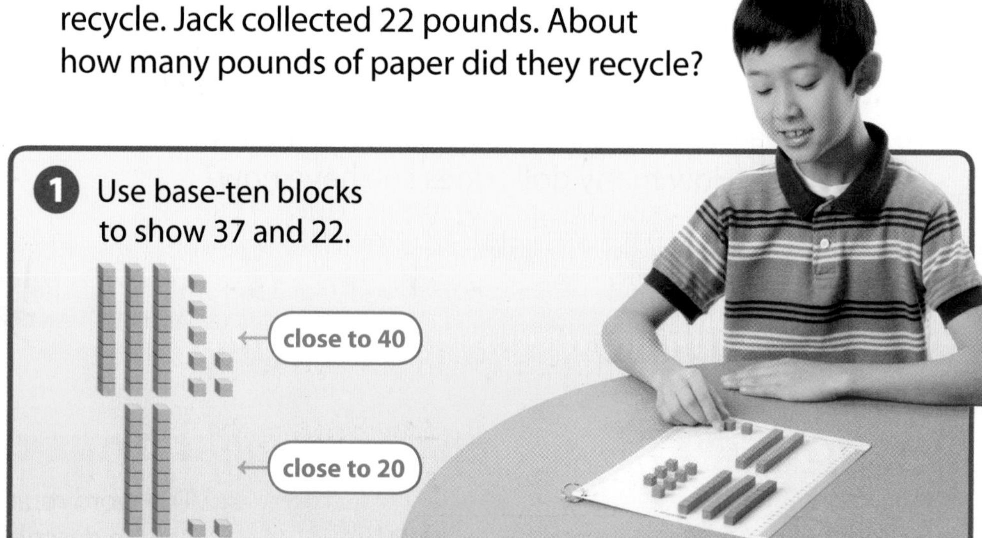

2 Round each number to the nearest 10. Use tens blocks to show 40 and 20.

37 rounds to 40.
22 rounds to 20.

3 To estimate the sum of 37 and 22, use 40 and 20. Count the number of tens blocks.

$$\begin{array}{r} 40 \\ +\ 20 \\ \hline 60 \end{array}$$

4 Draw a quick picture to show your work.

|||| + || = ||||||

Solution: Todd and Jack recycled about 60 pounds of newspaper.

Suppose you want to estimate the sum of 3 numbers. Lisa, Lakeisha, and Pat collected 25 bottles, 46 bottles, and 32 bottles. About how many bottles did they collect in all?

1. Use base-ten blocks to model each number.
2. Round each number to the nearest ten.
3. Estimate the sum.
4. Draw a quick picture to show your work.

Extend

Estimate the sum. You may use base-ten blocks to help.

1. 16 + 32 + 14 + 41

2. 9 + 29 + 13 + 17

3. 234 + 125 + 366

4. 98 + 480 + 216

5. 91 + 348 + 287

6. 11 + 34 + 15 + 49

Choose the best estimate. Explain your strategy.

7. 82 + 3 + 17
- **A** 90
- **B** 200
- **C** 100

8. 235 + 456 + 290
- **A** 1000
- **B** 600
- **C** 1500

9. 540 + 662 + 188
- **A** 1100
- **B** 2000
- **C** 1400

Todd's little sister, Lisa, gave him these exercises to check. Use them to answer Problems 10–11.

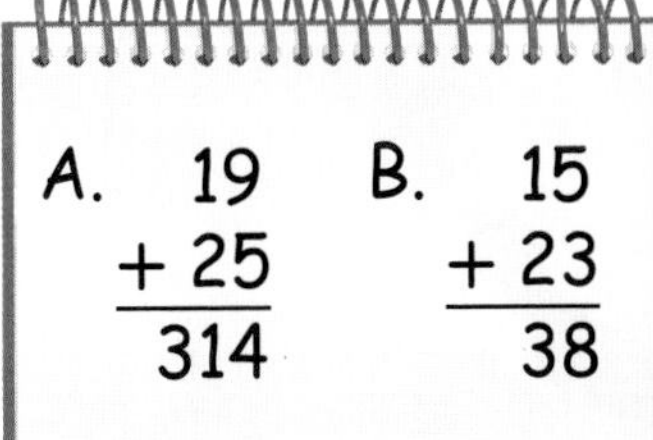

10. **Challenge** Are any exercises wrong? If so, which ones?

11. **Explain** How can estimation help Lisa find her mistake?

Writing Math

Explain Taro estimated the sum of 34 and 53. Look at his work. Would the estimate be different if he rounded the addends first?

$$\begin{array}{r} 34 \\ +\ 53 \\ \hline 87 \end{array} \longrightarrow 90$$

Estimate: 90

CA Standards

KEY NS 3.1 Demonstrate an understanding of, and the ability to use, standard algorithms for the addition and subtraction of multidigit numbers.

AF 1.0 Students use and interpret variables, mathematical symbols, and properties to write and simplify expressions and sentences.

Also KEY NS 3.0, KEY AF 1.2, MR 1.0, MR 2.0, MR 2.3, MR 3.0, MR 3.3

Vocabulary

$15 + 0 = 15$

addends → 15, 0; sum → 15

Zero Property of Addition

Commutative Property of Addition

Associative Property of Addition

Addition Properties

Objective Recognize and apply properties of addition.

Learn by Example

In this lesson, you will learn some addition properties that can help you add.

Addition Properties

Zero Property of Addition

When you add zero to a number, the **sum** is that number.

$12 + 0 = 12$

Commutative Property of Addition

When you change the order of the **addends**, the sum stays the same.

$8 + 7 = 15$

$7 + 8 = 15$

Associative Property of Addition

When you change the way the addends are grouped, the sum stays the same.

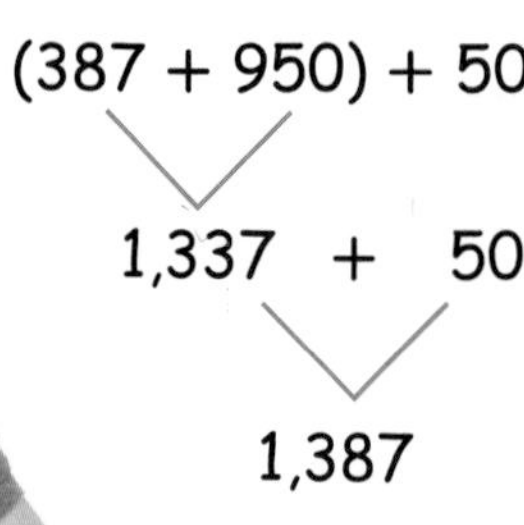

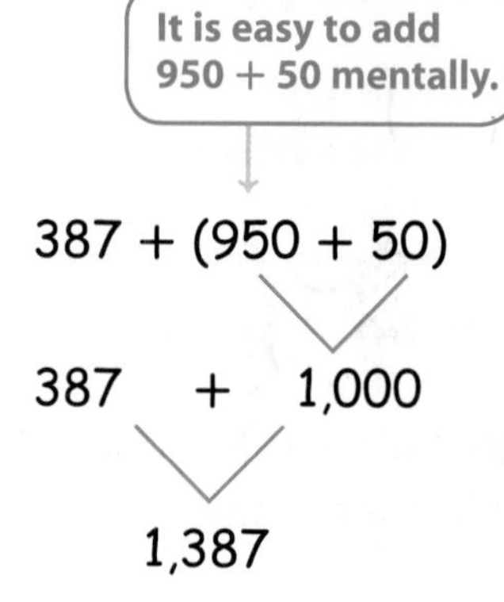

It is easy to add 950 + 50 mentally.
387 + (950 + 50)
387 + 1,000
1,387

Guided Practice

Algebra Properties

Find the number that makes the number sentence true. Tell which property of addition you used.

1. $11 + 0 = \square$

2. $\square + 21 = 21 + 15$

3. $19 + \square = 19$

4. $6 + (7 + 12) = (6 + \square) + 12$

Ask Yourself

- Is one of the numbers zero?
- Will changing the order of addends make the addition easier?

Group the addends so you can add mentally. Then find the sum. Show your work.

5. $67 + 33 + 29$

6. $24 + 98 + 2$

7. $760 + 40 + 134$

8. $102 + 298 + 14$

9. $33 + 17 + 83$

10. $785 + 130 + 15$

Math Talk How did you group the addends in Exercise 6 so it was easier to add? Tell what property you used.

Practice and Problem Solving

Algebra Properties

Find the number that makes each number sentence true. Tell which property of addition you used.

11. $34 + 99 = \square + 34$

12. $342 + 0 = \square$

13. $\square + 62 = 62$

14. $18 + (12 + 4) = (\square + 12) + 4$

15. $24 + (4 + 9) = (24 + \square) + 9$

16. $(7 + 3) + 67 = 7 + (3 + \square)$

17. $\square + 36 = 36 + 17$

Group the addends so you can add mentally. Then find each sum. Show your work.

18. $75 + 25 + 46$

19. $92 + 421 + 8$

20. $511 + 473 + 89$

21. $490 + 84 + 10$

22. $382 + 291 + 9$

23. $820 + 78 + 80$

Solve.

24. Victoria collected 29 bundles of newspaper to recycle. Kumar and Marc each collected 25 bundles. Use mental math to find the total bundles of newspaper they collected.

25. Students made 24 bug bookmarks, 45 flower bookmarks, and 66 animal bookmarks. Use mental math to find the total. What property did you use?

26. **Generalize** Does the Commutative Property work for subtraction? Support your answer and include an example. What about the Zero Property?

Science Link

Use the picture to solve.

27. What is the total resistance of the circuit on the right? Explain how to find the total easily using mental math and the properties of addition.

28. A series circuit has two resistors of 37 Ω and 24 Ω. Does it or the circuit shown have a lesser resistance?

29. If the light bulbs in a series circuit were arranged in a different order, would the total resistance remain the same? Explain why or why not.

30. If another resistor of 42 Ω is added to the series circuit shown, what is its total resistance?

Electricity

- Electricity flows in a circuit, or loop.
- A resistor reduces the flow of electricity in a circuit.
- A light bulb is one example of a resistor.
- Resistance is measured in *ohms* (Ω).
- In a series circuit such as the one shown here, with more than one resistor, the total resistance equals the sum of the individual resistances.

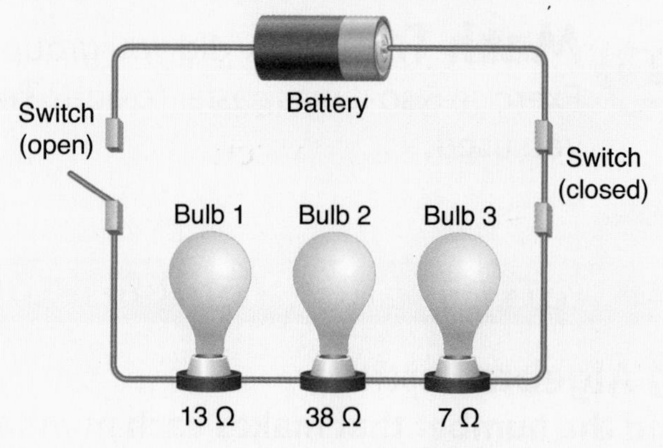

Science PS 1.a

Spiral Review and Test Practice

Round the number to the nearest ten thousand. KEY NS 1.3 pages 32, 34

31. 47,259 **32.** 24,842 **33.** 539,025 **34.** 1,266,487

Round the number to the nearest hundred thousand. KEY NS 1.3 pages 32, 34

35. 587,284 **36.** 731,538 **37.** 4,523,881 **38.** 7,459,032

Write the letter of the correct answer. KEY AF 1.2

39. Which is the value of the expression $(12 + 3) - (4 + 1)$?

A 10 **B** 12 **C** 15 **D** 20

Extra Practice See page 67, Set A.

Key Standards Review

Need Help?
See Key Standards Handbook.

Round the number to the nearest hundred thousand. KEY NS 1.3

1. 34,768,320
2. 12,465,200
3. 523,407
4. 863,480
5. 72,982,119
6. 264,000

Round the number to the nearest hundred. KEY NS 1.3

7. 7,876,340
8. 362,141
9. 148,723
10. 256,899
11. 8,999,111
12. 46,929

Write the numbers in order from least to greatest. KEY NS 1.2

13. 732,400 723,400 700,230

14. On Friday 62,478 people attended a concert. On Saturday 65,893 people attended a concert. On which day did more people attend a concert?

Algebraic Thinking

Always, Sometimes, or Never?

Use *always, sometimes,* or *never* to answer the question. AF 1.0, AF 1.1

1. Choose a number for n. When does the value of $n + 0$ equal the value of $0 + n$?
2. Choose a number for x. When does the value of $x + 1$ equal the value of $x - 1$?
3. Choose a number for r. When does the value of $r + 5$ equal the value of $5 + r$?
4. Choose a number for z. When does the value of z equal the value of $2 + z$?
5. Choose a number for y. When does the value of y equal the value of $y + y$?

CA Standards
KEY NS 1.3 Round whole numbers through the millions to the nearest ten, hundred, thousand, ten thousand, or hundred thousand.

KEY NS 3.0 Students solve problems involving addition, subtraction, multiplication, and division of whole numbers and understand the relationships among the operations.

Also NS 1.0, KEY NS 1.4, MR 1.0, MR 2.0, MR 2.3, MR 2.5, MR 3.1

Estimate Sums

Objective Round numbers to estimate sums.

Learn by Example

The Community Center has space for 675 students in an after-school arts program. 478 grade-school students and 188 middle-school students sign up. Does the center have enough space for all who signed up?

To answer this question, you do not need an exact sum. Since you only need to know if the number of students who signed up is 675 or less, you can estimate the sum.

1 Round each addend to the nearest hundred. Then add the rounded numbers.

478	rounds to	500
+ 188	rounds to	+ 200
		700

Both addends were rounded up, so the actual sum will be less than 700.

2 To get a closer estimate, round to the nearest ten. Then add.

478	rounds to	480
+ 188	rounds to	+ 190
		670

Both addends were rounded up, and their sum is less than 675. So the actual sum is less than 675.

Solution: The Community Center has enough room for all the students.

Other Examples

A. Round each number to the nearest thousand. Then estimate the sum.

5,742	rounds to	6,000
+ 1,575	rounds to	+ 2,000
		8,000

B. Round each number to the nearest ten thousand. Then estimate the sum.

73,465	rounds to	70,000
+ 19,287	rounds to	+ 20,000
		90,000

Guided Practice

Round each number to the nearest hundred. Estimate the sum.

1. 365 + 732 **2.** 586 + 198 **3.** 4,567 + 1,111

Round each number to the nearest thousand. Estimate the sum.

4. $\begin{array}{r} 4{,}522 \\ +\ 3{,}726 \\ \hline \end{array}$ **5.** $\begin{array}{r} 8{,}173 \\ +\ 2{,}566 \\ \hline \end{array}$ **6.** $\begin{array}{r} 6{,}359 \\ +\ 1{,}703 \\ \hline \end{array}$

Round each number to the nearest ten thousand. Estimate the sum.

7. $\begin{array}{r} 16{,}723 \\ +\ 24{,}119 \\ \hline \end{array}$ **8.** $\begin{array}{r} 76{,}897 \\ +\ 47{,}129 \\ \hline \end{array}$ **9.** $\begin{array}{r} 15{,}096 \\ +\ 32{,}749 \\ \hline \end{array}$

Ask Yourself

- To what place am I rounding?
- Is the digit in the place to the right greater than or less than 5?

Guided Problem Solving

Use the questions to solve this problem.

10. The Community Center has a sports program with activities for 450 students. If 242 boys and 233 girls sign up, will the center need to add more activities?

a. **Understand** The center has space for how many students? How many have signed up?

b. **Plan** Do you need an exact answer to solve the problem? Explain. What place should you round to, to get the best estimate?

c. **Solve** Round each number to the nearest ten, and find the sum. Then write the answer.

d. **Look Back** Can you use your estimate instead of the exact sum to answer the question? Explain.

Math Talk In Problem 10 above, suppose you had rounded to the nearest 100. Could you use that estimate to solve the problem? Explain your answer.

Practice and Problem Solving

Round each number to the nearest hundred. Estimate the sum.

11. 941 + 386 **12.** 256 + 371 **13.** 682 + 921

Round each number to the nearest thousand. Estimate the sum.

14. 1,752 + 973

15. 8,426 + 778

16. 12,493 + 2,178

17. 7,623 + 4,401

Round each number to the nearest ten thousand. Estimate the sum.

18. 28,984 + 13,218

19. 25,103 + 86,273

20. 99,452 + 9,749

21. 33,679 + 54,231

History-Social Science Link

Use the table to solve.

22. Estimate, to the nearest hundred, the sum of the distances shown in the table.

23. Is your estimate from Problem 22 greater than or less than the actual length? Explain your answer without finding the actual length.

24. Explain Look back at Problem 23. What are the advantages of estimating the solution? Of finding an exact solution?

The Pony Express Trail

State	Wyoming	Utah	Nevada	California
Miles	540	241	404	223

- The Pony Express was a system of horse-and-rider teams that carried mail.
- The trail ran about 2,000 miles between Missouri and California, passing through 8 states.
- It took about 10 days to deliver mail from one end of the trail to the other.

History-Social Science 4.4.1

Spiral Review and Test Practice

Compare. Write $>$ or $<$ for the ⬭. KEY NS 1.2 page 28

25. 254,920 ⬭ 537,951 **26.** 2,647,018 ⬭ 2,467,108

Write the letter of the correct answer. KEY NS 1.3, KEY NS 3.0

27. In 2005, Fresno had 461,116 residents and Long Beach had 474,014. About how many people live in these two cities?

A 925,000 **B** 935,000 **C** 945,000 **D** 950,000

Extra Practice See page 67, Set B.

Use a Pattern

Consecutive whole numbers are whole numbers that increase by 1 at each step. For example, 7, 8, 9, and 10 are consecutive whole numbers.

When you add an even number of consecutive whole numbers, there is an interesting pattern. Look at these examples.

Find 7 + 8 + 9 + 10.

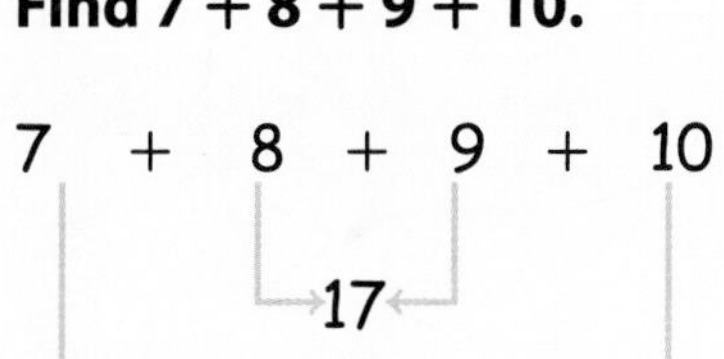

17 + 17 = 34

The sum is 34.

Find 10 + 11 + 12 + 13 + 14 + 15.

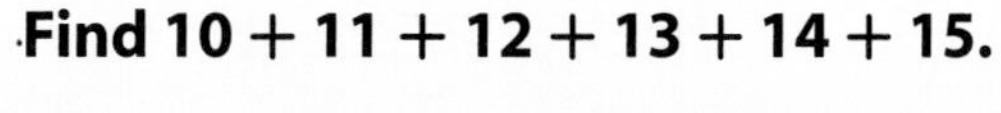

25

25

25

25 + 25 + 25 = 75

The sum is 75.

Find each sum using the pattern above. Use estimation to check if your answers are reasonable.

1. 16 + 17 + 18 + 19
2. 4 + 5 + 6 + 7 + 8 + 9
3. 30 + 31 + 32 + 33
4. 97 + 98 + 99 + 100
5. 4 + 5 + 6 + 7 + 8 + 9 + 10 + 11
6. 57 + 58 + 59 + 60
7. What is the sum of the first ten consecutive whole numbers?
8. Which four consecutive whole numbers have a sum of 90? Explain how you found your answer.

CA Standards
KEY (NS 3.1) Demonstrate an understanding of, and the ability to use, standard algorithms for the addition and subtraction of multidigit numbers.

KEY (NS 3.0) Students solve problems involving addition, subtraction, multiplication, and division of whole numbers and understand the relationships among the operations.

Also MR 1.0, MR 1.2, MR 2.0, MR 2.1, MR 2.3

Vocabulary

regroup

Navajo woman with sheep on her sheep farm

Add Whole Numbers

Objective Find whole number sums using regrouping.

Learn by Example

You already know three addition properties that can help you add. In this lesson, you will learn one way to add large numbers.

The Navajo use the wool from their sheep to weave cloth. Suppose a family has one flock of 129 sheep and another flock of 97 sheep. How many sheep do they have in all?

Add. 129 + 97

1 Add the ones.

$9 + 7 = 16$

$$\begin{array}{r} {\scriptstyle 1} \\ 129 \\ +\ 97 \\ \hline 6 \end{array}$$

Regroup 16 tens as 1 ten and 6 ones

2 Add the tens.

$1 + 2 + 9 = 12$

$$\begin{array}{r} {\scriptstyle 11} \\ 129 \\ +\ 97 \\ \hline 26 \end{array}$$

Regroup 12 tens as 1 hundred and 2 tens

3 Add the hundreds.

$1 + 1 = 2$

$$\begin{array}{r} {\scriptstyle 11} \\ 129 \\ +\ 97 \\ \hline 226 \end{array}$$

Solution: The family has 226 sheep in all.

Other Examples

A. Add Large Numbers.

$$\begin{array}{r} {\scriptstyle 111} \\ 535{,}293 \\ +\ 82{,}048 \\ \hline 617{,}341 \end{array}$$

B. Add More Than Two Addends.

$$\begin{array}{r} {\scriptstyle 1\ 21} \\ 23{,}578 \\ 1{,}564 \\ +\ \ \ 387 \\ \hline 25{,}529 \end{array}$$

Guided Practice

Add. Use estimation to verify your answer.

1. 583 + 54

2. 6,582 + 298

3. 2,793 + 524

4. 24,571 + 192,714

5. 36,305 + 9,221 + 115,872

Ask Yourself

- Are the digits lined up correctly?
- Do I need to regroup?
- Did I use estimation to verify my answer?

Math Talk Suppose you are adding 674 + 318. Why do you place the regrouped 1 ten over the 7 in 674 and not over the 6 or the 4?

Practice and Problem Solving

Add. Use estimation to verify your answer.

6. 6,714 + 8,600

7. 5,195 + 3,261

8. 12,894 + 34,710

9. 275,182 + 463,957

10. 9,832 + 661

11. 8,623 + 782 + 47,958

12. 1,058 + 209 + 29,623

Solve.

13. **Multistep** Carolyn had a box of 1,549 colored beads. She traded 1,125 of them for 869 wooden beads. How many beads does she have now?

14. Jim removed 83 tiny beads from a long necklace. Then he added 62 larger beads. The necklace now has 545 beads. How many beads did the necklace have before?

Spiral Review and Test Practice

Write the value of the underlined digit. NS 1.0 pages 8, 12

15. 782,390 (underlined digit: 2)

16. 39,886,264 (underlined digit: 3)

17. 2,659,300 (underlined digit: 6)

Write the letter of the correct answer. KEY NS 3.1

18. 3,578 + 1,585

A 5,063 **B** 5,153 **C** 5,163 **D** 4,163

Extra Practice See page 67, Set C.

CA Standards
MR 2.1, MR 2.5, MR 1.1, MR 2.3, MR 2.4, MR 1.0, MR 2.0, KEY NS 1.3, KEY NS 3.0, KEY NS 3.1

Problem Solving

Objective Use skills and strategies to solve word problems.

Visitors work on art projects at a painting booth at the Sawdust Art Festival.

The Sawdust Art Festival is a popular summer festival at Laguna Beach. You can view craft demonstrations, such as glass blowing, or take an art workshop.

Solve. Tell which strategy or method you used.

1. A balloon artist at the festival has a box of 1,295 red balloons, 976 blue balloons, 1,147 green balloons, and 1,037 yellow balloons.
   a. Round each number to the nearest hundred. Then estimate the total number of balloons.
   b. Find the exact number of balloons. Is this number close to your estimate?
   c. **Analyze** Round the exact number of balloons to the nearest hundred. Is this rounded sum the same as your estimate?

2. **Draw a Picture** A small skimboard is about 48 inches long and 18 inches wide. The skimboarders want to display their skimboards for the festival by laying them out on a patch of beach that is 100 inches long and 80 inches wide. How many skimboards will fit?

Skimboarder

Problem Solving on Tests

Select a Strategy

- Make an Organized List
- Estimate
- Guess and Check
- Make a Table
- Work Backward

1. A library has one hundred sixty-two thousand books, magazines, tapes, and CDs. What is this number in standard form?

A 16,200
B 126,000
C 160,200
D 162,000

NS 1.0 page 8

2. Heidi wrote a number as 1,000,000 + 600 + 5,000 + 50,000 + 9 + 300,000,000. What is this number in standard form?

A 301,556,009
B 301,055,609
C 130,550,609
D 130,609,550

Test Tip
You can sketch a place-value chart to help solve the problem.

KEY NS 1.1 page 16

3. Magda looked up the populations of four California cities. Which of the following populations has the greatest value?

A 382,369
B 283,936
C 238,936
D 328,036

KEY NS 1.2 page 28

4. Mr. Miller drove his car 204,375 miles before he sold it. What is 204,375 rounded to the nearest thousand?

A 205,000
B 204,400
C 204,000
D 200,000

KEY NS 1.3 page 32

5. A popular magazine sold 7,626,088 copies in one year. What is 7,626,088 rounded to the nearest hundred thousand?

A 7,000,000
B 7,600,000
C 8,626,088
D 8,000,000

KEY NS 1.3 page 34

6. A stadium has 60,000 seats. There is a baseball game in the stadium every day. About 40,000 people were at the game on Tuesday. The number of people at each game increased by 2,000 every day. About how many people were at the game on Saturday?

A 42,000 people
B 48,000 people
C 50,000 people
D 68,000 people

Test Tip
Which information in the problem helps you find the answer?

KEY NS 3.1 page 62

Education Place
Visit www.eduplace.com/camap/ for **Test-Taking Tips** and **Extra Practice**.

Reading & Writing 

Vocabulary

Three **properties of addition** are the **Zero Property**, the **Commutative Property**, and the **Associative Property**.

Complete the word web.

Properties of Addition

Zero Property of Addition
When you add zero to a number, the **sum** is that number.
6 + 0 = ▢
0 + ▢ = 29

Commutative Property
When you change the order of the **addends**, the **sum** stays the same.
5 + 4 = 5 + ▢

Associative Property
When you change the way the **addends** are grouped, the **sum** stays the same.
3 + (2 + 6) = (3 + 2) + 6
3 + ▢ = ▢ + 6
11 = ▢

Writing How does knowing these addition properties help you when you add?

Reading Look for this book in your library.
Math-Terpieces, by Greg Tang and Greg Paprocki

CA Standards
MR 2.3 Use a variety of methods, such as words, numbers, symbols, charts, graphs, tables, diagrams, and models, to explain mathematical reasoning.
Also AF 1.0

Standards-Based Extra Practice

Set A

AF 1.0 page 54

Find the number that makes each number sentence true. Tell which property of addition you used.

1. 13 + 0 = ■
2. (4 + 2) + 5 = 4 + (■ + 5)
3. 2 + (8 + 5) = (2 + ■) + 5
4. 22 + ■ = 31 + 22
5. **Explain** Xavier collected stamps from all over the United States. He has 25 stamps in one book, 55 in another book, and 64 in his last book. Which addition property would work best to find how many stamps he has in all? Explain.

Set B

KEY NS 1.3, KEY NS 1.4 page 58

Round each number to the greatest place. Then estimate the sum.

1. 321 + 734
2. 263 + 193
3. 924 + 268
4. 1,620 + 1,440
5. 1,620 + 2,300
6. 54,823 + 45,592
7. 25,983 + 18,235
8. 64,987 + 35,764
9. A community center has an arts program with activities for 650 students. If 307 boys and 292 girls sign up, will the center need to add more activities?

Set C

KEY NS 3.1 page 62

Add. Use estimation to verify your answer.

1. $\begin{array}{r} 592 \\ +\ 45 \\ \hline \end{array}$
2. $\begin{array}{r} 3,582 \\ +\ 298 \\ \hline \end{array}$
3. $\begin{array}{r} 22,430 \\ +\ 3,340 \\ \hline \end{array}$
4. $\begin{array}{r} 3,203 \\ +\ 3,203 \\ \hline \end{array}$
5. **Explain** Tim wants to know how far his family will drive on their vacation this summer. They will travel from Palm Springs to Phoenix (258 miles), from Phoenix to Salt Lake City (500 miles), and then back to Palm Springs (543 miles). How far will they drive? Explain how you got your answer.

Education Place
Visit www.eduplace.com/camap/ for **Extra Practice**.

Chapter Review/Test

Vocabulary and Concepts — AF 1.0, MR 2.3

Write the best word to complete the sentence.

1. When one addend is 0, the other addend is the same as the sum, describes the ______ Property of Addition.
2. A number that is close to an exact amount is called an ______.

Skills — AF 1.0, KEY NS 3.1, KEY NS 3.0, KEY NS 1.3

Find the number that makes the number sentence true. Tell which property of addition you used.

3. $38 + \blacksquare = 38$
4. $(5 + 6) + 7 = 5 + (\blacksquare + 7)$
5. $61 + 18 = \blacksquare + 61$
6. $\blacksquare + 15 = 15 + 400$

Round each number to the greatest place. Estimate the sum.

7. 78,032 + 2,389
8. 38,436 + 2,921
9. 281,342 + 289,342

Add. Use estimation to verify your answer.

10. 1,593 + 359
11. 57,562 + 1,899
12. 1,266,892 + 950,205
13. 252,563 + 292,195
14. 4,837 + 4,111
15. 23,231 + 15,943
16. 3,784 + 42,573
17. 11,695 + 12,204
18. 295 + 708 + 11,866

Problem Solving and Reasoning — KEY NS 3.1, MR 2.1, MR 2.3

Solve.

19. Last year, 189,002 people attended the Sawdust Art Festival. If 1,985 more people attend this year, what will the attendance be?
20. If the population of a city is 2,705,107, is twenty-seven million a good estimate? Explain.

Writing Math When might estimation not be a good way to solve a problem?

Spiral Review and Test Practice

1. Which of these is the number 812,190,000?

   A eight hundred twelve million, one hundred nine thousand

   B eight hundred twelve million, one hundred ninety thousand

   C eight hundred twelve million, nine hundred ten thousand

   D eight hundred twenty-one million, one hundred ninety thousand

KEY NS 1.1 page 12

2. Which is 3,000 + 20 + 5,000,000 + 100,000 + 600 + 200,000,000 + 90,000 in standard form?

   A 250,193,620

   B 205,193,620

   C 205,193,602

   D 205,139,620

KEY NS 1.1 page 16

3. Which of the following has the greatest value?

   A 7,456,102 **C** 7,327,906

   B 7,448,298 **D** 7,392,321

KEY NS 1.2 page 28

4. What is 25,187,709 rounded to the nearest ten million?

   A 20,000,000

   B 25,190,000

   C 25,200,000

   D 30,000,000

Test Tip
Look at the place to the right of the place you are rounding to.

KEY NS 1.3 page 34

5. Find the number that makes the sentence true.

   $94 + (12 + 6) = (94 + \_\_) + 6$

   A 94 **C** 18

   B 88 **D** 12

AF 1.0 page 54

6. Last year, 345,987 new homes were built. This year 525,345 new homes were built. To the nearest thousand, about how many new homes were built in these two years?

   A 872,000 new homes

   B 871,340 new homes

   C 871,000 new homes

   D 870,000 new homes

KEY NS 1.3 page 58

Education Place
Visit www.eduplace.com/camap/ for **Test-Taking Tips** and **Extra Practice.**

Chapter 4

Subtraction

A bowl of brightly colored beads

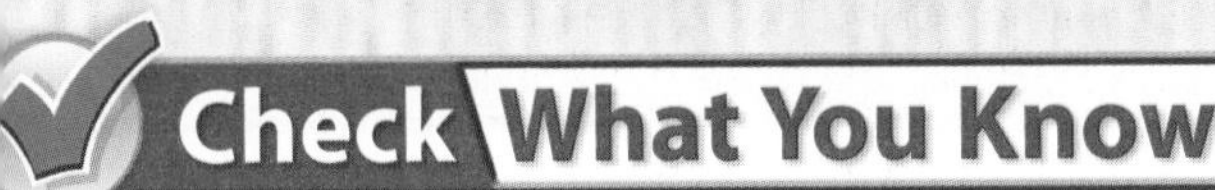

Check What You Know

Word Bank
difference
estimate
round
sum

Vocabulary and Concepts GRADE 3 KEY NS 2.1, MR 2.3

Choose the best word to complete the sentence.

1. When you subtract 2 from 6, the _____ is 4.
2. You can round numbers to _____ a difference.

Skills GRADE 3 KEY NS 2.1

Write a related subtraction sentence.

3. 25 + 27 = 52
4. 17 + 28 = 45
5. 42 + 37 = 79
6. 62 + 19 = 81

Find the difference.

7. 96 −32
8. 916 − 716
9. 150 − 128

Problem Solving and Reasoning GRADE 3 KEY NS 2.1

10. Evaline wants to fill her photo album. The album holds 245 photos. Evaline already has 197 photos in the album. How many more photos does she need to put in the album to fill it?

Vocabulary

Visualize It!

regroup

to use place value to exchange equal amounts when renaming a number

Regrouping can occur in addition and subtraction.

Regrouping in Addition	Regrouping in Subtraction
1 1 278 + 634 912	8 10 12 ~~912~~ − 634 278

Addition and subtraction are opposite or **inverse operations**.

Language Tips

The word *difference* has many meanings. It can mean a noticeable change. In mathematics, *difference* is what the answer in subtraction is called.

Words that look alike in English and Spanish often have the same meaning.

English	Spanish
regroup	reagrupar
operation	operación

See **English-Spanish Glossary** pages 644–666.

Education Place Visit www.eduplace.com/camap/ for the **eGlossary** and **eGames**.

CA Standards MR 2.3 Use a variety of methods, such as words, numbers, symbols, charts, graphs, tables, diagrams, and models, to explain mathematical reasoning. Also **KEY** NS 3.1

Hands On
Model Subtraction from 2,000

Objective Find whole number differences using models.

CA Standards
KEY NS 3.1 Demonstrate an understanding of, and the ability to use, standard algorithms for the addition and subtraction of multidigit numbers.
Also KEY NS 3.0, MR 2.0, MR 2.3, MR 2.4

Vocabulary

regroup

Materials
- Learning Tool 10 ($1,000 Bills)
- dollar bill set

Explore

In Chapter 3, you learned about addition using regrouping. Now you will learn about subtraction using regrouping.

Mrs. Silva had $2,000. She bought a new bicycle for $350. How much money does Mrs. Silva have left?

Question How can you use play money to find the answer?

Work with a partner to subtract $2,000 − $350.

1 Show $2,000.

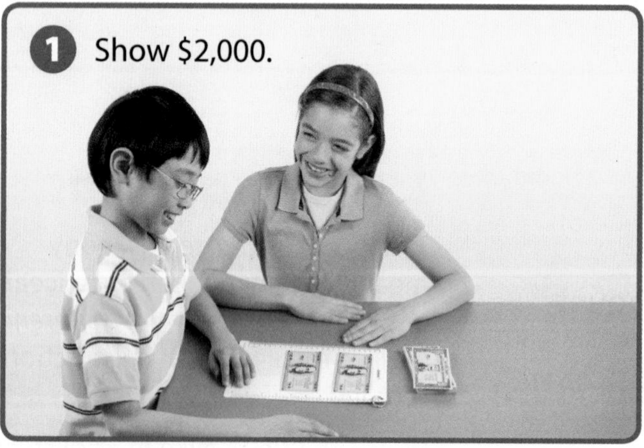

2 You need to **regroup** before you can take away $350. Regroup one $1000 bill as ten $100 bills.

$1000 | $100 $100 | $100 $100 | $100 $100 | $100 $100 | $100 $100

$1000

3 Now you can take away $300 but not $50. Regroup one $100 bill as ten $10 bills.

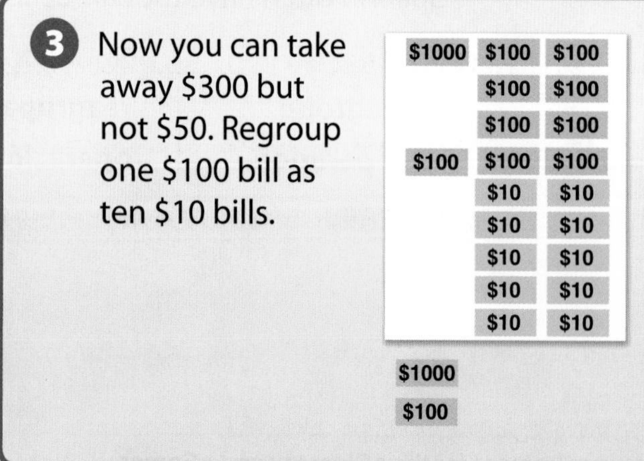

4 Take away $350 from $2,000. Write a subtraction problem to show your answer.

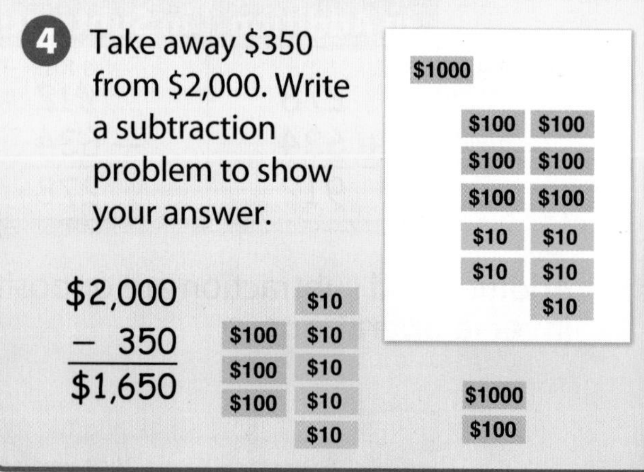

$$\begin{array}{r} \$2,000 \\ -\ \ 350 \\ \hline \$1,650 \end{array}$$

Solution: Mrs. Silva has $1,650 left.

Another Example

A tailor has $2,000. He buys a new sewing machine for $682. How much money does he have left?

1 Show $2,000.

$1000
$1000

2 You need to regroup before you can take away $682. Regroup $1,000.

$1000 $100 $100
$100 $100
$100 $100
$100 $100
$100 $100

3 Then regroup $100.

$1000 $100 $100
$10 $10 $100 $100
$10 $10 $100 $100
$10 $10 $100 $100
$10 $10 $100
$10 $10

4 Then regroup $10. Now you can take away $682. Record your work.

$1000 $100 $100
$10 $10 $100 $100
$10 $10 $100 $100
$10 $10 $100 $100
$10 $10 $100
$10 $1 $1 $1
$1 $1 $1
$1 $1 $1 $1

Solution: The tailor has $1,318 left.

Extend

Use play money to help you subtract.

1. $2,000 − 600

2. $2,000 − 700

3. $2,000 − 350

4. $2,000 − 790

5. $2,000 − 162

6. $2,000 − 365

7. $2,000 − $670 **8.** $2,000 − $230 **9.** $2,000 − $570 **10.** $2,000 − $220

11. $2,000 − $540 **12.** $2,000 − $730 **13.** $2,000 − $400 **14.** $2,000 − $516

15. $2,000 − $253 **16.** $2,000 − $795 **17.** $2,000 − $857 **18.** $2,000 − $99

Writing Math

Explain Explain all the steps you took to solve Exercise 18.

Estimate Differences

Objective Round numbers to estimate differences.

CA Standards
KEY NS 1.3 Round whole numbers through the millions to the nearest ten, hundred, thousand, ten thousand, or hundred thousand.

Also NS 1.0, KEY NS 1.4, KEY NS 3.0, KEY NS 3.1, MR 1.0, MR 1.1, MR 1.2, MR 2.0, MR 2.3, MR 2.5

Vocabulary

estimate

difference

Learn by Example

Mr. Lucas has \$1,143. He buys an easel for \$867. Does Mr. Lucas have enough money left to buy extra paints for \$259?

To answer this question, you do not need an exact answer. Since you only need to know if Mr. Lucas has at least \$259 left, you can **estimate** the **difference** between \$1,143 and \$867.

1 Round each amount to the nearest hundred.

\$1,143	rounds to	\$1,100
\$ 867	rounds to	− 900
		\$ 200

Since the amount of Mr. Lucas's money was rounded down, and the price was rounded up, we know the difference is at least \$200.

You need a closer estimate to solve the problem.

2 To get a closer estimate, round to the nearest ten.

\$1,143	rounds to	\$1,140
\$ 867	rounds to	− 870
		\$ 270

Since the amount of Mr. Lucas's money was rounded down, and the price was rounded up, we know the difference is at least \$270.

Solution: \$270 > \$259, so Mr. Lucas has enough money left to buy extra paints.

Other Examples

A. Round each number to the nearest thousand. Then estimate the difference.

5,669	rounds to	6,000
− 2,168	rounds to	− 2,000
		4,000

B. Round each number to the nearest hundred. Then estimate the difference.

24,309	rounds to	24,300
− 12,087	rounds to	− 12,100
		12,200

Guided Practice

Round each number to the nearest hundred. Then estimate the difference.

1. 5,826 − 1,739 **2.** 76,284 − 31,086

Round each number to the nearest thousand. Then estimate the difference.

3. 9,804 − 7,169 **4.** 57,536 − 24,811

Ask Yourself

- To what place am I rounding?
- What is the digit to the right of that place?

Guided Problem Solving

Use the questions to solve this problem.

5. Mr. Mayer paid for a new woodcarving set with $100. The set cost $83. Does Mr. Mayer have enough money left to buy a $25 stain kit?

a. **Understand** How much did Mr. Mayer have? How much did he spend?

b. **Plan** Does Mr. Mayer need an exact answer? Explain. To what place should he round?

c. **Solve** Find the estimated difference. Then write the answer to the problem.

d. **Look Back** Why can you use the estimated difference to answer the question?

Wood carver

Math Talk Look back at Exercise 4. Which gives a closer estimate—rounding each number to the nearest thousand or to the nearest hundred? Why?

Practice and Problem Solving

Round each number to the nearest hundred. Then estimate the difference.

6. 9,463 − 2,938 **7.** 7,652 − 3,708 **8.** 8,653 − 4,172

9. 38,354 − 24,137 **10.** 96,848 − 52,765 **11.** 79,977 − 58,941

Round each number to the nearest thousand. Then estimate the difference.

12. 8,731 − 3,194

13. 4,199 − 1,733

14. 7,652 − 4,576

15. 63,084 − 31,692

16. 76,523 − 42,687

17. 29, 863 − 14,097

Real World Data

Solve. Use the price list for Problems 19 and 20.

18. At the start of the model train show, there were 63,822 train cars for sale. At the end of the show, there were 16,481 unsold cars. Estimate the number of cars sold by rounding to the nearest thousand and then by rounding to the nearest hundred.

19. Multistep Ramon bought a boxcar kit and a passenger car kit. He paid with a $20 and a $10 bill. About how much change should Ramon get back? Explain how you solved the problem.

20. Right or Wrong? Emma has $50. She wants to buy a freight car, a diesel locomotive, and a caboose kit. She estimates the individual costs by rounding to the nearest ten dollars and says she has enough money. Is Emma correct? Explain.

Plastic Model Kits

Type of Car	Price
Boxcar	$8.95
Caboose	$32.99
Freight	$11.29
Locomotive, Diesel Steam	 $14.29 $18.70
Passenger	$15.95
Stake-sided	$35.99

Spiral Review and Test Practice

Order from least to greatest. KEY NS 1.2 page 28

21. 16,304,802 16,403,208 999,899

22. 3,321,904 3,231,904 3,132,904

23. 6,398,437 6,938,437 6,847,201

24. 9,076,442 9,706,446 9,706,445

Write the letter of the correct answer. KEY NS 3.0, KEY NS 1.3

25. Which number is an estimate for the difference between 19,003 and 5,714 when both numbers are rounded to the nearest thousand?

A 25,000 **B** 15,000 **C** 14,000 **D** 13,000

Extra Practice See page 87, Set A.

Key Standards Review

Need Help?
See Key Standards Handbook.

Write the numbers in order from least to greatest. KEY NS 1.2

1. 11,376 11,386 10,984 12,999

2. 564,300 399,111 654,300 65,489

3. 611,372 919,569 13,471 15,490

Compare. Use > or <. KEY NS 1.2

4. 78,623 ⬭ 78,923

5. 93,425 ⬭ 93,452

6. 110,999 ⬭ 999,110

7. 201,333 ⬭ 846,117

8. 9,011 ⬭ 1,109

9. 4,836 ⬭ 3,804

10. 32,590 ⬭ 35,290

11. 46,295 ⬭ 43,295

Challenge — Algebraic Thinking

Population Counts

Use the table to solve. NS 1.0, KEY NS 1.2, KEY NS 1.3

City	Population
San Francisco	751,682
San Jose	898,349
Long Beach	475,460
Fresno	451,455

1. Find the city using these clues for its population: It has a 5 in the ten thousands place, a 6 in the hundreds place, and the number in the tens place is 4 times the number in the ones place.

2. Round the populations of Fresno and Long Beach to the nearest hundred thousand. Can you tell which population is larger from the rounded population? What could you do to find rounded populations that would show which of these two populations is larger?

3. Write the greatest number you can make using each digit from the population of San Jose only once.

CA Standards

KEY (NS 3.1) Demonstrate an understanding of, and the ability to use, standard algorithms for the addition and subtraction of multidigit numbers.

KEY (NS 3.0) Students solve problems involving addition, subtraction, multiplication, and division of whole numbers and understand the relationships among the operations.

Also MR 1.0, MR 1.1, MR 1.2, MR 2.0, MR 2.1, MR 2.3, MR 2.4, MR 2.6, MR 3.0, MR 3.3

Vocabulary

inverse operations

Subtract Whole Numbers

Objective Find whole number differences.

Learn by Example

In Lesson 2, you estimated differences. In this lesson, you will learn how to find exact differences.

Suppose a domino line has 2,865 dominoes in it. If 868 dominoes are knocked down, how many dominoes are left standing?

Subtract. 2,865 − 868

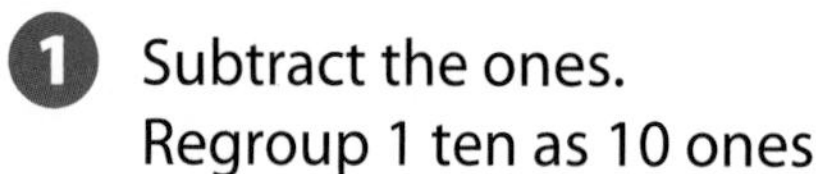

1 Subtract the ones. Regroup 1 ten as 10 ones.

```
       5 15
  2,8  6  5
−   8  6  8
-----------
          7
```

2 Subtract the tens. Regroup 1 hundred as 10 tens.

```
        15
      7  5 15
  2,  8  6  5
−     8  6  8
-------------
         9  7
```

3 Subtract the hundreds. Regroup 1 thousand as 10 hundreds.

```
     17 15
  1   7  5 15
  2,  8  6  5
−     8  6  8
-------------
      9  9  7
```

4 Subtract the thousands.

```
     17 15
  1   7  5 15
  2,  8  6  5
−     8  6  8
-------------
  1,  9  9  7
```

Check

Use estimation to check that your answer is reasonable.

```
  2,900
−   900    1,997 is close
  2,000    to 2,000.
```

Use addition to check that your answer is correct.

```
  2,865      1,997
−   868    +   868    The numbers are the same,
  1,997      2,865    so the difference is correct.
```

You can check subtraction by adding because addition undoes subtraction. Addition and subtraction are opposite or **inverse operations**.

Solution: 1,997 dominoes are left standing.

Another Example

Subtract 5-Digit Numbers

```
   2  12
  6 3̸, 2̸ 8 5
– 4 1, 6 7 4
  2 1, 6 1 1
```

Check.

60,000	21,611 is close to 20,000.
− 40,000	So, the answer is reasonable.
20,000	

Guided Practice

Subtract. Use addition to check your answer.

1. 483 − 262

2. 4,674 − 1,833

3. 6,572 − 4,981

4. 7,816 − 5,281

Ask Yourself

- Did I line up the digits correctly?
- Do I need to regroup before I subtract?

5. 839 − 45 **6.** 5,359 − 348 **7.** 5,314 − 2,763

8. 8,120 − 5,316 **9.** 7,692 − 1,387 **10.** 9,243 − 6,185

Algebra Equations

Use inverse operations to find the missing number.

11. 39 + ■ = 58 **12.** ■ − 178 = 113 **13.** 962 + ■ = 4,887

Math Talk In subtraction, when do you need to regroup? Include examples in your answer.

Practice and Problem Solving

Subtract. Use addition to check your answer.

14. 967 − 815

15. 8,397 − 5,067

16. 9,748 − 4,627

17. 2,813 − 924

18. 9,526 − 8,410 **19.** 8,361 − 6,175 **20.** 7,927 − 2,639

21. 5,188 − 1,434 **22.** 7,359 − 2,684 **23.** 9,634 − 4,967

Algebra Equations

Use inverse operations to find the missing number.

24. ■ − 247 = 429 **25.** 342 + ■ = 829 **26.** ■ − 276 = 634

27. ■ − 3,823 = 2,059 **28.** ■ − 9,628 = 3,987 **29.** ■ + 3,689 = 5,618

Solve.

30. The domino club has 1,985 dominoes. A group used 928 of the dominoes to make a domino line. How many of the dominoes were not used? Use inverse operations to check your answer.

31. **Multistep** Josh and Meg started with 2,658 dominoes. They each used 350 dominoes. Write and simplify an expression that shows how many dominoes were not used.

Science Link

Use the picture to solve.

32. On March 1, an electric meter at Bench School showed the number at the right.

a. On March 31, the meter showed 53,407. How many kilowatt-hours of electricity were used that March?

b. Ortiz School used 15,398 kilowatt-hours of electricity in March. Which school used less electricity, Ortiz or Bench?

c. In April, Ortiz School used 14,453 kilowatt-hours of electricity. How many kilowatt-hours did the school save compared to the previous month?

Electricity

- Electrical energy can be converted to heat, light, and motion.
- In your home, electrical energy may heat your stove, make the lights come on, or turn a fan.
- An electric meter measures the amount of electricity used in units of kilowatt-hours.
- Another unit used to measure electricity is the joule (J).

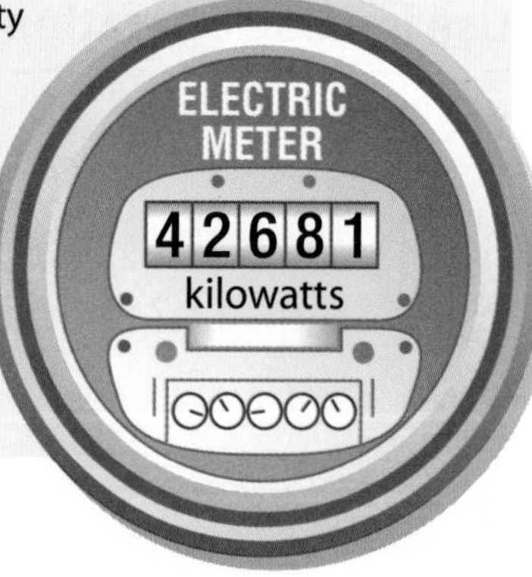

Science PS 1.g

Spiral Review and Test Practice

Round the number to the nearest hundred thousand. KEY NS 1.3 pages 32, 34

33. 5,678,123 **34.** 14,349,687 **35.** 42,986,375

36. 5,748,123 **37.** 16,349,687 **38.** 42,886,375

Write the letter of the correct answer. KEY NS 3.1

39. 79,231 − 38,641

A 40,590 **B** 40,690 **C** 41,590 **D** 41,690

Extra Practice See page 87, Set B.

Practice Game

Get the Least

Object of the Game Try to get the least difference.

Materials

- Learning Tool 11 (*Get the Least* Game Board)
- number cube labeled 1–6

Set Up

Each player gets a game board.

Number of Players 2 or more

How to Play

1. On each turn, a player rolls the number cube and then writes the digit rolled in one of the boxes on the playing board. Once a digit has been written in a box, it may not be changed.

2. After the players' boards have been filled, players find the difference between their two numbers.

   The player with the least difference is the winner.

CA Standards

KEY NS 3.1 Demonstrate an understanding of, and the ability to use, standard algorithms for the addition and subtraction of multidigit numbers.

Education Place

Visit www.eduplace.com/camap/ for **Brain Teasers** and **eGames** to play.

Subtract Across Zeros

Objective Subtract when some digits are zeros.

CA Standards
KEY NS 3.1 Demonstrate an understanding of, and the ability to use, standard algorithms for the addition and subtraction of multidigit numbers.
KEY NS 3.0 Students solve problems involving addition, subtraction, multiplication, and division of whole numbers and understand the relationships among the operations.
Also MR 1.1, MR 1.2, MR 2.0, MR 2.1, MR 2.2, MR 2.3, MR 2.6, MR 3.0, MR 3.3

Learn by Example

Leah estimates that she has 2,500 stamps in her collection. The actual count is 2,206 stamps. What is the difference between Leah's estimate and the actual number of stamps?

Subtract. 2,500 − 2,206

1 Subtract the ones. 6 > 0, so you need to regroup. There are no tens to regroup. So, regroup 1 hundred as 10 tens.

$$\begin{array}{r} {\scriptstyle 4\ 10} \\ 2,\!\not{5}\not{0}0 \\ -\ 2,\!206 \\ \hline \end{array}$$

2 Regroup 1 ten as 10 ones.

$$\begin{array}{r} {\scriptstyle 9} \\ {\scriptstyle 4\ \not{10}\ 10} \\ 2,\!\not{5}\not{0}\not{0} \\ -\ 2,\!206 \\ \hline \end{array}$$

3 Then subtract.

$$\begin{array}{r} {\scriptstyle 9} \\ {\scriptstyle 4\ \not{10}\ 10} \\ 2,\!\not{5}\not{0}\not{0} \\ -\ 2,\!206 \\ \hline 294 \end{array}$$

Check

Use estimation to check that your answer is reasonable.

$$\begin{array}{r} 2,500 \\ -2,200 \\ \hline 300 \end{array}$$

294 is close to 300.

Use addition to check that your answer is correct.

$$\begin{array}{r} {\scriptstyle 1\,1} \\ 2,206 \\ +\ 294 \\ \hline 2,500 \end{array}$$

It checks.

Solution: There are 294 fewer stamps than Leah estimated.

Guided Practice

Subtract. Use estimation or addition to check.

1. 306 − 94

2. 802 − 488

3. 4,055 − 1,572

4. 7,046 − 2,315

5. 500 − 156

6. 9,070 − 2,305

7. 6,003 − 2,346

Ask Yourself

Do I need to regroup more than once before I can subtract?

Math Talk When subtracting from a 4-digit number with zeros in the ones, tens, and hundreds places, where would you start regrouping? When would you start subtracting?

Practice and Problem Solving

Subtract. Use estimation or addition to check.

8. 404 − 159

9. 710 − 572

10. 900 − 748

11. 7,038 − 3,251

12. 2,004 − 1,413

13. 8,080 − 637

14. 7,000 − 5,394

15. 5,050 − 3,256

16. 9,055 − 8,215

17. 6,000 − 4,120

18. 8,009 − 5,506

Solve.

19. **Multistep** An Internet site has 6,500 keychains for sale. One week, 2,494 keychains sold. The next week, 1,973 keychains sold. How many keychains are left?

Spiral Review and Test Practice

Find the number that makes the number sentence true. Tell which property of addition you used. AF 1.0 page 54

20. 4,392 + 0 = ■

21. 1,934 + 1,975 = 1,975 + ■

22. (603 + 9730) + 644 = ■ + (9730 + 644)

Write the letter of the correct answer. KEY NS 3.1

23. 47,000 − 8,935

A 37,165 **B** 37,065 **C** 38,165 **D** 38,065

Extra Practice See page 87, Set C.

Problem Solving Plan
Too Much or Too Little Information

Objective Find the information needed to solve a problem.

CA Standards
MR 1.1 Analyze problems by identifying relationships, distinguishing relevant from irrelevant information, sequencing and prioritizing information, and observing patterns.

KEY NS 3.1 Demonstrate an understanding of, and the ability to use, standard algorithms for the addition and subtraction of multidigit numbers.

Also KEY NS 3.0, MR 1.0, MR 1.2, MR 2.0, MR 2.1, MR 2.3, MR 2.4, MR 3.0, MR 3.1, MR 3.2, MR 3.3

Learn Through Reasoning

Some problems have too many facts, and others do not have enough. You must read a problem carefully to find the information you need.

Coast redwoods are among the tallest and oldest living things on Earth. A coast redwood called the Stratosphere Giant is approximately 370 feet tall. Its girth (distance around the trunk) is 50 feet. The Rockefeller Tree is 362 feet tall. The oldest coast redwood on record is about 2,200 years old.

Big Basin Redwoods State Park, California

Think
Read the problem carefully. Find the information you need to solve the problem.

Too Much Information

How much taller is the Stratosphere Giant than the Rockefeller Tree?

Find the facts you need.

- height of the Stratosphere Giant (370 ft)
- height of the Rockefeller Tree (362 ft)

There is more information in the problem, but it is not needed.

Subtract to find the difference.

The Stratosphere Giant is 8 feet taller than the Rockefeller Tree.

$$\begin{array}{r} 370 \text{ ft} \\ -\ 362 \text{ ft} \\ \hline 8 \text{ ft} \end{array}$$

Too Little Information

How much bigger around is the Stratosphere Giant than the Rockefeller Tree?

Find the facts you need.

- girth of the Stratosphere Giant (50 ft)
- girth of the Rockefeller Tree (not given)

The distance around the trunk of the Rockefeller Tree is not given, so there is not enough information to solve the problem.

Guided Problem Solving

Solve using the Ask Yourself questions. Use the information on page 84 for Problem 1.

Ask Yourself

- What does the question ask?
- What facts do I need to use?

1. A cypress tree in Mexico measures 140 feet around its trunk and is 130 feet tall. How much bigger around is this tree than the Stratosphere Giant?

2. The bristlecone pine called Methuselah is about 4,767 years old. Pine Alpha is about 4,000 years old, and the Patriarch pine is even younger. The Patriarch is how many years younger than Methuselah?

Math Talk Why is it important to read the question carefully?

Independent Problem Solving

Solve. If not enough information is given, tell what information is needed to solve the problem. Explain why your answer makes sense.

3. Omar lives 290 miles from a redwood reserve. It takes him 6 hours to drive to the reserve. If Omar drives to the reserve and back, how many miles will he drive?

4. One forest trail is a 10-mile loop. The trail reaches a height of 1,800 feet. Another trail reaches 1,200 feet. How much longer is the first trail than the second?

5. The Redwoods National and State Parks cover 131,983 acres of land and include 37 miles of coastline. An acre is 43,560 square feet, about the size of a football field. The state park land covers 60,268 acres. How many acres does the national park land cover?

6. **Multistep** On Friday, Brad hiked a 1,380-foot trail. On Saturday, he hiked 850 feet on a different trail and rested. Then he hiked 470 feet and rested. Then he hiked 662 feet to the end of the trail. How long was the trail he hiked on Saturday? Use estimation to check.

7. **Challenge** Zack took 15 pictures of birds. Tina took twice as many pictures as Meiko did. If Tina and Meiko took 36 pictures in all, how many pictures did each girl take?

8. **Create and Solve** Write two word problems, one with too much information and one with too little information.

Steller's jay

Vocabulary

Sometimes when you **subtract** you will need an exact answer. Sometimes you will not. There are different ways of subtracting that fit each situation.

If you *do not* need to know the exact difference, you may be able to estimate.

Round to the nearest hundred.

$1,375 → $1,400
$682 → − 700
■

Ellis is buying a guitar for $682. He has saved $1,375. Will he have enough to buy a $700 amplifier, too?

If you *do* need to know the exact difference, you will have to subtract. You may even have to regroup.

$1,375
− 682
■

Answer the questions.

1. Can Ellis afford the amplifier, too?
2. Of the two subtraction methods shown here, which one should Ellis use? Explain.

Writing Suppose Ellis sees a guitar he likes better for $539. Can he afford to buy this one *and* the amplifier, too? Estimate to find the answer.

Reading Check out this book in your library.
Panda Math, by Hua Mei and Mei Sheng

CA Standards
MR 2.3 Use a variety of methods, such as words, numbers, symbols, charts, graphs, tables, diagrams, and models, to explain mathematical reasoning.
Also KEY NS 3.1, KEY NS 1.3

Standards-Based Extra Practice

Set A

KEY NS 1.3 page 74

Round each number to the greatest place. Then estimate the difference.

1. 5,936 − 1,853

2. 56,274 − 34,036

3. 4,382 − 2,305

4. 1,394 − 1,365

5. 9,790 − 7,321

6. 67,538 − 23,811

7. 34,987 − 28,500

8. 8,932 − 2,345

9. 23,501 − 1,935

10. **Explain** Victoria has $150 for her trip to Washington D.C. She spends $137 on a camera. Does she have enough money left to buy 3 rolls of film for $13.50? Explain how you know.

Set B

KEY NS 3.1 page 78

Subtract. Use addition to check your answer.

1. 493 − 262

2. 4,685 − 1,933

3. 6,683 − 4,932

4. 8,761 − 7,932

5. 2,832 − 998

6. 3,234 − 2,382

7. 845 − 56

8. 5,472 − 481

9. **Compare** Jacob started with 3,747 state quarters. He spent 1,865 of them. Kelly started with 3,068 state quarters. She used 1,185 of them. Compare how many quarters they each have left.

Set C

KEY NS 3.1 page 82

Subtract. Estimate or add to check.

1. 406 − 94

2. 703 − 488

3. 5,043 − 1,544

4. 8,035 − 7,236

5. 3,002 − 2,233

6. 601 − 156

7. 9,070 − 7,565

8. 12,903 − 11,342

9. **Explain** Joshua has collected 5,900 stamps. He trades 65 of them for 25 collectable state stamps. How many stamps does he have now? Explain how you can check you answer with addition.

Education Place
Visit www.eduplace.com/camap/ for more **Extra Practice**.

Chapter Review/Test

Vocabulary and Concepts

KEY NS 3.0, MR 2.3

Write the best word to complete the sentence.

1. Rewriting 23 as 2 tens and 3 ones is an example of ______.
2. Addition and subtraction are ______ operations.

Skills

KEY NS 3.1, KEY NS 3.0, KEY NS 1.3

Round each number to the nearest hundred. Then estimate the difference.

3. 6,195 − 3,462
4. 886 − 885
5. 84,312 − 62,568

Round each number to the nearest thousand. Then estimate the difference.

6. 8,562 − 3,020
7. 2,193 − 999
8. 23,532 − 16,392

Subtract. Use addition to check your answers.

9. 5,306 − 2,224
10. 5,638 − 2,823
11. 800 − 487
12. 8,532 − 4,900
13. 5,965 − 3,230
14. 940 − 208
15. 7,000 − 1,255
16. 87 − 45
17. 2,500 − 1,500
18. 800 − 420

Problem Solving and Reasoning

KEY NS 3.1, MR 2.3

Solve. Explain if there is too much or too little information.

19. A group planned to hike 3,567 feet in one day. At 1,938 feet they had to stop because the trail was blocked. What is the difference between how far they wanted to go and how far they went?
20. The bristlecone pine called Methuselah is about 4,767 years old. Pine Alpha is about 4,000 years old. Round to the nearest hundred and estimate the difference in age.

Writing Math How can inverse operations help you check a subtraction exercise?

Spiral Review and Test Practice

1. Which of these is the number 120,678,000?

   A two hundred ten million, six hundred seventy-eight thousand

   B one hundred two million, six hundred seventy-eight thousand

   C one hundred twenty million, six hundred seventy-eight thousand

   D one hundred twenty million, seven hundred sixty-eight thousand

Test Tip
Look at each period of the number separately.

KEY NS 1.1 page 12

2. What is 35,678,920 rounded to the nearest ten million?

   A 40,000,000 **C** 35,700,000

   B 36,000,000 **D** 30,000,000

KEY NS 1.3 page 34

3. Choose the best estimate.
   87 + 31 + 27

   A 130 **C** 145

   B 140 **D** 150

KEY NS 3.0 page 52

4. 4,693 + 2,317 =

   A 7,010

   B 7,000

   C 6,910

   D 6,010

KEY NS 3.1 page 62

5. Which is the difference between 14,620 and 3,295 when both numbers are rounded to the nearest thousand?

   A 18,000

   B 12,000

   C 11,000

   D 10,000

KEY NS 1.3 page 74

6. 40,528 − 23,679 =

   A 17,849

   B 16,849

   C 16,845

   D 16,749

Test Tip
Check your work using inverse operations.

KEY NS 3.1 page 78

Education Place
Visit www.eduplace.com/camap/ for **Test-Taking Tips** and **Extra Practice.**

Expressions and Equations

Brown pelicans are found along the entire length of California's coast.

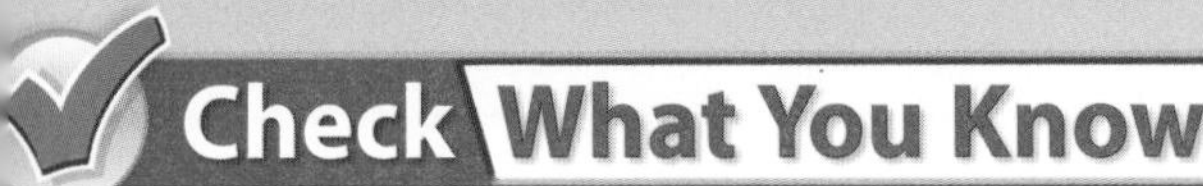

Check What You Know

Vocabulary and Concepts KEY NS 1.2, MR 2.3

Choose the best term to complete each sentence. pages 26, 28

Word Bank
- added to
- greater than
- equal to
- less than
- subtracted from

1. The > symbol in 73 > 41 means that 73 is _____ 41.

2. The = symbol in 24 + 12 = 36 means that 24 + 12 is _____ 36.

Skills KEY NS 3.1, KEY NS 1.2

Add or subtract. pages 62, 78

3. 23 + 24 **4.** 43 − 28 **5.** 71 − 39 **6.** 62 + 19

Write <, >, or = for the ⬭. page 28

7. 346 ⬭ 345 **8.** 1,432 ⬭ 496 **9.** 2,892 ⬭ 2,829

Problem Solving and Reasoning KEY NS 3.1

10. Mrs. Johnson's class collected 173 cans for the Food Drive. Mr. Burn's class collected 219 cans. How many more cans did Mr. Burn's class collect?

Vocabulary

Visualize It!

equation
a mathematical sentence with an equal sign

parentheses
grouping symbols that indicate which operations should be performed first

(45 + 67) − 28 = 84

simplify
to reduce an expression to a simpler form

(45 + 67) = 112

Language Tips

The word *expression* has many meanings. For example, it can mean a look that shows a feeling, as in *the expression on his face shows that he is happy*. In mathematics, an *expression* is a number or group of numbers with operation symbols.

Words that look alike in English and Spanish often have the same meaning.

English	Spanish
parentheses	**paréntesis**
equation	**ecuación**
simplify	**simplificar**

See **English-Spanish Glossary** pages 644–666.

Education Place Visit www.eduplace.com/camap/ for the **eGlossary** and **eGames**.

CA Standards MR 2.3 Use a variety of methods, such as words, numbers, symbols, charts, graphs, tables, diagrams, and models, to explain mathematical reasoning. **Also AF 1.0**

Hands On
Expressions with Parentheses

Objective Create and evaluate expressions that use parentheses.

CA Standards
KEY AF 1.2 Interpret and evaluate mathematical expressions that now use parentheses.

KEY AF 1.3 Use parentheses to indicate which operation to perform first when writing expressions containing more than two terms and different operations.

Also AF 1.0, MR 1.1, MR 2.0, MR 2.3, MR 3.0, MR 3.2

Vocabulary

evaluate
expression
parentheses

Materials
- Workmat 1
- Number Tiles
- Learning Tool 12 (Optional)

Explore

In this lesson, you will use number tiles to make expressions that have parentheses. Then you will **evaluate**, or find the value of, each **expression**.

Parentheses ( ) are used to show which operations in an expression should be done first.

Question What happens when you use parentheses in expressions?

Lita created the expression 6 − 1 + 2 with number tiles. Where can she draw parentheses so that the value of the expression is 3?

1 Use number tiles to make the expression 6 − 1 + 2 on Workmat 1.

2 Draw parentheses around a group of numbers. See if the value of the expression is 3.

(6 − 1) + 2
5 + 2
7

3 Move the parentheses to another group of numbers. Now see if the value of the expression is 3.

6 − (1 + 2)
6 − 3
3

Think
The position of the parentheses can change the value of the expression.

Use number tiles 3, 8, 9, +, −, and parentheses to make an expression with the value of 4.

1 Use number tiles to create an expression.

$3 + 8 - 9$

2 Draw parentheses and evaluate the expression.

$(3 + 8) - 9$

$11 - 9$

2

3 The expression does not have a value of 4.
Repeat Steps 1 and 2 trying different expressions.
Find an expression with a value of 4.

Extend

Copy the expression. Add parentheses to make an expression with the value of 5.

1. $8 - 5 + 2$

2. $12 - 3 + 4$

3. $16 - 3 + 8$

4. $12 - 10 + 3$

5. $10 - 2 + 3$

6. $15 + 6 - 16$

Use the numbers to make an expression with the value of 34. Use +, −, and parentheses when needed in each expression.

7. 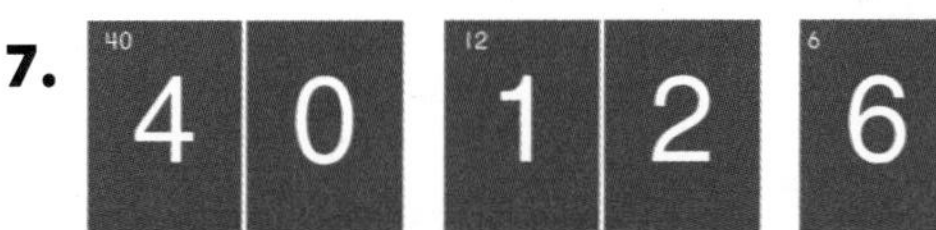

8. 

9. 

10. 

11. 

12. 

13. Create and Solve Use the numbers 13, 15, and 5 to write and evaluate three expressions with different values. Each expression should use addition, subtraction, and parentheses.

Writing Math

Right or Wrong? Marco says that $48 - (16 - 6)$ and $(48 - 16) - 6$ have the same value. Is he correct? Explain why or why not.

Write and Evaluate Expressions

Objective Write and evaluate expressions that use addition and subtraction.

CA Standards
KEY AF 1.2 Interpret and evaluate mathematical expressions that now use parentheses.
AF 1.0 Students use and interpret variables, mathematical symbols, and properties to write and simplify expressions and sentences.
Also KEY AF 1.3, MR 1.0, MR 1.1, MR 2.0, MR 2.4, MR 3.0, MR 3.2, MR 3.3

Vocabulary

expression
simplify

Learn by Example

An **expression** may be just one number, or it may consist of numbers and operation symbols. Sometimes an expression contains parentheses.

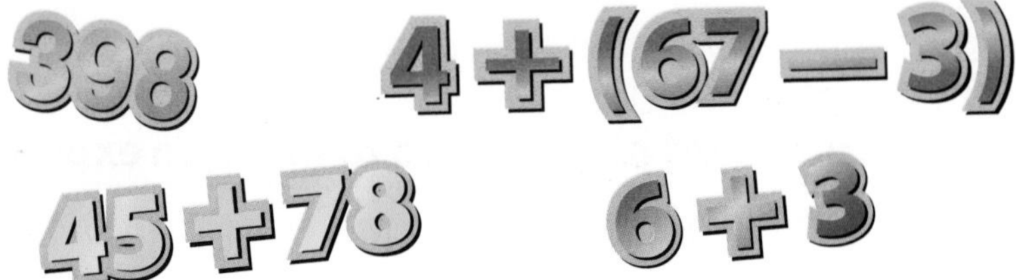

When you evaluate, or **simplify**, an expression, you do all of the operations and write the result.

Simplify the expression (87 − 57) + (85 − 65) − 10.

1 Do the operations inside the parentheses.

(87 − 57) + (85 − 65) − 10
30 + 20 − 10

2 Simplify the rest of the operations from left to right.

50 − 10
40

Ask Yourself
- What operations are inside the parentheses?
- What direction do I start adding and subtracting from?

Guided Practice

Simplify the expression.

1. (18 − 7) + 3

2. (83 − 3) + (14 + 6)

3. (19 − 6) + 32

4. (64 − 37) + (29 − 17)

5. 9 + (33 − 11)

6. 82 − (19 + 51)

7. $72 - (60 - 2)$

8. $16 + (49 + 49)$

9. $(19 - 8) + (36 - 5)$

10. $(24 + 62) - (42 + 18)$

11. $(22 + 53) - (74 - 59)$

12. $(38 - 18) - (90 - 80)$

Guided Problem Solving

Use the questions to solve this problem.

13. Alyssa bought the two books shown. She gave the cashier a $20 bill. Write an expression to show the change that Alyssa should receive.

a. **Understand** How much did the books cost? How much did Alyssa pay the cashier?

b. **Plan/Solve** Write an expression to show the total cost of the books.

Write an expression to show how much Alyssa paid.

Combine the two expressions to show how much change Alyssa should get back.

c. **Look Back** Simplify the expression. Read the word problem again. Does your answer make sense?

Math Talk Describe how you would simplify the expression $30 + (150 + 140) - 20$.

Practice and Problem Solving

Simplify the expression.

14. $(15 + 3) + (20 - 10)$

15. $(52 - 2) - 15$

16. $(25 + 75) + (6 + 9)$

17. $(48 - 2) + 18$

18. $(16 - 1) - (13 + 2)$

19. $(14 + 10) - (8 - 3)$

20. $(89 + 22) - (57 - 14)$

21. $(62 - 12) - (33 + 3)$

22. $(70 - 60) - (50 - 40)$

23. $(46 + 99) + (81 - 6)$

Think
Remember, always do operations in parentheses first.

Write and evaluate an expression to solve.

24. Jodie had a set of 24 cups. She dropped and broke 8 of them. Then she went to the store and bought 6 more cups. How many cups does she have now?

25. Kenny earned $16 cutting grass. Then he earned $35 raking leaves. He spent $25 on a gift for his sister. How much money does Kenny have now?

Science Link

Use the table. Write and evaluate expressions to solve Problems 26–27.

26. How many pounds did the seal pup gain in 4 weeks?

27. **Challenge** When the seal was 2 years old, he weighed 2,000 pounds more than he weighed at 4 weeks. Then he lost 350 pounds. How much does he weigh now?

Elephant Seals

- The elephant seal lives in the northern Pacific and is the largest seal in the world.
- An adult male elephant seal can grow to more than 16 feet in length and 5,000 pounds in weight!
- Elephant seals are carnivores, which means they only eat meat. They eat a lot of fish and squid.

Age	Weight (pounds)
birth	75
1 week	155
2 weeks	225
3 weeks	300
4 weeks	390

Elephant seal pup

Science LS 2.b

Spiral Review and Test Practice

Copy and complete the equation. Tell which property of addition you used. KEY NS 3.0 page 54

28. 82 + 97 = ▢ + 82

29. (36 + 42) + 9 = 36 + (▢ + 9)

Write the letter of the correct answer. KEY AF 1.2

30. What is the value of the expression below?

22 − (14 + 6) + 7

A 9 **B** 21 **C** 37 **D** 49

Extra Practice See page 107, Set A.

Key Standards Review

Need Help?
See Key Standards Handbook.

Round the following numbers to the nearest ten thousand. KEY NS 1.3

1. 8,967,300
2. 14,374,321
3. 48,599
4. 742,514
5. 946,112
6. 10,311

Find the sum or difference. KEY NS 3.0, KEY NS 3.1

7. 36,457 + 23,451 + 18,931
8. 1,254 + 7,823 + 5,899
9. 2,371 + 5,984 + 3,112
10. 87,936 − 64,572 = ■
11. 6,789 − 3,457 = ■
12. 53,390 − 3,490 = ■
13. 8,452 − 6,533 = ■
14. 9,408 − 4,619 = ■
15. 77,203 − 6,454 = ■

Algebraic Thinking

Make It 5!

Use the numbers to write an expression with a value of 5. You may use +, −, and parentheses. KEY AF 1.2, KEY AF 1.3

1. 10 3 2
2. 5 4 6 2
3. 13 7 1
4. 9 6 3 1

CA Standards

KEY AF 1.2 Interpret and evaluate mathematical expressions that now use parentheses.

AF 1.0 Students use and interpret variables, mathematical symbols, and properties to write and simplify expressions and sentences.

Also AF 1.1, MR 1.0, MR 1.1, MR 2.0, MR 2.2, MR 2.3, MR 3.0, MR 3.3

Vocabulary

equation

inequality

Expressions, Equations, and Inequalities

Objective Write and solve equations and inequalities.

Learn by Example

In Lesson 2, you learned how to write and evaluate expressions. In this lesson, you will learn how to use expressions to write and solve equations and inequalities.

Example 1

Sometimes two different expressions have the same value.

When you simplify $(10 + 20) - 5$, the result is 25.

When you simplify $18 + (2 + 5)$, the result is 25.

In this case, you can write an **equation** with the $=$ symbol.

An equation is a number sentence that says two expressions have the same value.

$$(10 + 20) - 5 = 18 + (2 + 5)$$

Example 2

Sometimes two expressions have different values.

When you simplify $(2 + 13) + 30$, the result is 45.

When you simplify $(10 + 4) - (3 + 1)$, the result is 10.

In this case, you can write an **inequality** with the $<$ or $>$ symbols.

An inequality is a number sentence that says two expressions do not have the same value.

$$(2 + 13) + 30 > (10 + 4) - (3 + 1)$$

$$(10 + 4) - (3 + 1) < (2 + 13) + 30$$

Think

$>$ means ***is greater than***

$<$ means ***is less than***

Guided Practice

Write whether the number sentence is an *expression*, an *equation*, or an *inequality*.

1. $(50 + 3) + 3 = 56$ **2.** $75 > 45$ **3.** 79

4. $(64 - 5) + 4 < 86 + 3$

Copy and complete by using >, <, or =.

5. $82 \bigcirc 48 + (39 - 1)$ **6.** $16 - (3 + 8) \bigcirc 42$

7. $(50 + 15) + 1 \bigcirc 66$ **8.** $(16 - 4) + 25 \bigcirc 25 + 11$

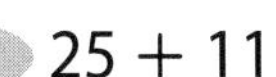

> ### Ask Yourself
> - What are the differences between an expression, an equation, and an inequality?
> - Which operation should I do first?

Math Talk Describe how equations and inequalities are similar and how they are different.

Practice and Problem Solving

Write whether the number sentence is an *expression*, an *equation*, or an *inequality*.

9. $19 + (5 - 4) = 20$ **10.** $94 + 36$ **11.** $(15 + 3) + 20 > 52 - 25$

Copy and complete by using >, <, or =.

12. $6 + (145 - 18) \bigcirc (145 - 18) + 6$ **13.** $(17 - 10) + 3 \bigcirc (100 + 90) - 1$

14. $8 + (140 - 10) \bigcirc 100 + 24$ **15.** $6 + (86 + 9) \bigcirc (6 + 86) + 9$

16. $42 + (18 - 7) \bigcirc 22 + 33$ **17.** $(21 - 8) + 6 \bigcirc 10 + (6 - 4)$

Solve.

18. Write one equation and one inequality using the expressions to the right.

$14 + (6 + 8)$ $(10 + 4) - 7$

$21 - (8 + 6)$

19. **Challenge** Pick a number from those to the right to make each number sentence true. Use each number only once.

a. $(9 + 3) - 8 > 2 + \square$

b. $\square + 6 < 37 - (25 + 5)$

c. $48 + 3 > \square + 36$

d. $12 + \square < (16 - 13) + 15$

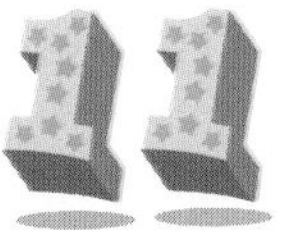

20. Gwen walked 18 miles last week. This week, she walked 4 fewer miles than last week. Write an inequality that compares how far Gwen walked in the two weeks.

21. **Create and Solve** Write a word problem that can be solved by simplifying the expression $(18 - 2) + 6$. Then solve the problem.

Real World Data

Use the table for Problems 22–25.

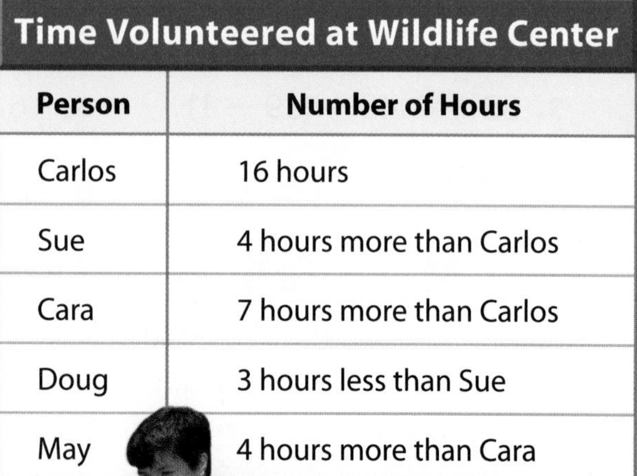

Time Volunteered at Wildlife Center	
Person	**Number of Hours**
Carlos	16 hours
Sue	4 hours more than Carlos
Cara	7 hours more than Carlos
Doug	3 hours less than Sue
May	4 hours more than Cara

22. Write expressions to show how many hours each person volunteered at the wildlife center.

23. Who volunteered more hours at the center, Cara or Doug?

24. Write and simplify an expression to find how many hours Carlos, Sue, and Cara volunteered altogether.

25. Write an inequality that compares the number of hours Carlos and Sue volunteered to the number of hours Doug and May volunteered.

Spiral Review and Test Practice

Round each number to the greatest place. Then estimate the difference. KEY NS 1.3, KEY NS 3.0 page 74

26. $729 - 489$

27. $9{,}876 - 6{,}789$

28. $829 - 648$

29. $22{,}846 - 12{,}405$

30. $318{,}242 - 179{,}845$

Write the letter of the correct answer. AF 1.1, KEY AF 1.2

31. What number goes in the box to make this number sentence true?

$(8 - 2) + 3 = 6 + \square$

A 3 **B** 6 **C** 9 **D** 13

Test Tip
Start by finding the value of the expression on the left side of the equation.

Extra Practice See page 108, Set B.

Number Sense

Will the Value Change?

You can use the operations in an expression to help you predict whether the value will change if you move the parentheses.

Addition Only

$(5 + 4) + 6$ ◯ $5 + (4 + 6)$

$9 + 6$ ◯ $5 + 10$

15 ◯ 15

$15 = 15$

If the expression contains only addition, then moving the parentheses will not change the value.

Subtraction Only

$12 - (4 - 3)$ ◯ $(12 - 4) - 3$

$12 - 1$ ◯ $8 - 3$

11 ◯ 5

$11 \neq 5$

If the expression contains only subtraction, then moving the parentheses may change the value.

Addition Followed by Subtraction

$(7 + 6) - 5$ ◯ $7 + (6 - 5)$

$13 - 5$ ◯ $7 + 1$

8 ◯ 8

$8 = 8$

If the expression contains addition followed by subtraction, then moving the parentheses does not change the value.

Subtraction Followed by Addition

$(10 - 2) + 3$ ◯ $10 - (2 + 3)$

$8 + 3$ ◯ $10 - 5$

11 ◯ 5

$11 \neq 5$

If the expression contains subtraction followed by addition, then moving the parentheses may change the value.

1. If all the numbers in an expression are added together, why does the value stay the same if the parentheses are moved?

2. If an expression contains a minus sign followed by parentheses, the value may change if the parentheses are moved. Why?

CA Standards

KEY AF 2.0 Students know how to manipulate equations.

KEY AF 2.1 Know and understand that equals added to equals are equal.

Also AF 1.1, KEY AF 1.2, MR 1.1, MR 2.0, MR 2.3, MR 2.4, MR 3.0, MR 3.3

Add Equals to Equals

Objective Understand that equals added to equals are equal.

Learn by Example

In this lesson, you will learn what happens when you add the same number to both sides of an equation.

Will both sides of the equation $15 + 30 = 45$ still have the same value if 25 is added to both sides?

1 Simplify both sides of the equation.

The expressions on both sides of the equation have the same value.

$$15 + 30 = 45$$
$$45 = 45$$

2 Now rewrite the equation adding 25 to each side.

$$(15 + 30) + 25 = 45 + 25$$

3 Simplify both sides.

The expressions on both sides of the equation still have the same value.

$$(15 + 30) + 25 = 45 + 25$$
$$45 + 25 = 45 + 25$$
$$70 = 70$$

Solution: Both sides of the equation will still have the same value if 25 is added to both sides.

Guided Practice

Copy and complete.

1. $(59 - 32) + 15 = 27 + 15$
$\square + 15 = \square$
$\square = \square$

2. $(59 - 32) + 41 = 27 + 41$
$\square + \square = \square$
$\square = \square$

Ask Yourself

Do the expressions on both sides of the equal sign have the same value?

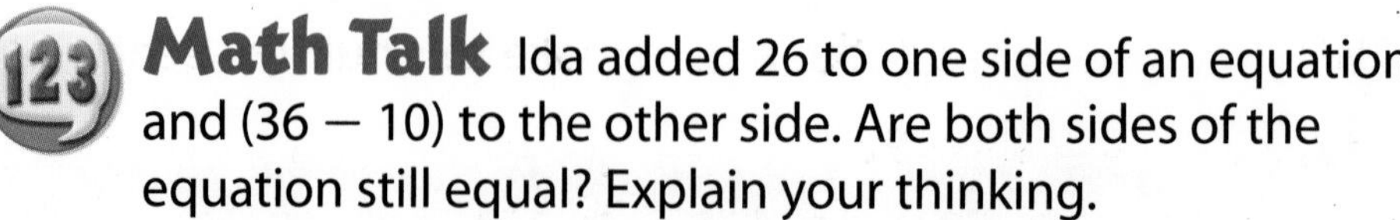

Math Talk Ida added 26 to one side of an equation and (36 − 10) to the other side. Are both sides of the equation still equal? Explain your thinking.

Practice and Problem Solving

Think

In an equation, both sides of the = must have the same value.

Copy and complete.

3. $56 + 29 = 85$
$\square = 85$

4. $11 + (56 + 29) = 11 + 85$
$11 + \square = \square$
$\square = \square$

5. $50 + (56 + 29) = 50 + 85$
$\square + \square = \square$
$\square = \square$

6. $75 - 38 = \square$
$\square = \square$

7. $(75 - 38) + 15 = 37 + 15$
$\square + 15 = \square$
$\square = \square$

8. $(75 - 38) + 28 = 37 + 28$
$\square + \square = \square$
$\square = \square$

Hint

$\neq$ means ***not equal to.***

Compare the expressions. Write $\neq$ or = for each ⬭.

9. $15 + 3$ ⬭ 18
$4 + (15 + 3)$ ⬭ $4 + 18$

10. $48 + 15$ ⬭ $32 + 26 + 10$
$(48 + 15) + 5$ ⬭ $(32 + 26 + 10) + 5$

11. $150 - 125$ ⬭ $12 + 13 + 8$
$6 + (150 - 125)$ ⬭ $6 + (12 + 13 + 8)$

12. $50 - 16$ ⬭ $17 + 17$
$5 + (50 - 16)$ ⬭ $10 + (17 + 17)$

Solve.

13. Justify Mike says that equals subtracted from equals are equal. Is he correct? Give an example to support your thinking.

14. Analyze What do you know about the value of the ★ and the ▲ in this equation?

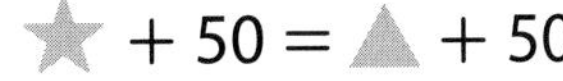

★ + 50 = ▲ + 50

Spiral Review and Test Practice

Solve. KEY NS 1.1 page 16

15. Write the number 4,002,329 in expanded notation.

16. Write the number 800,000 + 7,000 + 300 + 2 in standard form.

Write the letter of the correct answer. KEY AF 2.1

What number goes in the box to make this number sentence true?

17. $92 + 59 = \square + 92$

A 33 **B** 59 **C** 92 **D** 151

Extra Practice See page 109, Set C.

Problem Solving Strategy
Break a Problem into Parts

Objective Represent a multistep problem by writing and evaluating an expression that uses parentheses.

CA Standards
MR 1.2 Determine when and how to break a problem into simpler parts.

KEY AF 1.3 Use parentheses to indicate which operations to perform first when writing expressions containing more than two terms and different operations.

Also KEY AF 1.2, KEY NS 3.0, MR 1.0, MR 1.1, MR 2.0, MR 2.3, MR 2.4, MR 3.0, MR 3.1, MR 3.2, MR 3.3

Learn by Example

In the morning, the nature club spotted 42 cranes in the east marsh and 35 cranes in the south marsh. In the evening, they saw 54 cranes in the east marsh and 27 cranes in the south marsh. How many more cranes did they see in the evening than in the morning?

UNDERSTAND

You know how many cranes were seen in the morning and the evening. You want to find out how many more cranes were seen in the evening than in the morning.

PLAN

Write an expression with parentheses to represent the situation.

1. number of cranes seen in the morning: $42 + 35$
2. number of cranes seen in the evening: $54 + 27$
3. Then write an expression that shows how many more cranes were seen in the evening than in the morning. Use parentheses to show what operations to do first.

$$(54 + 27) - (42 + 35)$$

SOLVE

Evaluate the expression.

The Nature Club saw 4 more cranes in the evening than in the morning.

$$(54 + 27) - (42 + 35)$$

$$81 - 77$$

$$4$$

LOOK BACK

Did you answer the question that was asked?

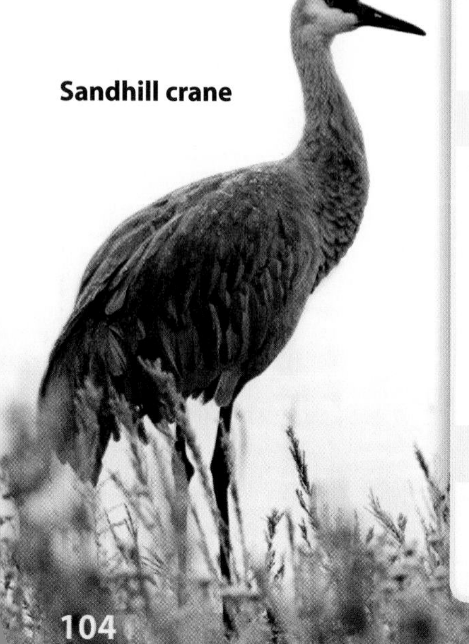
Sandhill crane

Guided Problem Solving

Solve using the Ask Yourself questions.

1. A scientist found 129 scorpions. Of these, 32 were found under rocks and 17 were found under branches. The rest were seen entering burrows. Write and evaluate an expression to find out how many scorpions were seen entering burrows.

Ask Yourself
- Should I add or subtract?
- Do I need to use parentheses?

Math Talk Does the expression 129 − 32 + 17 represent Problem 1? Why or why not?

Independent Problem Solving

Choose the expression that represents the problem. Then solve the problem. Explain why your answer makes sense.

2. On an island are 834 pelican nests. On a nearby island, are 784 pelican nests. During a storm, 15 nests on one island and 8 nests on the other are destroyed. How many nests are left on the two islands?

A (834 + 784) + (15 − 8) **B** (834 + 784) − (15 + 8)

3. Yosemite onion is a rare plant. Only 13 of these plants were last counted in California. Suppose 5 more plants are discovered, but 2 of the original 13 do not survive. How many Yosemite onion plants will there be?

A (13 − 2) + 5 **B** (13 + 2) − 5

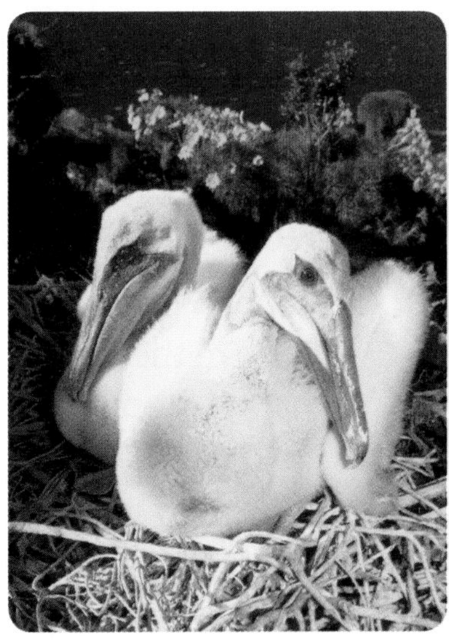

Brown pelican chicks on Anapaca Island in Channel Islands National Park, CA

Write an expression with parentheses for each problem. Then solve the problem. Explain why your answer makes sense.

4. Last year, a conservation group saved 25 acres of land for animals and 12 acres for plants. This year, they saved 63 acres for animals and 18 acres for plants. How many more acres were saved for animals?

5. **Challenge** Ricardo raised $120 to donate to a wildlife group. His brother raised $28 dollars less than Ricardo. How much money did they raise together?

6. **Create and Solve** Write a word problem that can be solved using this expression: 20 − (6 + 5).

Reading & Writing

Vocabulary

When you **simplify** an **expression**, you evaluate it. Sometimes expressions contain **parentheses** ( ). To evaluate the expression, do the operations in the parentheses first.

(64 – 54) + (80 – 67)	
Step 1: Do the operations inside the parentheses ( ).	(64 – 54) → 64 – 54 → 10 (80 – 67) → 80 – 67 → 13
Step 2: Then add or subtract from left to right.	Add 10 and 13. 10 + 13 → 23
So, (64 – 54) + (80 – 67) is 23.	

Solve.

Stephen bought two books. One cost $9 and the other cost $5. He gave the cashier a $20 bill. Write an expression to show the change Stephen should receive.

1. Write an expression to show the total cost of the books.
2. Write an expression to show how much Stephen gave the cashier.
3. Write an expression to show how much change Stephen should get back.
4. Simplify the expression. Read the word problem again. Does your answer make sense?

Writing Write and evaluate an expression to describe 245 minus the sum of 62, 8, and 43.

Reading Check out this book in your library.
The King's Chessboard, by David Birch

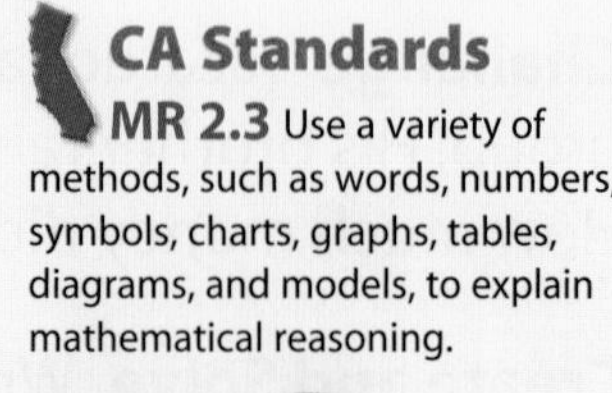

CA Standards
MR 2.3 Use a variety of methods, such as words, numbers, symbols, charts, graphs, tables, diagrams, and models, to explain mathematical reasoning.

Also KEY AF 1.3

Standards-Based Extra Practice

Set A KEY AF 1.2, KEY AF 1.3 page 94

Simplify the expression.

1. (83 − 36) + 3
2. (42 + 53) + 28
3. (29 − 23) − 2
4. (45 − 32) + 26
5. (19 − 11) + 10
6. (99 − 5) − 12
7. (250 − 29) + 40
8. (300 − 159) + 67
9. (20 + 3) + (15 − 10)
10. (54 − 4) − 15
11. (50 + 50) + (7 + 3)
12. (45 + 62) − 45
13. (24 − 14) + (24 + 12)
14. (34 − 12) + 34
15. 78 − (34 + 32)
16. (345 − 230) + (345 − 200)
17. 89 + (34 − 19)
18. (35 + 53) − 21
19. (342 + 97) + (385 − 342)
20. 78 + (76 − 76)

Write and evaluate an expression to solve.

21. Carly had a set of 25 dolls. She gave 10 of them to a children's home. Then her mother and father bought her 4 new dolls. How many dolls does she have now?

22. Erica had 52 pencils. She gave 30 to her teacher. Then her sister gave her 5 more. How many pencils does she have now?

23. Kathy earned $15 baby-sitting. Then she earned $18 baby-sitting. She spent $14 on school supplies. How much money does Kathy have now?

Education Place
Visit www.eduplace.com/camap/ for more **Extra Practice**.

Standards-Based Extra Practice

Set B

KEY AF 1.2 page 98

Write whether the number sentence is an *expression*, an *equation*, or an *inequality*.

1. $(28 + 2) + 5 = 35$
2. $38 < 79$
3. $13 + 62$
4. $(28 - 10) + 6 < 35 - 6$
5. $221 + (63 - 8) = 276$
6. $21 - 3 > 11 + 5$
7. $53 > 21 - 5$
8. $1467 - 578$
9. $62{,}367{,}521 > 62{,}367{,}520$
10. $357 - (26 + 45) = 286$
11. $21 - 3 < 11 + (21 + 3)$
12. $3{,}592{,}390 + (21 - 6)$

Copy and complete by using >, < or =.

13. $85 \bigcirc 28 + (32 - 1)$
14. $26 + 5 \bigcirc 38 - 7$
15. $(16 - 3) + 26 \bigcirc 27 + 9$
16. $8 + (147 - 18) \bigcirc (144 - 17) + 6$
17. $10 + (82 + 9) \bigcirc (10 + 82) + 9$
18. $266 - 54 \bigcirc 392 + 28$
19. $(13 - 3) + 10 \bigcirc 20 + (6 - 0)$
20. $100 - (16 + 34) \bigcirc 40 + (15 - 5)$
21. $30 \bigcirc (20 + 16) - 6$
22. $18 + 1 \bigcirc (10 - 2) + 9$

Solve.

23. Chandra ran 13 miles last week. This week she ran 2 more miles than last week. Write an inequality that compares how far Chandra ran each week.

24. **Evaluate** Joseph's family spent 6 hours driving to their vacation spot. Juan's family traveled 4 hours more than Joseph's family. Brandon's family traveled 2 hours less than Joseph's family. Write and simplify an expression to find how many total hours were spent driving by the three families.

Standards-Based Extra Practice

Set C KEY AF 2.0, KEY AF 2.1, KEY AF 1.2 page 102

Copy and complete.

1. $34 + 25 = 59$
$\square = 59$

2. $81 = 62 + 19$
$81 = \square$

3. $(32 + 21) + 11 = 53 + 11$
$\square + 11 = \square$
$\square = \square$

4. $50 + (71 + 39) = 50 + 110$
$50 + \square = \square$
$\square = \square$

5. $(73 - 21) + 10 = 52 + 10$
$\square + 10 = \square$
$\square = \square$

6. $82 - 38 = \square$
$\square = \square$

7. $(33 - 16) + 2 = 17 + 2$
$\square + 2 = \square$
$\square = \square$

8. $63 + (21 - 11) = 63 + 10$
$63 + \square = \square$
$\square = \square$

9. $(16 + 28) - 5 = 44 - 5$
$\square - 5 = \square$
$\square = \square$

10. $(12 - 5) + 52 = 7 + 52$
$\square + 52 = 59$
$\square = \square$

Compare the expressions. Write ≠ or = for each ◯.

11. $18 + 3$ ◯ 21
$4 + (18 + 3)$ ◯ $4 + 21$

12. $30 - 6$ ◯ $34 + 2$
$5 + (30 - 6)$ ◯ $5 + (34 + 2)$

13. $21 + 62$ ◯ $3 + 50 + 20$
$(21 + 62) - 3$ ◯ $(3 + 50 + 20) - 3$

14. $72 - 36$ ◯ $18 + 18$
$7 + (72 - 36)$ ◯ $7 + (18 + 18)$

15. $45 - 3$ ◯ $42 + 10$
$6 + (45 - 3)$ ◯ $6 + (42 + 10)$

16. $38 - 8$ ◯ $25 + 5$
$(38 - 8) - 6$ ◯ $(25 + 5) - 6$

17. $36 - 16$ ◯ $10 + 10$
$25 - (36 - 16)$ ◯ $25 - (10 + 10)$

18. $55 - 32$ ◯ $25 + 10$
$21 + (55 - 32)$ ◯ $21 + (25 + 10)$

19. **Compare** Mike has collected 32 of a set of 50 postage stamps. Marc has 2 pages of 16 postage stamps. If they each get 8 more stamps, do they have equal or unequal amounts of stamps? Write an equation or inequality to show your answer.

Education Place
Visit www.eduplace.com/camap/ for more **Extra Practice**.

Chapter Review/Test

Vocabulary and Concepts

KEY AF 1.2, AF 1.0, MR 2.3

Write the best word to complete the sentence.

1. When you evaluate an expression, first do the operations in _______.

2. When you carry out the operations in an expression and write the answer, you evaluate or _______ the expression.

Skills

AF 1.0, KEY AF 1.2, KEY AF 2.0, KEY AF 2.1

Write an expression for the situation.

3. 36 fewer than 54

4. 320 minus the sum of 180 and 32

5. 21 more than the difference of 60 and 15

Simplify the expression.

6. $(21 + 15) + (32 + 3)$

7. $(68 - 22) - 30$

8. $(37 + 5) - (22 + 5)$

Complete by writing >, <, or = for each ⬭.

9. $79 + 1$ ⬭ 80

10. $(63 - 4) + 4$ ⬭ $68 + 4$

11. $100 - 56$ ⬭ $100 - 55$

Copy and complete.

12. $60 + (54 + 21) = 60 + 75$

$\square + \square = \square$

$\square = \square$

13. $(64 - 19) + 15 = 50 + 10$

$\square + \square = \square$

$\square = \square$

Problem Solving and Reasoning

MR 2.3, MR 2.2, KEY AF 1.2, KEY AF 1.3

Solve.

14. Marcia found 22 shells. Lucy found 5 more than Marcia. Write an expression for the total number of shells they found.

15. Carlos collected 10 sports cards. He bought 12 more. Then he gave his friend 7 of the cards. How many cards did he have left?

Writing Math Explain the difference between an inequality using the > or < and an inequality using the ≠ symbol.

Spiral Review and Test Practice

1. Which is 20,000 + 9 + 600,000,000 + 40,000,000 + 300,000 + 400 + 1,000 in standard form?

A 604,321,409

B 604,321,490

C 640,321,409

D 640,312,409

KEY NS 1.1 page 16

2. Which of the following has the greatest value?

A 5,695,934

B 5,908,432

C 5,009,876

D 5,237,879

Test Tip
Only compare two answer choices at a time.

KEY NS 1.2 page 28

3. Which is the value of the expression (15 + 4) − (8 + 2)?

A 29

B 19

C 13

D 9

KEY AF 1.2 page 54

4. 2,567 + 5,434 =

A 7,001

B 7,901

C 7,991

D 8,001

KEY NS 3.1 page 62

5. 23,000 − 5,296 =

A 18,704

B 17,714

C 17,704

D 17,104

KEY NS 3.1 page 82

6. What is the value of the expression below?

34 − (13 + 7) + 8

A 6

B 14

C 22

D 36

Test Tip
Pay attention to all operation symbols.

KEY AF 1.2 page 92

Education Place
Visit www.eduplace.com/camap/ for **Test-Taking Tips** and **Extra Practice.**

Unit 2 Test

Vocabulary and Concepts

AF 1.0, KEY AF 1.2, MR 2.3 Chapters 3–5

Write *true* or *false* to the statements below.

1. The Commutative Property of Addition says you may change the way the addends are grouped.
2. Addition and subtraction are inverse operations.
3. A number or a group of numbers and operation symbols is called an equation.
4. The Associative Property of Addition is when the order of the addends is changed.

Computation

KEY NS 1.3, KEY NS 3.1, KEY AF 1.2, KEY AF 2.1 Chapter 3, Lesson 3

Round each number to the given place value. Estimate the sum or difference.

Round to thousands. **5.** 3,643 − 2,432 **6.** 3,287 + 2,643

Round to ten thousands. **7.** 28,493 − 21,304 **8.** 83,203 + 23,032

Add or subtract. Use estimation or addition to check your answers. Chapters 3 and 4

9. $\begin{array}{r} 582 \\ +\,438 \\ \hline \end{array}$ **10.** $\begin{array}{r} 9{,}040 \\ -\,7{,}228 \\ \hline \end{array}$ **11.** $\begin{array}{r} 8{,}403 \\ -\,6{,}242 \\ \hline \end{array}$

Copy and complete by writing >, <, or =. Write whether each is an *equation* or an *inequality*. Chapter 5, Lesson 3

12. 105 + 10 ⬤ 115 **13.** (21 + 2) − 9 ⬤ 32 **14.** 235 + 22 ⬤ 275 − 25

Copy and complete. Chapter 5, Lesson 4

15. (48 + 32) + 11 = 80 + 11
■ + 11 = ■
■ = ■

16. (24 − 21) + 5 = 3 + 5
■ + 5 = ■
■ = ■

Solve.

17. Joshua stated that: "If 6 + 1 + 8 = 15, then 8 + 1 + 6 = 15." Is Joshua correct? Explain.
18. Emily has 156 quarters. About one half of them are state quarters. She says she has 80 state quarters. Is this a good estimate? Explain.

Problem Solving and Reasoning

KEY NS 3.1, AF 1.1, KEY AF 1.3, MR 2.3 Chapters 3–5

Solve.

19. Sonya spent $7 and $9 at the trading post. She gave the cashier a $20 bill. Write and simplify an expression to show the change that Sonya should receive.

20. Carlos earned $10 doing chores and $5 helping a neighbor. He spent $12 at the hobby shop. Write and solve an equation to show how much money Carlos has left.

Writing Math Explain the difference between an expression, an equation, and an inequality.

Performance Assessment

KEY AF 1.2, KEY AF 1.3, MR 1.1, MR 2.3

Are We There Yet?

Sam's family is driving from San Diego to Yosemite National Park. His father wants to have an answer when Sam asks, "Are we there yet?" To have the answer, Sam's father needs to figure out some driving times along the way.

Task	Information You Need		
Use the information above and to the right. Write and simplify expressions to show how long it will take to drive to each city. Write and simplify an expression to find the driving time for the entire trip.	**Estimated Driving Time**		
	From	**To**	**Time**
	San Diego	Los Angeles	2 hours
	Los Angeles	San Francisco	4 hours more than San Diego to Los Angeles
	San Francisco	Yosemite	2 hours less than Los Angeles to San Francisco
	Yosemite	San Diego	5 hours less than the sum of the first three distances

Greg Tang's **Go Fast, Go Far**

Unit 2 Mental Math Strategies

Make 99

A simple strategy of mine, is first to make a 99!

I have a fast way to do 100 – 36. First I subtract 1 from 100 to make 99. Then I subtract 1 from 36 to get 35. Now I can subtract 35 from 99. Making 99 means no regrouping. The answer is 64!

1. 100 – 36. Take 1 from 100. → 99; Take 1 from 36. → –35; 64

2. 300 – 43. Take 1 from 300. → ▢; Take 1 from 43. → – ▢; ▢

3. 500 – 72. Take ▢ from 500. → ▢; Take ▢ from 72. → – ▢; ▢

4. 100 – 27. Take ▢ from ▢. → ▢; Take ▢ from ▢. → – ▢; ▢

You are doing great!

5. 200 – 18 → ▢ – ▢ = ▢

6. 400 – 81 → ▢ – ▢ = ▢

7. 700 – 13 → ▢ – ▢ = ▢

8. 200 – 39 → ▢ – ▢ = ▢

9. 400 – 54 → ▢ – ▢ = ▢

10. 800 – 41 → ▢ – ▢ = ▢

Take It Further!

Now try doing all the steps in your head!

Doing Great!

11. 100 – 44

12. 400 – 86

13. 500 – 92

14. 800 – 71

Unit 3

Multiplication and Division

BIG IDEAS!

- Multiplication and division are related operations.
- The order of operations tells how to simplify an expression.
- Equals multiplied by equals are equal.

Chapter 6
Relate Multiplication and Division

Chapter 7
More Expressions and Equations

Songs and Games

Math Music Track 3: *40 Cookies*
eGames at
www.eduplace.com/camap/

Math Readers

Get Ready **Game**

Know Your Facts

Object of the Game Use multiplication and division facts to reach a target score.

Materials
- Learning Tool 13 (Multiplication and Division Fact Cards)
- number cube labeled 1–6

Set Up
Place all the Multiplication Fact Cards in a stack face up on the left. Place all the Division Fact Cards in a stack face up on the right.

Number of Players 2

How to Play

1. Player 1 rolls the number cube. If 1, 3, or 5 is rolled, the player chooses a Multiplication Fact Card. If 2, 4, or 6 is rolled, the player chooses a Division Fact Card.
2. Player 1 finds the product or quotient and writes the answer on a piece of paper.
3. Player 2 repeats Steps 1-2. Players continue taking turns. Each answer is added to the previous total.
4. When the fact cards run out, players use the cards they have already chosen to set up two new stacks.
5. The first player to reach or pass 200 wins.

CA Standards
KEY NS 3.0 Students solve problems involving addition, subtraction, multiplication, and division of whole numbers and understand the relationships among the operations.

Education Place
Visit www.eduplace.com/camap/ for **Brain Teasers** and **eGames** to play.

Reading To get the right answer to a mathematics problem, you need to make sure you understand the question.

Problem 1
There are 25 students in Mr. Mack's classroom. Students sit in groups of 5. Which number sentence can be used to find the number of groups?

A $25 + 5 = \square$
B $5 \times 25 = \square$
C $25 \div 5 = \square$
D $25 - 5 = \square$

Thinking Through Problem 1

Think about the question.
Should the number sentence show addition, multiplication, division, or subtraction?

Think about what you know. You know the total number of students and the number in each group.

Think about what you don't know. You don't know the number of groups. You can divide 25 into groups of 5 to find out.

The correct answer is **C.**

Writing Now it's your turn. Solve Problem 2. Then write about how you solved the problem, step by step.

Problem 2
To raise money for a class trip, the students in Mr. Mack's class sell cards. The table shows how much money they can raise depending on what they sell.

Number of boxes sold	Dollars raised
2	$5
4	$10
6	$15
8	$20
10	?

If Seth sells 10 boxes, how much money would he raise?

A $20
B $22
C $25
D $30

I always check to see if I answered the question that was asked.

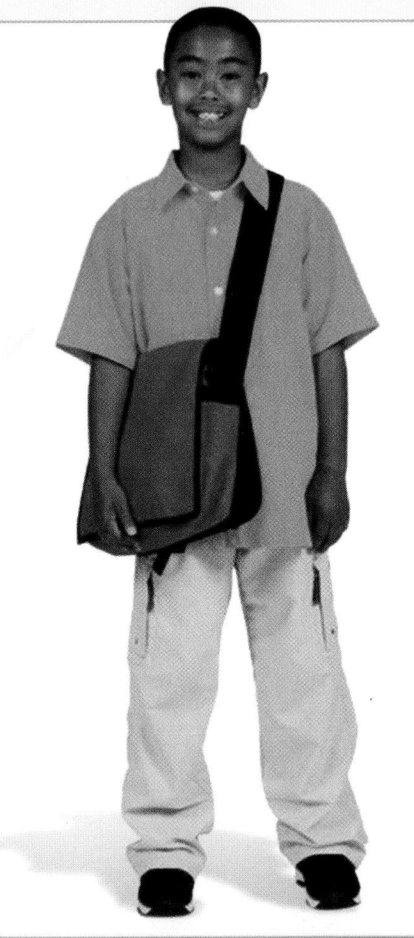

Relate Multiplication and Division

Check What You Know

Vocabulary and Concepts GRADE 3 NS 2.0, MR 2.3

Choose the best word to complete the sentence.

1. The answer to a division problem is a _____.

2. Multiplication and _____ are inverse operations.

Word Bank
- divide
- division
- multiply
- product
- quotient

Skills GRADE 3 KEY NS 2.3

Complete the number sentence. Use the drawing to help.

3. ●●●●●

$1 \times \square = 5$

$5 \div \square = 5$

4. ●●●●
●●●●

$\square \times 4 = 8$

$\square \div 2 = 4$

Problem Solving and Reasoning GRADE 3 KEY NS 2.3

Solve.

5. Write a multiplication and division sentence for the array.

●●●●●
●●●●●
●●●●●

Vocabulary

Visualize It!

Commutative Property of Multiplication
$4 \times 8 = 8 \times 4$

Identity Property of Multiplication
$8 \times 1 = 8$
$1 \times 8 = 8$

Properties of Multiplication

Associative Property of Multiplication
$(4 \times 3) \times 2 =$
$4 \times (3 \times 2)$

Zero Property of Multiplication
$9 \times 0 = 0$
$0 \times 9 = 0$

Language Tips

A *pair* of shoes is two shoes. A *pair* of socks is two socks. In mathematics, a *pair* is also always two. A *pair* of factors is two factors.

Words that look alike in English and Spanish often have the same meaning.

English	Spanish
factor	factor
product	producto

See **English-Spanish Glossary** pages 644–666.

Education Place Visit www.eduplace.com/camap/ for the **eGlossary** and **eGames**.

CA Standards MR 2.3 Use a variety of methods, such as words, numbers, symbols, charts, graphs, tables, diagrams, and models, to explain mathematical reasoning. **Also AF 1.0**

LESSON 1

Hands On
Relate Multiplication and Division

Objective Understand the relationship between multiplication and division.

CA Standards
KEY NS 3.0 Students solve problems involving addition, subtraction, multiplication, and division of whole numbers and understand the relationships among the operations.

MR 2.3 Use a variety of methods, such as words, numbers, symbols, charts, graphs, tables, diagrams, and models, to explain mathematical reasoning.

Also MR 1.1, MR 2.4, MR 3.0, MR 3.2

Vocabulary

inverse operations

array

Materials
- Workmat 1
- number cubes
- counters
- eManipulatives (optional) eduplace.com/camap

Explore

Multiplication and division are **inverse operations**. Division "undoes" multiplication.

Question How can you use an array to show the relationship between multiplication and division?

Tomás used 35 counters to make an **array**. What equations can he write for this array?

1 Use counters to make the array.

Write a multiplication equation.

5 rows × 7 columns = 35 total

2 Turn the array sideways. Now there are 7 rows and 5 columns.

Write a multiplication equation.

7 rows × 5 columns = 35 total

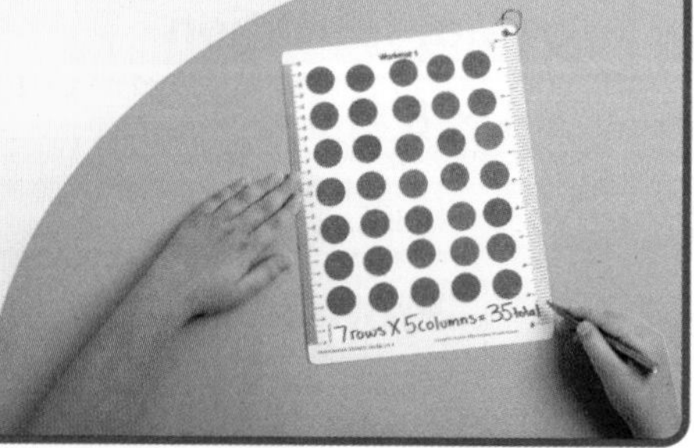

3 Write a division equation.

35 total ÷ 5 columns = 7 rows

Write a division equation for the other array.

35 total ÷ 7 columns = 5 rows

Work with a partner to make an array.

1 Toss number cubes to get two numbers that will be the number of rows and the number of columns in the array.

2 Make the array with counters on Workmat 1. Then turn the array on Workmat 1 sideways.

3 Write all the multiplication and division equations for the array.

Extend

Write all the multiplication and division equations for the array.

1. 

2. 

3. 

4. 

5. 

6. 

Use counters or a sketch to make one array for each product.

7. 12

8. 10

9. 18

10. Look at Exercises 7–9. Are there any products for which you can make more than one array? If so, which ones?

11. **Analyze** Why can you only write one multiplication equation and one division equation for the array in Exercise 3?

12. **Challenge** Draw another array that has only one multiplication equation and one division equation.

Math Journal

Writing Math

What's Wrong? Seth used 36 counters to make the arrangement shown. Why is this not an array? Draw at least two different arrays Seth could have made with the 36 counters.

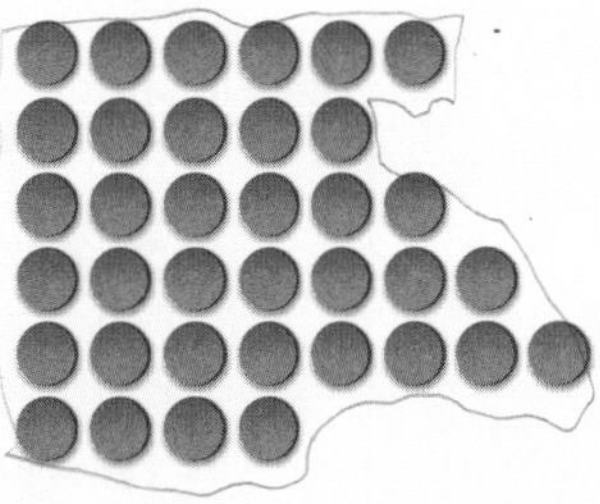

CA Standards
KEY NS 3.0 Students solve problems involving addition, subtraction, multiplication, and division of whole numbers and understand the relationships among the operations.

Also AF 1.1, MR 1.1, MR 2.0, MR 2.3

Vocabulary

array

fact family

Relate Multiplication and Division

Objective Use multiplication facts to help you divide.

Learn by Example

Darren arranged 18 state quarters in an **array** with the same number of coins in each row.

Darren wrote two multiplication equations about the array.

$$\underset{\text{rows}}{3} \times \underset{\text{columns}}{6} = \underset{\text{total}}{18}$$

$$\underset{\text{columns}}{6} \times \underset{\text{rows}}{3} = \underset{\text{total}}{18}$$

Darren also wrote two division equations about the array.

$$\underset{\text{total}}{18} \div \underset{\text{columns}}{6} = \underset{\text{rows}}{3}$$

$$\underset{\text{total}}{18} \div \underset{\text{rows}}{3} = \underset{\text{columns}}{6}$$

The equations that can be written by using the numbers 3, 6, and 18 form a **fact family**. Fact families show that multiplication and division are related.

Ask Yourself
- Which are the factors?
- What is the product?

Guided Practice

Complete the fact family.

1. $3 \times 5 = \square$ $\quad 15 \div 3 = \square$
   $5 \times 3 = \square$ $\quad 15 \div 5 = \square$

Write the fact family for the set of numbers.

2. 4, 4, 16
3. 5, 6, 30
4. 2, 5, 10

Math Talk How can knowing $7 \times 4 = 28$ help you find $28 \div 4$?

Practice and Problem Solving

Complete the fact family.

5. $4 \times 6 = \square$ $\quad$ $24 \div 4 = \square$
$6 \times 4 = \square$ $\quad$ $24 \div 6 = \square$

6. $8 \times 9 = \square$ $\quad$ $72 \div 8 = \square$
$9 \times 8 = \square$ $\quad$ $72 \div 9 = \square$

Write the fact family for the set of numbers.

7. 3, 6, 18 $\quad$ **8.** 4, 9, 36 $\quad$ **9.** 5, 9, 45 $\quad$ **10.** 6, 8, 48

11. 4, 8, 32 $\quad$ **12.** 8, 8, 64 $\quad$ **13.** 7, 9, 63 $\quad$ **14.** 9, 9, 81

Algebra Equations

Use a related division equation to find the missing number. Write the equation you used.

15. $8 \times \square = 64$ $\quad$ **16.** $\square \times 6 = 54$ $\quad$ **17.** $\square \times 9 = 36$ $\quad$ **18.** $\square \times 9 = 45$

19. $7 \times \square = 49$ $\quad$ **20.** $20 \times \square = 20$ $\quad$ **21.** $5 \times \square = 30$ $\quad$ **22.** $\square \times 8 = 16$

23. $3 \times \square = 27$ $\quad$ **24.** $6 \times \square = 36$ $\quad$ **25.** $1 \times \square = 7$ $\quad$ **26.** $\square \times 4 = 40$

27. $8 \times \square = 24$ $\quad$ **28.** $\square \times 3 = 27$ $\quad$ **29.** $\square \times 7 = 42$ $\quad$ **30.** $5 \times \square = 25$

Solve.

31. Can you form a fact family using 2, 7, and 27? Explain why or why not.

32. **Algebra** There are two fact families that contain 3, 6, and another number. Write the equations for both fact families.

Spiral Review and Test Practice

Add. Use estimation to support your answer. KEY NS 3.1 page 58

33. 9,374 + 2,550 $\quad$ **34.** 35,296 + 11,593 $\quad$ **35.** 73,180 + 26,324 $\quad$ **36.** 350,137 + 416,582

Write the letter of the correct answer. KEY NS 3.0

37. If $8 \times 5 = 40$, then what is $40 \div 8$?

A 5 $\quad$ **B** 8 $\quad$ **C** 32 $\quad$ **D** 48

Extra Practice See page 137, Set A.

CA Standards

KEY NS 3.0 Students solve problems involving addition, subtraction, multiplication, and division of whole numbers and understand the relationships among the operations.

AF 1.0 Students use and interpret variables, mathematical symbols, and properties to write and simplify expressions and sentences.

Also KEY AF 1.2, AF 1.1, MR 1.0, MR 1.1, MR 2.0, MR 2.3, MR 3.0, MR 3.3

Vocabulary

Commutative Property of Multiplication

Identity Property of Multiplication

Zero Property of Multiplication

Associative Property of Multiplication

Think

Remember, the parentheses tell you which numbers to multiply first.

Multiplication Properties and Division Rules

Objective Use multiplication properties and division rules.

Learn by Example

In Lesson 2, you used arrays to write fact families. In this lesson, you will use arrays to learn about multiplication properties and division rules.

Multiplication Properties

Commutative Property of Multiplication
When you change the order of the factors, the product stays the same.

$3 \times 2 = 6$ $2 \times 3 = 6$

Identity Property of Multiplication
When you multiply any number by 1, the product is equal to that number.

$6 \times 1 = 6$

Zero Property of Multiplication
When you multiply any number by 0, the product is 0.

$4 \times 0 = 0$

Associative Property of Multiplication
When you group factors in different ways, the product stays the same.

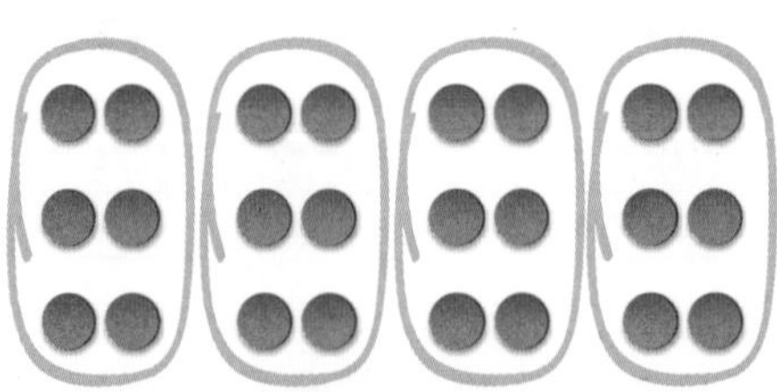

$(3 \times 2) \times 4$

$6 \times 4 = 24$

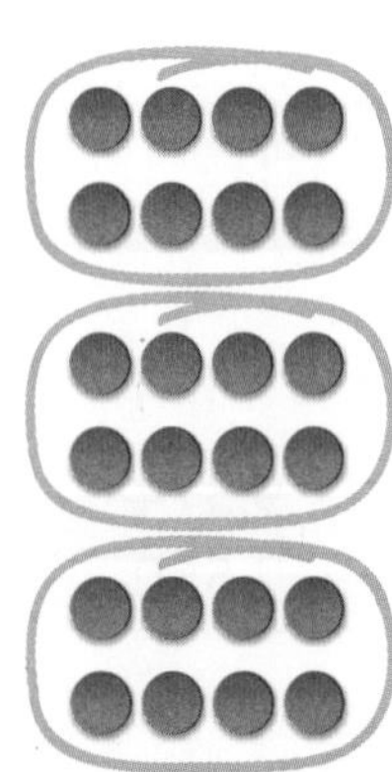

$3 \times (2 \times 4)$

$3 \times 8 = 24$

Division rules can help you divide with 1 or 0.

Division Rules

When you divide a number by itself, the quotient is 1. This is true for all numbers except 0.	$5 \div 5 = 1$ or $5\overline{)5}$ = 1
When you divide a number by 1, the quotient is the same as the dividend.	$5 \div 1 = 5$ or $1\overline{)5}$ = 5
When you divide 0 by a number other than 0, the quotient is 0.	$0 \div 5 = 0$ or $5\overline{)0}$ = 0
You cannot divide a number by 0.	~~$5 \div 0$~~ ~~$0\overline{)5}$~~

Guided Practice

Use properties and rules to solve. If there is no solution, explain why.

Ask Yourself

What property or rule can I use?

1. $1 \times 93 = \square$ **2.** $(2 \times \square) \times 4 = 16$ **3.** $0 \div 3 = \square$

4. $9 \div 9 = \square$ **5.** $4 \times \square = 0$ **6.** $8 \div 0 = \square$

7. $\square \div 15 = 0$ **8.** $9 \times \square = 7 \times 9$ **9.** $10 \div \square = 10$

10. $7 \times 0 = \square$ **11.** $\square \times 5 = 5$ **12.** $4 \div \square = 1$

Math Talk Do you need to know the value of 6×9 to find $(6 \times 9) \times 0$? Use multiplication properties to explain.

Practice and Problem Solving

Use properties and rules to solve. If there is no solution, explain why.

13. $5 \times 8 = \square \times 5$

14. $4 \div 1 = \square$

15. $9 \div \square = 1$

16. $0 \div 72 = \square$

17. $\square \times 1 = 5$

18. $(3 \times 2) \times 4 = 3 \times (\square \times 4)$

Solve.

19. **Analyze** Terry divided a non-zero number by 1. What do you know about the quotient? How do you know?

20. **Reasoning** Tiara is thinking of three whole numbers. The product of the three numbers is 8. Their sum is 7. What are the numbers? Explain.

Science Link

Use the Fun Facts to solve.

21. For each number in the Fun Facts, tell if it has been rounded or if it is exact.

22. About how many of the earthquakes detected each year cannot be felt?

23. Sonja wrote $(2 \times 5) \times 10$ to show the number of earthquakes that cause damage each year. Michael wrote $2 \times (5 \times 10)$ to show the number. Who is correct? Explain.

Earthquakes

- Scientists detect around 500,000 earthquakes each year. About 100,000 of them can be felt and about 100 of them cause damage.
- From 1975 to 1995, only 4 states did not have any earthquakes—Florida, Iowa, North Dakota, and Wisconsin.
- The southern California area has about 10,000 earthquakes every year.

Science ES 5.a

Spiral Review and Test Practice

Evaluate the expression. KEY AF 1.2 pages 94, 98

24. $(4 + 5) - 3$

25. $(8 + 2) - (4 + 2)$

26. $9 + (10 - 4)$

Write the letter of the correct answer. KEY AF 1.3

27. Which of these is another way to write $(2 \times 3) \times 5$?

A $2 \times (3 \times 5)$ **B** $(2 + 3) + 5$ **C** $(2 \times 5) + 3$ **D** $(2 \times 4) \times 4$

Extra Practice See page 137, Set B.

Key Standards Review

Need Help?
See Key Standards Handbook.

Find the sum or difference. KEY NS 3.0, KEY NS 3.1

1. $4{,}593 - 2{,}697 =$ ▢
2. $497 + 3{,}478 =$ ▢
3. $23{,}999 - 6{,}782 =$ ▢
4. $876{,}502 + 304{,}502 =$ ▢
5. $395 + 421 + 789 =$ ▢
6. $11{,}111 - 10{,}999 =$ ▢
7. $16{,}735 - 9{,}043 =$ ▢
8. $23 + 547 + 1{,}693 =$ ▢

Evaluate the expression. KEY AF 1.2

9. $(12 + 2) - 4$
10. $11 + (3 - 2)$
11. $(29 + 4) - (31 + 2)$
12. $(15 - 3) + (15 - 3)$
13. $9 + (36 - 7)$
14. $(14 - 2) - 11$
15. $14 + (25 - 5)$
16. $(27 + 3) - 10$
17. $(8 + 4) - (11 - 7)$
18. $(30 + 8) - (15 + 3)$
19. $7 + (29 - 8)$
20. $(14 + 9) - 8$
21. $(33 - 4) - (15 + 4)$
22. $43 - (16 + 3)$
23. $37 + (12 - 7)$

Challenge — Algebraic Thinking

How Do They Relate?

Complete the sentence. KEY NS 3.0, KEY AF 1.2, AF 1.0

1. 3×4 is to 4×3 as 6×7 is to _____ .
2. $0 \div 13$ is to 0 as _____ $\times 13$ is to 0.
3. $(4 \times 5) \times 7$ is to $4 \times (5 \times 7)$ as $(6 \times 8) \times 2$ is to _____ .
4. 9×1 is to 9 as _____ $\times 1$ is to 12.
5. $5 \div 5$ is to 1 as $6 \div$ _____ is to 1.
6. 8×5 is to 5×8 as 4×9 is to _____ .

CA Standards
KEY NS 3.0 Students solve problems involving addition, subtraction, multiplication, and division of whole numbers and understand the relationships among the operations.
MR 2.3 Use a variety of methods, such as words, numbers, symbols, charts, graphs, tables, diagrams, and models, to explain mathematical reasoning.
Also KEY NS 3.2, NS 4.1, MR 1.1, MR 2.0, MR 2.3, MR 3.2

Vocabulary

multiple

square number

Materials
Learning Tool 14 (Multiplication Table)

Hands On
Patterns in Multiplication and Division

Objective Use a multiplication table to multiply and divide.

Explore

In this lesson, you will use patterns on a multiplication table to multiply and divide.

Question What number relationships can you find on a multiplication table?

1 Use the table to find 5 × 6. Find the square where the row for 5 and the column for 6 meet.

The product is 30.

×	0	1	2	3	4	5	6	7
0	0	0	0	0	0	0	0	0
1	0	1	2	3	4	5	6	7
2	0	2					12	
3	0	3					18	
4	0	4					24	
5	0	5	10	15	20	25	30	
6	0	6						
7	0	7						

column ↓ (6); row → (5); product ↑ (30)

2 A **multiple** of a number is the product of that number and any whole number. The row for 5 shows some multiples of 5.

List three multiples of 5 that continue the row.

3 A **square number** is the product of two factors that are the same.

$4 \times 4 = 16$, so 16 is a square number.
$7 \times 7 = 49$, so 49 is a square number.

- Find other square numbers in the table.
- Describe how you found them.

4 To find 40 ÷ 8, look down the column for 8 until you find 40. Follow that row to the left to find the quotient.

- What is the quotient of 40 ÷ 8?
- Use your table to find 21 ÷ 7. Describe how you found it.

×	0	1	2	3	4	5	6	7	8
0	0	0	0	0	0	0	0	0	0
1	0	1	2	3	4	5	6	7	8
2	0	2	4	6	8	10	12	14	16
3	0	3	6	9	12	15	18	21	24
4	0	4	8	12	16	20	24	28	32
5	0	5	10	15	20	25	30	35	40

Extend

Use your multiplication table to solve.

1. Find the number 24 in four different places in the table. Write a division sentence for each 24 you find. How are the equations the same? How are they different?
2. Write a division sentence using a square number as a dividend. Write the fact family for the 3 numbers in your division sentence. How many number sentences are in the fact family? Explain why.
3. What multiplication property does the column for 0 show? What multiplication property does the column for 1 show?
4. What division rule does the row for 0 show? What division rule does the row for 1 show?
5. Fill in the products in your table. Then extend the table to show the multiples of 10.

Writing Math

Analyze Look at the multiples of 3 and 6 in the table. What do you notice? What other pairs of multiples have the same relationship?

CA Standards
KEY NS 3.2 Demonstrate an understanding of, and the ability to use, standard algorithms for multiplying a multidigit number by a two-digit number and for dividing a multidigit number by a one-digit number; use relationships between them to simplify computations and to check results.

Also MR 1.0, MR 1.1, MR 2.0, MR 2.2, MR 2.3, MR 3.0, MR 3.3

Vocabulary

quotient
remainder

$$7\overline{)15}\ \ 2\text{ R}1$$

divisor (7)
dividend (15)
quotient → 2; remainder → R1

Division with Remainders

Objective Divide when there are remainders.

Learn by Example

You already know how to divide using multiplication facts. In this lesson, you will learn how to divide when there are remainders.

The Shanghai Acrobats use plates when they perform. Suppose there are 9 acrobats who each use the same number of plates. If there are 56 plates, how many plates does each acrobat use? How many plates are left?

To find the size of equal groups, divide. The number that is left over is the remainder. The remainder is always less than the divisor.

Divide. $56 \div 9 = \bigcirc$ or $9\overline{)56}$ (quotient: $\bigcirc$)

Example

1 Think of a 9 multiplication fact that is close to 56.

$9 \times \blacksquare = 56$
$9 \times 7 = 63$ ← **7 is too many. Try 6 as the quotient.**
$9 \times 6 = 54$

2 Divide.

```
   6
9)56
 -54   ← Multiply. 9 × 6 = 54
   2   ← Subtract. 56 − 54 = 2
```

3 Show the remainder.

```
   6 R2
9)56
 -54
   2   ← remainder
```

Solution: Each acrobat gets 6 plates. There are 2 plates left.

Check

- Multiply the quotient by the divisor.
  $6 \times 9 = 54$
- Add the remainder.
  $54 + 2 = 56$

The sum equals the dividend, so the answer is correct.

Guided Practice

Divide.

1. $2\overline{)11}$ **2.** $4\overline{)7}$ **3.** 32 ÷ 8 **4.** 25 ÷ 3

Ask Yourself

- What multiplication facts can help me?
- Is there a remainder? Is it less than the divisor?

Guided Problem Solving

Use the questions to solve this problem.

5. Suppose 9 acrobats are balancing sets of candles. Are 46 sets of candles enough for each of the acrobats to balance 5 sets? Explain your thinking.

a. **Understand** How many sets of candles are there? How many acrobats are there?

b. **Plan** What numbers should you divide? Why? What will the quotient tell you?

c. **Solve** Divide. Then write the answer to the problem.

d. **Look Back** Did you answer the question? Does your answer make sense?

Math Talk Why must the remainder always be less than the divisor?

Practice and Problem Solving

Divide. Then check your answer.

6. $4\overline{)6}$ **7.** $2\overline{)9}$ **8.** $5\overline{)12}$ **9.** $2\overline{)17}$ **10.** $4\overline{)23}$

11. $6\overline{)16}$ **12.** $9\overline{)91}$ **13.** $8\overline{)32}$ **14.** $3\overline{)23}$ **15.** $2\overline{)19}$

16. 69 ÷ 7 **17.** 44 ÷ 9 **18.** 36 ÷ 7 **19.** 39 ÷ 6 **20.** 20 ÷ 4

Work backward. Find the missing number.

21. 3 ÷ ▢ → 1 R1 **22.** 9 ÷ 4 → 2 R▢ **23.** 26 ÷ 9 → 2 R▢

24. 15 ÷ 3 → ▢ **25.** ▢ ÷ 8 → 2 R4 **26.** 17 ÷ 5 → ▢ R2

27. 34 ÷ ▢ → 4 R2 **28.** ▢ ÷ 7 → 4 **29.** 78 ÷ ▢ → 8 R6

Solve.

30. Suppose 9 acrobats each balance 8 plates. If there are 75 plates in all, how many plates will be left over?

31. What's Wrong? Chang is packing 53 glasses into boxes. He says he can divide them evenly into 8 boxes. Explain why he is wrong.

32. Seventy-six students are going on a field trip to the circus. They are traveling in vans that hold 9 students each. How many vans will they need to take all the students to the circus? Will each van be full?

33. Rhonda has 63 stickers. If she wants to place an equal number of stickers on 9 pages of her sticker book, how many stickers will go on each page?

History-Social Science Link

Use the Fun Facts to solve.

34. If Ashley has 38¢, how many tickets could she buy at the nickelodeon? How much money would she have left over?

35. How much longer was the longest nickelodeon show than the shortest show?

36. Analyze Suppose Charlie Chaplin was only paid in $100 bills. How many bills would he have received in 1917?

Moving Pictures

- The first moving-picture theaters in the United States opened in 1905. They were called nickelodeons because it cost a nickel to buy a ticket.
- The shows were 15 minutes to 90 minutes long.
- In 1917, Charlie Chaplin signed a one-million-dollar contract for his silent films.

Charlie Chaplin, silent film star

History-Social Science 4.4.9

Spiral Review and Test Practice

Write the value of the digit 5 in each number. NS 1.0 pages 8, 12

37. 120,857 **38.** 562,379,480 **39.** 16,050,000 **40.** 35,764

Write the letter of the correct answer. KEY NS 3.2

41. Tiffany solved the problem below. Which expression could be used to check her answer?

$32 \div 5 \rightarrow 6$ R2

A $(6 \times 5) \times 2$ **B** $(32 - 5) + 6$ **C** 6×5 **D** $(6 \times 5) + 2$

Extra Practice See page 137, Set C.

Practice **Game**

Remainder Face-Off

Object of the Game Find the remainder in division problems and compare to find the greater remainder.

Materials
Learning Tool 15 (*Remainder Face-Off Game Cards*)

Set Up
Deal all the cards so that each player has 12 cards face down in a pile.

Number of Players 2

How to Play

1. Players place one card from their pile face up at the same time. As each card is put down, players think quickly and find the quotient and the remainder.
2. The player who has the division problem with the greater remainder takes both cards.
3. If the remainders match, each player places three cards face down on the table and a fourth card face up. The player with the greater remainder on the fourth card takes all of the cards on the table.
4. The game is over when one of the players has all of the cards in the deck.

CA Standards
KEY NS 3.0 Students solve problems involving addition, subtraction, multiplication, and division of whole numbers and understand the relationships among the operations.

Education Place
Visit www.eduplace.com/camap/ for **Brain Teasers** and **eGames** to play.

CA Standards
MR 1.0, MR 2.0,
MR 2.4, MR 2.6,
KEY NS 3.0, KEY NS 3.1,
KEY NS 3.2, KEY AF 1.2,
KEY AF 1.3,
History-Social Science 4.4.3

Problem Solving

Objective Use skills and strategies to solve word problems.

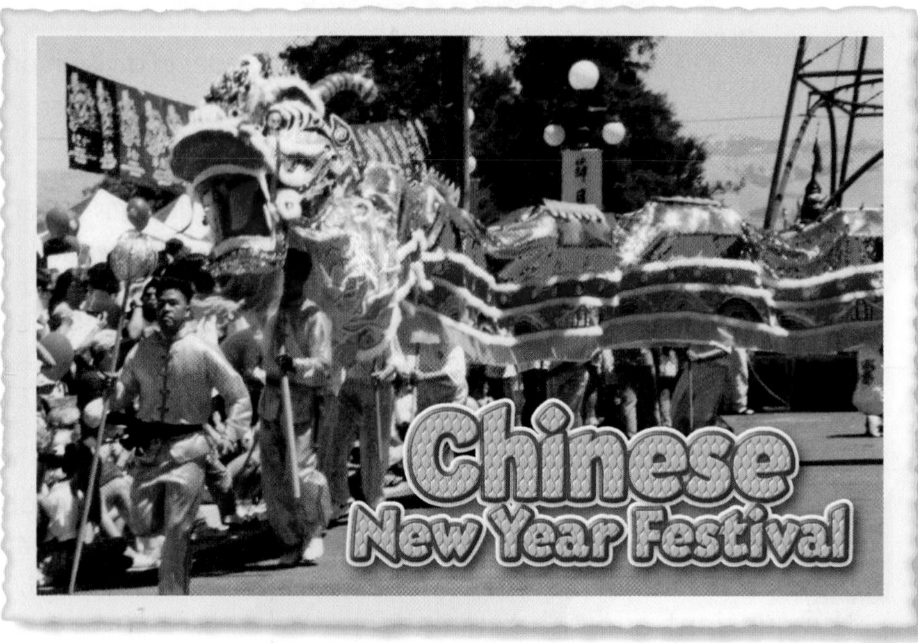

The Golden Dragon dances through the streets of San Jose.

At the start of the new year on the lunar calendar, street festivals honor and celebrate the city's Chinese heritage.

Solve. Tell which strategy or method you used.

1. Suppose Mr. Chu bought 4 times as many spring rolls as steamed buns. If he bought 36 spring rolls, how many steamed buns did he buy? Use multiplication to check.

2. In the Lion Dance, one dancer holds the head of the lion costume. A second dancer leans over to support the lion's tail. How many dancers would be needed if the dance included 6 lions? 10 lions? 20 lions?

3. **Create and Solve** Bubble tea is a Taiwanese drink sold at the festival. You can buy a large bubble tea for $3 and a small bubble tea for $2.
   a. Write an expression using parentheses that shows the cost of 4 large bubble teas and 3 small bubble teas.
   b. Evaluate the expression to find the total cost.

Lion head

Problem Solving on Tests

Select a Strategy

- Make an Organized List
- Estimate
- Choose the Operation
- Draw a Picture

1. In an election, four candidates received the following number of votes. Which is the least number of votes?

A 37,089

B 42,259

C 32,259

D 32,195

KEY NS 1.2 page 28

2. Joe and Jenny wrote expressions with the same value. Joe wrote $(3 \times 4) \times 2$. Which is the equation Jenny wrote?

A $(3 + 4) \times 2$

B $3 \times (4 \times 2)$

C $3 + (4 \times 2)$

D $(3 \times 4) + 2$

AF 1.0 page 124

3. Juan did 4 math problems in the morning and 11 in the afternoon. Kate did 9 problems in the morning and 3 in the afternoon. To find how many more problems he did than Kate, Juan wrote the expression $(4 + 11) - (9 + 3)$. What is the value of the expression?

A 27

B 9

C 5

D 3

KEY AF 1.2 page 94

4. A movie theater has an afternoon show and an evening show. There were 396 people at the afternoon show. What information do you need to find how many more people were at the evening show than the afternoon show?

A No more information is needed.

B There were 412 people at the afternoon show the next day.

C There were 515 people at the evening show.

D The theater has 550 seats.

KEY NS 3.0, MR 1.1 page 62

5. Marcus had 31 sports cards. He gave his sister 8 baseball and 7 basketball cards. Then he bought 5 more cards. He writes the expression below to represent the number of cards he has now. What is the value of the expression?

$$31 - (8 + 7) + 5$$

A 21

B 35

C 37

D 41

Test Tip

Does your answer make sense? Draw a picture to check your answer.

KEY AF 1.2 page 94

Education Place
Visit www.eduplace.com/camap/ for **Test-Taking Tips** and **Extra Practice.**

Vocabulary

Like addition and subtraction, **multiplication** and **division** are related operations. You can use the properties of multiplication and fact families to help solve problems.

Choose a term from the word bank to complete each sentence.

Word Bank
Commutative Property of Multiplication
Zero Property of Multiplication
Associative Property of Multiplication
fact family
factor
array

1. $(2 \times 4) \times 3 = 2 \times (4 \times 3)$ is an example of the ________.
2. $3 \times 6 = 6 \times 3$ is an example of the ________.
3. $3 \times 6 = 18, 6 \times 3 = 18, 18 \div 3 = 6, 18 \div 6 = 3$ is an example of a ________.

Read both problems and answer the questions that follow.

Problem A	Problem B
At their family reunion, the Evans family fills 4 picnic tables. There are 6 people at each table. How many family members attend the Evans family reunion?	There are 24 people at the Evans family reunion. If 6 people can sit at a picnic table, how many tables will the Evans family fill?

4. Which problem shows **multiplication**? Write the number sentence to solve the problem.
5. Which problem shows **division**? Write the number sentence to solve the problem.
6. Write a fact family for 4, 6, and 24.

Writing Write a word problem that can be solved by multiplying. Then write a related word problem that can be solved by dividing.

Reading Look for this book in your library.
Anno's Mysterious Multiplying Jar, by Masaichiro and Mitsumasa Anno

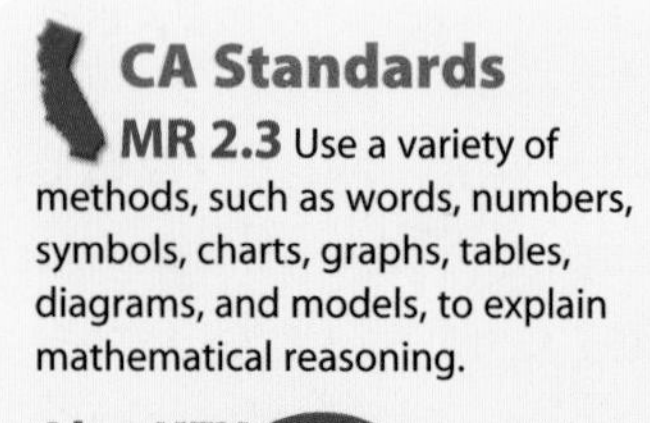

CA Standards
MR 2.3 Use a variety of methods, such as words, numbers, symbols, charts, graphs, tables, diagrams, and models, to explain mathematical reasoning.
Also KEY NS 3.0

Standards-Based Extra Practice

Set A

KEY NS 3.0 page 122

Write the fact family for the set of numbers.

1. 3, 4, 12 **2.** 7, 9, 63 **3.** 4, 7, 28 **4.** 6, 7, 42

5. 9, 9, 81 **6.** 7, 8, 56 **7.** 4, 8, 32 **8.** 6, 8, 48

9. 4, 4, 16 **10.** 5, 6, 30 **11.** 8, 8, 64 **12.** 6, 9, 54

13. Explain How can $4 \times 8 = 32$ help you find $32 \div 4$?

Set B

KEY NS 3.0, AF 1.0 page 124

Use properties and rules to solve. If there is no solution, explain why.

1. $41 \times 1 = \square$ **2.** $7 \div \square = 1$ **3.** $(4 \times 1) \times 9 = \square \times (1 \times 9)$

4. $12 \div 0 = \square$ **5.** $(3 \times \square) \times 5 = 45$ **6.** $0 \div 6 = \square$

7. $\square \div 1 = 32$ **8.** $(4 \times 8) \times \square = 0$ **9.** $\square \times (8 \times 8) = (5 \times 8) \times 8$

10. $9 \times \square = 6 \times 9$ **11.** $\square \div 24 = 0$ **12.** $\square \div 18 = 1$

13. Justify Why can 0 be divided by any other number, but any number cannot be divided by 0?

Set C

KEY NS 3.2 page 130

Divide. Then check your answer.

1. $11 \div 3$ **2.** $40 \div 7$ **3.** $27 \div 5$ **4.** $65 \div 7$ **5.** $17 \div 3$

6. $9\overline{)91}$ **7.** $4\overline{)32}$ **8.** $7\overline{)25}$ **9.** $8\overline{)48}$ **10.** $8\overline{)65}$

11. $6\overline{)53}$ **12.** $6\overline{)33}$ **13.** $9\overline{)26}$ **14.** $3\overline{)29}$ **15.** $5\overline{)46}$

16. $91 \div 10$ **17.** $69 \div 7$ **18.** $13 \div 3$ **19.** $21 \div 6$ **20.** $66 \div 9$

21. Explain Mr. Cruz is planning to give each of his students 2 pencils for their math test. Pencils come in packs of 8. If he has 32 students, can he open enough packs to give all his students pencils but have none left over? Explain.

Education Place
Visit www.eduplace.com/camap/ for more **Extra Practice.**

Chapter Review/Test

Vocabulary and Concepts

KEY NS 3.0, MR 2.3

Write the best term to complete the sentence.

1. A(n) _______ is the product of two factors that are the same.
2. A(n) _______ shows objects arranged in equal rows and columns.
3. A(n) _______ of a number is the product of that number and a whole number.

Skills

KEY NS 3.0, AF 1.0, AF 1.1

Write the fact family for the set of numbers.

4. 4, 8, 32
5. 3, 6, 18
6. 7, 7, 49
7. 5, 9, 45

Use properties and rules to solve. If there is no solution, explain why.

8. $5 \times \square = 8 \times 5$
9. $36 \div 0 = \square$
10. $(6 \times 3) \times 19 = \square \times (3 \times 19)$

Divide. Then check your answer.

11. $2\overline{)7}$
12. $6\overline{)21}$
13. $72 \div 9$
14. $38 \div 7$

Work backward. Find the missing number.

15. $30 \div \square \longrightarrow 5$
16. $53 \div 7 \longrightarrow \square$ R4
17. $69 \div \square \longrightarrow 9$ R6
18. $83 \div 8 \longrightarrow 10$ R$\square$

Problem Solving and Reasoning

MR 2.3, KEY NS 3.0

Solve.

19. A family orders 2 large pizzas. If a large pizza has 8 slices, can they share equally among 5 people and finish the pizza? Explain.
20. Eighty-one students signed up for baseball. How many teams of 9 will there be? Will anyone be left out?

Writing Math Why are fact families smaller for square numbers? Explain.

Spiral Review and Test Practice

1. Which of these is the number 896,000,549?

A nine hundred eighty-six million, five hundred forty-nine

B eight hundred ninety-six million, five hundred forty-nine

C eight hundred ninety-six million, five hundred forty-nine thousand

D eight hundred ninety-six million, five hundred ninety-four

2. Which of the following has the greatest value?

A 789,069,143 **C** 798,082,043

B 789,620,456 **D** 798,420,111

3. 6,432 + 2,568 =

A 9,000

B 8,990

C 8,900

D 8,000

Test Tip
Check your answer using inverse operations.

KEY NS 3.1 page 62

4. 53,251 − 14,673 =

A 48,578

B 38,678

C 38,588

D 38,578

KEY NS 3.1 page 78

5. What number goes in the box to make this number sentence true?

$(9 - 3) + 2 = 5 + \square$

A 3

B 6

C 8

D 9

Test Tip
Check that the complete values on both sides of the equal sign are the same.

KEY AF 1.2 page 98

6. If $9 \times 6 = 54$, then what is $54 \div 9$?

A 5

B 6

C 9

D 45

Education Place
Visit www.eduplace.com/camap/ for **Test-Taking Tips** and **Extra Practice.**

More Expressions and Equations

California produces enough wind energy to light a city the size of San Francisco.

Check What You Know

Word Bank
- expression
- equation
- inequality
- parentheses

Vocabulary and Concepts AF 1.0, MR 2.3

Choose the best word to complete the sentence. pages 94, 98

1. $25 + 27 \neq 54$ is an example of an _____.
2. $(34 + 27) - 21$ is an example of an _____.

Skills KEY NS 3.0, KEY AF 1.3

Multiply or divide. pages 124, 130

3. $3 \times 4 \times 8$
4. $49 \div 8$
5. $71 \div 9$
6. $3 \times 2 \times 5$

Copy the expression. Then insert parentheses so that the expression equals 6. page 92

7. $10 + 5 - 9$
8. $18 \div 6 \div 2$
9. $2 + 2 \times 2$

Problem Solving and Reasoning KEY NS 3.0

10. Michael is putting baseball cards in an album. If he arranges the cards horizontally, he can fit 3 rows of 4 cards on a page. If he arranges the cards vertically, he can fit 5 rows of 2 cards. Which way would he get the most cards in his album?

Vocabulary

Visualize It!

order of operations

Operations must be performed in a specific order to arrive at the correct answer.

Simplify $2 \times (11 - 2) \div 3 + 4$.

- First do the operations in parentheses.
- Then multiply and divide in order from left to right.
- Finally, add and subtract in order from left to right.

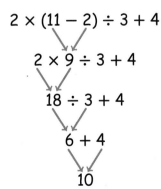

$2 \times (11 - 2) \div 3 + 4$

$2 \times 9 \div 3 + 4$

$18 \div 3 + 4$

$6 + 4$

10

Language Tips

Look for prefixes at the beginning of words to help you understand what the words mean. The prefixes, *in-* and *un-* usually change the meaning of the word to its opposite. For example, *equality* means *equal* while *inequality* means *not equal*.

Words that look alike in English and Spanish often have the same meaning.

English	Spanish
parentheses	paréntesis
equation	ecuación
simplify	simplificar

See **English-Spanish Glossary** pages 644–666.

Education Place Visit www.eduplace.com/camap/ for the **eGlossary** and **eGames**.

CA Standards MR 2.3 Use a variety of methods, such as words, numbers, symbols, charts, graphs, tables, diagrams, and models, to explain mathematical reasoning. **Also AF 1.0, KEY AF 1.2**

LESSON 1

Hands On
Expressions with All Four Operations

Objective Use order of operations to evaluate expressions.

CA Standards
KEY AF 1.2 Interpret and evaluate mathematical expressions that now use parentheses.

KEY AF 1.3 Use parentheses to indicate which operation to perform first when writing expressions containing more than two terms and different operations.

Also KEY NS 3.0, MR 1.1, MR 2.0, MR 2.3

Vocabulary

expression

order of operations

Materials
- Workmat 1
- number tiles

Explore

You already know that when evaluating **expressions**, you simplify what is in the parentheses first. In this lesson, you will learn more rules about evaluating expressions. The **order of operations** tells you the order in which you must do the operations.

Question How can you use the order of operations to evaluate an expression?

What is the value of $(18 - 4) \div 2 \times 8 + 3$?

1 Show the expression with number tiles on your Workmat. Draw parentheses around $18 - 4$.

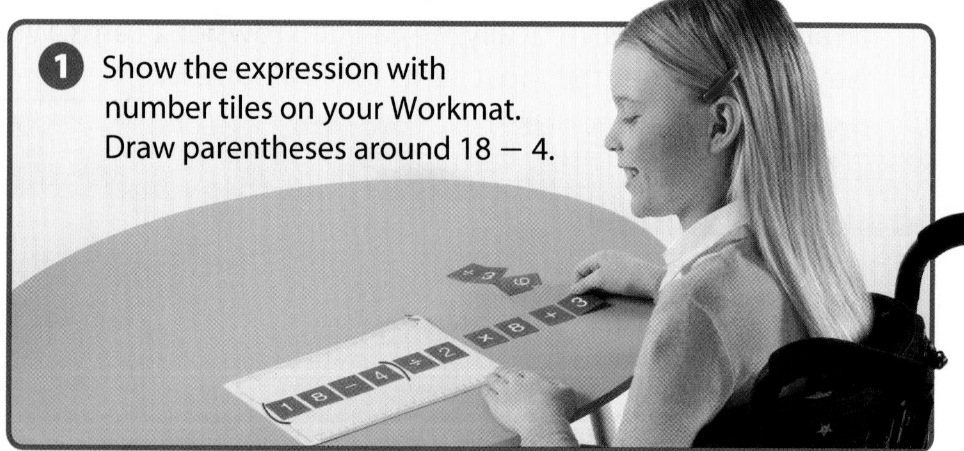

2 Simplify the operation inside the parentheses.

$(18 - 4) \div 2 \times 8 + 3$
$14 \div 2 \times 8 + 3$

3 Simplify the multiplication and division in order from left to right.

$14 \div 2 \times 8 + 3$
$7 \times 8 + 3$
$56 + 3$

4 Simplify the addition and subtraction in order from left to right.

$56 + 3$
59

Solution: The value of $(18 - 4) \div 2 \times 8 + 3$ is 59.

Suppose there were no parentheses. Would the value of the expression change? Use order of operations to find out.

Find the value of $18 - 4 \div 2 \times 8 + 3$.

1 Multiply and divide in order from left to right.

2 Add and subtract in order from left to right.

Use the numbers and operation symbols below to make an expression with a value of 5. Remember to follow the order of operations.

1.

2.

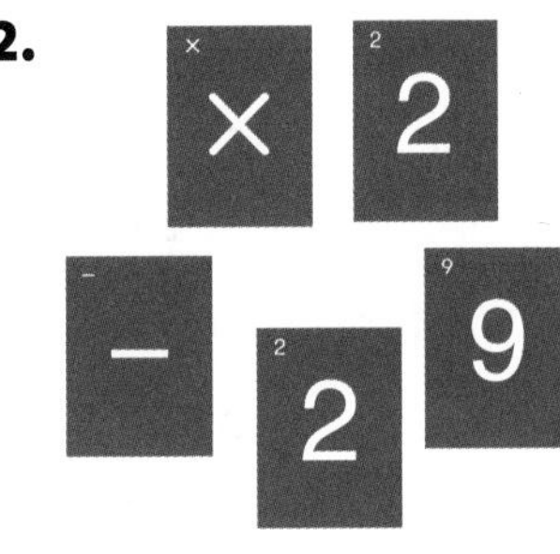

3. Write the expression shown at the right four times. Add one set of parentheses to each expression to get four different values.

4. **Challenge** Use your results from Problem 3. Which expression with parentheses has the same value as the expression without parentheses? Why?

5. **Create and Solve** Write and evaluate an expression. Then add parentheses to change the value of the expression.

Writing Math

What's Wrong? Jerry wrote $7 - 2 \times 3$ on the board. He said the value of the expression was 15. What did he do wrong? What is the value of the expression?

Expressions with All Four Operations

Objective Write and evaluate expressions.

CA Standards
KEY AF 1.2 Interpret and evaluate mathematical expressions that now use parentheses.

KEY AF 1.3 Use parentheses to indicate which operation to perform first when writing expressions containing more than two terms and different operations.

Also AF 1.0, KEY NS 3.0, MR 1.0, MR 1.1, MR 1.2, MR 2.0, MR 2.3, MR 2.4

Vocabulary

order of operations

Learn by Example

Juanita is selling environment posters for the Children's Earth Parade in San Diego. Each poster is \$2 each. If Ryan bought 3 posters and paid with a \$10 bill, how much change should he get back?

Write an expression to show how much change Ryan should get. \$10 − (3 × \$2)

To evaluate, or simplify, the expression, follow the **order of operations**.

Order of Operations

1. Simplify the operations inside the parentheses.
2. Simplify multiplication and division in order from left to right.
3. Simplify addition and subtraction in order from left to right.

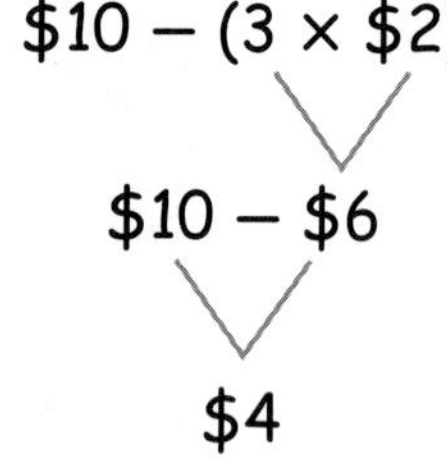

Solution: Ryan should get \$4 in change.

Ask Yourself
- What operation should I do first?
- What operation should I do next?

Guided Practice

Write an expression with parentheses for the situation. Follow the order of operations.

1. 24 fewer than 3 times 9

2. 35 more than 40 divided by 8

3. 3 times the sum of 49, 58, and 60

Simplify the expression.

4. $11 - 2 \times 5$

5. $(11 - 2) \times 5$

6. $\left(2 + \frac{12}{4}\right) \times 3$

Hint

$\frac{12}{4}$ is another way to write $12 \div 4$.

Guided Problem Solving

Use the questions to solve this problem.

7. Liz's class is collecting cans. The teacher collected 25 cans. The first group of students collected 9 bags of cans with 8 cans in each bag. The second group collected twice as many cans as the teacher. How many cans were collected?

   a. **Understand** What do you want to know? What information do you need to find out?

   b. **Plan** Write three expressions to show how many cans the teacher and each group collected.

   c. **Solve** Use parentheses to combine the three expressions into one expression showing the total number of cans collected. Then evaluate.

   d. **Look Back** Would the answer change if there were no parentheses? Explain.

Math Talk Does the expression $9 + (4 \times 5)$ have the same value as $9 + 4 \times 5$? Why or why not?

Practice and Problem Solving

Write an expression with parentheses for the situation. Follow the order of operations.

8. 36 more than 45 divided by 9

9. 28 fewer than 6 times 9

10. the sum of 12 and the product of 4 and 5

Simplify the expression.

11. $(20 - 8) \div 4$

12. $38 - 4 \times (3 + 5)$

13. $60 \div 6 - 2 \times 3$

14. $6 + 40 - 9 \times 4$

15. $\left(13 - \frac{9}{3}\right) + (9 - 3)$

16. $(16 - 15) \times (13 + 2)$

Write and evaluate an expression to solve.

17. Richard's family recycled 80 cans in July. They recycled twice as many in August. How many cans did they recycle in the two months?

18. Kaya has 2 boxes of green bottles with 6 in each box. She has 3 boxes of blue bottles with 8 in each box. How many bottles does she have altogether?

19. **Multistep** There are 1,235 cans on a recycling truck. Every time the driver goes around a corner, 2 cans fall off. This happens 5 times. Then the driver picks up 50 more cans. How many cans are on the truck now?

Science Link

Use the graph to solve Problems 20–22.

20. To study mold, Mrs. Light's class placed 12 soggy bread crumbs under glass. The bar graph shows how many of the bread crumbs were moldy each day. Make a table to show this information.

21. How many more crumbs turned moldy from Thursday to Friday than from Tuesday to Wednesday? Write and evaluate an expression to find the answer.

22. Donald studies the graph and adds the number of crumbs recorded for each day. He counts 26 crumbs, a value much greater than 12 crumbs. Explain this difference.

Mold Growth

Decomposers break down once-living matter and return nutrients to the soil. Mold is a decomposer.

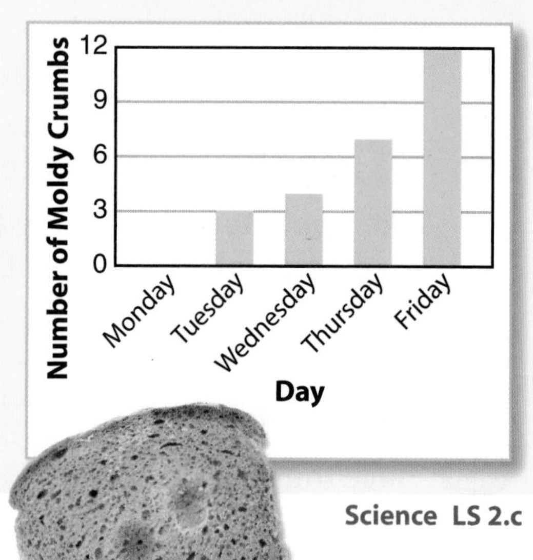

Science LS 2.c

Spiral Review and Test Practice

Find the difference. KEY NS 3.1 pages 78, 82

23. 4,963 − 2,479
24. 307,422 − 183,533
25. 400,325 − 211,485
26. 8,009 − 3,456
27. 307,405 − 255,545
28. 803,405 − 682,473

Write the letter of the correct answer. KEY AF 1.2

29. What is the value of the expression? $10 \times (4 + 2)$

A 42 **B** 60 **C** 16 **D** 20

Extra Practice See page 157, Set A.

Key Standards Review

Need Help?
See Key Standards Handbook.

Write an expression for the problem. Then simplify the expression to solve the problem. KEY AF 1.3

1. Jamie ran 9 miles in one week. She ran twice as many miles the next week. How many miles did she run in all?

2. Peter rode the bus to school 10 times in January. He rode the bus half as many times in February, and twice as many times as January, in March. How many times did Peter ride the bus in the three months?

3. On Monday, Jasmine collected 8 tickets for the school raffle. On Tuesday, she collected 3 times as many. On Wednesday, she gave 28 tickets to her friend. How many tickets does Jasmine have?

Find the difference. Use addition to check your answer. KEY NS 3.0

4. 234 − 68 = ▢
5. 1,111 − 999 = ▢
6. 42,509 − 3,699 = ▢
7. 10,550 − 9,637 = ▢

Algebraic Thinking

You Make It Up!

Use the numbers to write an expression with the given value. You may use +, −, ×, ÷, and parentheses. KEY AF 1.2, KEY AF 1.3

1. 2 6 1 8 — value = 27
2. 10 7 5 — value = 15
3. 2 3 6 4 — value = 24

LESSON 3

CA Standards
AF 1.0 Students use and interpret variables, mathematical symbols, and properties to write and simplify expressions and sentences.

Also KEY AF 1.2, KEY AF 1.3, KEY NS 3.0, MR 1.0, MR 1.1, MR 1.2, MR 2.0, MR 2.3

Vocabulary

equation

inequality

Equations and Inequalities with All Four Operations

Objective Write equations and inequalities by comparing the values of two expressions using =, <, or >.

Learn by Example

In Chapter 5, you wrote equations and inequalities. Remember that an **equation** is two expressions that have the same value. An **inequality** compares two expressions that do not have the same value.

Volunteers knit tiny wool sweaters to help penguins affected by oil spills. Eva knit 8 sweaters. Lynn knit 3 times as many sweaters as Eva. Scott knit 16 more sweaters than Eva. Write a number sentence that compares how many sweaters Lynn knit to how many sweaters Scott knit.

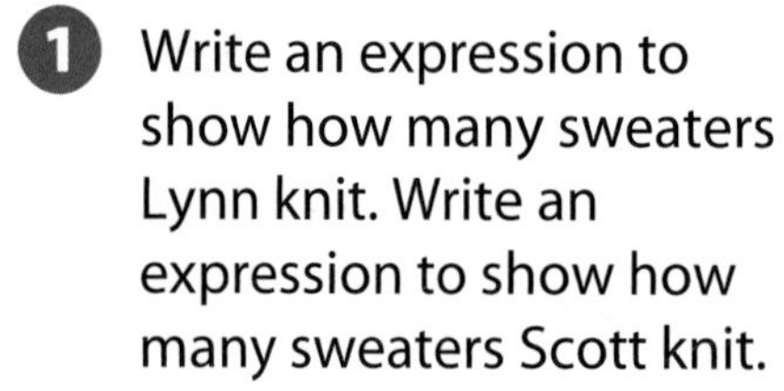

Example 1

1 Write an expression to show how many sweaters Lynn knit. Write an expression to show how many sweaters Scott knit.

sweaters Lynn knit	sweaters Scott knit
8×3	$8 + 16$

2 Evaluate each expression.

8×3	$8 + 16$
24	24

3 Compare the two expressions. Use =, <, or >.

$8 \times 3 = 8 + 16$

$24 = 24$

Solution: $8 \times 3 = 8 + 16$.

Example 2

1 Write an expression to show how many sweaters Eva knit and an expression to show how many sweaters Scott knit. Evaluate each expression. 8 $8 + 16$

2 Compare the two expressions. Use $=$, $<$, or $>$ to write a number sentence.

Solution: $8 < (8 + 16)$, or $8 < 24$.

Guided Practice

Ask Yourself
- Which operations should I do first?
- Which operations should I do next?

Copy and complete. Use $>$, $<$, or $=$.

1. $45 \div 9 + 15$ ⬭ 3×8 **2.** $16 - (8 + 3)$ ⬭ $\frac{36}{9} \times 5$

3. $(55 + 1) \div 8$ ⬭ $\frac{42}{6}$ **4.** $(3 + 6) \times 4$ ⬭ $3 + 6 \times 4$

5. $4 - 2 \times 1$ ⬭ $(4 - 2) \times 1$ **6.** $13 + (4 \times 3) - 10$ ⬭ $(10 \times 10) \div 10$

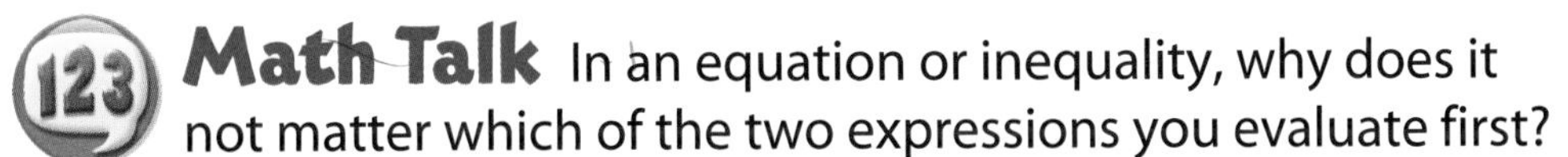

Math Talk In an equation or inequality, why does it not matter which of the two expressions you evaluate first?

Practice and Problem Solving

Hint
When there are no parentheses, do the multiplication and division before the addition and subtraction.

Copy and complete. Use $>$, $<$, or $=$.

7. $2 + 5 \times 4$ ⬭ $77 \div 7$ **8.** $(56 \div 7) + 15$ ⬭ 3×8

9. $32 + 5$ ⬭ $35 - 3 \times 5$ **10.** $7 \times 6 + 7$ ⬭ $4 \times 2 \times 6$

11. $(3 \times 4) \div (0 + 6)$ ⬭ $3 \times (4 + 6)$ **12.** $(3 \times 9) + (5 - 2)$ ⬭ $63 \div 7 \times 4$

Write $+$, $-$, $\times$, or $\div$ in each ⬭ to make the number sentence true.

13. 5 ⬭ $6 = 56 - 26$ **14.** $\frac{27}{9} + 7 = 12$ ⬭ $3 - 5$

15. $4 \times 3 = 22$ ⬭ $(20 \div 2)$ **16.** $2 + (21$ ⬭ $3) = 2 \times 4 + 1$

Write equations or inequalities to solve.

17. Sara saw 8 penguins. Max saw 4 times the number of penguins that Sara did. Alice saw 17 more penguins than Sara. Write a number sentence that compares how many penguins Max saw to how many penguins Alice saw.

18. One penguin weighs 7 pounds. Another weighs three times as much. A third penguin weighs 15 pounds more than the first penguin. Write a number sentence that compares the weights of the second and third penguins.

Real World Data

Use the table to solve. Show your work.

19. Write an inequality that compares the number of spills in the Atlantic and Pacific Oceans to the number of spills in the Gulf of Mexico.

20. The Gulf of Mexico had 36 more oil spills than all the U.S. rivers and canals. How many oil spills were there in rivers and canals that year?

Oil Spills in Some U.S. Waters in One Year

Body of Water	Number of Spills
Atlantic Ocean	83
Pacific Ocean	493
Gulf of Mexico	1,728

Spiral Review and Test Practice

Copy and complete. KEY AF 2.1, KEY AF 2.0 page 102

21. $(19 - 3) + 6 = 16 + \square$

22. $5 + (4 + 20) = \square + (12 + 12)$

23. $10 + (25 + 3) = 10 + \square$

24. $(44 - 5) + 50 = (36 + 3) + \square$

Write the letter of the correct answer. KEY AF 1.2

25. Which statement is true?

A $(12 - 6) \times 2 = 12 - (6 \times 2)$

B $(12 - 6) \times 2 < 12 - (6 \times 2)$

C $(12 - 6) \times 2 > 12 - (6 \times 2)$

D $(12 - 6) \times 2 = 12 - 6 \times 2$

Extra Practice See page 157, Set B.

Math Works! Physical Education Teacher

Teach Sports

Mrs. Brown is a physical education teacher. She uses expressions to help her order equipment and organize games.

Write an expression for each problem. Then solve the problem.

1. To make teams, Mrs. Brown divides the students into 4 equal groups. How many students would be on each team if there were 36 students in a class?

2. Mrs. Brown is ordering jump ropes. She wants to order one short jump rope for every 10 students in the school, and 18 long jump ropes. How many jump ropes does Mrs. Brown need to order if there are 100 students in the school?

3. **Multistep** Mrs. Brown wants to buy some barrels. Each barrel holds 6 basketballs or 8 soccer balls. How many barrels does Mrs. Brown need to hold 54 basketballs and 56 soccer balls?

CA Standards
KEY AF 1.3, MR 1.0, MR 1.1, MR 2.4

Multiply Equals by Equals

Objective Understand that equals multiplied by equals are equal.

CA Standards
KEY AF 2.2 Know and understand that equals multiplied by equals are equal.

KEY AF 2.0 Students know how to manipulate equations.

Also AF 1.1, KEY AF 1.2, MR 1.1, MR 2.0, MR 2.3, MR 2.4, MR 2.6, MR 3.0, MR 3.3

Learn by Example

In this lesson, you will learn what happens when you multiply both sides of an equation by the same number.

Will both sides of the equation $5 \times 2 = 10$ still have the same value if both sides are multiplied by 3?

1 Simplify both sides of the equation. Check that they are equal.

$$5 \times 2 = 10$$
$$10 = 10$$

2 Now rewrite the equation multiplying each side by 3.

$$(5 \times 2) \times 3 = 10 \times 3$$

3 Simplify both sides.

$$(5 \times 2) \times 3 = 10 \times 3$$
$$10 \times 3 = 30$$
$$30 = 30$$

Equals multiplied by equals are equal.

Solution: Both sides of the equation will still have the same value if both sides are multiplied by 3.

Guided Practice

Copy and complete.

1. $2 \times (6 + 1) = 2 \times$ ▢

2. $3 \times (5 \times 4) = 3 \times$ ▢

3. $(4 + 7) \times$ ▢ $= 11 \times 6$

4. $(5 - 1) \times$ ▢ $= (8 - 4) \times 5$

Ask Yourself
Did I evaluate the complete expression first?

Math Talk Arun multiplied one side of an equation by 2 and the other side of the equation by 3. Does he still have an equation? Give an example to support your thinking.

Practice and Problem Solving

Copy and complete.

5. $3 \times (12 - 5) = 3 \times \square$
6. $9 \times (36 \div 4) = \square \times 9$
7. $(8 + 3) \times \square = 11 \times 5$
8. $2 \times (13 + 7) = 2 \times \square$
9. $\square \times (8 \times 4) = 4 \times 32$
10. $5 \times (40 \div 5) = 5 \times \square$
11. $4 \times (\square - 4) = 4 \times 6$
12. $2 \times (15 \div \square) = 2 \times 5$

Compare the expressions. Write ≠ or = for the ⬭.

13. 6×2 ⬭ 12
    $3 \times (6 \times 2)$ ⬭ 3×12
14. 5×3 ⬭ 8
    $9 \times (5 \times 3)$ ⬭ 9×8
15. $18 \div 2$ ⬭ 8
    $6 \times (18 \div 2)$ ⬭ 6×8
16. $63 \div 9$ ⬭ 7
    $4 \times (63 \div 9)$ ⬭ 4×7

Solve.

17. **Justify** Stephen multiplied both sides of an inequality by 4. Does he still have an inequality? Give an example to support your thinking.
18. **Analyze** What do you know about the value of the ▲ and the ★ in this equation? ▲ × 4 = 4 × ★

Think
In an equation, both sides of the = must have the same value.

Spiral Review and Test Practice

Write the quotient and the remainder. KEY NS 3.2 page 130

19. 7)41
20. 8)34
21. 6)39
22. 6)16
23. 5)47
24. 8)67
25. 4)23
26. 9)26
27. 2)15
28. 5)37

Write the letter of the correct answer. KEY AF 2.2, KEY AF 2.0

29. What number goes in the box to make this number sentence true? $10 \times (3 + 6) = \square \times 9$

A 3 **B** 6 **C** 10 **D** 90

Extra Practice See page 157, Set C.

LESSON 5

CA Standards

MR 2.4 Express the solution clearly and logically by using the appropriate mathematical notation and terms and clear language; support solutions with evidence in both verbal and symbolic work.

KEY AF 1.3 Use parentheses to indicate which operation to perform first when writing expressions containing more than two terms and different operations.

Also AF 1.0, KEY AF 1.2, KEY NS 3.0, MR 1.1, MR 1.2, MR 2.0, MR 2.3, MR 3.0, MR 3.1, MR 3.2, MR 3.3

Problem Solving Strategy
Write an Expression

Objective Write and evaluate expressions that use all four operations to solve problems.

Learn by Example

At a craft sale, Mrs. Greene buys 6 bead bracelets. She pays for them with a $20 bill. How much change should she receive?

JEWELRY FOR SALE

Bead Bracelets	$3
Necklaces	$5
Rings	$1

UNDERSTAND

You want to find the change Mrs. Greene should receive.

This is what you know:

- Bead bracelets cost $3 each.
- Mrs. Greene buys 6 bracelets.
- She pays with a $20 bill.

PLAN

Write an expression with parentheses to represent the situation.

1 First, show the total cost of the bracelets.

6 × $3 ← cost of bracelets

2 Then subtract the total cost from $20.

$20 – (6 × $3)

SOLVE

Evaluate the expression.

Mrs. Greene should receive $2 in change.

$20 – (6 × $3)
20 – 18
2

LOOK BACK

Did you answer the question that was asked?

Think

The parentheses are not necessary because of the order of operations. However, they help make it clear what operation to do first.

Guided Problem Solving

Use the Ask Yourself questions and price list to write an expression for the problem. Then solve.

1. During the first hour of a pottery sale, Mr. Gelfand sold 2 large bowls and 3 painted tiles. How much money did he make in the first hour?

Ask Yourself

- Did I use the right numbers in my expression?
- Did I place the parentheses correctly?

Math Talk Could you use the expression $2 \times \$10 + 3 \times \$7$ to represent Problem 1? Why or why not?

Independent Problem Solving

Write an expression to represent each problem. Solve the problem. Explain why your answer makes sense.

POTTERY FOR SALE
Small bowl $3
Large bowl $10
Painted tile $7
Plate $8
Buy 3 small bowls, get 1 free!

2. Paulo bought 2 small bowls. He paid for them with a \$10 bill. How much change did Paulo receive?

3. Together, Rena and Bo bought 3 plates for their aunt. They each paid half the cost of the pottery. How much did each person pay?

4. Maddie spent \$28 on painted tiles and \$24 on plates. How many items did Maddie buy?

5. For each large bowl that Mr. Gelfand makes, he uses 4 pounds of clay. How many pounds of clay will he use for an order of large bowls that costs \$40?

6. **Challenge** Mr. Gelfand told a customer that for every 3 small bowls bought, she would get 1 for free. The customer spent \$18 on small bowls. How many small bowls did she get for free?

7. **Create and Solve** Use the information on the price list to write a word problem that you can solve by writing and evaluating an expression with parentheses.

Vocabulary

When evaluating an expression, the rules of the **order of operations** tells you the order in which you do the operations.

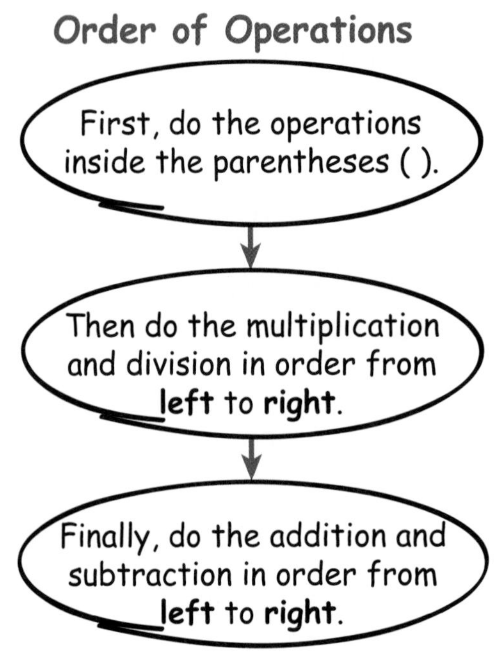

Order of Operations
First, do the operations inside the parentheses ( ).
Then do the multiplication and division in order from left to right.
Finally, do the addition and subtraction in order from left to right.

Simplify. Follow the order of operations.

(28 − 4) ÷ 3 × 4

Do what is in the parentheses first.

1. What is (28 − 4)?

Then multiply and divide in order from left to right.

2. What is 24 ÷ 3?
3. What is 8 × 4?
4. What is the value of the expression (28 − 4) ÷ 3 × 4?

Writing Show how to simplify 16 + 4 ÷ 4 − 2.

Reading Look for this book in your library.
Math Curse, by Jon Scieszka

CA Standards
MR 2.3 Use a variety of methods, such as words, numbers, symbols, charts, graphs, tables, diagrams, and models, to explain mathematical reasoning.

Also KEY 

Standards-Based Extra Practice

Set A

KEY AF 1.2, KEY AF 1.3 page 144

Write an expression with parentheses for the situation. Follow the order of operations.

1. 14 fewer than 7 times 4
2. 25 more than 16 divided by 4

Simplify the expression.

3. $40 \div 5 \times 6 - 1$
4. $(36 \div 4) \div 3 + 2$
5. $(11 + 9) \div 5$
6. $10 \times 5 - 30 + 7$
7. $2 \div 2 + 4 \times 11$
8. $26 + 18 \div (6 - 3)$
9. **Explain** Evaluate the expression $(12 - 4) \times (2 + 1)$. Would the value change if there were no parentheses?

Set B

AF 1.0, KEY AF 1.2 page 148

Copy and complete using >, <, or =.

1. $5 \times 6 - 15$ ⬭ $32 \div 4$
2. 72 ⬭ $(4 \times 2) \times (3 \times 3)$

Write +, −, ×, or ÷ in each ⬭ to make the number sentence true.

3. $\frac{64}{8} + 4 = 6$ ⬭ 2
4. 18 ⬭ $3 = 25 \div 5 + 1$
5. **Compare** Jamal lives 8 blocks from school. Bethany lives 3 times as far from school as Jamal. Michael lives 4 times as far as Jamal and Bethany combined. Write a number sentence that compares how far from school Bethany lives to how far from school Michael lives.

Set C

KEY AF 2.0, KEY AF 2.2 page 152

Copy and complete.

1. $3 \times (16 \div 4) = \square \times 3$
2. $(12 - 7) \times 10 = \square \times 2$
3. $(32 - 16) \div 2 = \square \times 4$
4. $\square \times (6 \times 6) = 9 \times 4$
5. **Analyze** If you multiply both sides of an equality by 8 do you still have an equality? Give an example.

Education Place
Visit www.eduplace.com/camap/ for more **Extra Practice.**

Chapter Review/Test

Vocabulary and Concepts

MR 2.3, KEY AF 1.3

Write the best term to complete the sentence.

1. To evaluate an expression, follow the ______.

2. A number sentence that gives two expressions that have the same value is a(n) ______.

Skills

KEY AF 1.2, KEY AF 1.3, KEY AF 2.2, KEY AF 2.0

Write an expression for the situation.

3. 14 fewer than 4 times 9

4. 30 more than 10 divided by the sum of 2 and 3

Simplify the expression.

5. $(22 - 13) \times (27 \div 3)$

6. $42 - 4 \times (7 + 2)$

7. $60 - (7 \times 8) + 7$

8. $48 \div 8 - (0 \times 9)$

Copy and complete using >, <, or =.

9. $(2 \times 4) + 6$ ⬭ $28 - 0 \div 2$

10. $10 - (2 \times 5)$ ⬭ $(10 - 2) \times 5$

Copy and complete.

11. $\square \times (6 \times 7) = 2 \times 42$

12. $6 \times (20 \div 4) = 6 \times \square$

13. $(28 \div 4) + 13 = 7 + \square$

Problem Solving and Reasoning

MR 2.4, MR 2.3, KEY NS 3.0, KEY AF 1.3

Solve.

14. A human baby weighs 7 pounds. A baby rhino weighs 93 pounds more. A baby elephant weighs twice as much as a baby rhino. Write an expression to find a baby elephant's weight.

15. Carmen raised \$18 to adopt an animal at the zoo. Niko raised \$3 less than half of what Carmen raised. Write an expression to find how much Niko raised.

Writing Math Mikaela says that $4 \times (5 + 3)$ is the same as $4 \times 5 + 3$. Is she right? Why or why not?

Spiral Review and Test Practice

1. Which is 60,000 + 70 + 300,000,000 + 500 + 20,000,000 + 100,000 + 4,000 in standard form?

A 320,164,750

B 320,614,570

C 320,164,570

D 230,164,570

KEY NS 1.1 page 16

2. Which is the value of the expression (14 + 5) − (8 − 2)?

A 29

B 19

C 13

D 9

Test Tip
Make sure to pay attention to all operational symbols.

KEY AF 1.2 page 94

3. Which is the difference between 35,490 and 6,764 when both numbers are rounded to the nearest thousand?

A 28,000

B 29,000

C 30,000

D 42,000

KEY NS 1.3, KEY NS 3.1 page 74

4. 67 + 58 = 58 + □

A 125

B 67

C 58

D 9

AF 1.1 page 54

5. Which of these is another way to write (2 × 4) × 3?

A (2 × 3) + 4

B (2 + 3) + 4

C 2 × (4 × 3)

D (2 + 3) × 4

Test Tip
Check your answer by comparing the value of the expression of your answer choice to the value of the expression in the problem.

KEY AF 1.2 page 124

6. What is the value of the expression below?

(20 − 8) ÷ 2

A 6

B 10

C 16

D 26

KEY AF 1.2 page 144

Education Place
Visit www.eduplace.com/camap/ for **Test-Taking Tips** and **Extra Practice.**

Unit 3 Test

Vocabulary and Concepts

KEY NS 3.0, MR 2.3 Chapters 6–7

Complete each sentence with a vocabulary term from this unit.

1. The rules for _______ tell you the order in which you must do the operations.

2. A number sentence showing two expressions that have the same value is called a(n) ______.

3. A(n) ______ of a number is the product of that number and any whole number.

Computation

KEY NS 3.0, AF 1.1, KEY NS 3.2, KEY AF 1.2, KEY AF 2.2 Chapter 6, Lesson 2

Write the fact family for each set of numbers.

4. 5, 5, 25
5. 7, 9, 63
6. 5, 8, 40
7. 6, 7, 42

Use properties and rules to solve. If there is no solution, explain why. Chapter 6, Lesson 3

8. $16 \div 0 = \blacksquare$
9. $7 \times \blacksquare = 8 \times 7$
10. $(6 \times 2) \times 1 = \blacksquare \times (2 \times 1)$

Divide. Then check your answer. Chapter 6, Lesson 5

11. $4\overline{)7}$
12. $7\overline{)43}$
13. $5\overline{)38}$
14. $3\overline{)29}$
15. $9\overline{)94}$
16. $7\overline{)42}$

Simplify each expression. Chapter 7, Lessons 1–2

17. $(63 - 54) \times (18 \div 9)$
18. $79 - 6 \times (1 + 7)$
19. $81 - 9 \times 9 + 12$

Copy and complete. Chapter 7, Lesson 4

20. $\blacksquare \times (5 \times 7) = 9 \times 35$
21. $5 \times (20 \div 4) = 5 \times \blacksquare$

Problem Solving and Reasoning

AF 1.0, KEY AF 1.2, KEY AF 1.3, KEY NS 3.0 Chapters 6–7

Solve.

22. Selma has 12 tomatoes. She has 18 more carrots than tomatoes. She has twice as many squash as tomatoes. Write an inequality that compares carrots to squash.

23. Copy this expression four times.

    $4 + 16 \div 4 \times 2 - 1$

    Then add one set of parentheses to each expression to get four different values.

Solve.

24. Paulina has 38 tarts to place on 6 plates. If each plate has the same number of tarts, how many tarts are on each plate? How many tarts are leftover?

25. Write a division sentence using a square number as a dividend. Write the fact family for the 3 numbers in your division sentence.

Writing Math Explain how multiplication facts can help you solve the division problem 47 ÷ 6?

Performance Assessment

Recycling Drive

KEY NS 3.0, KEY AF 1.2, MR 1.1

The 4th grade classes at King Elementary School are having a competition to see which class can collect the most glass bottles in one month. The classes will redeem their bottles for cash to help pay for their annual camping trip.

Class	Number of Bags	Bottles per Bag
Ms. Lufkin	10	
Mr. Caporal	9	
Mr. Parker		8
Ms. Guerrero		7

Task	Information You Need
Use the information above and at the right to complete the chart above. Explain your strategy. Then write two different expressions that represent the total number of bottles collected.	Ms. Lufkin's class collected 60 bottles.
	Mr. Caporal's class collected 81 bottles.
	Mr. Parker's class collected 56 bottles.
	Ms. Guerrero's class collected 63 bottles.

Greg Tang's Go Fast, Go Far

Unit 3 Mental Math Strategies

Multiply by 6

A group of 6 is quick to see, if you think in groups of 3!

I have a fast way to multiply 6 × 8. Since it's just 6 groups of 8, I add 3 groups of 8 to another 3 groups of 8 and get 24 + 24 = 48. Multiplication is just repeated addition in smart and easy groups!

1. 6 × 8 = 24 + 24 = 48
(3 × 8, 3 × 8)

2. 6 × 9 = ☐ + ☐ = ☐
(3 × 9, 3 × 9)

3. 6 × 5 = ☐ + ☐ = ☐
(3 × 5, 3 × 5)

4. 6 × 6 = 18 + ☐ = ☐
(3 × 6, 3 × 6)

You are doing fine!

5. 6 × 10 = ☐ + ☐ = ☐

6. 6 × 7 = ☐ + ☐ = ☐

7. 6 × 3 = ☐ + ☐ = ☐

8. 6 × 12 = ☐ + ☐ = ☐

Good For You!

Take It Further!

Now try doing all the steps in your head!

9. 6 × 20

10. 6 × 11

Unit

Algebra and Functions

BIG IDEAS!

- A letter or symbol used to stand for a number is called a variable.
- An equation with two variables can describe the rule for a function table.

Chapter 8
Variables

Chapter 9
Equations with Two Variables

Songs and Games

Math Music Track 4: *20 Kids Go Camping*
eGames at
www.eduplace.com/camap/

Math Readers

This is a close-up of a mosaic from Nuestro Pueblo in the Watts district of Los Angeles, CA.

Get Ready **Game**

Expression Match

Object of the Game Evaluate expressions and try to have more cards than the other player at the end of the game.

Materials
Learning Tool 16 (Expression and Value Cards) (2 sets)

Set Up
Place the expression cards in a stack face down and the matching value cards in another stack face down.

Number of Players 2

How to Play

1. Player 1 turns over one card from each pile and places them face up next to each other.

2. If the cards match, and Player 2 agrees, Player 1 takes the cards. If the cards do not match, Player 1 leaves the cards where they are.

3. Player 2 repeats Steps 1 and 2.

During play, if either player does not agree that a pair of cards makes a match, he or she may challenge. Then the values must be checked before the cards can be taken.

4. If a player does not notice a match, the other player may say "Match" and take the cards before taking a turn. "Matches" may be made with any cards that are face-up.

5. When all the cards in the face-down piles have been played, the game is over. The player with more cards is the winner.

CA Standards
KEY AF 1.2 Interpret and evaluate mathematical expressions that now use parentheses.

AF 1.0 Students use and interpret variables, mathematical symbols, and properties to write and simplify expressions and sentences.

Education Place
Visit www.eduplace.com/camap/ for **Brain Teasers** and **eGames** to play.

Reading In both reading and math, you should ask yourself, "What's the point?" or "What is this all about?" If you can answer the question, you know the big idea.

Sharon takes notes to help her understand the big ideas in math. She has just started to take notes on Unit 4.

Big Idea	Notes/Examples
• A letter or symbol used to stand for a number is a variable.	In $(n - 3) \times 6$, n is a variable. You can use any letter or symbol to stand for a number. When the value of the variable changes, the value of the expression changes.
• An equation with two variables can describe the rule for a function table.	

My notes help me understand the big ideas.

Writing Copy the Big Idea Chart for Unit 4. Take notes as you work through the unit. If you have any questions you can also write them down. At the end of the unit, share your notes with a classmate. Compare your work and try to answer any questions you still have.

Variables

Check What You Know

Word Bank
equation
expression
parentheses
inequality

Vocabulary and Concepts AF 1.0, MR 2.3

Choose the best word to complete the sentence. pages 92, 98

1. To evaluate $(3 + 6) - 4$, you first simplify what is in the ____.
2. $45 + 53 \neq 108$ is an example of an ____.
3. $135 = 96 + 39$ is an example of an ____.

Skills KEY NS 3.0

Solve. pages 62, 78, 82, and 122

4. $145 + 357$
5. $276 - 148$
6. $309 - 132$
7. 8×7
8. $54 \div 6$
9. $81 \div 9$

Problem Solving and Reasoning GRADE 3 NS 2.5

10. Carla is putting 126 books into 6 boxes. If she puts the same number of books in each box, how many books will be in each box?

Vocabulary

Visualize It!

variable
a letter or a symbol that represents a number in an algebraic expression

$$2x + 8y + 9$$

algebraic expression
an expression that includes one or more variables and operations

Language Tips

The word *variable* means *likely to change or vary*. In mathematics, a *variable* is a letter or symbol that represents a number in an algebraic expression.

Words that look alike in English and Spanish often have the same meaning.

English	Spanish
variable	variable
equation	ecuación
expression	expresión

See **English-Spanish Glossary** pages 644–666.

Education Place Visit www.eduplace.com/camap/ for the **eGlossary** and **eGames**.

CA Standards MR 2.3 Use a variety of methods, such as words, numbers, symbols, charts, graphs, tables, diagrams, and models, to explain mathematical reasoning. **Also AF 1.1**

Hands On
Variables

Objective Understand the concept of variables.

CA Standards
AF 1.1 Use letters, boxes, or other symbols to stand for any number in simple expressions or equations (e.g., demonstrate an understanding and the use of the concept of a variable).

AF 1.0 Students use and interpret variables, mathematical symbols, and properties to write and simplify expressions and sentences.

Also KEY AF 1.2, MR 1.1, MR 2.0, MR 2.3, MR 3.0, MR 3.3

Vocabulary

variable

Materials
- Workmat 1
- number tiles

Explore

A letter or a symbol that is used to stand for an unknown number is called a **variable**. The value of an expression with a variable depends on the value of the variable.

Question How does the value of an expression change when the value of the variable changes?

Evaluate $(n - 3) \times 6$ when $n = 8$.

1 Write the expression on Workmat 1.

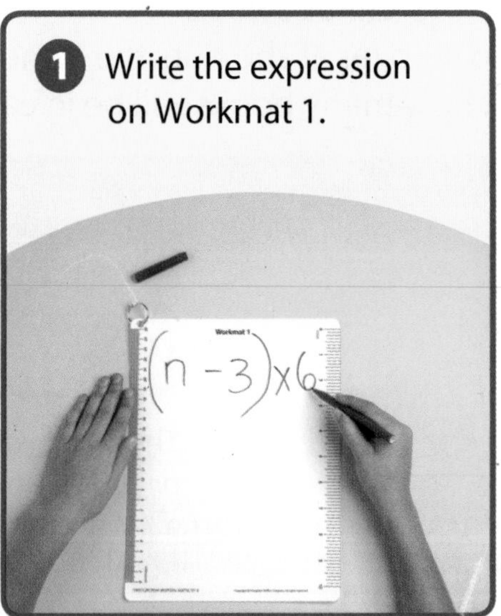

2 Cover the variable n in the expression with the number tile 8.

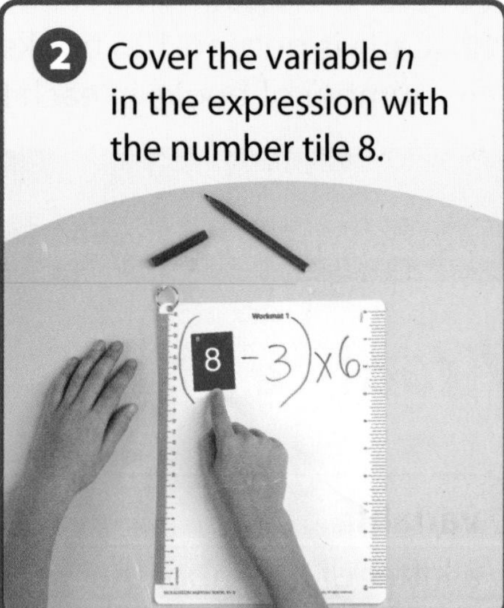

3 Evaluate the expression on the workmat.
- First, do what's in the parentheses.
- Then multiply.
- Write the value of the expression.

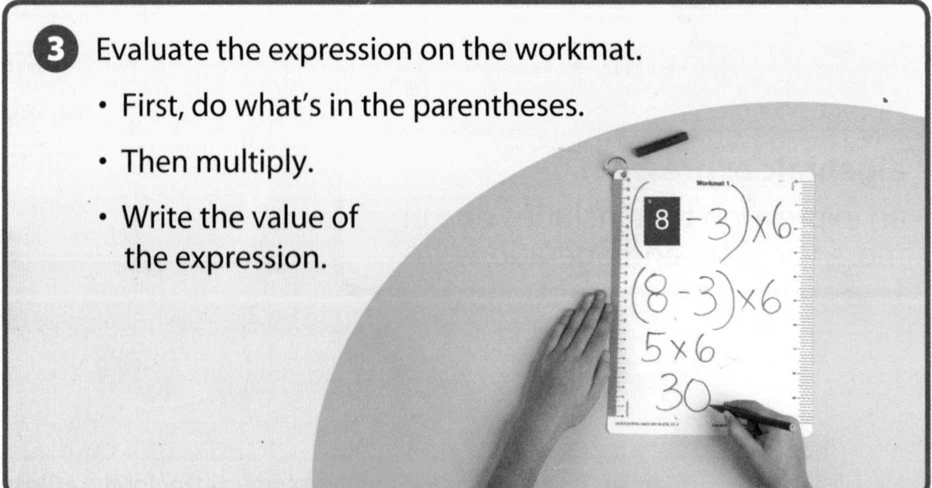

Solution: When $n = 8$, the expression $(n - 3) \times 6$ has a value of 30.

What would the value of the same expression be if the variable had a value of 9?

1. Write the expression on Workmat 1 again. This time, cover the variable n with the number tile 9.
2. Evaluate the expression. Write the value of the expression.

Use Workmat 1 and number tiles to evaluate the expression.

	Expression	Value when $y = 2$	Value when $y = 5$
1.	$(y + 2) \times 10$		
2.	$12 + y - 4$		
3.	$50 - (6 \times y)$		
4.	$(10 - y) + 8$		
5.	$3 \times 3 \times (y + 4)$		
6.	$(10 \div y) \times (5 + 3)$		
7.	$9 \times (y - 2)$		
8.	$(10 - y) \times (y \times 2)$		
9.	$(y \times 3) + (y \times 5)$		

Evaluate each expression. Use Workmat 1 and number tiles to help.

10. $2x + 5$ when $x = 6$

11. $3 + (15 \div n)$ when $n = 5$

12. $75 - 3m$ when $m = 8$

13. $(p + 3) \times 6$ when $p = 6$

14. $2 \times (c + 4) - 8$ when $c = 4$

15. $(z + 7) \times (7 - z)$ when $z = 3$

16. **Challenge** Evaluate this expression when $n = 6$. Show your work.

$(n + 3) \times (n - 4) \div (3 + n)$

Writing Math

Generalize Does it matter what letter or symbol you use for a variable? Explain.

Write and Evaluate Algebraic Expressions

Objective Write and evaluate expressions containing variables.

CA Standards

AF 1.1 Use letters, boxes, or other symbols to stand for any number in simple expressions or equations (e.g., demonstrate an understanding and the use of the concept of a variable).

AF 1.0 Students use and interpret variables, mathematical symbols, and properties to write and simplify expressions and sentences.

Also MR 1.0, MR 1.1, MR 2.0, MR 2.2, MR 2.3, MR 2.4

Vocabulary

algebraic expression

variable

Learn by Example

Many people have worked to help the grizzly bears that live in Yellowstone National Park. Suppose a park ranger saw 2 cubs in each of the dens she found. How many cubs did she see?

Since you don't know how many dens the ranger found, you can write an **algebraic expression** using a **variable** to stand for that number.

Expressions that contain variables are called algebraic expressions.

Example 1

Write an algebraic expression for the number of cubs the ranger saw.

- Let n stand for the number of dens. ← **You may choose any letter or symbol for the variable.**
- Then express the number of cubs.

$2 \times n$ or $2 \bullet n$ or $2n$ ← **You read all these expressions as "2 times *n*."**

Solution: The ranger saw $2n$ cubs.

Now suppose the ranger found 3 dens. How many bear cubs did she see?

Evaluate $2n$ when $n = 3$.

Example 2

1 Write the expression.	2 Replace n with 3.	3 Simplify the expression.
$2n$	$2n$ 2×3	$2n$ 2×3 6

Solution: If the ranger found 3 dens, she saw 6 cubs.

Suppose the ranger saw 2 more cubs this week than last week. Let the variable y stand for the number of cubs the ranger saw last week. Which expression stands for the number of cubs the ranger saw this week?

$2y$ $y - 2$ $y \div 2$ $y + 2$

Example 3

- $2y$ means twice the number seen last week.
- $y - 2$ means 2 fewer than the number seen last week.
- $y \div 2$ means half the number seen last week.
- $y + 2$ means 2 more than the number seen last week.

Solution: The ranger saw $y + 2$ cubs this week.

Guided Practice

- What is the variable?
- Do I add, subtract, multiply, or divide?

Choose the expression that matches the words. Let p stand for the number of bears.

1. 5 more than the number of bears

A $5p$ **B** $5 + p$

2. half as many bears

A $p \div 2$ **B** $p - 2$

Evaluate the expression when $n = 6$.

3. $n \div 3$ **4.** $n + 7$ **5.** $2n - 3$ **6.** $12 \div n$ **7.** $3 + 4n$

Math Talk When writing an expression, how do you know when to use a variable?

Practice and Problem Solving

Write an expression that matches the words. Let n stand for the number of bear cubs seen yesterday.

8. 5 fewer cubs than seen yesterday

9. half as many cubs as seen yesterday

10. four times the number seen yesterday

Evaluate the expression when $p = 7$.

11. $3p$ **12.** $p - 7$ **13.** $2 \times p + 5$ **14.** $6 + 2p$

15. $0 + p$ **16.** $2p \div 7$ **17.** $7p - 4$ **18.** $28 + p$

Write an expression for the problem. Choose your own variables.

19. There are 3 more bear dens this year than last year. How many bear dens are there this year?

20. Bob and Joe collect animal figures. Bob has half as many figures as Joe. How many figures does Bob have?

Science Link

Use the Fun Facts to solve.

21. Let p stand for the weight of a male penguin when an egg is laid. Write an expression to show how little the male penguin might weigh when the egg hatches.

22. Let x stand for the total number of penguin eggs.

a. Suppose 8 of the eggs hatched. Write an expression to show how many eggs have not yet hatched.

b. Suppose $x = 13$. How many eggs have not yet hatched?

Emperor Penguins

- Penguin eggs survive in Antarctica's harsh environment because male penguins keep the eggs on their feet for up to 9 weeks to keep the eggs warm.
- During this time, the male penguin doesn't eat at all. So he may lose up to half of his body weight.

Science LS 3.b

Spiral Review and Test Practice

Copy and complete by using >, <, or =. KEY AF 1.2 pages 94, 98

23. $7 + (45 + 8)$ ⬭ $8 + 45 + 7$

24. $(50 - 13) + 5$ ⬭ $95 - 45$

25. $36 - (5 + 9)$ ⬭ $18 + 3$

26. $(25 + 6) - 3$ ⬭ $25 + 5$

Write the letter of the correct answer. AF 1.1

27. What is the value of the expression below if $n = 6$?

$18 - n \div 3$

A 4 **B** 16 **C** 12 **D** 2

Extra Practice See page 183, Set A.

Key Standards Review

Need Help?
See Key Standards Handbook.

Insert parentheses to show which operation to perform first.
KEY AF 1.3

1. $4 + 8 \times 2 = 20$
2. $10 \div 5 + 24 = 26$
3. $20 - 2 \times 6 = 8$
4. $9 \times 3 - 4 = 23$

Find the sum or difference. KEY NS 3.0, KEY NS 3.1

5. 6,783 − 256 = ▢
6. 893 + 4,999 = ▢
7. 10,572 + 2,345 = ▢
8. 1,756,900 − 87,423 = ▢
9. 1,508,333 − 115, 300 = ▢
10. 29,347 − 11, 862 = ▢
11. 2,439,200 − 54,627 = ▢
12. 3,080,754 − 2,620,530 = ▢
13. 5,273,612 + 3,810,365 = ▢
14. 73,654 + 8,154 = ▢
15. 473,294 − 8,562 = ▢
16. 3,273 − 999 = ▢

Math Reasoning

Using Vocabulary

Match each statement with the correct algebraic expression. AF 1.0, AF 1.1

1. When n is 6, the value of the expression is 8. — **a.** $n - 4$
2. When n is 6, the value of the expression is 2. — **b.** $n + 2$
3. When n is 2, the value of the expression is 6. — **c.** $n - 2$
4. When n is 8, the value of the expression is 6. — **d.** $n + 4$
5. When n is 4, the value of the expression is 10. — **e.** $n - 6$
6. When n is 10, the value of the expression is 4. — **f.** $n + 6$

Solve Addition and Subtraction Equations

Objective Write and solve equations involving addition and subtraction.

CA Standards
KEY AF 2.0 Students know how to manipulate equations.
KEY AF 2.1 Know and understand that equals added to equals are equal.
Also KEY NS 3.0, AF 1.0, AF 1.1, MR 1.0, MR 1.1, MR 2.3, MR 2.4, MR 2.6, MR 3.0, MR 3.2

Vocabulary

solve

equation

Think
An equation is like a balanced scale. Both sides are equal. So whatever you do to one side, you need to do to the other side.

Learn by Example

In this lesson, you will **solve** algebraic **equations**. You will find a value for the variable that makes the equation true.

Monica and Kayla have 7 dogs to walk. If Kayla walks 4 dogs, how many dogs does Monica need to walk?

Since there is an unknown number, you can write an equation with a variable to solve this problem.

1 Write an equation that describes the situation.

Use the variable d to stand for the number of dogs that Monica walks.

number of dogs Monica walks
total number of dogs

$$d + 4 = 7$$

number of dogs Kayla walks

2 Use inverse operations to find the value of the variable. Addition and subtraction are inverse operations.

Subtract 4 from both sides of the equation, so that d is alone on one side.

$$d + 4 = 7$$
$$d + 4 - 4 = 7 - 4$$
$$d = 3$$

Equals added to equals are equal. So, equals subtracted from equals are equal.

Check
To check, substitute the variable with the solution. Then simplify the equation.

Both sides of the equation are the same, so the solution is correct.

$$d + 4 = 7$$
$$3 + 4 = 7$$ ← Substitute 3 for d.
$$7 = 7$$

Solution: Since $d = 3$, Monica needs to walk 3 dogs.

Guided Practice

Solve the equation. Tell what number you added to or subtracted from both sides.

1. $k - 14 = 2$ **2.** $35 = p + 20$ **3.** $4 = y - 7$

Solve the equation. Check the solution.

4. $m + 10 = 35$ **5.** $r + 7 = 43$ **6.** $c - 10 = 10$

Ask Yourself

- Do I need to add or subtract to get the variable alone?
- Did I do the same operation to both sides of the equation?

Math Talk You know that equals added to equals are equal. How does this help you solve equations?

Practice and Problem Solving

Solve the equation. Tell what number you added to or subtracted from both sides.

7. $x - 4 = 14$ **8.** $17 = m + 16$ **9.** $a + 5 = 15$ **10.** $24 = q - 10$

Solve the equation. Check the solution.

11. $w + 2 = 7$ **12.** $20 = y + 15$ **13.** $t - 6 = 10$ **14.** $30 = g - 18$

Write and solve an equation for the problem.

15. Akio just put 4 new fish in his fish tank. He now has a total of 12 fish in his tank. How many fish did Akio start with?

16. Four people were on a bus. Two people got off at the first stop and some people got on. If there are now 9 people on the bus, how many people got on?

Spiral Review and Test Practice

Solve. KEY NS 3.0 page 128

17. Write the multiples of 10 from 10 to 100.

18. Write the multiples of 5 from 5 to 50.

Write the letter of the correct answer. KEY AF 2.0, KEY AF 2.1

19. What is the value of x?

$x - 18 = 23$

A 5 **B** 23 **C** 31 **D** 41

Extra Practice See page 184, Set B.

CA Standards

KEY (AF 2.0) Students know how to manipulate equations.

KEY (AF 2.2) Know and understand that equals multiplied by equals are equal.

Also KEY (NS 3.0), **AF 1.1, MR 1.0, MR 1.1, MR 2.0, MR 2.3, MR 2.4, MR 2.6, MR 3.0, MR 3.2, MR 3.3**

Solve Multiplication and Division Equations

Objective Write and solve equations involving multiplication and division.

Learn by Example

When there is an unknown number, you can write an equation with a variable to solve the problem.

Mia has 8 goldfish, which is twice as many as Dwight has. How many goldfish does Dwight have?

1 Write an equation that describes the situation.

Use the variable g to stand for the number of goldfish that Dwight has.

twice as many → 2; number of fish Mia has → 8

$$2g = 8$$

number of fish Dwight has → g

2 Use inverse operations to find the value of the variable. Multiplication and division are inverse operations.

Divide each side of the equation by 2, so that g is alone on one side.

$$2g = 8$$
$$g \times 2 \div 2 = 8 \div 2$$
$$g = 4$$

Equals multiplied by equals are equal. So, equals divided by equals are equal.

Check

Substitute the variable with the solution. Then simplify the equation.

Both sides of the equation are the same, so the solution is correct.

$$2g = 8$$
$$2 \times 4 = 8 \quad \leftarrow \text{Substitute 4 for } g.$$
$$8 = 8$$

Solution: Since $g = 4$, Dwight has 4 goldfish.

Guided Practice

Solve the equation. Tell what number you multiplied or divided both sides by. Check the solution.

1. $5 \times p = 20$ **2.** $4 = m \div 6$ **3.** $21 = 7n$

4. $6b = 36$ **5.** $k \div 9 = 3$ **6.** $y \div 4 = 7$

Ask Yourself

- Do I need to multiply or divide to get the variable alone?
- Did I do the same operation to both sides of the equation?

Guided Problem Solving

Use the questions to solve this problem.

7. Kendi had 5 times as many CDs as DVDs. Then she gave 3 CDs away. She has 32 CDs now. Write an equation to show how many DVDs Kendi has.

a. **Understand** How is the number of CDs related to the number of DVDs?

b. **Plan** Choose a variable to stand for the number of DVDs and write an equation.

c. **Solve** Perform inverse operations to find the value of the variable. How many DVDs does Kendi have?

d. **Look Back** How can you check your answer?

8. Suppose Kendi has 47 CDs. Use your equation from Problem 7 to find out how many DVDs she has.

Math Talk You know that equals multiplied by equals are equal. How does this help you solve equations?

Practice and Problem Solving

Solve the equation. Tell what number you multiplied or divided both sides by. Check the solution.

9. $4p = 40$ **10.** $b \div 2 = 9$ **11.** $c \div 6 = 7$

12. $3 \cdot k = 15$ **13.** $n \div 7 = 3$ **14.** $15 = 5 \cdot x$

15. $7 + 2 = m \div 3$ **16.** $4p = 10 + 6$ **17.** $2 \cdot 3 \cdot m = 24$

Think

$4p$, $4 \times p$, and $4 \cdot p$ all mean "4 times p".

Write and solve an equation for the problem.

18. The pet store has three times as many cats as dogs. If there are 15 cats, how many dogs are there?

19. **Analyze** There are 7 angelfish in a small tank. That is half as many as are in the large tank. How many angelfish are in the large tank?

History-Social Science Link

Solve.

20. The tallest coast redwood is about 375 feet tall. One of the largest giant sequoia trees is about 285 feet tall. How much taller is the tallest redwood?

21. California redwood trees once covered about 2 million acres. Now the trees cover about 95,000 acres. Write and solve an equation to show how many acres of redwoods have been cut down.

22. Suppose one redwood tree is 500 years old. It is expected to live 4 times as long as its current age. Write and solve an equation to show how long the tree is expected to live.

Redwood Trees

- The redwood trees of Humboldt County in northern California are some of the tallest trees on Earth.
- Because of the durability of their wood, many redwoods were cut down by timber companies.
- The coast redwood, or sequoia, is the world's tallest tree. The sierra redwood, or giant sequoia, is shorter, but wider.

History-Social Science 4.1.3

Spiral Review and Test Practice

Simplify the expression. KEY AF 1.2 page 144

23. $5 \times (8 + 3)$ **24.** $16 \div (5 - 3)$ **25.** $(8 + 2) \times 8$ **26.** $(16 - 9) \times 6$

Copy and complete using $>$, $<$, or $=$. KEY AF 1.2 page 148

27. $56 \div (8 - 1)$ ⬭ $16 \div 2$ **28.** $29 - 3 \times 4$ ⬭ $(16 - 6) \times 10$

Write the letter of the correct answer. KEY AF 2.0

29. Which number is represented by n?

$4n + 3 = 23$

A 3 **B** 5 **C** 20 **D** 26

Extra Practice See page 185, Set C.

Practice **Game**

Equation Match-Up

Object of the Game To check the solutions of equations.

Materials

- Learning Tool 17 (*Equation Match-Up* Game Cards)
- index cards (optional)

Set Up

Shuffle the cards. Place them face down in any order in a 4 × 4 array.

Number of Players 2

How to Play

1. A player turns over any two cards. If the cards show an equation and its solution, the player keeps both cards. If not, the player turns the cards face down in the same positions.

2. Players take turns repeating Step 1 until all 8 matches have been made. The player with the greater number of cards is the winner.

$x + 6 = 9$	$x = 8$	$x \div 4 = 6$	$x = 2$
$4 + x = 10$	$x = 3$	$2x = 8$	$x = 24$
$x - 8 = 2$	$x = 6$	$5x = 10$	$x = 36$
$x + 1 = 9$	$x = 10$	$x \div 6 = 6$	$x = 4$

CA Standards
AF 1.0 Students use and interpret variables, mathematical symbols, and properties to write and simplify expressions and sentences.

Education Place
Visit www.eduplace.com/camap/ for **Brain Teasers** and **eGames** to play.

Problem Solving Plan
Use Equations for Comparison Problems

Objective Use equations and comparison bars to solve comparison problems.

CA Standards
MR 2.3 Use a variety of methods, such as words, numbers, symbols, charts, graphs, tables, diagrams, and models, to explain mathematical reasoning.

KEY AF 2.0 Students know how to manipulate equations.

Also KEY AF 2.1, KEY AF 2.2, AF 1.1, MR 1.0, MR 1.1, MR 1.2, MR 2.0, MR 2.4, MR 3.0, MR 3.1, MR 3.2

Learn Through Reasoning

You can use equations to solve problems that involve one amount that is greater than or less than another amount. Comparison bars can help you write equations to find an unknown amount in a comparison problem.

Example 1

On her farm, Kristin has 9 horses and 5 cows. How many more horses than cows does Kristin have? Let x stand for the unknown amount.

Equation	Explanation
$5 + x = 9$	Write an equation that describes the situation.
$5 + x - 5 = 9 - 5$ $x = 4$	Use inverse operations to find the value of the variable. Subtract 5 from both sides of the equation, so that x is alone on one side.

Kristin has 4 more horses than cows.

Example 2

Kristin has four times more chickens than ducks. If she has 20 chickens, how many ducks does she have?

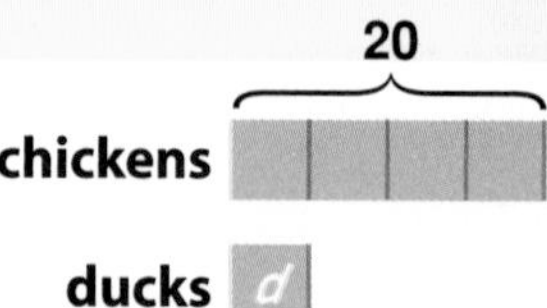

Equation	Explanation
$4d = 20$	Write an equation that describes the situation.
$d \times 4 \div 4 = 20 \div 4$ $d = 5$	Use inverse operations to find the value of the variable. Divide each side of the equation by 4, so that d is alone on one side.

Kristin has 5 ducks.

Guided Problem Solving

Solve using the Ask Yourself questions.

1. Rick has 6 rabbits. Hayley has 4 rabbits. How many more rabbits does Rick have than Hayley? Write an equation to solve the problem.

Ask Yourself

- What does the question ask?
- How can I use comparison bars to solve the problem?

Math Talk Explain how you can check your solution.

Independent Problem Solving

Draw comparison bars and write an equation to solve. Then check your solution.

2. On a bird watching trip, Charlie saw five times more eagles than condors. If he saw 10 eagles, how many condors did he see?
3. Kiva collected 12 different types of leaves for her science project. Len collected 9 more different types of leaves than Kiva. How many different types of leaves did Len collect?
4. Cindy's dog weighs 7 pounds. Matilda's dog weighs 5 times as much as Cindy's. How much does Matilda's dog weigh?
5. **Multistep** In a vase, there are 12 more red roses than the number of yellow and white roses combined. If there are 4 yellow roses and 8 white roses in the vase, how many red roses are in the vase?
6. **Challenge** At an animal shelter, the number of tiger cats plus the number of calico cats is three times greater than the number of white cats. If there are 4 white cats and 4 calico cats at the shelter, how many tiger cats are at the shelter?
7. **Create and Solve** Write and solve a word problem that can be represented by these comparison bars.

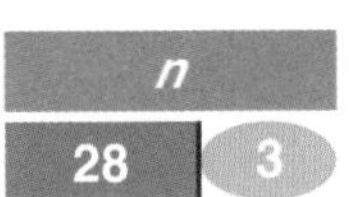

Reading & Writing 

Vocabulary

When you solve equations with **variables**, you perform the same operation to both sides of the equation.

Choose a term from the word bank to complete each sentence.

Word Bank
algebraic expression
equals
equation
evaluate
expression
inequality
variable

1. A mathematical sentence with an equal sign is called an ________.
2. A letter that stands for a number is called a ________.
3. An expression with a variable is called an ________.
4. Equals multiplied by ________ are equal.

Complete the chart. Evaluate each expression when $y = 2$ and $y = 5$.

	Expression	Value when $y = 2$	Value when $y = 5$
5.	$(y + 3) \times 8$		
6.	$(12 + y) - 4$		
7.	$63 - (5 \times y)$		
8.	$(10 - y) + 6$		
9.	$(3 \times 2) \times (y + 4)$		
10.	$(10 \div y) \times (2 + 5)$		

Writing Choose one of the expressions from the chart. Write the value when $y = 10$.

Reading Check out this book in your library. *Famous Flights: Understanding and Using Variables*, by Greg Roza

CA Standards
MR 2.3 Use a variety of methods, such as words, numbers, symbols, charts, graphs, tables, diagrams, and models, to explain mathematical reasoning.

Also KEY AF 1.2

Standards-Based Extra Practice

Set A

AF 1.0, AF 1.1 page 170

Choose the expression that matches the words.

1. 4 more than p
   A $4p$ **B** $p - 4$ **C** $4 \div p$ **D** $4 + p$

2. half of d
   A $d \div 2$ **B** $d - 2$ **C** $d + 2$ **D** $2d$

3. 7 times x
   A $7 - x$ **B** $7x$ **C** $7 + x$ **D** $7 \div x$

4. 8 fewer than 2 times n
   A $2 + n - 8$ **B** $2 - n \div 8$ **C** $2 \div n - 8$ **D** $2n - 8$

Evaluate the expression when $x = 8$.

5. $14 - x$
6. $x + 2 - 5$
7. $6x$
8. $32 - 2x$
9. $24 - 3x$
10. $2x + 2$
11. $40 \div x - 2$
12. $x + 4 - 10$

Evaluate the expression when $y = 5$.

13. $50 \div y$
14. $8y + 12$
15. $20 - y \times 3$
16. $y + 6 \div 2$
17. $y \div 5$
18. $5 + 2y$
19. $y - 12 \div 12$
20. $6y - 14$

Write an expression for the problem. Choose your own variables.

21. James brought some pencils on the first day of school. Kaylin brought half as many pencils as James. How many pencils does Kaylin have?

22. Some students in Ms. Traina's class bring their lunch to school. There are 14 more students who buy their lunch than bring their lunch. How many students buy their lunch?

23. **Explain** Mr. Good asked his students to write an expression for "two times q." Jarrod wrote $2q$. Janelle wrote $2 \cdot q$. Arno wrote $2 \times q$. Which student wrote the expression correctly? Why?

Education Place
Visit www.eduplace.com/camap/ for more **Extra Practice**.

Standards-Based Extra Practice

Set B

KEY AF 2.0, KEY AF 2.1 page 174

Solve the equation. Tell what number you added to or subtracted from both sides.

1. $s - 8 = 12$
2. $22 + y = 31$
3. $40 = n + 25$
4. $b - 4 = 4$
5. $5 = q - 66$
6. $y + 14 = 48$
7. $a - 33 = 19$
8. $12 = c - 9$
9. $72 = y + 36$
10. $28 = d - 8$
11. $9 + x = 30$
12. $f + 11 = 42$
13. $r - 18 = 4$
14. $65 = h + 25$
15. $42 + t = 42$
16. $16 = b - 8$
17. $j + 16 = 4 + 12$
18. $x - 9 = 36 - 7$
19. $82 + y = 100$
20. $t + 2 + 2 = 14$

Solve the equation. Check the solution.

21. $8 + f = 23$
22. $40 = h + 32$
23. $t - 15 = 65$
24. $18 = r - 11$
25. $q - 4 = 14$
26. $12 + c = 21$
27. $27 = 9 + s$
28. $50 + b = 85$
29. $4 + 8 + p = 18$
30. $g + 7 - 5 = 20$
31. $k - 10 + 3 = 32$
32. $y + 6 = 12 - 5$
33. $21 - 11 = y - 9$
34. $5 + 13 = 8 + t$
35. $7 + y = 62 - 38$
36. $b + 43 - 13 = 36$
37. $60 = h + 9 - 5$
38. $7 + 10 + b = 34$
39. $j - 14 + 3 = 18$
40. $32 - 15 = x + 5$

Write and solve an equation for the problem.

41. Finn is baking cookies for his 27 classmates. He bakes 12 cookies in the first batch and 12 cookies in the second batch. How many more cookies does he need to bake to have enough cookies for all his classmates?

42. Craig's football team scored 24 points in their first game and 14 points in their second game. The score in their third game is 10 less than the sum of their first two games' scores. What was their score in their third game?

43. Eleven birds were nesting in a tree. Five birds flew away. Some other birds landed in the tree. If there are now 20 birds in the tree, how many birds landed in the tree?

44. Jermaine just added 4 new video games to his collection. He now has a total of 38 games. How many games did Jermaine start with?

45. **Explain** What does it mean to "solve" an equation?

Standards-Based Extra Practice

Set C KEY AF 2.0, KEY AF 2.2 page 176

Solve the equation. Tell what number you multiplied or divided both sides by. Check the solution.

1. $5p = 25$ **2.** $x \div 3 = 8$ **3.** $9 = f \div 4$ **4.** $63 = 7g$

5. $6 \cdot b = 36$ **6.** $3y = 24$ **7.** $2 = n \div 2$ **8.** $q \div 5 = 8$

9. $\frac{s}{3} = 5$ **10.** $2 \times 2 = 2m$ **11.** $9 = \frac{k}{8}$ **12.** $4t = 28$

13. $h \div 3 = 4 \times 2$ **14.** $64 = 8c$ **15.** $45 = p \cdot 9$ **16.** $\frac{x}{7} = 6$

17. $4 \times 5 = 2z$ **18.** $w \div 2 = 5$ **19.** $y \div 6 = 2 \times 5$ **20.** $t \div 9 = 9$

Solve the equation. Check the solution.

21. $7x = 21$ **22.** $w \div 6 = 9$ **23.** $2 = p \div 4$ **24.** $70 = 7k$

25. $9 \cdot r = 18$ **26.** $6n = 30$ **27.** $3 = 3n$ **28.** $g \div 10 = 8$

29. $\frac{m}{5} = 10$ **30.** $8 \times 2 = 2y$ **31.** $7 = \frac{c}{8}$ **32.** $9f = 81$

33. $j \div 5 = 2 \times 3$ **34.** $72 = 9x$ **35.** $50 = h \cdot 50$ **36.** $\frac{d}{3} = 7$

37. $5 \times 8 = 4z$ **38.** $t \div 7 = 7$ **39.** $k \div 9 = 3 \times 3$ **40.** $r \div 8 = 2$

Write and solve an equation for each problem.

41. The local animal shelter is housing 27 cats. If the cats are split evenly into 9 cages, how many cats are in each cage?

42. A pet store has 8 angelfish. That is half the number of koi they have. How many koi do they have?

43. Hannah's rabbit had babies last spring. This spring, her rabbit had 5 times as many babies. If Hannah's rabbit had 15 babies this spring, how many babies did she have last spring?

44. Reagan and her dog run 2 miles each afternoon. On the weekend they run a total of 3 times as far. How far do Reagan and her dog run on the weekend?

45. **Explain** How can you check that $x = 2$ is the solution to $4x = 8$?

Education Place
Visit www.eduplace.com/camap/ for more **Extra Practice**.

Chapter Review/Test

Vocabulary and Concepts

MR 2.3, AF 1.0

Write the best word to complete the sentence.

1. A letter or a symbol that is used to stand for an unknown number is called a ______.

2. When you ______ an algebraic equation, you find the value for the variable that makes the equation true.

Skills

KEY AF 2.0, KEY AF 2.1, KEY AF 2.2, AF 1.1, MR 1.0

Evaluate the expression when $a = 9$.

3. $4a$
4. $36 \div a$
5. $50 - a$
6. $6 + 2a$

Solve the equation. Tell what you did to both sides.

7. $x + 7 = 21$
8. $32 = m + 24$
9. $55 = p - 12$
10. $r - 13 = 59$
11. $7d = 63$
12. $q \div 21 = 1$
13. $y \div 3 = 6$
14. $9f = 54$

Solve the equation. Check the solution.

15. $8 + 1 = x \div 2$
16. $3b = 8 + 19$
17. $n - 4 = 3$
18. $20 = x + 12$

Problem Solving and Reasoning

AF 1.1, MR 2.3, MR 1.1

Write an expression for the problem. Choose your own variables.

19. There are 4 fewer students in Nati's class this year than last year. How many students are there in Nati's class this year?

20. Some students in Nati's class went swimming this summer. Three times as many students went to the movies. How many students went to the movies this summer?

Writing Math How do you know which operation to use when you solve an equation?

Spiral Review and Test Practice

1. One museum has 465,287 paintings. Another museum has 347,821 paintings. To the nearest thousand, about how many paintings are in the two museums combined?

A 117,000 paintings

B 812,000 paintings

C 813,000 paintings

D 814,000 paintings

Test Tip
Make a plan. What do you need to do before solving the problem?

KEY NS 1.3, KEY NS 3.1 page 58

2. 92,231 − 45,685 =

A 36,546

B 46,546

C 46,556

D 46,646

KEY NS 3.1 page 78

3. What is the value of the expression below?

35 − (12 + 3) + 5

A 55

B 31

C 25

D 15

KEY AF 1.2 page 94

4. What is 690,564 rounded to the nearest hundred?

A 691,000

B 690,600

C 690,560

D 690,500

KEY NS 1.3 page 32

5. Which statement is true?

A $(15 - 5) \times 2 > 15 - (5 \times 2)$

B $(15 - 5) \times 2 < 15 - (5 \times 2)$

C $(15 - 5) \times 2 = 15 - (5 \times 2)$

D $(15 - 5) \times 2 = 15 - 5 \times 2$

KEY AF 1.2, AF 1.0 page 148

6. What is the value of the expression below if $n = 8$?

$22 - n \div 2$

A 4

B 7

C 14

D 18

Test Tip
Rewrite the expression using 8 for the variable.

AF 1.1 page 168

Education Place
Visit www.eduplace.com/camap/ for **Test-Taking Tips** and **Extra Practice.**

Equations with Two Variables

Check What You Know

Word Bank
equation
expression
inequality
variable

Vocabulary and Concepts AF 1.1, AF 1.0, MR 2.3

Choose the best word to complete the sentence. pages 98, 168

1. In the expression $3m + 6$, the letter m is a ____.
2. Both sides of an ____ have the same value.
3. $58 < 46 + 36$ is an example of an ____.

Skills KEY NS 3.0

Multiply or divide. page 122

4. 5×6
5. 8×2
6. 6×10
7. $36 \div 9$
8. $28 \div 7$
9. $56 \div 7$

Problem Solving and Reasoning KEY NS 3.0

10. Janelle wants to make necklaces for her 3 best friends. If she puts 9 beads on each necklace, how many beads will she need? How many beads will she need if she puts 10 beads on each necklace?

Vocabulary

Visualize It!

function rule
a rule that gives exactly one output value for each input value

function table
a table that matches each input value with a unique output value

Rule: $y = x + 45$	
Input (x)	Output (y)
5	50
6	51
7	52
8	53

Language Tips

Looking at the prefixes for the words *input* and *output* will help you know what the words mean. The word *input* means *something that is put in*. The word *output* means *something that is put out*.

Words that look alike in English and Spanish often have the same meaning.

English	Spanish
variable	variable
expression	expresión
function	funcion

See **English-Spanish Glossary** pages 644–666.

Education Place Visit www.eduplace.com/camap/ for the **eGlossary** and **eGames**.

CA Standards MR 2.3 Use a variety of methods, such as words, numbers, symbols, charts, graphs, tables, diagrams, and models, to explain mathematical reasoning. **Also KEY AF 1.5**

CA Standards
Prepares for
KEY AF 1.5 Understand that an equation such as $y = 3x + 5$ is a prescription for determining a second number when a first number is given.

MR 1.1 Analyze problems by identifying relationships, distinguishing relevant from irrelevant information, sequencing and prioritizing information, and observing patterns.

Also AF 1.0, AF 1.1, MR 2.3, MR 2.4, MR 3.0, MR 3.2, MR 3.3

Vocabulary

function table

Materials
- Workmat 1
- counters
- eManipulatives (optional) www.eduplace.com/camap/

Hands On
Function Tables

Objective Understand the concept of a function table.

Explore

A **function table** lists pairs of numbers. Each input value has exactly one output value.

Question How can you use a function table to show a pattern?

Ms. Thompson is hanging posters on her bulletin board. She uses tacks to hang the posters in the pattern shown below. How many tacks does she use to hang 8 posters next to each other?

Input: Number of posters	Output: Number of tacks
1	
2	
3	
4	
5	
6	
7	
8	

1 poster
4 tacks

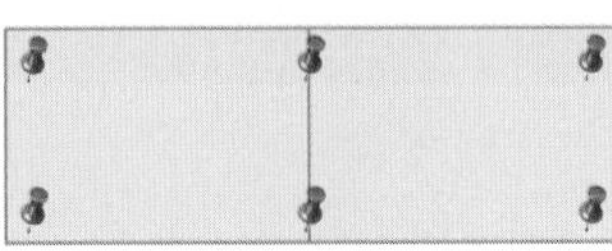
2 posters
6 tacks

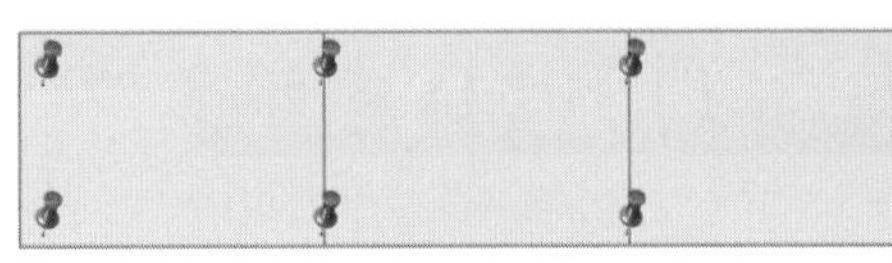
3 posters
8 tacks

1. Copy the function table. Fill in the first 3 rows using the pictures above.

2. Show how the pattern continues. Draw 4 posters on Workmat 1. Use counters to show where the tacks are placed. Record the number of counters in the function table.

3. Continue to draw and use counters to show the pattern. Complete the last 4 rows of the function table.

Solution: Ms. Thompson uses 18 tacks to hang 8 posters.

Extend

Draw the next two figures of the pattern.
Copy and complete the function table.

1.

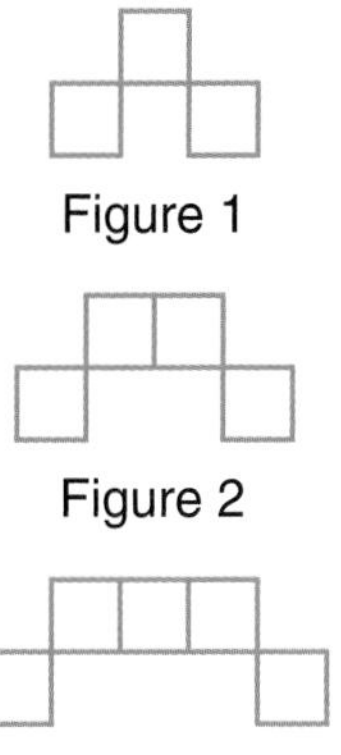

Figure 1

Figure 2

Figure 3

Figure number	Number of squares
1	
2	
3	
4	
5	

2.

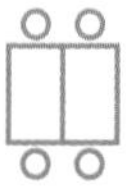

Figure 1

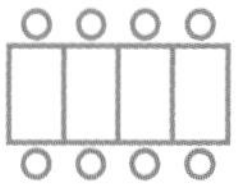

Figure 2

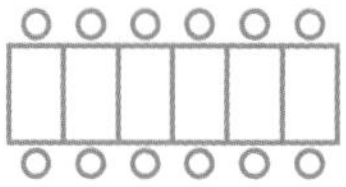

Figure 3

Figure number	Number of circles
1	
2	
3	
4	
5	

3.

Figure 1

Figure 2

Figure 3

Figure number	Number of circles
1	
2	
3	
4	
5	

4.

Figure 1

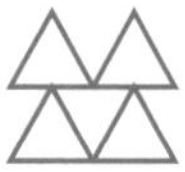

Figure 2

Figure 3

Figure number	Number of triangles
1	
2	
3	
4	
5	

Solve.

5. A school has 5 new vans. Each van has 9 seat belts. Complete the function table to show how many seat belts there are in all the vans.

Number of vans	Number of seat belts
1	
2	
3	
4	
5	

6. **Challenge** Look back at Problem 5. If the number of vans is *n*, write an expression for the number of seat belts.

Writing Math

Create and Solve Create your own pattern. Make and complete a function table to match your pattern.

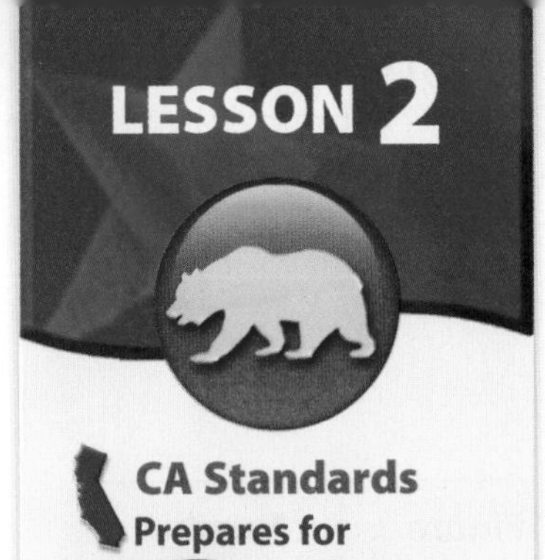

Write Function Rules Using One Variable

Objective Write function rules using one variable.

CA Standards
Prepares for
KEY AF 1.5 Understand that an equation such as $y = 3x + 5$ is a prescription for determining a second number when a first number is given.

AF 1.1 Use letters, boxes, or other symbols to stand for any number in simple expressions or equations (e.g., demonstrate an understanding and the use of the concept of a variable).

Also AF 1.0, MR 1.1, MR 2.0, MR 2.3, MR 2.4, MR 3.0, MR 3.2, MR 3.3

Learn by Example

In Lesson 1, you used function tables to show patterns. In this lesson, you will use a variable to write a rule for a function table.

The Bicycle Club of Irvine buys water bottles in packages of 6. The function table shows the relationship between the number of packages and the number of water bottles.

Input: Number of packages	Output: Number of water bottles
1	6
2	12
3	18
4	■

Use a variable to write a function rule for the table. Then use the rule to find the number of water bottles in 4 packages.

Think

Remember, a **function table** is a table that matches each input value with exactly one output value.

1 Use a variable to represent the input value. The input value in the function table is the number of packages. Let *n* stand for the number of packages. So 6*n* stands for the number of water bottles.

The rule is Output $= 6n$. ← **The number of water bottles is always 6 times the number of packages.**

2 The output value in the function table is the number of water bottles. You can use the rule to find the number of bottles in 4 packages.

Number of bottles $= 6n$

$= 6 \times 4$ ← **Substitute 4 for *n*.**

$= 24$

Solution: There are 24 water bottles in 4 packages.

Guided Practice

Algebra Functions

Copy and complete.

	Rule: Output = $6m - 2$	
	Input (m)	Output
1.	4	■
2.	6	■
3.	8	■

4.

Rule: ___?___	
Input (b)	Output
10	40
6	24
3	12

Ask Yourself

- What is the rule?
- Does the rule work for every pair of numbers in the table?

Guided Problem Solving

Use the questions to solve this problem.

5. Marissa bikes 8 miles each day. Make a function table to show how many total miles she bikes in 2 days, 5 days, and 7 days. Use the variable n to stand for the number of days. Write an equation to show the function rule.

a. **Understand** What does the variable n stand for? How many miles does Marissa bike each day?

b. **Plan** What will the input and output columns in your function table represent? How many rows should be in the table?

c. **Solve** Make and complete the function table. What will the rule for the function table be?

d. **Look Back** Does your rule work for every pair of numbers in the table?

6. Look back at Problem 5. If another row was added to the function table, what could the input and output be?

Math Talk Do you need to look at all the numbers in a function table to write the rule? Explain.

Practice and Problem Solving

Algebra Functions

Copy and complete.

	Rule: Output = $20 \div n$	
	Input (n)	Output
7.	2	■
8.	5	■
9.	10	■

	Rule: Output = $9 + 4d$	
	Input (d)	Output
10.	5	■
11.	7	■
12.	9	■

13.

Rule: ____?____	
Input (a)	Output
10	5
14	7
24	12

Make a function table. Write the rule using one variable.

14. The cycling team always has 5 more bikes than riders, in case some bikes need repair. Show how many bikes they have if there are 6, 7, 8, or 9 riders.

15. **Challenge** The output values in a function table are 0, 4, and 8. The rule for the table is Output = $2m - 6$. What are the input values?

Real World Data

Solve. Use the Fun Facts for Problem 16.

16. Was the first Tour de France race greater or less than 2,200 miles? How do you know?

17. Suppose each team had 9 riders. Make a function table to show the relationship between the number of teams and the number of riders. Use your rule to find the number of riders on 6 teams.

Tour de France

- The Tour de France is a famous bicycle race that was first held in 1903. That race was 2,428 kilometers long.
- The total length of the race in 2006 was 3,657 kilometers or about 2,200 miles.
- 189 riders competed in the Tour de France race in 2006.

Spiral Review and Test Practice

Copy and complete. KEY AF 1.3 page 148

18. $(9 + 8) \times 6 = 17 \times$ ■

19. $(18 - 14) \times$ ■ $= (20 \div 5) \times 3$

Write the letter of the correct answer. AF 1.1

20. ▲ = ■ + 6 If ■ = 4, what is ▲?

A 2 **B** 4 **C** 6 **D** 10

Extra Practice See page 203, Set A.

Key Standards Review

Need Help?
See Key Standards Handbook.

Fill in the box to make the number sentence true. KEY AF 2.0, KEY AF 2.2

1. $(8 - 1) \times 3 = 7 \times \square$
2. $(4 \times 4) \times (2 \times 3) = \square \times 6$
3. $(3 + \square) \times 3 = 15 \times 3$
4. $6 \times 7 = 6 \times \square$
5. $(2 + \square) \times 9 = 6 \times 9$

Solve. Tell whether you used an estimate.
Explain your thinking. KEY NS 1.4

6. Angela has \$387. She buys a bicycle for \$293. Does she have enough money left to buy a lock for her bike, for \$46?
7. There are 608 seats in the school auditorium. There are 452 students attending an assembly. Are there enough seats for the 116 teachers that will also attend the assembly?

Cricket Chirps

If you count the number of cricket chirps in a fifteen-second period, you can find the temperature outside in degrees Fahrenheit.

Write the rule and complete the function table. AF 1.0, AF 1.1, KEY AF 1.5

Rule: ____?____	
Number of chirps (*n*)	**Temperature (*T*)**
2	39
3	40
	41
8	
11	
	51
17	
	58
	79

Write Function Rules Using Two Variables

Objective Write function rules using two variables.

CA Standards

KEY AF 1.5 Understand that an equation such as $y = 3x + 5$ is a prescription for determining a second number when a first number is given.

AF 1.1 Use letters, boxes, or other symbols to stand for any number in simple expressions or equations (e.g., demonstrate an understanding and the use of the concept of a variable).

Also AF 1.0, MR 1.1, MR 2.2, MR 2.3, MR 2.4, MR 3.2, MR 3.3, MR 3.0

Vocabulary

two-variable equation

Learn by Example

In this lesson, you will learn how to use an equation with two variables to represent a function table.

Cora and two of her friends like to go rollerblading. Each skate has 4 wheels. The function table at the right shows the relationship between the number of skates and the number of wheels.

Write a rule for the function table.

Input: Number of skates	Output: Number of wheels
1	4
2	8
3	12
4	16
5	20
6	24

Different Ways to Write a Function Rule

Way 1 **Use one variable.**

- Let s stand for the number of skates, the input.
- $4s$ can stand for the number of wheels, the output.

The rule for the function table can be written as Output $= 4s$.

Way 2 **Use two variables.**

- Let s stand for the number of skates.
- Let w stand for the number of wheels.

The rule for the function table can be the equation $w = 4s$.

When you use two different variables to write the rule, you are writing a **two-variable equation**.

Solution: The rule is Output $= 4s$ or $w = 4s$.

Guided Practice

Copy and complete.

	Rule: $y = 3x - 7$	
	Input (x)	Output (y)
1.	5	■
2.	7	■
3.	10	■

4.

Rule: ?	
Input (x)	Output (y)
16	4
36	9
40	10

Ask Yourself

- What is the rule?
- Does the rule work for every pair of numbers in the table?

	Rule: $q = 6 + 2p$	
	Input (p)	Output (q)
5.	4	■
6.	6	■
7.	8	■

	Rule: $b = 3a + 3$	
	Input (a)	Output (b)
8.	2	■
9.	3	■
10.	4	■

11.

Rule: ?	
Input (c)	Output (d)
10	20
30	40
50	60

Math Talk Think about the two equations $b = 6 + 2a$ and $b = 2a + 6$. Would the values of a and b be the same for both equations? Explain.

Practice and Problem Solving

Copy and complete.

	Rule: $y = 9 + 4x$	
	Input (x)	Output (y)
12.	1	■
13.	6	■
14.	8	■

	Rule: $b = 4a - 2$	
	Input (a)	Output (b)
15.	6	■
16.	8	■
17.	12	■

	Rule: $n = 2m + 3$	
	Input (m)	Output (n)
18.	3	■
19.	6	■
20.	9	■

21.

Rule: ?	
Input (w)	Output (p)
15	5
27	9
36	12

22.

Rule: ?	
Input (a)	Output (b)
20	4
35	7
50	10

23.

Rule: ?	
Input (n)	Output (m)
10	30
8	24
4	12

Solve.

24. Maria and her dog take a trip to the mall every day. The distance to the mall and back is 3 miles.

a. Make a function table to show how many miles she travels in 1, 5, and 10 days. Use a two-variable equation for the rule. Let x stand for the number of days. Let y stand for the number of miles.

b. Suppose Maria traveled a total of 27 miles to the mall and back. How many days was this? Explain.

Science Link

Use the table to solve.

A vitamin shop sells bottles of *Lactobacillus acidophilus*, a bacteria that helps people digest milk. The store calculates the price according to the rule $y = 6x + 20$, where x stands for the number of bottles and y stands for the price in dollars.

25. Copy and complete the function table to the right.

26. Will an order ever cost $47? Explain.

27. A customer wants 3 bottles. Should she buy them in 3 separate orders, 2 separate orders, or all at once? Explain.

Bacteria

- Microorganisms are very tiny living things—too tiny to see without a microscope. Bacteria are microorganisms.
- Some microorganisms can cause disease and spoil food. But some can be helpful.

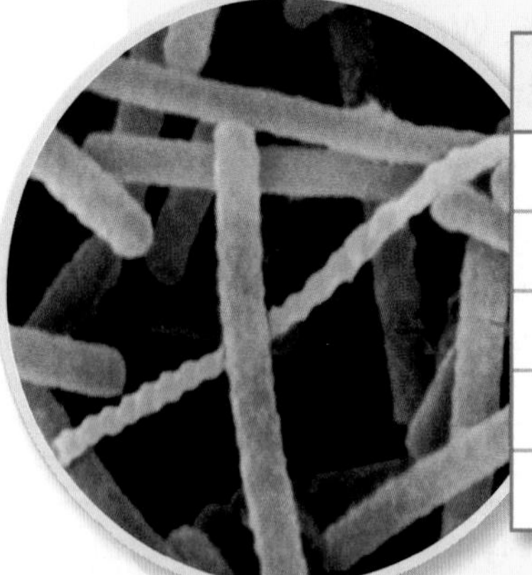

Bottles (x)	Price (y)
1	$26
2	
3	
4	
5	

Science LS 3.d

Spiral Review and Test Practice

Evaluate the expression when $a = 8$. AF 1.1 page 170

28. $6a$ **29.** $\frac{a}{2}$ **30.** $a + 45$ **31.** $50 - a$ **32.** $a \times 4$

Write the letter of the correct answer. KEY AF 1.5

33. The sum of x plus y equals 10. If $x = 2$, which equation can be used to find the value of y?

A $y - 2 = 10$ **B** $2 + y = 10$ **C** $x - y = 10$ **D** $x + 2 = 10$

Extra Practice See page 203, Set B.

Math Works! Caterer

Party Time

Mavis is a caterer. She prepares food for events and parties. Mavis uses equations to figure out how much food to bring based on the number of people at an event. The table shows some of the equations she uses.

Type of Food	Equation x = number of people y = number of items
strawberries	$y = 5x$
cookies	$y = 2x$
rolls	$y = 2x + 12$

Use the table for Problems 1–3.

1. If Mavis is serving strawberries to 8 people, how many strawberries will she bring?
2. If she is baking cookies for a party of 9, how many cookies will she bake?
3. If 10 people are coming to an event, how many rolls does Mavis need?

Solve.

4. Mavis charges $25 an hour for each event plus a $9 service charge. If T is the total charge and h is the number of hours, write an equation to find the total charge when you know the number of hours.

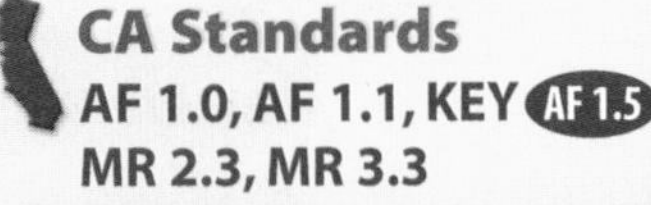
CA Standards
AF 1.0, AF 1.1, KEY AF 1.5, MR 2.3, MR 3.3

LESSON 4

Field Trip...

CA Standards
MR 1.0, MR 1.1, MR 2.0, MR 2.3, MR 2.4, KEY NS 3.0, KEY NS 3.1, AF 1.0, AF 1.1, KEY AF 2.0, KEY AF 2.1

Problem Solving

Objective Use skills and strategies to solve word problems.

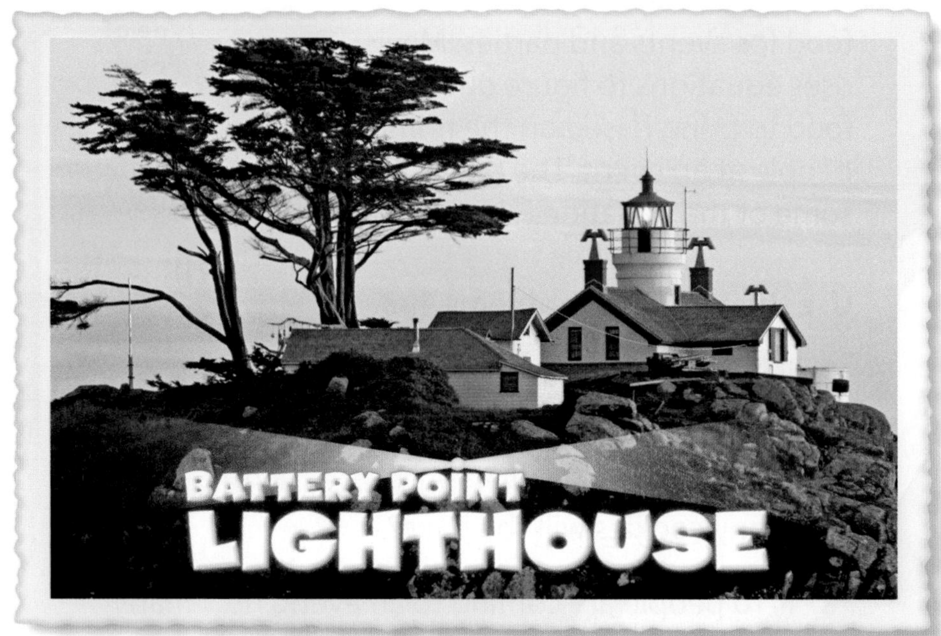

The lighthouse helps protect ships as they move south to San Francisco along the rocky coast.

Solve. Tell which strategy or method you used.

1. A white light in the lighthouse tower flashes once every 30 seconds.
   a. Use this information to complete the table.
   b. **Find a Pattern** How many times does the light flash in 5 minutes? Show your work. Remember, there are 60 seconds in 1 minute.

Input: Number of flashes (x)	Output: Number of seconds (y)
0	0
1	30
2	60
3	
4	

2. Use the timeline. For how many years did the U.S. Coast Guard (USCG) operate the lighthouse?

3. **Create and Solve** Write a word problem that could be solved using the timeline and this equation: $1856 + x = 1964$. Then solve your problem.

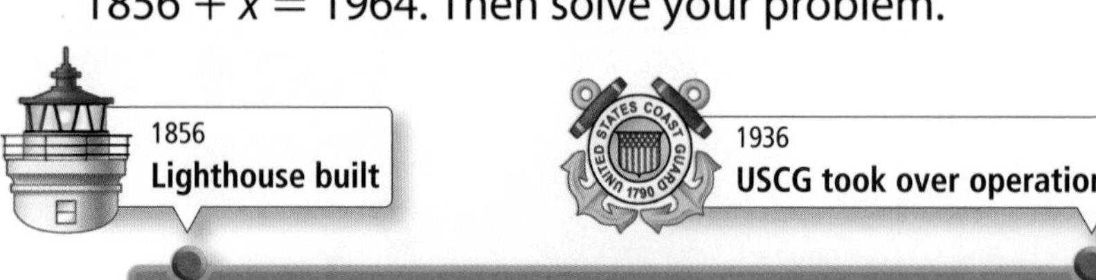

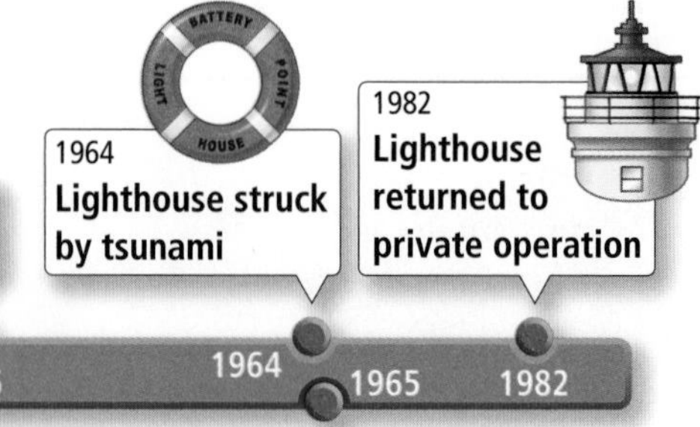

Problem Solving on Tests

Select a Strategy
- Choose the Operation
- Estimate
- Write an Equation
- Guess and Check
- Work Backward

1. Mount Whitney in California is 14,494 feet tall. Mount Katahdin in Maine is 9,175 feet shorter than Mount Whitney. Approximately how tall is Mount Katahdin?

A 23,000 feet **C** 6,000 feet
B 24,000 feet **D** 5,000 feet

KEY NS 1.4 page 74

2. Clara had \$18. After buying two pairs of socks, she has \$10 left. One pair of socks costs \$4. In the number sentence below, the $\square$ represents how much she spent on the other pair of socks. What number goes in the box to make the number sentence true?

$$18 - (\square + 4) = 10$$

A 4 **B** 6 **C** 8 **D** 12

KEY AF 2.1 page 174

3. Last year, there were 13 boys and 22 girls in Mrs. Soto's class. This year, there are 15 boys and 21 girls. Which expression will tell you how many more students are in the class this year than last year?

A $(13 + 22) - (15 + 21)$
B $(15 + 21) - (13 + 22)$
C $(22 + 21) - (13 + 15)$
D $(15 + 21) + (13 + 22)$

KEY AF 1.2 page 92

Test Tip
Think about the order of operations. Perform operations inside the parentheses first.

4. Emily solved the problem below. Which expression could be used to check her answer?

$$\begin{array}{r} 4\text{ R2} \\ 6\overline{)26} \end{array}$$

A $(4 \times 6) \times 2$ **C** $(4 \times 6) + 2$
B $(4 \times 6) + 6$ **D** $(4 \times 2) \times 6$

KEY NS 3.2 page 130

5. Latoya wants to make the following number sentence a true statement. What number should she put in the box?

$$15 \times (3 + 2) = \square \times 5$$

A 15 **B** 3 **C** 2 **D** 75

KEY AF 2.2 page 152

6. Shirts are on sale for \$3 off the original price of \$11. The expression $n \times (\$11 - \$3)$ shows the cost of buying n shirts on sale. What is the cost of buying 4 shirts on sale?

A \$56 **C** \$32
B \$44 **D** \$12

Test Tip
Think about using multiplication properties to help you.

KEY AF 1.2 page 192

Education Place
Visit www.eduplace.com/camap/ for **Test-Taking Tips** and **Extra Practice**.

Reading & Writing 

Vocabulary

When you use two different variables to write a **function rule**, you are writing a **two-variable equation**.

Solve.

Nick is recording the growth of a sunflower plant. It is one inch tall today. If the plant grows 2 inches each day, how tall will it be by the end of five days?

The function table shows the relationship between the number of days of growth and the plant's height in inches.

Input: Days	Output: Height in inches
1	2
2	4
3	6
4	8
5	■
6	■

Answer these questions about Nick's sunflower plant.

1. What variable can you use to represent the number of days?
2. What variable can you use to represent the height in inches?
3. What is the rule for the function table?
4. How tall will Nick's sunflower plant be at the end of Day 6?

Writing Tom's sunflower plant grows three inches every day. Write a two-variable equation to show the relationship between days and height in inches. Use the equation to give the height of the plant in 5 days.

Reading Check out this book in your library. *Rabbits Rabbits Everywhere: A Fibonacci Tale*, by Ann McCallum

CA Standards
MR 2.3 Use a variety of methods, such as words, numbers, symbols, charts, graphs, tables, diagrams, and models, to explain mathematical reasoning.

Also KEY  AF 1.5

Standards-Based Extra Practice

Set A

KEY AF 1.5 page 192

Algebra Functions

Copy and complete.

Rule: Output $= x + 7$	
Input (x)	Output
10	■
5	■
1	■

1.
2.
3.

Rule: Output $= 3b$	
Input (b)	Output
3	■
6	■
9	■

4.
5.
6.

7.

Rule: ____?____	
Input (g)	Output
9	54
7	42
4	24

8. **Explain** Would it be easier to find the rule for a function table with 2 pairs of numbers or 4 pairs of numbers?

Set B

KEY AF 1.5 page 196

Algebra Functions

Copy and complete.

1.
2.
3.

Rule: $t = 4s$	
Input (s)	Output (t)
4	■
6	■
8	■

4.
5.
6.

Rule: $f = 3 + 8d$	
Input (d)	Output (f)
6	■
4	■
2	■

7.
8.
9.

Rule: $n = 5m \div 3$	
Input (m)	Output (n)
3	■
6	■
0	■

10.

Rule: ____?____	
Input (j)	Output (k)
12	3
20	5
32	8

11.

Rule: ____?____	
Input (x)	Output (y)
13	4
11	2
9	0

12.

Rule: ____?____	
Input (p)	Output (q)
3	21
4	28
5	35

13. **Justify** According to the rule in Problem 12, why is there no whole number that can be used as an input value to get an output of 32?

Education Place
Visit www.eduplace.com/camap/ for more **Extra Practice**.

Chapter Review/Test

Vocabulary and Concepts

KEY AF 1.5, AF 1.1, MR 2.3

Write the best term to complete the sentence.

1. A _______ is a table that matches each input value with exactly one output value.

2. A _______ is a letter or a symbol that is used to stand for an unknown number.

3. In a function, each _______ value has exactly one output value.

Skills

KEY AF 1.5, AF 1.1

Copy and complete.

	Rule: $m = n - 4$	
	Input (n)	Output (m)
4.	4	
5.	6	
6.	8	
7.	10	
8.	12	

	Rule: $f = 8 + e$	
	Input (e)	Output (f)
9.	11	
10.	13	
11.	15	
12.	17	
13.	19	

	Rule: $m = 5n$	
	Input (n)	Output (m)
14.	4	
15.	6	
16.	8	
17.	10	
18.	1	

Problem Solving and Reasoning

MR 1.1, MR 2.3, KEY AF 1.5, AF 1.1

Solve.

19. Subway cars can hold up to 25 people. Make a function table to show how many people fit in a 2-, 3-, or 4-car train. Write the rule using one variable. Let x stand for the number of cars.

20. Hal rides his bike 4 miles to school and back every day. Make a function table to show how many miles he rides in 2, 5, and 10 days. Write the rule using one variable. Let d stand for the number of days.

Writing Math How does a function rule help you fill out a function table?

Spiral Review and Test Practice

1. $1{,}398 + 3{,}742 =$

A 4,140

B 5,040

C 5,130

D 5,140

KEY NS 3.1 page 62

2. What number goes in the box to make this number sentence true?

$(9 - 4) + 5 = 4 + \square$

A 18

B 10

C 6

D 5

Test Tip
Find the value of the left side of the equation. Then solve to find the missing number on the right.

KEY AF 2.1 page 98

3. Maria solved the problem below. Which expression could be used to check her answer?

$52 \div 8 \rightarrow 6$ R4

A 8×6

B $(8 \times 6) + 4$

C $(52 - 8) + 6$

D $(8 \times 6) \times 4$

KEY NS 3.2 page 130

4. $5 \times (4 + 3) = \square \times 7$

A 35

B 5

C 4

D 3

KEY AF 2.2 page 152

5. What is the value of *x*?

$x - 14 = 20$

A 34

B 25

C 20

D 6

Test Tip
Remember, the values of each side of an equation are always equal.

KEY AF 2.0 page 174

6. Look at the problem below.

$\triangle = \square + 8$

If $\square = 3$, what is $\triangle$?

A 3

B 5

C 8

D 11

KEY AF 1.5 page 196

Education Place
Visit www.eduplace.com/camap/ for **Test-Taking Tips** and **Extra Practice.**

Unit 4 Test

Vocabulary and Concepts — AF 1.1, MR 2.3 Chapters 8–9

Write *true* or *false* for the statements.

1. An algebraic expression contains one or more variables.
2. To solve an algebraic equation, find the value for the variable that makes the equation true.

Computation — AF 1.1, KEY AF 2.0, KEY AF 2.1, KEY AF 2.2, KEY AF 1.5 Chapter 8, Lessons 1–2

Evaluate each expression when $y = 4$.

3. $7y$
4. $15 + y$
5. $y + 7 \times 2$
6. $28 \div y$
7. $(10 \times 3) - (3 \times y)$
8. $80 + (5 \times y)$

Solve the equation. Tell what number you added to or subtracted from both sides. Chapter 8, Lesson 3

9. $x + 14 = 32$
10. $45 = m + 9$
11. $38 = p - 12$

Solve the equation. Tell what number you multiplied or divided each side by. Chapter 8, Lesson 4

12. $9d = 63$
13. $p \div 54 = 1$
14. $c \div 6 = 6$

Copy and complete. Chapter 9, Lessons 2–3

	Rule: Output = $k - 10$	
	Input (k)	Output
15.	16	
16.	20	
17.	24	

	Rule: $h = g \div 6$	
	Input (g)	Output (h)
18.	24	
19.	36	
20.	48	

21.

Rule: ___?___	
Input (s)	Output (t)
5	40
8	64
10	80

Problem Solving and Reasoning — KEY AF 2.1, KEY AF 1.5, KEY AF 2.2, MR 2.3 Chapter 9, Lesson 4

Write an equation to solve. Show your work.

22. There were 18 people in the book club. Four people moved away. Then some new people joined the book club. If there are 17 people in the book club now, how many new people joined?

23. A dog walker walks 6 small dogs and 4 large dogs. Another dog walker walks twice as many small dogs and half as many large dogs. How many dogs d does the second dog walker walk?

24. Jen charges \$8 an hour to pet sit. Write a rule and make a function table to show how much she makes after pet sitting for 2, 4, and 6 hours. Let a equal the hours worked.

25. Derek orders books from his favorite series over the Internet. Each book b costs \$6 and the shipping charge is \$2 per order. Use the rule $c = 6b + 2$ and a function table to find c, the cost of 4, 6, and 10 books.

BIG IDEA!

Writing Math The output values (y) in a function table are 13, 16, and 19. The rule for the table is $y = 3x + 1$. What are the input values (x)? Explain how you got your answers.

Performance Assessment

Which Puppy? AF 1.0, KEY AF 1.5

Haley can adopt a puppy as long as it weighs less than 25 pounds when it is half-grown at 6 months old. Which puppy should Haley adopt?

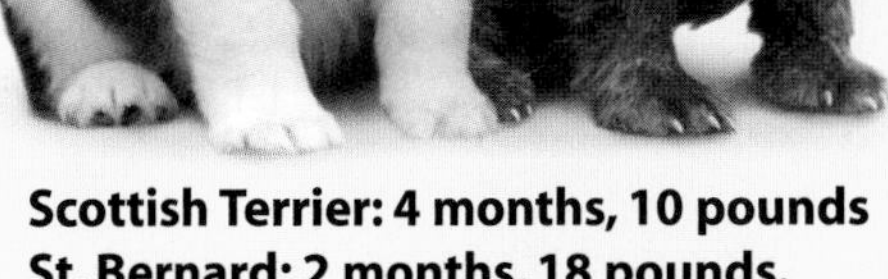

Scottish Terrier: 4 months, 10 pounds
St. Bernard: 2 months, 18 pounds.

Task	Information You Need
Use the information above and on the right to decide which puppy Haley should adopt. Use function tables to help you find the answer.	The puppy must weigh less than 25 pounds when it is 6 months old.
	The Scottish Terrier's weight will increase by 3 pounds per month until it is 6 months old.
	The St. Bernard's weight will increase by 4 pounds per month until it is 6 months old.

Greg Tang's Go Fast, Go Far

Unit 4 Mental Math Strategies

Multiply by 9

A group of 9 requires tact, start with 10 and then subtract!

I have a fast way to multiply 9 × 8. Instead of 9 groups of 8, I start with 10 groups of 8 because it's easier. 10 × 8 = 80, then to get 9, I subtract one 8 to get 72. A group of 9 is easier as 10 take away 1!

1. 9 × 8 = [80] − [8] = [72]
(10 × 8) (1 × 8)

2. 9 × 12 = ■ − ■ = ■
(10 × 12) (1 × 12)

3. 9 × 6 = ■ − ■ = ■
(10 × 6) (1 × 6)

4. 9 × 7 = [70] − ■ = ■
(10 × 7) (1 × 7)

Great work!

5. 9 × 3 = ■ − ■ = ■

6. 9 × 9 = ■ − ■ = ■

7. 9 × 11 = ■ − ■ = ■

8. 9 × 20 = ■ − ■ = ■

Doing Great!

Take It Further!

Now try doing all the steps in your head!

9. 9 × 5

10. 9 × 10

11. 9 × 4

12. 9 × 40

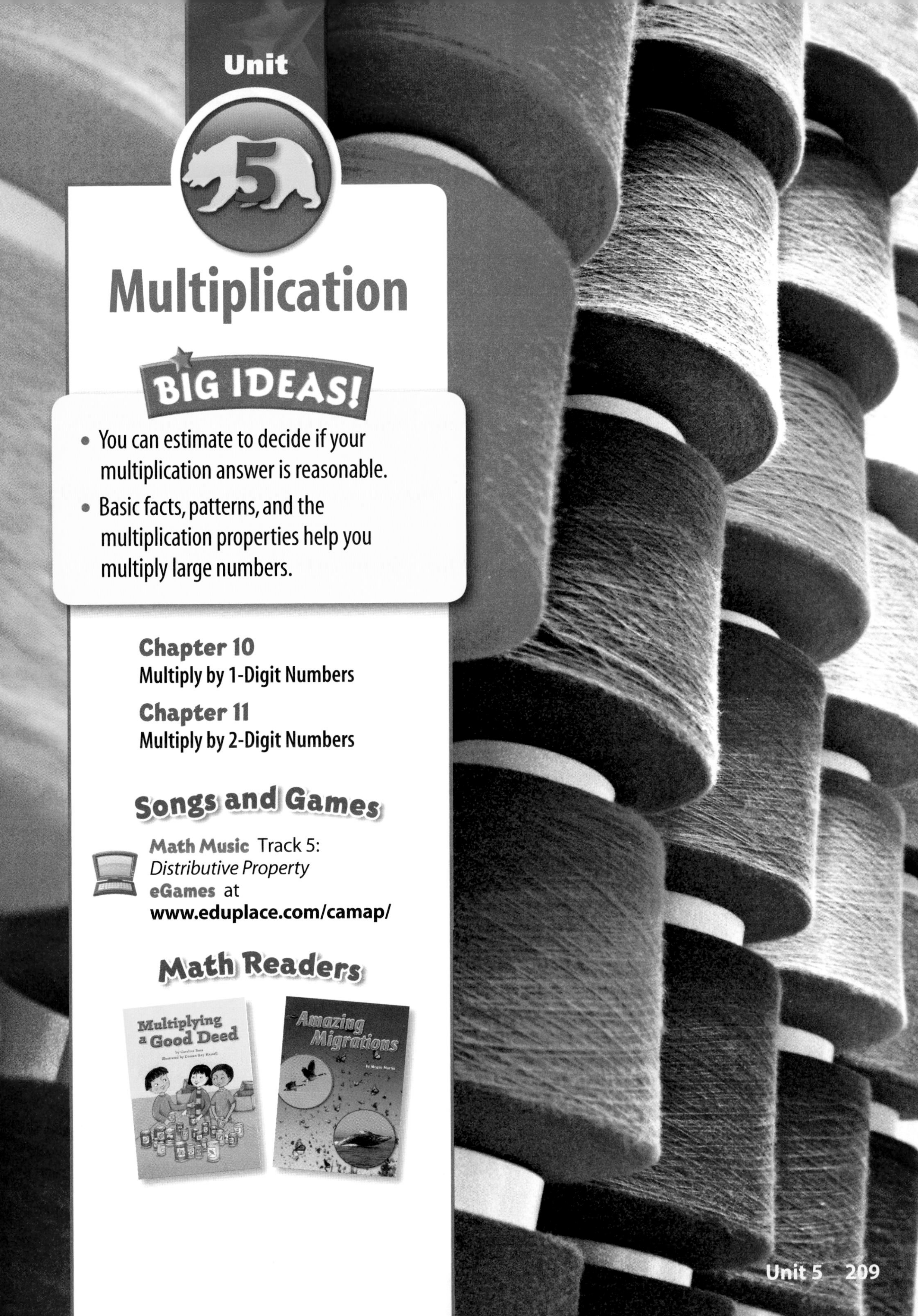

Unit 5

Multiplication

BIG IDEAS!

- You can estimate to decide if your multiplication answer is reasonable.
- Basic facts, patterns, and the multiplication properties help you multiply large numbers.

Songs and Games

Math Music Track 5: *Distributive Property*
eGames at
www.eduplace.com/camap/

Math Readers

Get Ready **Game**

Multiply and Add!

Object of the Game Multiply one-digit numbers and add one-digit numbers to earn ten points first.

Materials

- Learning Tool 12 (Digit and Symbol Cards) (1 set of digit cards 0–9)
- Learning Tool 18 (*Multiply and Add!* Game Board)

Set Up

Shuffle and make a stack of all the digit cards.

Number of Players 2–4

How to Play

1. Each player takes three cards from the stack. Players fill in the boxes on their game boards with the numbers they chose.
2. Players find the value of their expressions.
3. Players compare values. The player who has the greatest value gets one point. If players are tied for the greatest value, then each gets one point.
4. Shuffle the cards again and continue. The first player to reach 10 points is the winner.

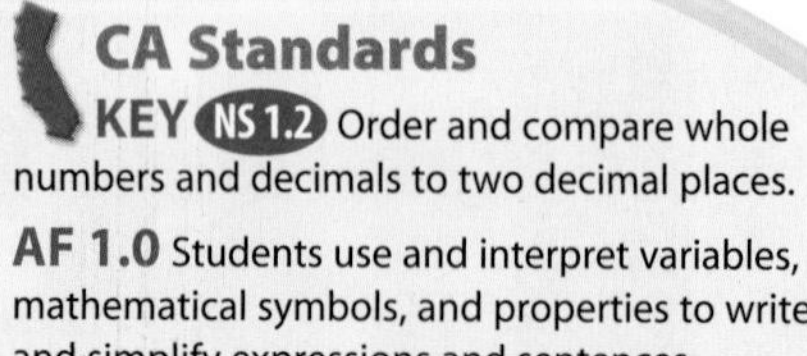

CA Standards

KEY NS 1.2 Order and compare whole numbers and decimals to two decimal places.

AF 1.0 Students use and interpret variables, mathematical symbols, and properties to write and simplify expressions and sentences.

Education Place

Visit www.eduplace.com/camap/ for **Brain Teasers** and **eGames** to play.

Reading & Writing Math

Reading When you read a story, you can look at the illustrations to help you visualize or picture what is happening. You can use pictures or models to help you visualize math.

Read the problem. Use the sketch to help you visualize.

Rosie helps out at her mom's store on Saturdays. She earns $15 each time! If she works for 6 Saturdays, how much will she earn?

$10	$5
$10	$5
$10	$5
$10	$5
$10	$5
$10	$5

I can sketch the bills to visualize the problem and find a way to solve it.

Writing Here's a sketched picture. Work with a partner to write at least 2 different word problems the sketch suggests.

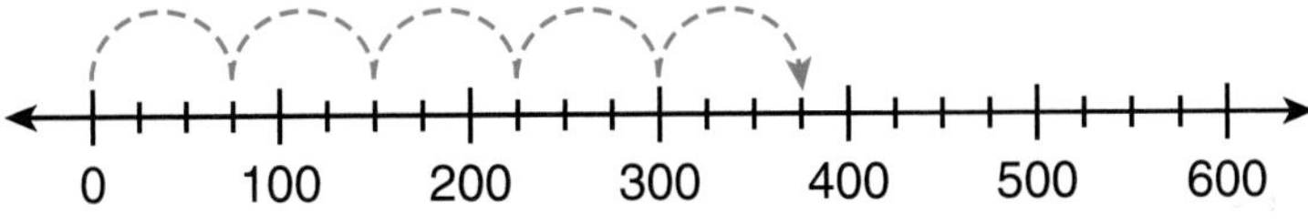

Chapter 10

Multiply by 1-Digit Numbers

Check What You Know

Word Bank
addends
factors
regrouping
skip counting
sum
product

Vocabulary and Concepts GRADE 3 NS 2.0, MR 2.3

Choose the best word or term to complete the sentence.

1. When you multiply two numbers, the answer is the ____.
2. When you rename a number using place value, you are ____.
3. The numbers that you multiply are called ____.

Skills GRADE 3 NS 2.0

Write a multiplication sentence for each.

4. $25 + 25 + 25 = 75$
5. $40 + 40 + 40 + 40 + 40 = 200$
6. $302 + 302 + 302 + 302 = 1{,}208$

Find the product.

7. 23×2
8. 3×300
9. $6 \times 2{,}000$

Problem Solving and Reasoning GRADE 3 KEY NS 2.2

10. When you use Jake's favorite number as a factor, the product is always twice the other factor. What is Jake's favorite number?

Vocabulary

Visualize It!

multiply
to combine equal groups

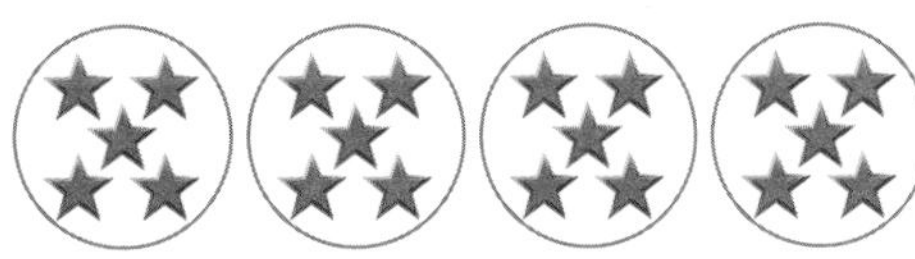

$4 \times 5 = 20$

factors
the numbers used in a multiplication problem

product
the answer in a multiplication problem

Language Tips

Factor has many meanings. For example, it can mean *something that contributes to an outcome*, as in *hard work is often the greatest factor in success.* In mathematics, a *factor* is a number that is used in a multiplication problem.

Words that look alike in English and Spanish often have the same meaning.

English	Spanish
sum	suma
product	producto
multiply	multiplicar
factor	factor

See **English-Spanish Glossary** pages 644–666.

Education Place Visit www.eduplace.com/camap/ for the **eGlossary** and **eGames**.

CA Standards MR 2.3 Use a variety of methods, such as words, numbers, symbols, charts, graphs, tables, diagrams, and models, to explain mathematical reasoning. **Also KEY NS 3.2**

CA Standards
KEY NS 3.0 Students solve problems involving addition, subtraction, multiplication, and division of whole numbers and understand the relationships among the operations.

Prepares for KEY NS 3.2 Demonstrate an understanding of, and the ability to use, standard algorithms for multiplying a multidigit number by a two-digit number and for dividing a multidigit number by a one-digit number; use relationships between them to simplify computations and to check results.

Also MR 1.0, MR 1.1, MR 1.2, MR 2.0, MR 2.2, MR 2.3, MR 2.4, MR 3.0, MR 3.3

Materials
- Workmat 2
- base-ten blocks
- eManipulatives (optional) www.eduplace.com/camap/

Hands On
Multiply 2-Digit Numbers by 1-Digit Numbers

Objective Use base-ten blocks to model multiplication.

Explore

In Chapter 6, you learned about the relationship between multiplication and division. In this lesson, you will model multiplying a 2-digit number by a 1-digit number.

Question How can you use base-ten blocks to find a product?

Yo-Yo-Mania received 3 boxes of yo-yos. Each box holds 32 yo-yos. How many yo-yos did the store receive?

Work with a partner to find 3×32.

1 Use base-ten blocks to show 3 groups of 32.

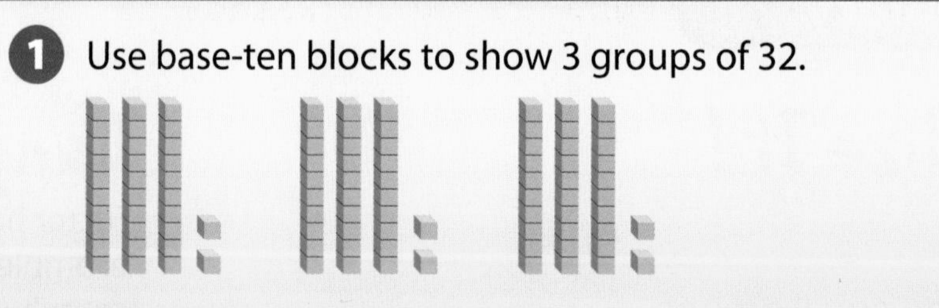

2 Count the tens blocks. 3×3 tens $= 9$ tens, or 90

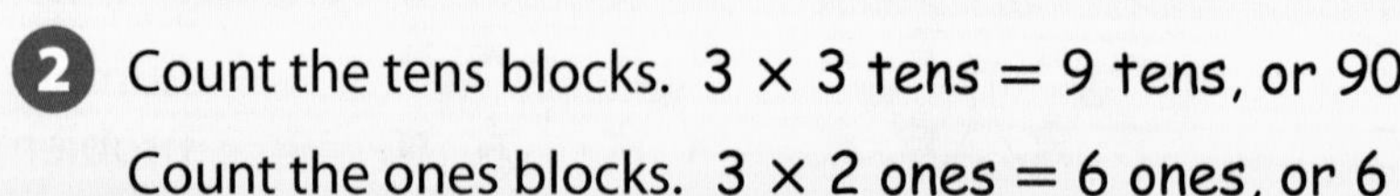

Count the ones blocks. 3×2 ones $= 6$ ones, or 6

3 Record your work on Workmat 2.

$3 \times 32 = 96$

tens	ones
9	6

Solution: The store received 96 yo-yos.

Suppose the store received 2 boxes of 26 yo-yos.
How many yo-yos did the store receive?

Now find 2 × 26.

1 Use base-ten blocks to show 2 groups of 26.

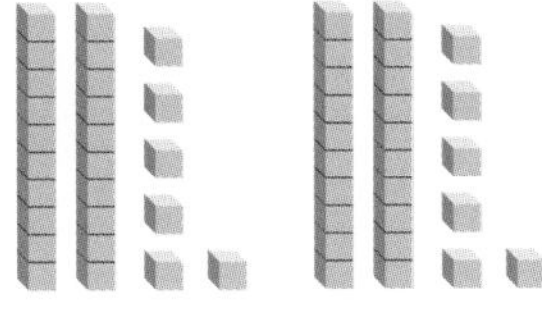

2 × 2 tens = 4 tens

2 × 6 ones = 12 ones

2 Put the tens together. Put the ones together. Regroup 10 ones as 1 ten.

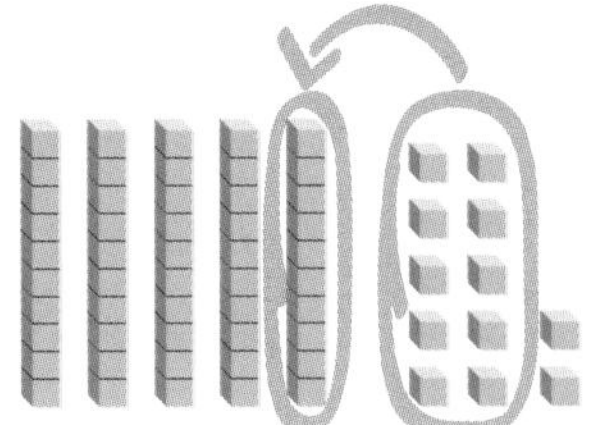

3 Record your work on Workmat 2.

2 × 26 = 52

Solution: The store received 52 yo-yos.

Extend

Tell what multiplication sentence the blocks show.

1. 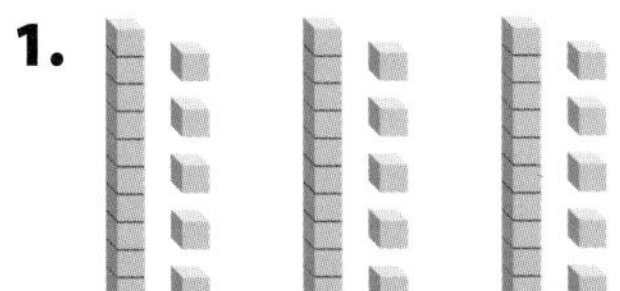

2. 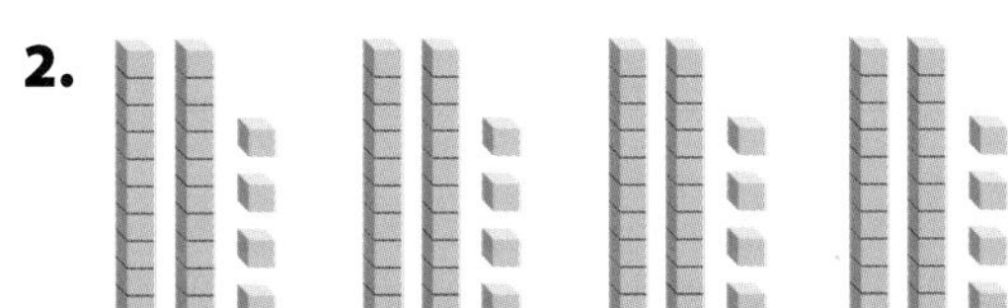

Use base-ten blocks to find the product.

3. 3 × 31 **4.** 2 × 18 **5.** 4 × 21 **6.** 3 × 22

7. 5 × 15 **8.** 2 × 27 **9.** 7 × 13 **10.** 4 × 16

11. **Multistep** (3 + 2) × (9 + 5)

12. **Challenge** How can you use the product of 3 × 15 to find the product of 9 × 15? Use a drawing to help you explain your answer.

Writing Math

Generalize Can you tell if you will need to regroup just by looking at the numbers in the problem? Support your answer.

Estimate Products

Objective Estimate products by rounding factors.

CA Standards
KEY NS 1.4 Decide when a rounded solution is called for and explain why such a solution may be appropriate.

MR 2.5 Indicate the relative advantages of exact and approximate solutions to problems and give answers to a specified degree of accuracy.

Also KEY NS 1.3, KEY NS 3.0, MR 1.0, MR 1.1, MR 1.2, MR 2.0, MR 2.3, MR 2.4, MR 3.0, MR 3.1, MR 3.2, MR 3.3

Vocabulary

5 ← **factors**
× 8 ←
40 ← **product**

Learn by Example

In Lesson 1, you explored multiplication. In this lesson, you will learn how to estimate **products**.

Simon's hometown of Marysville is having a Peach Festival. Suppose last year, 7,911 visitors came to the festival. The market's director expects about twice as many to come this year. About how many visitors are expected this year?

Since the question asks *about* how many, you do not need to find an exact product. You can estimate the product by rounding the 4-digit **factor**, 7,911, to its greatest place.

1 Round 7,911 to the nearest thousand.

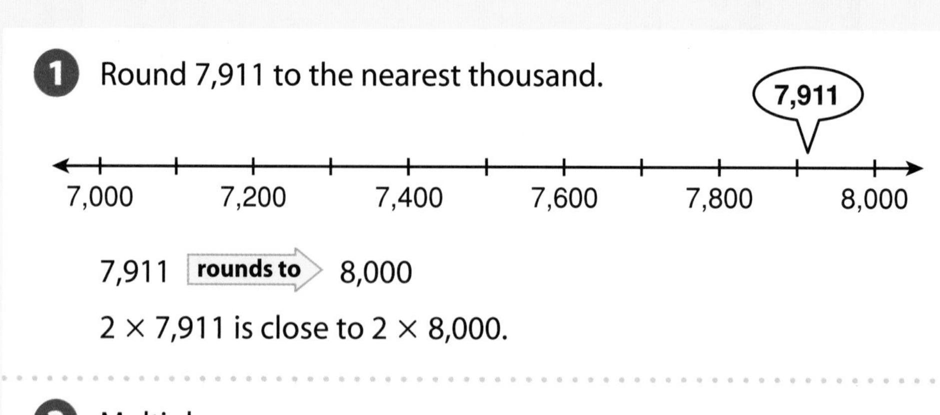

7,911 **rounds to** 8,000

2 × 7,911 is close to 2 × 8,000.

2 Multiply.

2 × 8 = 16, so

2 × 8,000 = 16,000.

16,000 is a high estimate because 7,911 was rounded up to 8,000. The actual product is *less than* 16,000.

The actual product is *greater than* 2 × 7,000, or 14,000.

So, it is between 14,000 and 16,000.

Solution: Fewer than 16,000 visitors are expected to come this year.

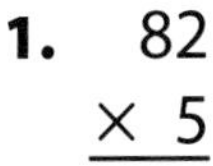

Guided Practice

Round the larger factor to the greatest place. Then estimate the product.

1. 82×5 **2.** 423×9 **3.** 781×6 **4.** 817×8

5. 28×2 **6.** 186×4 **7.** $1{,}995 \times 7$

Ask Yourself

What does the larger factor round to?

Guided Problem Solving

Use the questions to solve this problem.

8. Mr. Lai has 4 boxes with 144 clementines in each. Mr. Lai says the total number of clementines is 576. Use estimation to decide if his total is reasonable.

- **a. Understand** What are you asked to find out? Do you need an exact answer or an estimate?
- **b. Plan** Make two estimates for the total number of clementines. Find a low and a high estimate.
- **c. Solve** Is 576 between your two estimates? Is Mr. Lai's total reasonable?
- **d. Look Back** Is your low estimate or your high estimate closer to the actual total number of clementines? How did you decide?

9. Suppose Mr. Lai had said the total number of clementines was 986. Would this total be reasonable? Why or why not?

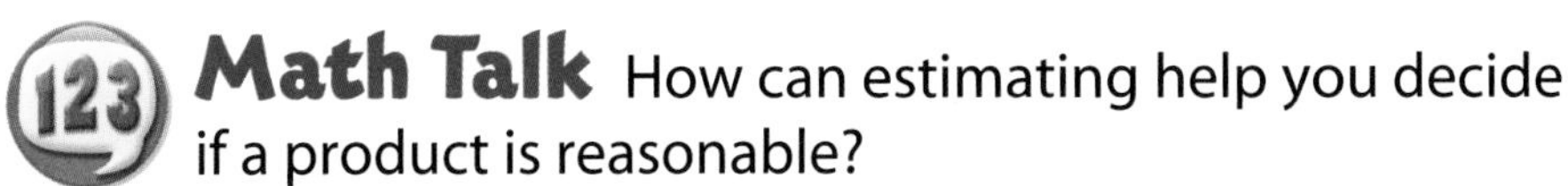

Math Talk How can estimating help you decide if a product is reasonable?

Practice and Problem Solving

Round the larger factor to the greatest place. Then estimate the product.

10. 55×4 **11.** 939×2 **12.** $4{,}598 \times 3$ **13.** 874×6 **14.** 737×8

15. 73×7 **16.** $1{,}914 \times 3$ **17.** 735×3 **18.** 993×6

Science Link

Solve.

19. A sunflower seed sprouted in Ming's garden. At the end of 2 weeks, the plant was 19 cm tall. After 3 months, the plant was 9 times as tall. About how tall was the plant after 3 months?

20. Multistep Roberto's garden has 4 sunflowers with 18 heads each and 3 sunflowers with 12 heads each. About how many sunflower heads is this in all?

21. One sunflower head on Ming's plant has 628 seeds.

a. Ming estimates that the total number of seeds on 3 of the sunflower heads is about 1,800. Is her estimate lower or higher than the actual number?

b. Ming's brother estimates that there are about 2,100 seeds in total. Is his estimate lower or higher than the actual number?

c. Analyze Do you think the actual total is closer to 1,800 seeds or to 1,900 seeds? Explain.

Sunflowers

- Sunflowers are native to North America.
- Some sunflowers can have 20 or more heads (flowers) on the same stalk.
- Bees and other insects pollinate sunflowers.
- Sunflower seeds are an important food source for birds and other wildlife.

Science LS 3.c

Spiral Review and Test Practice

Use multiplication properties and division rules to solve. AF 1.1, KEY NS 3.0 page 124

22. $7 \times 4 = 4 \times \square$

23. $\square \times 6 = 6$

24. $15 \div \square = 1$

Write the letter of the correct answer. KEY NS 1.3

25. Chris sold 4 crates of golf balls. Each crate held 4,896 golf balls. Approximately how many golf balls did Chris sell?

A 5,000 **B** 15,000 **C** 20,000 **D** 25,000

Extra Practice See page 229, Set A.

Key Standards Review

Need Help?
See Key Standards Handbook.

Solve. KEY AF 2.1, AF 1.0

1. $62 + 7 = 62 + \square$
2. $46 + 823 = \square + 40 + 6$
3. $52 + 915 = \square + 50 + 2$
4. $93 + 15 = \square + 93$

If $S = T$, tell whether each statement is true or false. KEY AF 2.1, AF 1.0

5. $S + 6 = T + 6$
6. $S + 3 = 9 + T$
7. $S > T$
8. $S < T$
9. $S + 1 = T \times 1$
10. $S - T = T - S$

Algebra Functions

Complete each function table. KEY AF 1.5

11.

Rule: $y = 2x + 4$	
x	y
5	14
■	18
9	■
11	■
■	30

12.

Rule: $y = 4x - 1$	
x	y
3	11
5	■
7	■
■	35
■	43

Number Sense

Greater Than or Less Than?

Choose the correct answer. Try to use mental math. KEY NS 3.0

1. Which product is less than 1,500?

   2×812 or 4×369

2. Which product is greater than 2,500?

   3×875 or 6×275

3. Which product is greater than 1,000?

   5×220 or 9×99

4. Which product is less than 3,000?

   4×701 or 5×689

CA Standards
KEY NS 3.0 Students solve problems involving addition, subtraction, multiplication, and division of whole numbers and understand the relationships among the operations.

MR 2.1 Use estimation to verify the reasonableness of calculated results.

Also AF 1.1, KEY AF 1.5, MR 1.0, MR 1.2, MR 2.0, MR 2.2, MR 2.3, MR 2.4, MR 2.6, MR 3.1

Multiply Greater Numbers

Objective Multiply 3- and 4-digit numbers by 1-digit numbers.

Learn by Example

You can use what you learned in Lessons 1 and 2 to find the product of greater numbers.

A music store has 1,952 CDs and DVDs on sale for $3 each. What is the value of these CDs and DVDs?

Multiply. $3 \times 1{,}952 = n$

1 Multiply the ones.
3×2 ones $= 6$ ones

$$\begin{array}{r} 1{,}952 \\ \times \quad 3 \\ \hline 6 \end{array}$$

2 Multiply the tens.
3×5 tens $= 15$ tens

$$\begin{array}{r} \scriptstyle 1 \quad \\ 1{,}952 \\ \times \quad 3 \\ \hline 56 \end{array}$$

Regroup 15 tens as 1 hundred and 5 tens.

3 Multiply the hundreds.
3×9 hundreds $= 27$ hundreds

Add the 1 regrouped hundred.
$27 + 1 = 28$ hundreds

$$\begin{array}{r} \scriptstyle 2\ 1 \quad \\ 1{,}952 \\ \times \quad 3 \\ \hline 856 \end{array}$$

Regroup 28 hundreds as 2 thousands and 8 hundreds.

4 Multiply the thousands.
3×1 thousand $= 3$ thousands

Add the 2 regrouped thousands.
$3 + 2 = 5$ thousands

$$\begin{array}{r} \scriptstyle 2\ 1 \quad \\ 1{,}952 \\ \times \quad 3 \\ \hline 5{,}856 \end{array}$$

Check

Estimate to check the reasonableness of your answer.

1,952 **rounds to** 2,000 $3 \times 2{,}000 = \$6{,}000$

The value must be less than $6,000, so $5,856 is a reasonable answer.

Think

The value must be greater than $3 × 1,000, or $3,000. So, the actual product is between $3,000 and $6,000, but closer to $6,000.

Solution: The value of the CDs and DVDs is $5,856.

Guided Practice

Multiply. Use estimation to check.

1. 112×2
2. 952×3
3. $4{,}126 \times 8$
4. $2{,}211 \times 6$
5. $3{,}786 \times 5$
6. $5{,}991 \times 4$

Ask Yourself

- Do I need to regroup the ones, tens, or hundreds?
- Do I need to add any regrouped tens, hundreds, or thousands?

Math Talk When multiplying larger numbers, do you always need to regroup? Explain your answer.

Practice and Problem Solving

Multiply. Use estimation to check.

7. 321×2
8. $7{,}342 \times 9$
9. $7{,}195 \times 3$
10. $7{,}492 \times 4$
11. $9{,}225 \times 6$
12. $5{,}562 \times 7$
13. $14{,}218 \times 5$
14. $21{,}254 \times 8$

Copy and complete.

	Rule: $b = a \times 3$	
	Input (a)	Output (b)
15.	243	
16.	596	
17.	721	

	Rule: $q = p \times 7$	
	Input (p)	Output (q)
18.	329	
19.	776	
20.	2,128	

	Rule: $w = v \times 4$	
	Input (v)	Output (w)
21.	1,415	
22.	2,632	
23.	4,998	

Solve.

24. Tahni buys 2 rolls of blue streamers and 4 rolls of red streamers at the party store. Each roll is 1,124 inches long. How many inches of streamers are in the 6 rolls?

25. Would the answer to Problem 24 change if there were 4 rolls of blue streamers and 2 rolls of red streamers?

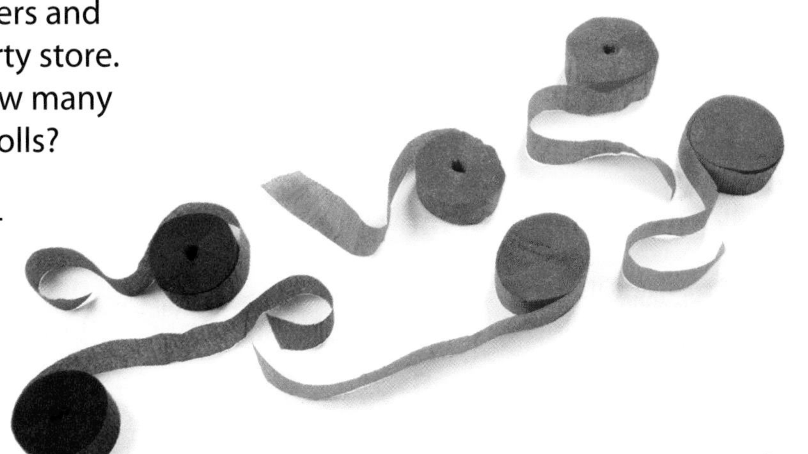

26. Multistep A grocery store is raising money for a local charity. If 1,173 shoppers each contributed \$2 and 946 shoppers each contributed \$3, how much money was raised?

27. Explain The mall is open from 10 A.M. until 8 P.M. every day. About 125 people per hour enter the mall on a weekday. If twice as many people enter on the weekend, about how many people enter the mall on a Saturday? Explain.

Real World Data

Use the table to solve.

Driving Distance from Los Angeles	
City	**Distance (miles)**
Sacramento, CA	385
Seattle, WA	1,145
Salt Lake City, UT	688
Portland, OR	964

28. Algebra Ann lives in Los Angeles. Her brother lives three times as far from Ann as Ann lives from Sacramento. Write and solve an equation that shows the distance from Ann's house to her brother's house. Let *m* stand for the number of miles.

29. Multistep Last year, Ann made four round trips to Seattle. How many miles did she drive on these four trips altogether? Hint: To find a round-trip distance, multiply the one-way distance by 2.

30. Multistep Ann will go to either Salt Lake City or Portland for a vacation. How much farther will she drive round trip if she chooses Portland?

Spiral Review and Test Practice

Solve the equation. Check the solution. KEY AF 2.0, KEY AF 2.1, KEY AF 2.2 pages 174, 176

31. $x + 13 = 25$ **32.** $6p = 42$ **33.** $h \div 3 = 6$ **34.** $a - 57 = 41$

Write the letter of the correct answer. KEY NS 3.0

35. Tickets to a sports event cost \$5. If 9,749 people attend the event, what is the total amount spent on tickets?

A \$48,545 **B** \$48,745 **C** \$45,745 **D** \$48,705

Extra Practice See page 229, Set B.

Plan a Wedding

Event planners are hired to put together events such as large parties or weddings. If you become an event planner, every day can be a party!

Solve.

1. One hundred eighteen people will be at a wedding dinner. Each person will need a salad fork, a dinner fork, a dessert fork, a spoon, and a knife. How many pieces of silverware will the planner need?

2. Invitations to a wedding are sent to guests with an outer envelope, a decorative envelope, and a return envelope. If 146 invitations are sent out, how many envelopes will be needed?

3. A band performs at weddings for $215 an hour. If they perform for 6 hours, how much will they be paid?

4. **Multistep** The wedding planner has 9 boxes of place cards. Each box holds 125 cards. How many will he have left after he uses 198 for a wedding?

CA Standards
KEY NS 3.0 Students solve problems involving addition, subtraction, multiplication, and division of whole numbers and understand the relationships among the operations.
MR 2.1 Use estimation to verify the reasonableness of calculated results.
Also AF 1.0, AF 1.1, MR 1.2, MR 2.0, MR 2.2, MR 2.3, MR 2.4, MR 2.6

Multiply with Zeros

Objective Multiply numbers that have zeros.

Learn by Example

A t-shirt company inventory shows 2,007 t-shirts each in 6 sizes: XS, S, M, L, XL, and XXL. How many t-shirts are in the warehouse?

Vocabulary Tip
An **inventory** is a list of the number of kinds of items.

Multiply. $6 \times 2,007 = n$

1 Multiply the ones.
$6 \times 7 = 42$ ones

$$\begin{array}{r} \scriptstyle 4 \\ 2,007 \\ \times \quad 6 \\ \hline 2 \end{array}$$

Regroup 42 ones as 4 tens and 2 ones.

2 Multiply the tens.
$6 \times 0 = 0$ tens

Add the 4 regrouped tens.
$0 + 4 = 4$ tens

$$\begin{array}{r} \scriptstyle 4 \\ 2,007 \\ \times \quad 6 \\ \hline 42 \end{array}$$

3 Multiply the hundreds.
$6 \times 0 = 0$ hundreds

$$\begin{array}{r} \scriptstyle 4 \\ 2,007 \\ \times \quad 6 \\ \hline 042 \end{array}$$

4 Multiply the thousands.
$6 \times 2 = 12$ thousands

$$\begin{array}{r} \scriptstyle 4 \\ 2,007 \\ \times \quad 6 \\ \hline 12,042 \end{array}$$

Regroup 12 thousands as 1 ten thousand and 2 thousands.

Check
Estimate to check the reasonableness of your answer.
2,007 **rounds to** 2,000 $\qquad 6 \times 2,000 = 12,000$
The number of t-shirts must be greater than 12,000, so 12,042 is a reasonable answer.

Think
The number of t-shirts must be less than $6 \times 3,000$, or 18,000. So, the actual product is between 12,000 and 18,000, but much closer to 12,000.

Solution: There are 12,042 t-shirts in the warehouse.

Guided Practice

Multiply. Use estimation to check.

1. 790×3 **2.** 205×4 **3.** $3,205 \times 2$ **4.** $4,900 \times 9$

Ask Yourself

- Do I need to do any regrouping?
- Do I need to add any regrouped numbers?

Math Talk If you multiply 3,406 by 3, will the product have a zero in the tens place? Why or why not?

Practice and Problem Solving

Multiply. Use estimation to check.

5. 109×2 **6.** 705×5 **7.** $6,003 \times 8$ **8.** $3,860 \times 3$ **9.** $5,900 \times 6$

10. 908 × 8 **11.** 1,076 × 6 **12.** 6,040 × 5 **13.** 8,900 × 7 **14.** 9,095 × 9

Solve.

15. In the summer, a store sells 8 times as many shorts as pants.

a. **Multistep** If the store sold 1,019 pants one summer, how many shorts and pants did the store sell in all?

b. **Challenge** Complete the expression to show the total number of shorts and pants sold that summer.

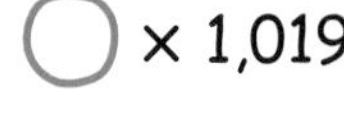

Spiral Review and Test Practice

Copy and complete. AF 1.1, KEY AF 1.5 page 196

	Rule: $b = a + 3$	
	Input (a)	Output (b)
16.	3	
17.	5	

	Rule: $n = 2m$	
	Input (m)	Output (n)
18.	2	
19.	7	

	Rule: $q = p \div 4$	
	Input (p)	Output (q)
20.	12	
21.	20	

Write the letter of the correct answer. KEY NS 3.0

22. There are 8 shelves in a bookstore. Each shelf has 2,500 books. How many books is this in all?

A 2,000 **B** 26,000 **C** 20,000 **D** 200,000

Extra Practice See page 229, Set C.

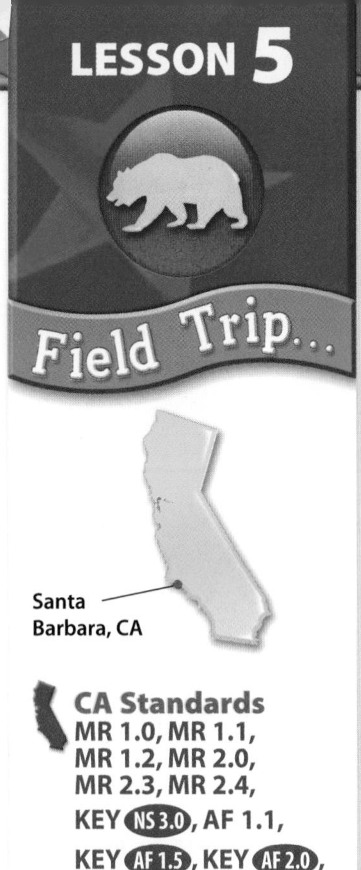

CA Standards
MR 1.0, MR 1.1, MR 1.2, MR 2.0, MR 2.3, MR 2.4, KEY NS 3.0, AF 1.1, KEY AF 1.5, KEY AF 2.0, KEY AF 2.2

Problem Solving

Objective Use skills and strategies to solve word problems.

At a farmer's market, you can meet the farmers who grow the food you buy!

The Santa Barbara Certified Farmer's Market sells only organically grown, local produce.

- **Organically grown** means there were no harmful chemicals used.
- About 75 million acres are farmed organically worldwide.

Solve. Tell which strategy or method you used.

1. **Multistep** In the morning, a farmer has 3 baskets of avocados with 135 avocados in each. At the end of the day, he has 68 avocados left. How many did he sell?

2. Use the function table.
   a. Write a two-variable equation that shows how b and c are related.
   b. What would be the cost of 12 bags?

Input: Number of bags of chard (b)	Output: Cost of chard in dollars (c)
1	\$3
2	\$6
3	\$9

3. **Write an Equation** Maneesh buys tomatoes for his homemade tomato sauce. The equation $c = 2p$ shows how the cost (c) and the pounds of tomatoes (p) are related.
   a. Make a function table that shows the price of 1, 2, 3, 4, 5, and 6 pounds of tomatoes.
   b. If Maneesh bought \$16 of tomatoes, how many pounds did he buy? Write and solve an equation.

Problem Solving on Tests

Select a Strategy
- Choose the Operation
- Estimate
- Write an Equation
- Guess and Check
- Work Backward

1. The U.S. Census Bureau estimated that about 9,720,000 people under the age of 18 lived in California in 2005. Which of these is the number 9,720,000?

A nine million, seven hundred two thousand

B nine million, seven hundred twenty thousand

C ninety million, seven hundred twenty thousand

D nine million, seven hundred twenty

KEY NS 1.1 page 12

2. On Monday Carrie read 117 pages of her book. On Tuesday she read 95 pages, and on Wednesday she read 87 pages. Approximately how many pages did Carrie read in the three days?

A 100 pages　**C** 300 pages

B 200 pages　**D** 400 pages

KEY NS 1.4 page 58

3. The Perez family drove 2,040 miles one-way on a trip. On the return trip, they shortened their route by 618 miles. How many miles was their return trip?

A 1,638 miles　**C** 1,432 miles

B 1,622 miles　**D** 1,422 miles

KEY NS 3.1 page 82

4. Naomi is packing her collection of animal figurines in 17 boxes. Each box holds 9 figurines. How many figurines is she packing?

A 26

B 163

C 153

D 8

KEY NS 3.0 page 214

5. John's brother always takes 8 minutes more to get ready for school than John does. In the sentence below, $\triangle$ is John's time and $\square$ is his brother's time.

$$\square = \triangle + 8$$

If $\square = 25$, what is $\triangle$?

A 16

B 17

C 33

D 44

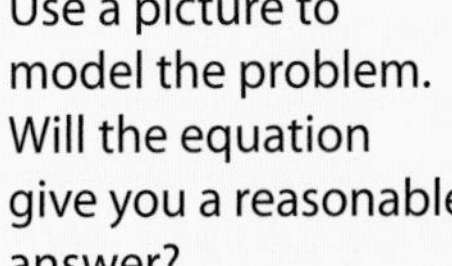

Test Tip
Use a picture to model the problem. Will the equation give you a reasonable answer?

KEY AF 1.5 page 196

Education Place
Visit www.eduplace.com/camap/ for **Test-Taking Tips** and **Extra Practice**.

Vocabulary

Sometimes when you multiply greater numbers, you can **estimate** the **product** by rounding factors to the greatest place value.

A movie theater is expanding its 218 seats to three times that number. About how many seats will the theater have?

Fill in the chart to estimate the product of 3 × 218.

Step 1: Round 218 to the nearest hundred.	218 ⟶ ______ 3 × 218 is close to ______
Step 2: Multiply.	If 3 × 2 = 6, then 3 × 200 = ______
So, the movie theater will have about ______ seats. Is the actual product *greater than* or *less than* the estimate?	

Fill in the chart to estimate the product of 4 × 4,908.

Step 1: Round 4,908 to the nearest thousand.	4,908 ⟶ ______ 4 × 4,908 is close to ______
Step 2: Multiply.	If 4 × 5 = 20, then 4 × 5,000 = ______
So, the product of 4 × 4,908 is about ______. Is the actual product is *greater than* or *less than* the estimate?	

Writing Write down a 1-digit and a 4-digit number and estimate the product. Is your estimation *greater than* or *less than* the actual product? Explain.

Reading Look for this book in your library.
Great Estimations, by Bruce Goldstone

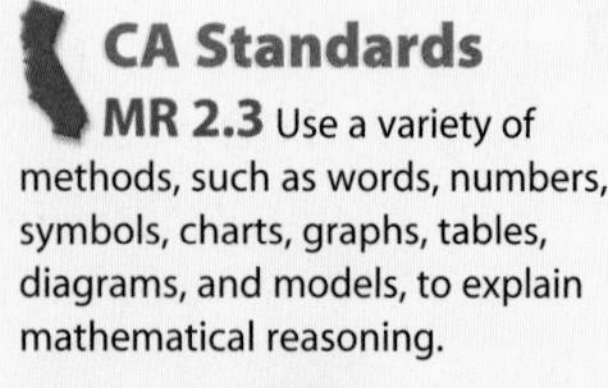
CA Standards
MR 2.3 Use a variety of methods, such as words, numbers, symbols, charts, graphs, tables, diagrams, and models, to explain mathematical reasoning.

Also KEY NS 3.0

Standards-Based Extra Practice

Set A

KEY NS 1.4, MR 2.5 page 216

Round the larger factor to the greatest place. Then estimate the product.

1. 25 × 7
2. 89 × 5
3. 153 × 8
4. 3,832 × 6
5. 786 × 4
6. 77 × 4
7. 2,304 × 9
8. 339 × 2
9. 5,911 × 8
10. 9,099 × 5
11. **Analyze** Supreme Sports Store has just received a shipment of 7 boxes of baseballs. Each box contains 140 baseballs. Give a high and low estimate of the number of baseballs in the shipment. Tell which estimate is closer.

Set B

KEY NS 3.0, MR 2.1 page 220

Multiply. Use estimation to check.

1. 997 × 2
2. 119 × 3
3. 5,863 × 3
4. 9,211 × 9
5. 4,848 × 6
6. **Compare** During summer months, Maryanne works 24 hours a week at Yummy's Bakery for $8 an hour. During school months she works 15 hours a week at Music Mania for $9 an hour. Does Maryanne earn more money per week during the summer or during school? Why?

Set C

KEY NS 3.0, MR 2.1 page 224

Multiply. Use estimation to check.

1. 406 × 5
2. 2,007 × 3
3. 1,099 × 2
4. 903 × 7
5. 5,008 × 5
6. **Analyze** The Fresh Plus grocery store's biggest seller during the summer is six-packs of root beer. Last summer Fresh Plus sold 5,096 six-packs. How many cans did Fresh Plus sell last summer?

Education Place
Visit www.eduplace.com/camap/ for more **Extra Practice.**

Chapter Review/Test

Vocabulary and Concepts

MR 2.3, KEY NS 3.0

Write the best word to complete the sentence.

1. The numbers you multiply in a multiplication sentence to get a product are called ______.
2. To ______ is to find a number close to the exact amount.

Skills

KEY NS 1.3, KEY NS 3.0, MR 2.1

Round the larger factor to the greatest place. Then estimate the product.

3. 97×3
4. 55×5
5. 413×2
6. $4{,}982 \times 8$
7. $7 \times 1{,}307$
8. 4×788
9. 480×5
10. 6×932

Multiply. Use estimation to check.

11. 980×9
12. 406×4
13. $5{,}002 \times 8$
14. $3{,}936 \times 6$
15. 4×750
16. $2{,}247 \times 3$
17. $8 \times 1{,}090$
18. $7 \times 6{,}438$

Problem Solving and Reasoning

MR 2.1, MR 2.5, MR 2.3, KEY NS 3.0

Solve. Use estimation to check.

19. The craft store sells packages of yarn for $4. How much money will the store take in by selling 88 red and 75 blue packages?
20. Janice drives 1,004 miles each month for work. How many miles will she drive in 6 months?

Writing Math How do you know when to regroup ones, tens, and hundreds?

Spiral Review and Test Practice

1. $23 + 68 = 68 + \square$

A 91

B 68

C 45

D 23

AF 1.0 page 54

2. If $5 \times 6 = 30$, then what is $30 \div 5$?

A 35

B 25

C 6

D 5

Test Tip
Remember, multiplication and division are inverse operations.

KEY NS 3.0 page 122

3. What is the value of the expression below?

$24 \div (6 + 2)$

A 3

B 4

C 6

D 32

KEY AF 1.2 page 144

4. Which letter is represented by n?

$2n - 7 = 9$

A 16

B 8

C 7

D 2

KEY AF 2.0 page 176

5. The sum of x plus y equals 15. If $x = 6$, which equation can be used to find the value of y?

A $x + 6 = 15$

B $x - y = 15$

C $y - 6 = 15$

D $6 + y = 15$

KEY AF 1.5 page 196

6. Mr. Lemone owns 3 apple orchards. There are 5,235 trees growing in each orchard. Approximately how many trees are in all of the orchards?

A 18,000 trees

B 15,705 trees

C 15,000 trees

D 10,000 trees

Test Tip
Remember, *approximately* means to find an estimate.

KEY NS 1.3 page 216

Education Place
Visit www.eduplace.com/camap/ for **Test-Taking Tips** and **Extra Practice.**

Multiply by 2-Digit Numbers

Check What You Know

Word Bank
compare
estimate
number line
round

Vocabulary and Concepts KEY NS 1.3, MR 2.1

Choose the best word or term to complete the sentence. pages 32, 216

1. When you _____ 28 to the nearest ten, the answer is 30.
2. You can use a(n) _____ to see if an answer is reasonable.

Skills KEY NS 3.0

Estimate. Then multiply. pages 214, 216

3. 13×5
4. 7×37
5. 3×84

Multiply. page 220

6. 125×6
7. 164×4
8. 325×8
9. 244×5

Problem Solving and Reasoning KEY NS 3.0

10. A baker placed 16 rolls on each of 5 trays. How many rolls did he place on the trays?

Vocabulary

Visualize It!

Distributive Property

the property which states that when two addends are multiplied by a factor, the product is the same as if each addend is multiplied by the factor and those products are added.

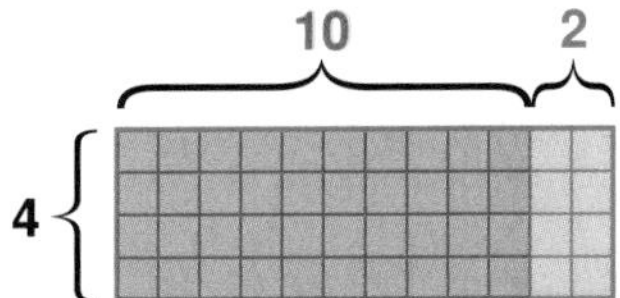

$4 \times 12 = \bigcirc$

$4 \times (10 + 2) = \bigcirc$

$(4 \times 10) + (4 \times 2) = \bigcirc$

$40 + 8 = 48$

Language Tips

When you *distribute* something, you separate it into parts and give the parts away. When you use the *Distributive Property*, you separate a number into parts and then multiply the parts.

Words that look alike in English and Spanish often have the same meaning.

English	Spanish
strategy	estrategia
factor	factor

See **English-Spanish Glossary** pages 644–666.

Education Place Visit www.eduplace.com/camap/ for the **eGlossary** and **eGames**.

CA Standards MR 2.3 Use a variety of methods, such as words, numbers, symbols, charts, graphs, tables, diagrams, and models, to explain mathematical reasoning. **Also AF 1.0**

Hands On
Multiply by Multiples of 10

Objective Use basic multiplication facts and patterns of zeros to multiply mentally.

CA Standards
KEY NS 3.0 Students solve problems involving addition, subtraction, multiplication and division of whole numbers and understand the relationships among the operations.

KEY NS 3.3 Solve problems involving multiplication of multidigit numbers by two-digit numbers.

Also MR 1.0, MR 1.1, MR 1.2, MR 2.0, MR 2.2, MR 2.3, MR 2.4, MR 3.0, MR 3.2, MR 3.3

Materials
- Workmat 1
- Learning Tool 19 ($50 Bills) (2 copies per team)

Explore

Mrs. Phillips sells tickets at the concert hall. Tickets for Saturday night's show are $50. She sold 3,000 tickets. How much money did she collect?

Question How can you use basic facts and patterns to find 3,000 × 50?

Divide your class into 10 teams.

1 Count out thirty $50 bills. Then count the money by making piles of $100.

2 Make a table like the one shown. Record the product for 30 × 50.

Number of $50 Bills	Multiplication Equation
3	3 × 50 = 150
30	30 × 50 = ◯
300	300 × 50 = ◯
3,000	3,000 × 50 = ◯

3 Combine all the money from the 10 teams in your class so that there are three hundred \$50 bills. Then count all the money. Record the product for 300 × 50 in the table.

4 Suppose 10 classes combine all their money so that there are three thousand \$50 bills. Find a pattern of zeros in the table. Use your pattern to find 3,000 × 50. Record the product in the table.

Solution: Mrs. Phillips collected \$150,000.

Extend

Use basic facts and patterns to find the products.

1. 3 × 20
30 × 20
300 × 20
3,000 × 20

2. 6 × 40
60 × 40
600 × 40
6,000 × 40

3. 4 × 50
40 × 50
400 × 50
4,000 × 50

4. 7 × 40
70 × 40
700 × 40
7,000 × 40

5. 8 × 60
80 × 60
800 × 60
8,000 × 60

6. 9 × 30
90 × 30
900 × 30
9,000 × 30

7. **Analyze** Look back at Exercise 3. Each product has one more zero than found in the factors. Explain why.

Find the product. Show the basic fact.

8. 30 × 2

9. 30 × 20

10. 300 × 20

11. 3,000 × 20

12. 200 × 30

13. 60 × 60

14. 70 × 90

15. 600 × 60

16. 3,000 × 80

17. 900 × 20

18. 80 × 40

19. 60 × 50

20. 200 × 50

21. 6,000 × 10

22. 400 × 90

23. 40 × 50

24. 30 × 60

25. 700 × 40

26. 8,000 × 20

27. 400 × 30

Writing Math

What's Wrong? Inez wrote 80 × 50 = 400. Explain what she might have done wrong.

LESSON 2

CA Standards
AF 1.0 Students use and interpret variables, mathematical symbols, and properties to write and simplify expressions and sentences.

KEY NS 3.3 Solve problems involving multiplication of multidigit numbers by two-digit numbers.

Also KEY NS 3.0, MR 1.1, MR 1.2, MR 1.0, MR 3.2, MR 3.0, MR 2.0, MR 2.2, MR 2.3, MR 2.4

Vocabulary

Distributive Property

Materials
- colored pencils, 4 colors
- grid paper

Hands On
Multiply 2-Digit Numbers by 2-Digit Numbers

Objective Use models and the Distributive Property to multiply two 2-digit numbers.

Explore

In this lesson, you will use the **Distributive Property** to multiply 2-digit numbers by 2-digit numbers.

Question How can you use the Distributive Property to multiply greater numbers?

Carla is a baker. Each of her trays holds 21 muffins. If she fills 15 trays, how many muffins will she bake?

Work with a partner. Use models and the Distributive Property to find 15×21.

1 Draw a rectangle on grid paper to show 15×21.

You should have 15 rows with 21 squares in each row.

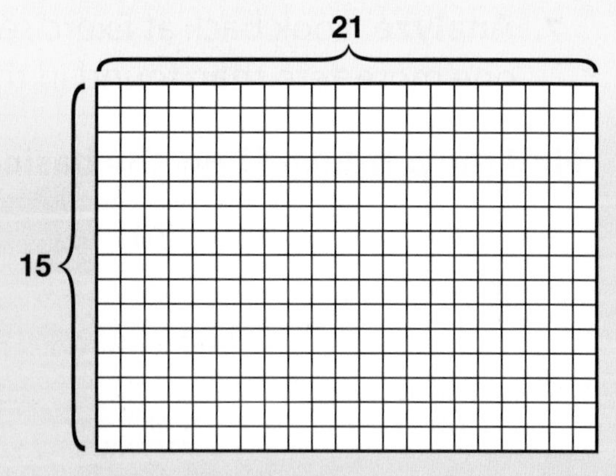

2 $15 = 10 + 5$
Draw a line to separate the factor 15 into the tens place and the ones place.

Now you have two rectangles.

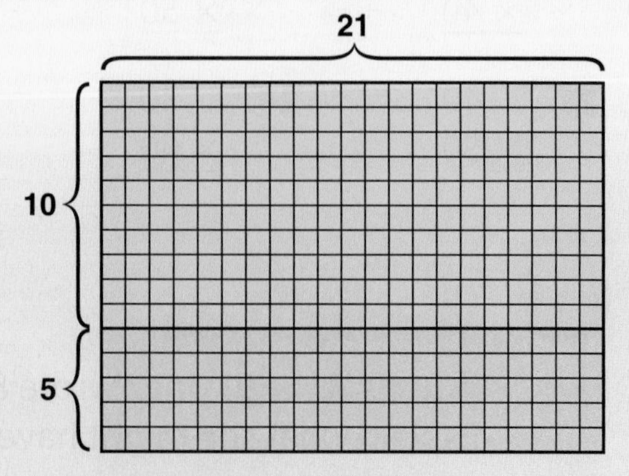

Think

To use the Distributive Property:

1. Write each factor in expanded notation.
2. Multiply each addend by the addends of the other factor.

3 $21 = 20 + 1$

Draw another line to separate the factor 21 into the tens place and the ones place. Label the grid.

Show the multiplication 15×21.

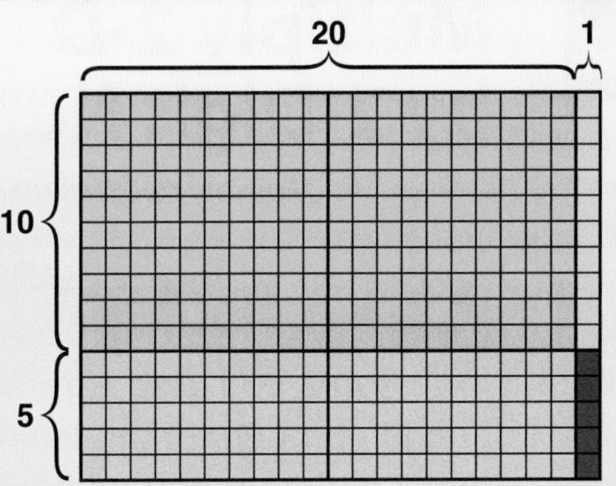

4 Multiply to find all the products. Then add the products.

The sum of the products is equal to the number of squares, 315.

10 rows of 20 →	$10 \times 20 =$	200
10 rows of 1 →	$10 \times 1 =$	10
5 rows of 20 →	$5 \times 20 =$	100
5 rows of 1 →	$5 \times 1 =$	+ 5
		315

5 Use the Distributive Property to record your work.

$(10 \times 20) + (10 \times 1) + (5 \times 20) + (5 \times 1) = \bigcirc$

$200 + 10 + 100 + 5 = 315$

$15 \times 21 = 315$

Solution: Carla will make 315 muffins.

Extend

Use models and the Distributive Property to find the product. Record your work.

1. 23×11 **2.** 13×15 **3.** 20×22 **4.** 12×12 **5.** 18×28

6. Challenge $(10 \times 30) + (10 \times 6) + (4 \times 30) + (4 \times 6) = \blacksquare \times 36$

Writing Math

Connect Write the multiplication equation that the model represents. Then write the equation as the sum of four products.

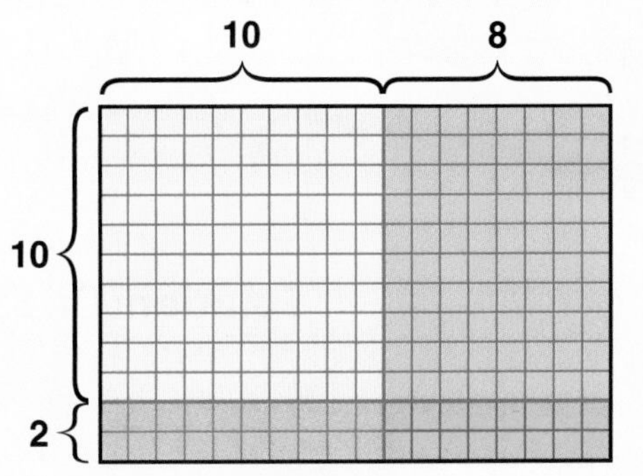

Extra Practice See page 249, Set A.

Multiply 2-Digit Numbers by 2-Digit Numbers

Objective Multiply two 2-digit numbers.

CA Standards
KEY NS 3.2 Demonstrate an understanding of, and the ability to use, standard algorithms for multiplying a multidigit number by a two-digit number and for dividing a multidigit number by a one-digit number; use relationships between them to simplify computations and to check results.

KEY NS 3.3 Solve problems involving multiplication of multidigit numbers by two-digit numbers.

Also KEY NS 3.0, AF 1.0, AF 1.1, KEY AF 1.2, KEY AF 2.0, KEY AF 2.1, MR 1.0, MR 1.1, MR 1.2, MR 2.0, MR 2.2, MR 2.3, MR 2.4, MR 3.0, MR 3.2

Learn by Example

In Lesson 2, you used a model to multiply two 2-digit numbers. In this lesson, you will multiply two 2-digit numbers without using grid paper.

Dr. Sanchez is a geologist. He is putting minerals in a display case for a science exhibit. There are 14 rows in the case. Each row will hold 13 minerals. How many minerals can Dr. Sanchez place in the case?

Multiply. $14 \times 13 = n$

1 Multiply 14 by 3 ones.

$$\begin{array}{r} \overset{1}{14} \\ \times\ 13 \\ \hline 42 \end{array} \leftarrow 14 \times 3$$

2 Multiply 14 by 1 ten.

$$\begin{array}{r} \overset{1}{14} \\ \times\ 13 \\ \hline 42 \\ 140 \end{array} \begin{array}{l} \\ \\ \leftarrow 14 \times 3 \\ \leftarrow 14 \times 10 \end{array}$$

3 Add the products.

$$\begin{array}{r} \overset{1}{14} \\ \times\ 13 \\ \hline 42 \\ +140 \\ \hline 182 \end{array} \begin{array}{l} \\ \\ \leftarrow 14 \times 3 \\ \leftarrow 14 \times 10 \\ \leftarrow (14 \times 3) + (14 \times 10) \end{array}$$

The **Distributive Property** shows why this works.

$14 \times 13 = 14 \times (3 + 10)$

$14 \times 13 = (14 \times 3) + (14 \times 10)$

Solution: Dr. Sanchez can place 182 minerals in the case.

Guided Practice

Multiply.

1. $\begin{array}{r} 31 \\ \times 23 \\ \hline \end{array}$ **2.** $\begin{array}{r} 49 \\ \times 17 \\ \hline \end{array}$ **3.** $\begin{array}{r} 52 \\ \times 36 \\ \hline \end{array}$ **4.** $\begin{array}{r} 22 \\ \times 45 \\ \hline \end{array}$

5. $\begin{array}{r} 68 \\ \times 25 \\ \hline \end{array}$ **6.** $\begin{array}{r} 15 \\ \times 43 \\ \hline \end{array}$ **7.** $\begin{array}{r} 27 \\ \times 79 \\ \hline \end{array}$ **8.** $\begin{array}{r} 19 \\ \times 63 \\ \hline \end{array}$

9. 54×96 **10.** 16×33 **11.** 81×81

Ask Yourself

- What numbers are multiplied first?
- What numbers are multiplied next?
- What do I add to find the product?

Use the Distributive Property to find the value of *n*.

12. $12 \times 5 = (10 \times n) + (2 \times 5)$

13. $(n + 4) \times 15 = 14 \times 15$

Math Talk How does the Distributive Property show how each step works when you multiply?

Fun Fact

Obsidian is a mineral formed when volcanic lava comes in contact with water. It has a dark, glassy appearance.

Practice and Problem Solving

Multiply.

14. $\begin{array}{r} 26 \\ \times 16 \\ \hline \end{array}$ **15.** $\begin{array}{r} 21 \\ \times 31 \\ \hline \end{array}$ **16.** $\begin{array}{r} 34 \\ \times 24 \\ \hline \end{array}$ **17.** $\begin{array}{r} 84 \\ \times 42 \\ \hline \end{array}$ **18.** $\begin{array}{r} 71 \\ \times 63 \\ \hline \end{array}$

19. $\begin{array}{r} 52 \\ \times 25 \\ \hline \end{array}$ **20.** $\begin{array}{r} 63 \\ \times 53 \\ \hline \end{array}$ **21.** $\begin{array}{r} 89 \\ \times 92 \\ \hline \end{array}$ **22.** $\begin{array}{r} 65 \\ \times 29 \\ \hline \end{array}$ **23.** $\begin{array}{r} 25 \\ \times 78 \\ \hline \end{array}$

24. $\begin{array}{r} 37 \\ \times 24 \\ \hline \end{array}$ **25.** $\begin{array}{r} 17 \\ \times 53 \\ \hline \end{array}$ **26.** $\begin{array}{r} 62 \\ \times 31 \\ \hline \end{array}$ **27.** $\begin{array}{r} 14 \\ \times 56 \\ \hline \end{array}$ **28.** $\begin{array}{r} 47 \\ \times 72 \\ \hline \end{array}$

29. 18×30 **30.** 41×50 **31.** 93×70 **32.** 55×60 **33.** 98×90

Use the Distributive Property to find the value of *n*.

34. $21 \times 18 = (20 \times n) + (1 \times 18)$

35. $(n + 7) \times 12 = 17 \times 12$

36. $34 \times 19 = (30 \times 10) + (30 \times 9) + (n \times 10) + (n \times 9)$

Solve.

37. **Analyze** Dr. Sanchez has 214 rock samples. A storage box has space for 12 rows of 16 rocks. Will all of Dr. Sanchez's rocks fit in the box? Explain your answer.

38. **Challenge** Write a multiplication sentence with the greatest possible product. Use the digits 2, 3, 4, and 5 once to make 2 two-digit numbers.

Science Link

Use the Fun Facts to solve.

39. In 55 years, about how many millimeters will the San Andreas Fault move?

40. The Wasatch Fault in Utah is 914 kilometers shorter than the San Andreas Fault. Which equation would you use to find the length of the Wasatch Fault: $n + 914 = 1,300$ or $n - 914 = 1,300$? Solve the equation.

41. You cannot see 175 miles of the San Andreas Fault because it is below the surface of the earth. How many miles of the fault can be seen?

San Andreas Fault

- The San Andreas Fault Zone is more than 1,300 kilometers (800 miles) long.
- During the past 3 million years, the San Andreas Fault Zone has moved about 56 millimeters a year. That is 2 inches a year. This is about how fast your fingernails grow!
- Movement along the fault causes earthquakes.

Science ES 5.a

Spiral Review and Test Practice

Copy and complete. KEY AF 1.5 page 196

	Rule: $s = 3r + 8$	
	Input (r)	Output (s)
42.	6	■
43.	9	■
44.	12	■

	Rule: $b = a \div 4$	
	Input (a)	Output (b)
45.	20	■
46.	24	■
47.	28	■

48.

Rule: ___?___	
Input (p)	Output (q)
2	14
4	28
6	42

Write the letter of the correct answer. KEY NS 3.3

49. Each of 76 art students will decorate 15 ceramic tiles for a mural. How many tiles will be in the finished mural?

A 91 **B** 456 **C** 1,110 **D** 1,140

Extra Practice See page 249, Set B.

Key Standards Review

Need Help?
See Key Standards Handbook.

Solve. Tell whether you used an estimate or an exact answer. Explain your thinking. KEY NS 1.4

1. Eliza has $74. She buys a microscope for $37. Does she have enough money left to buy extra slides for $23?

2. Harry has 309 buttons in his art box. He uses 111 buttons in each full-page collage he makes, and 82 buttons in each half-page collage. Does he have enough buttons to make 2 full-page collages and 1 half-page collage?

3. Charlie has 435 stamps in his collection. He gives 247 stamps to his sister. If his empty stamp book holds 150 stamps, does he have enough stamps left to fill the book?

4. Arthur is reading a 509-page book. So far, he has read 346 pages. How many pages does he have left to read?

Challenge Number Sense

Greatest Product

Arrange each set of digits into two 2-digit numbers whose product is the greatest possible. KEY NS 3.2

1. 9, 0, 2, 3
2. 7, 8, 9, 0
3. 2, 6, 4, 9
4. 0, 1, 5, 9
5. 5, 1, 3, 9
6. 7, 3, 5, 1
7. 4, 0, 6, 8
8. 2, 4, 6, 8
9. 9, 7, 5, 3
10. 6, 0, 8, 8

Multiply 3-Digit Numbers by 2-Digit Numbers

Objective Multiply 3-digit numbers by 2-digit numbers.

CA Standards

KEY NS 3.2 Demonstrate an understanding of, and the ability to use, standard algorithms for multiplying a multidigit number by a two-digit number and for dividing a multidigit number by a one-digit number; use relationships between them to simplify computations and to check results.

KEY NS 3.3 Solve problems involving multiplication of multidigit numbers by two-digit numbers.

Also KEY NS 1.1, KEY NS 3.0, KEY AF 1.5, KEY AF 2.0, KEY AF 2.1, KEY AF 2.2, MR 3.1, MR 1.0, MR 1.2, MR 2.0, MR 2.1, MR 2.2, MR 2.3, MR 2.4, MR 2.6, MR 3.0, MR 3.2, MR 3.3

Learn by Example

In Lesson 3, you learned how to multiply two 2-digit numbers. In this lesson, you will use the same process to multiply greater numbers.

Some people get their exercise while they work! A mail carrier walks 116 miles each month.

How many miles does the mail carrier walk in a year?

Multiply. $116 \times 12 = n$

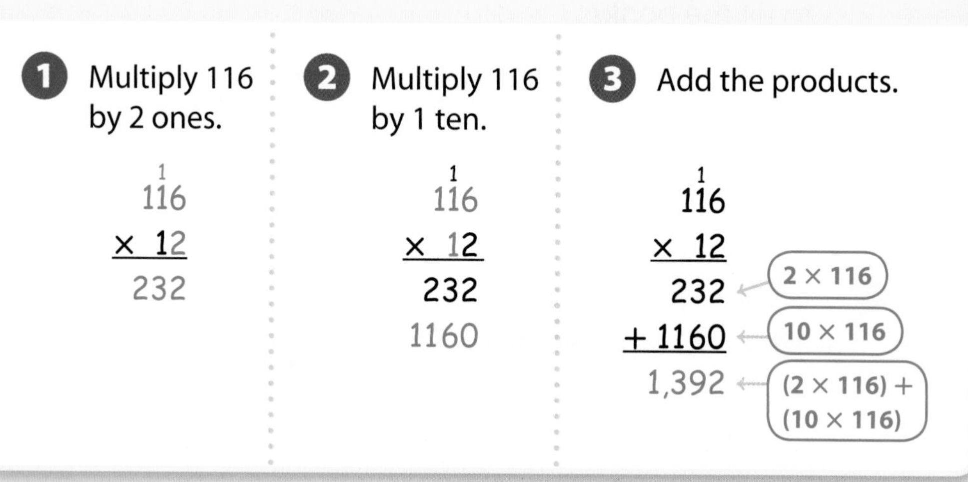

Solution: The mail carrier walks 1,392 miles in a year.

Other Examples

A. Zero in the Tens Place

$$\begin{array}{r} 205 \\ \times\ 59 \\ \hline 1845 \\ +\ 10250 \\ \hline 12{,}095 \end{array}$$

B. Zero in the Ones Place

$$\begin{array}{r} 490 \\ \times\ 63 \\ \hline 1470 \\ +\ 29400 \\ \hline 30{,}870 \end{array}$$

C. Multiple of 10

$$\begin{array}{r} 135 \\ \times\ 20 \\ \hline 0 \\ +\ 2700 \\ \hline 2{,}700 \end{array}$$

Guided Practice

Multiply. Estimate to make sure your answer is reasonable.

1. 241×14

2. 305×32

3. 132×60

4. 574×82

Ask Yourself

- What numbers are multiplied first?
- What numbers are multiplied next?
- What do I add to find the product?

Guided Problem Solving

Use the questions to solve this problem.

5. Officer Jones rides 136 miles each month for her job. How many miles will she ride in 2 years?

a. **Understand** How many months are in a year? How many months are in 2 years?

b. **Plan** What operation will you use?

c. **Solve** Use the operation you named to solve the problem. Write the answer to the question.

d. **Look Back** Solve the problem another way. Do you get the same answer?

6. Look back at Problem 5.

a. How many miles does Officer Jones ride in 4 years?

b. **Analyze** Compare the total number of miles for 2 years with the total for 4 years. What do you notice? Is this reasonable?

c. **Generalize** How does the total number of miles change when the number of years is doubled?

Math Talk When you multiply a 3-digit number by a 2-digit number, what is the greatest number of digits possible in the product? What is the least number of digits?

Practice and Problem Solving

Multiply. Estimate to make sure your answer is reasonable.

7. 132×20

8. 121×43

9. 208×52

10. 496×71

11. 500×85

Algebra Equations

Find the value of *n*.

12. $n \div 82 = 430$ **13.** $n \div 36 = 263$ **14.** $n \div 90 = 157$

History-Social Science Link

Solve.

15. In 1972, the value of the California avocado crop was $24,608,846. By 2005, it had increased to $275,034,420. How much did it increase?

16. Avocados are packed in boxes. One box holds 24 pounds. If a pallet holds 105 boxes, how many pounds of avocadoes does the pallet hold?

17. Avocados were firmly established in California by 1871. Write and solve an equation to find *y*, the number of years ago this was.

18. **Multistep** Each tree in one avocado grove yields about 150 avocados per year. How many avocados would 89 trees yield in two years?

Avocados

- Avocados are fruit that grow on trees.
- There are over 1,000 avocado varieties, but only seven are grown commercially.
- California produces most of the avocados grown in the United States.

History-Social Science 4.4.6

Spiral Review and Test Practice

Round the larger number to the greatest place. Then estimate the product. KEY NS 3.0, KEY NS 1.3 page 216

19. 59×5 **20.** 43×7 **21.** 678×8 **22.** 8×532 **23.** 6×388

Write the letter of the correct answer. KEY NS 3.3

24. The store has 663 boxes of pencils. If there are 24 pencils in each box, how many pencils are in the store?

A 687 **B** 3,978 **C** 15,912 **D** 16,012

Extra Practice See page 249, Set C.

Practice Game

Up, Up, and Away!

Object of the Game Multiply 3-digit numbers by 2-digit numbers and try to get the greater product.

Materials
- Learning Tool 20 (*Up, Up, and Away!* Game Board)
- number cube labeled 1–6

Set Up
Each player gets a game board.

Number of Players 2 or more

How to Play

1. Players take turns rolling the number cube and filling in the boxes on their playing boards with the number rolled. Once a digit has been written in a box, it may not be changed.

2. After the players' boards have been filled, each player finds the product of their two numbers. Whoever has the greatest product gets a point.

3. The first player to earn five points wins.

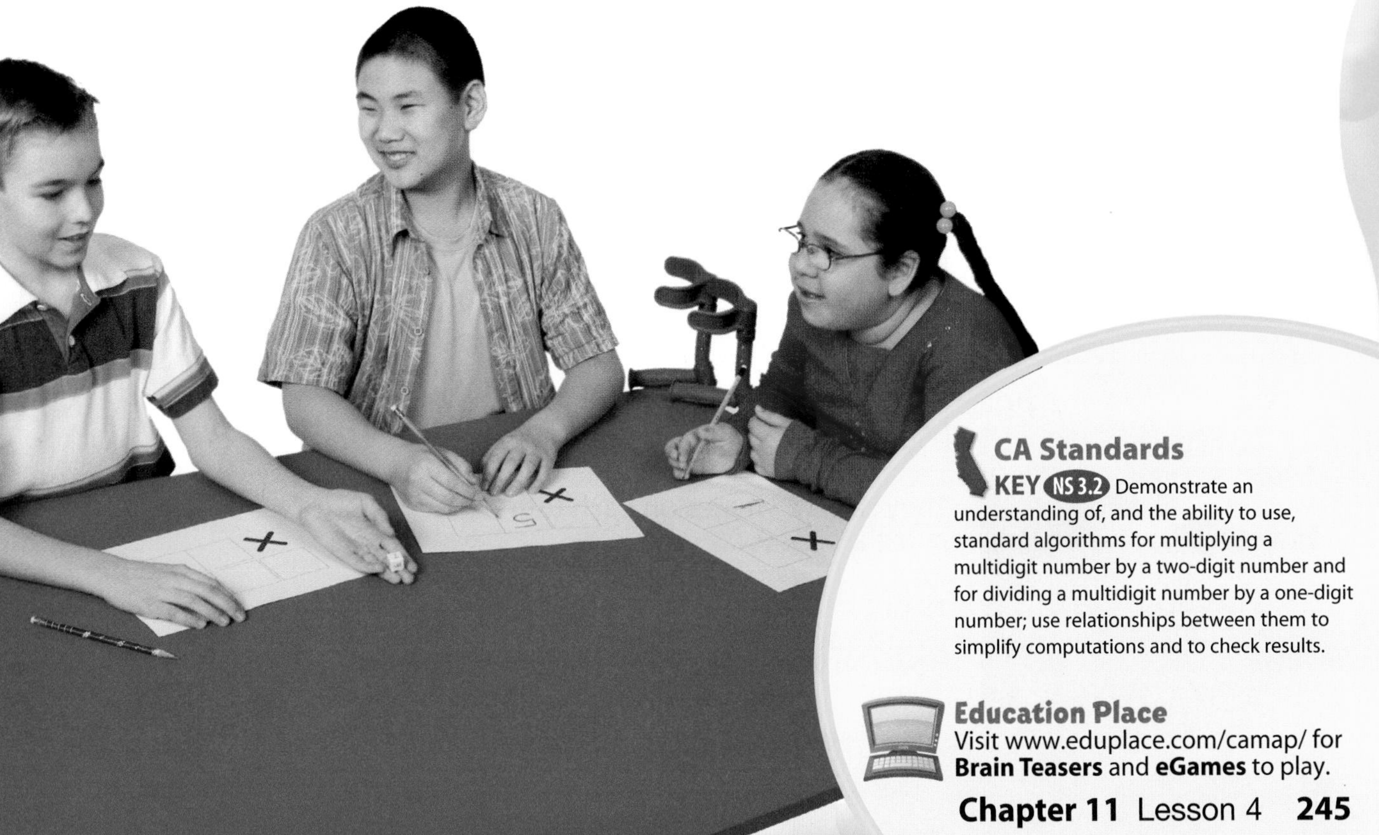

CA Standards
KEY NS 3.2 Demonstrate an understanding of, and the ability to use, standard algorithms for multiplying a multidigit number by a two-digit number and for dividing a multidigit number by a one-digit number; use relationships between them to simplify computations and to check results.

Education Place
Visit www.eduplace.com/camap/ for **Brain Teasers** and **eGames** to play.

LESSON 5

CA Standards
MR 1.0 Students make decisions about how to approach problems.

KEY NS 3.3 Solve problems involving multiplication of multidigit numbers by two-digit numbers.

Also KEY NS 3.0, MR 1.1, MR 2.0, MR 2.3, MR 2.4, MR 3.0, MR 3.1, MR 3.2, MR 3.3

Problem Solving Strategy
Guess and Check

Objective Guess and check to solve problems.

Learn by Example

One month, wildlife observers took 25 tours and reported 300 California gray whale sightings. If they saw the same number of whales each time, how many whales did they see on each tour?

UNDERSTAND

You want to find how many whales were seen on each tour.

This is what you know:

- There were 25 tours.
- Each tour had the same number of sightings.
- There were 300 whale sightings in total.

PLAN

Find a number that will make this equation true:

$\bigcirc \times 25 = 300$

Guess a number. Check to see if the equation is true.
If not, guess again.

SOLVE

Make a reasonable guess.

1st Guess	2nd Guess	3rd Guess
Try 10. $10 \times 25 = 250$ 10 is too few. Guess again.	Try 15. $15 \times 25 = 375$ 15 is too many. Guess again.	Try 12. $12 \times 25 = 300$ 12 is the answer.

They saw 12 whales on each tour.

LOOK BACK

How can you check to be sure the answer is correct?

California gray whale

Guided Problem Solving

Solve using the Ask Yourself questions.

1. Talya is thinking of two numbers. One number is 6 more than the other. The sum of the numbers is 30. What are the numbers?

Ask Yourself
- What should my first guess be?
- Was my first guess too big or too small?

Math Talk Will everyone have the same number of guesses? Explain.

Independent Problem Solving

Solve. Use the menu for Problems 6, 7, and 9. Explain why your answer makes sense.

2. A photographer said she took pictures of sow bugs that included 952 legs. A sow bug has 14 legs. How many sow bugs did she photograph?
3. Two numbers have a product of 64 and a difference of 0. What are the numbers?
4. Two numbers have a product of 36 and a difference of 5. What are the numbers?
5. The sum of 3 numbers is 11. The product of the numbers is 36. What are the numbers?
6. Marcus bought 2 items at the Snack Bar and spent $7. Which 2 items did he buy?
7. Courtney bought 3 items at the Snack Bar and spent $4. Which 3 items did she buy?
8. **Challenge** Eric collects $53 while working at the Snack Bar. The 14 bills he has are $1 bills, $5 bills, and $10 bills. How many of each kind of bill does he have?
9. **Create and Solve** Use the menu to write and solve a guess and check problem.

Fun Fact

Sow bugs are also known as "rollie-pollies" because they roll up when they are in danger.

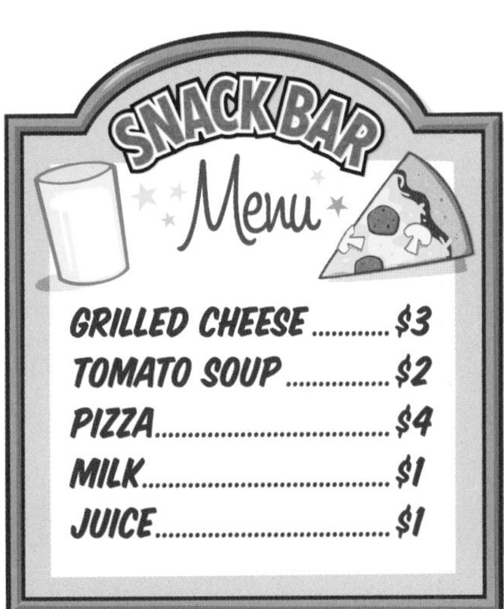

Reading & Writing 

Vocabulary

Vera is doing her math homework. Read the problem and study the way she solves it.

The florist shop is making up bouquets for a wedding. The shop made 12 bouquets. Each bouquet contains 18 flowers. How many flowers did the florist shop use?

$$\begin{array}{r} 12 \\ \times\ 18 \\ \hline 96 \\ 120 \\ \hline 216 \end{array}$$

The **Distributive Property** shows why Vera's steps worked.

Find the part of the problem that represents each step and write it in the chart.

1.	Multiply by ones.	
2.	Multiply by tens.	
3.	Add the partial products.	
4.	Estimate the product.	
5.	Check if the product is reasonable.	

Writing Show a different way to find 12×18.

Reading Look for this book in your library.
A Grain of Rice, by Helena C. Pittman.

CA Standards
MR 2.3 Use a variety of methods, such as words, numbers, symbols, charts, graphs, tables, diagrams, and models, to explain mathematical reasoning.

Also KEY NS 3.2, KEY NS 3.3

Standards-Based Extra Practice

Set A

AF 1.0, KEY NS 3.2 page 236

1. $21 \times 15 = (20 \times 10) + (20 \times \square) + (1 \times 10) + (1 \times \square)$
2. $42 \times 42 = (40 \times \square) + (40 \times 2) + (2 \times \square) + (2 \times 2)$
3. $\square \times 18 = (60 \times 10) + (60 \times 8) + (5 \times 10) + (5 \times 8)$

Set B

KEY NS 3.2, KEY NS 3.3 page 238

Multiply.

1. 21×41
2. 85×22
3. 62×38
4. 47×59
5. 67×42
6. 66×47
7. 74×72
8. 55×41
9. 89×87
10. 53×99
11. 12×40
12. 42×60
13. 92×80
14. 56×90
15. 88×60
16. **Analyze** Fast Track shoe store just received a shipment of 336 pairs of running shoes. The storage room has space for 15 rows of 21 shoe boxes. Will the shipment fit in the storage room?

Set C

KEY NS 3.2, KEY NS 3.3 page 242

Multiply. Estimate to make sure your answer is reasonable.

1. 252×12
2. 345×51
3. 189×34
4. 648×72
5. 571×36
6. 974×22
7. 764×48
8. 879×65
9. 46×295
10. 67×359
11. 25×736
12. 32×843
13. **Justify** All 1,242 students at Richards Elementary School are going to read a book about Martin Luther King, Jr. The teachers ordered the books, which arrived in 11 boxes. If each box holds 117 books, will there be enough books for every student?

Education Place
Visit www.eduplace.com/camap/ for more **Extra Practice**.

Chapter Review/Test

Vocabulary and Concepts

MR 2.3, AF 1.0, KEY NS 3.0

Write the best word to complete the sentence.

1. When you multiply two numbers, your outcome is a ______.

2. You can use the ______ Property to help you multiply greater numbers by 2-digit numbers.

Skills

KEY NS 3.0, KEY NS 3.2

Use basic facts and patterns to find the products.

3. 7×60
4. 7×600
5. $9 \times 3{,}000$
6. $6 \times 9{,}000$

Use the Distributive Property to find the value of *n*.

7. $15 \times 16 = (10 \times 10) + (10 \times n) + (5 \times 10) + (5 \times n)$

8. $28 \times n = (20 \times 10) + (20 \times 3) + (8 \times 10) + (8 \times 3)$

Multiply.

9. 19×12
10. 55×23
11. 98×79
12. 43×50
13. 110×49

14. 21×50
15. 33×20
16. 67×30
17. 48×70
18. 80×57

Problem Solving and Reasoning

KEY NS 3.3, MR 1.0, MR 2.3

Solve.

19. Dr. Harvey uses 24 bottles of solution in his lab each month. How many bottles of solution will he use in 10 months?

20. Tough Truck Builders built 23 trucks this year. If 18 tires were put on each truck, how many tires did Tough Truck Builders use this year?

Writing Math Kara used the Distributive Property to multiply 41×22. She rewrote the problem as $(4 \times 2) + (4 \times 2) + (1 \times 2) + (1 \times 2)$. Explain what she did wrong.

Spiral Review and Test Practice

1. $6,535 + 2,676 =$

A 8,211 **C** 9,201

B 9,111 **D** 9,211

KEY NS 3.1 page 62

2. $26,000 - 8,249 =$

A 17,751

B 17,761

C 17,851

D 27,751

KEY NS 3.1 page 82

3. A restaurant bought 125,735 paper tablecloths. What is this number in word form?

Test Tip
Read each answer choice before choosing one.

A one hundred fifty-two thousand, seven hundred thirty-five

B one hundred twenty-five thousand, seven hundred thirty-five

C one hundred twenty-five thousand, three hundred seventy-five

D one hundred twenty-five thousand, three hundred fifty-seven

KEY NS 1.1 page 12

4. What is the value of *s*?

$20 = s + 12$

A 32 **C** 8

B 20 **D** 6

KEY AF 2.0 page 174

5. Plants at a plant sale cost $6 each. If 3,547 plants are sold, how much money is spent on plants?

A $21,282

B $21,242

C $21,082

D $18,282

Test Tip
Estimate to check that your answer is reasonable.

KEY NS 3.0 page 220

6. For the school trip, 15 buses were needed. There were 45 students riding on each bus. How many students were on all of the buses?

A 60 students

B 225 students

C 270 students

D 675 students

KEY NS 3.3 page 238

Education Place
Visit www.eduplace.com/camap/ for **Test-Taking Tips** and **Extra Practice**.

Unit 5 Test

Vocabulary and Concepts

MR 2.3 Chapters 10–11

Complete each sentence with a word that will make the sentence true.

1. To ______ is to find a number close to the exact amount.

2. When you multiply two numbers, the outcome is a ______.

3. A ______ is a number multiplied to get a product.

4. $12 \times 15 = (2 \times 15) + (10 \times 15)$ is an example of the ______ Property.

Computation

MR 2.1, KEY NS 3.0, MR 1.1, KEY NS 3.2 Chapter 10, Lessons 2–3

Multiply. Check by estimation.

5. 49×5

6. 71×6

7. 892×9

8. $6{,}898 \times 8$

Use basic facts and patterns to find the products. Chapter 11, Lessons 1–2

9. 40×4

10. 800×6

11. $9{,}000 \times 7$

Use the Distributive Property to find the product. Chapter 11, Lesson 2

12. 12×14

13. 13×12

Multiply. Chapters 10–11

14. 109×4

15. 777×3

16. 393×6

17. $2{,}735 \times 5$

18. 19×11

19. 42×15

20. 79×67

21. 98×31

Problem Solving and Reasoning

KEY NS 3.0, AF 1.0, MR 2.3 Chapters 10–11

Solve. Write an expression to represent each problem.

22. Gill Elementary School received 6 boxes of math books with 35 books in each box. After each student received a book, there were 12 books left. How many students received books?

23. Carlton jogs an average of 120 miles per month. If he continues jogging at this rate, how many miles will he jog over the next year? Over the next 3 years?

Solve. Write an expression to represent each problem.

24. A baseball cap company has 5 outlet stores. In June, July, and August, each store sells 1,025 caps per month. How many caps do the five stores sell over the three-month period?

25. A factory packs pottery mugs in boxes to ship them to stores. Each box contains 6 rows of 8 mugs. How many pottery mugs will be in 10 boxes? In 25 boxes?

Writing Math Use a model to show how you can use the Distributive Property to find the product of 11 × 12. Explain how the model works.

Performance Assessment

Over Budget?

KEY NS 3.2, KEY NS 3.3, AF 1.0, MR 1.1

The city is having a festival in a city park. Allison's Bakery has agreed to donate $1,200 in baked goods.

Price List

Baked Goods	Group Size
Holiday Bread	$23
Biscuits	$12/dozen
Bagels	$28/dozen
Multigrain Rolls	$22/dozen

Task	Information You Need
Use the information above and at the right. Is the cost of the order under the $1,200 donation? Write an expression to represent the problem. If yes, what could the city add to the order? If no, what could the city remove from the order?	The city wants to order: 12 loaves of holiday bread 15 dozen biscuits 12 dozen bagels 14 dozen multigrain rolls

Greg Tang's Go Fast, Go Far

Unit 5 Mental Math Strategies

Half Then Double

Even numbers are no trouble.
First do half and then just double!

I have a fast way to multiply 8 × 14.
I start with half of 14 and multiply
8 × 7 = 56. Since this is only half,
I double to get the answer 2 × 56 = 112.
Two steps are easier than one!

1. 8 × 14 → 56 → 112
8 × 7, Double.

2. 7 × 12 → 42 → ▢
7 × 6, Double.

3. 6 × 18 → ▢ → ▢
6 × 9, Double.

4. 9 × 16 → ▢ → ▢
9 × 8, Double.

Very nice work! Keep it up!

5. 5 × 16 → ▢ → ▢

6. 9 × 12 → ▢ → ▢

7. 6 × 14 → ▢ → ▢

8. 7 × 16 → ▢ → ▢

9. 7 × 18 → ▢ → ▢

10. 8 × 18 → ▢ → ▢

Go Faster!

Take It Further!

Now try doing all the steps in your head!

11. 8 × 12 **12.** 5 × 22 **13.** 9 × 18 **14.** 6 × 24

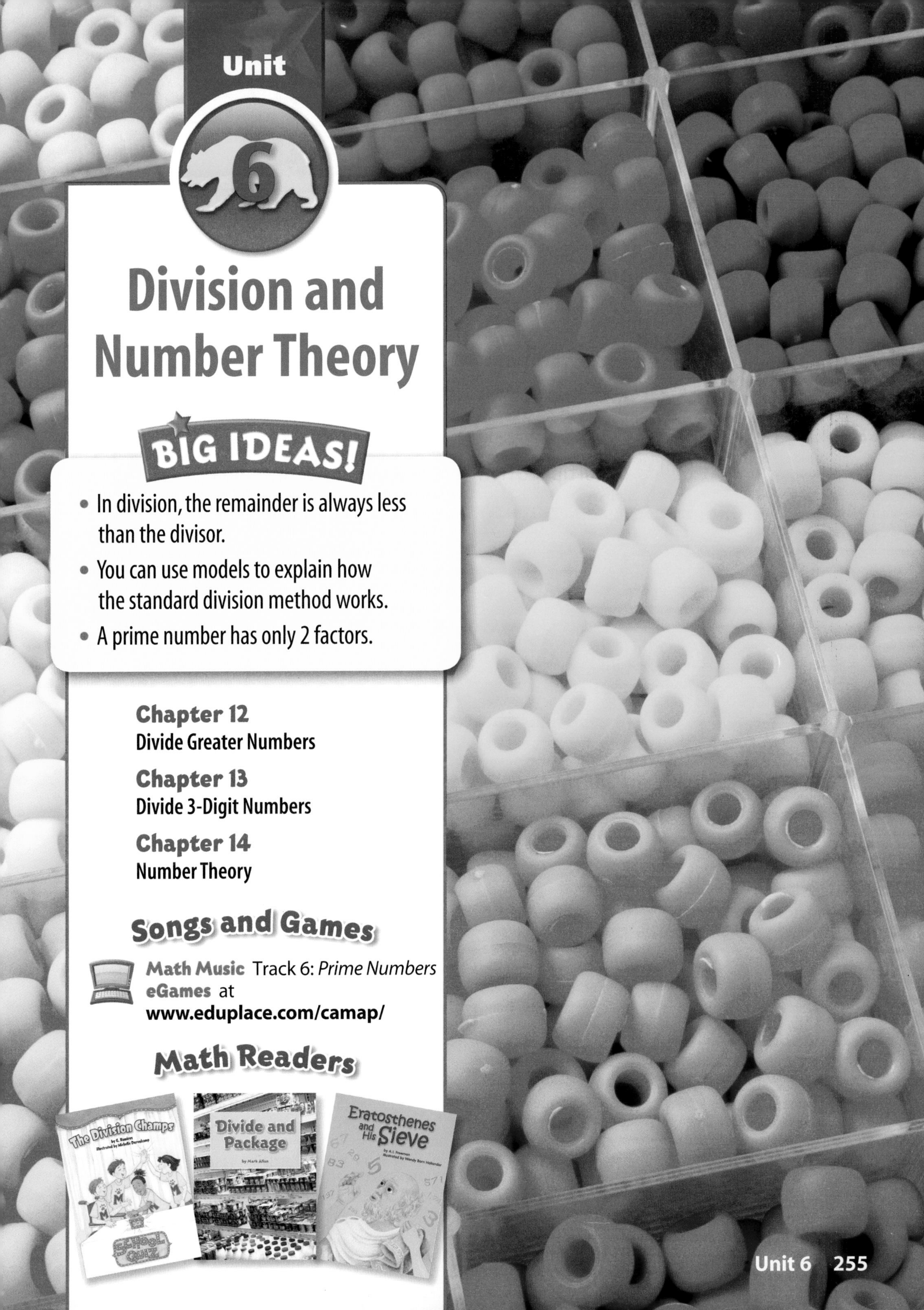

Unit 6

Division and Number Theory

BIG IDEAS!

- In division, the remainder is always less than the divisor.
- You can use models to explain how the standard division method works.
- A prime number has only 2 factors.

Songs and Games

Math Music Track 6: *Prime Numbers*
eGames at
www.eduplace.com/camap/

Math Readers

Get Ready Game

Math Scramble

Object of the Game Use tiles to make as many equations as possible.

Materials

number tiles (5 sets)

Set Up

Make a stack of all the $\times$ and $\div$ symbol tiles. Deal all of the number tiles.

Number of Players 2–4

How to Play

1. Player 1 builds a multiplication or division equation using his or her tiles.

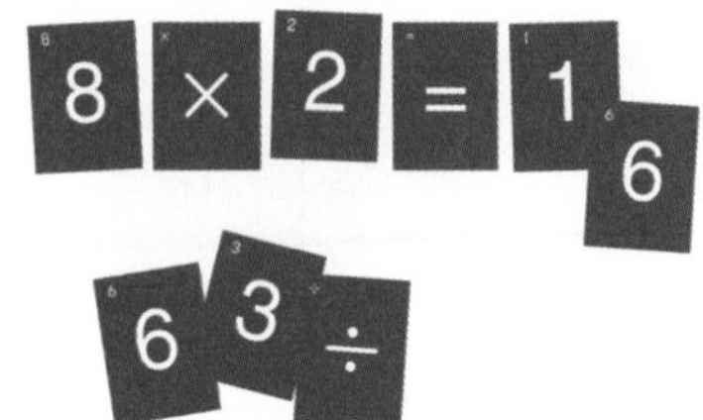

2. Player 2 builds an equation onto Player 1's equation.

3. Players take turns until neither player can build another equation.

4. The player with fewer tiles left wins.

CA Standards

AF 1.0 Students use and interpret variables, mathematical symbols, and properties to write and simplify expressions and sentences.

KEY NS 3.0 Students solve problems involving addition, subtraction, multiplication, and division of whole numbers and understand the relationships among the operations.

Education Place

Visit www.eduplace.com/camap/ for **Brain Teasers** and **eGames** to play.

Reading You can use a **K-W-L** chart to help you understand a reading selection. To help you solve a math problem, you can use a **K-W-P-L** chart. The chart shows important facts without extra information. Here is an example:

Liz spent $17 on souvenirs at Only Australia. She bought a stuffed kangaroo for herself and stuffed koalas for her sisters. How many koalas did Liz buy?

Stuffed Animal Prices	
Kangaroo	$5
Wombat	$3
Koala	$4
Platypus	3 for $12
Wallaby	2 for $12

What Do I Know?	What Do I Want to Know?	What's My Plan to Find Out?	What Did I Learn?
• Liz spent $17 on 1 kangaroo and some koalas. • Kangaroos cost $5 each. • Koalas cost $4 each.	• How many koalas did Liz buy?	• Subtract $5 to find out how much Liz spent on koalas. • Divide by $4 to find how many koalas she bought.	

$17 − $5 = $12.
$12 ÷ $4 = 3.
Liz bought 3 koalas.

Writing Write another question that can be solved with the information in the price list. Trade questions with a classmate and use the K-W-P-L chart to help you solve it.

What Do I Know?	What Do I Want to Know?	What's My Plan to Find Out?	What Did I Learn?

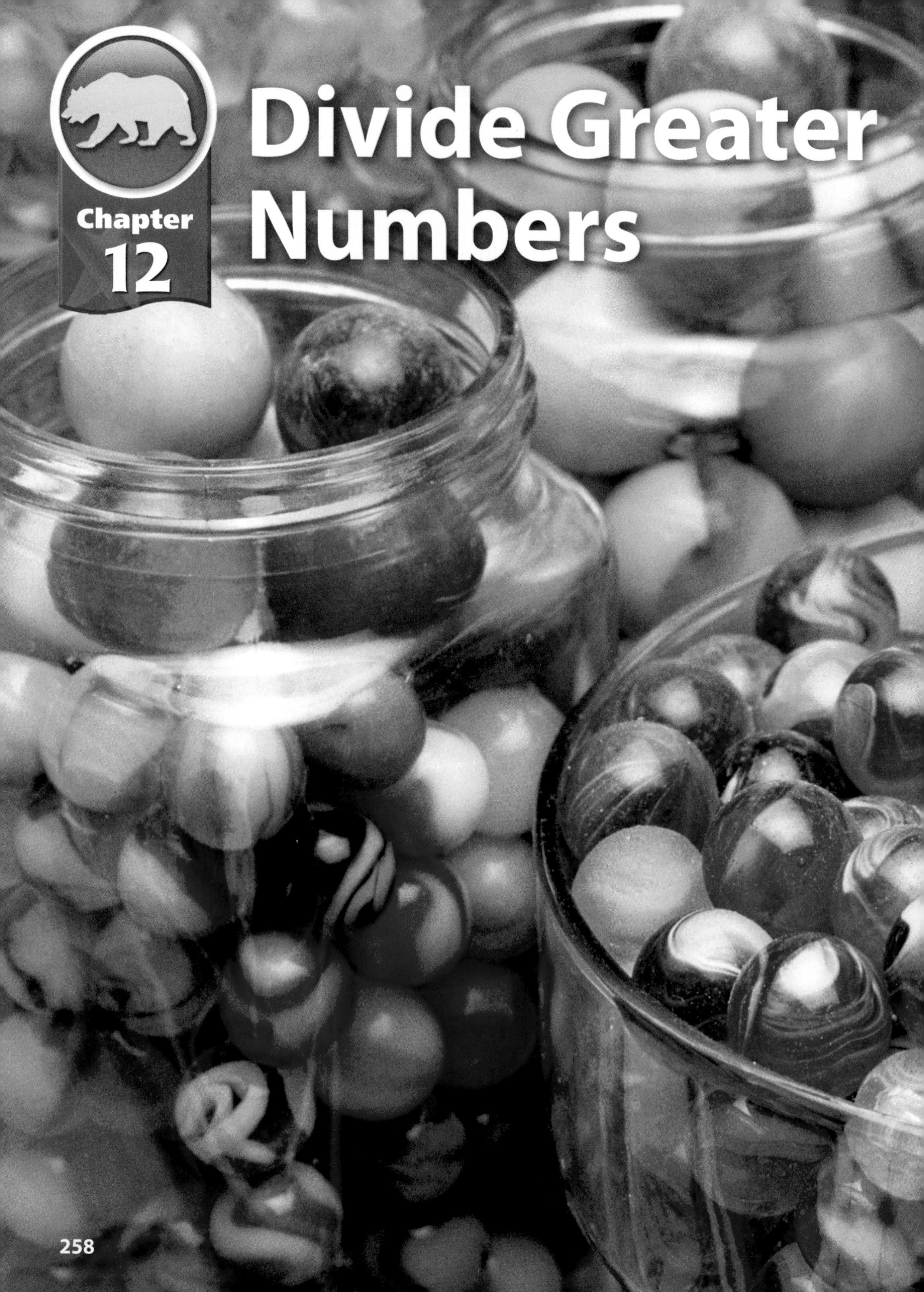

Chapter 12

Divide Greater Numbers

Check What You Know

Vocabulary and Concepts KEY NS 3.0, MR 2.3

Choose the best word or term to complete the sentence. pages 120, 124

Word Bank
one
equal groups
unequal parts
zero

1. In division, items are separated into ____.
2. When you divide zero by a number, the answer is always ____.

Skills KEY NS 3.2

Write two related multiplication facts for each division fact. page 122

3. $56 \div 8 = 7$
4. $42 \div 6 = 7$
5. $54 \div 9 = 6$

Divide. page 130

6. $6\overline{)19}$
7. $8\overline{)27}$
8. $9\overline{)41}$
9. $7\overline{)37}$

Problem Solving and Reasoning GRADE 3 NS 2.5, MG 1.4

10. Felipe has a long board. After he cuts a 2-foot piece off the board, he has 60 inches remaining. How many feet long was the original board?

Vocabulary

Visualize It!

$$\begin{array}{r} 21\text{ R}3 \\ 4\overline{)87} \\ -8 \\ \hline 07 \\ -4 \\ \hline 3 \end{array}$$

quotient
the answer in division

divisor
the number you are dividing by

dividend
the number that is being divided

remainder
the number that is left over

Language Tips

Many common words have very specific mathematical meanings. A *remainder* is something that is left over after other parts have been taken away. In mathematics, a *remainder* is what is left over after you have divided a number into equal parts.

Words that look alike in English and Spanish often have the same meaning.

English	Spanish
dividend	dividendo
divisor	divisor
quotient	cociente

See **English-Spanish Glossary** pages 644–666.

Education Place Visit www.eduplace.com/camap/ for the **eGlossary** and **eGames**.

CA Standards MR 2.3 Use a variety of methods, such as words, numbers, symbols, charts, graphs, tables, diagrams, and models, to explain mathematical reasoning. **Also KEY NS 3.4**

Hands On
Model Division

Objective Use base-ten blocks to model division.

CA Standards
KEY NS 3.0 Students solve problems involving addition, subtraction, multiplication, and division of whole numbers and understand the relationships among the operations.
Also KEY NS 3.4, MR 2.2, MR 2.3, MR 2.4, MR 2.0

Materials
- Workmat 1
- base-ten blocks
- eManipulatives (optional) www.eduplace.com/camap/

Explore

You will use what you learned in Chapter 6 about dividing smaller numbers with a remainder to model division with larger numbers with a remainder.

Question How can you use base-ten blocks to divide larger numbers?

Camila and Nicholas use bottle caps to make pictures. They share 47 bottle caps equally. How many caps do they each get? How many are left over?

1. Use base-ten blocks to show 47.

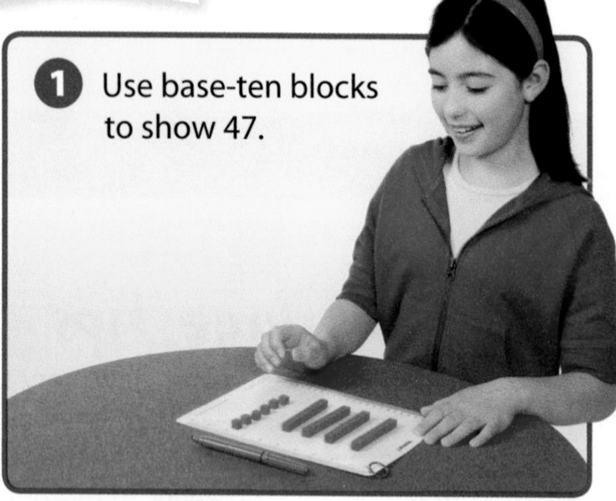

2. Divide the tens blocks into 2 groups. Your groups must be
   - equal in size.
   - as large as possible.

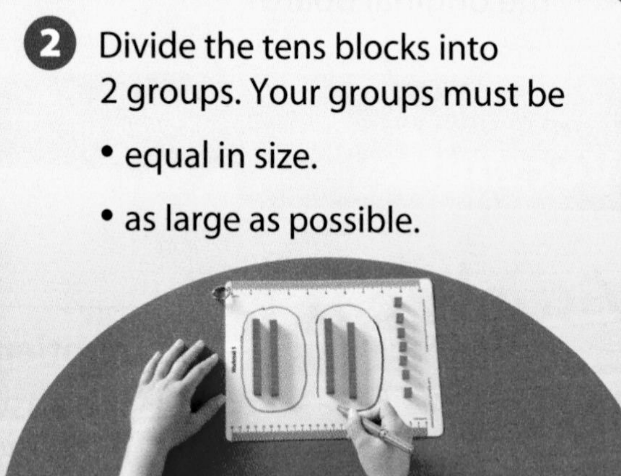

3. Divide the ones blocks into 2 equal groups. How many are
   - in each group?
   - left over?

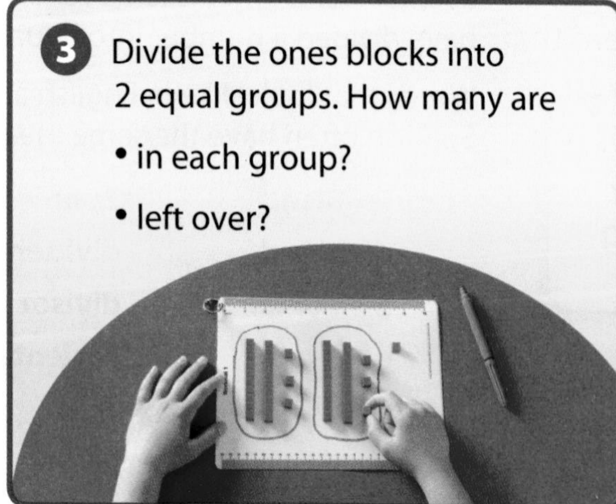

4. Draw a quick picture to show your work with blocks.

Solution: Camila and Nicholas each get 23 bottle caps. There is 1 bottle cap left over.

What if 3 students want to share 37 bottle caps equally?

1 Use base-ten blocks to show 37.

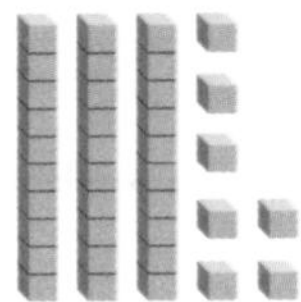

2 Divide the tens blocks into 3 equal groups. How many tens are in each group? Are there any left over?

3 Divide the ones blocks into 3 equal groups. How many ones are in each group? Are there any left over?

4 Draw a quick picture to show your work.

Solution: The 3 students would each get 12 bottle caps. There would be 1 bottle cap left over.

Extend

Use base-ten blocks to complete the table. Draw quick pictures to show your work.

	Number	Number of Equal Groups	Number in Each Group	Number Left	Show the Division
1.	85	4		1	85 ÷ 4 → 21 R1
2.	63	3			
3.	28		14		
4.	49		24		
5.	83			1	

6. Create and Solve Write a word problem that can be solved using your solution to Exercise 4. What do the numbers in each group represent?

Writing Math

What's Wrong? Bena divided 25 bottle caps into 2 groups as shown. She says that 25 ÷ 2 has an answer of 11 R3. Explain what she did wrong.

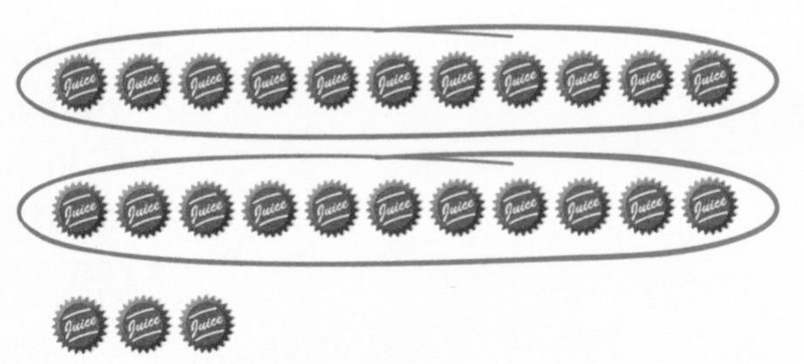

Extra Practice See page 275, Set A.

CA Standards

KEY NS 3.0 Students solve problems involving addition, subtraction, multiplication, and division of whole numbers and understand the relationships among the operations.

KEY NS 3.2 Demonstrate an understanding of, and the ability to use, standard algorithms for multiplying a multidigit number by a two-digit number and for dividing a multidigit number by a one-digit number; use relationships between them to simplify computations and to check results.

Also KEY NS 3.4, MR 1.0, MR 1.2, MR 2.0, MR 2.2, MR 2.3, MR 2.4, MR 2.6, MR 3.0, MR 3.1, MR 3.2, MR 3.3

Vocabulary

quotient

remainder

$$\begin{array}{r} 13 \text{ R1} \\ 2\overline{)27} \end{array}$$

divisor

dividend

Divide Larger Numbers with Remainders

Objective Find two-digit quotients with and without remainders.

Learn by Example

In Lesson 1, you used models to find 37 ÷ 3. Here is how to use quick pictures and numbers to find 37 ÷ 3.

Draw It	Write It

1 There are 3 groups. You can draw 1 ten in each group.

You drew 3 × 1, or 3 tens. There are 0 tens left over.

$$\begin{array}{r} 1 \\ 3\overline{)37} \\ -3 \\ \hline 0 \end{array}$$

Divide. 3 tens ÷ 3
Multiply. 1 ten × 3
Subtract. 3 tens − 3 tens
Compare. $0 < 3$

2 You can draw 2 ones in each group.

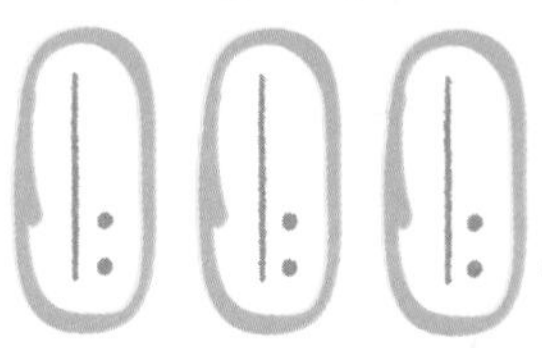

You drew 3 × 2, or 6 ones. There is 1 one left over.

$$\begin{array}{r} 12 \\ 3\overline{)37} \\ -3\downarrow \\ \hline 07 \\ -\ 6 \\ \hline 1 \end{array}$$

Bring down 7 ones.
Divide. 7 ones ÷ 3
Multiply. 2 ones × 3
Subtract. 7 ones − 6 ones
Compare. $1 < 3$

3 You can write the division in two different ways.

$$\begin{array}{r} 12 \text{ R1} \\ 3\overline{)37} \end{array} \quad \text{or} \quad 37 \div 3 \rightarrow 12 \text{ R1}$$

Both ways show:

- 37 in all (**dividend**)
- 3 equal groups (**divisor**)
- 12 in each group (**quotient**)
- **remainder** of 1

Check

- Multiply the quotient by the divisor. $12 \times 3 = 36$
- Add the remainder. $36 + 1 = 37$

The sum equals the dividend, so the answer is correct.

Guided Practice

Divide. Use multiplication to check.

1. $3\overline{)39}$ **2.** $2\overline{)85}$ **3.** $2\overline{)47}$ **4.** $5\overline{)59}$

5. $68 \div 6$ **6.** $95 \div 3$ **7.** $34 \div 3$ **8.** $94 \div 3$

Ask Yourself

- Can I divide the tens?
- Can I divide the ones?
- Are there any ones left over?

Guided Problem Solving

Use the questions to solve this problem.

9. At the museum, 68 students wait to visit the butterfly room. Only 3 people can enter at a time. How many full groups will visit the butterfly room? How many students will be in the last group?

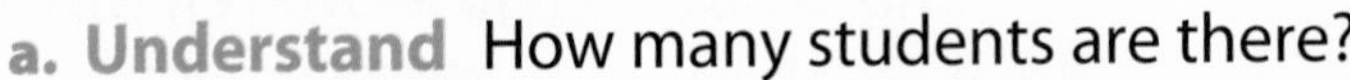

a. Understand How many students are there?

b. Plan What are you trying to find? Explain why you can divide to solve the problem.

c. Solve Solve the problem, and write the answer.

There are ◯ groups of 3 students.

There will be ◯ students in the last group.

d. Look Back Does your answer make sense?

10. Look back at Problem 9. What if 6 students were allowed in the room at once? How many full groups would there be? How many students would be in the last group?

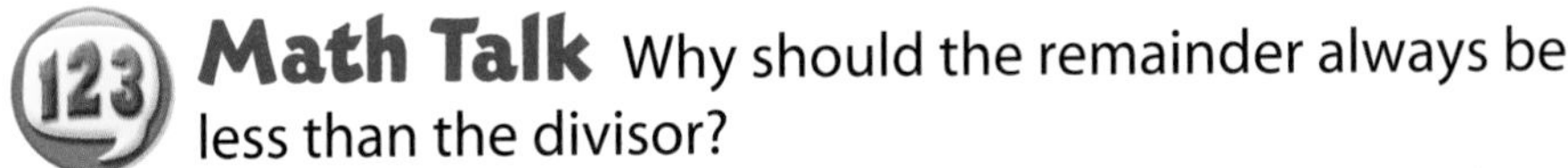

Math Talk Why should the remainder always be less than the divisor?

Practice and Problem Solving

Divide. Use multiplication to check.

11. $4\overline{)87}$ **12.** $3\overline{)62}$ **13.** $2\overline{)63}$ **14.** $4\overline{)89}$ **15.** $3\overline{)96}$

16. $91 \div 3$ **17.** $27 \div 2$ **18.** $46 \div 2$ **19.** $56 \div 5$ **20.** $97 \div 3$

Solve.

21. Badri has 67 butterflies in his collection. He wants to place an equal number in each of the 3 boxes. How many butterflies will each box hold? How many butterflies will be left over?

22. **Multistep** A shop sold 25 butterfly nets for $9 each. It also sold 35 butterfly carriers for $10 each. How much more did the shop receive for the carriers than for the nets?

23. **Money** Jennifer has $29. She buys 2 butterfly kites. Each kite costs the same amount. She has $1 left. How much does each kite cost?

24. **Challenge** When a customer buys 4 butterfly stickers, he or she gets a fifth one for free. How many stickers will Tara pay for if she wants a total of 80 stickers?

Science Link

Solve. Use the Fun Facts for Problem 25.

25. Monarchs that migrate south live about 8 times longer than those that migrate north. About how long does a butterfly that migrates north live?

26. A monarch butterfly migrating south can travel the entire distance in about 80 days. How many full weeks does this migration take?

Migration of the Monarch Butterfly

- Monarch butterflies migrate south in the fall and north in the spring to stay in a warm environment.
- Monarchs that migrate south live about 32 weeks.
- Monarch butterflies can travel up to 50 miles a day at 12 miles per hour.

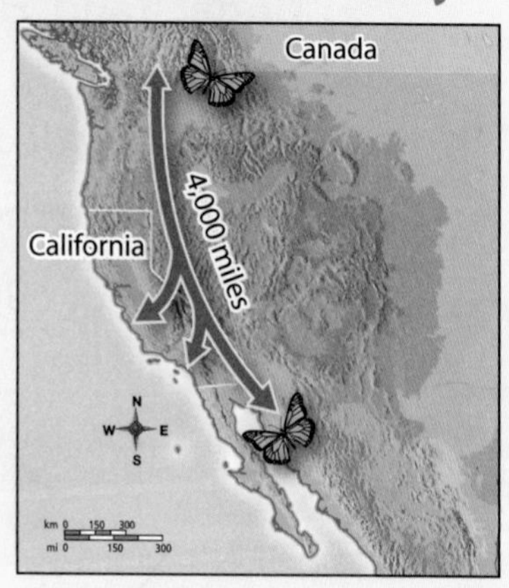

Science LS 3.b

Spiral Review and Test Practice

Copy and complete using >, <, or =. KEY AF 1.2 pages 144, 148

27. $(2 \times 9) + (5 - 4)$ ⬭ $63 \div 9 \times 3$

28. $3 \times (16 - 4)$ ⬭ $30 + (1 \times 6)$

29. $(3 + 1) \times 8$ ⬭ $3 + (1 \times 8)$

30. $(9 \times 5) - (6 - 2)$ ⬭ $(8 - 7) + (8 \times 5)$

Write the letter of the correct answer. KEY NS 3.2

31. $49 \div 4$

A 11 R3 **B** 12 **C** 12 R1 **D** 13

Extra Practice See page 275, Set B.

Key Standards Review

Need Help?
See Key Standards Handbook.

Solve. KEY NS 3.0, KEY NS 3.2

1. 32 × 15 = ▢
2. 64 × 12 = ▢
3. 183 × 10 = ▢
4. 453 × 13 = ▢
5. 631 × 26 = ▢
6. 400 × 35 = ▢
7. 534 × 60 = ▢
8. 216 × 58 = ▢
9. 111 × 36 = ▢

Solve. KEY NS 3.3

10. The fourth grade is collecting buttons for a class project. Each time a student collects 250 buttons they bring them into school and put them in a jar. So far, 12 students have added buttons to the jar. How many buttons are in the jar?

11. Each summer, 18 groups of 34 children attend a summer camp. How many campers are there in all?

12. The museum welcomes 427 guests each day on average. How many people will visit the museum in two weeks?

Challenge Math Reasoning

Digit Detective

Use each digit exactly once to make the sentence true. KEY NS 3.0

1. ▢▢ ÷ ▢ → 31 R2

  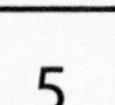

9 | 3 | 5

2. ▢▢ ÷ ▢ → 21 R3

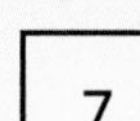 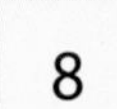 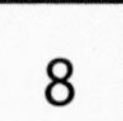  

7 | 8 | 4

3. ▢▢ ÷ ▢ → 22 R2

 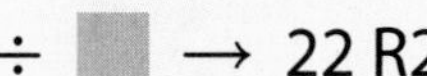  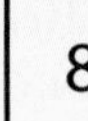

3 | 8 | 6

4. ▢▢ ÷ ▢ → ▢▢ R2

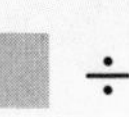 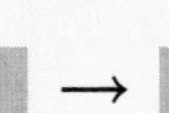    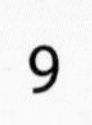  

3 | 9 | 2 | 8 | 3

LESSON 3

CA Standards

KEY NS 3.2 Demonstrate an understanding of, and the ability to use, standard algorithms for multiplying a multidigit number by a two-digit number and for dividing a multidigit number by a one-digit number; use relationships between them to simplify computations and to check results.

KEY NS 3.0 Students solve problems involving addition, subtraction, multiplication, and division of whole numbers and understand the relationships among the operations.

Also KEY NS 3.4, KEY NS 1.2, MR 2.0, MR 2.2, MR 2.3, MR 2.4, MR 2.6

Vocabulary

regroup

- Regroup 1 ten as 10 ones.

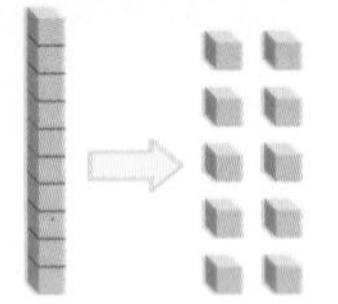

- Regroup 10 ones as 1 ten.

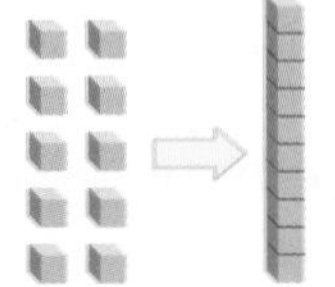

Materials

- base-ten blocks
- eManipulatives (optional) www.eduplace.com/camap/

Hands On
Regroup in Division

Objective Regroup to divide two-digit numbers.

Learn With Manipulatives

Jamie collected 54 postcards. He wants to store the same number of postcards in 4 albums. How many postcards will be in each album? How many postcards will be left over?

You want to find the size of the equal groups, so divide.

Model It	Write It
1 Use base-ten blocks to show 54. 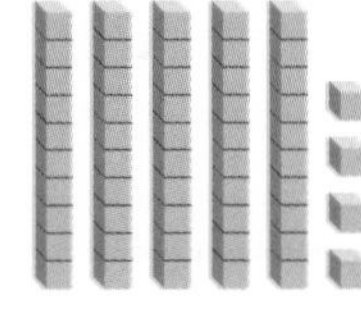	• How many equal groups are there? • How many tens are there? • How many ones are there? $4\overline{)54}$

2 Divide the 5 tens blocks into 4 equal groups.

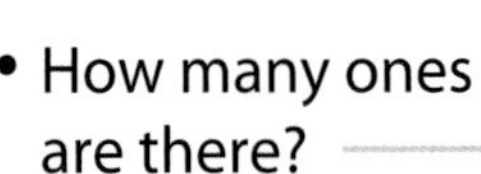

- How many tens are in each group? → 1
- How many tens did you use? → −4
- How many tens are left? → 1

$$\begin{array}{r} 1 \\ 4\overline{)54} \\ -4 \\ \hline 1 \end{array}$$

Divide. 5 tens ÷ 4
Multiply. 1 ten × 4
Subtract. 5 tens − 4 tens

3 **Regroup** the 1 ten block left as 10 ones blocks.

How many ones do you have now? → 14

$$\begin{array}{r} 1 \\ 4\overline{)54} \\ -4\downarrow \\ \hline 14 \end{array}$$

Bring down 4 ones.

Model It	Write It
 Divide the 14 ones blocks.	
• How many ones are in each group?	13 R2 4)54 −4 14 Divide. 14 ones ÷ 4
• How many ones did you use?	−12 Multiply. 3 ones × 4
• How many ones are left?	2 Subtract. 14 ones − 12 ones

Solution: There will be 13 postcards in each album. There will be 2 postcards left.

Check
54 ÷ 4 ⟶ 13 R2
$(13 \times 4) + 2 = 54$
So the answer is correct.

Another Example

```
  12 R6
7)90
 −7
  20
 −14
   6
```

Even though there is a zero here, there are still ones to divide. You need to divide the ones that you regrouped.

Check
90 ÷ 7 ⟶ 12 R6
$(12 \times 7) + 6 = 90$
So the answer is correct.

Guided Practice

Divide. Use base-ten blocks if you need help. Use multiplication to check.

1. 5)74 **2.** 4)73 **3.** 3)81 **4.** 2)57

5. 92 ÷ 6 **6.** 63 ÷ 4 **7.** 98 ÷ 7 **8.** 59 ÷ 3

Ask Yourself
- When I divide the tens, are there any left over?
- What should I do with any tens that are left over?

Practice and Problem Solving

Divide. Use multiplication to check.

9. 4)62 **10.** 8)98 **11.** 6)74 **12.** 7)94 **13.** 3)61 **14.** 5)63

15. 8)96 **16.** 4)79 **17.** 2)52 **18.** 3)97 **19.** 2)37 **20.** 3)43

21. 80 ÷ 6 **22.** 99 ÷ 7 **23.** 65 ÷ 3 **24.** 81 ÷ 7 **25.** 64 ÷ 4 **26.** 76 ÷ 5

Solve.

27. Sally, Marshall, and Enda are placing 86 postcards into 3 equal piles. How many postcards will be in each pile? How many postcards will be left over?

28. Rahul has 39 stamps to put on 19 postcards. He will put 2 stamps on each postcard. How many stamps will he have left over?

29. **What's Wrong?** Kelly did the division shown. What mistake did she make? Show how she should have completed the division.

$$\begin{array}{r} 10 \text{ R}3 \\ 4\overline{)70} \\ -4 \\ \hline 3 \end{array}$$

History-Social Science Link

Use the table to solve.

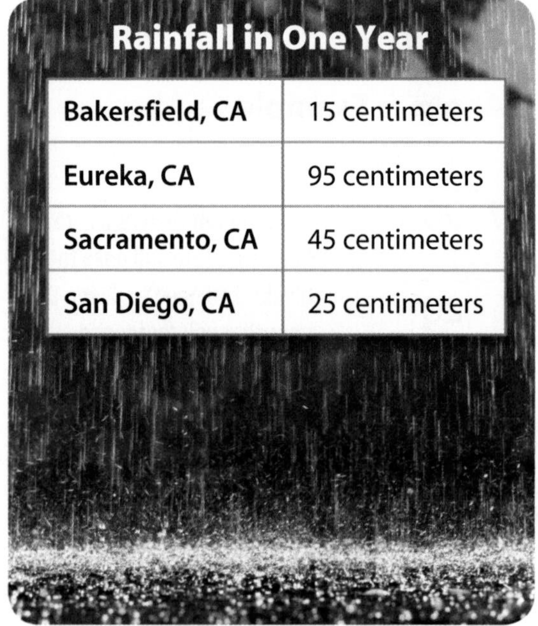

Rainfall in One Year

Bakersfield, CA	15 centimeters
Eureka, CA	95 centimeters
Sacramento, CA	45 centimeters
San Diego, CA	25 centimeters

30. Order the cities in the table from least amount of rain to greatest amount of rain.

31. Which city got three times as much rain as Bakersfield?

32. Eureka got four times as much rain as Fresno. About how many centimeters of rain did Fresno get?

33. **Challenge** Make a bar graph of the data in the table.

History-Social Science 4.1.3

Spiral Review and Test Practice

Multiply. Check by estimation. KEY NS 3.0 pages 220, 224

34. 272 × 3 **35.** 6,625 × 5 **36.** 4,537 × 8

37. 6,081 × 4 **38.** 9,009 × 9 **39.** 5,060 × 7

Write the letter of the correct answer. KEY NS 3.0

40. Jason divides his 59 toy cars in 4 boxes. If each of the boxes has the same number of cars, how many cars are left over?

A 0 **B** 1 **C** 2 **D** 3

Practice Game

Race for the Remainder

Object of the Game Practice division and try to be the first player to get 30 points.

Materials
- number cube labeled 1–6
- number cube labeled 4–9
- paper

Set Up
Each player gets paper for division and to keep score.

Number of Players 2

How to Play

1. The first player rolls both number cubes to make a 2-digit dividend.
2. The first player rolls a number cube labeled 4 to 9 to make a divisor.
3. The first player then divides the dividend by the divisor. The second player checks that the quotient is correct. The remainder is the number of points the first player receives.
4. Player 2 repeats Steps 1 to 3. Have the players take turns. The first player to reach a total of 30 or more points wins.

CA Standards
KEY NS 3.2 Demonstrate an understanding of, and the ability to use, standard algorithms for multiplying a multidigit number by a two-digit number and for dividing a multidigit number by a one-digit number; use relationships between them to simplify computations and to check results.

Education Place
Visit www.eduplace.com/camap/ for **Brain Teasers** and **eGames** to play.

CA Standards
KEY NS 3.2 Demonstrate an understanding of, and the ability to use, standard algorithms for multiplying a multidigit number by a two-digit number and for dividing a multidigit number by a one-digit number; use relationships between them to simplify computations and to check results.

MR 1.1 Analyze problems by identifying relationships, distinguishing relevant from irrelevant information, sequencing and prioritizing information, and observing patterns.

Also KEY NS 3.4, KEY NS 3.0, AF 1.1, MR 1.0, MR 1.2, MR 2.0, MR 2.2, MR 2.3, MR 2.4, MR 2.6, MR 3.0

Divide Multiples of 10

Objective Use basic division facts and patterns of zeros to divide mentally.

Learn by Example

The Delmar family collected pennies. When the jar was full, Mrs. Delmar gave the pennies to her three sons. They counted 1,500 pennies and shared them equally. How many pennies did each boy get?

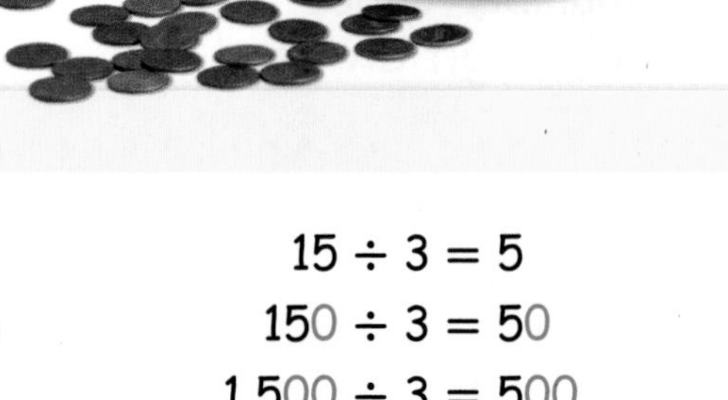

Divide.
1,500 ÷ 3 = ◯ or 3)1,500

Use the basic fact 15 ÷ 3 = 5.

What do you notice about the pattern of zeros?

15 ÷ 3 = 5
150 ÷ 3 = 50
1,500 ÷ 3 = 500

2 zeros — 2 zeros

Check
1,500 ÷ 3 = 500
500 × 3 = 1,500
So the answer is correct.

Solution: Each boy got 500 pennies.

Guided Practice

Divide. Use basic facts and patterns to help you. Use multiplication to check.

1. 48 ÷ 8 = 6
480 ÷ 8 = 60
4,800 ÷ 8 = ■

2. 21 ÷ 7 = 3
210 ÷ 7 = ■
2,100 ÷ 7 = ■

3. 4,500 ÷ 9

4. 900 ÷ 3

5. 5,400 ÷ 9

6. 4,000 ÷ 5

Ask Yourself
- What basic fact can I use?
- How many zeros should be in the quotient?

Math Talk Look at Exercise 6. Why does the quotient have 2 zeros and not 3?

Practice and Problem Solving

Divide. Use multiplication to check.

7. $8 \div 4 = \square$
$80 \div 4 = \square$
$800 \div 4 = \square$

8. $9 \div 3 = \square$
$90 \div 3 = \square$
$900 \div 3 = \square$

9. $6 \div 2 = \square$
$60 \div 2 = \square$
$600 \div 2 = \square$

10. $270 \div 3 = \square$

11. $120 \div 2 = \square$

12. $160 \div 4 = \square$

13. $240 \div 8 = \square$

14. $120 \div 3 = \square$

15. $350 \div 7 = \square$

x Algebra Equations

Solve the equation.

16. $3{,}200 \div 4 = n$

17. $5{,}600 \div 8 = s$

18. $2{,}500 \div 5 = p$

19. $320 \div 8 = x$

20. $420 \div 6 = d$

21. $m \div 5 = 90$

Solve.

22. Sela has 6 times as many coins now as she had four months ago. If Sela has 240 coins now, how many coins did she have four months ago?

23. **Explain** A rare 1937 penny costs $210 in a store. If Dae Youn saves $3 every week, will he have enough money to buy the coin after one year?

24. **Multistep** Chip collected 289 dimes. Sue collected 191 dimes. They put their dimes together and then divided them into 8 stacks. If each stack had an equal number of dimes, how many dimes were in each stack?

Spiral Review and Test Practice

Multiply. KEY NS 3.2 pages 238, 242

25. 52×11 **26.** 68×34 **27.** 621×63 **28.** 857×79 **29.** 292×52

Write the letter of the correct answer. KEY NS 3.4

30. There are 4 jars of coins on the counter. Each jar has the same number of coins. If there is a total of 1,600 coins, how many coins are in each jar?

A 40 **B** 400 **C** 800 **D** 40,000

Extra Practice See page 275, Set C.

CA Standards
MR 1.0 Students make decisions about how to approach problems.

KEY NS 3.4 Solve problems involving division of multidigit numbers by one-digit numbers.

Also KEY NS 3.2, KEY NS 3.0, MR 1.1, MR 1.2, MR 2.0, MR 2.3, MR 2.4, MR 3.0, MR 3.1, MR 3.2

Problem Solving Plan
Interpret Remainders

Objective Understand the meaning of the quotient and remainder in a division problem.

Learn by Example

You can use the same division to solve each word problem below. You have to understand what the quotient and remainder mean to answer the question in the problem.

Increase the Quotient

Mrs. Ross puts 7 postcards on each page of her scrapbook. How many pages does she need for 79 postcards?

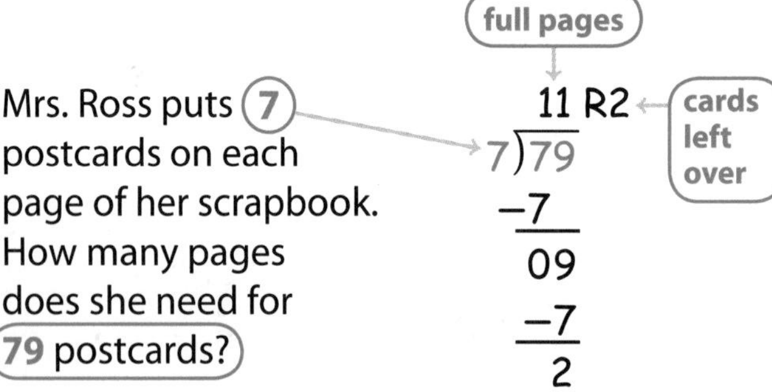

Since Mrs. Ross wants to place all the cards, she will need 12 pages—11 full pages plus 1 page for the 2 extras.

Use the Remainder

Mrs. Ross divides her 79 postcards equally among 7 children. If she keeps the extras, how many postcards does she keep?

cards for each child → 11 R2 ← cards left over

```
 11 R2
7)79
 −7
  09
  −7
   2
```

The remainder tells how many postcards Mrs. Ross keeps, so the remainder is the solution.

Drop the Remainder

An exhibit of old postcards is on display at a museum for 79 days. How many full weeks is that?

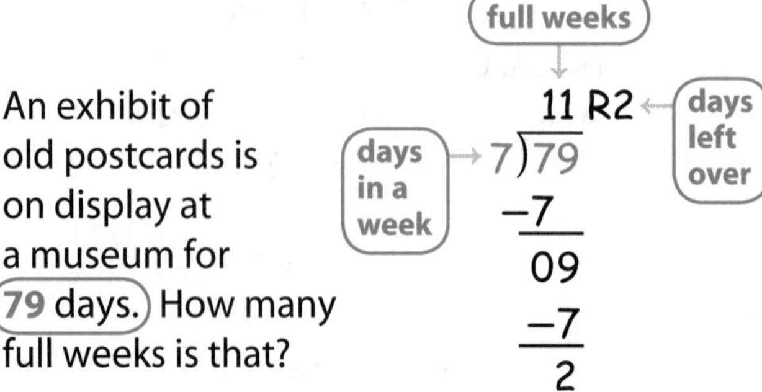

Since the question asks about full weeks, drop the remainder. The quotient is the solution.

IN THE MARIPOSA BIG TREE GROVE
YOSEMITE NATIONAL PARK, CALIFORNIA

Guided Problem Solving

Solve using the Ask Yourself questions.

1. Every day, Mr. Lun displays exactly 6 postcards. If Mr. Lun has 68 postcards, how many days will he display postcards?

Ask Yourself

- Should I increase the quotient or drop the remainder?
- Is the remainder the answer?

Math Talk Explain how you know what to do with the remainder in the problem above.

Independent Problem Solving

Solve. Explain why your answer makes sense.

2. Mrs. Webster wants to buy 68 postcards. Postcards come in packages of 6. How many packages does Mrs. Webster need to buy?

3. **Money** Mr. Seng buys as many \$6 postcard books as he can with \$68. How much money does Mr. Seng have left after he buys the postcard books? Use multiplication to check.

4. Suzanne is placing postcards in her scrapbook, beginning with page 1. She puts 3 postcards on each page. She is placing the ninety-fifth postcard. Which page is it on?

5. Fifty-nine fourth graders visit a pet shop. Only 5 students can see a dog-training demonstration at one time. How many times does the demonstration have to be given so that all 59 students can see it? Use multiplication to check.

6. **Challenge** Freddie and his sister Marcella want to earn money to buy two bikes. Each bike costs \$35. They charge \$3 to wash a dog. How many dogs do they need to wash to earn enough money?

7. **Create and Solve** Write two word problems, one that you solve by dropping the remainder and one in which the remainder is the answer.

Vocabulary

When you **divide**, you take numbers and separate them into smaller, **equal groups**. When a number is left after a whole number is divided by another, it is called a **remainder**.

Kelly is making necklaces to sell at a craft fair. Each necklace is made with 3 glass beads and 4 stone beads. She has a package of 46 glass beads to use. How many necklaces can she make?

$$\begin{array}{r} 15 \\ 3\overline{)46} \\ -3 \\ \hline 16 \\ -15 \\ \hline 1 \end{array}$$

Use this problem and solution to complete the word web below. Each part of the word web has the word, an example, and a number.

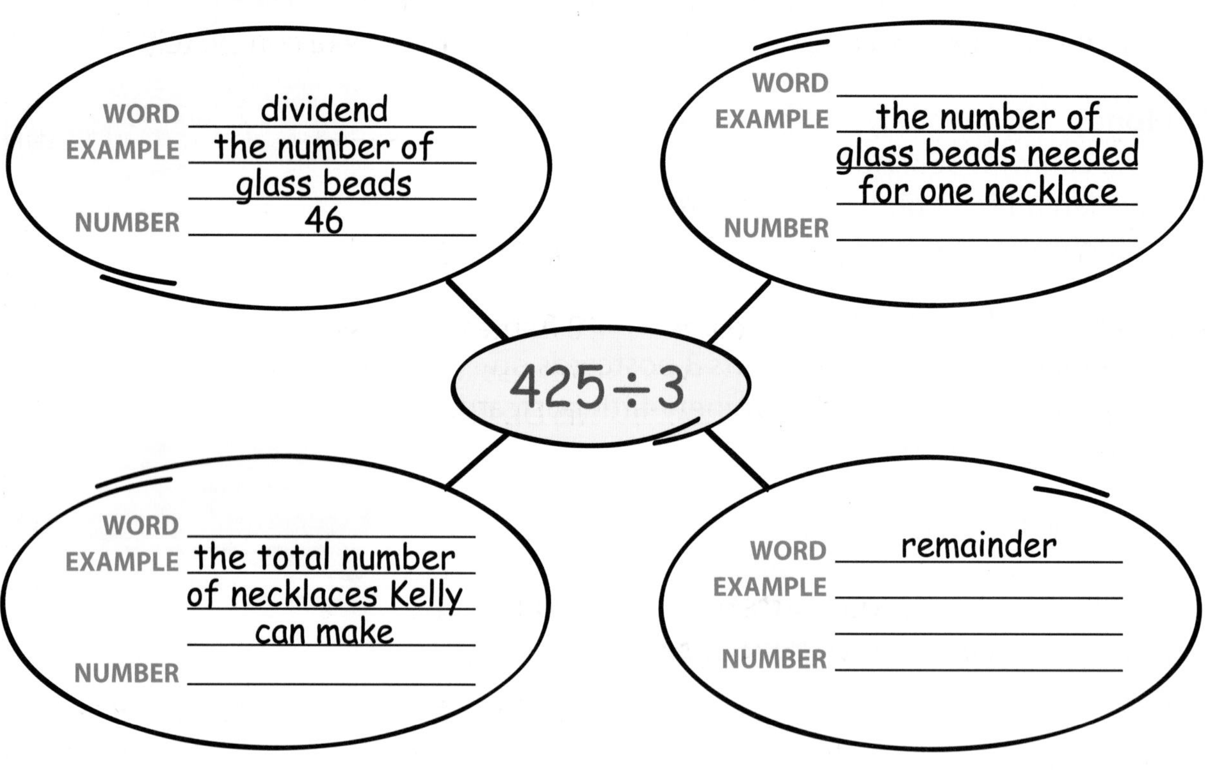

Kelly can make ________ necklaces with ________ glass bead(s) left over.

Writing Write a problem that can be solved by division. Make a word web like this one for the problem.

Reading Check out this book in your library.
Math Man, by Teri Daniels

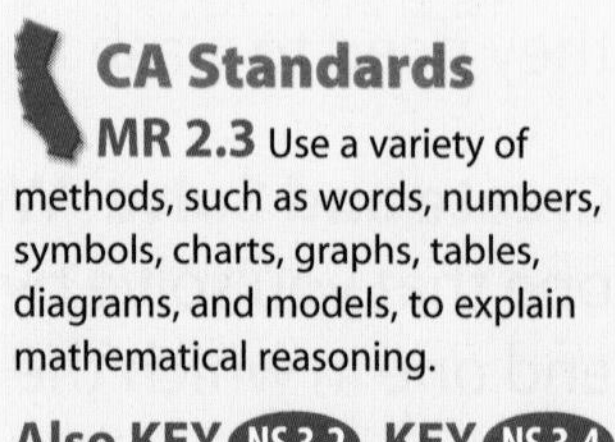
CA Standards
MR 2.3 Use a variety of methods, such as words, numbers, symbols, charts, graphs, tables, diagrams, and models, to explain mathematical reasoning.
Also KEY NS 3.2, KEY NS 3.4

Standards-Based Extra Practice

Set A

KEY NS 3.0, MR 2.3 page 260

Use base-ten blocks to complete the table. Draw quick pictures to show your work.

	Number	Number of Equal Groups	Number in Each Group	Number Left	Show the Division
1.	32	5			32 ÷ 5 → 6 R2
2.	78		9		
3.	61	6			

4. Explain Olivia contacted 16 businesses for job descriptions. If she places 5 job descriptions in each binder, how many binders will she completely fill?

Set B

KEY NS 3.0, KEY NS 3.2 page 262

Divide. Use multiplication to check.

1. 47 ÷ 5 **2.** 63 ÷ 8 **3.** 71 ÷ 7 **4.** 34 ÷ 6

5. Justify Dr. Chan has 8 cases to arrange 68 frames for glasses. She thinks she needs to purchase one more case in order to hold them all. If each case can hold 8 frames, will Dr. Chan need to make a purchase?

Set C

KEY NS 3.2, MR 1.1 page 270

Divide. Use basic facts and patterns to help you. Use multiplication to check your answers.

1. 63 ÷ 7 =
630 ÷ 7 =
6300 ÷ 7 =

2. 36 ÷ 6 =
360 ÷ 6 =
3600 ÷ 6 =

3. 18 ÷ 6 =
180 ÷ 6 =
1800 ÷ 6 =

4. 45 ÷ 9 =
450 ÷ 9 =
4500 ÷ 9 =

Solve the equation.

5. $540 \div 6 = d$ **6.** $t \times 2 = 600$ **7.** $h \times 9 = 8100$

8. Analyze Gloria has 5 times as many stickers as she did at the beginning of the school year. If she has 400 stickers now, how many did she have at the start of the school year?

Education Place
Visit www.eduplace.com/camap/ for more **Extra Practice.**

Chapter Review/Test

Vocabulary and Concepts — KEY NS 3.0, MR 2.3

Write the best word to complete the sentence.

1. In a division equation, the answer is also called the ______.
2. When a problem says "590 is divided by 6", the number 590 is the ______.
3. You can check a division problem by multiplying the ______ by the quotient.

Skills — KEY NS 3.0, KEY NS 3.2

Divide.

4. $67 \div 7$
5. $28 \div 6$
6. $37 \div 9$
7. $31 \div 6$
8. $6\overline{)46}$
9. $3\overline{)86}$
10. $8\overline{)74}$
11. $5\overline{)93}$
12. $50 \div 5$
13. $480 \div 8$
14. $6{,}400 \div 8$
15. $70 \div 10$

Solve each equation.

16. $350 \div 7 = m$
17. $2{,}100 \div 3 = f$
18. $360 \div 9 = t$

Problem Solving and Reasoning — MR 1.0, MR 1.1, MR 2.3, MR 2.6, KEY NS 3.0, KEY NS 3.4

Solve.

19. Jordan has 47 model planes. Each day he brings in 6 planes to show the class. How many days will Jordan be bringing in planes?
20. Jackie's school of 300 is visiting an art museum. Groups of 3 students are viewing each painting. How many paintings are being viewed?

Writing Math How is checking a division problem with a remainder different from checking a different problem that has no remainder? Explain.

Spiral Review and Test Practice

1. What is 13,457,500 rounded to the nearest ten million?

   A 10,000,000

   B 13,000,000

   C 13,500,000

   D 20,000,000

KEY NS 1.3 page 34

2. □ + 61 = 61 + 125

   A 61

   B 64

   C 125

   D 186

KEY AF 2.1 page 102

3. The sum of *a* plus *b* equals 14. If $a = 8$, which equation can be used to find the value of *b*?

   A $8 + a = 14$

   B $8 + b = 14$

   C $a - b = 14$

   D $8 - b = 14$

Test Tip
Check that you have substituted the correct value for the known variable.

KEY AF 1.5 page 196

4. Mr. Patel packs 5 boxes of paper. Each box holds 3,600 sheets of paper. How many sheets of paper does he pack in all?

Test Tip
Remember to use zero as a place holder when multiplying.

   A 1,800 sheets of paper

   B 15,000 sheets of paper

   C 18,000 sheets of paper

   D 180,000 sheets of paper

KEY NS 3.0 page 224

5. Sara has 34 packets of wildflower seeds. If there are 229 seeds in each packet, how many seeds does Sara have?

   A 7,786 seeds
   C 1,603 seeds

   B 7,756 seeds
   D 263 seeds

KEY NS 3.3 page 242

6. $62 \div 4 =$

   A 15
   C 16

   B 15 R2
   D 16 R2

KEY NS 3.2 page 262

Education Place
Visit www.eduplace.com/camap/ for **Test-Taking Tips** and **Extra Practice.**

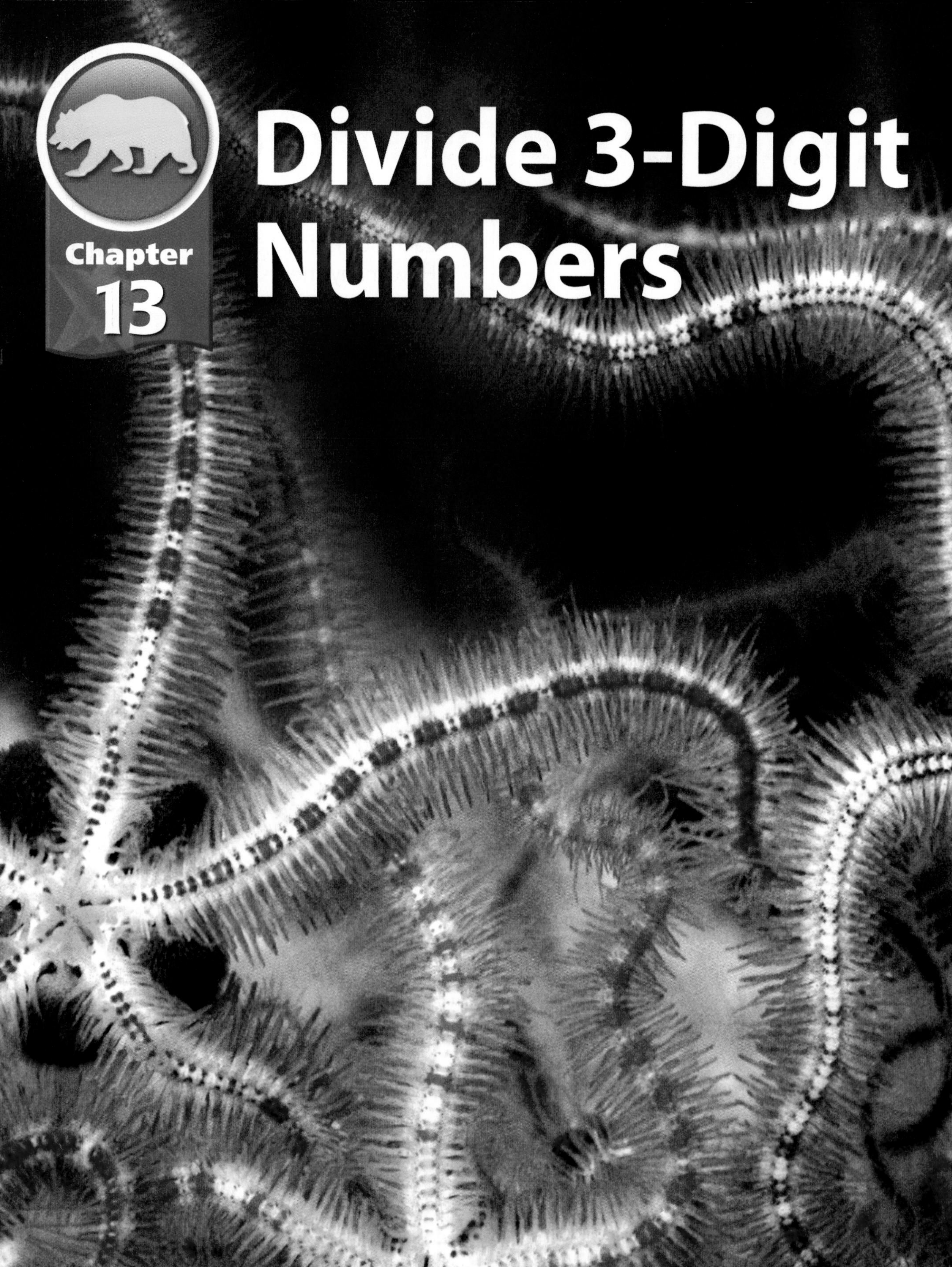

Divide 3-Digit Numbers

In the waters near La Jolla, CA, millions of spiny brittle stars can be seen along the ocean floor.

Check What You Know

Word Bank
dividend
divisor
quotient
regroup
remainder

Vocabulary and Concepts KEY NS 3.0, MR 2.3

Choose the best word to complete the sentence. page 130

1. The answer in division is called the _____.
2. If equal groups cannot be made when you divide, you will have a _____.
3. When you divide, the _____ is divided into equal groups.

Skills KEY NS 3.0

Divide. page 262

4. $4\overline{)48}$
5. $5\overline{)65}$
6. $3\overline{)77}$
7. $40 \div 3$
8. $20 \div 7$
9. $42 \div 3$

Problem Solving and Reasoning KEY NS 3.0

10. Suppose a number is divided by 6. What numbers could the remainder be? Explain how you know?

Vocabulary

Visualize It!

average
the number found by dividing the sum of a group of numbers by the number of addends

Jake's Test Scores	
Test 1	89
Test 2	91
Test 3	78
Test 4	86

Find the average of Jake's scores.

First add the test scores to find the total.

$$\begin{array}{r} 89 \\ 91 \\ 78 \\ +\ 86 \\ \hline 344 \end{array}$$

Then divide by the number of tests.

$$\begin{array}{r} 86 \\ 4\overline{)344} \\ -\ 32 \\ \hline 24 \\ -\ 24 \\ \hline 0 \end{array}$$

Language Tips

Many common words have very specific mathematical meanings. For example, when something is *average*, it is *ordinary*. But in mathematics, an *average* is the sum of a group of numbers divided by the number of addends in the group.

Words that look alike in English and Spanish often have the same meaning.

English	Spanish
dividend	dividendo
divisor	divisor
quotient	cociente

See **English-Spanish Glossary** pages 644–666.

Education Place Visit www.eduplace.com/camap/ for the **eGlossary** and **eGames**.

CA Standards MR 2.3 Use a variety of methods, such as words, numbers, symbols, charts, graphs, tables, diagrams, and models, to explain mathematical reasoning. **Also KEY NS 3.4**

Hands On
Model Division: 3-Digit Dividends

Objective Use base-ten blocks to model division of a 3-digit number by a 1-digit number.

CA Standards
KEY NS 3.4 Solve problems involving division of multidigit numbers by one-digit numbers.
MR 2.3 Use a variety of methods, such as words, numbers, symbols, charts, graphs, tables, diagrams, and models, to explain mathematical reasoning.
Also KEY NS 3.2, KEY NS 3.0, MR 2.0, MR 2.2, MR 2.4, MR 2.6

Materials
- base-ten blocks
- eManipulatives (optional) www.eduplace.com/camap/

Explore

Question How can you use base-ten blocks to divide a 3-digit number?

At a farm, 3 horses are fed 375 pounds of hay each week. If the horses all receive the same amount of hay, how many pounds of hay does each horse get?

Work in groups to divide 375 into three equal groups.

1 Use base-ten blocks to show 375.

Divide the hundreds blocks into 3 equal groups.

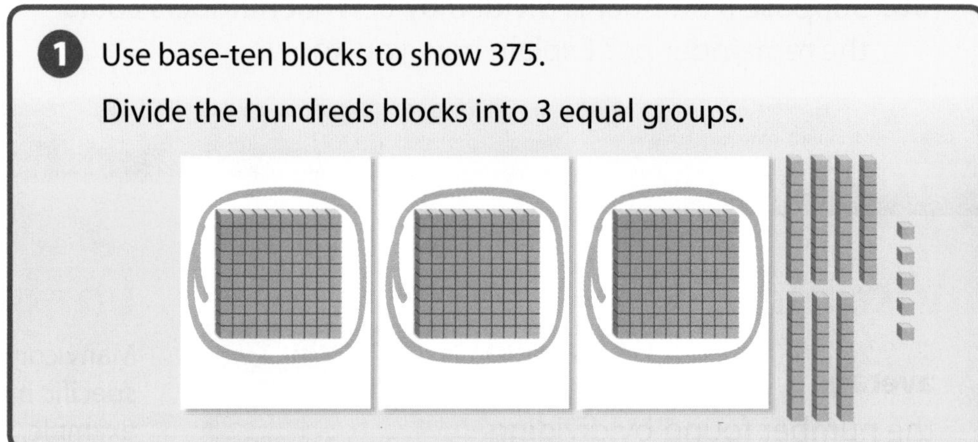

2 Divide the tens blocks into 3 equal groups.
There is 1 tens block left over.

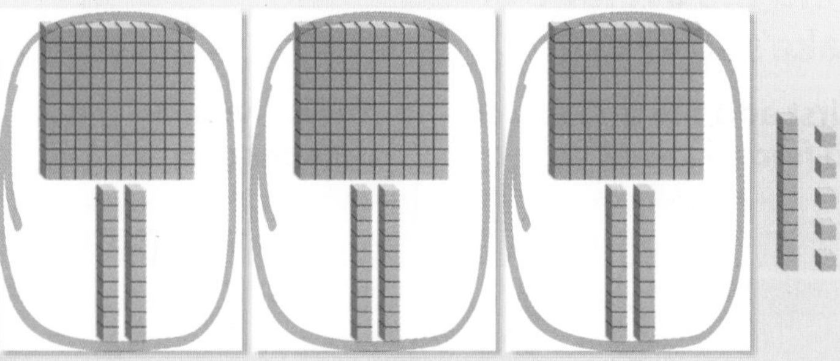

 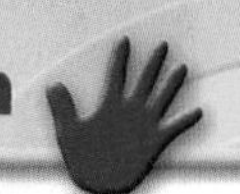

3 Regroup 1 tens block as 10 ones blocks. Add these to the 5 ones blocks you already have.

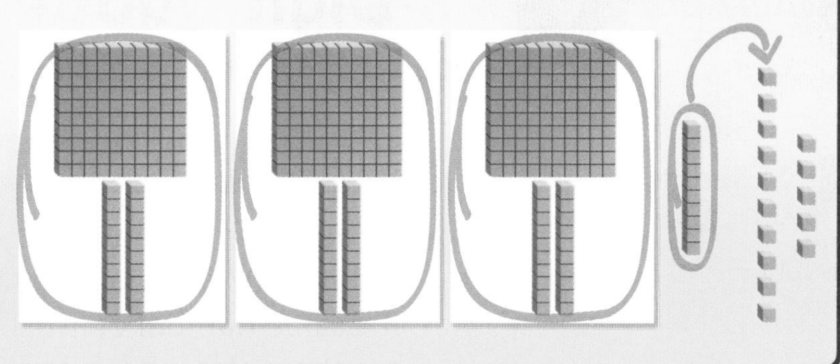

4 Divide the ones blocks into 3 equal groups.

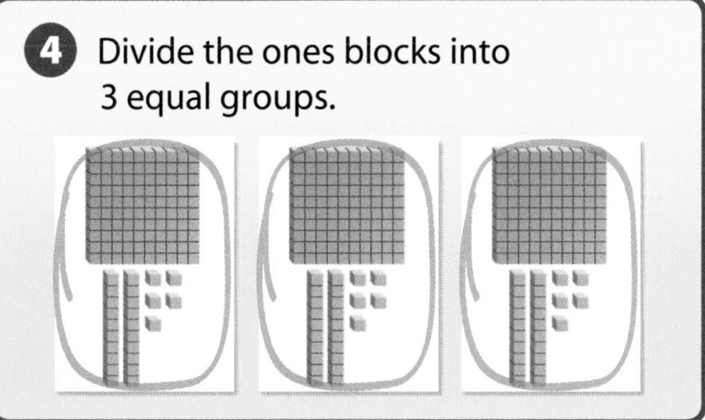

5 Draw a quick picture to show your work.

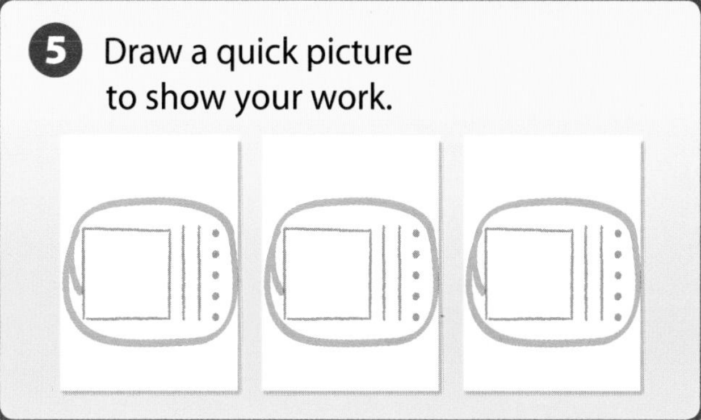

Solution: Each horse gets 125 pounds of hay.

Extend

Use base-ten blocks to complete the table. Draw quick pictures to show your work.

	Number	Number of Equal Groups	Number in Each Group	Number Left	Show the Division
1.	253	2		1	253 ÷ 2 → 126 R1
2.	317	3			
3.	426		142		
4.	489	4			
5.	541	2		1	

Writing Math

Explain Candace and Darrel are solving the division problem 662 ÷ 2. Candace says there will be a remainder. Darrel says there will not be a remainder. Who is correct?

3-Digit Quotients

Objective Divide a 3-digit number by a 1-digit number.

CA Standards
KEY NS 3.0 Students solve problems involving addition, subtraction, multiplication, and division of whole numbers and understand the relationships among the operations.
KEY NS 3.4 Solve problems involving division of multidigit numbers by one-digit numbers.
Also KEY NS 3.2, KEY AF 2.0, KEY AF 2.2, MR 1.0, MR 1.1, MR 1.2, MR 2.0, MR 2.2, MR 2.3, MR 2.4, MR 2.6, MR 3.0, MR 3.1, MR 3.2, MR 3.3

Vocabulary

quotient
remainder
12 R1
$4\overline{)49}$
divisor
dividend

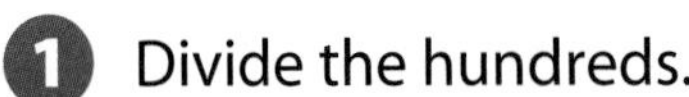

Learn by Example

An aquarium is setting up a new exhibit. Aquarium workers will put 407 fish into 3 different tanks. If each tank will hold the same number of fish, how many fish will be in each tank? Are there any fish left over?

Divide. $407 \div 3 = \bigcirc$ or $3\overline{)407}$

1 Divide the hundreds.

```
    1
3)407
 -3     Multiply. 1 × 3
  1     Subtract. 4 − 3
        Compare. 1 < 3
```

After you divide the hundreds, tens, or ones place, the remainder should **always** be less than the divisor.

2 Bring down the tens. Divide the tens.

```
   13
3)407
 -3
  10    Bring down the tens.
 - 9    Multiply. 3 × 3
   1    Subtract. 10 − 9
        Compare. 1 < 3
```

3 Bring down the ones. Divide the ones.

```
  135
3)407
 -3
  10
 - 9
   17   Bring down the ones.
 - 15   Multiply. 5 × 3
    2   Subtract. 17 − 15
        Compare. 2 < 3
```

Check
Multiply. Then add the remainder.
$3 \times 135 = 405$
$405 + 2 = 407$
The sum equals the dividend, so the answer is correct.

Solution: Each tank will hold 135 fish.
There are 2 fish left over.

Guided Practice

Divide. Use multiplication to check.

1. $2\overline{)394}$ **2.** $2\overline{)962}$ **3.** $775 \div 2$ **4.** $697 \div 6$

Ask Yourself

Can I divide the hundreds? The tens? The ones?

Guided Problem Solving

Use the questions to solve this problem.

5. An aquarium had a dolphin show. Ninety-eight people went to the show on Friday, 179 people went on Saturday, and 146 went on Sunday. What was the **average** number of people who saw the show each day?

a. **Understand** What are you trying to find?

b. **Plan** What numbers will you add? What number will you divide by?

c. **Solve** Follow your plan. Write the answer.

d. **Look Back** Use multiplication to check your division.

An **average** is a number that represents a group of numbers. To find an average, divide the sum of the group of numbers by the number of addends.

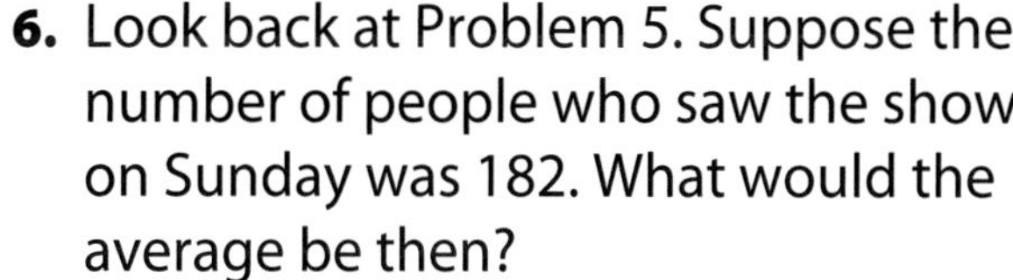

6. Look back at Problem 5. Suppose the number of people who saw the show on Sunday was 182. What would the average be then?

Math Talk Think about $482 \div 4$. Without dividing, how do you know the quotient will have 3 digits?

Practice and Problem Solving

Divide. Use multiplication to check.

7. $2\overline{)836}$ **8.** $4\overline{)709}$ **9.** $3\overline{)519}$ **10.** $3\overline{)404}$

11. $5\overline{)762}$ **12.** $6\overline{)913}$ **13.** $8\overline{)923}$ **14.** $8\overline{)889}$

15. $578 \div 3$ **16.** $710 \div 5$ **17.** $535 \div 2$ **18.** $864 \div 5$

Algebra Equations

Find the value of *n*.

19. $n \times 8 = 408$ **20.** $7 \times n = 329$ **21.** $n \cdot 3 = 750$

22. $4 \cdot n = 852$ **23.** $9n = 639$ **24.** $6n = 270$

Solve.

25. The aquarium workers use 4 carts to deliver packs of food to the tanks. Each cart carries the same number of packs. If there are 464 packs in all, how many packs are on each cart?

26. Multistep Fran and Kichi volunteer at the aquarium. Fran passed out 306 brochures in 2 days. Kichi passed out 420 brochures in 3 days. If the two girls continue at their rates, who will pass out the most brochures the next day?

Real World Data

Use the table for Problems 27–28.

27. The length of a truck is 36 feet. How many sea wasp jellyfish laid end-to-end would equal the length of the truck?

28. Analyze Which of the jellyfish in the table are longer than you are tall?

Lengths of Jellyfish

Jellyfish	Length
Sea wasp	9 feet
Sea nettle	20 feet
Lion's mane	7 feet
Box jellyfish	16 feet

Sea nettle

Spiral Review and Test Practice

Complete the fact family. KEY NS 3.0 page 122

29. $3 \times 7 = \square$ $21 \div 3 = \square$
$7 \times 3 = \square$ $21 \div 7 = \square$

30. $6 \times 9 = \square$ $54 \div 6 = \square$
$9 \times 6 = \square$ $54 \div 9 = \square$

Write the letter of the correct answer. KEY NS 3.4

31. There are 9 rows of seats in an aquarium's outdoor theater. Each row has the same number of seats. If there is a total of 216 seats, how many seats are in each row?

A 22 **B** 23 **C** 24 **D** 25

Extra Practice See page 295, Set A.

Key Standards Review

Need Help?
See Key Standards Handbook.

Explain your thinking. KEY NS 3.0, KEY NS 3.2

1. Alvin and Arlene each solve the problem 834 × 27 = ? They use different methods. Explain why both methods work and give the same answer.

Alvin

834	834	5,838
× 7	× 20	+ 16,680
5,838	16,680	22,518

Arlene

834
× 27
5,838
+ 16,680
22,518

Problem Solving

What Is the Number?

Use the clues to find each number. KEY NS 3.0

1. **Clues:**
   - The divisor is 4.
   - The dividend is 127.
   - The quotient is 31.

   What is the remainder?

2. **Clues:**
   - The dividend is 363.
   - The remainder is 3.
   - The quotient is 90.

   What is the divisor?

3. **Clues:**
   - The remainder is 5.
   - The quotient is 547.
   - The divisor is 8.

   What is the dividend?

4. **Clues:**
   - The dividend is 287.
   - The remainder is 3.
   - The divisor is 4.

   What is the quotient?

Place the First Digit of the Quotient

Objective Decide where to write the first digit in the quotient.

CA Standards
KEY NS 3.2 Demonstrate an understanding of, and the ability to use, standard algorithms for multiplying a multidigit number by a two-digit number and for dividing a multidigit number by a one-digit number; use relationships between them to simplify computations and to check results.

KEY NS 3.4 Solve problems involving division of multidigit numbers by one-digit numbers.

Also KEY NS 3.0, KEY AF 1.5, MR 1.0, MR 2.0, MR 2.2, MR 2.3, MR 2.4, MR 2.6

Learn by Example

Reggie has 237 trading cards of zoo animals. If he puts these cards into 5 equal piles, how many trading cards will be in each pile? How many will be left over?

Sometimes when you divide a 3-digit number by a 1-digit number, you get a 2-digit quotient.

Divide. $237 \div 5 = \bigcirc$ or $5\overline{)237}$ (quotient: $\bigcirc$)

1 Decide where to place the first digit.

$5\overline{)237}$

Since $2 < 5$, there will be no hundreds in the quotient. The first digit will be in the tens place.

2 Regroup the hundreds as tens. Divide the tens.

Think: $5\overline{)23 \text{ tens}}$ → ? tens

```
   4
5)237
 - 20   Multiply. 4 × 5
    3   Subtract. 23 − 20
        Compare. 3 < 5
```

3 Bring down the ones. Divide the ones.

Think: $5\overline{)37 \text{ ones}}$ → ? ones

```
   47 R2
5)237
 - 20↓
    37   Bring down the ones.
  - 35   Multiply. 7 × 5
     2   Subtract. 37 − 35
         Compare. 2 < 5
```

Check
Multiply. Then add.
$(5 \times 47) + 2 = 237$
The sum equals the dividend, so the answer is correct.

Solution: There will be 47 trading cards in each pile. Two cards will be left over.

Guided Practice

Divide. Use multiplication to check.

1. $6\overline{)384}$ **2.** $8\overline{)672}$ **3.** $7\overline{)542}$ **4.** $4\overline{)348}$

5. $437 \div 6$ **6.** $235 \div 5$ **7.** $341 \div 9$ **8.** $473 \div 6$

Ask Yourself

Can I divide the hundreds? The tens? The ones?

Math Talk When you divide a 3-digit dividend by a 1-digit divisor, what is the least number of digits that can be in the quotient?

Practice and Problem Solving

Divide. Use multiplication to check.

9. $4\overline{)396}$ **10.** $8\overline{)272}$ **11.** $5\overline{)394}$ **12.** $3\overline{)485}$

13. $2\overline{)162}$ **14.** $4\overline{)284}$ **15.** $6\overline{)532}$ **16.** $8\overline{)889}$

17. $134 \div 2$ **18.** $504 \div 3$ **19.** $317 \div 9$ **20.** $587 \div 6$

Algebra Functions

Copy and complete.

	Rule: $y = x \div 3$	
	Input (x)	**Output (y)**
21.	209	■
22.	361	■
23.	577	■

	Rule: $b = a \div 4$	
	Input (a)	**Output (b)**
24.	209	■
25.	361	■
26.	577	■

Solve.

27. There are 452 insect trading cards arranged in 4 equal groups. How many cards are in each group?

28. Stuart wants to sort 242 sea animal photos into 5 equal groups. How many photos will he have left over?

Science Link

Solve.

29. Otis has photos of pygmy marmosets. If he puts them into 4 equal groups, there will be 84 photos in each group. How many photos does Otis have? Use division to check your answer.

30. A nickel has a mass of 5 grams. How many nickels would it take to balance a 120-gram pygmy marmoset on a scale?

31. Sandy sees a pygmy marmoset at the Santa Ana Zoo at Prentice Park. The marmoset is 34 centimeters long from head to tail. If the marmoset's body is 16 centimeters long, how long is its tail?

32. **Challenge** A pygmy marmoset can jump vertically up to 192 inches. There are 12 inches in 1 foot. Can a marmoset jump up to a tree branch that is 14 feet above it? Explain your answer.

Fun Facts

The Pygmy Marmoset

- Pygmy marmosets are native to rainforests.
- They are the smallest monkeys in the world! They range from 14–16 cm in length. And that's without their 15–20 cm tails! They generally have a mass between 120 and 190 grams.
- They eat mostly tree sap but also eat fruit and insects. They spend most of each day chewing tree bark to reach the sap or looking for other food.

Science LS 3.c

Spiral Review and Test Practice

Copy and complete. KEY AF 1.5 page 196

	Rule: $y = 3x + 9$	
	Input (x)	Output (y)
33.	1	▒
34.	2	▒
35.	3	▒

	Rule: $b = 2a - 5$	
	Input (a)	Output (b)
36.	5	▒
37.	7	▒
38.	9	▒

39.

Rule: ___?___	
Input (w)	Output (p)
18	3
24	4
30	5

Write the letter of the correct answer. KEY NS 3.2

40. 587 ÷ 6

A 96 **B** 96 R5 **C** 97 **D** 97 R5

Extra Practice See page 295, Set B.

Math Works! Carpenter

Build a Half-Pipe

Cecilia is a carpenter who is building half-pipes for a new skate park.

Solve.

1. Cecilia has a board that is 186 inches long. She cuts it into two equal pieces to build part of the half-pipe wall. How long will each piece be?

2. Look at the diagram of the half-pipe. The support beams are evenly spaced. How many inches will there be between the centers of its support beams?

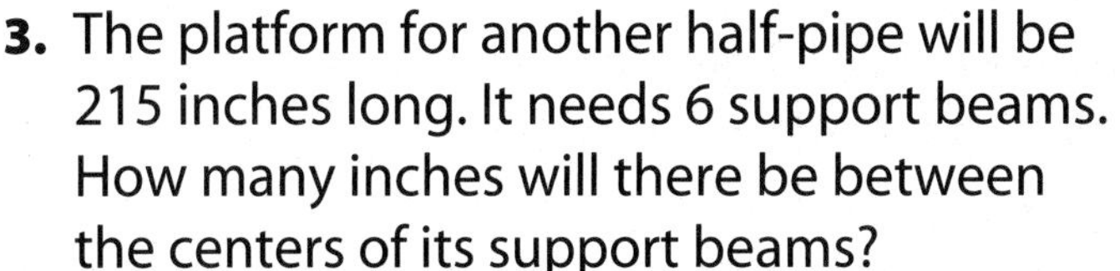

3. The platform for another half-pipe will be 215 inches long. It needs 6 support beams. How many inches will there be between the centers of its support beams?

National Inline Skate Series (NISS) Finals, Venice Beach, CA

CA Standards
KEY NS 3.0, KEY NS 3.2, KEY NS 3.4

Zeros in the Quotient

Objective Decide when to place zeros in the quotient.

CA Standards
KEY NS 3.2 Demonstrate an understanding of, and the ability to use, standard algorithms for multiplying a multidigit number by a two-digit number and for dividing a multidigit number by a one-digit number; use relationships between them to simplify computations and to check results.

KEY NS 3.4 Solve problems involving division of multidigit numbers by one-digit numbers.

Also KEY NS 3.0, AF 1.0, AF 1.1, KEY AF 1.2, MR 2.0, MR 2.2, MR 2.3, MR 2.4, MR 2.6

Learn by Example

A whale watch company buys binoculars in boxes of 8. If the tour manager orders 824 binoculars, how many boxes should she receive?

Divide. $824 \div 8 = \bigcirc$ or $8\overline{)824}$

1 Decide where to place the first digit. Divide the hundreds.

Think: $8\overline{)8 \text{ hundreds}}$ = ? hundreds

$$\begin{array}{r} 1 \\ 8\overline{)824} \\ -8 \\ \hline 0 \end{array}$$

Multiply. 1×8
Subtract. $8 - 8$
Compare. $0 < 8$

2 Bring down the tens. Divide the tens.

Think: $8\overline{)2 \text{ tens}}$ = ? tens

$$\begin{array}{r} 10 \\ 8\overline{)824} \\ -8 \\ \hline 02 \end{array}$$

Since $2 < 8$, there will be no tens in the quotient. Write a zero in the tens place.

3 Bring down the ones. Divide the ones.

Think: $8\overline{)24 \text{ ones}}$ = ? ones

$$\begin{array}{r} 103 \\ 8\overline{)824} \\ -8 \\ \hline 024 \\ -24 \\ \hline 0 \end{array}$$

Multiply. 3×8
Subtract. $24 - 24$
Compare. $0 < 8$

Check
Multiply.
$8 \times 103 = 824$
The product equals the dividend.

Solution: The manager should receive 103 boxes.

Ask Yourself
Can I divide the hundreds? The tens? The ones?

Guided Practice

Divide. Use multiplication to check.

1. $3\overline{)924}$ **2.** $4\overline{)832}$ **3.** $5\overline{)547}$ **4.** $6\overline{)639}$

Math Talk Look back at Exercise 1. Why must you remember to write the zero in the quotient?

Practice and Problem Solving

Divide. Use multiplication to check.

5. $4\overline{)804}$ **6.** $2\overline{)412}$ **7.** $7\overline{)756}$ **8.** $6\overline{)361}$

9. $7\overline{)840}$ **10.** $2\overline{)613}$ **11.** $9\overline{)992}$ **12.** $5\overline{)754}$

13. $612 \div 3$ **14.** $963 \div 8$ **15.** $947 \div 9$ **16.** $910 \div 7$

Algebra Expressions

Find the value of each expression when $n = 3$.

17. $66 \div n$ **18.** $96 \div n$ **19.** $849 \div n$ **20.** $342 \div n$

21. $848 \div (n - 1)$ **22.** $(8 \times n) \div 2$ **23.** $742 \div (n + 4)$ **24.** $342 \div (n \times 3)$

Solve.

25. The whale watch company sailed 3 times last Saturday, with the same number of tourists each time. If 324 tourists sailed on Saturday, how many people were on each tour?

Gray whale

26. **Explain** Think about the problem $968 \div 8 = 121$. Without dividing, decide whether there would be a remainder if you divided by 4. Explain your reasoning.

Spiral Review and Test Practice

Divide. Use multiplication to check. KEY NS 3.2 pages 262, 266

27. $87 \div 4$ **28.** $93 \div 2$ **29.** $54 \div 3$

Write the letter of the correct answer. KEY NS 3.4

30. Jamie divides 321 books equally into 3 boxes. How many books are in each box?

A 17 **B** 107 **C** 648 **D** 3,752

Extra Practice See page 295, Set C.

LESSON 5

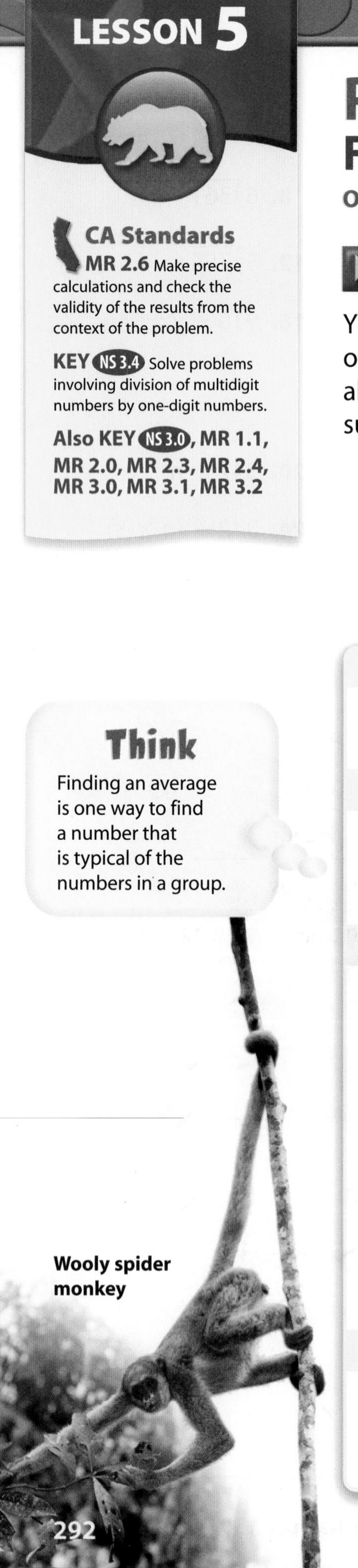

CA Standards
MR 2.6 Make precise calculations and check the validity of the results from the context of the problem.

KEY NS 3.4 Solve problems involving division of multidigit numbers by one-digit numbers.

Also KEY NS 3.0, MR 1.1, MR 2.0, MR 2.3, MR 2.4, MR 3.0, MR 3.1, MR 3.2

Think
Finding an average is one way to find a number that is typical of the numbers in a group.

Wooly spider monkey

Problem Solving Plan
Find an Average

Objective Use division to find an average.

Learn by Example

You can use division to find the average, or mean, of a group of numbers. To find an average, first add all the numbers in the group, and then divide the sum by the number of addends.

At America's Teaching Zoo in Moorpark, CA, you can adopt an animal to help pay for its upkeep. The cost to adopt a tortoise is $100, an owl is $85, a spider monkey is $125, a fox is $75, and a bald eagle is $125. What is the average cost to adopt an animal?

UNDERSTAND

You want to find the average cost to adopt an animal.

PLAN

To find the average cost, add all the costs together, and then divide the sum by the number of animals, which is five.

SOLVE

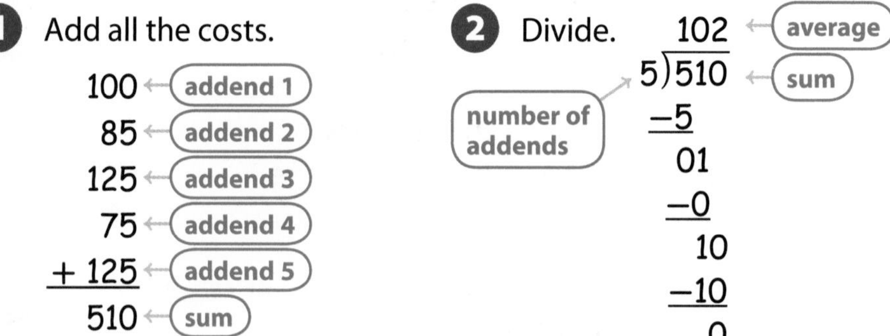

The average cost to adopt an animal is $102.

LOOK BACK

Is the average cost a reasonable representation of the individual costs? Why or why not?

Guided Problem Solving

Solve using the Ask Yourself questions.

1. A zoo has three lions. The male lion weighs 444 pounds. One female lion weighs 265 pounds. The other female lion weighs 278 pounds. What is the average weight of the lions?

Ask Yourself

- What numbers should I add to find the total weight?
- What number should I use as a divisor to find the average?

Math Talk Is the average weight a reasonable representation of the individual weights? Why or why not?

Independent Problem Solving

Solve. Use the table for Problems 2–3.

2. The table shows the amount of food eaten by each elephant for five days. What was the average amount of food eaten by the male elephant each day?

3. **Multistep** How much greater is the average amount of food eaten by the male elephant each day than the average amount eaten by the female?

Food eaten per day (lbs)		
	Male elephant	**Female elephant**
Monday	135 pounds	125 pounds
Tuesday	125 pounds	130 pounds
Wednesday	125 pounds	115 pounds
Thursday	120 pounds	120 pounds
Friday	130 pounds	125 pounds

4. **Challenge** There are three tigers at a zoo. One tiger weighs 259 pounds. Another tiger weighs 326 pounds. If the average weight of the three tigers is 294 pounds, what is the weight of the third tiger?

5. **Create and Solve** Write two word problems that involve finding a 3-digit average of three numbers. In one problem, the average should be a reasonable representation of the individual numbers. In the other problem, the average should be very different from each of the individual numbers.

Reading & Writing 

Vocabulary

An **average** is a number that represents a group of numbers. To find an average, divide the sum of the group of numbers by the number of addends.

A computer class for senior citizens has three students. The table shows their names and ages. What is the average age of the students in the computer class?

Name	Age
Mr. Hall	71
Mrs. Williams	62
Mrs. O'Hare	80

Use the questions to solve this problem.

Understand What are you trying to find? __________ __________ __________	Plan What numbers will you add? What number will you divide by? __________ __________ __________
Solve Follow your plan. Write the answer to the question. __________ __________	Look Back Use multiplication to check your division. __________ __________

Writing A fourth student registers for the computer class. She is 95 years old. What do you think this will do to the average age of the class? Check to see if you are right.

Reading Check out this book in your library.
The Doorbell Rang, by Pat Hutchins

CA Standards
MR 2.3 Use a variety of methods, such as words, numbers, symbols, charts, graphs, tables, diagrams, and models, to explain mathematical reasoning.

Also KEY NS 3.2, KEY NS 3.4

Standards-Based Extra Practice

Set A

KEY NS 3.0, KEY NS 3.4 page 282

Divide. Use multiplication to check.

1. 884 ÷ 8 **2.** 789 ÷ 7 **3.** 578 ÷ 4 **4.** 684 ÷ 5

5. 916 ÷ 4 **6.** 285 ÷ 2 **7.** 856 ÷ 6 **8.** 637 ÷ 3

9. A class visited the zoo. For admission, the students paid a total of $115. If a student ticket cost $5, how many students went to the zoo?

Set B

KEY NS 3.2, KEY NS 3.4 page 286

Copy and complete each table.

	Rule: $y = x \div 6$	
	Input (x)	Output (y)
1.	738	
2.	402	
3.	522	

	Rule: $y = x \div 4$	
	Input (x)	Output (y)
4.	352	
5.	612	
6.	892	

7. There are 396 goldfish that need to be divided equally into 9 tanks. How many fish will be in each tank?

Set C

KEY NS 3.2, KEY NS 3.4 page 290

Divide. Use multiplication to check.

1. $8\overline{)834}$ **2.** $7\overline{)649}$ **3.** 408 ÷ 4 **4.** 521 ÷ 5

5. 345 ÷ 7 **6.** $4\overline{)595}$ **7.** 609 ÷ 3 **8.** $3\overline{)289}$

9. **Analyze** Look at the problem 366 ÷ 6 = 61. Without actually dividing, would there be a remainder if the divisor was changed to 2? Explain your thinking.

Education Place
Visit www.eduplace.com/camap/ for more **Extra Practice.**

Chapter Review/Test

Vocabulary and Concepts

KEY NS 3.0, KEY NS 3.4, MR 2.3

Write the best word to complete the sentence.

1. The _______ is the number that you are dividing.
2. The _______ is the number of even groups in a division problem.
3. A number that is "left over" in a quotient is called a _______.
4. Use _______ to check your division.

Skills

KEY NS 3.2

Divide. Use multiplication to check your answers.

5. 689 ÷ 3
6. 1,456 ÷ 2
7. 951 ÷ 9
8. 434 ÷ 2
9. $8\overline{)564}$
10. 760 ÷ 2
11. $6\overline{)497}$
12. $8\overline{)630}$
13. $3\overline{)444}$

Problem Solving and Reasoning

MR 2.3, MR 2.6, KEY 

Solve.

14. Maria has a collection of 153 animal magnets. If she arranged them in rows of 9, how many rows will she have?
15. The aquarium gift shop sold $540 worth of stuffed animal whales in one day. If each stuffed whale costs $9, how many stuffed whales did the gift shop sell?

Writing Math When doing a division problem, why is it helpful to use multiplication to check your answer?

Spiral Review and Test Practice

1. $82{,}000 - 3{,}812 =$

A 88,188

B 79,188

C 78,198

D 78,188

Test Tip
Remember, you always need to regroup when subtracting from a zero.

KEY NS 3.1 page 82

2. Which statement is true?

A $12 \div (2 \times 3) = 12 \div 2 \times 3$

B $12 \div (2 \times 3) = (12 \div 2) \times 3$

C $12 \div (2 \times 3) < (12 \div 2) \times 3$

D $12 \div (2 \times 3) > (12 \div 2) \times 3$

KEY AF 1.2, AF 1.0 page 148

3. What is the value of the expression below if $t = 8$?

$20 + t \div 4$

A 6

B 7

C 22

D 28

AF 1.1 page 170

4. Tamar ordered 5 boxes of napkins. Each box contained 3,429 napkins. Approximately how many napkins did Tamar order?

A 10,000 napkins

B 15,000 napkins

C 18,145 napkins

D 20,000 napkins

KEY NS 1.3 page 216

5. Jonah divides his 45 books onto 6 shelves. If each shelf has the same number of books, how many books are left over?

A 39 books

B 7 books

C 6 books

D 3 books

Test Tip
Make sure you understand what the question is asking. Are there any words or phrases that are clues?

KEY NS 3.4 page 262

6. There are 8 people sitting at each table at a large party. If there are 232 people at the party, how many tables are there?

A 1,856 tables

B 240 tables

C 29 tables

D 28 tables

KEY NS 3.4 page 282

Education Place
Visit www.eduplace.com/camap/ for **Test-Taking Tips** and **Extra Practice**.

Number Theory

The Ferris wheel and roller coaster are popular rides at the Orange County Fair in Costa Mesa, CA.

Check What You Know

Word Bank
- factor
- divisor
- quotient
- product
- dividend

Vocabulary and Concepts KEY NS 3.0, MR 2.3

Choose the best word to complete the sentence. page 130

1. In the equation $63 \div 7 = 9$, the number 7 is the ____.
2. In the equation $32 \div 4 = 8$, the number 32 is the ____.

Skills GRADE 3 AF 2.2, KEY NS 2.3

Skip count to find the missing numbers.

3. 15, 20, 25, __ , __ , __
4. 40, 50, __ , __ , 80
5. 4, 8, 12, __ , __ , __
6. __ , 12, 18, __ , __

Write a division sentence and a multiplication sentence for the array.

7.
8.
9.

Problem Solving and Reasoning KEY NS 3.0

10. Hannah scored 76, 82, 88, and 94 on four math tests. What was her average test score?

Vocabulary

Visualize It!

3 is a **prime number**. It has exactly two factors: 1 and 3.	$1 \times 3 = 3$
6 is a **composite number**. It has more than two factors: 1, 2, 3, and 6.	$1 \times 6 = 6$ $2 \times 3 = 6$
3 is a **common factor** of 3 and 6. 3 is a factor of both 3 and 6.	$1 \times 3 = 3$ $2 \times 3 = 6$

Language Tips

If you have *common interests* with someone, it means you both have the same interests. If two numbers have *common factors,* it means both numbers share some or all factors.

Words that look alike in English and Spanish often have the same meaning.

English	Spanish
prime number	número primo
composite number	número compuesto
common factor	factor común

See **English-Spanish Glossary** pages 644–666.

Education Place Visit www.eduplace.com/camap/ for the **eGlossary** and **eGames**.

CA Standards MR 2.3 Use a variety of methods, such as words, numbers, symbols, charts, graphs, tables, diagrams, and models, to explain mathematical reasoning. **Also KEY NS 4.2**

CA Standards

NS 4.0 Students know how to factor small whole numbers.

NS 4.1 Understand that many whole numbers break down in different ways (e.g., $12 = 4 \times 3 = 2 \times 6 = 2 \times 2 \times 3$).

Also KEY NS 4.2, MR 1.1, MR 2.2, MR 2.3, MR 2.4, MR 3.0, MR 3.3

Vocabulary

factor

Materials
- Workmat 1
- Workmat 5
- counters
- eManipulatives (optional) www.eduplace.com/camap/

Think

Remember, an **array** is an arrangement of numbers, objects, or pictures in columns and rows.

Hands On
Find Factors of a Number

Objective Find factors of numbers to 50.

Explore

Question How can you use arrays to find all the factors of a number?

Nathan earned 8 blue ribbons at a county fair. He wants to display the ribbons in an array. What are all the different arrays he can make?

To answer this problem, find all the factors of 8. A **factor** is one of two or more numbers that are multiplied to give a product.

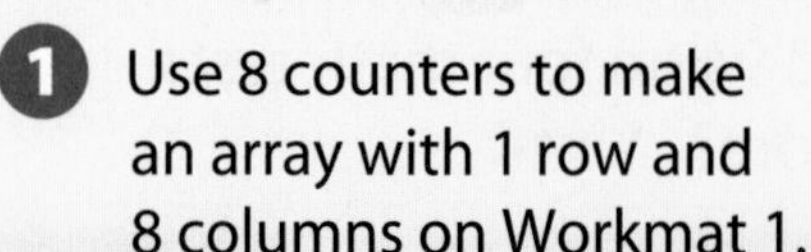

1 Use 8 counters to make an array with 1 row and 8 columns on Workmat 1.

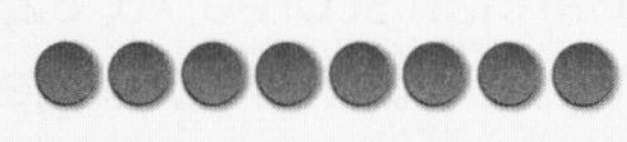

2 Record your array on Workmat 5.
- Label the number of rows and the number of columns.
- Write a multiplication sentence that represents the array.

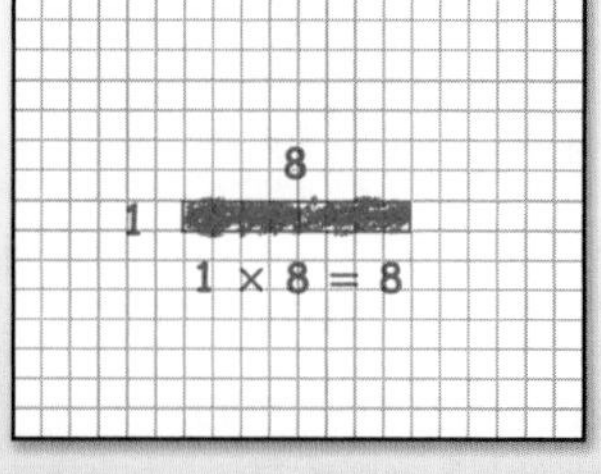

3 Repeat Steps 1 and 2 using arrays with 2 rows, 4 rows, and 8 rows. You cannot make 3, 5, 6, or 7 equal rows with 8 ribbons.

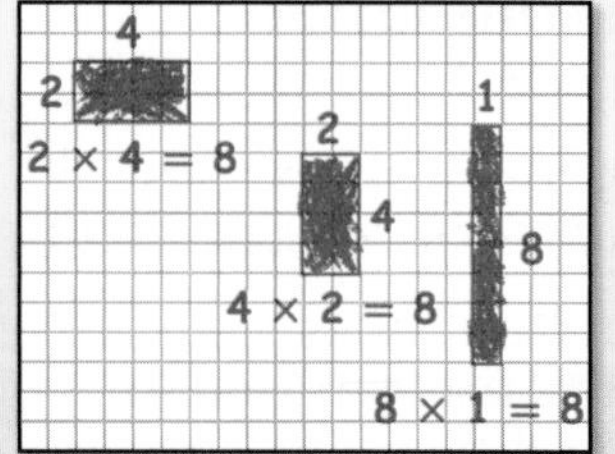

Solution: Nathan can arrange his 8 blue ribbons in four different arrays.

1×8 2×4 4×2 8×1

The factors of 8 are 1, 2, 4, and 8.

For some numbers, there are only 2 arrays, a single row and a single column. These numbers have exactly two factors: the number itself and 1.

What if Nathan has 5 blue ribbons to put into an array?

Vocabulary Tip
Numbers that have exactly two factors are called **prime numbers**.

1. Show an array for the 5 ribbons on Workmat 5. Write a multiplication sentence for the array using the number of rows and columns as factors.

2. Try to make arrays with 2 rows, 3 rows, and so on until you find all the possible arrays.

Solution: Nathan can arrange the 5 ribbons in only two arrays.

$1 \times 5 \qquad 5 \times 1$

The factors of 5 are 1 and 5.

Extend

Use Workmat 1 and counters to complete the table.

	Number	Multiplication Expressions	Factors
1.	9		
2.	10		
3.	12		
4.	23		
5.	36		

6. **Create and Solve** Add another row to the table above. Choose a number between 12 and 50 that is not already in the table. Complete the table for the number you choose.

Writing Math

Generalize Does a larger number always have more factors than a smaller number? Support your answer with an example.

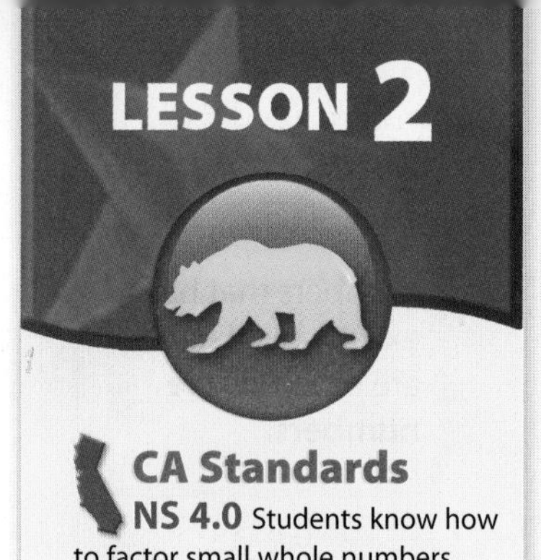

CA Standards
NS 4.0 Students know how to factor small whole numbers.

NS 4.1 Understand that many whole numbers break down in different ways (e.g., 12 = 4 × 3 = 2 × 6 = 2 × 2 × 3).

Also KEY NS 3.2, AF 1.0, AF 1.1, MR 1.0, MR 1.1, MR 2.0, MR 2.3, MR 2.4, MR 3.0, MR 3.2, MR 3.3

Vocabulary

factor
divisible
even number
odd number

Divisibility Rules

Objective Use divisibility rules to find factors.

Learn by Example

In Lesson 1, you used arrays to find the **factors** of numbers. In this lesson, you will learn to use divisibility rules to find factors of numbers.

A number is **divisible** by another number if it can be divided with no remainder.

Divisibility Rules	Examples
Even numbers are divisible by 2. Even numbers end with 0, 2, 4, 6, or 8 in the ones place.	Numbers divisible by 2: 630 632 634 636 638
Numbers that end with 0 or 5 in the ones place are divisible by 5.	Numbers divisible by 5: 630 635 640 645 650
Numbers that end with 0 in the ones place are divisible by 10.	Numbers divisible by 10: 600 610 620 630 640
If the sum of the digits of a number is divisible by 3, the number is divisible by 3.	630 is divisible by 3: 630 → $6 + 3 + 0 = 9$; $9 \div 3 = 3$
If the sum of the digits of a number is divisible by 9, the number is divisible by 9.	648 is divisible by 9: 648 → $6 + 4 + 8 = 18$; $18 \div 9 = 2$

Vocabulary Tip

Odd numbers end with 1, 3, 5, 7, or 9 in the ones place and are *not* divisible by 2.

Tickets for fair rides come in booklets of 40. Can 40 tickets be shared equally by 2 friends? 3 friends? 5 friends? 9 friends? 10 friends?

You want to know if 40 is divisible by 2, 3, 5, 9, or 10.

40	
Even. Ends in 0.	Divisible by 2. Divisible by 5 and 10.

Solution: Forty tickets can be shared equally by 2, 5, or 10 friends.

Guided Practice

28 120 46 75

Use divisibility rules to answer.

1. Which numbers have 2 as a factor? Which numbers have 9 as a factor? Tell how you know.
2. Which numbers have 5 as a factor? 10? Both 5 and 10?

Ask Yourself
What digit is in the ones place?

Guided Problem Solving

Use the questions to solve this problem.

3. Glenda took 186 photos at the California State Fair. Her photo album holds 5 photos per page. Will all the pages she uses for the photos be full?
   a. **Understand** How can you use divisibility rules and factors to solve this problem?
   b. **Plan** What digit in 186 will you look at?
   c. **Solve** Use divisibility rules. Write the answer to the question.
   d. **Look Back** Use division to check your answer.

4. Suppose Glenda decides to put only 3 photos on each page. Will each page she uses be full? Explain.

Math Talk Explain the relationship between divisibility and factors. Include an example in your answer.

Practice and Problem Solving

Use divisibility rules to tell if 2, 3, 5, 9, and 10 are factors of the given numbers.

5. 30
6. 45
7. 84
8. 95
9. 130
10. 180
11. 502
12. 2,000

Solve.

13. **Generalize** Can a number be too large to tell if it has 2, 5, or 10 as a factor? Explain your answer.

14. **Challenge** If a number is divisible by both 2 and 3, will it have 6 as a factor? Support your answer with examples.

Science Link

Solve. Show your work.

15a. Suppose one panda eats x pounds of bamboo in a day. If the panda weighs 3 times the amount it eats in a day, write an algebraic expression for its weight in pounds.

b. Suppose the panda eats 82 pounds of bamboo in a day. Use your expression from Part a to find what the panda weighs. Use division to check your answer.

16. The 36 students in the nature club went to see the pandas at the zoo. Could the students be placed in equal groups of 2? 3? 5? 9? 10? Use divisibility rules to support your answers.

Fun Facts

Giant Pandas

- Giant pandas are native to China.
- They have adapted to live mostly on bamboo shoots and leaves.
- Adult pandas spend 10 to 16 hours each day eating!
- The San Diego Zoo has the largest number of pandas in the U.S.

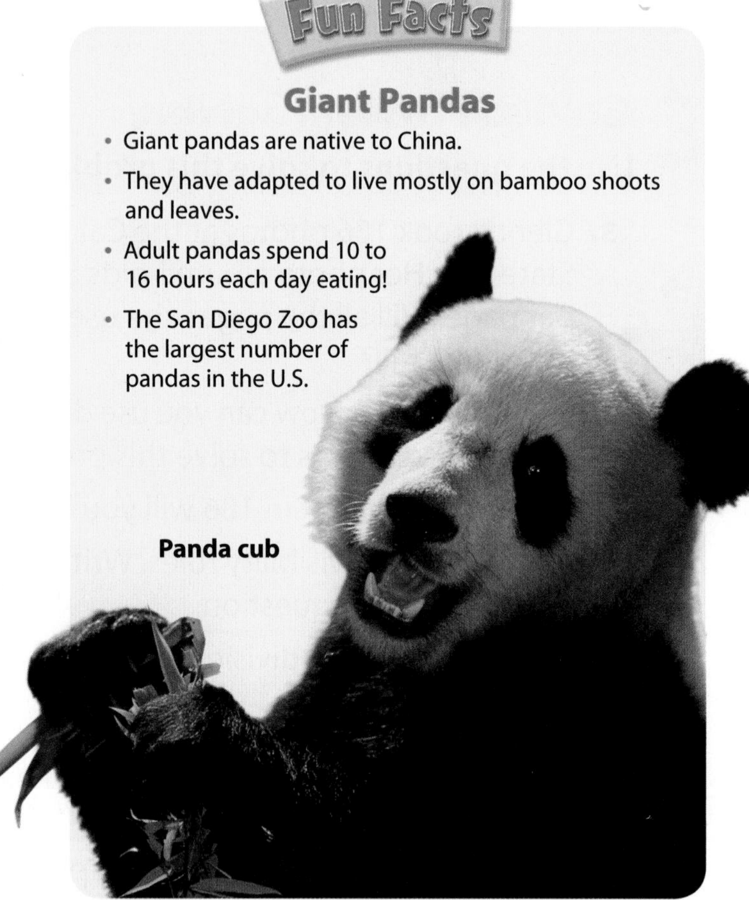

Panda cub

Science LS 3.c

Spiral Review and Test Practice

Solve the equation. KEY AF 2.0, KEY AF 2.1, KEY AF 2.2 pages 174, 176

17. $s + 4 = 7$

18. $20 = x - 12$

19. $7p = 49$

20. $\frac{h}{9} = 8$

Write the letter of the correct answer. KEY NS 4.2, NS 4.0

21. Which statement is true?

A The only factors of 12 are 1 and 12.

B The only factors of 13 are 1 and 13.

C The only factors of 14 are 1 and 14.

D The only factors of 15 are 1 and 15.

Extra Practice See page 315, Set A.

Key Standards Review

Need Help?
See Key Standards Handbook.

Solve. KEY NS 3.4

1. Tim has 137 grapes. He wants to share them equally with 5 friends. How many grapes will each friend get? How many grapes will be left over?

2. There are 264 seats in the auditorium. If there are 8 rows of seats, how many seats are in each row?

Which factors are prime numbers in these different representations of 36? KEY NS 4.2

a. 3×12

b. $2 \times 2 \times 3 \times 3$

c. 1×36

d. $2 \times 3 \times 6$

e. $4 \times 3 \times 3$

f. 4×9

Challenge Problem Solving

Why Do We Leap? KEY NS 3.0

Earth takes a little more than 365 days to orbit the sun, but our calendars usually have only 365 days. After several hundred years, the extra time would build up, and our seasons would be turned around.

Long ago, people came up with a solution—leap year. Every fourth year, an extra day is added to February.

- You can use division to find out which years are leap years. Pick any five years from 1904 to 2015. If you can divide the year evenly by 4, it is a leap year.
- How many leap years did you pick?

The Aztecs calculated a year as about 365 days.

Prime and Composite Numbers

Objective Decide whether a number is prime or composite.

CA Standards
NS 4.1 Understand that many whole numbers break down in different ways (e.g., 12 = 4 × 3 = 2 × 6 = 2 × 2 × 3).
KEY NS 4.2 Know that numbers such as 2, 3, 5, 7, and 11 do not have any factors except 1 and themselves and that such numbers are called prime numbers.
Also NS 4.0, MR 1.0, MR 1.1, MR 2.0, MR 2.3, MR 2.4

Vocabulary

prime number

composite number

Think

Since the number 1 has only one factor, it is neither prime nor composite.

Learn by Example

If you know what the factors of a number are, you can tell whether the number is *prime* or *composite*.

A **prime number** is a number that has exactly two factors, 1 and itself.

Number	Factors
19	1, 19
29	1, 29

A **composite number** is a number that has more than two factors.

Number	Factors
15	1, 3, 5, 15
18	1, 2, 3, 6, 9, 18

Is 7 a prime or composite number?

Identifying Prime and Composite Numbers

Way 1 **Use arrays to find factors.**

Draw as many arrays as you can for 7.

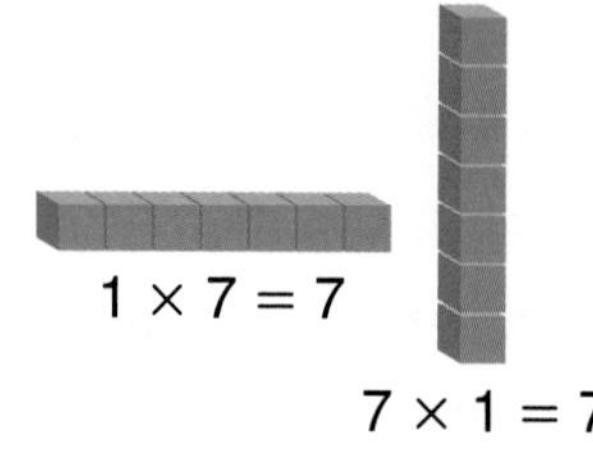

Way 2 **Use division or divisibility rules to find factors.**

You already know that 1 and 7 are factors of 7.

7 is not even, so 2 is not a factor.

7 ÷ 3 and 7 ÷ 4 have remainders in their quotients, so 3 and 4 are not factors.

7 does not have a 0 or a 5 in the ones places, so 5 is not a factor.

7 ÷ 6 has a remainder, so 6 is not a factor.

Solution: Since 7 has only two factors, 1 and itself, 7 is prime.

Guided Practice

Copy and complete the table.

	Number	Factors	Prime or Composite
	1	1	Neither
	2	1, 2	Prime
1.	3		
2.	4		
3.	5		

Ask Yourself

- Have I found all of the factors?
- Does the number have factors besides 1 and itself?

Math Talk Is the product of two prime numbers a prime or a composite number? Explain using an example.

Practice and Problem Solving

4. Extend and complete the table for 6 through 30.

Number	Factors	Prime or Composite
6		
7		
8		

Solve.

5. Right or Wrong? Aurora says that 51, 53, 55, 57, and 59 are all prime numbers. Use divisibility rules to find out if she is correct.

6. Challenge Name a 2-digit odd number that is prime. Name a 2-digit odd number that is composite.

Spiral Review and Test Practice

Divide. KEY NS 3.2 page 270

7. $80 \div 4$ **8.** $800 \div 4$ **9.** $8{,}000 \div 4$ **10.** $6{,}000 \div 6$

Write the letter of the correct answer. KEY NS 4.2

11. Which is a prime number?

A 6 **B** 9 **C** 11 **D** 15

Extra Practice See page 315, Set B.

Factor Trees

Objective Find prime factors of whole composite numbers.

CA Standards
KEY NS 4.2 Know that numbers such as 2, 3, 5, 7, and 11 do not have any factors except 1 and themselves and that such numbers are called prime numbers.

NS 4.1 Understand that many whole numbers break down in different ways (e.g., 12 = 4 × 3 = 2 × 6 = 2 × 2 × 3).

Also NS 4.0, KEY NS 3.1, MR 1.0, MR 1.1, MR 1.2, MR 2.0, MR 2.2, MR 2.3, MR 2.4, MR 3.0, MR 3.3

Vocabulary

prime factors

factor tree

Learn by Example

You already know how to find factors of a number. In this lesson, you will learn how to show a number as the product of its **prime factors** by making a **factor tree**.

1 Write any pair of factors for 24.

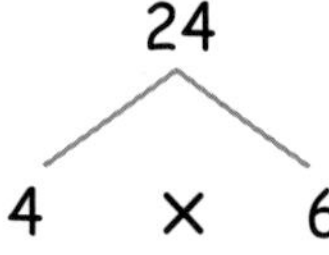

A factor tree is complete when each branch ends with a prime number.

2 Write a pair of factors for each factor until all factors are prime numbers.

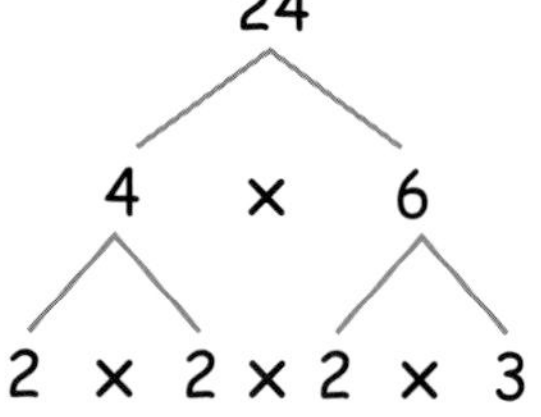

You can make different factor trees for one number.

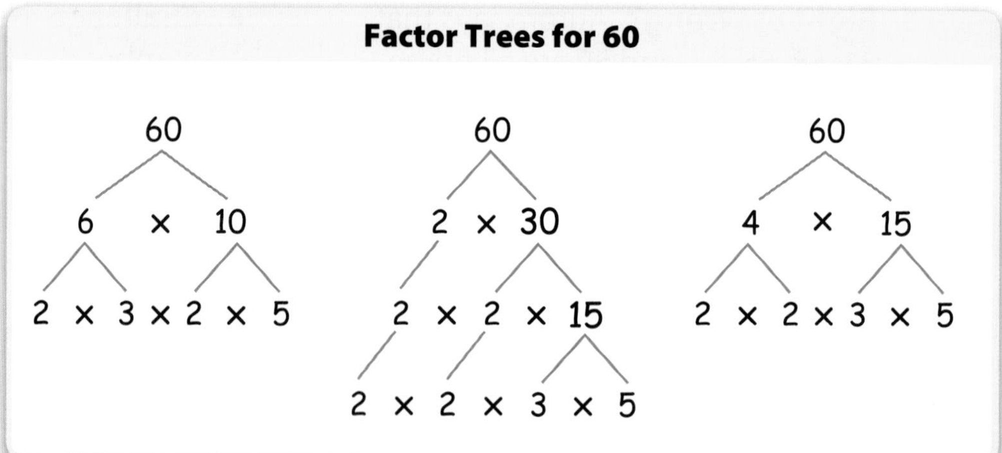

No matter which factors you start with, the last row of the factor tree will show the number as the product of the same prime factors.

Guided Practice

Copy and complete the factor trees for the number 36.

1. 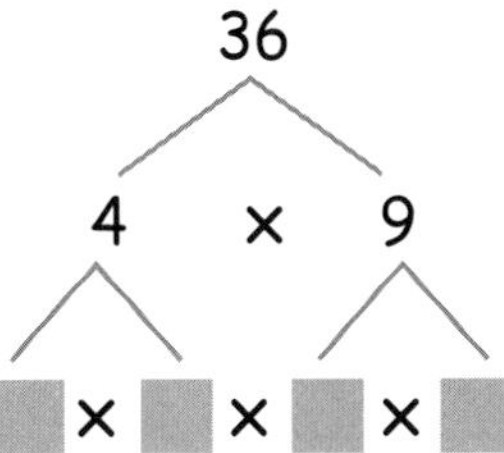

2. 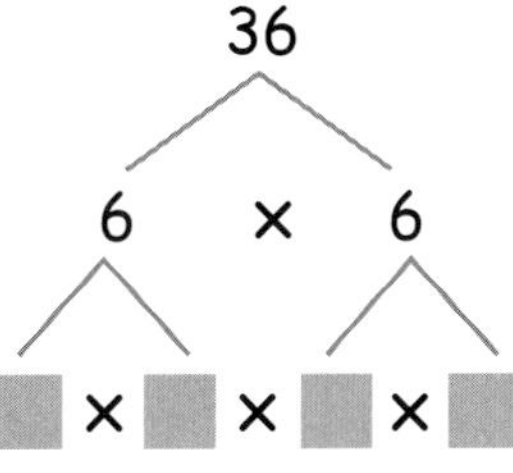

Ask Yourself

Are all the numbers at the bottom of my factor tree prime?

Make a factor tree for each number.

3. 12 **4.** 27 **5.** 50 **6.** 42

Math Talk Look at the factor trees for 60 on page 308. Would starting with 3×20 result in the same prime factors at the end of the branches? Explain.

Practice and Problem Solving

Copy and complete the factor trees for the number 48.

7. 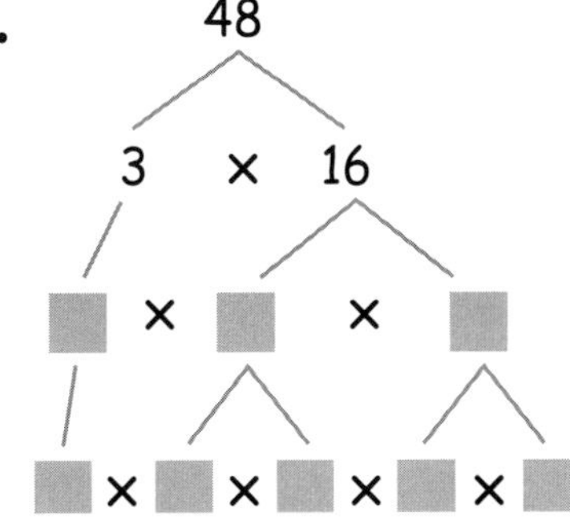

8. 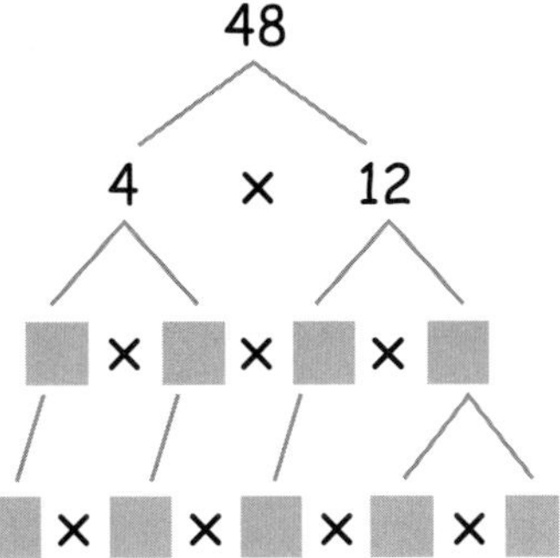

9. 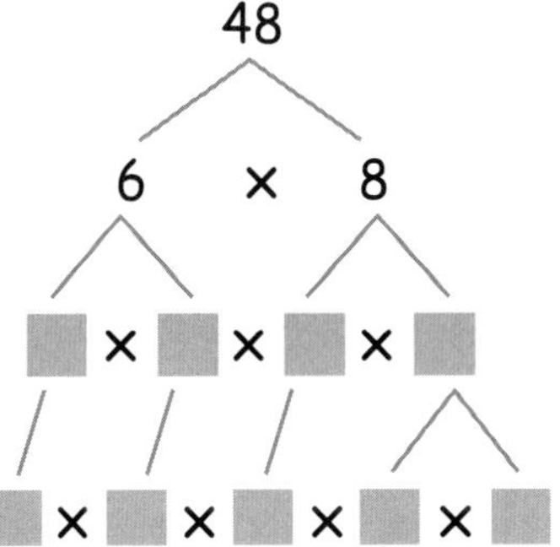

Make a factor tree for each number.

10. 65 **11.** 90 **12.** 18 **13.** 56

Solve.

14. Show three ways you could start a factor tree for 72, without using 1 or 72.

15. Show three ways you could start a factor tree for 40, without using 1 or 40.

16. Draw two different factor trees for the number 64.

17. Draw three different factor trees for the number 30.

18. **Explain** Why can you make several different factor trees for some numbers but only one or two factor trees for other numbers?

19. **Challenge** The numbers 2, 2, 3, 5, and 7 are on the last row of a factor tree. Draw a factor tree to find the number at the top of the tree.

History-Social Science Link

Solve. Show your work.

20. Mr. Graham has a photo of each of the 21 missions. He wants to post them on his classroom wall in an array. What are all the different arrays can he make?

21. Mission San Diego once covered 50,000 acres. By 1862, only 22 acres were left. How many fewer acres did the mission cover in 1862?

22. **Challenge** In 1809, Mission Santa Barbara had about 5,200 head of cattle. Use a factor tree to find the prime factors of 5,200. (Hint: Start with 52 × 100.)

California Missions

- The first mission was established in 1769.
- The 21 missions stretch from San Diego to Sonoma.
- The missions were placed one day's ride apart, some along old Indian trails.
- The missions introduced agriculture to the native Indian people.
- Many of California's largest cities started as part of the mission system.

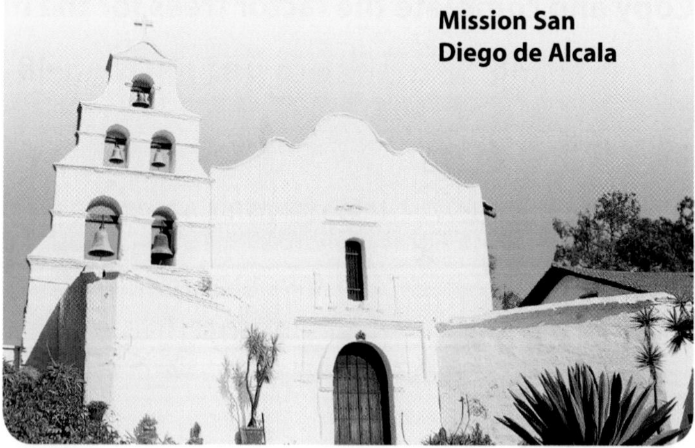

Mission San Diego de Alcala

History-Social Science 4.2.4

Spiral Review and Test Practice

Divide. KEY NS 3.2 pages 282, 286, 290

23. $\frac{430}{2}$ 24. 845 ÷ 5 25. $\frac{468}{8}$ 26. 201 ÷ 5

Write the letter of the correct answer. KEY NS 4.2

27. Which of these is another way to write the product of 15 × 4?

A 1 × 5 × 4 **B** 5 × 2 × 4 **C** 3 × 5 × 4 **D** 4 × 11 × 4

Extra Practice See page 315, Set C.

Factor Trees

Complete the factor trees.

1. 105

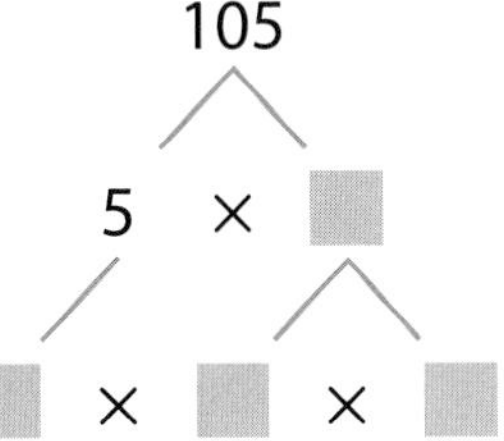

2. 98

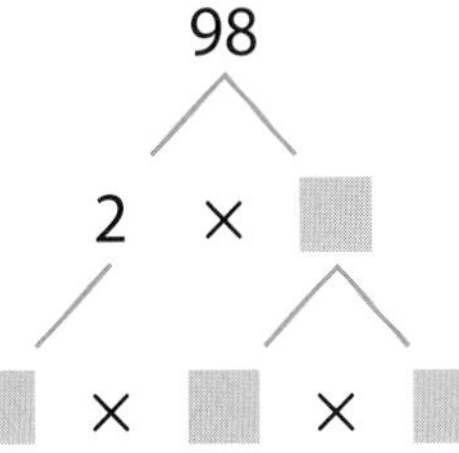

3. 81

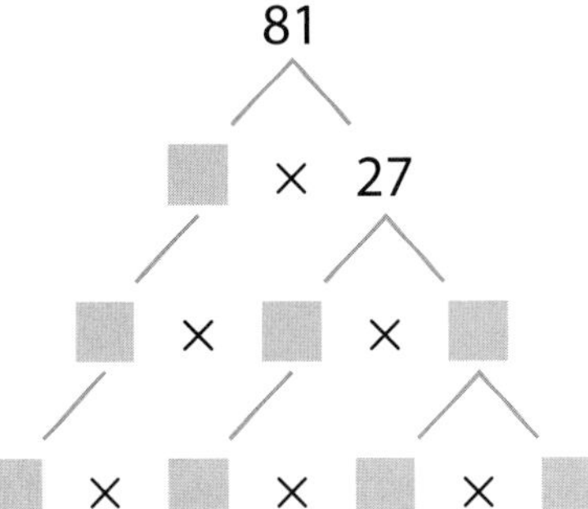

4. 140

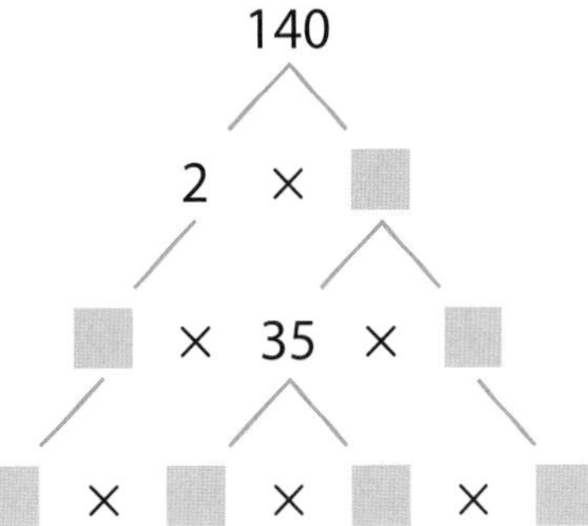

Make a factor tree to find the prime factors of each number.

5. 77 **6.** 85 **7.** 400 **8.** 144

9. Explain How do you know that a number is prime?

10. Analyze Han says that greater numbers have more prime factors than lesser numbers. Is Han correct? Use examples to explain your thinking.

LESSON 5
Field Trip...
Del Mar, CA
CA Standards
MR 1.0, MR 1.1,
MR 2.0, MR 2.3,
MR 3.0, MR 3.3,
NS 4.0, NS 4.1,
KEY NS 4.2

Problem Solving

Objective Use skills and strategies to solve word problems.

The fair features a variety of musicians, animal events, and children's activities.

The San Diego County Fair, started in 1880, brought county farmers together. Today, the fair attracts over a million visitors every year.

Solve. Tell which strategy or method you used.

1. The 2006 San Diego County Fair ran for 25 days. Is 25 a prime number? Draw a factor tree to explain.

2. **Draw a Picture** A baker wanted to display 5 pies.
   - **a.** Into how many different arrays can she arrange the pies? Draw pictures to show each array.
   - **b.** Suppose she sells one of her pies. Into how many different arrays can she arrange the pies that are left? Draw pictures to show each array.
   - **c.** **Generalize** For what number of pies will there be exactly 2 possible arrays? Explain.
   - **d.** **Challenge** For what number of pies will there be exactly 1 possible array?

A poster from the 2006 San Diego County Fair

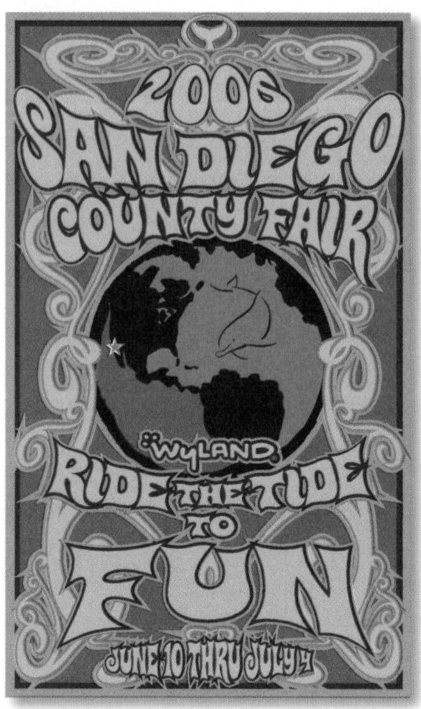

Problem Solving on Tests

Select a Strategy
- Choose the Operation
- Estimate
- Write an Equation
- Guess and Check
- Work Backward

1. The population of Orange County, California, in 2005 was estimated at 2,988,072. What is 2,988,072 rounded to the nearest hundred thousand?

A 2,000,000 **C** 3,000,000
B 2,988,000 **D** 2,990,000

KEY NS 1.3 page 34

2. Brett bought 12 whole wheat bagels and 6 sesame bagels every Sunday for 5 weeks. The expression $5 \times (12 + 6)$ represents the total number of bagels he bought in 5 weeks. How many bagels did Brett buy in 5 weeks?

A 66 bagels **C** 23 bagels
B 42 bagels **D** 90 bagels

KEY AF 1.2 page 144

3. Fiona has watered 11 of her plants. She has 19 more plants to water. In the equation below, x represents the total number of plants Fiona has to water. What is the value of x?

$x - 11 = 19$

A 8 **C** 30
B 20 **D** 209

Test Tip
Think about inverse operations when you solve an equation.

KEY AF 2.0 page 175

4. Chris made 4 number cards and asked Erica to pick the prime number. Which number should Erica choose?

A 35 **B** 36 **C** 37 **D** 38

KEY NS 4.2 page 306

5. Max earns $50 a month. He saves part of his earnings and spends the rest. Let x represent how much Max saves and y represent how much Max spends. If $x = 10$, which equation can be used to find the value of y?

A $y - 10 = 50$ **C** $x - y = 50$
B $10 + y = 50$ **D** $x + 10 = 50$

KEY AF 1.5 page 196

6. Jorge built 4 cabinets to hold CDs. Each cabinet can hold 1,080 CDs. How many CDs will the 4 cabinets hold?

A 4,320 CDs **C** 3,200 CDs
B 4,032 CDs **D** 1,320 CDs

KEY NS 3.0 page 224

7. Each lecture hall at a university can seat 505 people. How many people can 28 lecture halls seat?

A 5,050 people
B 1,540 people
C 14,140 people
D 4,140 people

Test Tip
Use estimation to check your answer for reasonableness.

KEY NS 3.3 page 242

Education Place
Visit www.eduplace.com/camap/ for **Test-Taking Tips** and **Extra Practice.**

Reading & Writing 

Vocabulary

Knowing the definitions of mathematical terms can help you to solve problems.

Choose a term from the word bank to complete each sentence.

Word Bank
prime number
composite
factor
divisible
odd
even

1. Each number used in a multiplication expression is a called a ________.
2. A whole number that has exactly two factors, 1 and itself, is called a ________.
3. Numbers that end with 0, 2, 4, 6, or 8 in the ones place and are divisible by 2 are called ________ numbers.
4. A number that can be divided by another number into equal parts with no remainder is ________ by that number.
5. Numbers that end with 1, 3, 5, 7, or 9 in the ones place and are *not* divisible by 2 are called ________ numbers.
6. A whole number that has more than two factors is called a ________ number.

You can show a number as the product of its prime factors by making a **factor tree**.

7. Make a factor tree for the number 48.
8. The prime factors for 48 are ________.

Writing Explain why the number 1 is neither a prime nor a composite number.

Reading Check out this book in your library. *Fourscore and Seven*, by Betsy Franco

CA Standards
MR 2.3 Use a variety of methods, such as words, numbers, symbols, charts, graphs, tables, diagrams, and models, to explain mathematical reasoning.
Also NS 4.0, NS 4.1, KEY NS 4.2

Standards-Based Extra Practice

Set A

NS 4.0, NS 4.1 page 302

Use divisibility rules to tell if 2, 3, 5, 9, and 10 are factors. Write *yes* or *no*.

1. 56
Divisible by 2?
Divisible by 3?
Divisible by 5?
Divisible by 9?
Divisible by 10?

2. 118
Divisible by 2?
Divisible by 3?
Divisible by 5?
Divisible by 9?
Divisible by 10?

3. 120
Divisible by 2?
Divisible by 3?
Divisible by 5?
Divisible by 9?
Divisible by 10?

4. 72
Divisible by 2?
Divisible by 3?
Divisible by 5?
Divisible by 9?
Divisible by 10?

5. Generalize When looking at a large number, can you easily tell if it is divisible by 2, 5, or 10? Explain.

Set B

NS 4.1, KEY NS 4.2 page 306

List all factors for each number. Decide if each number is prime or composite; write *P* if prime and *C* if composite.

1. 24
Factors:

Prime or composite:

2. 35
Factors:

Prime or composite:

3. 57
Factors:

Prime or composite:

4. 17
Factors:

Prime or composite:

5. Analyze Gabbi thinks 51 is a prime number. Jonathon thinks she is incorrect. Who is correct and why?

Set C

NS 4.1, KEY NS 4.2 page 308

Make a factor tree for each number.

1. 32 **2.** 14 **3.** 64 **4.** 56 **5.** 42

6. Compare Justin and Ruth both created a factor tree for the number 24. Justin's tree looked like this: $2 \times 2 \times 2 \times 3$. Ruth's looked like this: $2 \times 3 \times 2 \times 2$. Who is correct?

Education Place
Visit www.eduplace.com/camap/ for more **Extra Practice.**

Chapter Review/Test

Vocabulary and Concepts

KEY NS 4.2, MR 2.3

Write the best word to complete the sentence.

1. A _______ number does not have any factors other than 1 and itself.

2. Numbers that have more than two factors are called _______ numbers.

Skills

NS 4.1, KEY NS 3.0

Use divisibility rules to tell if 2, 3, 5, 9, and 10 are factors of the given numbers.

3. 32
4. 78
5. 135

Make a factor tree for the number.

6. 30
7. 70
8. 126

Problem Solving and Reasoning

MR 2.0, MR 2.3, NS 4.1, KEY NS 3.0

Solve.

9. The school is planning a graduation ceremony. If there are 395 students in the class, can 3 students at a time walk side-by-side into the auditorium and have no students left to walk alone or in a pair? Explain.

10. One hundred sixty-two students want to play baseball this year. Are there enough students to fill up teams of 9 students without leaving anyone out? Explain.

Writing Math Why is it helpful to use divisibility rules when dividing?

Spiral Review and Test Practice

1. Sabrina solved the problem below. Which expression could be used to check her answer?

$46 \div 7 \rightarrow 6\ R4$

A 7×6

B $(7 \times 6) \times 4$

C $(7 \times 6) + 4$

D $46 - 7 + 6$

KEY NS 3.2 page 130

2. Which number is represented by *r*?

$2r = 7 + 9$

A 2

B 8

C 16

D 32

Test Tip
Before choosing an answer, make sure that the expression is completely simplified.

KEY AF 2.0 page 176

3. There are 435 tires in each garage. If there are 16 garages, how many tires are there?

A 69,600 tires

B 6,960 tires

C 3,045 tires

D 451 tires

KEY NS 3.3 page 242

4. There are 6 movies playing at a theater. The same number of tickets was bought for each movie. If a total of 1,200 tickets were bought, how many tickets were bought for each movie?

A 7,200 tickets

B 1,206 tickets

C 1,194 tickets

D 200 tickets

Test Tip
Make a plan. What operation should you use?

KEY NS 3.4 page 270

5. $433 \div 6 =$

A 72 R2

B 72 R1

C 72

D 71

KEY NS 3.2 page 286

6. Which statement is true?

A The only factors of 17 are 1 and 17.

B The only factors of 16 are 1 and 16.

C The only factors of 15 are 1 and 15.

D The only factors of 10 are 1 and 10.

KEY NS 4.2 page 308

Education Place
Visit www.eduplace.com/camap/ for **Test-Taking Tips** and **Extra Practice**.

Unit 6 Test

Vocabulary and Concepts — KEY NS 3.0, MR 2.3, AF 1.1, MR 3.3, NS 4.1, KEY NS 4.2 Chapter 12, Lesson 2

Complete each sentence with a vocabulary word from this unit.

1. When dividing a number, the answer is called the ______.
2. The number left after a whole number is divided equally is the ______.
3. The number that is divided in a division problem is called the ______.

Computation — KEY NS 3.2 Chapters 12–13

Divide. Use multiplication to check.

4. $7\overline{)58}$
5. $5\overline{)37}$
6. $9\overline{)85}$
7. $6\overline{)51}$
8. $431 \div 4$
9. $583 \div 5$
10. $821 \div 6$
11. $626 \div 3$

Solve each equation. Chapter 12, Lesson 4

12. $80 \div 8 = f$
13. $240 \div 6 = d$
14. $7{,}200 \div 9 = t$
15. $5{,}400 \div 6 = g$

Use divisibility rules to tell if 2, 3, 5, 9, and 10 are factors of the given numbers. Chapter 14, Lesson 1

16. 64
    Divisible by 2?
    Divisible by 3?
    Divisible by 5?
    Divisible by 9?
    Divisible by 10?
17. 135
    Divisible by 2?
    Divisible by 3?
    Divisible by 5?
    Divisible by 9?
    Divisible by 10?
18. 150
    Divisible by 2?
    Divisible by 3?
    Divisible by 5?
    Divisible by 9?
    Divisible by 10?

Complete the table. List all factors for each number. Chapter 14, Lesson 1

		Factors	Prime or Composite
19.	24		
20.	25		
21.	19		

Problem Solving and Reasoning

KEY NS 3.4 Chapters 12–13

Solve.

22. Sam has 6 times more fantail goldfish today as she did 5 years ago. If she has 300 fantails now, how many did she have five years ago?

23. Nancy has 620 stamps. She can fit 8 stamps on each page of her stamp album. How many pages will she need for the stamps?

24. There are four labs at the aquarium. If a group of 118 students visit the labs, can there be an equal number of students in each lab? If not, how can they be grouped as evenly as possible?

25. Jessica is responsible for keeping animal fact sheets at 5 different locations at the zoo. If she has 440 fact sheets, how many can she place in each of the 5 locations?

Writing Math How can you tell when you need a 0 in a quotient? Include an example with your answer.

Performance Assessment

Where's Ian?

NS 4.1, KEY NS 3.4, MR 3.3

Laura is going to visit her cousin Ian. She says you can use Ian's area code to tell where he lives.

Task	Information You Need
Use the information above and at the right. In what city does Cousin Ian live? Use a factor tree to support your answer.	Ian's area code is divisible by 2.
	Ian's area code is divisible by 3.
	Ian's area code is divisible by 5.

Chico 530
Oakland 510
San Jose 408
Fresno 559
Santa Barbara 805
Burbank 818
Palm Springs 760
Santa Monica 310
San Diego 619

Greg Tang's Go Fast, Go Far

Unit 6 Mental Math Strategies

Divide by 5

No need for paper or a pen, just double and divide by 10!

I have a fast way to find 45 ÷ 5. First double 45 to get 90. Next divide 90 by 10 to get 9. Dividing by 5 is the same as multiplying the dividend by 2 then dividing by 2 × 5 or 10.

1. 45 ÷ 5 → [90] ÷ [10] → [9]
Double 45. Divide by 10.

2. 55 ÷ 5 → ▢ ÷ [10] → ▢
Double 55. Divide by 10.

3. 75 ÷ 5 → ▢ ÷ ▢ → ▢
Double 75. Divide by 10.

4. 85 ÷ 5 → ▢ ÷ ▢ → ▢
Double 85. Divide by 10.

You are doing great!

5. 65 ÷ 5 → ▢ ÷ ▢ → ▢

6. 95 ÷ 5 → ▢ ÷ ▢ → ▢

7. 110 ÷ 5 → ▢ ÷ ▢ → ▢

8. 135 ÷ 5 → ▢ ÷ ▢ → ▢

Go Faster!

Take It Further!

Now try doing all the steps in your head!

9. 150 ÷ 5

10. 225 ÷ 5

11. 330 ÷ 5

12. 415 ÷ 5

Unit 7

Measurement and Negative Numbers

BIG IDEAS!

- When you convert larger units to smaller units, you multiply. When you convert smaller units to larger units, you divide.
- For every positive number, there is an opposite negative number.

Chapter 15
Units of Measurement

Chapter 16
Temperature and Negative Numbers

Songs and Games

Math Music Track 7:
How's the Weather?
eGames at
www.eduplace.com/camap/

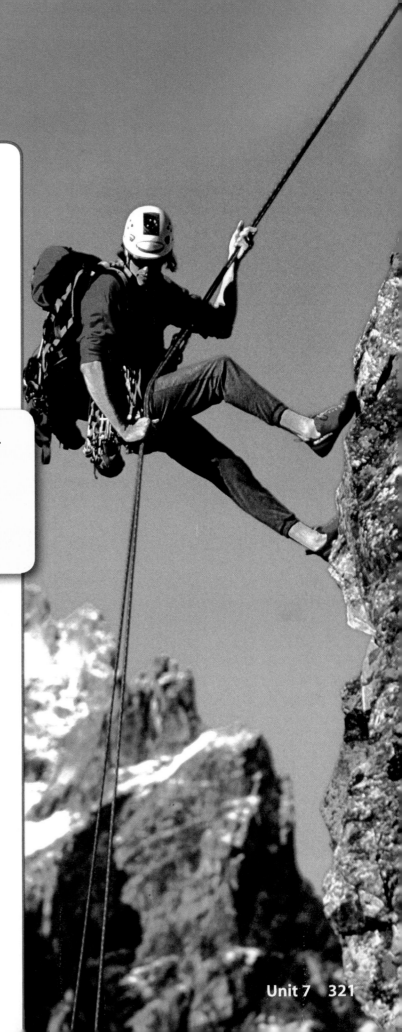

Math Readers

Get Ready Game

What's the Perimeter?

Object of the Game Calculate perimeter to earn more points than the other player.

Materials
Learning Tool 21 (Perimeter and Area Cards)

Set Up
Place the cards face down in a stack.

Number of Players 2

How to Play

1. Players take turns drawing cards from the stack and finding the perimeters of the rectangles.
2. Players earn the number of points equal to the perimeter. Record the points.
3. When all the cards have been drawn, players add all of their points and compare the totals.
4. The player with more points is the winner.

CA Standards
MG 1.0 Students understand perimeter and area.

Education Place
Visit www.eduplace.com/camap/ for **Brain Teasers** and **eGames** to play.

Reading When you are doing homework, make use of nearby help. Check out the Glossary and the Table of Measures at the back of the book.

In the next two chapters, you will learn about measurement. You will read some words you know. You will see some new words.

Which of these words do you know?
Which should you look up in the Glossary?

Customary System	Metric System
inch, mile, yard, foot	millimeter, centimeter, decimeter, meter, kilometer

It's easy to use the Glossary. The words are listed in alphabetical order.

Writing Sometimes you may be able to use a Table of Measures to help you answer questions. Use the portion of the table below to help you solve this problem.

Francine measured the width of the door. It is 1 yard, 3 inches wide. How many inches wide is the door?

Customary Units of Length
1 foot (ft) = 12 inches (in.)
1 yard (yd) = 36 inches
1 yard = 3 feet
1 mile (mi) = 5,280 feet
1 mile = 1,760 yards

Units of Measurement

Pumpkins in a field, Half Moon Bay, CA

Check What You Know

Word Bank
- inch
- yard
- meter
- millimeter

Vocabulary and Concepts GRADE 3 MG 1.1, MR 2.3

Choose the best word to complete the sentence.

1. The standard unit of length that equals 100 centimeters is called a ____.
2. In customary units of measurement, 3 feet are equal to 1 ____.

Skills GRADE 3 MG 1.1

Measure the length of the object to the nearest centimeter.

3. your pencil
4. your math book
5. your shoe

Choose the unit you would use to measure the weight of each. Write *ounce* or *pound*.

6. a cell phone
7. a computer

Choose the better estimate of the object's capacity.

8. a soup bowl 1 pt or 1 gal
9. a drinking glass 1 c or 1 qt

Problem Solving and Reasoning GRADE 3 KEY MG 1.3, KEY MG 2.3

10. What is the perimeter of a square whose side measures 10 feet?

Vocabulary

Visualize It!

Customary Measurement

Capacity
2 **cups** = 1 **pint**
2 pints = 1 **quart**

Weight
16 **ounces** = 1 **pound**
2000 pounds = 1 **ton**

Length
12 **inches** = 1 **foot**
3 feet = 1 **yard**

Language Tip

Words that look alike in English and Spanish often have the same meaning.

English	Spanish
pint	pinta
quart	cuarto
yard	yarda
ounce	onza

See **English-Spanish Glossary** pages 644–666.

Education Place Visit www.eduplace.com/camap/ for the **eGlossary** and **eGames**.

CA Standards MR 2.3 Use a variety of methods, such as words, numbers, symbols, charts, graphs, tables, diagrams, and models, to explain mathematical reasoning. **Also KEY NS 3.0**

LESSON 1

CA Standards

KEY NS 1.9 Identify on a number line the relative position of positive fractions, positive mixed numbers, and positive decimals to two decimal places.

Also NS 1.5, MR 1.1, MR 2.0, MR 2.3, MR 2.4, MR 2.5

Vocabulary

number line

inch

Materials

- Learning Tool 22 (Student-Made Ruler)
- Scissors

Hands On
Measure Length

Objective Measure length using an inch ruler.

Explore

In this lesson, you will make and use a ruler to measure the lengths of objects.

A ruler is a type of **number line**. The longest marks on the ruler show the location of whole **inches**. The shorter marks show parts of an inch.

Question How can you use a ruler to measure the length of an object to the nearest inch? To the nearest half inch?

Make a ruler and find the length of the pea pod.

Hint
Some rulers do not have a zero. These rulers use the left edge of the ruler as a starting point.

1. On Learning Tool 22, the longest marks represent 0 and the whole inches 1–6. Add the labels for 3–6.

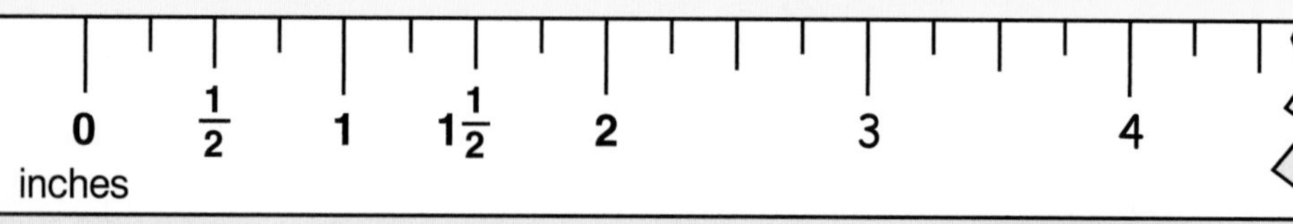

2. Locate the shorter marks that are halfway between the whole inches. These are the half-inch marks. They show the point that is halfway between two whole inches.

   Add the labels for $2\frac{1}{2}$, $3\frac{1}{2}$, $4\frac{1}{2}$, and $5\frac{1}{2}$.

   Then cut out your ruler.

Think
The $3\frac{1}{2}$ inch mark is exactly in the middle of, or halfway between, 3 and 4.

3 Use the ruler to measure the pea pod to the nearest inch. Use the half-inch mark to decide if the pea pod is closer to 3 or 4 inches.

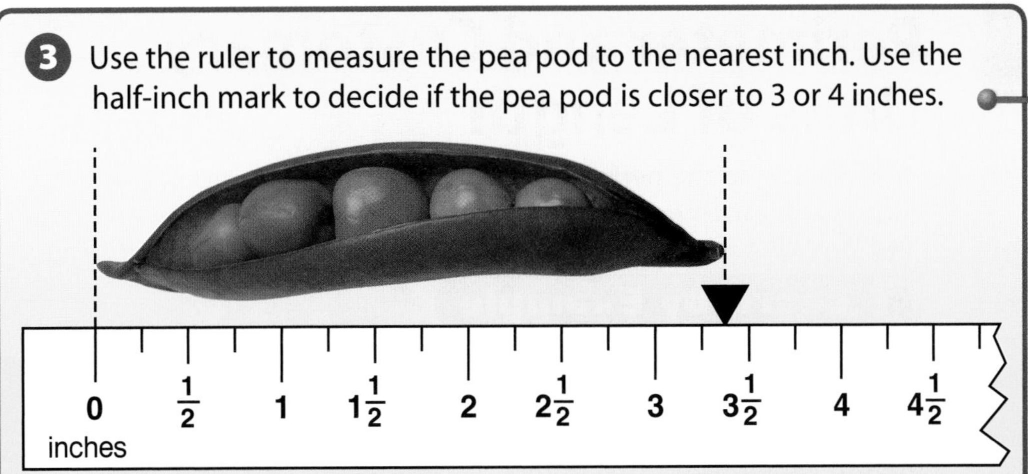

Hint

If the end of an object is exactly halfway between two whole numbers, round to the next whole inch.

4 The shortest marks show the points halfway between a half inch and a whole inch. Use the shortest mark to decide if the pea pod is closer to 3 inches or to $3\frac{1}{2}$ inches.

Solution: To the nearest inch, the pea pod is about 3 inches long. To the nearest half inch, the pea pod is about $3\frac{1}{2}$ inches long.

Extend

Measure the length to the nearest inch and to the nearest half inch.

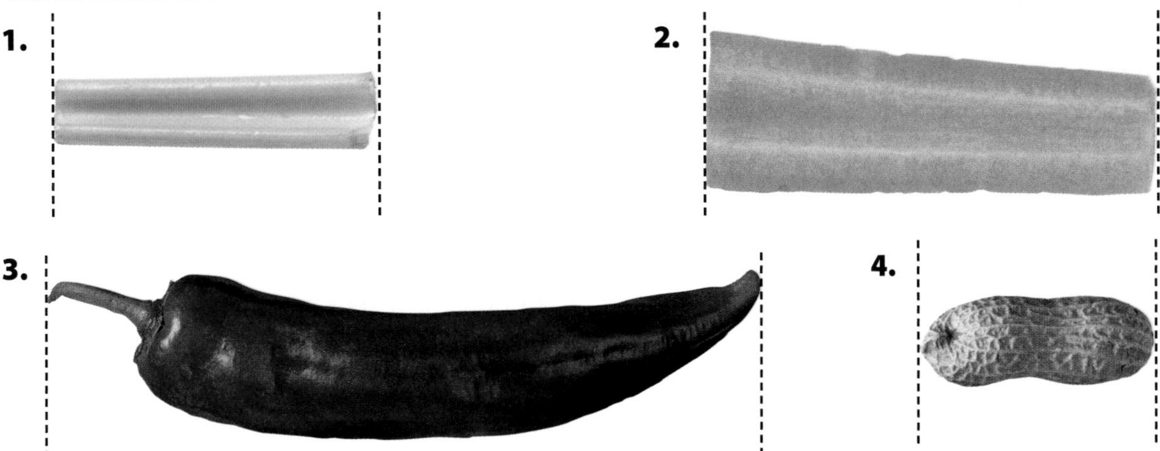

Writing Math

Analyze One green bean is less than 5 inches long, and another is more than 5 inches long. To the nearest inch, both beans measure about 5 inches long. Explain how this is possible.

Perimeter and Customary Units of Length

Objective Find the perimeter of a rectangle and convert customary units of length.

CA Standards
KEY NS 3.2 Demonstrate an understanding of, and the ability to use, standard algorithms for multiplying a multidigit number by a two-digit number and for dividing a multidigit number by a one-digit number; use relationships between them to simplify computations and to check results.

MG 1.0 Students understand perimeter and area.

Also AF 1.4, KEY AF 1.5, KEY NS 3.4, KEY NS 3.0, MR 1.0, MR 1.1, MR 1.2, MR 2.0, MR 2.3, MR 2.4, MR 3.0, MR 3.2

Vocabulary

perimeter

customary system

Customary Units of Length
1 **foot** (ft) = 12 **inches** (in.)
1 **yard** (yd) = 3 feet
1 yard (yd) = 36 inches
1 **mile** (mi) = 5,280 feet
1 mile (mi) = 1,760 yards

Learn by Example

The distance around a figure is called its **perimeter**.

Inches, feet, yards, and miles are units of the **customary system** used to measure length.

What is the perimeter of the rectangular sign in feet?

Add the lengths of the sides.

6 feet + 9 feet + 6 feet + 9 feet = 30 feet

Convert Feet to Inches

What is the perimeter in inches?

When you convert from larger units to smaller units, the number of units increases. So multiply.

Multiply by the number of inches in 1 foot.

$30 \times 12 = 360$

30 = number of feet; 12 = inches in 1 foot; 360 = inches in 30 feet

The perimeter of the sign is 360 inches.

Convert Feet to Yards

What is the perimeter in yards?

When you convert from smaller units to larger units, the number of units decreases. So divide.

Divide by the number of feet in 1 yard.

$30 \div 3 = 10$

30 = number of feet; 3 = feet in 1 yard; 10 = yards in 30 feet

The perimeter of the sign is 10 yards.

Guided Practice

Copy and complete the table. Write the rule.

1. Rule: ___?___

Input: ft (x)	2	3	5	8	9	12
Output: in. (y)	24	36				

Ask Yourself

- Am I converting to a larger or smaller unit?
- Should I multiply or divide?

Find the perimeter, in feet, of the rectangle.

2. 12 ft, 5 ft

3. 4 yd, 1 yd

4. 6 in., 6 in.

Guided Problem Solving

Use the questions to solve this problem.

5. Multistep Joan wants to put a fence around each of her two rectangular gardens. One garden measures 8 yd by 10 yd. The other measures 3 yd by 4 yd. How many feet of fencing does Joan need?

a. **Understand** Draw a sketch to represent what you know. What unit did you use?

b. **Plan** Decide which to do first: convert units or find perimeters.

c. **Solve** Follow your plan. Write the answer.

d. **Look Back** Solve the problem in a different way. Show your work. Is the answer the same?

Math Talk Explain why you multiply when converting from a larger to a smaller unit.

Practice and Problem Solving

Copy and complete the table. Write the rule.

6. Rule: ___?___

Input: ft (x)	3	6	9	12	15	30
Output: yd (y)	1		3			

7. Rule: ___?___

Input: mi (a)	1	2	3	4	5	6
Output: yd (b)	1,760	3,520				

Find the perimeter, in feet, of the rectangle.

8. 28 ft by 85 ft

9. 13 in. by 5 in.

10. 2 mi by 1 mi

Use the Fun Facts to solve.

11. Draw a number line that shows the range of ages of fossils in Dove Spring Formation. Then show a point for a fossil that is nine million, five hundred thousand years old.

12. Some of the cliffs at the canyon are 300 feet in height. There are 3 feet in 1 yard. What is this height in yards?

13. One hiking trail at the canyon is 4 miles long. There are 5,280 feet in 1 mile. What is this distance in feet?

Red Rock Canyon, Kern County

The cliffs of Red Rock Canyon are formed mostly of sandstone, a sedimentary rock.

- Sandstone feels grainy because it is made up of sand-sized pieces of rocks and minerals.
- The canyon's Dove Spring Formation contains fossils of plants and animals that lived 7 to 12 million years ago.

Science ES 4.a

Spiral Review and Test Practice

Simplify the expression. KEY AF 1.2 page 144

14. $6 - 2 \times 3$ **15.** $(6 - 2) \times 3$ **16.** $(14 - 9) \div 5$

Copy and complete, using >, <, or =. KEY AF 1.2 page 148

17. $66 \div 6$ ⬭ $(1 + 2) \times 5 - 4$ **18.** $9 + 4$ ⬭ $22 - 11 \times 2$

Write the letter of the correct answer. MG 1.0, AF 1.4

19. Which equation below represents the perimeter (P) of the rectangle?

A $7 + 11 = P$ **C** $7 \times 11 \times 7 \times 11 = P$

B $11 \times 7 = P$ **D** $7 + 11 + 7 + 11 = P$

11 in. by 7 in.

Extra Practice See page 343, Set A.

Key Standards Review

Need Help?
See Key Standards Handbook.

Divide. Use multiplication to check. KEY NS 3.2

1. 341 ÷ 7
2. 826 ÷ 9
3. 228 ÷ 3
4. 632 ÷ 4
5. 913 ÷ 6

Copy and complete the function table. KEY AF 1.5

	Rule: $y = 3x - 1$	
	x	y
	2	5
6.	7	
7.		26
8.		29

	Rule: $y = 5x + 4$	
	x	y
	1	9
9.	3	
10.	7	
11.		54

12.

Rule: ___?___	
x	y
4	20
6	30
8	40
10	50

Challenge — Number Sense

A Snail's Pace KEY NS 3.0

A snail is climbing a 5-meter fence. Every day the snail climbs 1 meter, but slides back 50 centimeters every night. How long does it take the snail to climb to the top of the fence?

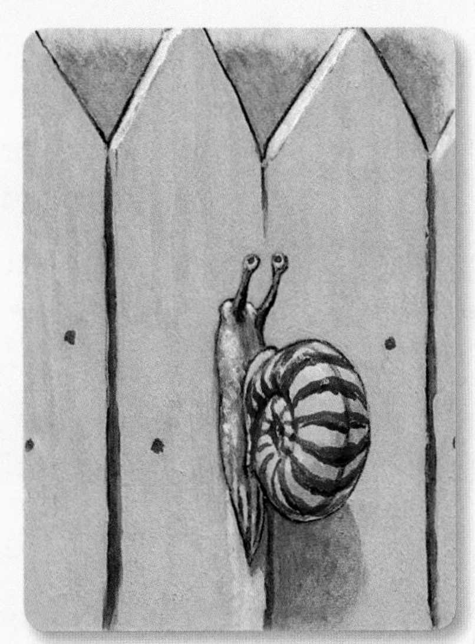

CA Standards
KEY NS 3.2 Demonstrate an understanding of, and the ability to use, standard algorithms for multiplying a multidigit number by a two-digit number and for dividing a multidigit number by a one-digit number; use relationships between them to simplify computations and to check results.

Also KEY NS 3.0, KEY NS 3.3, KEY NS 3.4, AF 1.1, MR 1.0, MR 1.1, MR 1.2, MR 2.0, MR 2.3, MR 2.4

Vocabulary

capacity

weight

Customary Units of Capacity
1 **pint** (pt) = 2 **cups** (c)
1 **quart** (qt) = 2 pints
1 quart (qt) = 4 cups
1 **gallon** (gal) = 4 quarts
1 gallon (gal) = 16 cups

Customary Units of Weight
1 **pound** (lb) = 16 **ounces** (oz)
1 **ton** (T) = 2,000 pounds

Customary Units of Capacity and Weight

Objective Convert customary units of capacity and weight.

Learn by Example

In Lesson 2, you converted customary units of length. In this lesson, you will convert customary units of capacity and weight.

Cups, pints, quarts, and gallons are customary units used to measure **capacity**, the amount a container can hold. Ounces, pounds, and tons are customary units used to measure **weight**, how heavy an object is.

Convert Quarts to Gallons

Angela's watering can holds 8 quarts of water. How many gallons is that?

When you convert from smaller units to larger units, the number of units decreases. So divide.

Divide by the number of quarts in 1 gallon.

$$8 \div 4 = 2$$

8: number of quarts; 4: quarts in 1 gallon; 2: gallons in 8 quarts

The watering can holds 2 gallons of water.

Convert Pounds to Ounces

Angela grew a watermelon that weighs 10 pounds. How many ounces is that?

When you convert from larger units to smaller units, the number of units increases. So multiply.

Multiply by the number of ounces in 1 pound.

$$10 \times 16 = 160$$

10: number of pounds; 16: ounces in 1 pound; 160: ounces in 10 pounds

The watermelon weighs 160 ounces.

Guided Practice

Find the missing number.

1. 8 c = ___ pt **2.** 16 pt = ___ qt **3.** 2 qt = ___ c

4. 20 qt = ___ gal **5.** 2 gal = ___ qt **6.** 64 oz = ___ lb

Ask Yourself

- Am I converting to a larger or smaller unit?
- Should I multiply or divide?

Math Talk Explain why you divide when converting from a smaller to a larger unit.

Practice and Problem Solving

Find the missing number.

7. 32 c = ___ gal **8.** 8 gal = ___ qt **9.** 9 pt = ___ c **10.** ___ gal = 16 pt

11. ___ lb = 3 T **12.** 48 oz = ___ lb **13.** 5T = ___ lb **14.** 32 qt = ___ gal

Solve.

15. **Multistep** Jane has 5 cups of water. Alberto has 3 pints. Ali has 1 quart. List the amounts in order from least to greatest.

It is usually easiest to order amounts using the smallest given unit.

16. **Challenge** Which is the better buy, a 4-ounce bag of plant food for \$12 or a half-pound bag for \$16? Explain your answer.

Spiral Review and Test Practice

Copy and complete. KEY AF 1.5 page 192

	Rule: Output = $x + 8$	
	Input (x)	**Output**
17.	2	___
18.	7	___
19.	22	___

	Rule: Output = $7m - 3$	
	Input (m)	**Output**
20.	4	___
21.	8	___
22.	9	___

23.

Rule: ___?___	
Input (p)	**Output**
5	15
8	24
12	36

Write the letter of the correct answer. KEY NS 3.3

24. Laura made 18 gallons of lemonade. There are 16 cups in 1 gallon. How many cups of lemonade did Laura make?

A 2 **B** 34 **C** 248 **D** 288

Metric Units of Length

Objective Convert metric units of length.

Learn by Example

In Lesson 2, you converted customary units of length. In this lesson, you will convert metric units of length.

Millimeters, centimeters, decimeters, meters, and kilometers are units of length in the **metric system**. A millimeter is about the width of the letter l on this page.

A corn kernel is about 1 centimeter long.

An ear of corn is about 2 decimeters long.

A young corn plant is about 1 meter tall.

A cornfield can be about 1 kilometer long.

CA Standards

KEY NS 3.2 Demonstrate an understanding of, and the ability to use, standard algorithms for multiplying a multidigit number by a two-digit number and for dividing a multidigit number by a one-digit number; use relationships between them to simplify computations and to check results.

KEY AF 1.5 Understand that an equation such as $y = 3x + 5$ is a prescription for determining a second number when a first number is given.

Also MG 1.0, KEY NS 3.0, KEY NS 3.3, AF 1.1, MR 1.0, MR 1.1, MR 1.2, MR 2.0, MR 2.3, MR 3.0

Vocabulary

metric system

Metric Units of Length
1 **centimeter** (cm) = 10 **millimeters** (mm)
1 **decimeter** (dm) = 10 centimeters
1 **meter** (m) = 10 decimeters
1 **kilometer** (km) = 1,000 meters

Convert Meters to Decimeters

How many decimeters are in 4,000 meters?

Multiply by the number of decimeters in 1 meter.

$4{,}000 \times 10 = 40{,}000$

(4,000: number of meters; 10: decimeters in 1 meter; 40,000: decimeters in 4,000 meters)

When you convert from larger units to smaller units, the number of units increases. So multiply.

There are 40,000 decimeters in 4,000 meters.

Convert Meters to Kilometers

How many kilometers are in 4,000 meters?

Divide by the number of meters in 1 kilometer.

$4{,}000 \div 1{,}000 = 4$

(4,000: number of meters; 1,000: meters in 1 kilometer; 4: kilometers in 4,000 meters)

When you convert from smaller units to larger units, the number of units decreases. So divide.

There are 4 kilometers in 4,000 meters.

Think

kilo- means 1,000.
centi- means 100.
deci- means 10.
milli- means $\frac{1}{1000}$.

Guided Practice

Find the missing number.

1. 40 cm = ▢ mm
2. 200 cm = ▢ m
3. 50 cm = ▢ dm
4. 3 km = ▢ m
5. ▢ mm = 9 cm
6. 5,000 m = ▢ km

Ask Yourself

- Am I converting to a larger or smaller unit?
- Should I multiply or divide?

Math Talk How is converting metric units the same as converting customary units? How is it different?

Practice and Problem Solving

Find the missing number.

7. 50 km = ▢ m
8. 600 mm = ▢ cm
9. 3 m = ▢ cm
10. ▢ dm = 40 cm

Copy and complete. Write the rule using *x* and *y*.

11. Rule: ______?______

Input: cm (*x*)	10	50	90	100	220
Output: dm (*y*)	1	▢	▢	▢	▢

12. Rule: ______?______

Input: m (*x*)	1	3	60	120	260
Output: dm (*y*)	10	▢	▢	▢	▢

Solve.

13. **Multistep** A rectangular sign is 2 meters high and 4 meters wide. What is the perimeter of the sign in centimeters? In millimeters?

14. **Challenge** A 3-km road has signs every 250 meters, including both ends of the road. How many signs are on the road?

Spiral Review and Test Practice

Multiply. KEY NS 3.2 pages 238, 242

15. 54 × 17
16. 729 × 12
17. 310 × 40
18. 529 × 53

Write the letter of the correct answer. KEY NS 3.3

19. Pedro drove 60 kilometers. There are 1,000 meters in 1 kilometer. How many meters did he drive?

A 60 m **B** 6,000 m **C** 60,000 m **D** 600,000 m

Extra Practice See page 343, Set C.

CA Standards
KEY NS 3.2 Demonstrate an understanding of, and the ability to use, standard algorithms for multiplying a multidigit number by a two-digit number and for dividing a multidigit number by a one-digit number; use relationships between them to simplify computations and to check results.

MR 3.2 Note the method of deriving the solution and demonstrate a conceptual understanding of the derivation by solving similar problems.

Also KEY NS 3.0, KEY NS 3.3, KEY NS 3.4, AF 1.1, KEY AF 1.5, MR 1.0, MR 1.1, MR 1.2, MR 2.0, MR 2.3

Vocabulary

liter
milliliter
gram
kilogram
mass

Metric Units of Capacity and Mass

Objective Convert metric units of capacity and mass.

Learn by Example

In Lesson 3, you converted customary units of capacity and weight. In this lesson, you will convert metric units of capacity and mass.

Liters and **milliliters** are metric units used to measure capacity. **Grams** and **kilograms** are metric units of **mass**, the amount of matter in an object.

Convert Grams to Kilograms

Ben grew a pumpkin that weighs 3,000 grams. How many kilograms is that?

Metric Units of Mass
1 kilogram (kg) = 1,000 grams (g)

Divide by the number of grams in 1 kilogram.

$$3{,}000 \div 1{,}000 = 3$$

3,000 → number of grams; 1,000 → grams in 1 kilogram; 3 → kilograms in 3,000 grams

Think: $3 \times 1{,}000 = 3{,}000$

Solution: There are 3 kilograms in 3,000 grams.

Convert Liters to Milliliters

Ben's bucket holds 8 liters of water. How many milliliters is that?

Metric Units of Capacity
1 liter (L) = 1,000 milliliters (ml)

Multiply by the number of milliliters in 1 liter.

$$8 \times 1{,}000 = 8{,}000$$

8 → number of liters; 1,000 → milliliters in 1 liter; 8,000 → milliliters in 8 liters

Solution: There are 8,000 milliliters in 8 liters.

Guided Practice

Find the missing number.

1. 9 L = ▢ mL
2. ▢ L = 5,000 mL
3. 8 kg = ▢ g
4. ▢ kg = 2,000 g

Ask Yourself

- Are the units for capacity or mass?
- Should I multiply or divide to convert units?

Copy and complete the table. Write the rule using *x* and *y*.

5. Rule: ____?____

Input: L (*x*)	3	7	9	12	13	15
Output: mL (*y*)	3,000	7,000	▢	▢	▢	▢

Math Talk How can you use mental math to convert between kilograms and grams and between liters and milliliters?

Practice and Problem Solving

Find the missing number.

6. 4 L = ▢ mL
7. ▢ L = 6,000 mL
8. ▢ mL = 10 L
9. 5,000 g = ▢ kg
10. ▢ g = 3 kg
11. 44 kg = ▢ g
12. 8 L = ▢ mL
13. ▢ kg = 31,000 g
14. ▢ mL = 15 L

Copy and complete the table. Write the rule using *x* and *y*.

15. Rule: ____?____

Input: g (*x*)	2,000	5,000	6,000	9,000	11,000	14,000
Output: kg (*y*)	2	▢	▢	▢	▢	▢

16. Rule: ____?____

Input: mL (*x*)	1,000	4,000	7,000	10,000	12,000	13,000
Output: L (*y*)	1	▢	▢	▢	▢	▢

Solve.

17. **Multistep** Susan has 4 bottles of water to take to the garden. Each bottle has a capacity of 500 mL. How many liters of water can the 4 bottles hold?

18. **Analyze** Allie can lift 25 kg. Michelle can lift 20,000 g. There are 1,000 grams in 1 kilogram. Who can lift more? By how many grams?

19. Cory buys four 3-kg boxes of flower bulbs. Each bulb has a mass of 60 g. There are 1,000 grams in 1 kilogram. How many bulbs did Cory buy?

20. Jared's empty canvas bag has a mass of 3 kg. He doesn't want to carry more than 7 kg. There are 1,000 grams in 1 kilogram. How many grams of equipment can he pack in the bag?

Real World Data

Use the graph to solve.

21. How many more liters of water are used for a bath than for a five-minute shower?

22. There are 1,000 milliliters in 1 liter. How many milliliters of water does a 5-minute shower use?

23. **Multistep** One day in the Domney home, the shower ran for 30 minutes, 2 baths were taken, and the dishwasher ran 3 loads. How much water was used?

24. **Challenge** The Domneys switched to a new, low-flow showerhead that uses 35 liters during a 5-minute shower. How many liters of water will be saved after 20 showers?

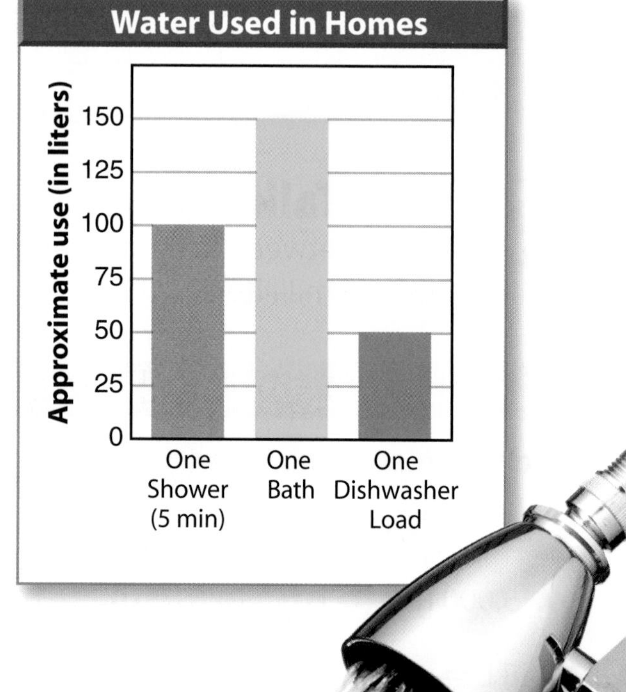

Spiral Review and Test Practice

Use divisibility rules to tell if 2, 3, 5, 9, and 10 are factors of the given numbers. NS 4.0 page 302

25. 135
26. 290
27. 6003

Write the letter of the correct answer. KEY NS 3.0

28. Bryan drinks half a liter of water after jogging. There are 1,000 milliliters in 1 liter. How many milliliters did he drink?

A 1,000 mL **B** 100 mL **C** 500 mL **D** 200 mL

Extra Practice See page 343, Set D.

Practice Game

Tick-Tack-Toe Measurement

Object of the Game Practice using metric units of measure. Try to get three counters in a row.

Materials

- 10 counters
- meterstick
- balance scale with metric units of measure
- Learning Tool 23 (*Tick-Tack-Toe Measurement* Game Board)

Set Up

Each player takes 5 counters. Player 1 uses the counters yellow-side-up. Player 2 uses the counters red-side-up.

Number of Players 2

How to Play

1. One player chooses any square on the board. Each player writes an estimate for the item in the square using metric units.

2. Players work together to measure the item. The player whose estimate comes closer to the actual measurement places his or her counter on the square.

3. Take turns repeating Steps 1 and 2. The first player to get 3 counters in a row horizontally, vertically, or diagonally wins!

the length of your classroom	the mass of your math book	the width of your chair
the width of your desk	the mass of your shoe	the length of your math book
the mass of a stapler	the length of a chalk eraser	the height of your desk

CA Standards

MR 2.0 Students use strategies, skills, and concepts in finding solutions.

Education Place

Visit www.eduplace.com/camap/ for **Brain Teasers** and **eGames** to play.

LESSON 6

Problem Solving Plan
Estimated or Exact Amounts

Objective Decide whether an estimate or an exact number is needed to solve a problem.

CA Standards
MR 2.5 Indicate the relative advantages of exact and approximate solutions to problems and give answers to a specified degree of accuracy.

KEY NS 1.4 Decide when a rounded solution is called for and explain why such a solution may be appropriate.

Also KEY NS 1.3, KEY NS 3.1, KEY NS 3.2, KEY NS 3.4, KEY NS 3.0, MR 1.0, MR 1.1, MR 1.2, MR 2.0, MR 2.3, MR 2.4, MR 2.6, MR 3.0, MR 3.1, MR 3.2

Learn Through Reasoning

One year, a farmer harvested 1,248 pounds of tomatoes, 890 pounds of squash, 1,527 pounds of pumpkins, and 1,238 pounds of apples. The next year, the farmer harvested 5,206 pounds of produce altogether.

Sometimes you need to use exact amounts.

How many more pounds of pumpkins than of apples did the farmer **harvest**?

The question asks *how many*, so you need an exact answer.

$$\begin{array}{r} 1{,}527 \\ -\ 1{,}238 \\ \hline 289 \end{array}$$

There were 289 more pounds of pumpkins than apples.

Sometimes a problem asks for an estimate.

About how many pounds of tomatoes and squash were harvested?

Since the question asks *about how many*, you can use estimates.

1,248	rounds to	1,200
+ 890	rounds to	+ 900
		2,100

The farmer harvested about 2,100 pounds of tomatoes and squash.

Sometimes an estimate is all you need.

Did the farmer harvest more the first year or the second year?

Use high and low estimates to find the total in the first year.

	Low Estimate				High Estimate
Tomatoes	1,200		1,248		1,300
Squash	800	←	890	→	900
Pumpkins	1,500		1,527		1,600
Apples	+ 1,200		1,238		+ 1,300
	4,700				5,100

Since the high estimate for the first year is less than 5,206, the farmer harvested more in the second year.

Harvesting tomatoes

Guided Problem Solving

Solve using the Ask Yourself questions. Explain why you used estimates or exact numbers.

1. Look at the problems on page 340. Suppose in the third year, the farmer harvested 5,020 pounds of produce. In which of the 3 years did he harvest the least produce?

Ask Yourself

- What is the question asking?
- Do I need an estimated or an exact answer?

Math Talk Were you able to use estimates to solve Problem 1?

Independent Problem Solving

Solve. Explain why you used estimates or exact numbers.

2. **Multistep** Mrs. Gallagher buys a wheelbarrow for $56 and clippers for $28. She pays for them with a $100 bill. Does Mrs. Gallagher have enough money left to buy a $9 hose?

3. The botanical garden ordered 5,000 plants. They received 2,098 pansies, 780 birds of paradise, 1,190 petunias, and 672 snapdragons. A gardener rounded to the nearest 100 and said that some plants were missing. Is she correct?

4. André plants 9 rows with the same number of lemon trees. If he plants 126 trees, how many trees are in each row? Use multiplication to check.

5. **Multistep** The perimeter of Ila's garden is 100 feet. She plans to put a stone border around it. If each stone is 8 inches long, how many stones will she need for the border?

6. **Challenge** For Problem 5, Kevin rounded 8 inches to 10 inches before finding the number of stones needed. Jessica rounded 8 inches to 5 inches. By how many stones is Kevin's estimate too small? By how many stones is Jessica's estimate too big?

7. **Create and Solve** Write three word problems, one that needs an exact answer, one that asks for an estimate, and one that can be solved by using estimated amounts.

Bird of paradise

Vocabulary

When measuring, you can use the **unit of measure** from the **customary system** or the **metric system**.

Choose the more appropriate unit of measure for each item.

1. 

a box of cereal:
grams **meters**

2. 

a sunflower:
feet **inches**

3. 

a can of soup:
milliliters **kilometers**

Find the missing number.

4. 

the length of a pencil:
18 cm = ▢ mm

5. 

the capacity of a fish tank: 3 gal = ▢ qt

6. 

the distance you and your family traveled on vacation: 300 mi = ▢ ft

Write an item you would measure in each of the following units.

7. kilometers ________ **8.** centimeters ________ **9.** meters ________

Writing Find a plant in your home, backyard, or in a local park. Measure its height and the length of one leaf. Explain what units you used and why.

Reading Look for this book in your library.
Measuring Penny, by Loreen Leedy

CA Standards
MR 2.3 Use a variety of methods, such as words, numbers, symbols, charts, graphs, tables, diagrams, and models, to explain mathematical reasoning.
Also KEY NS 3.0

Standards-Based Extra Practice

Set A

KEY NS 3.2, MG 1.0 page 328

Find the missing number.

1. 18 feet = ▒ yards
2. ▒ ft = 2 mi
3. 7 feet = ▒ in.
4. **Explain** Gary bought 30 feet of fencing for his flower garden. Will he have enough fencing to surround his garden if the measures of each side of the garden are 4 feet, 5 feet, 8 feet, and 9 feet? Explain your answer.

Set B

KEY NS 3.2 page 332

Find the missing number.

1. 4 cups = ▒ pints
2. 2 gal = ▒ c
3. 64 oz = ▒ lbs
4. **Compare** Gracie and Ellie are each filling fish tanks of equal size. If Gracie uses a gallon container and Ellie uses a cup container, who will finish first?

Set C

KEY NS 3.2 page 334

Find the missing number.

1. 20 cm = ▒ mm
2. 6,000 m = ▒ km
3. 500 cm = ▒ m
4. 3 dm = ▒ cm
5. **Analyze** Polly has 200 centimeters of ribbon to tie bundles of flowers together. If each bundle requires 2 decimeters of ribbon, how many bundles can Polly tie?

Set D

KEY NS 3.2 page 336

Find the missing number.

1. 7,000 mL = ▒ L
2. 4 kg = ▒ g
3. 47 L = ▒ mL
4. 6,000 g = ▒ kg
5. **Analyze** Roger measured out 4,000 mL of fertilizer. Clara measured out 3 liters. What is the total amount of fertilizer the two have together? State your answer in both milliliters and liters.

Education Place
Visit www.eduplace.com/camap/ for more **Extra Practice**.

Chapter Review/Test

Vocabulary and Concepts

MG 1.0, MR 2.3

Write the best word to complete the sentence.

1. The ______ system uses units such as meters, kilometers, and centimeters to measure length.
2. The distance around the outside of a figure is called the ______.

Skills

KEY NS 3.0, KEY NS 3.2

Find the missing number.

3. 18 ft = ▢ yd
4. ▢ in. = 4 ft
5. 3 mi = ▢ ft
6. 9 yd = ▢ ft
7. 4 c = ▢ pt
8. ▢ gal = 12 qt
9. 2 lb = ▢ oz
10. 3 T = ▢ lb
11. 4 L = ▢ mL
12. 12 m = ▢ dm
13. ▢ km = 4,000 m
14. 6 kg = ▢ g
15. 20 dm = ▢ m
16. 3 m = ▢ cm
17. ▢ mm = 23 cm
18. 4 m = ▢ cm

Problem Solving and Reasoning

KEY NS 3.0, MG 1.0, MR 1.0, MR 2.3

Solve. Explain the method you used.

19. Dorian is purchasing materials to fence in his garden. The length of the garden is 12 ft and the width is 18 feet. How many yards of fence will he need?
20. Harvey has 1 quart and 1 pint of juice. He needs 6 cups for a punch recipe. Does he have enough juice?

Writing Math When measuring long distances in customary units, you should use miles. What metric unit of measure would you use for the same distance? Justify your answer.

Spiral Review and Test Practice

1. Which of these is another way to write $(5 \times 2) \times 4$?

A $(5 + 2) + 4$

B $(5 \times 2) + 4$

C $(5 \times 4) \times 2$

D $(5 \times 3) \times 3$

Test Tip
Evaluate each expression to see which one equals $(5 \times 2) \times 4$.

KEY AF 1.2 page 124

2. Look at the problem below.

$\square = \triangle + 3$

If $\triangle = 2$, what is $\square$?

A 1 **C** 3

B 2 **D** 5

KEY AF 1.5 page 192

3. A grocery store has 226 crates of oranges. If there are 32 oranges in each crate, how many oranges are in the store?

A 258 oranges

B 1,130 oranges

C 7,232 oranges

D 7,332 oranges

KEY NS 3.3 page 242

4. Ellen divides 416 marbles equally into 4 jars. How many marbles are in each jar?

A 14 marbles **C** 464 marbles

B 104 marbles **D** 1,664 marbles

KEY NS 3.4 page 290

5. Which is a prime number?

A 4

B 7

C 10

D 12

Test Tip
Test each number using the rules of divisibility.

KEY NS 4.2 page 306

6. Which equation below represents the perimeter (P) of the rectangle?

A $5 + 10 = P$

B $10 \times 5 = P$

C $5 + 10 + 5 + 10 = P$

D $5 \times 10 \times 5 \times 10 = P$

AF 1.4, MG 1.4 page 328

Education Place
Visit www.eduplace.com/camap/ for **Test-Taking Tips** and **Extra Practice.**

Temperature and Negative Numbers

Temperatures below zero are written as negative numbers.

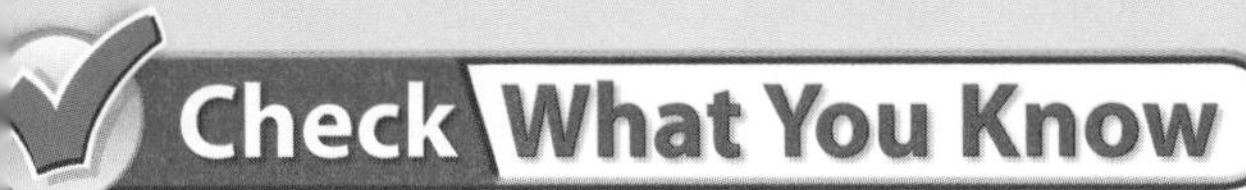

Word Bank
Celsius
Fahrenheit
temperature
thermometer

Vocabulary and Concepts GRADE 3 MG 1.0, MR 2.3

Choose the best word to complete the sentence.

1. The customary unit used to measure temperature is degrees _____.
2. A tool used to measure temperature is a _____.

Skills GRADE 3 MG 1.1, AF 1.0

Write the temperature using degrees Fahrenheit (°F).

3. 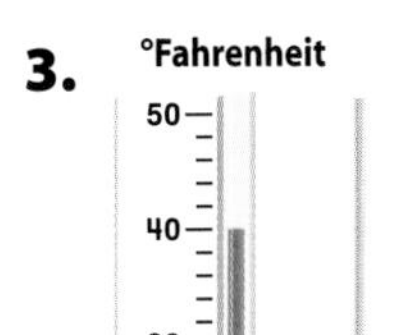

4. 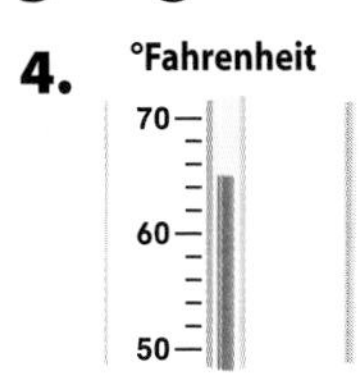

5. 

Compare. Write $>$, $<$, or $=$ for the ⬭.

6. 4,576 ⬭ 4,579
7. 325 ⬭ 235
8. 23 + 13 ⬭ 29 + 7
9. 24 − 13 ⬭ 35 − 21

Problem Solving and Reasoning GRADE 3 KEY NS 2.1

10. One morning, the temperature was 35°F. The temperature rose 12°F by noon. After the sun set, the temperature fell 21°F. What was the temperature after the sun set?

Vocabulary

Visualize It!

Integers are the set of positive whole numbers, their opposites (negative numbers), and 0.

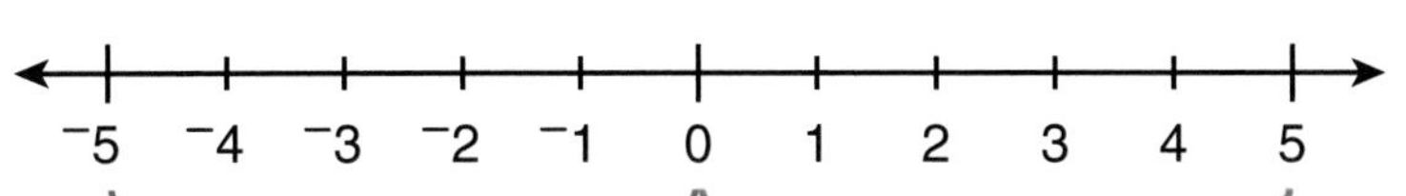

A **negative number** is less than 0.

A **positive number** is greater than 0.

Language Tips

When you are **positive** about something, you are very sure of it. In mathematics, if a number is **positive**, it is greater than zero.

Some words are alike in English and Spanish.

English	Spanish
Celsius	Centígrado
Fahrenheit	Fahrenheit
negative	negativo
positive	positivo

See **English-Spanish Glossary** pages 644–666.

Education Place Visit www.eduplace.com/camap/ for the **eGlossary** and **eGames**.

CA Standards MR 2.3 Use a variety of methods, such as words, numbers, symbols, charts, graphs, tables, diagrams, and models, to explain mathematical reasoning. **Also KEY NS 1.8**

LESSON 1

Hands On
Negative Numbers on the Number Line

Objective Use a number line to understand positive and negative integers.

CA Standards
KEY NS 1.8 Use concepts of negative numbers (e.g., on a number line, in counting, in temperature, in "owing").

NS 1.0 Students understand the place value of whole numbers and decimals to two decimal places and how whole numbers and decimals relate to simple fractions. Students use the concepts of negative numbers.

Also MR 1.1, MR 2.3, MR 3.0, MR 3.2, MR 3.3

Vocabulary

integers
negative
positive
opposite

Materials
- Workmat 4
- eManipulatives (optional) www.eduplace.com/camap/

Explore

You have used a number line that shows zero and numbers greater than zero. In this lesson, you will use a number line that includes numbers less than zero.

Question How can you make a number line to help you understand negative integers?

Carlos and Sara are playing a game at a party. In the first round, Carlos lost 4 points and Sara gained 5 points. How will they record their scores?

The numbers $^{-}4$ and 5 are **integers**.
$^{-}4$ is a **negative** integer. 5 is a **positive** integer.
Positive 5 can be written either as $^{+}5$ or as 5.

1 Use Number Line 2 on Workmat 4. Label the number 5 on the last mark at the right end of the number line. Count backwards from 5 to 0, labeling the marks on the number line as you count.

Think
Zero is also an integer. It is neither positive or negative.

2 The marks to the left of 0 represent negative numbers. Numbers that are the same distance from 0 on the number line are called **opposites**.

$^{-}1$ and 1 are opposites. Zero is its own opposite.

Label $^{-}1$ on the number line.

Label $^{-}2$, $^{-}3$, $^{-}4$, and $^{-}5$ on the number line.

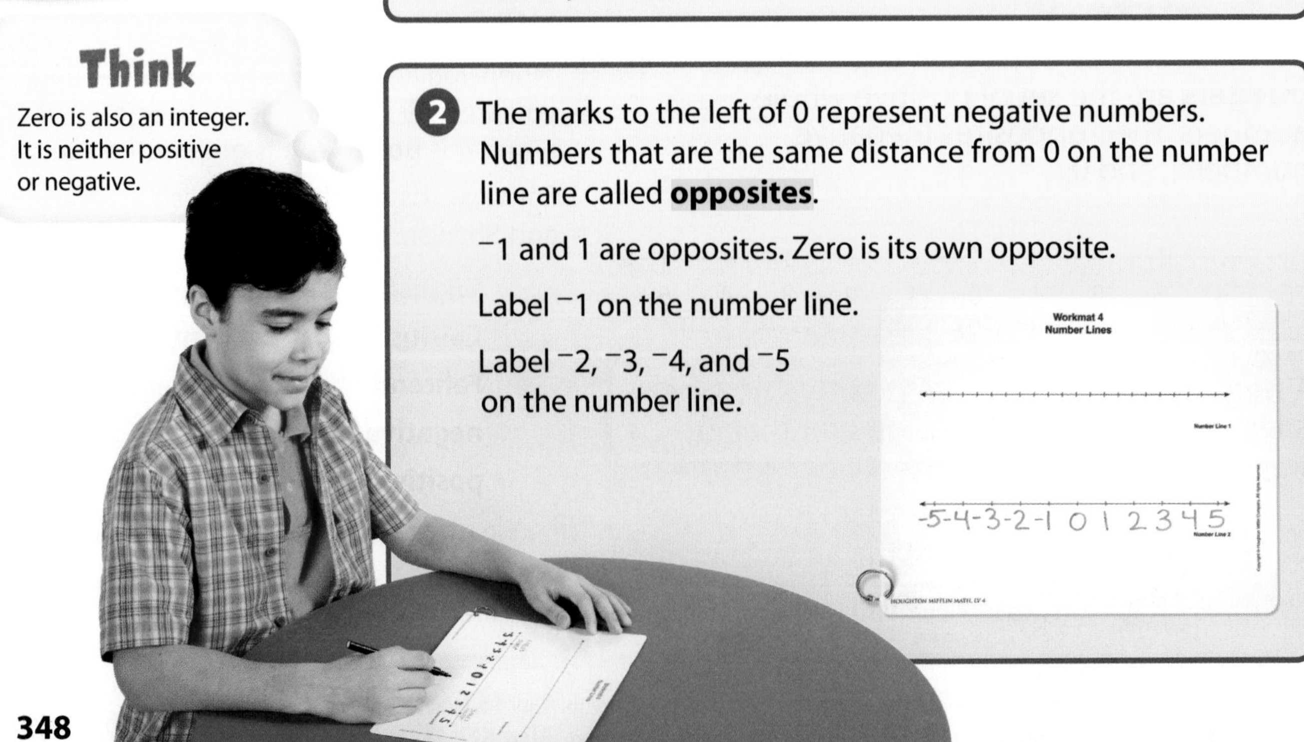

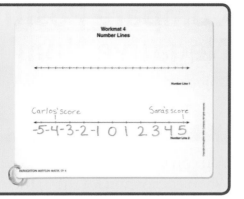

3 Label Carlos's score on the number line. Label Sara's score on the number line.

Solution: To show he lost 4 points, Carlos writes $^{-}4$.
To show she gained 5 points, Sara writes 5.

Extend

Write the integer for the letter on the number line.

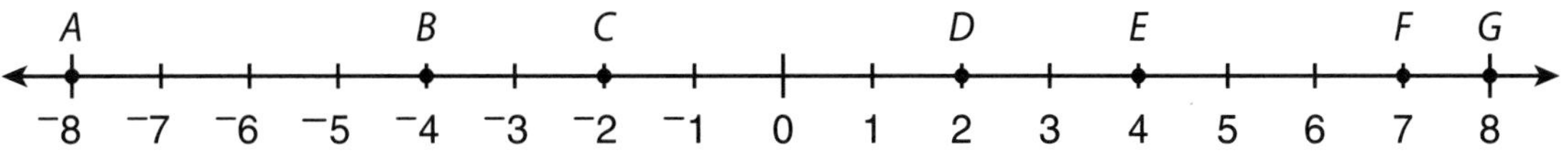

1. *A* **2.** *B* **3.** *C* **4.** *D* **5.** *E* **6.** *F* **7.** *G*

Write the integer for the situation.

8. 14 degrees below zero

9. 50 degrees above zero

10. 17 feet below sea level

11. 6 floors above street level

Use the number line you made to find the opposite of the number.

12. 2 **13.** $^{-}3$ **14.** 5 **15.** $^{-}1$ **16.** 4

Challenge Write the opposite for the number.

17. $^{-}34$ **18.** 98 **19.** 273 **20.** $^{-}5{,}423$ **21.** 0

Writing Math

Analyze What could the next three numbers in this pattern be? Explain your thinking.

9, 7, 5, 3, 1, ___, ___, ___

CA Standards
KEY NS 1.8 Use concepts of negative numbers (e.g., on a number line, in counting, in temperature, in "owing").
NS 1.0 Students understand the place value of whole numbers and decimals to two decimal places and how whole numbers and decimals relate to simple fractions. Students use the concepts of negative numbers.
Also AF 1.0, MR 1.1, MR 2.0, MR 2.3, MR 2.4

Vocabulary

temperature
degree

Compare Positive and Negative Numbers

Objective Compare positive and negative integers.

Learn by Example

You can use a number line to compare integers. When comparing integers, the number farther to the right is greater.

Which is greater, $^{-}5$ or $^{-}2$?

Compare Integers

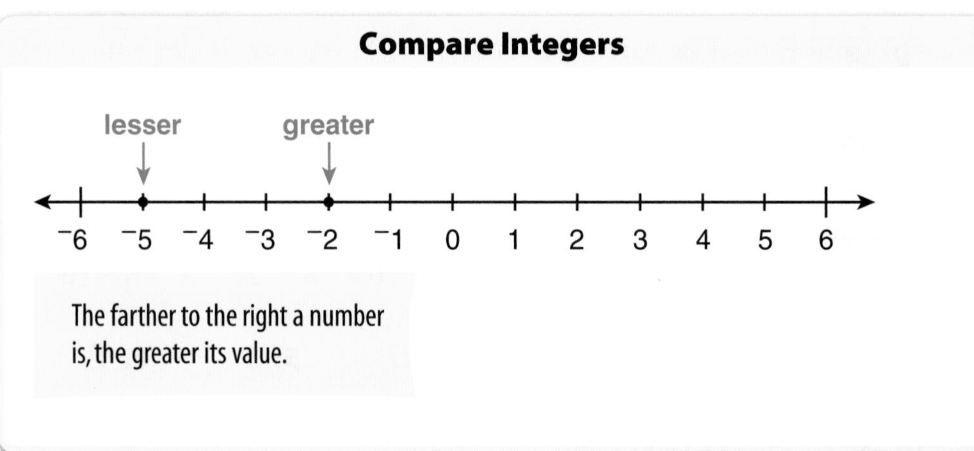

The farther to the right a number is, the greater its value.

Solution: $^{-}2 > {}^{-}5$. So, $^{-}2$ is greater.

Compare Temperatures

Vocabulary Tip
Degrees (°) are units used to measure temperature. °F stands for *degrees Fahrenheit*. °C stands for *degrees Celsius*.

The **temperature** at the base of a mountain is $^{-}1$°F, and the temperature at the top is $^{-}8$°F. Which is the lower temperature?

Think of a thermometer as a vertical number line. Temperatures above zero are positive numbers. Temperatures below zero are negative numbers. As you move up the thermometer, the temperatures increase.

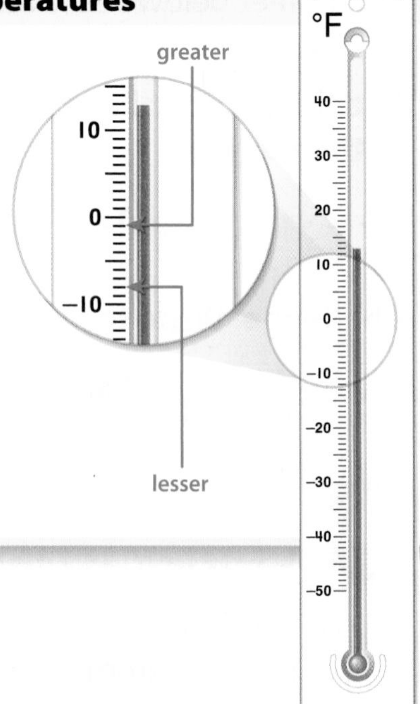

Solution: $^{-}8$°F < $^{-}1$°F. So, $^{-}8$°F is the lower temperature.

Guided Practice

Algebra Number Sentences

Use the number line on page 350. Choose >, <, or = to complete.

1. $^{-}6$ ◯ 6 **2.** $^{-}2$ ◯ $^{-}5$ **3.** 3 ◯ 3

> **Ask Yourself**
> - Are the numbers positive or negative?
> - Which number is farther right on the number line?

Math Talk **Right or Wrong?** Kim says that because 7 is greater than 4, $^{-}7$ is greater than 4. Is she correct? Explain.

Practice and Problem Solving

Algebra Number Sentences

Choose >, <, or = to complete.

4. 4 ◯ 4 **5.** $^{-}3$ ◯ $^{-}6$ **6.** $^{-}5$ ◯ 1 **7.** 5 ◯ $^{-}5$

Science Link

Use the Fun Facts to solve.

8. Date palms can survive temperatures as low as $^{-}15$°F. Write a number sentence to compare this temperature to Coachella Valley's lowest recorded temperature.

9. **Challenge** What is the difference between the highest and lowest temperatures in Coachella Valley?

Science LS 3.b

Coachella Valley

- California's Coachella Valley has a climate that is good for growing dates.
- The date palm grows best in areas with long, hot summers and little rainfall.
- The highest and lowest recorded temperatures for the valley are about 125°F and $^{-}13$°F.

Spiral Review and Test Practice

Identify the prime number in the list. KEY NS 4.2 page 306

10. 10, 11, 12 **11.** 47, 49, 51 **12.** 21, 23, 25

Write the letter of the correct answer. KEY NS 1.8

13. Which number sentence is true?

A $^{-}5 > ^{-}15$ **B** $^{-}4 < ^{-}9$ **C** $^{-}8 < ^{-}12$ **D** $^{-}20 > ^{-}10$

Extra Practice See page 359, Set A.

Use Negative Numbers

Objective Use concepts of negative numbers.

CA Standards
KEY NS 1.8 Use concepts of negative numbers (e.g., on a number line, in counting, in temperature, in "owing").
NS 1.0 Students understand the place value of whole numbers and decimals to two decimal places and how whole numbers and decimals relate to simple fractions. Students use the concepts of negative numbers.
Also MR 1.0, MR 2.2, MR 2.0, MR 2.3, MR 2.4, MR 3.0, MR 3.2, MR 3.3

Materials
eManipulatives (optional)
www.eduplace.com/camap/

Learn by Example

Taro owes his brother \$8. If Taro gives his brother \$2, how much will Taro owe?

Use a number line to find the answer.

Example 1

1 Since Taro owes \$8, start at $^{-}8$.

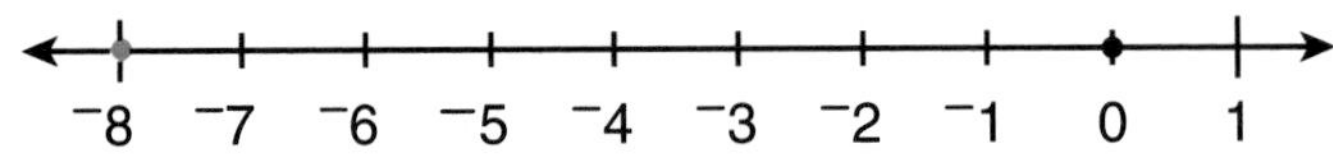

2 Because Taro gives back \$2, move 2 numbers to the right.

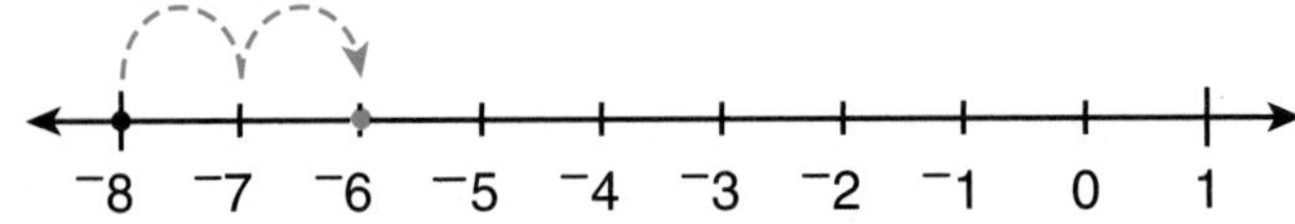

Solution: Taro will still owe \$6.

It was 3°C, and the temperature dropped 5 degrees. What is the temperature now?

Use a thermometer like a number line.

Example 2

1 Start at 3 degrees above 0.

2 Because the temperature dropped 5 degrees, move 5 degrees down from 3°C.

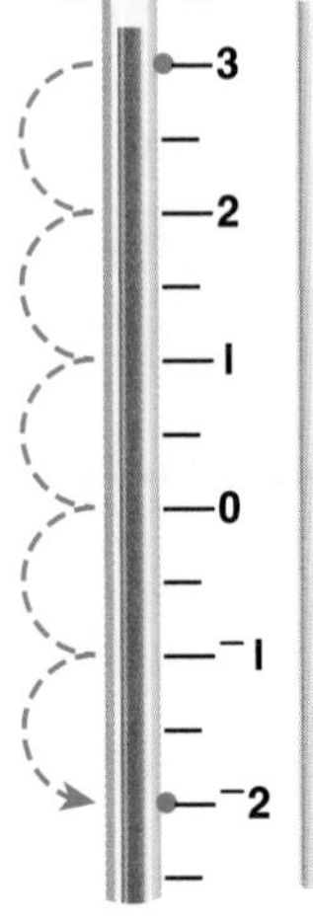

Solution: The temperature is $^{-}2$°C.

Guided Practice

Use the number line to find the answer.

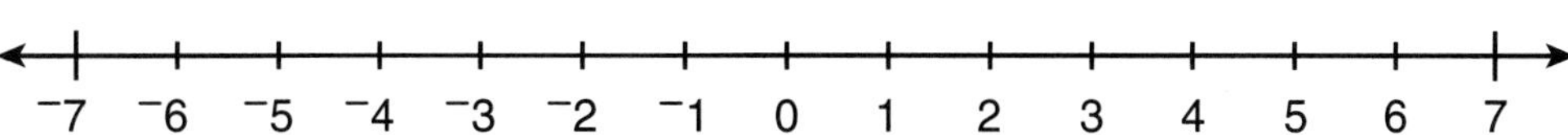

1. 2 more than ⁻5 **2.** 3 fewer than 1 **3.** 6 fewer than 6

Ask Yourself

Is the number greater or less than 0?

Guided Problem Solving

Use the questions to solve this problem.

4. After the first round of a game, Tom has ⁻5 points and Erica has 6 points. In the second round, Tom gets 7 points and Erica loses 2 points. Who has more points?

a. **Understand** What are you asked to find?

b. **Plan** Draw a number line to help you.

c. **Solve** Label marks to show the points after the first round. Then count up or down to find Tom's and Erica's scores after the second round. Answer the question.

d. **Look Back** Read the problem again. Does your number line match the problem?

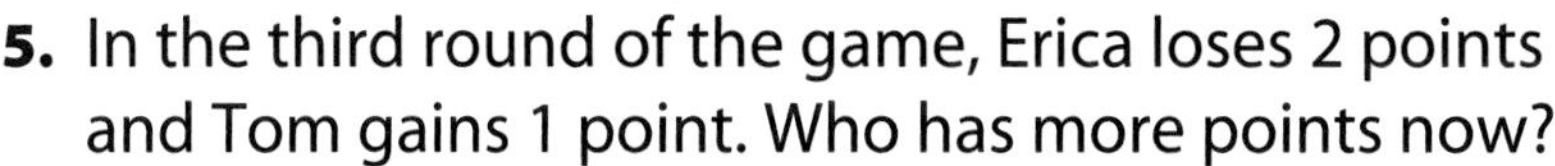

5. In the third round of the game, Erica loses 2 points and Tom gains 1 point. Who has more points now?

Math Talk Will "2 fewer than ⁻6" be ⁻4 or ⁻8? Explain.

Practice and Problem Solving

Use the number line above to find the answer.

6. 3 more than ⁻4 **7.** 2 fewer than ⁻3 **8.** 6 fewer than 3

9. 5 more than ⁻7 **10.** 4 fewer than ⁻4 **11.** 8 more than ⁻12

Solve.

12. Marc owes Adita $3. If Marc borrows another $4 from Adita, how much money does he owe Adita now?

History-Social Science Link

Solve.

13. One mile is 5,280 feet. If a boat travels 19 miles on the river, how many feet has it traveled?

14 a. A boat starts at point *A* and travels 8 miles north up the river. Then it turns around and goes south down the river for 12 miles. How far north or south is the boat from where it started?

b. The boat turns around again and travels 15 miles north up the river. Where is the boat now in relation to point *A*?

Sacramento River

The Sacramento River is the longest river in California. It is 382 miles long.

As settlers moved into California, the river became an easy way to travel and provided water for drinking and agriculture for settlers in the mid-1800s. The Sacramento River starts near Mount Shasta and empties into San Francisco Bay.

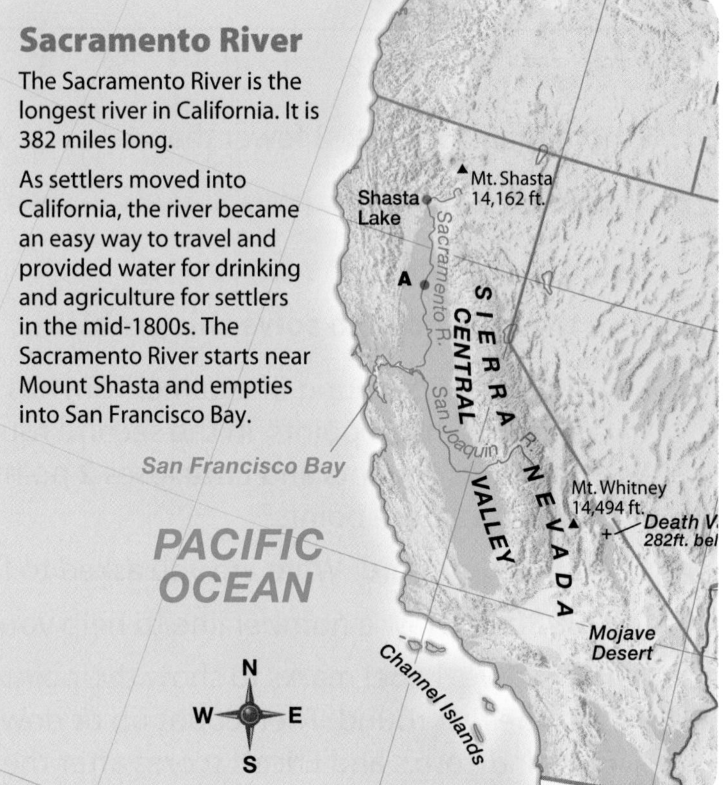

History-Social Science 4.1.4

Spiral Review and Test Practice

Find the perimeter, in feet, of the rectangle. MG 1.0 page 328

15. 15 ft; 4 ft

16. 5 yd; 2 yd

17. 3 yd; 2 yd

18. 10 in.; 2 in.

Write the letter of the correct answer. KEY NS 1.8

19. At 8:00 A.M., the temperature was $^{-}8$°F. By noon, the temperature was 6 degrees higher. What was the temperature at noon?

A $^{-}14$°F **B** $^{-}2$°F **C** 2°F **D** 14°F

Extra Practice See page 359, Set B.

Key Standards Review

Need Help? See Key Standards Handbook.

Write *true* or *false*. KEY NS 4.2

1. The only factors of 9 are 1 and 9.
2. The only factors of 2 are 1 and 2.
3. 3 is a prime number.
4. 15 is a prime number.
5. 12 is a composite number.
6. 8 is not a prime number.
7. 1 is a prime number.

Divide. KEY NS 3.2

8. $309 \div 6$
9. $472 \div 4$
10. $215 \div 5$
11. $684 \div 8$

Challenge — Number Sense

Low Score Wins KEY NS 1.8, NS 1.9

Bob uses his own method of keeping score in golf. Par is zero. One over par is 1, one under par is ⁻1, two over par is 2, two under par is ⁻2, and so on. Remember, the low score in golf wins. Use the scorecard and the number line to answer the questions.

Hole	Bob	Ruth	Ron	Roya
1	⁻2	1	⁻1	2
2	⁻1	2	1	1
3	0	⁻1	1	1
4	2	3	2	2
5	3	0	⁻1	⁻1
6	⁻1	1	2	2
7	0	⁻1	⁻1	⁻1
8	1	2	2	2
9	2	1	2	⁻2

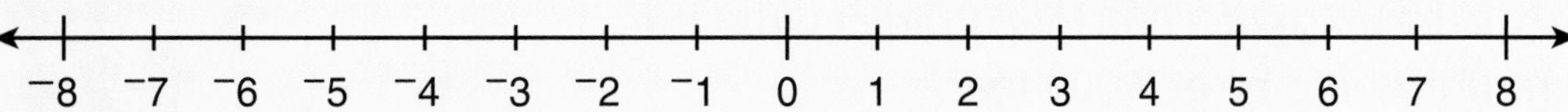

1. Use the number line to find each player's score at the end of the game.
2. Arrange the players by name from the lowest score to the highest score.
3. Which player had the lowest score? The highest?
4. If Bob and Ruth were partners and played Ron and Roya, which team would have won?

Problem Solving

Objective Use skills and strategies to solve word problems.

CA Standards
MR 1.0, MR 1.1, MR 1.2, MR 2.0, MR 2.3, MR 2.4, NS 1.0, NS 1.8, KEY NS 3.0, KEY NS 3.1

Death Valley is one of the hottest, driest places on Earth.

People come from around the world to visit Death Valley National Park. The park's Telescope Peak has a vertical drop from summit to floor twice as great as the depth of the Grand Canyon.

Fun Fact

Lizards in Death Valley cool their feet by lifting them off the ground, one or two at a time.

Side-blotched lizard

Solve. Tell which strategy or method you used.

1. **Multistep** The elevation of Telescope Peak is about 11,000 feet. Suppose on one day, the temperature was 39°F at the peak. Temperatures rise about 4°F with every decrease of 1,000 feet. Predict what the temperature would be at 7,000 feet.

2. The highest temperature recorded in California is 134°F in Death Valley. The lowest temperature of 45°F below zero was recorded at Boca in Nevada County. Express the lowest temperature as a negative integer.

3. The Furnace Creek Visitor Center has an elevation of $^{-}185$ feet. The Golden Canyon Trailhead has an elevation of $^{-}167$ feet. Which has the higher elevation?

Problem Solving on Tests

Select a Strategy

- Choose the Operation
- Estimate
- Work Backward
- Write an Equation
- Draw a Picture

1. Ethan and Ray spent 5 hours at a model train show. Boxcars were on sale for \$9 each and engines for \$48 each. Ethan bought 3 boxcars and Ray bought an engine. Which expression shows the total amount they spent?

A \$48 − (5 × \$9)

B \$48 + (3 × \$9)

C (\$48 × 3) + \$9

D (3 × \$9) − \$48

Test Tip
Look for information that is not needed to solve the problem.

KEY AF 1.2 page 144

2. Melissa is 8 years old. Karen is 40 years old. You can use the equation below to find how many times greater Karen's age is than Melissa's age. Which number is represented by *n*?

$$n \times 8 = 40$$

A 5 **C** 32

B 8 **D** 40

KEY AF 2.2 page 176

3. Think about a number line. Yesterday's temperature was 3 degrees Celsius. The temperature dropped 8 degrees overnight. What is today's temperature?

A 11°C **C** $^{-}5$°C

B 5°C **D** $^{-}11$°C

KEY NS 1.8 page 352

4. Nick's family has 7 boxes that hold 2,100 photos in all. Each box is filled with the same number of photos. How many photos are in each box?

A 30 **B** 40 **C** 300 **D** 400

5. Four students take piano lessons. One practices 50 minutes a day. Another practices 60 minutes a day. Two students each practice 35 minutes a day. What is the average number of minutes a day the four students practice the piano?

A 45 minutes **C** 50 minutes

B 48 minutes **D** 180 minutes

6. Dana has a collection of die-cast cars. The number of cars he has is a prime number. How many cars does Dana have?

A 18

B 21

C 23

D 25

Test Tip
You can draw a picture or use multiplication facts you know to help identify prime numbers.

KEY NS 4.2 page 306

Education Place
Visit www.eduplace.com/camap/ for **Test-Taking Tips** and **Extra Practice**.

Vocabulary

You can use a **number line** to write and **compare positive** and **negative integers**.

Write the **integer** located at each letter on the number line.

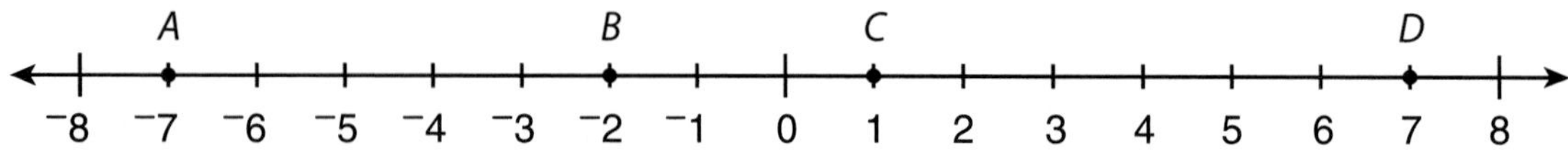

A ________ ***B*** ________

C ________ ***D*** ________

- When comparing two integers on a number line, the integer farther to the right is the ________ integer.
- Which points marked on the number line above are **opposites**?

A **thermometer** is like a vertical number line. Write the temperature indicated by the letter on the thermometer.

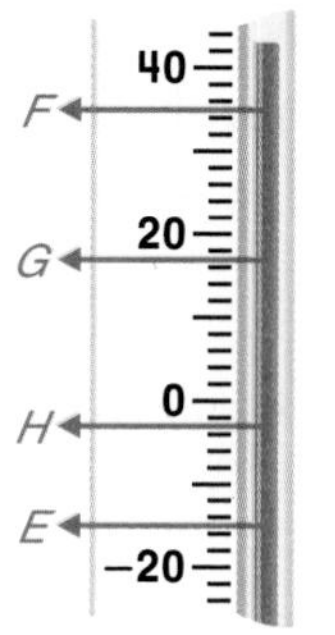

E ________ ***F*** ________

G ________ ***H*** ________

- The mercury climbs up the thermometer as the temperature (increases, decreases).
- Temperatures below zero are indicated by (positive, negative) numbers.

Writing How can you use negative numbers in the real world? Give an example.

Reading Look for this book in your library.
Temperature, by Brenda Walpole

CA Standards
MR 2.3 Use a variety of methods, such as words, numbers, symbols, charts, graphs, tables, diagrams, and models, to explain mathematical reasoning.

Also KEY NS 1.8

Standards-Based Extra Practice

Set A

KEY NS 1.8, NS 1.0 page 350

Use the symbols $>, <,$ or $=$ to complete the number sentence.

1. $^{-}11$ ___ $^{-}8$ **2.** 25 ___ 20 **3.** $^{-}14$ ___ 14

4. 21 ___ $^{-}43$ **5.** 1 ___ $^{-}15$ **6.** 26 ___ 26

Write the letter of the correct answer.

7. Which number sentence is true?

A $^{-}6 < {^{-}8}$ **B** $^{-}4 < {^{-}12}$ **C** $^{-}7 > {^{-}11}$ **D** $^{-}15 > {^{-}9}$

8. Which number sentence is **not** true?

A $^{-}5 < {^{-}3}$ **B** $^{-}7 > {^{-}12}$ **C** $^{-}15 < {^{-}14}$ **D** $^{-}20 > {^{-}16}$

9. **Justify** Alan says that the average temperature in his state is colder than in Joseph's state. Joseph disagrees. If the average temperature in Alan's state is $^{-}7$°F and in Joe's state is $^{-}5$°F, who is correct and why? Justify your answer.

Set B

KEY NS 1.8, NS 1.0 page 352

Think of a number line to help you find the amount.

1. 3 more than $^{-}7$ **2.** 5 fewer than 2 **3.** 8 fewer than 5

4. 3 more than $^{-}3$ **5.** 6 fewer than $^{-}3$ **6.** 8 fewer than 8

7. 4 more than $^{-}5$ **8.** 6 fewer than $^{-}2$ **9.** 1 fewer than 0

10. **Explain** Allie owes her mom \$4. If she babysits and earns \$6, what will her balance be after she pays her mom back? Explain.

11. **Justify** On a number line, Karl started at two, moved 5 spaces to the right, and then moved 8 spaces to the left. On what number did he end? Justify your answer.

Education Place
Visit www.eduplace.com/camap/ for more **Extra Practice**.

Chapter Review/Test

Vocabulary and Concepts — KEY NS 1.8, MR 2.3

Write the best word to complete the sentence.

1. Temperatures below zero are _______ numbers.

2. Numbers to the right of 0 on a number line are _______ integers.

Skills — NS 1.0, KEY NS 1.8

Write the integer for the situation.

3. 5 degrees below zero

4. 16 feet above sea level

5. 9 floors above ground

6. 8 degrees below zero

Use the number line. Choose >, <, or = to complete.

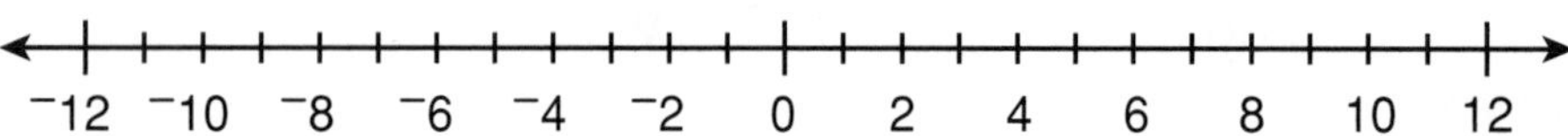

7. 5 ⬭ ⁻3

8. ⁻4 ⬭ ⁻5

9. ⁻7 ⬭ ⁻6

10. 0 ⬭ ⁻3

11. ⁻9 ⬭ ⁻1

12. 5 ⬭ ⁻2

13. 9 ⬭ 9

14. ⁻17 ⬭ ⁻14

Use the number line above to find the answer.

15. 4 more than ⁻3

16. 5 fewer than ⁻5

17. 7 more than ⁻12

18. 7 fewer than 9

Problem Solving and Reasoning — MR 2.3, NS 1.0, KEY NS 1.8

Think about a number line to solve.

19. One night in Maine, the temperature was ⁻5°F. It was 15° higher by 10 A.M. What was the temperature at 10 A.M.?

20. The temperature is 7°F and goes down by 11°. What temperature is it now?

Writing Math Explain why a negative integer is always less than a positive integer.

Spiral Review and Test Practice

1. Which is 6,000,000 + 3,000 + 2 + 800,000,000 + 40,000 + 700 in standard form?

A 860,043,702

B 806,043,702

C 806,403,702

D 800,643,702

KEY  NS 1.1 page 16

---

2. What number goes in the box to make this number sentence true?

$(6 - 3) + 4 = 2 + \square$

A 3

B 7

C 5

D 13

> **Test Tip**
> First find the value of the expression on the left side of the equation. Then find the missing number.

AF 1.1, KEY AF 1.2 page 94

---

3. Which number is represented by *n*?

$2n + 4 = 14$

A 5

B 4

C 10

D 18

KEY AF 2.1, **KEY** AF 2.2 page 176

---

4. Which of these is another way to write the product of 3×15?

A $3 \times 1 \times 5$

B $3 \times 5 \times 2$

C $3 \times 5 \times 3$

D $3 \times 4 \times 11$

> **Test Tip**
> Evaluate each expression to see which one equals 3×15.

NS 4.1 page 308

---

5. Pilar bought 15 gallons of milk. There are 16 cups in 1 gallon. How many cups of milk did Pilar buy?

A 1 cup

B 31 cups

C 160 cups

D 240 cups

KEY NS 3.3 page 332

---

6. Which number sentence is true?

A $^-3 < {}^-8$

B $^-12 > {}^-5$

C $^-7 < {}^-9$

D $^-10 > {}^-15$

KEY NS 1.8 page 350

Education Place
Visit www.eduplace.com/camap/ for **Test-Taking Tips** and **Extra Practice.**

Unit 7 Test

Vocabulary and Concepts — NS 1.0, KEY NS 1.8, KEY NS 1.9 Chapters 15–16

Complete each sentence with a vocabulary word from this unit.

1. Units of measure, such as foot, yard, and mile, are part of the _______ system of measure.

2. The distance around a figure is its _______.

3. The amount that a container can hold is the container's _______.

4. The set of whole numbers and their opposites and zero are called _______.

5. The symbol °F stands for _______ Fahrenheit and is used to measure _______.

Computation — NS 1.0, KEY NS 1.1, KEY NS 1.8, KEY NS 3.0, KEY NS 3.2, AF 1.1 Chapter 15, Lessons 2–4

Find the missing number.

6. 12 ft = ▢ yd **7.** 3 lb = ▢ oz **8.** 3 L = ▢ mL

9. 160 cm = ▢ mm **10.** 3,000 m = ▢ km **11.** 1 kg = ▢ g

Write the opposite of each integer. Chapter 16, Lessons 1–2

12. 15 **13.** $^{-}36$ **14.** 3 **15.** 24

Write the integer for the situation.

16. 4 degrees below zero **17.** 11 feet above sea level

Use $<$, $>$, or $=$ to complete each number sentence. Chapter 16, Lesson 2

18. $^{-}6$ ◯ $^{-}7$ **19.** 8 ◯ $^{-}1$ **20.** 11 ◯ eleven **21.** $^{-}18$ ◯ $^{-}14$

Problem Solving and Reasoning — KEY NS 1.8, KEY NS 3.0, AF 1.0 Chapter 15

Solve.

22. Jim plans to build a rectangular sandbox using wooden boards. The sandbox will measure 6 feet by 7 feet. How many feet of board will Jim need?

23. George has a bucket with a capacity of 5 gallons. Will the bucket be full if he pours two 10-quart containers of water into it? Explain your thinking.

Solve.

24. Nam and Mina are playing a game. Nam's score is 1 and Mina's score is 3. They play a round and now the score is $^{-}2$ and $^{-}2$. How many points did Nam and Mina gain or lose?

25. At 6 P.M. the temperature was 16°F. By 6 A.M. the next morning the temperature was $^{-}4$°F. How many degrees did the temperature drop in this twelve-hour period?

Writing Math When converting units, how do you know if you should multiply or divide? Support you answer with examples.

Performance Assessment

Pot of Gold!

KEY NS 1.8

Sonia is playing a board game. She is on Start and wants to land on the Pot of Gold on space 6.

Task	Information You Need
Use the information above and at the right. What set of 3 tosses will take Sonia to the Pot of Gold? What set of 4 tosses?	Sonia can take 3 or 4 turns.
	She tosses the number cube once per turn.
	The number cube can roll: 3, 5, 7, $^{-}1$, $^{-}2$, $^{-}3$.

Go Fast, Go Far

Unit 7 Mental Math Strategies

Divide by 6

The answer can be quick to see, divide by 2 and then by 3!

I have a fast way to do 24 ÷ 6. First, I divide 24 by 2 to get 12, then I divide 12 by 3 to get 4. Dividing in steps is easier than doing everything all at once.

1. 24 ÷ 6 → 12 → 4
Divide 24 by 2. Divide by 3.

2. 54 ÷ 6 → 27 → ▢
Divide 54 by 2. Divide by 3.

3. 42 ÷ 6 → ▢ → ▢
Divide 42 by 2. Divide by 3.

4. 90 ÷ 6 → ▢ → ▢
Divide 90 by 2. Divide by 3.

Nice work! Now try these!

5. 30 ÷ 6 → ▢ → ▢

6. 96 ÷ 6 → ▢ → ▢

7. 48 ÷ 6 → ▢ → ▢

8. 126 ÷ 6 → ▢ → ▢

9. 72 ÷ 6 → ▢ → ▢

10. 150 ÷ 6 → ▢ → ▢

Take It Further!

Now try doing all the steps in your head!

Good For You!

11. 84 ÷ 6

12. 90 ÷ 6

13. 180 ÷ 6

14. 240 ÷ 6

Fractions and Mixed Numbers

BIG IDEAS!

- Fractions can show parts of a whole, parts of a set, or the division of whole numbers by whole numbers.
- Equivalent fractions have the same value.
- You can compare and order fractions and mixed numbers on a number line.

Chapter 17
Fractions

Chapter 18
Compare and Order Fractions

Songs and Games

Math Music Track 8: *Four Red Marbles*
eGames at **www.eduplace.com/camap/**

Math Readers

Get Ready **Game**

Fraction Action!

Object of the Game Compare fractions and be the first player to get 8 points.

Materials
- fraction tiles (2 sets)
- Learning Tool 24 (Fraction Cards)

Number of Players 2

Set Up
Place the 1 whole fraction tile in front of the players; it will remain there for the game. Shuffle the fraction cards, and place them face down in a stack.

How to Play

1. Player 1 draws a card from the stack. He or she makes the fraction with the fraction tiles and places them under the 1 whole tile.
2. Player 2 draws a card from the pile. He or she makes the fraction with the fraction tiles and places them under Player 1's tiles.
3. Players decide whose fraction is greater. The player with the greater fraction gets one point. If the two fractions are equivalent, both players get one point.
4. The first player to earn 8 points is the winner.

CA Standards
NS 1.5 Explain different interpretations of fractions, for example, parts of a whole, parts of a set, and division of whole numbers by whole numbers.

Education Place
Visit www.eduplace.com/camap/ for **Brain Teasers** and **eGames** to play.

Reading You use strategies to help you in reading. You also use strategies to help you solve word problems. Read this problem:

You have two pizzas that are the same size. One pizza is cut into 6 equal slices. The other is cut into 8 equal slices. If you are very hungry, should you take one slice from the 6-piece pie or two slices from the 8-piece pie?

Before she solves the problem, Marta jots down problem-solving strategies that she knows.

Hmmm. I need to compare $\frac{1}{6}$ with $\frac{2}{8}$.

Problem-Solving Strategies

Break a problem into parts.

Write an expression.

Guess and check.

Make an organized list.

Draw a picture.

Use models to act it out.

Writing Copy the strategies Marta wrote down and add other strategies you know. Use one of the strategies to solve the problem. Describe how you solved the problem.

Fractions

Check What You Know

Word Bank
fraction
numerator
equivalent
denominator

Vocabulary and Concepts GRADE 3 NS 3.1, MR 2.3

Choose the best word to complete the sentence.

1. Different fractions that name the same part of a whole are _____.
2. The number in a fraction that names the total number of equal parts in the whole is the _____.

Skills GRADE 3 NS 3.1

Write the shaded part of the figure as a fraction of the whole.

3\.

4\. 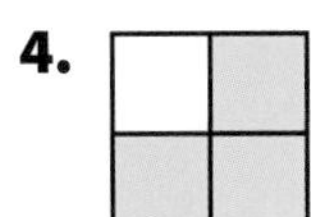

5\. 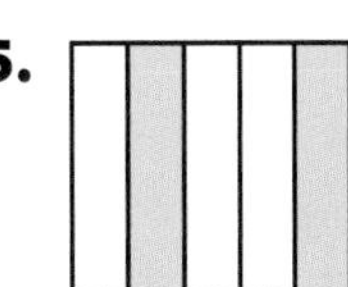

Compare. Write $>$, $<$, or $=$ for the ⬭.

6\. $\frac{3}{8}$ ⬭ $\frac{4}{8}$ 7. $\frac{2}{7}$ ⬭ $\frac{2}{9}$ 8. $\frac{2}{4}$ ⬭ $\frac{1}{2}$ 9. $\frac{1}{6}$ ⬭ $\frac{1}{2}$

Problem Solving and Reasoning GRADE 3 NS 3.1

10\. Elizabeth studied for $\frac{2}{4}$ hour, which was $\frac{1}{4}$ hour less than her sister studied. How long did Elizabeth's sister study?

Vocabulary

Visualize It!

A **fraction** is a number that names a part of a whole, a part of a set, or division by whole numbers.

$\frac{5}{12}$ of the stars are blue.

$\frac{5}{12}$

The **numerator** shows how many of the equal parts are blue.

The **denominator** shows the total number of equal parts.

Language Tip

Some words are similar in English and Spanish.

English	Spanish
fraction	fracción
numerator	numerador
denominator	denominador

See **English-Spanish Glossary** pages 644–666.

Education Place Visit www.eduplace.com/camap/ for the **eGlossary** and **eGames**.

CA Standards MR 2.3 Use a variety of methods, such as words, numbers, symbols, charts, graphs, tables, diagrams, and models, to explain mathematical reasoning. **Also NS 1.5**

CA Standards

NS 1.5 Explain different interpretations of fractions, for example, parts of a whole, parts of a set, and division of whole numbers by whole numbers; explain equivalence of fractions (see Standard 4.0).

NS 1.7 Write the fraction represented by a drawing of parts of a figure; represent a given fraction by using drawings; and relate a fraction to a simple decimal on a number line.

Also NS 1.0, MR 1.1, MR 2.0, MR 2.3, MR 2.4, MR 3.0, MR 3.2, MR 3.3

Vocabulary

fraction

numerator

denominator

Materials

- fraction tiles
- 2-color counters
- red and yellow colored pencils
- eManipulatives (optional) www.eduplace.com/camap/

Hands On
Model Fractions

Objective Model fractional parts of a whole and of a set.

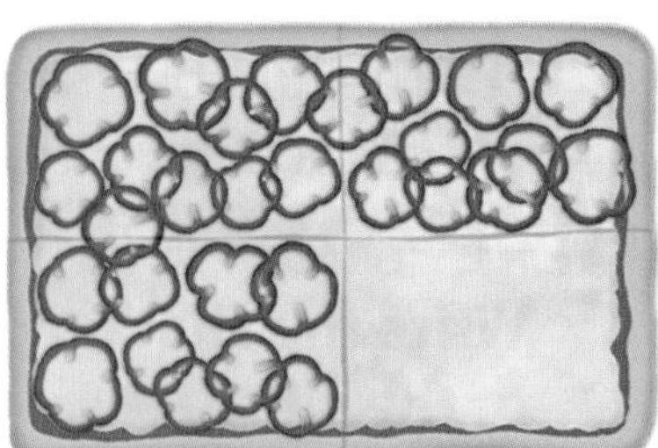

Explore

In this lesson, you will use fraction tiles to model equal parts of a whole and 2-color counters to model equal parts of a set.

John helped his dad make a rectangular pizza for dinner. They used green peppers as toppings on part of the pizza. You can use fractions to describe the pizza and the peppers.

A **fractions** can describe part of a whole.

slices with green peppers → $\frac{3}{4}$ ← **numerator**
total number of slices → ← **denominator**

This fraction is read as "three fourths."

Question How can you use fraction tiles to model how much of the pizza has green peppers?

1. To represent the whole pizza, choose a fraction tile to show one whole.

2. To show how many slices of pizza have green peppers, place three $\frac{1}{4}$ tiles under the whole.

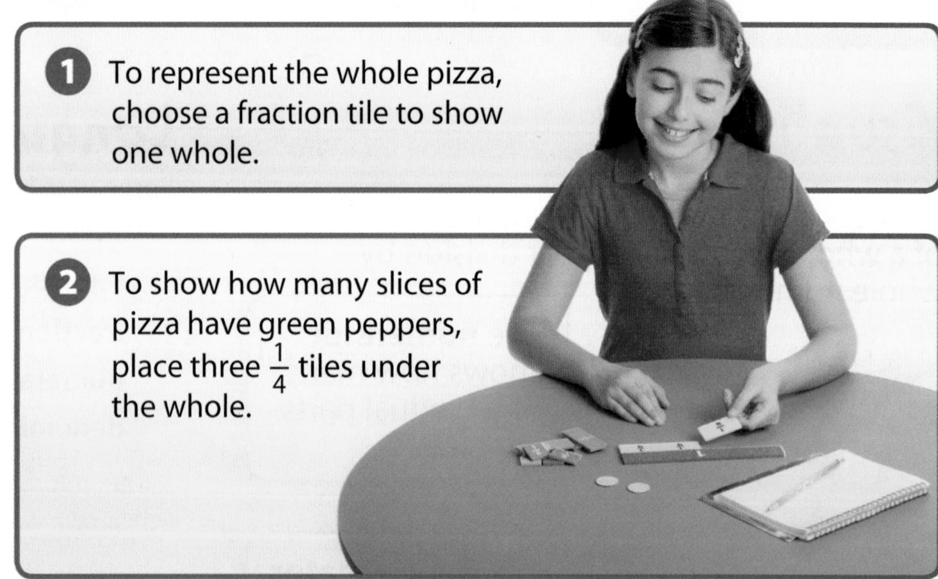

3. Draw and label a picture to show your work.

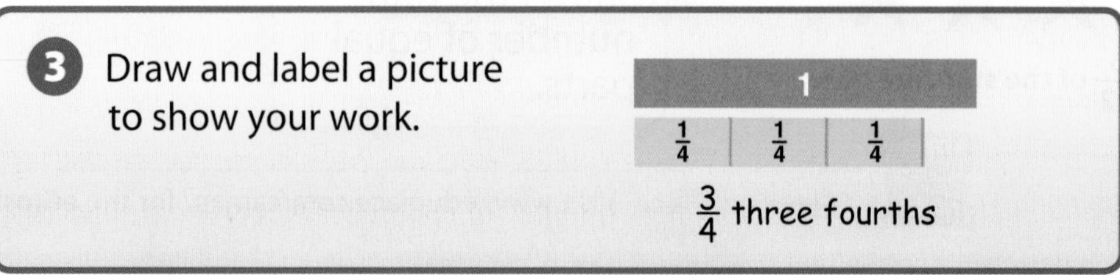

A fraction can describe part of a group.

number of yellow peppers ⟶ 4 ⟵ **numerator**
total number of peppers ⟶ 6 ⟵ **denominator**

$$\frac{4}{6}$$

This fraction is read as "four sixths."

Use 2-color counters to model how many peppers in the group are yellow.

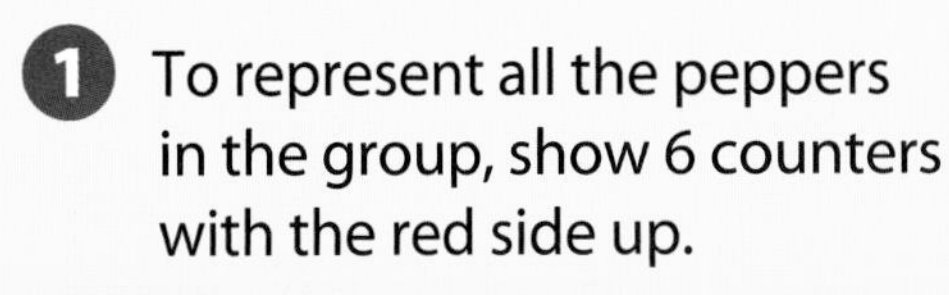

1 To represent all the peppers in the group, show 6 counters with the red side up.

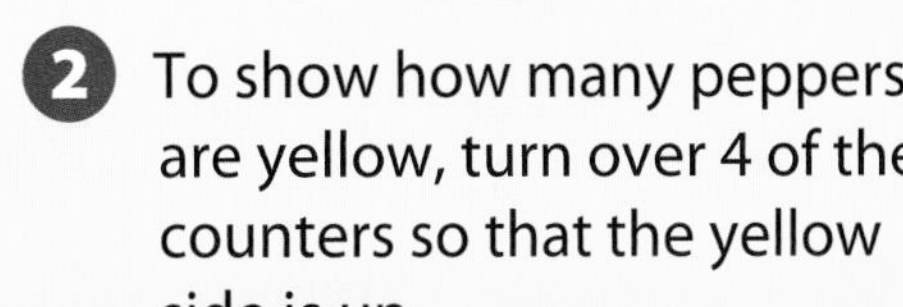

2 To show how many peppers are yellow, turn over 4 of the counters so that the yellow side is up.

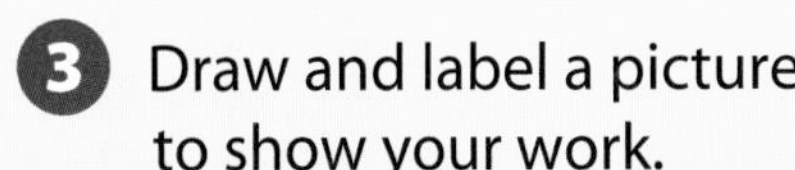

3 Draw and label a picture to show your work.

$\frac{4}{6}$

Extend

Use fraction tiles to model each fraction. Draw and label a picture to show your work.

1. $\frac{2}{3}$ **2.** $\frac{3}{8}$ **3.** $\frac{4}{4}$ **4.** $\frac{11}{12}$

5. $\frac{6}{10}$ **6.** $\frac{3}{5}$ **7.** $\frac{2}{2}$ **8.** $\frac{4}{6}$

Use counters to model each fraction. Draw and label a picture to show your work.

9. Use 3 counters to show $\frac{1}{3}$ red.

10. Use 5 counters to show $\frac{4}{5}$ yellow.

11. Use 8 counters to show $\frac{8}{8}$ yellow.

12. Use 12 counters to show $\frac{8}{12}$ red.

Writing Math

Generalize In the exercises above, which fractions equal one whole? How can you tell that a fraction equals one whole?

CA Standards
NS 1.5 Explain different interpretations of fractions, for example, parts of a whole, parts of a set, and division of whole numbers by whole numbers; explain equivalence of fractions (see Standard 4.0).

MR 2.3 Use a variety of methods, such as words, numbers, symbols, charts, graphs, tables, diagrams, and models, to explain mathematical reasoning.

Also NS 1.0, MR 1.0, MR 2.0, MR 2.3, MR 2.4

Prepares for NS 1.7

Vocabulary

numerator → 2

3 ← **denominator**

Fractional Parts of a Number

Objective Find fractional parts of a whole number.

Learn by Example

Natalia and her mother use 20 apples to make a pie. One fourth of the apples are green and three fourths are red. How many apples are red?

There are different ways to find $\frac{3}{4}$ of 20.

Different Ways to Find Fractional Parts of a Number

Way 1 **You can use a model.**

1. The **denominator**, 4, tells you to separate the 20 counters into 4 equal groups.
2. The **numerator**, 3, tells you to count the number in 3 groups.

$\frac{3}{4}$ of 20 is 15.

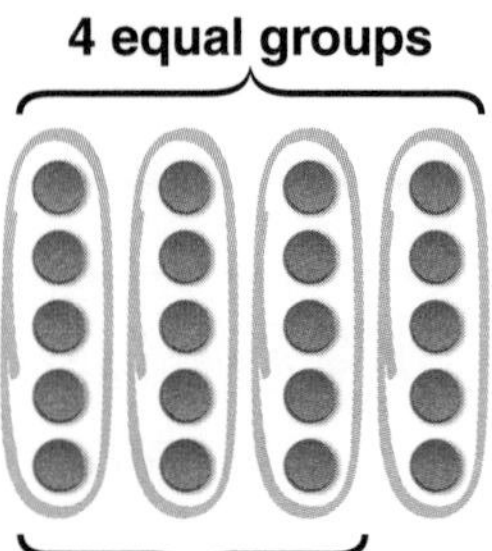

Way 2 **You can use division and multiplication.**

1. Divide 20 by 4 to find the number in each group.
2. Multiply the number in each group by 3.

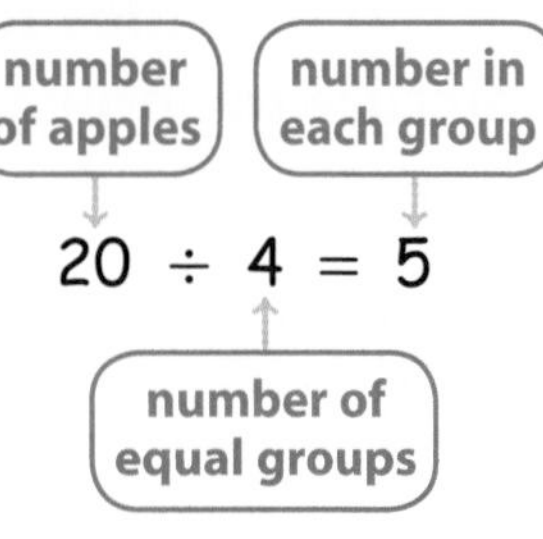

number in each group

$5 \times 3 = 15$

number of groups

$\frac{3}{4}$ of 20 is 15.

Solution: 15 apples are red.

Guided Practice

Find the fractional part of each number.

1. 

$\frac{1}{4}$ of 8

2. $\frac{3}{5}$ of 10

3. $\frac{2}{3}$ of 9 **4.** $\frac{1}{6}$ of 24 **5.** $\frac{2}{5}$ of 20 **6.** $\frac{3}{4}$ of 16

Ask Yourself

- How many equal parts are there?
- How many equal parts do I need to count?

Math Talk How does knowing $\frac{1}{5}$ of 10 help you find $\frac{2}{5}$ of 10?

Practice and Problem Solving

Find the fractional part of each number.

7. $\frac{2}{3}$ of 30 **8.** $\frac{3}{7}$ of 14 **9.** $\frac{7}{9}$ of 18 **10.** $\frac{5}{6}$ of 12 **11.** $\frac{3}{10}$ of 100

Solve.

12. Jerome has 21 apples. Two thirds of the apples are green. How many of the apples are green?

13. Keisha's family eats $\frac{3}{4}$ of an 8-piece apple pie. How many pieces are not eaten?

14. **Justify** Show why $\frac{2}{3}$ of 9 and $\frac{1}{3}$ of 18 name the same number. Use counters or draw a picture to explain your reasoning.

15. **Challenge** George's dad has 100 quarters. He tells George that he can have either $\frac{3}{4}$ or $\frac{6}{10}$ of them. Which should George choose? Explain.

Spiral Review and Test Practice

Make a factor tree for each number. NS 4.1 page 308

16. 14 **17.** 24 **18.** 12 **19.** 48 **20.** 36

Write the letter of the correct answer. NS 1.5

21. What is $\frac{2}{3}$ of 24?

A 8 **B** 16 **C** 32 **D** 40

Extra Practice See page 387, Set A.

Hands On
Model Equivalent Fractions

Objective Use models to identify equivalent fractions.

CA Standards
NS 1.7 Write the fraction represented by a drawing of parts of a figure; represent a given fraction by using drawings; and relate a fraction to a simple decimal on a number line.

KEY NS 1.9 Identify on a number line the relative position of positive fractions, positive mixed numbers, and positive decimals to two decimal places.

Also NS 1.5, MR 2.6, MR 1.0, MR 1.1, MR 2.3, MR 2.4, MR 3.3, MR 3.0, MR 2.0

Vocabulary

equivalent fractions

Materials

- Learning Tool 25 (Fractions Equivalent to $\frac{1}{2}$)
- fraction tiles
- eManipulatives (optional) www.eduplace.com/camap/

Explore

In Lesson 1, you used fraction tiles and 2-color counters to model fractions. In this lesson, you will use fraction tiles and number lines to model equivalent fractions.

Fractions that name the same amount are **equivalent fractions**.

Question How can you use models to find fractions that are equivalent to $\frac{1}{2}$?

Work with a partner.

1 Show one whole. Place a $\frac{1}{2}$ fraction tile below it. Then line up $\frac{1}{4}$ fraction tiles to fit below the $\frac{1}{2}$ fraction tile.

Two $\frac{1}{4}$ fraction tiles fit below a $\frac{1}{2}$ fraction tile, so $\frac{2}{4}$ names the same amount as $\frac{1}{2}$.

2 Line up $\frac{1}{8}$ fraction tiles to fit below the $\frac{1}{4}$ fraction tiles.

Four $\frac{1}{8}$ fraction tiles fit below the $\frac{1}{2}$ fraction tile, so $\frac{4}{8}$ names the same amount as $\frac{1}{2}$ and $\frac{2}{4}$.

$\frac{1}{2}$, $\frac{2}{4}$, and $\frac{4}{8}$ are equivalent fractions.

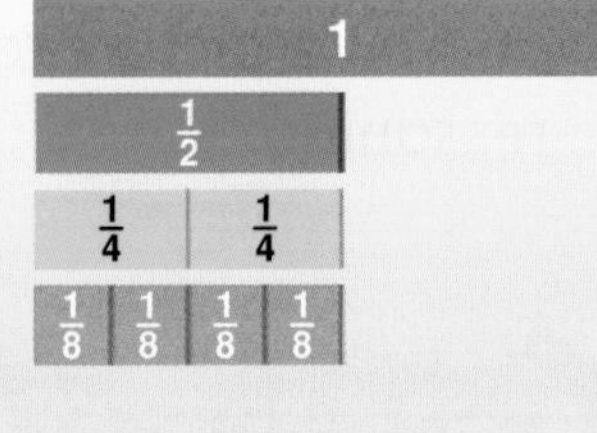

3 Use fraction tiles to find as many other fractions as you can that are equivalent to $\frac{1}{2}$. Record your work on Learning Tool 25.

Fraction Pieces	Quick Picture	How Many?	Equivalent Fractions
fourths			
sixths			
eighths			

You can also use number lines to find fractions equivalent to $\frac{1}{2}$.

Look at the number lines at the right.

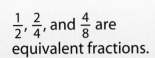

$\frac{1}{2}$, $\frac{2}{4}$, and $\frac{4}{8}$ are equivalent fractions.

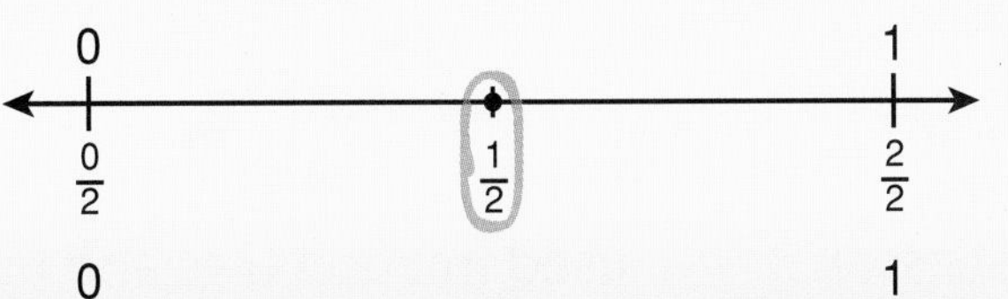

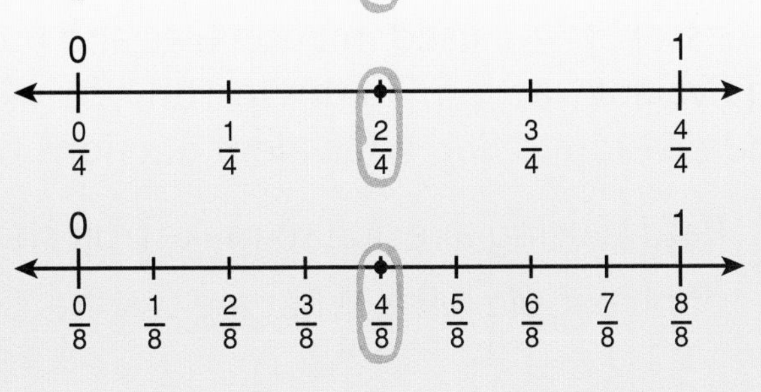

Extend

Decide whether the fractions are equivalent. Use fraction tiles to help you. Draw number lines to check your answers.

1. $\frac{3}{4}$ and $\frac{6}{8}$ **2.** $\frac{7}{10}$ and $\frac{5}{6}$ **3.** $\frac{8}{12}$ and $\frac{4}{6}$ **4.** $\frac{5}{6}$ and $\frac{10}{12}$

5. $\frac{3}{5}$ and $\frac{8}{16}$ **6.** $\frac{6}{9}$ and $\frac{4}{6}$ **7.** $\frac{3}{7}$ and $\frac{6}{14}$ **8.** $\frac{5}{9}$ and $\frac{4}{8}$

Find a fraction equivalent to each. Draw number lines or use fraction tiles to help you.

9. $\frac{2}{10}$ **10.** $\frac{4}{4}$ **11.** $\frac{1}{6}$ **12.** $\frac{4}{12}$

13. $\frac{3}{4}$ **14.** $\frac{2}{3}$ **15.** $\frac{1}{3}$ **16.** $\frac{2}{5}$

17. $\frac{9}{12}$ **18.** $\frac{3}{9}$ **19.** $\frac{10}{15}$ **20.** $\frac{3}{5}$

Writing Math

Generalize Describe the pattern you see in the equivalent fractions at the right. Then continue the pattern and find two more equivalent fractions.

$$\frac{4}{6} = \frac{6}{9} = \frac{8}{12} = \frac{10}{15}$$

Equivalent Fractions

Objective Find equivalent fractions.

CA Standards
NS 1.5 Explain different interpretations of fractions, for example, parts of a whole, parts of a set, and division of whole numbers by whole numbers; explain equivalence of fractions (see Standard 4.0).

KEY NS 1.9 Identify on a number line the relative position of positive fractions, positive mixed numbers, and positive decimals to two decimal places.

Also MR 1.1, MR 1.2, MR 1.0, MR 2.0, MR 2.3, MR 2.4, MR 2.6

Learn by Example

In Lesson 3, you used fraction tiles and number lines to find equivalent fractions. In this lesson, you will use multiplication and division to find equivalent fractions.

Patti is using a recipe to make fruit shakes. She needs $\frac{2}{6}$ cup of pineapple juice. What are two fractions equivalent to $\frac{2}{6}$?

Different Ways to Find Equivalent Fractions

Way 1 **You can use fraction tiles.**

$\frac{1}{3}$, $\frac{2}{6}$, and $\frac{4}{12}$ are equivalent fractions.

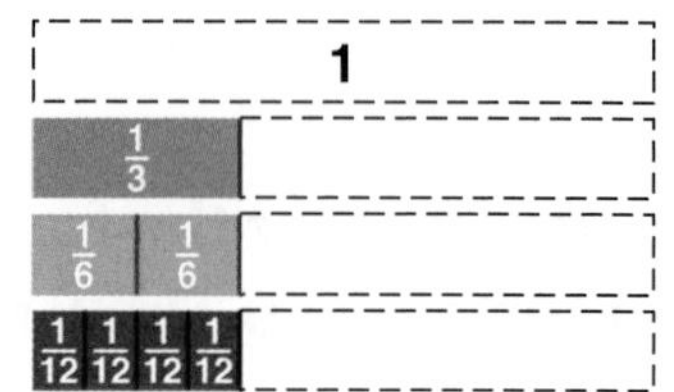

Way 2 **You can use number lines.**

$\frac{1}{3}$, $\frac{2}{6}$, and $\frac{4}{12}$ are equivalent fractions.

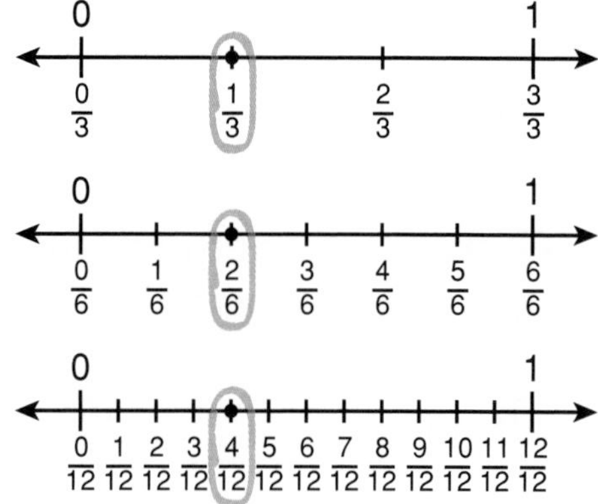

Way 3 **You can multiply.**

Multiply the numerator and denominator by the same number.

$$\frac{2}{6} = \frac{2 \times 2}{6 \times 2} = \frac{4}{12}$$

$\frac{2}{6}$ and $\frac{4}{12}$ are equivalent fractions.

Way 4 **You can divide.**

Divide the numerator and denominator by the same number.

$$\frac{2}{6} = \frac{2 \div 2}{6 \div 2} = \frac{1}{3}$$

$\frac{2}{6}$ and $\frac{1}{3}$ are equivalent fractions.

Solution: $\frac{1}{3}$ and $\frac{4}{12}$ are two fractions equivalent to $\frac{2}{6}$.

Guided Practice

Complete. Find the value of each ▢.

1. $\frac{3}{4} = \frac{3 \times 4}{4 \times 4} = \frac{▢}{16}$

2. $\frac{2}{3} = \frac{2 \times 3}{3 \times 3} = \frac{6}{▢}$

3. $\frac{2}{5} = \frac{2 \times ▢}{5 \times ▢} = \frac{8}{20}$

4. $\frac{1}{4} = \frac{1 \times ▢}{4 \times ▢} = \frac{5}{20}$

5. $\frac{12}{18} = \frac{12 \div 3}{18 \div 3} = \frac{▢}{▢}$

6. $\frac{8}{12} = \frac{8 \div 4}{12 \div 4} = \frac{▢}{▢}$

7. $\frac{3}{12} = \frac{▢}{4}$

8. $\frac{7}{14} = \frac{1}{▢}$

9. $\frac{4}{10} = \frac{2}{▢}$

Ask Yourself

- Should I multiply or divide?
- Which number should I multiply or divide by?

Guided Problem Solving

Use the questions to solve this problem.

10. Charlie has a bread recipe that uses $\frac{6}{8}$ cups of flour. How many $\frac{1}{4}$ cups is that?
    a. **Understand** Complete this sentence. You need to find a fraction equivalent to $\frac{6}{8}$ that has a denominator of ____.
    b. **Plan** Should you multiply or divide? Why?
    c. **Solve** Follow your plan. Write the answer to the problem.
    d. **Look Back** Use number lines to check your answer.

Math Talk Can you always multiply to find equivalent fractions? Can you always divide?

Practice and Problem Solving

Complete. Find the value of each ▢.

11. $\frac{2}{4} = \frac{2 \times 3}{4 \times ▢} = \frac{▢}{▢}$

12. $\frac{2}{4} = \frac{2 \div ▢}{4 \div 2} = \frac{▢}{▢}$

13. $\frac{2}{4} = \frac{2 \times 5}{4 \times ▢} = \frac{▢}{▢}$

14. Look at Exercises 11–13. What do you know about the three answers?

Solve.

15. Wanda makes trail mix that is $\frac{1}{3}$ raisins and $\frac{2}{3}$ granola. Describe her trail mix using 9 as a denominator.

16. **Challenge** The fractions $\frac{4}{5}$, $\frac{8}{10}$, $\frac{12}{15}$, and $\frac{16}{20}$ are all equivalent. The fraction $\frac{4}{5}$ is in **simplest form** because the numerator and denominator cannot both be evenly divided by any number other than 1. What is the simplest form of $\frac{4}{6}$?

Real World Data

Use the recipe to solve Problems 17–19.

17. Are the amounts of cranberry juice and pineapple juice equivalent? Explain.

18. Another recipe uses $\frac{6}{8}$ cup of cranberry juice. Does it use the same amount of cranberry juice as Patti's recipe? Explain.

19. **Challenge** For the California Strawberry Festival in Oxnard, Patti made 90 servings of her fruit shake. How many cups of pineapple juice did she use?

Patti's Fruit Shake

1 large banana	$\frac{3}{4}$ cup cranberry juice
1 cup strawberries	$\frac{1}{2}$ cup pineapple juice
1 mango cubed	1 cup ice cubes

Put all ingredients in blender.
Blend until thick and smooth.
Makes 3 servings.

Spiral Review and Test Practice

Use the number line to help you find the amount. KEY NS 1.8 page 352

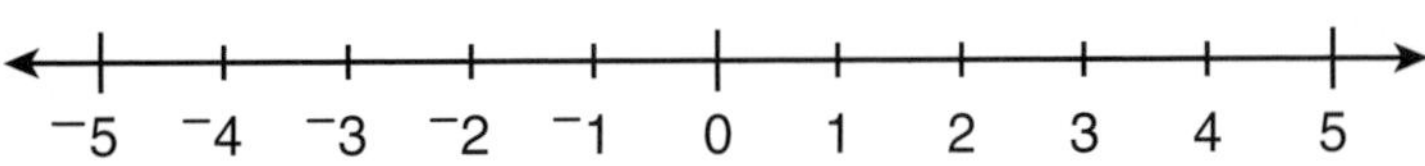

20. 4 more than $^{-}5$

21. 2 fewer than 1

22. 6 more than $^{-}2$

23. 3 fewer than $^{-}1$

Write the letter of the correct answer. NS 1.5

24. Which fraction is equivalent to $\frac{4}{16}$?

A $\frac{1}{4}$ **B** $\frac{4}{4}$ **C** $\frac{4}{8}$ **D** $\frac{12}{16}$

Extra Practice See page 387, Set B.

Practice Game

Fraction Match-Up

Object of the Game Match equivalent fractions.

Materials
16 index cards

Set Up
Make 16 cards like the ones shown.

Number of Players 2

How to Play

1. Shuffle the cards. Place them face down in any order in a 4 × 4 array.

2. A player turns over any two cards. If the cards show two equivalent fractions, the player keeps both cards. If not, the player turns the cards back over.

3. Players take turns repeating Step 2 until all 8 matches have been made. The player with the greater number of cards is the winner.

$\frac{3}{6}$	$\frac{1}{2}$	$\frac{4}{6}$	$\frac{2}{3}$
$\frac{15}{25}$	$\frac{3}{5}$	$\frac{14}{35}$	$\frac{2}{5}$
$\frac{9}{21}$	$\frac{3}{7}$	$\frac{3}{18}$	$\frac{1}{6}$
$\frac{12}{40}$	$\frac{3}{10}$	$\frac{15}{24}$	$\frac{5}{8}$

CA Standards
NS 1.5 Explain different interpretations of fractions, for example, parts of a whole, parts of a set, and division of whole numbers by whole numbers; explain equivalence of fractions.

Education Place
Visit www.eduplace.com/camap/ for **Brain Teasers** and **eGames** to play.

CA Standards

NS 1.5 Explain different interpretations of fractions, for example, parts of a whole, parts of a set, and division of whole numbers by whole numbers; explain equivalence of fractions (see Standard 4.0).

NS 1.7 Write the fraction represented by a drawing of parts of a figure; represent a given fraction by using drawings; and relate a fraction to a simple decimal on a number line.

Also AF 1.1, KEY AF 2.0, KEY AF 2.1, MR 1.0, MR 1.1, MR 2.0, MR 2.2, MR 2.3, MR 2.4

Vocabulary

like denominators

Add and Subtract Fractions

Objective Add and subtract fractions with like denominators.

Learn by Example

Lian is making a stir-fry. She plans to use the carrots and peas first. What fraction of the vegetables is this?

$\frac{4}{8}$ of the vegetables are carrots. $\frac{2}{8}$ of the vegetables are peas.

You can add $\frac{4}{8} + \frac{2}{8}$ to find the fraction she will use first.

The fractions $\frac{4}{8}$ and $\frac{2}{8}$ both have the same number in their denominators so, they have **like denominators**.

Add. $\frac{4}{8} + \frac{2}{8} = \bigcirc$

Example 1

Since the denominators are the same, you can add the numerators and keep the same denominator.

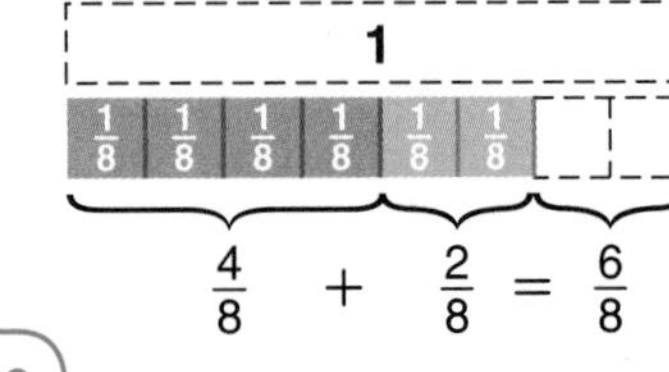

$$\frac{4}{8} + \frac{2}{8} = \frac{6}{8}$$

add numerators

denominator stays the same

Solution: Lian uses $\frac{6}{8}$ of the vegetables first.

Example 2

You can also subtract fractions with like denominators.

Subtract. $\frac{4}{8} - \frac{2}{8} = \bigcirc$

Since the denominators are the same, you can subtract the numerators and keep the same denominator.

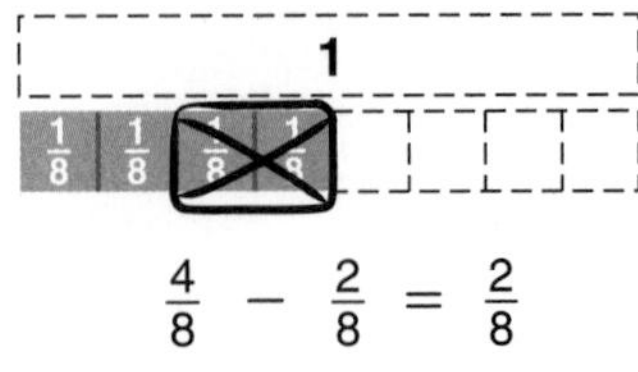

$$\frac{4}{8} - \frac{2}{8} = \frac{2}{8}$$

subtract numerators

denominator stays the same

Solution: $\frac{4}{8} - \frac{2}{8} = \frac{2}{8}$

Another Example

Sum equal to 1

$\frac{2}{6} + \frac{4}{6} = \frac{6}{6} = 1$

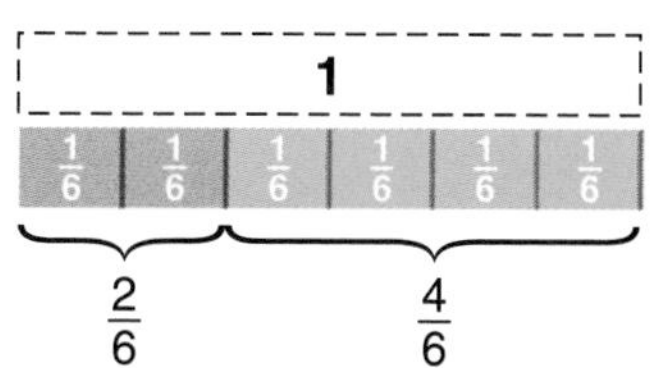

Guided Practice

Add or subtract. Use the fraction tiles to help you.

Ask Yourself

- Are there like denominators?
- Should I add or subtract the numerators?
- Do I need to simplify the answer?

1. $\frac{3}{8} + \frac{3}{8} = \square$

2. $\frac{3}{6} + \frac{4}{6} = \square$

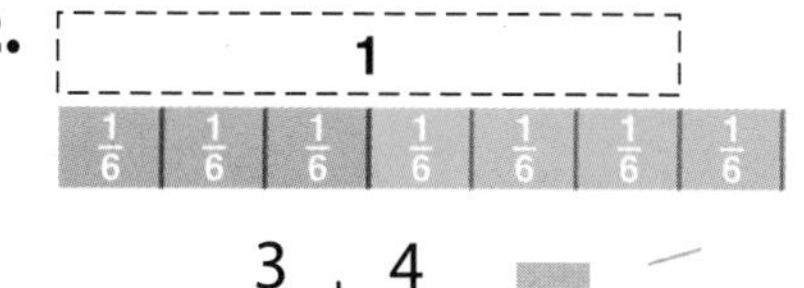

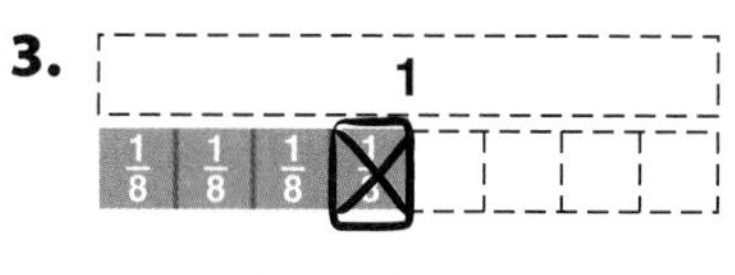

3. $\frac{4}{8} - \frac{1}{8} = \square$

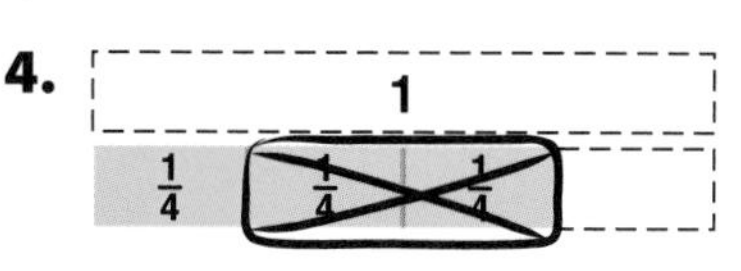

4. $\frac{3}{4} - \frac{2}{4} = \square$

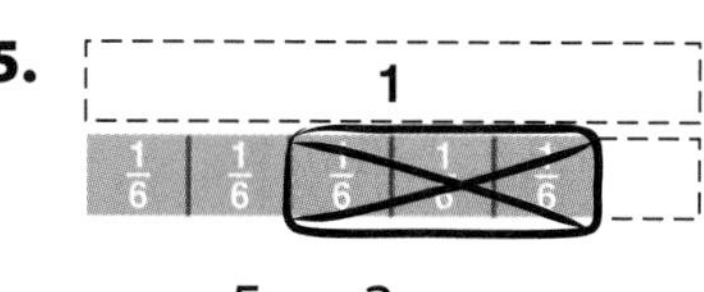

5. $\frac{5}{6} - \frac{3}{6} = \square$

Add or subtract.

6. $\frac{2}{9} + \frac{4}{9}$

7. $\frac{4}{6} - \frac{2}{6}$

8. $\frac{8}{10} + \frac{2}{10}$

9. $\frac{10}{11} - \frac{5}{11}$

10. $\frac{10}{12} - \frac{4}{12}$

Math Talk For fractions with like denominators, why can you add or subtract the numerators and keep the same denominator?

Algebra Variables

Find the value of *n*.

11. $\frac{n}{5} - \frac{4}{5} = \frac{1}{5}$

12. $\frac{5}{9} - \frac{n}{9} = \frac{0}{9}$

13. $\frac{n}{11} + \frac{6}{11} = \frac{11}{11}$

Practice and Problem Solving

Add or subtract.

14. $\frac{1}{4} + \frac{1}{4}$

15. $\frac{7}{8} - \frac{3}{8}$

16. $\frac{1}{3} + \frac{2}{3}$

17. $\frac{4}{9} - \frac{1}{9}$

18. $\frac{5}{6} - \frac{1}{6}$

19. $\frac{3}{8} + \frac{4}{8}$

20. $\frac{6}{10} - \frac{2}{10}$

21. $\frac{2}{10} + \frac{4}{10}$

Algebra Variables

Find the value of *n*.

22. $\frac{n}{8} + \frac{3}{8} = 1$

23. $\frac{9}{12} + \frac{n}{12} = 1$

24. $\frac{6}{7} + \frac{n}{7} = \frac{6}{7}$

25. Challenge $\frac{1}{8}$ and $\frac{1}{2}$ do not have like denominators. Use what you know about equivalent fractions to find the sum of $\frac{1}{8}$ and $\frac{1}{2}$.

Science Link

Mr. Copeland's class has two granite samples, A and B. Sample A is $\frac{6}{11}$ feldspar and $\frac{3}{11}$ quartz. The rest of the sample is mica.

Solve.

26. What fraction of sample A is made of feldspar or quartz?

27. What fraction is made of mica?

28. Challenge Granite sample B is $\frac{13}{22}$ feldspar. Is the amount of feldspar greater in sample A or B?

Granite

Different rocks with the same name may look quite different. Granite, for example, may look pink, gray, or black, depending on the different amounts of minerals that make it up. Feldspar, quartz, and mica are three minerals in granite.

Mica

Feldspar

Rose Quartz

Science ES 4.b

Spiral Review and Test Practice

Round the larger number to the greatest place. Then estimate the product. KEY NS 3.0 page 216

29. 56 × 3

30. 9 × 673

31. 286 × 4

32. 7,394 × 7

Write the letter of the correct answer. NS 1.5

33. $\frac{7}{10} - \frac{2}{10} = \blacksquare$

A $\frac{14}{10}$ **B** $\frac{9}{10}$ **C** $\frac{5}{10}$ **D** $\frac{7}{10}$

Extra Practice See page 387, Set C.

Key Standards Review

Need Help?
See Key Standards Handbook.

Write the integer for the symbol on the number line. KEY NS 1.8

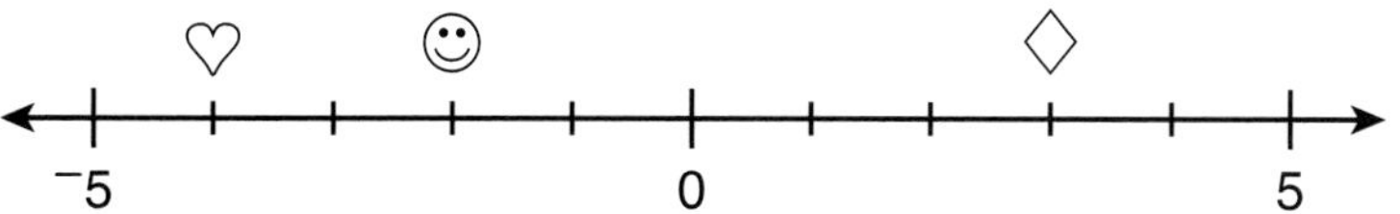

1. 

2. ◇

3. 

Use the thermometer to solve. KEY NS 1.8

°Fahrenheit

10
5
0
−5
−10

4. If it is 5°F, what will the temperature be after it drops 6°?

5. **Multistep** If it was −3°F, and the temperature dropped 2°, then increased 1°, what is the temperature now?

Challenge — Math Reasoning

Musical Fractions KEY NS 1.0

Fractions are used to name some of the notes in music.

All the notes in each measure below are equal to one whole note. But some notes are missing. Use the diagram at the right. Find the missing notes. The first measure has been started for you.

$\frac{1}{4} + \frac{1}{4} + \frac{1}{4} + \frac{1}{8} + ? = 1$

LESSON 6

Problem Solving Strategy
Use a Simpler Problem

Objective Use a simpler problem to help you add and subtract fractions.

CA Standards
MR 2.2 Apply strategies and results from simpler problems to more complex problems.
NS 1.5 Explain different interpretations of fractions, for example, parts of a whole, parts of a set, and division of whole numbers by whole numbers; explain equivalence of fractions (see Standard 4.0).
Also MR 1.0, MR 1.1, MR 1.2, MR 2.0, MR 2.3, MR 2.4, MR 2.6, MR 3.0, MR 3.1, MR 3.2

Learn by Example

You can solve a problem that involves adding and subtracting fractions by using a simpler problem that involves adding and subtracting whole numbers.

Karen and Raul both use diced jalapeño peppers when they make salsa. Karen uses $\frac{3}{8}$ cup of peppers. Raul uses $\frac{7}{8}$ cup of peppers. How many more cups of peppers does Raul use than Karen?

UNDERSTAND

You want to find out how many more cups of peppers Raul uses than Karen. You know:

- Karen uses $\frac{3}{8}$ cup of peppers.
- Raul uses $\frac{7}{8}$ cup of peppers.

PLAN

You can use easier numbers to help you decide how to solve the problem.

SOLVE

What if Raul used 7 cups of peppers and Karen used 3 cups of peppers? Subtract. $7 - 3 = 4$

Solve using the original numbers. Subtract. $\frac{7}{8} - \frac{3}{8} = \frac{4}{8}$ or $\frac{1}{2}$

So, Raul uses $\frac{4}{8}$, or $\frac{1}{2}$ cup more peppers than Karen.

LOOK BACK

Did you answer the question asked in the problem?

Guided Problem Solving

Solve using the Ask Yourself questions.

1. Nick used $\frac{3}{4}$ pound of tomatoes to make spaghetti sauce. Wendy used $\frac{1}{4}$ pound of tomatoes. How many fewer pounds of tomatoes did Wendy use than Nick?

Ask Yourself

- What simpler problem can I use?
- What operation can I use to solve the problem?

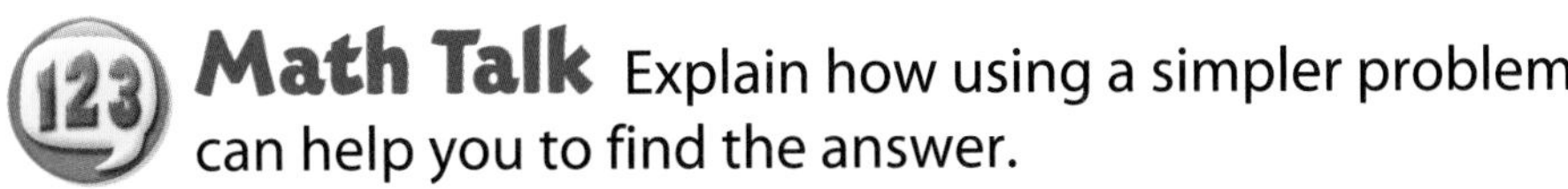

Math Talk Explain how using a simpler problem can help you to find the answer.

Independent Problem Solving

Use a simpler problem to solve. Explain why your answer makes sense.

2. Kate's recipe for fruit punch uses $\frac{5}{6}$ quart of cranberry juice. Barbara's recipe uses $\frac{1}{6}$ quart of cranberry juice. How much more cranberry juice does Kate's recipe use?

3. Roger uses three spices when he makes salad dressing. He uses $\frac{5}{16}$ teaspoon of basil, $\frac{3}{16}$ teaspoon of dill, and $\frac{1}{16}$ teaspoon of oregano. What is the total amount of spices Roger uses?

4. Sam wants to cook his soup for $\frac{11}{12}$ hour. He has already cooked the soup for $\frac{7}{12}$ hour. How many minutes longer must he cook the soup?

5. **Challenge** Maggy is using green, red, and yellow peppers in her salad. She uses $\frac{3}{8}$ cup of green peppers and $\frac{3}{8}$ cup of red peppers. If she wants to use a total of $\frac{7}{8}$ cup of peppers, how many cups of yellow peppers should she use?

6. **Create and Solve** Write a word problem that involves adding or subtracting fractions with like denominators.

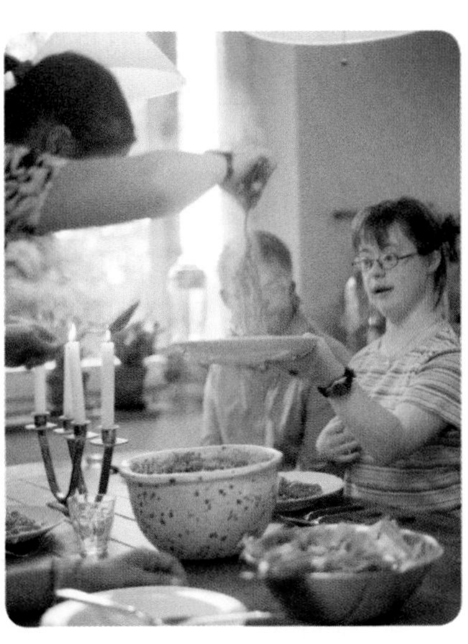

Reading & Writing 

Vocabulary

A **fraction** represents a part of a whole. The number below the line, called the **denominator**, tells how many equal parts the whole has been divided into. The number on top, called the **numerator**, tells how many of those equal parts there are.

Look at the drawings below. The fraction under each drawing represents the shaded part of the drawing.

For Questions 1–3, write the missing numerator and/or denominator.

1. 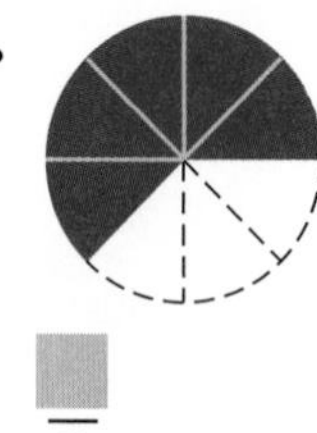

$\frac{\square}{8}$

2. 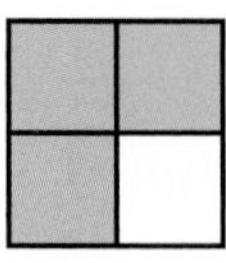

$\frac{3}{\square}$ 

3. 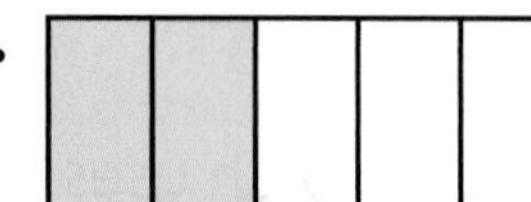

$\frac{\square}{\square}$

When two or more fractions have the same value, they are called **equivalent fractions**.

4. Name two **equivalent fractions** represented by the diagram.

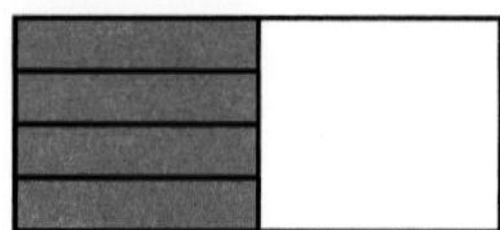

5. If a fraction is equivalent to $\frac{1}{2}$, its denominator must be ________ the value of its numerator.

Writing Write three fractions that are equivalent to $\frac{2}{8}$. Draw a picture to help you. How many times greater than the numerator is the denominator of each fraction?

Reading Check out this book in your library.
Fraction Fun, by David Adler

CA Standards
MR 2.3 Use a variety of methods, such as words, numbers, symbols, charts, graphs, tables, diagrams, and models, to explain mathematical reasoning.

Also NS 1.7

Standards-Based Extra Practice

Set A

NS 1.5 page 372

Find the fractional part of each number.

1. $\frac{1}{3}$ of 24
2. $\frac{5}{6}$ of 18
3. $\frac{4}{9}$ of 81
4. $\frac{3}{7}$ of 28
5. $\frac{6}{7}$ of 49
6. $\frac{1}{5}$ of 65
7. $\frac{2}{9}$ of 72
8. $\frac{8}{9}$ of 45
9. **Connect** Alberto mixed $\frac{3}{8}$ of 56 pints of chocolate milk with ice cream to make shakes for his party. How many pints of chocolate milk did Alberto use for the shakes?

Set B

NS 1.5 page 376

Complete. Find the value of each $\blacksquare$.

1. $\frac{3}{5} = \frac{3 \times 4}{5 \times 4} = \frac{\blacksquare}{20}$
2. $\frac{5}{6} = \frac{5 \times \blacksquare}{6 \times \blacksquare} = \frac{25}{30}$
3. $\frac{4}{7} = \frac{4 \times 6}{7 \times 6} = \frac{24}{\blacksquare}$
4. $\frac{9}{10} = \frac{9 \times \blacksquare}{10 \times \blacksquare} = \frac{45}{50}$
5. $\frac{72}{64} = \frac{72 \div \blacksquare}{64 \div \blacksquare} = \frac{9}{8}$
6. $\frac{2}{9} = \frac{2 \times 5}{9 \times 5} = \frac{10}{\blacksquare}$
7. **Explain** Emilio has $\frac{70}{80}$ pound of fish on his plate. What is the number of pounds of fish on Emilio's plate written in simplest form?

Set C

NS 1.5 page 380

Add or subtract.

1. $\frac{6}{8} - \frac{3}{8}$
2. $\frac{3}{7} + \frac{5}{7}$
3. $\frac{3}{9} + \frac{7}{9}$
4. $\frac{5}{6} + \frac{8}{6}$

Find the value of *n*.

5. $\frac{4}{7} + \frac{n}{7} = \frac{12}{7}$
6. $\frac{n}{6} + \frac{5}{6} = \frac{17}{6}$
7. $\frac{7}{8} - \frac{n}{8} = \frac{3}{8}$
8. $\frac{n}{9} - \frac{3}{9} = \frac{10}{9}$
9. **Analyze** Emma subtracts a certain number of sevenths from $\frac{15}{7}$ to make $\frac{6}{7}$. How many sevenths does she subtract?

Education Place
Visit www.eduplace.com/camap/ for more **Extra Practice**.

Chapter Review/Test

Vocabulary and Concepts

NS 1.5, MR 2.3

Write the best word to complete each sentence.

1. In the fraction $\frac{4}{5}$, the number 4 is called the ______.

2. $\frac{6}{8}$ and $\frac{3}{4}$ are examples of ______ fractions.

Skills

NS 1.5, AF 1.1

Find the fractional part of the number.

3. $\frac{1}{4}$ of 12

4. $\frac{2}{3}$ of 9

5. $\frac{7}{8}$ of 16

6. $\frac{4}{5}$ of 20

Complete. Find the value of the ■.

7. $\frac{2}{3} = \frac{2 \times 4}{3 \times 4} = \frac{■}{12}$

8. $\frac{4}{5} = \frac{4 \times ■}{5 \times ■} = \frac{12}{15}$

9. $\frac{18}{30} = \frac{18 \div 6}{30 \div 6} = \frac{■}{5}$

Add or subtract.

10. $\frac{3}{4} + \frac{1}{4} = ■$

11. $\frac{7}{8} - \frac{4}{8} = ■$

12. $\frac{4}{10} + \frac{3}{10} = ■$

13. $\frac{15}{16} - \frac{12}{16} = ■$

Problem Solving and Reasoning

NS 1.5, MR 2.2, MR 2.3

Solve.

14. Lien uses $\frac{1}{4}$ of a jar of paint for an art project. There are 12 ounces of paint in the jar. How many ounces does she use?

15. Sabrina walks $\frac{7}{20}$ mile to school. Lisa walks $\frac{3}{20}$ mile more than Sabrina. How far does Lisa walk to school?

Writing Math Explain how you would write a fraction that is equivalent to a given fraction.

Spiral Review and Test Practice

1. Tarek solved the problem below. Which expression could be used to check his answer?

$$5\overline{)23}$$ with quotient 4 R3

A (5 × 4) × 3

B (5 × 4) + 3

C 5 × 4

D (23 − 5) + 4

Test Tip
Evaluate each expression to see which one is equal to the dividend.

KEY NS 3.2 page 130

2. The sum of *x* plus *y* equals 12. If $x = 5$, which equation can be used to find the value of *y*?

A $y - 5 = 12$

B $5 + y = 12$

C $x - y = 12$

D $x + 5 = 12$

KEY AF 1.5 page 174

3. A bakery sold 8 boxes of muffins. Each box contained the same number of muffins. If there was a total of 192 muffins, how many muffins were in each box?

A 22 muffins

B 23 muffins

C 24 muffins

D 25 muffins

KEY NS 3.4 page 282

4. Alison ran 10 kilometers. There are 1,000 meters in 1 kilometer. How many meters did she run?

A 10 m

B 1,000 m

C 10,000 m

D 100,000 m

Test Tip
Check to make sure you have the correct number of zeroes in your answer.

KEY NS 3.3 page 334

5. At 8:00 A.M. the temperature was $^{-}6$°F. By noon the temperature was 5 degrees higher. What was the temperature at noon?

A $^{-}11$°F

B $^{-}1$°F

C 1°F

D 11°F

KEY NS 1.8 page 352

6. What is $\frac{3}{4}$ of 12?

A 3

B 4

C 9

D 15

NS 1.5 page 372

Education Place
Visit www.eduplace.com/camap/ for **Test-Taking Tips** and **Extra Practice.**

Chapter 18 Compare and Order Fractions

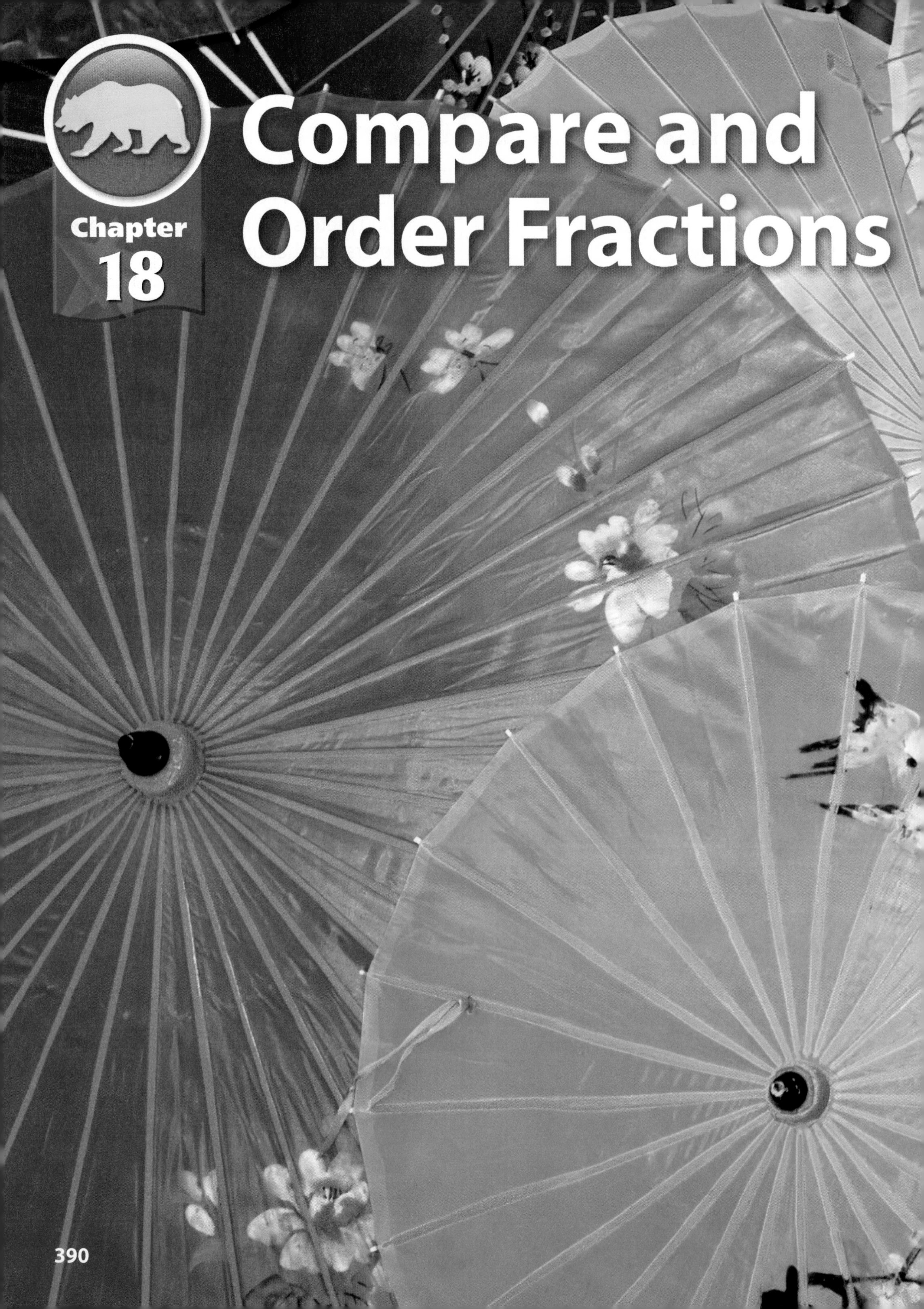

Check What You Know

Vocabulary and Concepts GRADE 3 NS 1.2, MR 2.3

Word Bank
- mixed number
- number line
- graph
- order

Choose the best term to complete the sentence.

1. You _____ numbers when you arrange them from greatest to least or from least to greatest.

2. A line that shows numbers as points in order from least to greatest is called a _____.

Skills GRADE 3 NS 3.1

Compare. Write >, <, or = for the ⬭.

3. \$0.35 ⬭ 29¢ **4.** \$0.77 ⬭ \$0.48 **5.** \$3.06 ⬭ \$3.50

Identify the fraction represented by the point.

6. 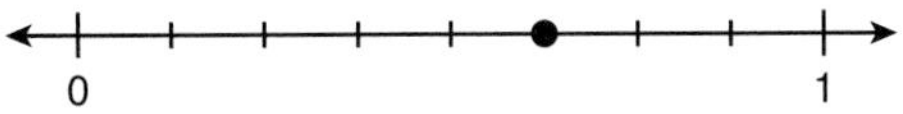

7. 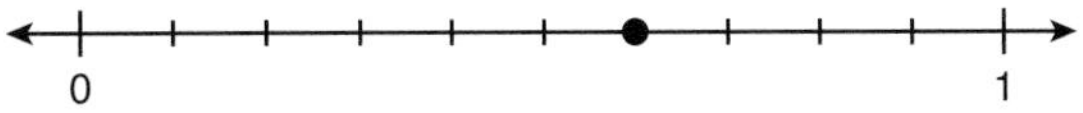

Write the fractions in order from least to greatest.

8. $\frac{4}{10}$ $\frac{2}{10}$ $\frac{4}{5}$

9. $\frac{7}{8}$ $\frac{6}{8}$ $\frac{6}{10}$

Problem Solving and Reasoning GRADE 3 NS 2.0

10. Jake came home with \$3. He had spent half his money on lunch and then \$5 on a book. How much did he start with?

Vocabulary

Visualize It!

A **fraction** shows a part of a whole, a collection, or a region.

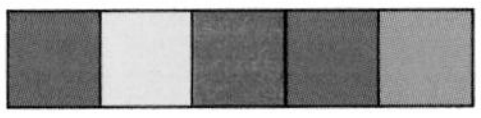

$\frac{2}{5}$ **are blue**

Ways to Show Numbers with Parts

An **improper fraction** has a numerator that is greater than or equal to its denominator.

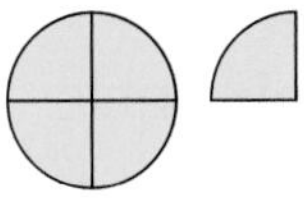

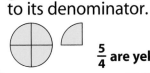

$\frac{5}{4}$ **are yellow**

A **mixed number** has a whole-number part and a fraction part.

There are $2\frac{1}{2}$ apples.

Language Tip

Some words are similar in English and Spanish.

English	Spanish
fraction	fracción
improper fraction	fracción impropia
mixed number	número mixto

See **English-Spanish Glossary** pages 644–666.

Education Place Visit www.eduplace.com/camap/ for the **eGlossary** and **eGames**.

CA Standards MR 2.3 Use a variety of methods, such as words, numbers, symbols, charts, graphs, tables, diagrams, and models, to explain mathematical reasoning. **Also NS 1.5 and NS 1.7**

Hands On
Compare Fractions

Objective Use models to compare fractions.

CA Standards
KEY NS 1.9 Identify on a number line the relative position of positive fractions, positive mixed numbers, and positive decimals to two decimal places.

Also NS 1.5, MR 1.0, MR 1.1, MR 2.0, MR 2.3, MR 2.4, MR 3.3, MR 3.0

Vocabulary

compare

Materials
- Learning Tool 26 (Fraction Number Lines)
- ruler
- fraction tiles
- eManipulatives (optional) www.eduplace.com/camap/

Explore

In Chapter 17, you used fraction tiles and number lines to show equivalent fractions. In this lesson, you will use those models to compare fractions.

Question How can you use fraction tiles or number lines to compare fractions?

Aidan and his uncle hiked $\frac{3}{8}$ of a mile and then stopped to rest. Then they hiked another $\frac{1}{8}$ of a mile. Did they hike more before they stopped to rest or after?

To answer this problem, you need to **compare** $\frac{3}{8}$ and $\frac{1}{8}$. When you compare fractions, you can tell which fraction is greater.

Use fraction tiles and a number line to compare $\frac{3}{8}$ and $\frac{1}{8}$.

1 Use fraction tiles.
- Show three $\frac{1}{8}$ tiles and one $\frac{1}{8}$ tile.
- Compare to find out which fraction is greater.

2 Use a number line on Learning Tool 26.
- Draw a circle around $\frac{3}{8}$.
  Draw a rectangle around $\frac{1}{8}$.
- The fraction farther to the right is greater.

Solution: Since $\frac{3}{8} > \frac{1}{8}$, Aidan and his uncle hiked more before they stopped to rest.

You can also use fraction tiles or number lines to compare fractions that have different denominators.

Compare $\frac{5}{8}$ and $\frac{1}{2}$.

1 Use fraction tiles.

- Show five $\frac{1}{8}$ tiles and one $\frac{1}{2}$ tile.
- Compare the lengths of the two fractions to find out which fraction is greater.

2 Use number lines that show eighths and halves.

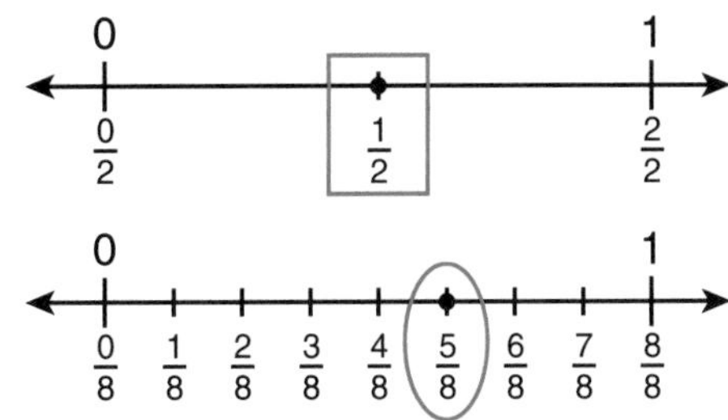

- Draw a circle around $\frac{5}{8}$. Draw a rectangle around $\frac{1}{2}$.
- The fraction farther to the right is greater.

Extend

Compare. Write >, <, or = for the ○. Use fraction tiles or number lines to help you.

1. $\frac{3}{8}$ ○ $\frac{5}{8}$ **2.** $\frac{3}{4}$ ○ $\frac{2}{4}$ **3.** $\frac{5}{10}$ ○ $\frac{9}{10}$ **4.** $\frac{4}{6}$ ○ $\frac{2}{6}$

5. $\frac{2}{5}$ ○ $\frac{4}{5}$ **6.** $\frac{2}{3}$ ○ $\frac{2}{3}$ **7.** $\frac{2}{5}$ ○ $\frac{5}{10}$ **8.** $\frac{4}{10}$ ○ $\frac{3}{5}$

9. $\frac{1}{2}$ ○ $\frac{4}{12}$ **10.** $\frac{8}{12}$ ○ $\frac{2}{3}$ **11.** $\frac{3}{6}$ ○ $\frac{1}{3}$ **12.** $\frac{3}{4}$ ○ $\frac{6}{8}$

13. Analyze Tony hiked $\frac{1}{8}$ of the Lady Bird Johnson Grove trail. Mindy hiked $\frac{3}{6}$ of it. Jonathan hiked $\frac{1}{4}$ of it. Who hiked the farthest? Explain.

Lady Bird Johnson Grove in Redwood National Park, Northern California

Writing Math

Generalize Why is it easier to compare fractions that have the same denominators than fractions that have different denominators?

Compare and Order Fractions

Objective Compare and order fractions.

CA Standards
KEY NS 1.9 Identify on a number line the relative position of positive fractions, positive mixed numbers, and positive decimals to two decimal places.

NS 1.5 Explain different interpretations of fractions, for example, parts of a whole, parts of a set, and division of whole numbers by whole numbers; explain equivalence of fractions (see Standard 4.0).

Also MR 1.0, MR 1.1, MR 2.2, MR 2.3, MR 2.4, MR 2.0

Vocabulary

unlike denominators
equivalent fractions
like denominators
order

Learn by Example

Mellie brings supplies to campers on an island. She uses $\frac{1}{6}$ of the storage space on her boat for life vests, $\frac{1}{2}$ for groceries, and $\frac{2}{6}$ for water. Is more space used for groceries or water?

Compare $\frac{1}{2}$ and $\frac{2}{6}$ to see which fraction is greater.

Since the two fractions have different denominators, or **unlike denominators**, you can use number lines or find **equivalent fractions** to compare.

Different Ways to Compare $\frac{1}{2}$ and $\frac{2}{6}$

Way 1 Use number lines.

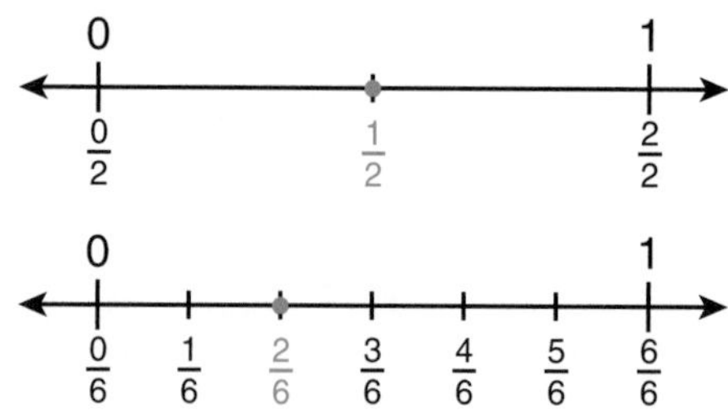

$\frac{1}{2}$ is farther to the right, so $\frac{1}{2} > \frac{2}{6}$.

Way 2 Find equivalent fractions with like denominators. Then compare the numerators.

- Find a fraction equivalent to $\frac{1}{2}$ with a denominator of 6.

$\frac{1}{2} = \frac{1 \times 3}{2 \times 3} = \frac{3}{6}$

so $\frac{1}{2} = \frac{3}{6}$.

- Since the fractions $\frac{3}{6}$ and $\frac{2}{6}$ have **like denominators**, compare the numerators.

$3 > 2$

$\frac{3}{6} > \frac{2}{6}$, so $\frac{1}{2} > \frac{2}{6}$.

Solution: Mellie uses more space for groceries than water.

Use what you know about comparing fractions to order fractions.

Order $\frac{1}{3}$, $\frac{1}{6}$, and $\frac{5}{6}$ from least to greatest.

Different Ways to Order Fractions

Way 1 **Use number lines.**

$\frac{1}{6}$ is farthest to the left.

$\frac{5}{6}$ is farthest to the right.

$\frac{1}{3}$ is in the middle.

So, $\frac{1}{6} < \frac{1}{3} < \frac{5}{6}$.

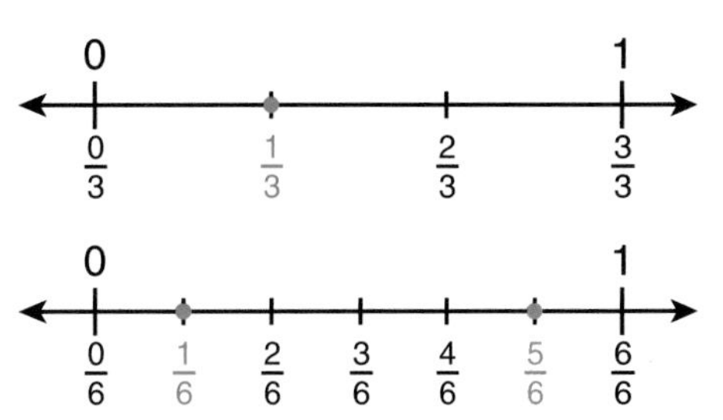

Way 2 **Find equivalent fractions with like denominators. Then compare the numerators.**

- Find a fraction equivalent to $\frac{1}{3}$ with a denominator of 6.

$$\frac{1}{3} = \frac{1 \times 2}{3 \times 2} = \frac{2}{6}$$

so $\frac{1}{3} = \frac{2}{6}$.

- Since the fractions $\frac{2}{6}$, $\frac{1}{6}$ and $\frac{5}{6}$ have like denominators, compare the numerators, and order the fractions.

$1 < 2 < 5$

$\frac{1}{6} < \frac{2}{6} < \frac{5}{6}$, so $\frac{1}{6} < \frac{1}{3} < \frac{5}{6}$.

Solution: The order of the fractions from least to greatest is $\frac{1}{6}$, $\frac{1}{3}$, $\frac{5}{6}$.

Guided Practice

Compare. Write >, <, or = for the ⬭.

1. $\frac{3}{5}$ ⬭ $\frac{1}{5}$

2. $\frac{2}{3}$ ⬭ $\frac{5}{6}$

3. $\frac{2}{2}$ ⬭ $\frac{4}{4}$

Order the fractions from greatest to least.

4. $\frac{2}{7}$ $\frac{6}{7}$ $\frac{4}{7}$

5. $\frac{3}{4}$ $\frac{7}{8}$ $\frac{5}{8}$

6. $\frac{1}{5}$ $\frac{1}{10}$ $\frac{4}{5}$

Ask Yourself

Do the fractions have like denominators? If not, how can I find equivalent fractions?

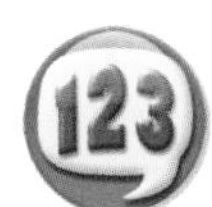

Math Talk Dax said that $\frac{4}{10}$ must be greater than $\frac{3}{5}$ since 4 is greater than 3. Explain why he is wrong.

Practice and Problem Solving

Compare. Write >, <, or = for the ⬭.

7. $\frac{2}{6}$ ⬭ $\frac{4}{6}$ **8.** $\frac{3}{8}$ ⬭ $\frac{1}{4}$ **9.** $\frac{4}{6}$ ⬭ $\frac{2}{3}$ **10.** $\frac{1}{2}$ ⬭ $\frac{2}{4}$

11. $\frac{3}{4}$ ⬭ $\frac{5}{8}$ **12.** $\frac{2}{8}$ ⬭ $\frac{1}{4}$ **13.** $\frac{1}{3}$ ⬭ $\frac{3}{9}$ **14.** $\frac{7}{10}$ ⬭ $\frac{3}{4}$

Order the fractions from least to greatest.

15. $\frac{4}{8}$ $\frac{7}{8}$ $\frac{1}{8}$ **16.** $\frac{7}{12}$ $\frac{10}{12}$ $\frac{3}{4}$ **17.** $\frac{4}{9}$ $\frac{5}{6}$ $\frac{5}{9}$ **18.** $\frac{2}{3}$ $\frac{7}{12}$ $\frac{5}{12}$

History-Social Science Link

Solve. Show your work.

19. How many years did it take to build the aqueduct?

20. a. About $\frac{1}{4}$ of the length of the first Los Angeles Aqueduct is tunnels. About $\frac{2}{5}$ is concrete conduits and about $\frac{1}{20}$ is steel and concrete pipeline. Order the fractions from least to greatest.

b. Challenge The remaining fraction of the aqueduct is channels. What is this fraction?

First Los Angeles Aqueduct

Construction of the first Los Angeles Aqueduct began in 1905 and was completed in 1913. The total length of the aqueduct was 223 miles.

History-Social Science 4.4.7

Spiral Review and Test Practice

Divide. Use multiplication and addition to check. KEY NS 3.2 pages 282, 286, 290

21. $4\overline{)484}$ **22.** $3\overline{)714}$ **23.** $6\overline{)258}$ **24.** $7\overline{)761}$ **25.** $5\overline{)208}$

Write the letter of the correct answer. NS 1.5

26. Which fraction represents the largest part of a whole?

A $\frac{1}{4}$ **B** $\frac{1}{5}$ **C** $\frac{1}{6}$ **D** $\frac{1}{8}$

Extra Practice See page 407, Set A.

Math Works! Architect

Plan a Clubhouse

Architects plan and design all types of buildings and structures. An architect designs a floor plan for a new building. Then blueprints are drawn as a model for the building.

A blueprint is more detailed than a floor plan. Blueprints tell the builder exactly where to put the walls, doors, windows, closets, and hallways in a building.

Use Workmat 5 to make a floor plan.

1. The outside edges of the large square are the outside walls of the clubhouse. Include a window and door in your plan. How many squares are inside your clubhouse floor plan?

2. Draw furniture or other objects that you want in your clubhouse. Label the objects.

3. What fraction of the squares in your clubhouse is covered by furniture or other objects?

4. What fraction of the squares in your clubhouse is not covered by furniture or other objects?

5. Compare the two fractions. Use $>$, $<$, or $=$.

CA Standards
NS 1.7, MR 1.1

CA Standards
KEY NS 1.9 Identify on a number line the relative position of positive fractions, positive mixed numbers, and positive decimals to two decimal places.

NS 1.7 Write the fraction represented by a drawing of parts of a figure; represent a given fraction by using drawings; and relate a fraction to a simple decimal on a number line.

Also NS 1.5, MR 1.1, MR 2.2, MR 2.3, MR 2.0, MR 1.0

Vocabulary

mixed number

improper fraction

Write Mixed Numbers and Improper Fractions

Objective Write mixed numbers and improper fractions.

Learn by Example

After a picnic, there were two whole sandwiches and one fourth of a sandwich left. You can write the amount of sandwiches as a mixed number or as an improper fraction.

Model It	Write It

A **mixed number** is made up of a whole number and a fraction.

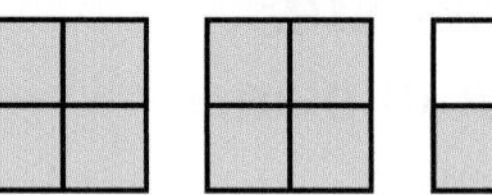

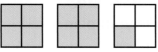

whole number → $2\frac{1}{4}$ ← fraction

Think: Count the wholes and parts.

An **improper fraction** has a numerator that is greater than or equal to its denominator.

2	3		6	7			
1	4		5	8		9	

improper fraction → $\frac{9}{4}$

Think: Count the parts. 9 fourths $= \frac{9}{4}$

The number line shows that $2\frac{1}{4}$ and $\frac{9}{4}$ represent the same number.

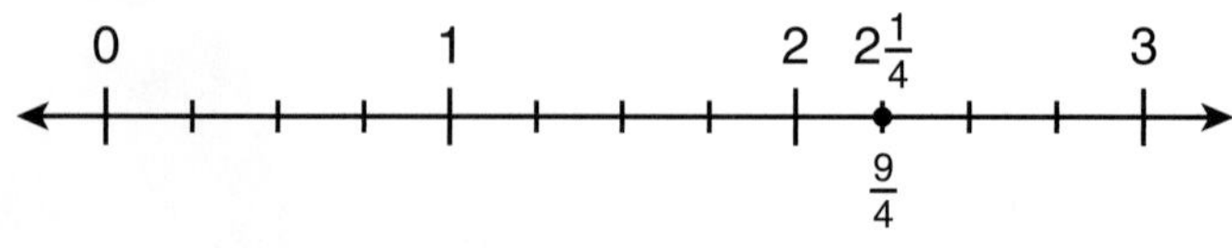

Other Examples

A. Convert Improper Fractions

$\frac{9}{4} = 2\frac{1}{4}$

$$\begin{array}{r} 2 \\ 4\overline{)9} \\ -8 \\ \hline 1 \end{array}$$

2 ← number of wholes

1 ← number of fourths

B. Convert Mixed Numbers

$2\frac{1}{4} = \frac{9}{4}$

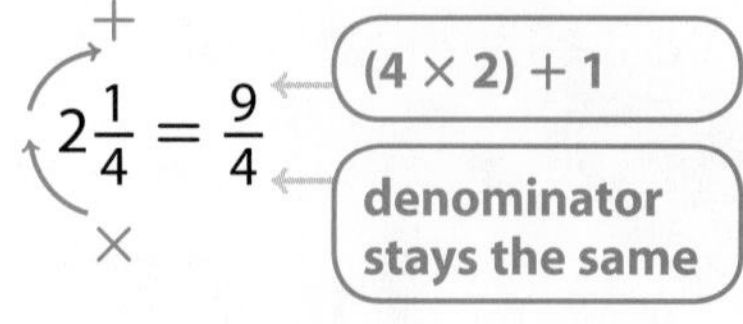

Think

The fraction bar stands for "divided by."

Guided Practice

Write an improper fraction and a mixed number or a whole number to describe the shaded parts.

1. 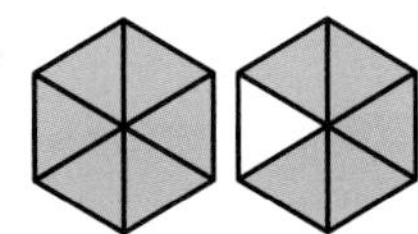

2. 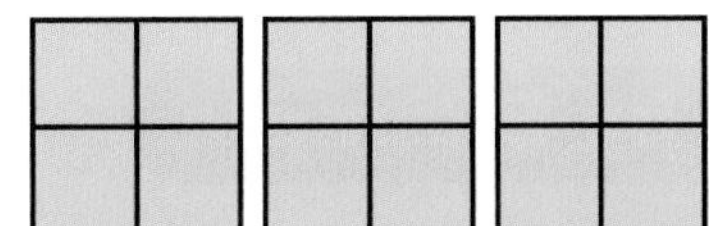

Ask Yourself
- Into how many equal parts is each figure divided?
- How many wholes are represented?

Write a mixed number and an improper fraction for the letter.

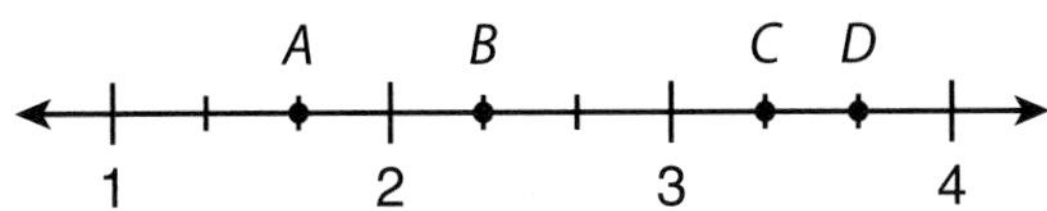

3. *C* **4.** *B* **5.** *D* **6.** *A*

Math Talk How can you tell whether a fraction can be rewritten as a mixed number or as a whole number?

Practice and Problem Solving

Write a mixed number and an improper fraction for the letter.

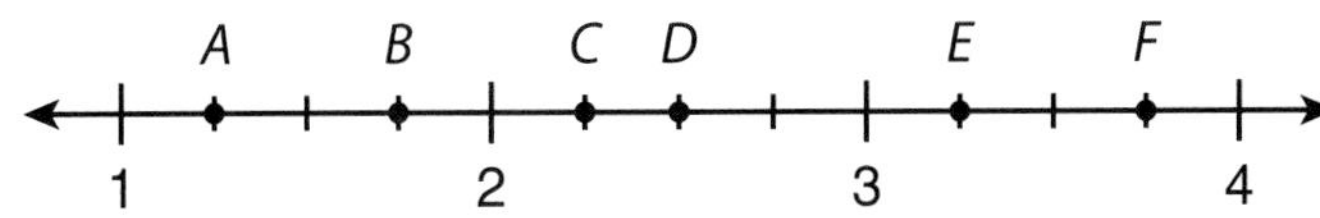

7. *A* **8.** *C* **9.** *F* **10.** *D* **11.** *B* **12.** *E*

13. Al had 5 oranges. He cut the oranges into halves. Each person ate one half. No oranges were left over. How many people ate oranges?

Spiral Review and Test Practice

Find the missing number. KEY NS 3.2 page 334

14. 5,000 m = ▢ km **15.** 4 m = ▢ cm **16.** 90 cm = ▢ mm

Write the letter of the correct answer. KEY NS 1.9

17. What number does point *P* represent?

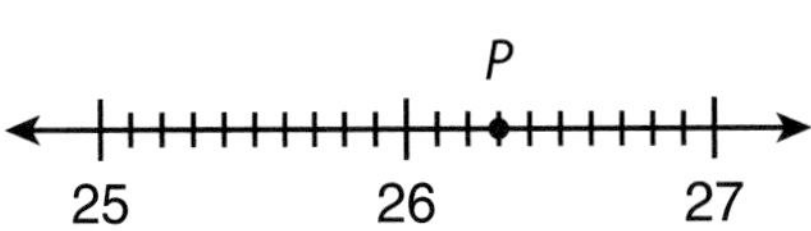

A $25\frac{3}{10}$ **B** $26\frac{3}{5}$ **C** $26\frac{3}{10}$ **D** $27\frac{7}{10}$

Extra Practice See page 407, Set B.

Compare and Order Fractions and Mixed Numbers

Objective Compare and order fractions and mixed numbers.

CA Standards
KEY NS 1.9 Identify on a number line the relative position of positive fractions, positive mixed numbers, and positive decimals to two decimal places.

NS 1.5 Explain different interpretations of fractions, for example, parts of a whole, parts of a set, and division of whole numbers by whole numbers; explain equivalence of fractions (see Standard 4.0).

Also MR 1.1, MR 2.2, MR 2.3, MR 2.0, MR 2.4, MR 1.0, MR 3.2, MR 3.0

Learn by Example

Look at the hiking sign.
Which trail is the longest?
Which trail is the shortest?

Since you want to find the longest and shortest trails, you need to compare and order the numbers.

Different Ways to Compare and Order $1\frac{1}{4}$, $1\frac{5}{8}$, and $\frac{1}{2}$

Way 1 Use number lines.

$\frac{1}{2}$ is farthest to the left.

$1\frac{5}{8}$ is farthest to the right.

$1\frac{1}{4}$ is in between.

So, $\frac{1}{2} < 1\frac{1}{4} < 1\frac{5}{8}$.

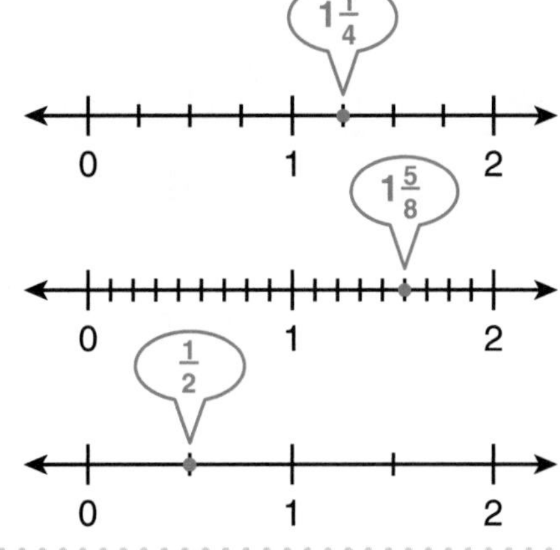

Way 2 Use equivalent fractions.

- Change the mixed numbers to improper fractions.

  $1\frac{1}{4} = \frac{5}{4}$ $\quad 1\frac{5}{8} = \frac{13}{8}$

- Write equivalent fractions with like denominators of 8.

  $\frac{5}{4} = \frac{10}{8}$ $\quad \frac{1}{2} = \frac{4}{8}$

- Since $\frac{10}{8}$, $\frac{13}{8}$, and $\frac{4}{8}$ now have like denominators, compare numerators, and order the fractions.

  $4 < 10 < 13$

  $\frac{4}{8} < \frac{10}{8} < \frac{13}{8}$, so $\frac{1}{2} < 1\frac{1}{4} < 1\frac{5}{8}$.

Solution: The longest trail is $1\frac{5}{8}$ miles. The shortest trail is $\frac{1}{2}$ mile.

Guided Practice

Compare. Write >, <, or = for the ⬭.

1. $3\frac{1}{3}$ ⬭ $2\frac{5}{6}$ **2.** $3\frac{1}{2}$ ⬭ $3\frac{5}{10}$ **3.** $1\frac{3}{4}$ ⬭ $1\frac{5}{9}$

Ask Yourself
- Do I need to find equivalent fractions?
- Can I use a number line to help me?

Order the numbers from greatest to least. Use number lines to help you.

4. $1\frac{5}{10}$ $1\frac{9}{10}$ $1\frac{4}{5}$ **5.** $\frac{9}{4}$ $1\frac{3}{8}$ $1\frac{1}{2}$ **6.** $2\frac{1}{3}$ $\frac{9}{6}$ $1\frac{5}{6}$

Guided Problem Solving

Use the questions to solve this problem.

7. Diego uses three different ropes for climbing. The first rope is $4\frac{5}{8}$ yards long, the second is $5\frac{3}{4}$ yards, and the third is $5\frac{1}{2}$ yards. Which is the longest rope?

a. **Understand** What do you need to find?

b. **Plan** Which rope is the shortest? Which two mixed numbers are left to compare?

c. **Solve** Find equivalent fractions to compare the two numbers. Which number is greater?

d. **Look Back** Use a number line to check your answer.

Math Talk Would you use a number line or find equivalent fractions to compare $1\frac{1}{2}$ and $1\frac{3}{8}$? Explain.

Practice and Problem Solving

Compare. Write >, <, or = for the ⬭.

8. $2\frac{7}{8}$ ⬭ $2\frac{3}{5}$ **9.** $2\frac{4}{5}$ ⬭ $\frac{28}{10}$ **10.** $1\frac{2}{3}$ ⬭ $1\frac{3}{4}$

Order the numbers from least to greatest. Use number lines to help you.

11. $2\frac{5}{12}$ $1\frac{2}{3}$ $2\frac{1}{3}$ **12.** $8\frac{2}{3}$ $8\frac{1}{2}$ $8\frac{3}{4}$ **13.** $\frac{18}{5}$ $2\frac{3}{10}$ $2\frac{4}{5}$

Solve.

14. Taka hikes $1\frac{1}{3}$ miles around a lake. Then she hikes $1\frac{2}{6}$ miles to a cabin. Which distance is greater?

15. What is the least denominator you can use to compare $\frac{1}{2}$, $\frac{3}{4}$, and $\frac{1}{6}$? Order the fractions from least to greatest.

16. **Generalize** Do you need to use equivalent fractions to compare mixed numbers with different whole number parts?

Science Link

Solve.

17. One year, the Calaveras Fault moved $5\frac{2}{5}$ mm. The next year, it moved $5\frac{2}{7}$ mm. Which distance is greater?

18. **Challenge** Misha can hike $1\frac{1}{2}$ km per hour. Josh can hike $\frac{3}{4}$ km per hour. Misha hikes for 2 hours and Josh hikes for 3 hours. Who hikes farther?

19. Three points on the central California fault zone are $10\frac{1}{2}$ km wide, $10\frac{1}{3}$ km wide, and $10\frac{5}{6}$ km wide. Order the points from narrowest to widest.

Calaveras Fault

- Breaks in the earth's crust, called faults, normally move slowly.
- Earthquakes occur when faults move very quickly.
- The Calaveras Fault in central California moves about 5 or 6 mm per year.

Science ES 5.a

Spiral Review and Test Practice

Find the value. NS 1.5 page 372

20. $\frac{1}{3}$ of 15 **21.** $\frac{3}{4}$ of 12 **22.** $\frac{5}{8}$ of 16 **23.** $\frac{4}{6}$ of 12 **24.** $\frac{2}{10}$ of 100

Write the letter of the correct answer. KEY NS 1.9

25. Which number is best represented by point M on this number line?

A $\frac{3}{5}$ **B** $\frac{8}{5}$ **C** $1\frac{3}{4}$ **D** $2\frac{2}{5}$

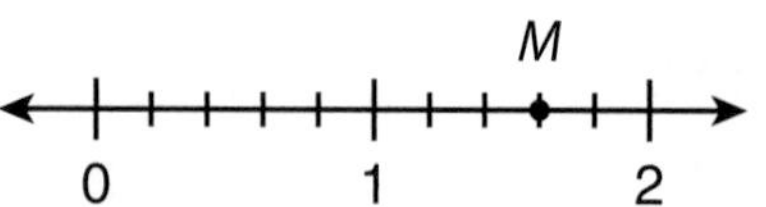

Extra Practice See page 407, Set C.

Key Standards Review

Need Help?
See Key Standards Handbook.

Solve. KEY NS 3.4

1. Mr. Blake wants to put his photos in an album. The album has 9 pages. If Mr. Blake has 207 photos, how many will go on each page of the album?

2. Alan watched a 168-minute long documentary in one week. He watched the program for the same amount of time each day. How many minutes did he watch each day?

3. There are 8 rows of seats in a theater. Each row has the same number of seats. If there is a total of 208 seats in the theater, how many seats are in each row?

4. Amilyn is planting tomato plants in her garden. She wants to plant the same number of tomato plants in each of four rows. If she has 112 tomato plants, how many will be in each row of her garden?

Logical Thinking

Silly Statements

What's wrong with each statement? NS 1.5

"I ate $\frac{3}{4}$ of a peach. You ate $\frac{1}{8}$ of a watermelon. Since $\frac{3}{4} > \frac{1}{8}$, I ate more fruit than you."

"I'm not very hungry. I only want 1 small slice of pizza. So cut one pizza into 4 slices instead of 8, please."

"I read $1\frac{2}{3}$ chapters of my book on Monday, $2\frac{1}{3}$ pages on Tuesday, and $3\frac{1}{2}$ paragraphs on Wednesday. I read the most on Wednesday because $3\frac{1}{2}$ is the largest mixed number."

Write your own silly statements.

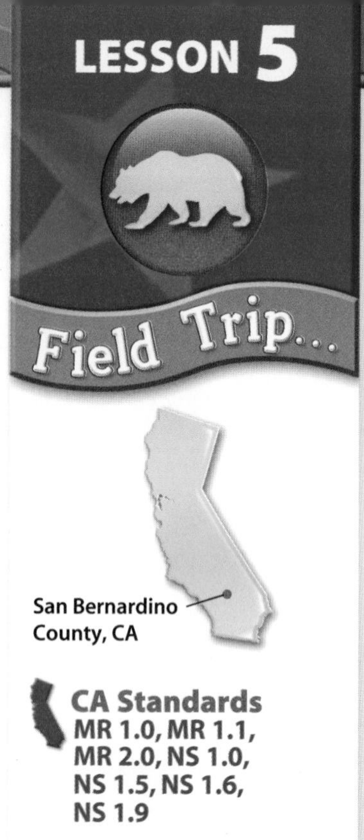

CA Standards
MR 1.0, MR 1.1, MR 2.0, NS 1.0, NS 1.5, NS 1.6, NS 1.9

Problem Solving

Objective Use skills and strategies to solve word problems.

You can enjoy the canyons, forests, lakes, and streams of the San Bernardino National Forest. Big Bear Lake is a popular recreation spot.

The San Bernardino National Forest has hiking and biking trails as well as beautiful campsites.

Trail Name	Difficulty Level	Round Trip (mi)
Bluff Mesa	Easy	$\frac{4}{5}$
Castle Rock	Difficult	$2\frac{2}{5}$
Champion Lodgepole Pine	Easy	$\frac{3}{5}$
Cougar Crest	Moderate	$5\frac{1}{2}$
Glory Ridge	Very Difficult	2
Pine Knot	Moderate	6
Woodland	Easy	$1\frac{1}{2}$

Use the table to solve. Tell which strategy or method you used.

1. What fraction of the trails listed are easy?
2. Order the trails from shortest to longest. Use a 0 to 6 number line to help you.
3. The total acreage of the San Bernardino National Forest is 671,686. Write this number in word form.
4. The Garcia family is going on a hike. Use these clues to find the trail they will hike.
   - The trail is not easy.
   - The trail is longer than 2 miles but less than 6 miles.
   - The trail is longer than 2.4 miles.

Problem Solving on Tests

Select a Strategy
- Choose the Operation
- Write an Equation
- Estimate
- Draw a Picture
- Make an Organized List

1. The lunch special at a diner has 3 types of salad—garden, vegetable, and fruit—and 2 types of soup—tomato and mushroom. How many possible combinations of soup and salad does the diner offer?

A 4

B 5

C 6

D 9

Test Tip
Make an organized list or draw a picture to help you.

SDAP 2.1 page 38

2. There are 8 fewer cans of peas than cans of beets in the school pantry. If n represents the number of cans of beets, which expression can be used to find how many cans of peas are in the school pantry?

A $8n$ **C** $n - 8$

B $8 - n$ **D** $n + 8$

AF 1.1 page 170

3. A party store has 517 packages of balloons. If there are 18 balloons in each package, how many balloons are in the store?

A 535 balloons **C** 9,206 balloons

B 4,653 balloons **D** 9,306 balloons

KEY NS 3.3 page 242

4. Marge is making a triple batch of muffins. One batch calls for $\frac{3}{4}$ of a cup of raisins, so a triple batch will require $\frac{9}{4}$ cups. What mixed number is equivalent to that amount?

A $2\frac{1}{9}$

B $2\frac{1}{4}$

C $2\frac{3}{4}$

D $3\frac{1}{4}$

NS 1.5 page 398

5. At 5:00 P.M. the temperature was 6°F. The temperature dropped 2°F every hour. What was the temperature at 11:00 P.M.?

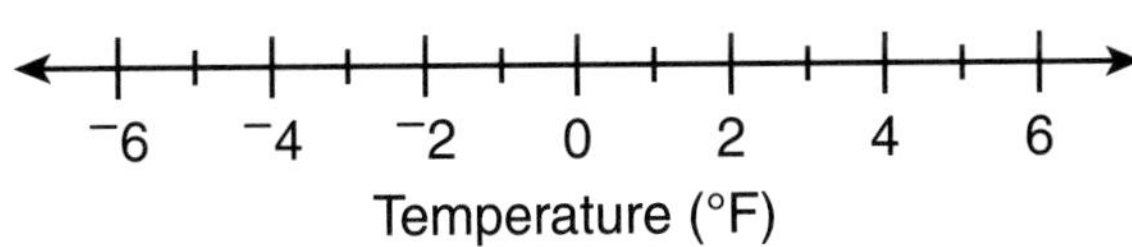

A ⁻4°F

B ⁻6°F

C 0°F

D 14°F

KEY NS 1.8 page 352

Education Place
Visit www.eduplace.com/camap/ for **Test-Taking Tips** and **Extra Practice**.

Reading & Writing 

Vocabulary

Match each definition with the correct term from the word bank. Some terms will be used more than once.

Word Bank
improper fraction
mixed number

1. A fraction that is greater than or equal to 1 is a(n) ________.
2. A fraction in which the numerator is greater than or equal to the denominator is a(n) ________.
3. A number containing a whole number part and a fraction part is a(n) ________.

Copy and complete the table, listing each number from the number box under its correct heading.

Improper Fractions	Mixed Numbers
________	________
________	________
________	________

Number Box

$3\frac{1}{3}$	$\frac{12}{7}$
$\frac{18}{6}$	$\frac{11}{8}$
$8\frac{2}{7}$	$6\frac{9}{10}$

4. Look at the list of improper fractions. Express each one as a mixed number.

Writing How can you tell if an improper fraction is equivalent to a whole number or a mixed number?

Reading Look for this book in your library.
Mega-Fun Fractions, by Marcia Miller and Martin Lee

CA Standards
MR 2.3 Use a variety of methods, such as words, numbers, symbols, charts, graphs, tables, diagrams, and models, to explain mathematical reasoning.

Also KEY NS 1.9

Standards-Based Extra Practice

Set A

KEY NS 1.9 page 394

Compare. Write >, <, or = for the ◯. Think about a number line.

1. $\frac{1}{3}$ ◯ $\frac{1}{5}$ **2.** $\frac{4}{6}$ ◯ $\frac{2}{3}$ **3.** $\frac{4}{4}$ ◯ $\frac{9}{8}$ **4.** $\frac{3}{6}$ ◯ $\frac{10}{12}$

5. $\frac{6}{4}$ ◯ $\frac{6}{8}$ **6.** $\frac{1}{3}$ ◯ $\frac{2}{9}$ **7.** $\frac{2}{6}$ ◯ $\frac{4}{12}$ **8.** $\frac{8}{5}$ ◯ $\frac{7}{10}$

9. Compare Compare $\frac{1}{3}$ and $\frac{1}{4}$. Both fractions have the same numerator. How can you tell which fraction is the smaller by looking at their denominators?

Set B

NS 1.5, KEY NS 1.9 page 398

Write a mixed number as an improper fraction or an improper fraction as a mixed number. Think about a number line.

1. $4\frac{5}{6}$ **2.** $\frac{25}{4}$ **3.** $7\frac{1}{8}$ **4.** $\frac{37}{5}$

5. $\frac{22}{3}$ **6.** $5\frac{1}{6}$ **7.** $\frac{31}{4}$ **8.** $3\frac{4}{5}$

9. Explain How do you write a mixed number as an improper fraction?

Set C

KEY NS 1.9 page 400

Compare. Write >, <, or = for the ◯. Think about a number line.

1. $1\frac{5}{4}$ ◯ $\frac{10}{4}$ **2.** $2\frac{2}{3}$ ◯ $\frac{7}{3}$ **3.** $3\frac{1}{3}$ ◯ $3\frac{2}{6}$ **4.** $2\frac{5}{8}$ ◯ $3\frac{1}{8}$

5. $\frac{7}{3}$ ◯ $3\frac{2}{3}$ **6.** $4\frac{1}{6}$ ◯ $2\frac{1}{6}$ **7.** $3\frac{1}{4}$ ◯ $7\frac{1}{2}$ **8.** $4\frac{5}{8}$ ◯ $5\frac{5}{8}$

Order the numbers from greatest to least.

9. $1\frac{4}{7}, \frac{12}{7}, \frac{25}{14}$ **10.** $\frac{26}{4}, 6\frac{1}{4}, 6\frac{3}{8}$

11. Analyze The mixed number $6\frac{2}{3}$ looks very similar to the improper fraction $\frac{62}{3}$. Which is larger?

Education Place
Visit www.eduplace.com/camap/ for more **Extra Practice.**

Chapter Review/Test

Vocabulary and Concepts

MR 2.3, KEY NS 1.9

Write the best word to complete the sentence.

1. A mixed number has a whole number part and a ______ part.
2. A fraction whose numerator is greater than its denominator is called a(n) ______ fraction.

Skills

MR 2.3, KEY NS 1.9, NS 1.7, NS 1.5

Compare. Write >, <, or = for the ⬭.

3. $\frac{1}{4}$ ⬭ $\frac{1}{5}$
4. $\frac{3}{5}$ ⬭ $\frac{4}{5}$
5. $\frac{3}{6}$ ⬭ $\frac{1}{2}$
6. $\frac{2}{3}$ ⬭ $\frac{3}{4}$
7. $\frac{3}{12}$ ⬭ $\frac{1}{6}$
8. $2\frac{1}{8}$ ⬭ $\frac{21}{8}$
9. $\frac{7}{3}$ ⬭ $2\frac{1}{3}$
10. $1\frac{1}{8}$ ⬭ $1\frac{1}{6}$

Write a mixed number and an improper fraction for the letter.

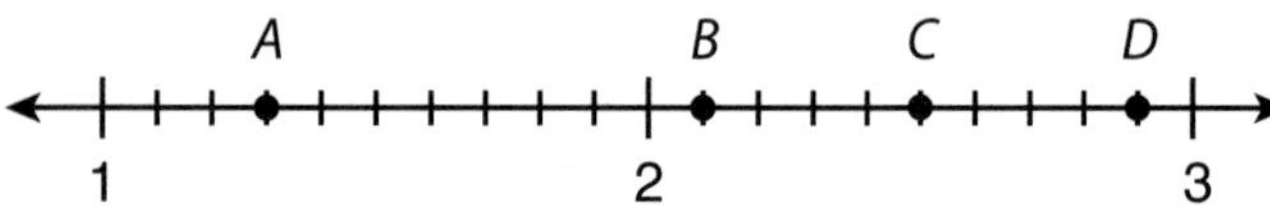

11. *A*
12. *B*
13. *C*
14. *D*

Order the fractions from least to greatest.

15. $\frac{2}{9}, \frac{5}{9}, \frac{1}{9}$
16. $\frac{1}{2}, \frac{1}{4}, \frac{3}{4}$
17. $\frac{3}{6}, \frac{4}{3}, \frac{5}{6}$
18. $\frac{1}{5}, \frac{2}{5}, \frac{3}{10}$

Problem Solving and Reasoning

MR 1.1, MR 2.3, KEY NS 1.9

Solve.

19. Andy hiked around Big Bear Lake. The trails were $\frac{3}{5}$ miles, $\frac{2}{3}$ miles, and $1\frac{1}{3}$ miles. Order the distances from least to greatest.
20. Bill came to a fork in the trail. An arrow showed $\frac{3}{8}$ mile to the nearest stream and $\frac{3}{4}$ mile to the dam. Which is the longer hike?

Writing Math Explain how you would compare fractions with unlike denominators.

Spiral Review and Test Practice

1. A stadium has 554 rows of seats. If there are 26 seats in each row, how many seats are in the stadium?

A 590 seats **C** 11,080 seats

B 4,432 seats **D** 14,404 seats

KEY NS 3.3 page 242

2. There are 3 boxes of buttons on a shelf. Each box has the same number of buttons. If there is a total of 1,500 buttons, how many buttons are in each box?

A 50 buttons

B 500 buttons

C 4,500 buttons

D 5,000 buttons

KEY NS 3.4 page 270

3. Which statement is true?

A The only factors of 15 are 1 and 15.

Test Tip
Use divisibility rules to test each number.

B The only factors of 16 are 1 and 16.

C The only factors of 17 are 1 and 17.

D The only factors of 18 are 1 and 18.

KEY NS 4.2 page 302

4. A bottle holds half a liter of juice. There are 1,000 milliliters in 1 liter. How many milliliters of juice are in the bottle?

A 1,000 mL

B 100 mL

C 500 mL

D 200 mL

KEY NS 3.4 page 336

5. The numbers in this pattern decrease by the same amount each time. What are the next two numbers in the pattern?

15, 12, 9, 6, 3, ____, ____

A 0, $^-1$

B 0, $^-3$

C 0, 3

D 0, 1

Test Tip
Find the pattern rule to determine the next two numbers in the pattern.

KEY NS 1.8 page 348

6. Which fraction represents the largest part of a whole?

A $\frac{1}{6}$ **C** $\frac{1}{3}$

B $\frac{1}{2}$ **D** $\frac{1}{4}$

NS 1.5 page 394

Education Place
Visit www.eduplace.com/camap/ for **Test-Taking Tips** and **Extra Practice.**

Unit 8 Test

Vocabulary and Concepts — NS 1.5, MR 2.3 Chapters 17–18

Complete each sentence with a vocabulary word from this unit.

1. ______ fractions have the same value.
2. A ______ ______ has a whole number part and a fraction part.
3. You can add and subtract fractions with ______ denominators.
4. A(n) ______ fraction has a numerator that is greater than or equal to its denominator.

Computation — NS 1.5, NS 1.6, NS 1.7, KEY NS 1.9, AF 1.1 Chapter 17, Lesson 2

Find the fractional part of each number.

5. $\frac{2}{3}$ of 33
6. $\frac{3}{5}$ of 30
7. $\frac{4}{7}$ of 35

Add, subtract or find the value of *n*. Chapter 17, Lesson 5

8. $\frac{3}{5} + \frac{4}{5} = n$
9. $\frac{4}{6} + \frac{1}{6} = n$
10. $\frac{6}{8} - \frac{n}{8} = \frac{3}{8}$

Compare. Write >, <, or = for the ⬭. Chapter 18, Lessons 1–4

11. $\frac{3}{5}$ ⬭ $\frac{2}{5}$
12. $\frac{2}{3}$ ⬭ $\frac{5}{6}$
13. $3\frac{1}{3}$ ⬭ $3\frac{2}{9}$
14. $\frac{25}{10}$ ⬭ $2\frac{1}{2}$

Order from greatest to least. Use a number line to help you. Chapter 18, Lessons 2 and 4

15. $\frac{1}{2}, \frac{5}{6}, \frac{1}{3}$
16. $1\frac{3}{4}, 1\frac{1}{2}, \frac{15}{8}$

Problem Solving and Reasoning — NS 1.5, NS 1.6, KEY NS 1.9, MR 3.1 Chapters 17–18

Solve. Check to see if your answer is reasonable.

17. One recipe uses $1\frac{2}{5}$ cups of nuts. A second recipe uses $\frac{14}{5}$ cups of nuts. Leah has $1\frac{1}{2}$ cups of nuts. Which recipe should she use? Explain.

18. A recipe calls for $1\frac{1}{4}$ cups of flour. Nelson is measuring the flour into a bowl. He has measured out $\frac{3}{4}$ cup of flour. How much more flour should he add to the bowl?

19. Hiro hiked three trails with these lengths at Big Bear Lake.

$3\frac{1}{10}$ mi $\frac{17}{5}$ mi $3\frac{1}{4}$ mi

Order the trails from shortest to longest. How far did Hiro hike altogether?

20. It took Jasmine $3\frac{3}{4}$ hours to hike Mountain View Trail. It took her friend Stacy $3\frac{5}{8}$ hours to hike the same trail. Who hiked the trail in the shorter amount of time?

Writing Math You can use a fraction to show each of the following.

- parts of a whole number
- parts of a set
- division of a whole number by a whole number

Give an example of each. Label your examples.

Performance Assessment

Band Breakfast

NS 1.5, MR 2.2, MR 2.6

The band is having a breakfast and will serve pancakes and biscuits with eggs. The cooking team needs to buy all of the ingredients.

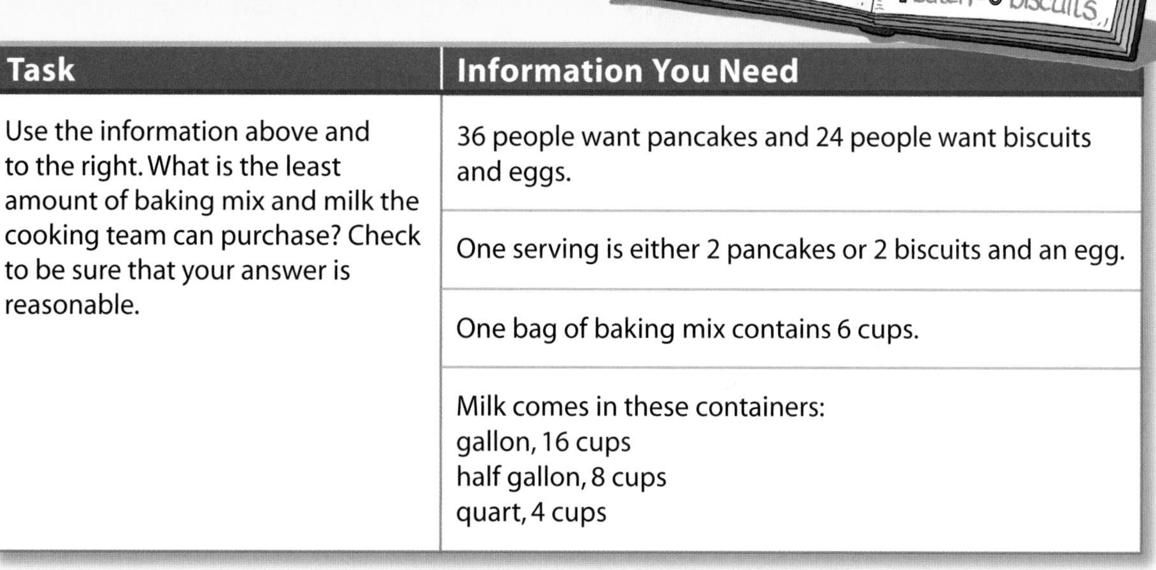

Task	Information You Need
Use the information above and to the right. What is the least amount of baking mix and milk the cooking team can purchase? Check to be sure that your answer is reasonable.	36 people want pancakes and 24 people want biscuits and eggs.
	One serving is either 2 pancakes or 2 biscuits and an egg.
	One bag of baking mix contains 6 cups.
	Milk comes in these containers: gallon, 16 cups half gallon, 8 cups quart, 4 cups

Greg Tang's Go Fast, Go Far

Unit 8 Mental Math Strategies

Multiply by 5

A group of 5 you'll find with ease.
Half of 10 is just a breeze!

I have a fast way to multiply 5 × 7. I want 5 groups of 7, but start with 10 groups of 7 because it's easier. 10 × 7 = 70, so to get 5 groups of 7, I take half of 70, which makes 35. A group of 5 is easier as half of 10!

1. 5 × 7 → half of [70] = [35]
   10 × 7
2. 5 × 38 → half of ▢ = ▢
   10 × 38
3. 5 × 18 → half of ▢ = ▢
   10 × 18
4. 5 × 9 → half of ▢ = ▢
   10 × 9

Way to go! Keep it up!

5. 5 × 16 → half of ▢ = ▢
6. 5 × 10 → half of ▢ = ▢
7. 5 × 6 → half of ▢ = ▢
8. 5 × 68 → half of ▢ = ▢

Take It Further!

Now try doing all the steps in your head!

9. 5 × 8
10. 5 × 12
11. 5 × 40
12. 5 × 65

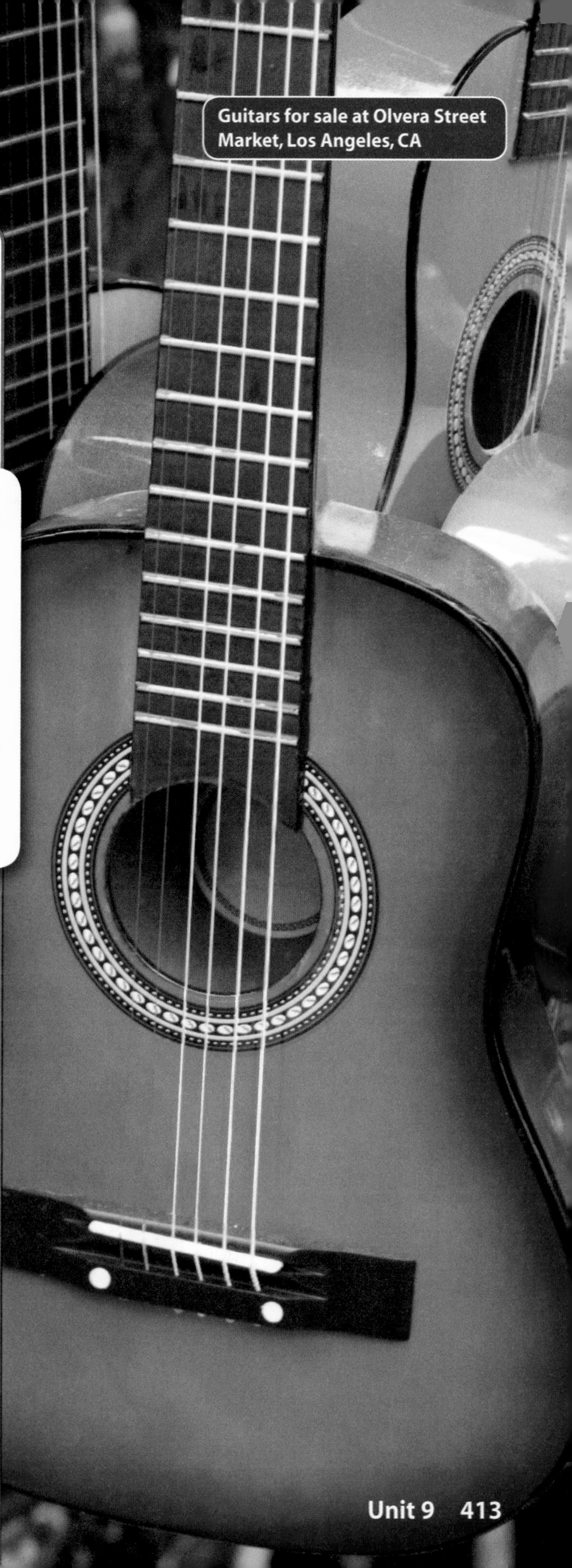

Guitars for sale at Olvera Street Market, Los Angeles, CA

Decimals

BIG IDEAS!

- Decimal place values get smaller as you read farther to the right of a decimal point.
- You can use a number line to compare decimals to whole numbers, fractions, and mixed numbers.
- You can add and subtract decimals like whole numbers if the decimal points are lined up.

Songs and Games

Math Music Track 9: *Decimals, It's Easy to Write*
eGames at
www.eduplace.com/camap/

Math Readers

Get Ready **Game**

Decimal Maze

Object of the Game Compare decimal numbers to earn more points than the other player.

Materials
- Workmat 4
- Learning Tool 27 (Decimal Cards)

Number of Players 2

Set Up
Shuffle the decimal cards and place them face down in a stack. Players label Number Line 1 on Workmat 4 as shown below.

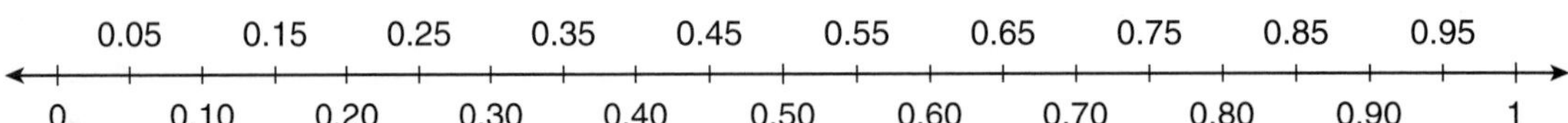

How to Play

1. Player 1 draws a card from the stack and places a dot on the number line to mark that decimal.
2. Player 2 repeats Step 1. Players compare the decimal numbers. Whoever marked the greater (closer to 1) decimal gets one point.
3. Erase the dot from the Workmat. Continue taking turns until all the cards in the deck have been drawn.
4. The player with more points wins.

CA Standards
KEY NS 1.2 Order and compare whole numbers and decimals to two decimal places.

Education Place
Visit www.eduplace.com/camap/ for **Brain Teasers** and **eGames** to play.

Reading In reading, thinking about what you already know helps you understand a new topic. You already know a lot about decimals. You can use what you know to move ahead.

Before beginning a lesson on fractions and decimals, Jake lists five things he already knows.

Topic: Fractions and Decimals

What do I already know?

1. Every decimal can be written as a fraction.
2. Decimals are based on tenths and hundredths.
3. 0.1 is $\frac{1}{10}$ or 1 of 10 equal parts.
4. 0.01 is $\frac{1}{100}$ or 1 of 100 equal parts.
5. 1 cent is $\frac{1}{100}$ of a dollar, or $0.01.

I remember using play money to show the value of coins.

Writing Work with a friend. Show how different coins are parts of a dollar. Write the value of each coin as a fraction with a denominator of 100 and as a decimal.

Coin	Number of Cents	Fraction of a Dollar	Value as a Decimal
penny	1¢	$\frac{1}{100}$	$0.01
nickel			
dime			
quarter			
half-dollar			

Understand Decimals

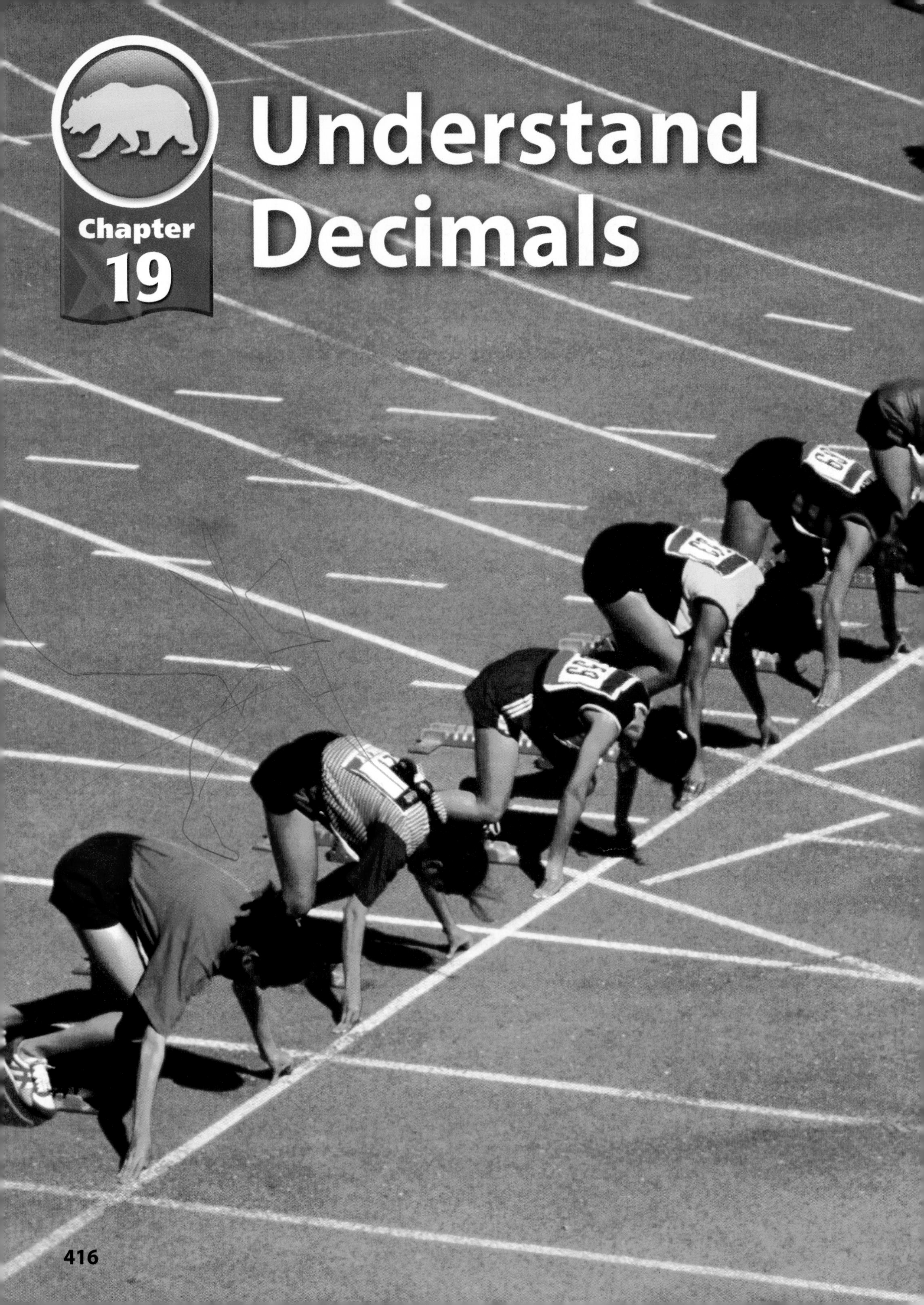

Check What You Know

Word Bank
fraction
hundredths
equivalent
tenths

Vocabulary and Concepts GRADE 3 NS 3.4, MR 2.3

Choose the best word to complete the sentence.

1. A whole can be divided into 100 equal parts called ____.
2. If two fractions name the same amount, they are called ____ fractions.

Skills GRADE 3 NS 3.4

Write a fraction and a decimal to describe the shaded part.

3. 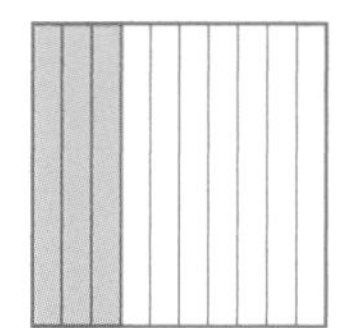
4. 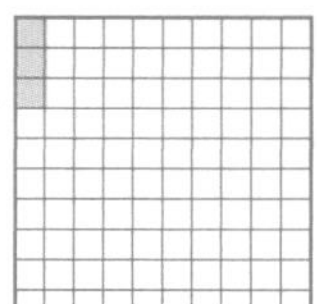
5. 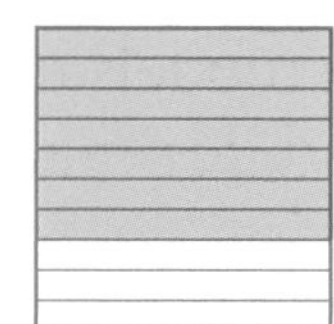
6. 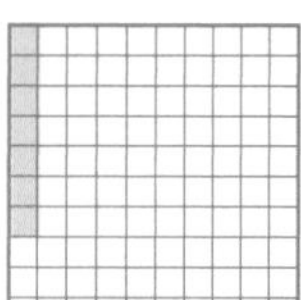

Write the fractions in order from least to greatest. page 394

7. $\frac{4}{10}$ $\frac{2}{10}$ $\frac{4}{5}$
8. $\frac{7}{8}$ $\frac{6}{8}$ $\frac{6}{10}$

Problem Solving and Reasoning GRADE 3 KEY NS 3.3, NS 3.4

9. Elizabeth had $0.25. What fraction of a dollar is $0.25?

Vocabulary

Visualize It!

A **decimal number** is a number with one or more digits to the right of a **decimal point**.

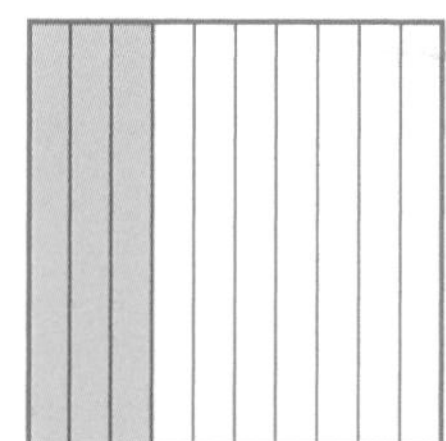

$\frac{3}{10} = 0.3$ ← $\frac{3}{10}$ can be written as a decimal.

↑ decimal point

Language Tips

The root of the word *decimal* means 10. In mathematics, the decimal place closest to the decimal point is *tenths*.

Some words are similar in English and Spanish.

English	Spanish
fraction	fracción
decimal	decimal
point	punto

See **English-Spanish Glossary** pages 644–666.

Education Place Visit www.eduplace.com/camap/ for the **eGlossary** and **eGames**.

CA Standards MR 2.3 Use a variety of methods, such as words, numbers, symbols, charts, graphs, tables, diagrams, and models, to explain mathematical reasoning. **Also NS 1.0**

CA Standards
NS 1.6 Write tenths and hundredths in decimal and fraction notations and know the fraction and decimal equivalents for halves and fourths (e.g., $\frac{1}{2}$ = 0.5 or 0.50; $\frac{7}{4} = 1\frac{3}{4} = 1.75$).

Also NS 1.0, NS 1.7, MR 1.1, MR 1.2, MR 2.0, MR 2.3, MR 2.4

Vocabulary

decimal number

decimal point

tenths

hundredths

Materials
- Learning Tool 28 (Tenths Grid)
- Learning Tool 29 (Hundredths Grid)
- Learning Tool 48 (Centimeter Grid Paper)
- crayons or colored pencils
- eManipulatives (optional) www.eduplace.com/camap/

Hands On
Fractions and Decimals

Objective Show tenths and hundredths in different ways.

Explore

Soccer Cards $\frac{7}{10}$ or $\frac{70}{100}$

Football Cards

In Chapter 17, you learned how to model fractions. In this lesson, you will use models to show how fractions and **decimal numbers** are related. Sometimes decimal numbers are just called decimals.

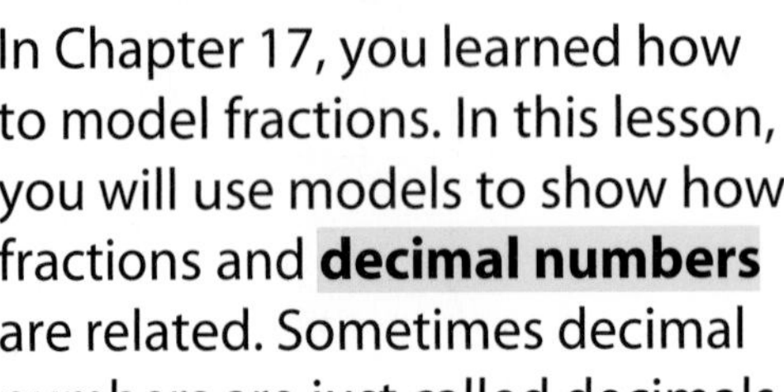

Question How can you use models to show how fractions and decimals are related?

A fraction with a denominator of 10 can be written as a decimal in **tenths**.

Fraction	Decimal	Word Form
$\frac{7}{10}$	0.7	seven tenths

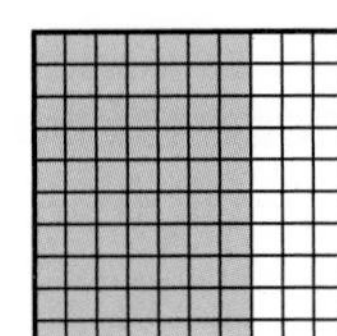

A fraction with a denominator of 100 can be written as a decimal in **hundredths**.

Fraction	Decimal	Word Form
$\frac{70}{100}$	0.70	seventy hundredths

Matt has the sports cards shown above. What part of Matt's collection is football cards?

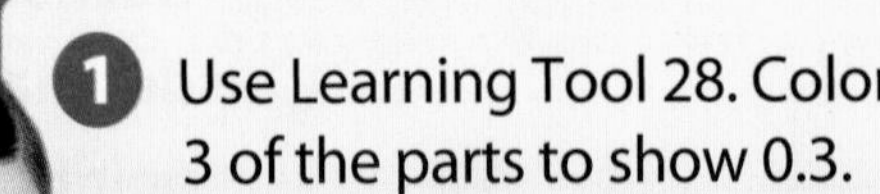

1. Use Learning Tool 28. Color 3 of the parts to show 0.3.

2. Use Learning Tool 29. Color 30 of the parts to show 0.30.

3. Compare the squares.
   - Is the same area colored in both squares?
   - How do you write $\frac{3}{10}$ as a decimal?
   - How do you write 0.30 as a fraction?

Another Example

Repeat Step 2 to show twenty-five hundredths.

Write $\frac{25}{100}$ as a decimal.

Write 0.25 as a fraction.

Extend

Write a fraction and a decimal to describe the model.

1. **2.** 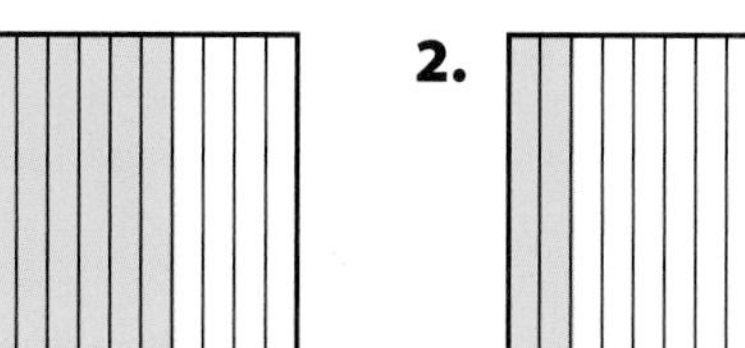

3. 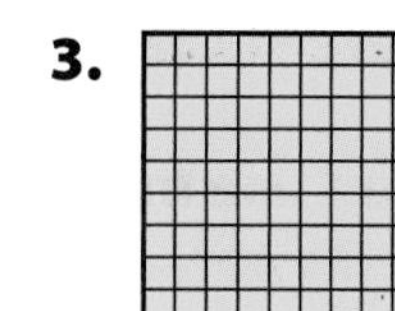

4. 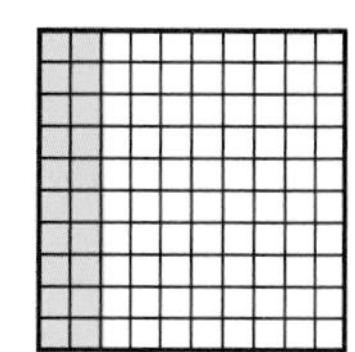

Use Learning Tool 48. Draw a model to show the fraction. Then write the fraction as a decimal.

5. $\frac{9}{10}$ **6.** $\frac{1}{10}$ **7.** $\frac{8}{10}$ **8.** $\frac{6}{10}$ **9.** $\frac{4}{10}$

10. $\frac{20}{100}$ **11.** $\frac{45}{100}$ **12.** $\frac{99}{100}$ **13.** $\frac{7}{100}$ **14.** $\frac{70}{100}$

Use Learning Tool 48. Draw a model to show the decimal. Then write the decimal as a fraction.

15. 0.3 **16.** 0.5 **17.** 0.7 **18.** 0.1 **19.** 0.8

20. 0.39 **21.** 0.83 **22.** 0.01 **23.** 0.76 **24.** 0.54

Solve.

25. **Multistep** In a bag of 100 marbles, there are 35 red marbles and 17 blue marbles. What fraction and decimal represent the part of the marbles that are neither red nor blue?

Writing Math

Explain Why is 0.1 greater than 0.01?

LESSON 2

CA Standards

NS 1.0 Students understand the place value of whole numbers and decimals to two decimal places and how whole numbers and decimals relate to simple fractions. Students use the concepts of negative numbers.

NS 1.6 Write tenths and hundredths in decimal and fraction notations and know the fraction and decimal equivalents for halves and fourths (e.g., $\frac{1}{2} = 0.5$ or 0.50; $\frac{7}{4} = 1\frac{3}{4} = 1.75$).

Also NS 1.7, MR 1.0, MR 1.1, MR 2.0, MR 2.3, MR 2.4

Mixed Numbers and Decimals

Objective Read, write, and model amounts greater than 1.

Learn by Example

Melanie and Elena jog down two paths. The Red Path is two and eight tenths kilometers long. The Blue Path is one and forty-four hundredths kilometers long.

Different Ways to Show Two and Eight Tenths

Way 1 **You can use models.**

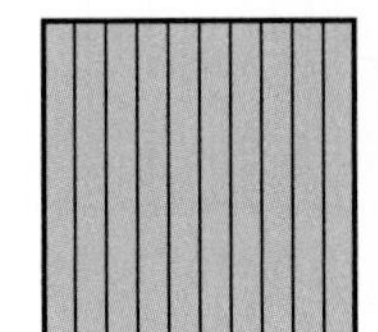
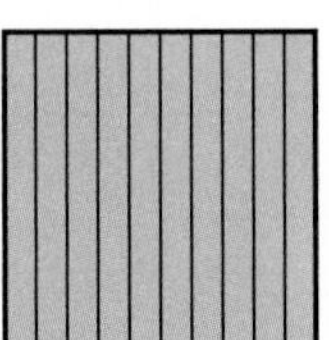
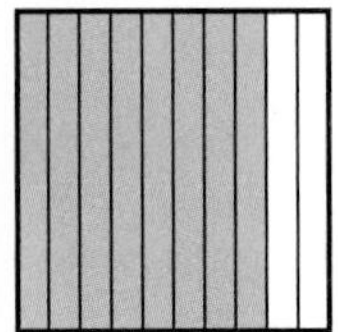

Way 2 **You can write a mixed number.** $2\frac{8}{10}$

Way 3 **You can write a decimal.**

Write: 2.8

Read: **two and eight tenths**

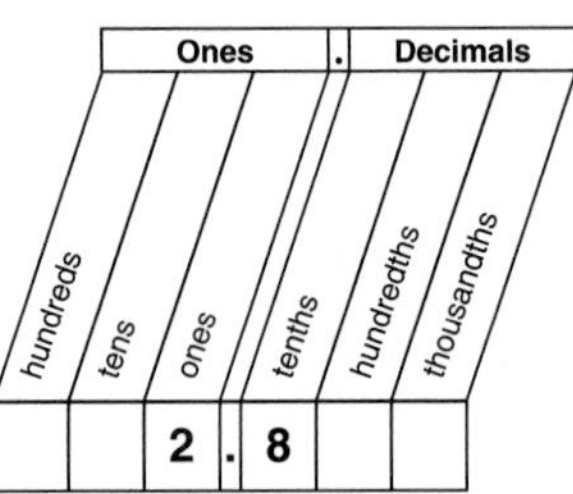

Different Ways to Show One and Forty-Four Hundredths

Way 1 **You can use models.**

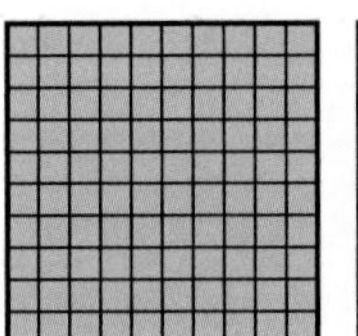
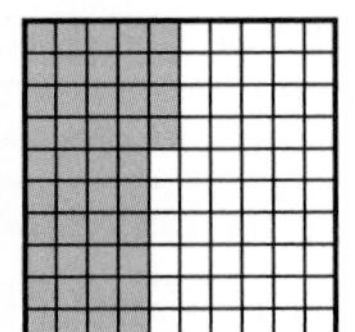

Way 2 **You can write a mixed number.** $1\frac{44}{100}$

Way 3 **You can write a decimal.**

Write: 1.44

Read: **one and forty-four hundredths**

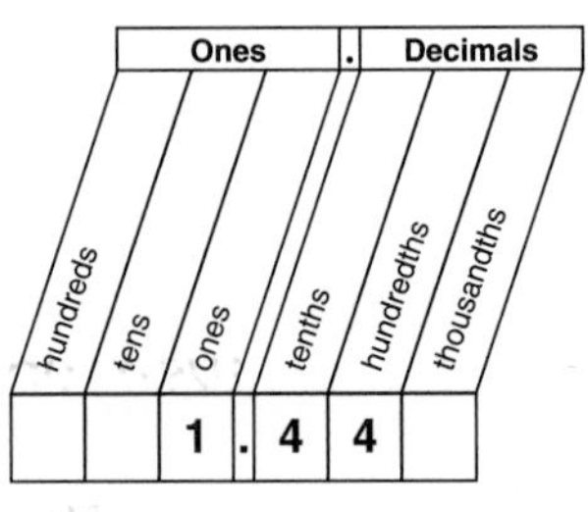

Guided Practice

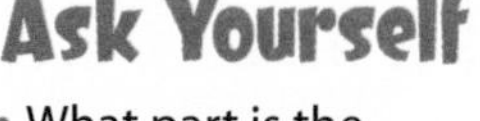

Ask Yourself

- What part is the whole number?
- What should the numerator be?
- What should the denominator be?

Write a mixed number and a decimal to describe the shaded part in the model.

1.

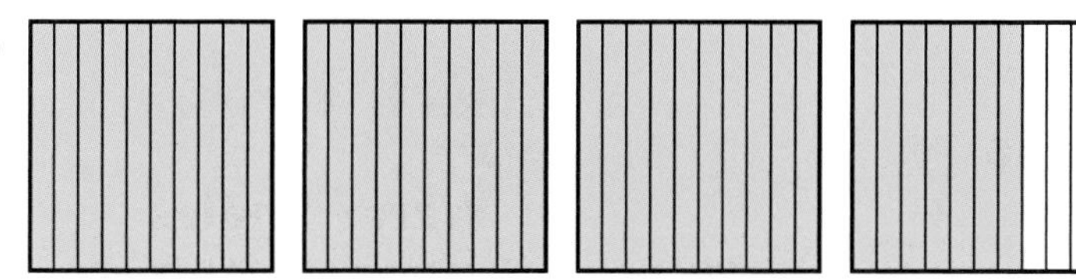

2.

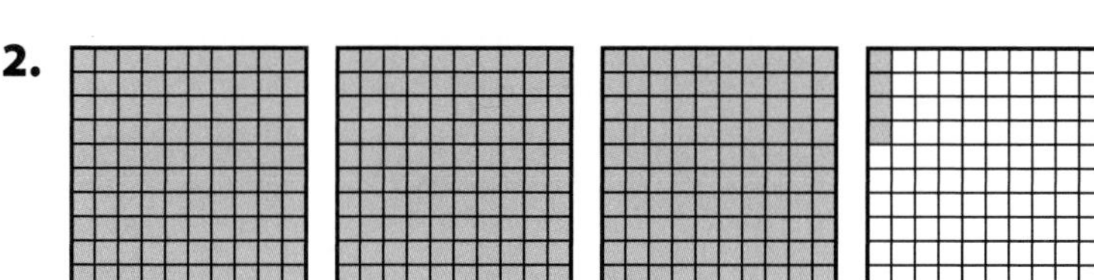

Write the number as a decimal.

3. $5\frac{3}{10}$ **4.** $9\frac{9}{10}$ **5.** $26\frac{7}{10}$ **6.** $15\frac{55}{100}$ **7.** $12\frac{5}{100}$ **8.** $2\frac{17}{100}$

9. seven tenths **10.** twenty-two hundredths **11.** one and five hundredths

Write the value of the digit 3 in the number.

12. 3.12 **13.** 5.03 **14.** 24.32 **15.** 351.29 **16.** 3,722.46

Math Talk Why is the value of each 4 in 1.44 different?

Practice and Problem Solving

Write a mixed number and a decimal to describe the shaded part in the model.

17.

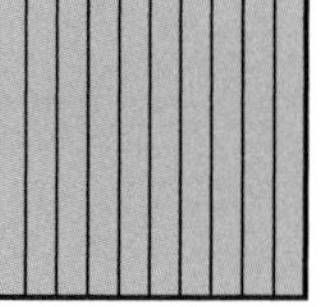

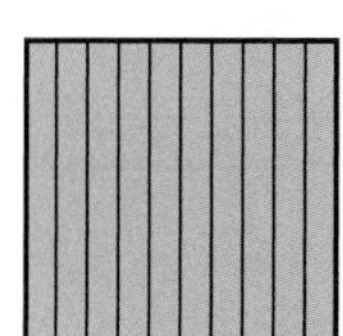

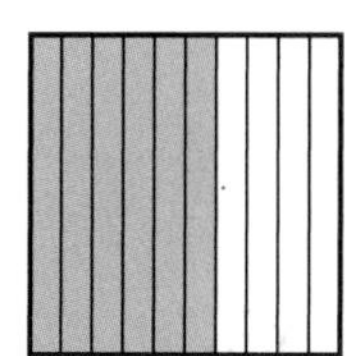

18.

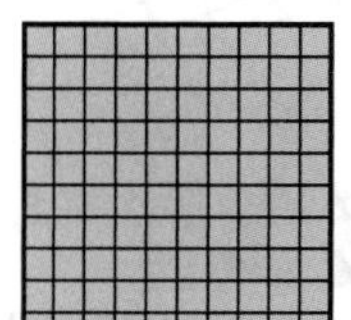

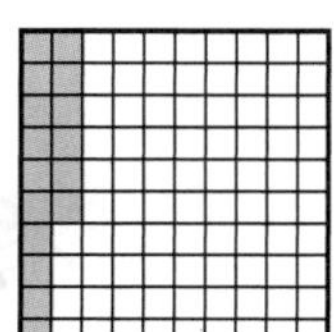

Write the number as a decimal.

19. $1\frac{2}{10}$ **20.** $7\frac{7}{100}$ **21.** $4\frac{54}{100}$ **22.** $5\frac{7}{10}$

23. $34\frac{6}{100}$ **24.** $158\frac{85}{100}$ **25.** $175\frac{9}{10}$ **26.** $19\frac{38}{100}$

27. five and seven tenths **28.** sixty-four hundredths

29. forty and four hundredths **30.** three and sixteen hundredths

Write the value of the digit 8 in the number.

31. 4.86 **32.** 6.08 **33.** 28.94 **34.** 856.25 **35.** 8,015.43

Science Link

Use the data in the table for Problems 36–39.

36. Mrs. Santos's class is doing an experiment to test types of insulation. Volunteers covered their hands and put them in cold water. How long did it take for the volunteer wearing a fleece glove to feel cold, in words?

37. Look at the number line below.

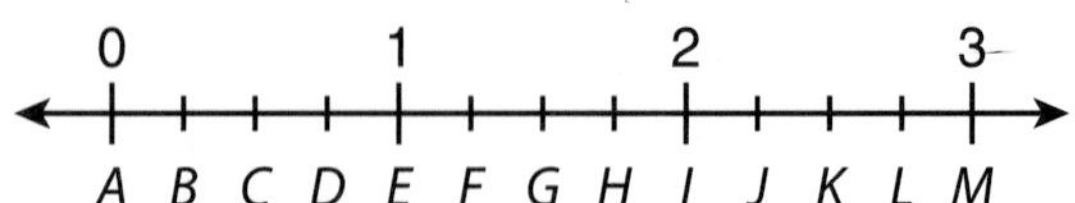

a. Which letter represents the time for the fleece gloves?

b. Which letter represents the time for the wool gloves?

c. Which letter represents the time for the blubber bags?

38. Explain Which gloves provided the best protection from the cold? How do you know?

39. Challenge Write the time for the blubber bags. Use a mixed number.

Warm Whales

Whales are able to survive in cold ocean waters because they have a thick layer of insulating fat, called blubber, just below the skin.

Type of Covering	Time Until Cold
Fleece Glove	$1\frac{1}{4}$ minute
Wool Glove	$\frac{3}{4}$ minute
Blubber Bag	2.5 minutes

Blue whale

Science LS 3.b

Spiral Review and Test Practice

Multiply. KEY NS 3.2 pages 238, 242

40. 55×22 **41.** 27×12 **42.** 123×42 **43.** 154×28

Write the letter of the correct answer. NS 1.6

44. What mixed number means the same as 5.45?

A $\frac{45}{100}$ **B** $5\frac{45}{100}$ **C** $5\frac{45}{1000}$ **D** $5\frac{45}{10}$

Extra Practice See page 435, Set A.

Key Standards Review

Need Help?
See Key Standards Handbook.

Use the number line to answer the questions. KEY NS 1.9

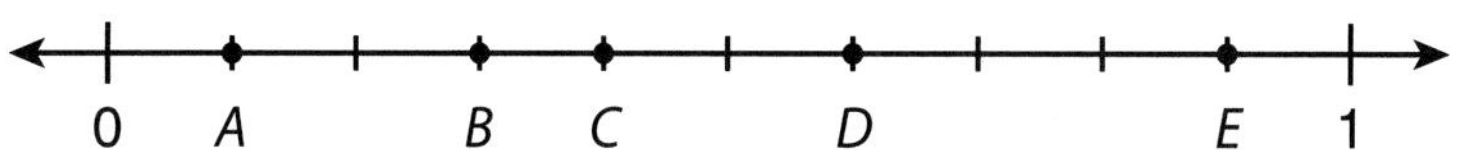

1. Write the fraction for *A*.
2. Write the fraction for *B*.
3. Write the fraction for *C*.
4. Write the fraction for *D*.
5. Write the fraction for *E*.

Use the number line to answer the questions. KEY NS 1.9

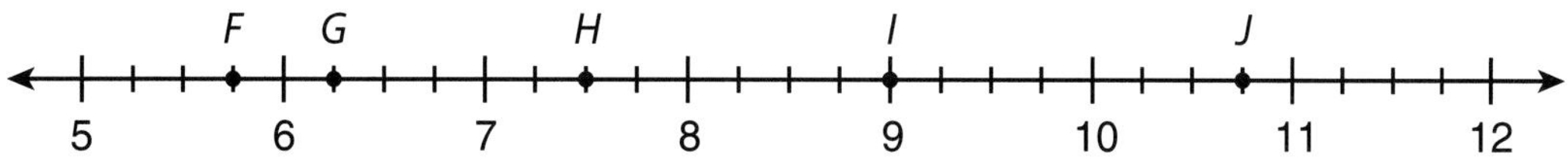

6. What number is represented by point *F*?
7. What number is represented by point *G*?
8. What number is represented by point *H*?
9. What number is represented by point *I*?
10. What number is represented by point *J*?

Challenge — Number Sense

What Number Is It?

Write a number that falls between the two numbers. NS 1.0

$1\frac{1}{4}$	?	1.5
$\frac{2}{3}$	?	0.75
$2\frac{3}{8}$	?	2.6

CA Standards
NS 1.6 Write tenths and hundredths in decimal and fraction notations and know the fraction and decimal equivalents for halves and fourths (e.g., $\frac{1}{2}$ = 0.5 or 0.50; $\frac{7}{4} = 1\frac{3}{4} = 1.75$)
NS 1.7 Write the fraction represented by a drawing of parts of a figure; represent a given fraction by using drawings; and relate a fraction to a simple decimal on a number line.
Also KEY NS 1.9, NS 1.0, NS 1.5, MR 2.2, MR 2.3, MR 2.4

Vocabulary

decimal equivalent

Fractions and Decimal Equivalents

Objective Write fractions, mixed numbers, and decimals that name the same amount.

Learn by Example

A decimal that names the same amount as a fraction is the fraction's **decimal equivalent**. One way to change a fraction to a decimal is to find an equivalent fraction with a denominator of 10 or 100.

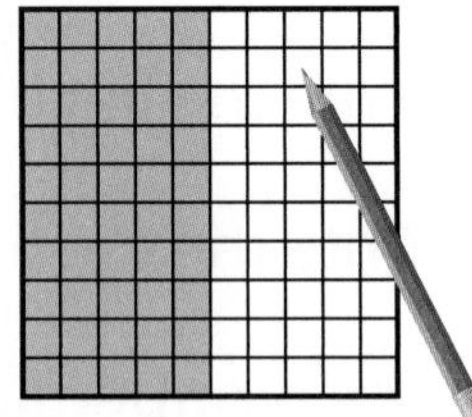

Jun says that $\frac{1}{2}$ of the grid is green. Noah says that $\frac{5}{10}$ is green. Manuel says that 0.5 is green, and Ben says that 0.50 of the grid is green. Are all four boys correct?

Different Ways to Show Equivalent Amounts

Way 1 **Use models.**

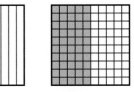

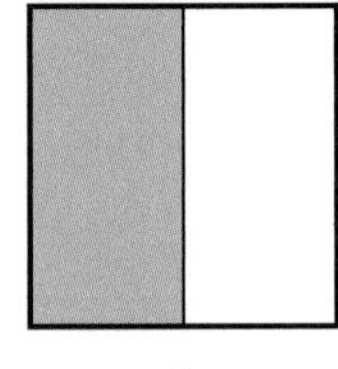

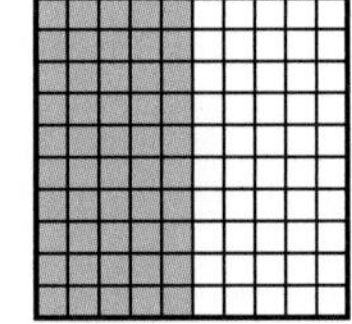

$\frac{1}{2}$ $\quad$ $\frac{5}{10}$ or 0.5 $\quad$ $\frac{50}{100}$ or 0.50

$$\frac{1}{2} = \frac{1 \times 5}{2 \times 5} = \frac{5}{10} = 0.5$$

$$\frac{1}{2} = \frac{1 \times 50}{2 \times 50} = \frac{50}{100} = 0.50$$

Way 2 **Use number lines.**

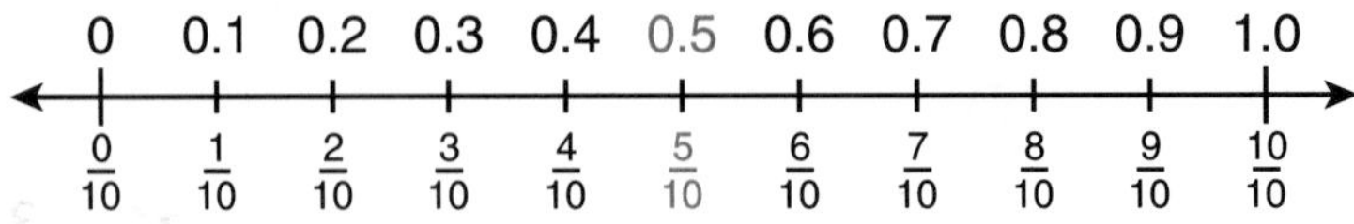

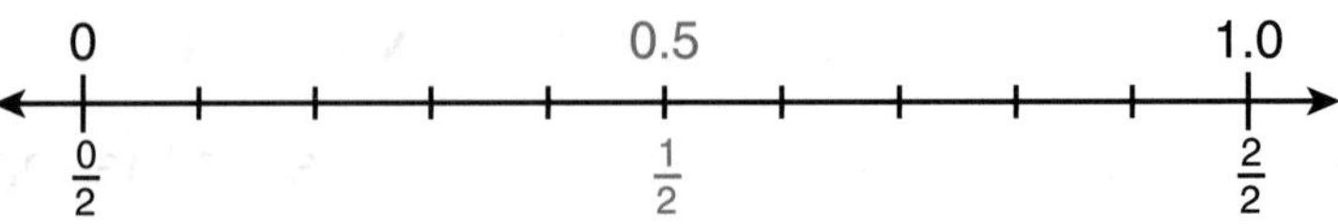

Solution: Yes, all four boys are correct.

Guided Practice

Write a fraction and a decimal to describe the shaded part.

1. 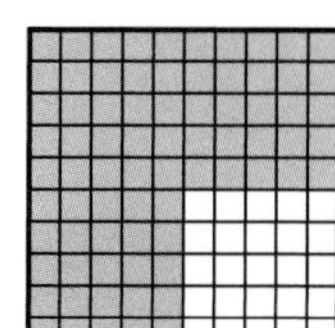

2. 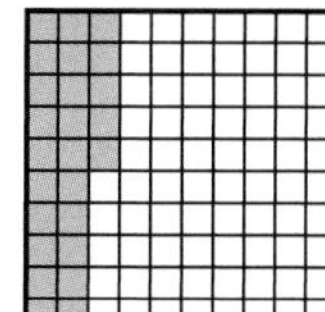

3. 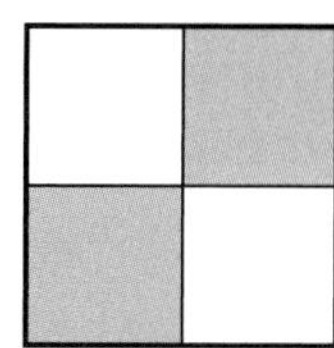

Ask Yourself

- What should the numerator and denominator be?
- Will the decimal have hundredths?

Write the decimal equivalent for each.

4. $\frac{1}{2}$ **5.** $2\frac{1}{4}$ **6.** $\frac{3}{2}$

Math Talk Describe how you would find the decimal equivalent for $\frac{1}{4}$.

Practice and Problem Solving

Use the number line for Exercise 7.

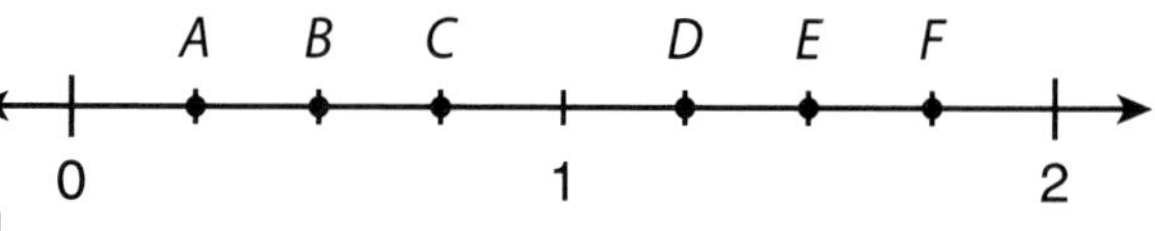

7. Write a fraction or mixed number for each point *A–F*. Then write the equivalent decimal.

Write the decimal equivalent for each.

8. $1\frac{1}{2}$ **9.** $\frac{1}{4}$ **10.** $\frac{3}{4}$ **11.** $1\frac{3}{4}$ **12.** $\frac{5}{4}$

Solve.

13. Analyze How can knowing that $\frac{1}{4}$ equals 0.25 help you find the decimal equivalent for $\frac{3}{4}$?

Spiral Review and Test Practice

Divide KEY NS 3.4 pages 262, 266

14. 45 ÷ 2 **15.** 49 ÷ 4 **16.** 93 ÷ 8 **17.** 90 ÷ 7

Write the letter of the correct answer. NS 1.6

18. Which fraction or mixed number means the same as 2.75?

A $2\frac{7}{5}$ **B** $2\frac{5}{7}$ **C** $2\frac{1}{4}$ **D** $2\frac{3}{4}$

Extra Practice See page 435, Set B.

LESSON 4

CA Standards
KEY (NS 1.2) Order and compare whole numbers and decimals to two decimal places.

KEY (NS 1.9) Identify on a number line the relative position of positive fractions, positive mixed numbers, and positive decimals to two decimal places.

Also NS 1.0, MR 1.0, MR 2.0, MR 2.2, MR 2.3,

Materials
- Workmat 2 (optional)
- Workmat 4 (optional)

Compare and Order Decimals

Objective Compare and order decimals.

Learn by Example

At a diving meet, Al earned these scores. What are his highest and lowest scores? What is the order of the scores from least to greatest?

4.6

3.9

4.8

4.0

Different Ways to Compare and Order Decimals

Way 1 **Use a place-value chart.**

- Line up the decimal points.
- Start comparing in the ones place. 3 < 4. So, 3.9 is the least.
- Continue comparing in the tenths place. 8 > 6 > 0. So, 4.8 is the greatest.

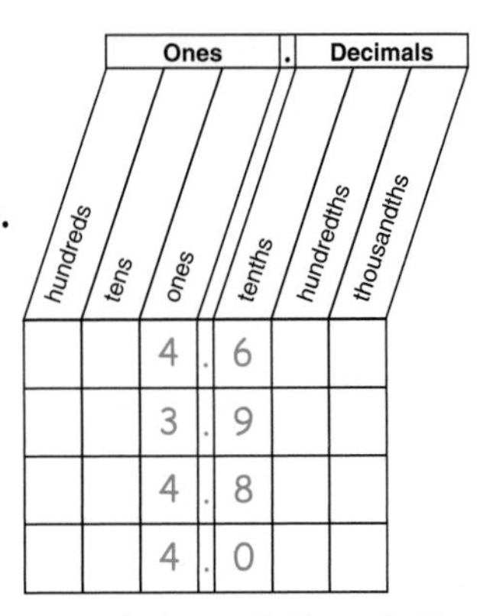

Ones			.	Decimals		
hundreds	tens	ones		tenths	hundredths	thousandths
		4	.	6		
		3	.	9		
		4	.	8		
		4	.	0		

4.8 > 4.6 > 4.0 > 3.9

Way 2 **Use a number line.**

Locate all the scores on a number line.

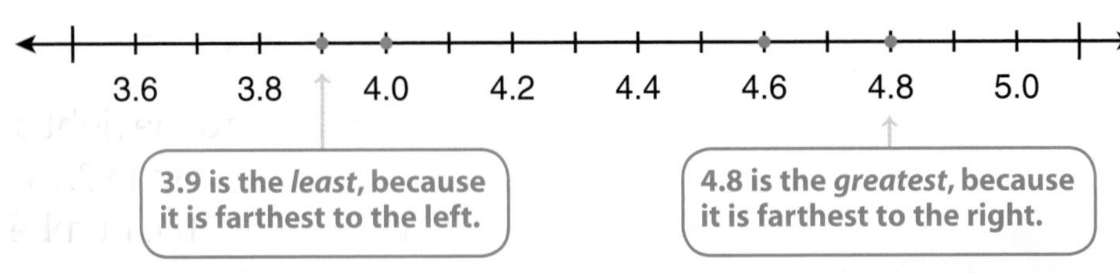
3.6
3.8
4.0
4.2
4.4
4.6
4.8
5.0
3.9 is the *least*, because it is farthest to the left.
4.8 is the *greatest*, because it is farthest to the right.

Solution: 4.8 is Al's highest score and 3.9 is his lowest score. The order of the scores is: 3.9, 4.0, 4.6, 4.8.

Another Example

Order 2.59, 2.5, and 2.12 from least to greatest.

- Line up the decimal points.
- Start comparing in the ones place.
- Continue until all are ordered.

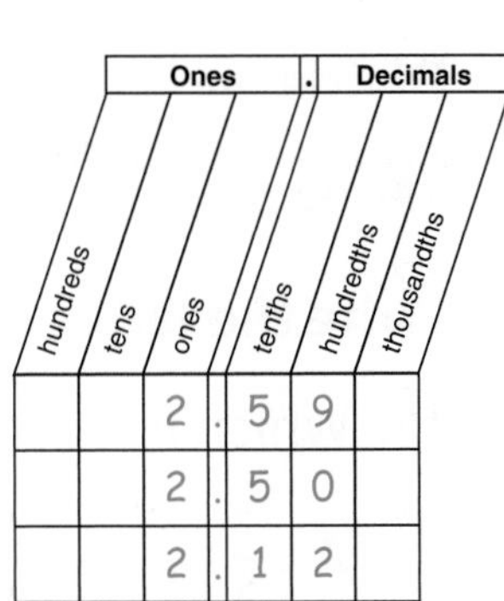

Ones			.	Decimals		
hundreds	tens	ones		tenths	hundredths	thousandths
		2	.	5	9	
		2	.	5	0	
		2	.	1	2	

2.12 < 2.5 < 2.59

Guided Practice

Compare. Write >, <, or = for the ⬭.

1. 3.2 ⬭ 3.6 **2.** 9.25 ⬭ 8.93 **3.** 12.5 ⬭ 12.50

Order the decimals from least to greatest.

4. 2.9 3.5 3.2 2.3 **5.** 4.7 4.78 4.73 4.67

Math Talk How is comparing decimals like comparing whole numbers?

Ask Yourself

- Where could each decimal be on a number line?
- What should I do if the numbers do not have the same number of decimal places?

Practice and Problem Solving

Compare. Write >, <, or = for the ⬭.

6. 7.8 ⬭ 8.7 **7.** 24.6 ⬭ 24.58 **8.** 6.9 ⬭ 6.90 **9.** 21.03 ⬭ 21.30

10. 4.9 ⬭ 5.1 **11.** 86.4 ⬭ 86.40 **12.** 17.25 ⬭ 16.93 **13.** 13.53 ⬭ 13.59

Order the decimals from greatest to least.

14. 2.13 2.14 2.24 2.42 **15.** 9.8 6.9 8.29 9.85 **16.** 4.73 4.82 4.38 4.9

17. 346.9 62.38 327.86 **18.** 32.87 87.3 82 28.32 **19.** 32.98 7 7.3 36.38 23.8

Solve.

20. Four teams have scores of 49.5, 50.0, 47.6, and 47.8. What is the order of the scores from least to greatest?

21. **Challenge** A decimal number has two digits to the right of the decimal point. It is less than 7.89 and greater than 7.58. The digit in the tenths place is odd. What might the number be?

Spiral Review and Test Practice

Find the missing number. KEY NS 3.2 page 336

22. 9 kg = ▢ g **23.** ▢ mL = 5 L **24.** 40,000 mL = ▢ L

Write the letter of the correct answer. KEY NS 1.2

25. Which of the following has the greatest value?

A 13.02 **B** 0.92 **C** 6.85 **D** 31.83

Extra Practice See page 435, Set C.

Compare and Order Fractions and Decimals

Objective Compare and order fractions, mixed numbers, and decimals.

CA Standards
KEY NS 1.2 Order and compare whole numbers and decimals to two decimal places.
KEY NS 1.9 Identify on a number line the relative position of positive fractions, positive mixed numbers, and positive decimals to two decimal places.
Also NS 1.6, NS 1.0, MR 1.0, MR 1.1, MR 2.0, MR 2.3, MR 2.4

Materials
- Workmat 2 (optional)
- Workmat 4 (optional)

Learn by Example

Tyrone rode his bike $1\frac{1}{2}$ miles to school. Then he rode 1.75 miles to the library. He then rode $\frac{5}{4}$ miles to his aunt's house. His ride home was $\frac{9}{10}$ mile. What is the order of all the distances from least to greatest?

Different Ways to Compare and Order Fractions and Decimals

Way 1 **Use a place-value chart.**

- Change the fractions to decimals.
- Write the decimals in hundredths.
- Compare.

Remember $\frac{5}{4} = 1\frac{1}{4}$.

	hundreds	tens	ones	.	tenths	hundredths	thousandths
$1\frac{1}{2}$ mi			1	.	5	0	
1.75 mi			1	.	7	5	
$\frac{5}{4}$ mi			1	.	2	5	
$\frac{9}{10}$ mi				.	9	0	

Way 2 **Use a number line.**

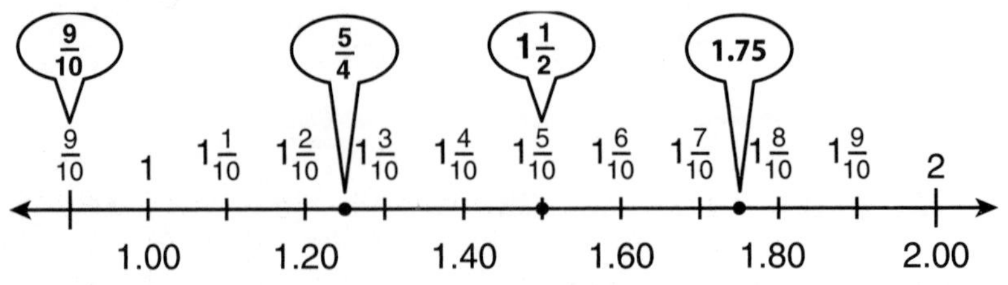

Solution: The order of the distances from least to greatest is:
$\frac{9}{10}$ mile $\quad \frac{5}{4}$ miles $\quad 1\frac{1}{2}$ miles $\quad$ 1.75 miles

Guided Practice

Compare. Write >, <, or = for the ⬭.

1. $\frac{7}{4}$ ⬭ 1.8
2. $3\frac{1}{2}$ ⬭ 3.21
3. $1\frac{1}{4}$ ⬭ 1.25

Order the numbers from least to greatest.

4. 1.4 $1\frac{9}{10}$ 1.05 $\frac{13}{10}$
5. $\frac{25}{100}$ 6.1 4.26 $\frac{8}{100}$

Ask Yourself

- Can I use a place-value chart or a number line?
- At which place should I start comparing digits?

Guided Problem Solving

Use the questions to solve this problem.

6. Four students raced to see how far they could ride their bikes in 10 minutes. The table shows the results. Write the names of the students in order from greatest to least distance traveled.

Student	Distance
Stanley	$\frac{12}{10}$ miles
Chloe	$\frac{3}{4}$ mile
Lucky	$1\frac{6}{10}$ miles
Aretha	1.95 miles

   a. **Understand** What are you asked to do?

   b. **Plan** Will you use a place-value chart or a number line to compare the numbers?

   c. **Solve** Use the plan you chose. Write the answer.
   - What is the order of the numbers from greatest to least?
   - Write the names of the students in the correct order.

   d. **Look Back** Solve the problem in a different way. Did you get the same answer?

Math Talk Would you use a number line or a place-value chart to order these numbers? Explain your choice.

18.3 83.24 $52\frac{1}{10}$ 79.67 $36\frac{14}{100}$

Practice and Problem Solving

Compare. Write >, <, or = for the ⬭.

7. 2.9 ⬭ $\frac{11}{4}$
8. 46.7 ⬭ $46\frac{1}{2}$
9. 35.7 ⬭ $153\frac{1}{4}$
10. $\frac{1}{2}$ ⬭ 0.50
11. $\frac{50}{100}$ ⬭ 0.05
12. $3\frac{1}{10}$ ⬭ 3.18
13. 5.9 ⬭ 5.90
14. 8.6 ⬭ $8\frac{3}{4}$

Order the numbers from greatest to least.

15. $\frac{15}{10}$ 1.9 $1\frac{36}{100}$ 1.63

16. 12.9 $12\frac{1}{4}$ 1.2 $\frac{1}{4}$

17. $\frac{18}{3}$ 3.18 31.8 318

18. 7.21 0.72 $\frac{21}{7}$ 0.07

History-Social Science Link

The California Gold Rush was an important time in California's history. Use the table for Problems 19–21.

19. How many years passed between the start of the Gold Rush and its end?

20. **Measurement** Gold nuggets can be measured in grams. Order these weights from least to greatest.

2.33 g 0.1 g 1.33 g 2 g

21. In 1848, a miner found $10 worth of gold. In 1848, a dollar was worth about 190 times what it was worth in 2005. What would $10 in 1848 have been worth in 2005?

California Gold Rush

Date	Historical Event
1848	Gold is discovered at Sutter's sawmill.
1849	The Gold Rush begins, attracting people from around the world.
1850	California becomes a state.
1852	Gold becomes scarce.
1859	Discovery of silver in Nevada ends the Gold Rush.

History-Social Science 4.3

Spiral Review and Test Practice

Show the set of numbers on a number line. Then order the numbers from least to greatest. KEY NS 1.9 pages 394, 398, 400

22. $\frac{1}{3}$ $\frac{5}{6}$ $\frac{4}{6}$

23. $2\frac{3}{4}$ $2\frac{3}{8}$ $1\frac{3}{4}$

Write the letter of the correct answer. KEY NS 1.9

24. On the number line below, what number does Point *M* represent?

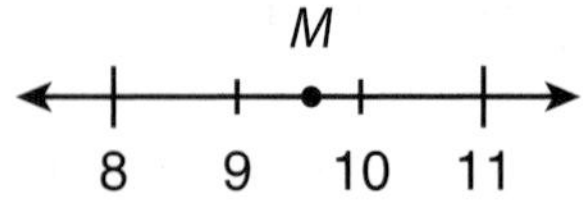

A 9.06 **B** 9.6 **C** 10.06 **D** 10.6

Extra Practice See page 435, Set D.

Practice **Game**

Roll a Fraction

Object of the Game Be the first to get three in a row.

Materials

- Learning Tool 30 (*Roll a Fraction* Game Board)
- 10 counters
- number cube labeled 0, $\frac{1}{10}$, $\frac{1}{4}$, $\frac{1}{2}$, $\frac{3}{4}$, 1

Set Up

Each player takes 5 counters. Player 1 uses the counters yellow side up. Player 2 uses the counters red side up.

Number of Players 2

How to Play

1. Player 1 rolls the number cube and places a counter on any square on the game board that contains a decimal greater than the fraction rolled.

2. Players take turns repeating Step 1. The first player to get 3 counters in a row horizontally, vertically, or diagonally is the winner.

CA Standards
NS 1.6 Write tenths and hundredths in decimal and fraction notations and know the fraction and decimal equivalents for halves and fourths (e.g., $\frac{1}{2}$ = 0.5 or 0.50; $\frac{7}{4}$ = $1\frac{3}{4}$ = 1.75).

KEY NS 1.2 Order and compare whole numbers and decimals to two decimal places.

Education Place
Visit www.eduplace.com/camap/ for **Brain Teasers** and **eGames** to play.

Problem Solving

Objective Use skills and strategies to solve word problems.

CA Standards
MR 1.0, MR 1.1, MR 2.0, NS 1.5, NS 1.6, KEY NS 3.3, AF 1.1, KEY AF 2.0, KEY AF 2.1

The National Yo-Yo Museum is the home of Big-Yo, a 256-pound working yo-yo.

The National Yo-Yo Museum has the world's largest display of yo-yos. Each October, the museum hosts the National Yo-Yo Contest.

Solve. Tell which strategy or method you used.

1. Suppose a display in the museum shows 2 blue, 4 green, and 6 red yo-yos. What fraction of the yo-yos are red? Express this fraction as a decimal.

2. In 1946, it was reported that the Duncan Company was producing 3,600 yo-yos every hour. How many yo-yos could the company make in 3 hours? 5 hours? A whole day?

3. The first time a yo-yo went into space was in 1985, aboard the Space Shuttle Discovery. The next trip into space for yo-yos was in 1992 aboard the Space Shuttle Atlantis. Choose and solve one of these equations to find out how many years passed between the two space trips.

   A $1985 + x = 1992$ **B** $1985 - x = 1992$

Fun Facts

- The first National Yo-Yo Contest was held in 1993.
- The contest is held annually in Chico, CA.

Problem Solving on Tests

Select a Strategy
- Write an Equation
- Choose the Operation
- Estimate
- Draw a Picture
- Work Backward

1. About 670,350,000 people visited a national park. What is this number in standard form?

A six hundred seven million, three hundred fifty thousand

B six hundred seventy million, three hundred fifty thousand

C six hundred seventy million, five hundred thirty thousand

D sixty seven million, three hundred fifty thousand

KEY NS 1.1 page 14

2. A bakery sold 4,362 bagels in June and 2,748 bagels in July. How many bagels were sold in June and July?

A 6,110 **C** 7,100

B 7,010 **D** 7,110

KEY NS 3.1 page 62

3. Talia read 6 pages of a book. Harry read 3 times as many pages as Talia. Olivia read 20 more pages than Talia. Which number sentence compares the number of pages that Harry and Olivia read?

A $3 \times 6 = 6 + 20$

B $3 \times 6 < 6 + 20$

C $3 \times 6 > 6 + 20$

D $3 + 6 < 6 + 20$

Test Tip
Work backward to find an expression that shows how much Olivia read.

AF 1.0 page 150

4. The temperature was $^{-}10$ °F in the morning. It was $^{-}2$ °F in the afternoon. Which number sentence compares the temperature in the morning to the temperature in the afternoon?

A $^{-}10 < {}^{-}2$

B $^{-}10 > {}^{-}2$

C $^{-}1 > {}^{-}2$

D $^{-}2 < {}^{-}10$

Test Tip
Draw a picture to help you understand the problem.

KEY NS 1.8 page 350

5. On the number line below, point *P* shows the number of muffins students ate for breakfast. What number is best represented by point *P* on this number line?

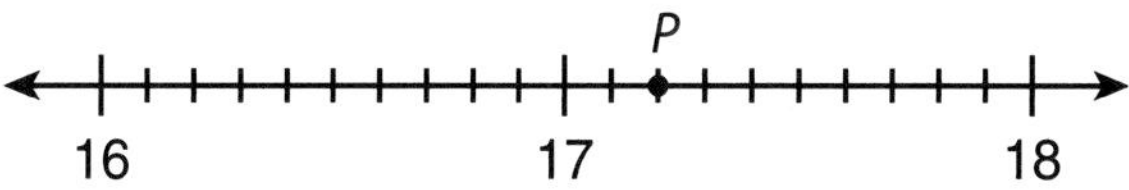

A 16.2

B 17

C 17.1

D 17.2

KEY NS 1.9 page 426

Education Place
Visit www.eduplace.com/camap/ for **Test-Taking Tips** and **Extra Practice**.

Vocabulary

A **decimal** is a number with one or more digits to the right of a **decimal point**. The decimal point separates the whole number part from the decimal part.

The **word form** for this number is six and eighty-three **hundredths**.

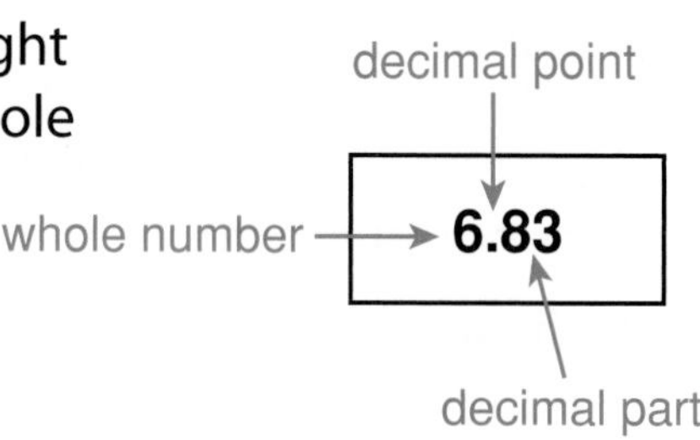

Copy the number lines. Then make a mark on your number line to show each number.

1. 0.4
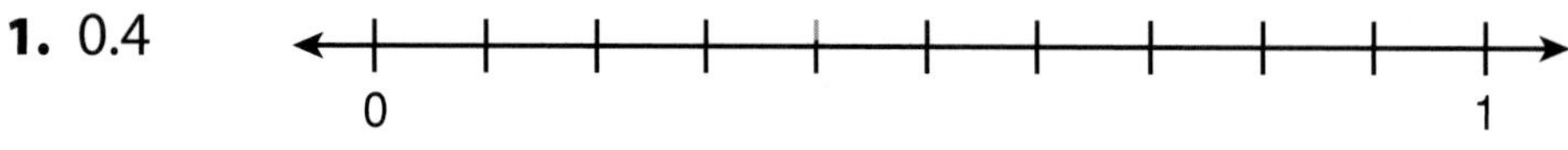

2. 0.40 (number line from 0 to 1)

3. $\frac{2}{5}$ (number line from 0 to 1)

4. $\frac{4}{10}$ (number line from 0 to 1)

Use the number lines above to help you answer Questions 5–7.

5. How are the decimals 0.4 and 0.40 different? How are they alike?

6. How are the fractions $\frac{2}{5}$ and $\frac{4}{10}$ different? How are they alike?

7. What do your number lines show about the four numbers?

Writing Explain how you could use a place-value chart to compare three decimals.

Reading Check out this book in your library.
The Go-Around Dollar, by Barbara Johnston Adams

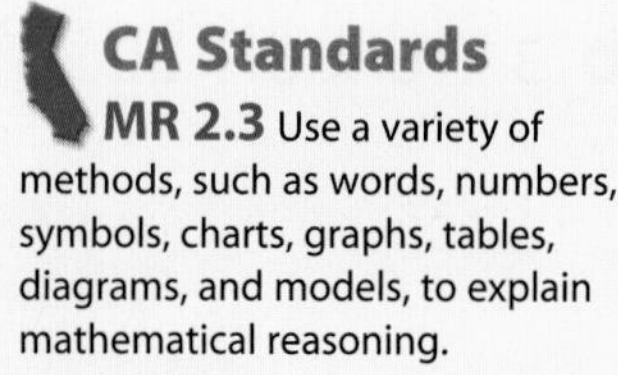

CA Standards
MR 2.3 Use a variety of methods, such as words, numbers, symbols, charts, graphs, tables, diagrams, and models, to explain mathematical reasoning.

Also NS 1.7

Standards-Based Extra Practice

Set A

NS 1.6 page 420

Write the number as a decimal.

1. $3\frac{4}{10}$ **2.** $11\frac{25}{100}$ **3.** $6\frac{8}{100}$ **4.** $7\frac{19}{100}$

5. Explain Leon has 2.07 cups of flour. His friend Kenesha has 2.7 cups of flour. Do they have the same amount? Explain.

Set B

NS 1.6 page 424

Write the decimal equivalent for each.

1. $4\frac{3}{10}$ **2.** $\frac{6}{4}$ **3.** $6\frac{3}{4}$ **4.** $6\frac{1}{2}$

5. Explain Ashley has $5\frac{1}{4}$ cartons of milk. She needs 5.5 cartons of milk. Does she have enough milk? Explain your reasoning.

Set C

KEY NS 1.2 page 426

Compare decimals. Write >, <, or = for the ⬭.

1. 1.6 ⬭ 1.7 **2.** 3.45 ⬭ 3.4 **3.** 3.76 ⬭ 3.75 **4.** 4.16 ⬭ 4.18

Order the decimals from least to greatest.

5. 1.49, 1.37, 1.56 **6.** 2.75, 1.92, 1.24 **7.** 2.35, 3.94, 2.46 **8.** 5.32, 4.39, 4.29

9. Compare Sam has $14.75 in his bank account. Sarah has $14.64 in her account. Which student has more money?

Set D

KEY NS 1.2 page 428

Order the numbers from least to greatest.

1. $1\frac{3}{4}$, 1.25, 1.01 **2.** 6.35, 6.3, 6.25 **3.** $3\frac{1}{4}$, 3.2, $\frac{7}{2}$ **4.** 4.15, $4\frac{1}{8}$, $\frac{17}{4}$

5. Explain Tao measures a table and finds it to be $5\frac{3}{4}$ feet long. Chen measures the same table and finds it to be 5.75 feet long. Do their measurements match? Explain.

Education Place
Visit www.eduplace.com/camap/ for more **Extra Practice.**

Chapter Review/Test

Vocabulary and Concepts — MR 2.3, NS 1.0, NS 1.6

Write the best word to complete the sentence.

1. When you write a fraction as a decimal, you write the decimal ______ of the fraction.

2. You can use a square with 100 equal sections to model ______.

Skills — NS 1.0, KEY NS 1.2, NS 1.6, KEY NS 1.9

Write the value of the digit 7 in the number.

3. 43.57 4. 78.353 5. 10.72 6. 0.475 7. 725.013

Write the number as a decimal.

8. $\frac{15}{100}$ 9. $4\frac{7}{10}$ 10. $\frac{1}{2}$ 11. $7\frac{19}{100}$ 12. $\frac{6}{4}$

Compare. Write >, <, or = for the ⬮.

13. 0.11 ⬮ 0.01 14. $\frac{3}{4}$ ⬮ 0.76 15. $1\frac{2}{5}$ ⬮ 1.4 16. 1.39 ⬮ $1\frac{1}{4}$

Order the numbers from least to greatest.

17. $\frac{16}{4}$, 2.6, $2\frac{53}{100}$, 1.53 18. $1\frac{9}{10}$, 1.09, $\frac{10}{2}$, $\frac{99}{100}$

Problem Solving and Reasoning — NS 1.0, KEY NS 1.2, MR 1.0, MR 2.3

Solve.

19. Suppose a display at the National Yo-Yo Museum shows a yo-yo that is 2.45 inches wide. Write that number as a fraction.

20. Two yo-yos Sandy saw at the museum measured $1\frac{3}{4}$ inches and 3.1 inches. Compare $1\frac{3}{4}$ and 3.1 using <, >, or =.

Writing Math How do you change a fraction to a decimal? Write instructions that other students can follow.

Spiral Review and Test Practice

1. What is the value of the expression below?

$5 \times (8 + 2)$

A 15 **C** 42

B 30 **D** 50

KEY AF 1.3 page 144

2. Look at the problem below.

$\square = 4 + \triangle$

If $\triangle = 5$, what is $\square$?

A 1

B 4

C 5

D 9

Test Tip
Substitute both values into the equation to check your answer.

KEY AF 1.5 page 192

3. Which number sentence is true?

A $^-6 > {}^-7$

B $^-9 > {}^-8$

C $^-1 < {}^-2$

D $^-5 < {}^-6$

KEY NS 1.8 page 350

4. $\frac{5}{8} - \frac{3}{8} =$

A $\frac{2}{8}$

B $\frac{3}{8}$

C $\frac{8}{8}$

D $\frac{1}{8}$

NS 1.5 page 380

5. On the number line below, what number does point *P* represent?

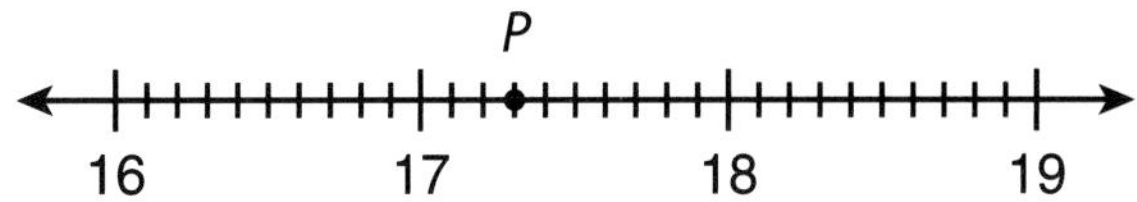

A $16\frac{3}{10}$ **C** $17\frac{3}{5}$

B $17\frac{3}{10}$ **D** $18\frac{7}{10}$

KEY NS 1.9 page 398

6. What mixed number means the same as 3.75?

A $\frac{75}{100}$ **C** $3\frac{75}{100}$

B $3\frac{75}{10}$ **D** $3\frac{75}{1000}$

NS 1.6 page 420

Education Place
Visit www.eduplace.com/camap/ for **Test-Taking Tips** and **Extra Practice.**

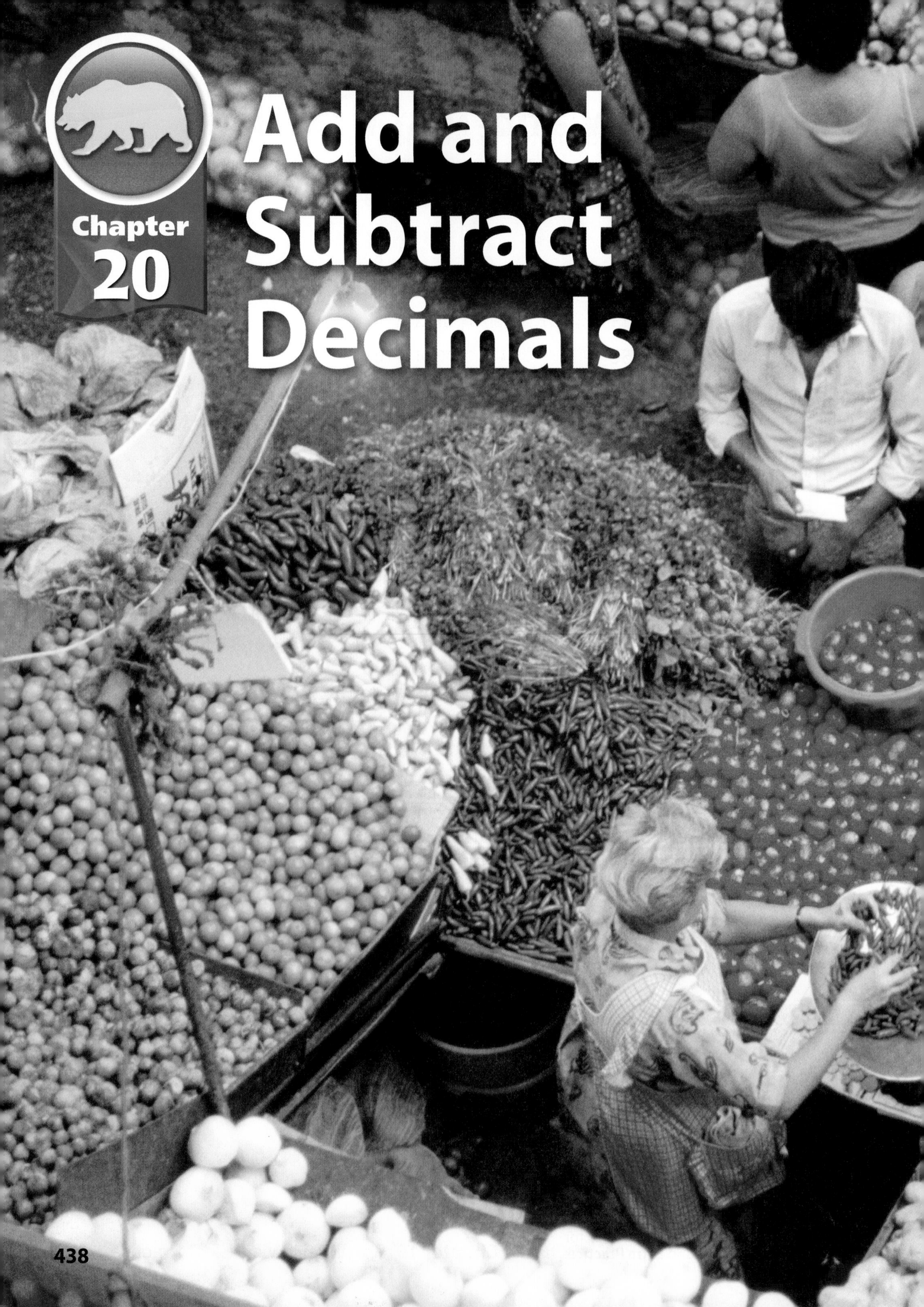

Chapter 20

Add and Subtract Decimals

Check What You Know

Word Bank
decimal
decimal point
hundredth
tenth

Vocabulary and Concepts NS 1.0, MR 2.3

Choose the best word to complete the sentence. page 418

1. A number with one or more digits to the right of the decimal point is a _____.
2. One of ten equal parts is a _____.

Skills NS 1.6

Write the fraction or mixed number as a decimal. page 420

3. one half
4. three and four tenths
5. three hundredths
6. twenty-one hundredths

Write the decimal as a fraction or mixed number. page 420

7. 4.2
8. 0.57
9. 1.01

Problem Solving and Reasoning KEY NS 1.9

10. Reynaldo lives 22.09 km from his aunt, 20.98 km from his grandparents, and 22.4 km from his uncle. Order the distances from least to greatest.

Vocabulary

Visualize It!

round
When you round a number you tell *about* how many or *about* how much.

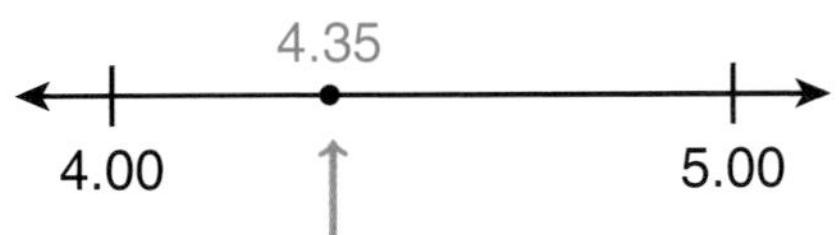

Look at the tenths place to round.
3 < 5, so 4.35 rounds down to 4.

Language Tip

Some words are alike in English and Spanish.

English	Spanish
decimal	**decimal**
decimal point	**punto decimal**
denominator	**denominador**

See **English-Spanish Glossary** pages 644–666.

Education Place Visit www.eduplace.com/camap/ for the **eGlossary** and **eGames**.

CA Standards MR 2.3 Use a variety of methods, such as words, numbers, symbols, charts, graphs, tables, diagrams, and models, to explain mathematical reasoning. **Also NS 1.0**

Hands On
Explore Addition and Subtraction of Decimals

Objective Use models to add and subtract decimals.

CA Standards
NS 2.0 Students extend their use and understanding of whole numbers to the addition and subtraction of simple decimals.

NS 2.1 Estimate and compute the sum or difference of whole numbers and positive decimals to two places.

Also MR 2.0, MR 2.2, MR 2.3, MR 2.4, MR 3.0, MR 3.2, MR 3.3

Materials
- Learning Tool 31 (Decimal Place-Value Charts and Grids)
- green and blue colored pencils
- eManipulatives (optional) www.eduplace.com/camap/

Explore

Question How can you use models to add and subtract decimals?

Mrs. Cortez bought the ribbon shown to decorate some baskets to sell at a craft fair. How much ribbon did Mrs. Cortez buy?

Use decimal models to find 1.5 + 0.75.

1 On Learning Tool 31, shade 1.5 decimal grids green. Then shade an additional 0.75 decimal grid blue.
How many decimal grids did you use? Why?

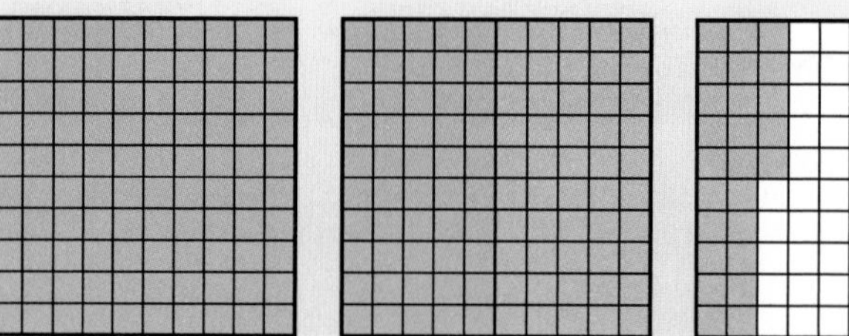

2 Record your work in the place-value chart.
- Why do you record 0 in the hundredths place for 1.5?
- What is the sum?

	ones	.	tenths	hundredths
	1	.	5	0
+	0	.	7	5
	2	.	2	5

Don't forget to line up the decimal points.

Solution: Mrs. Cortez bought 2.25 yards of ribbon.

You can also use models to subtract decimal numbers.

Use decimal models to find 2.1 − 1.45.

Think
Cross out part of the model to show subtraction.

1 On Learning Tool 31, shade 2.1 decimal grids green. Then outline 1.45 on the shaded part of the grids and cross it out.

How many hundredths are not crossed out?

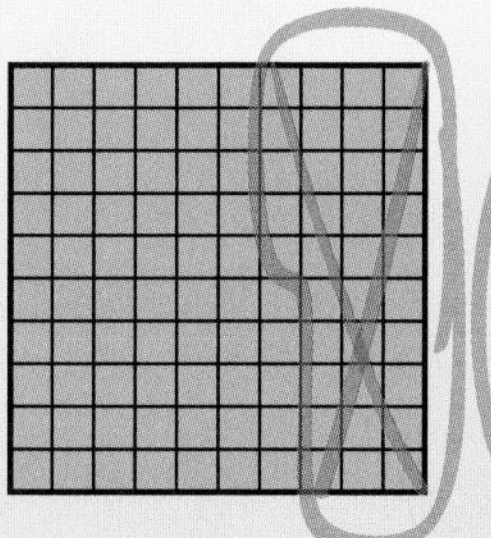
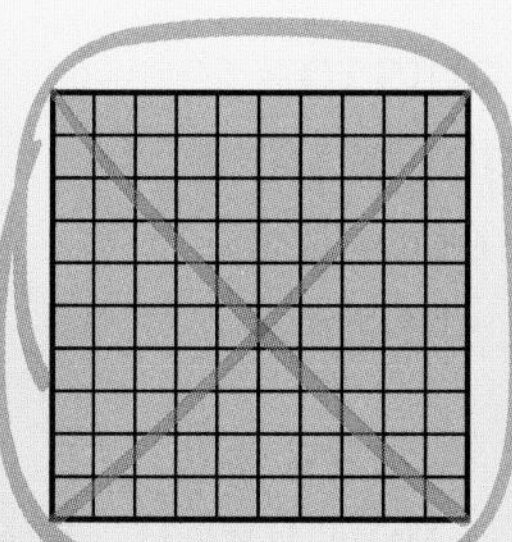
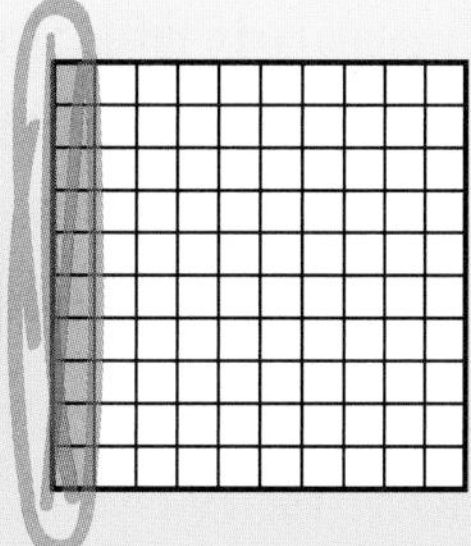

2 Record your work in the place-value chart.

- How should you line up the numbers?
- What is the difference?

	ones	.	tenths	hundredths
	2	.	1	0
−	1	.	4	5
	0	.	6	5

Extend

Find the sum or difference. Use grid paper if you need help.

1. 3 + 1.7 **2.** 3.2 − 1.4 **3.** 2.9 + 3.5 **4.** 4.5 − 2.9

5. 3.71 − 1.47 **6.** 1.04 + 1.18 **7.** 2.36 − 1.12 **8.** 3.27 + 4.96

Writing Math

Generalize Look at how the decimals are lined up in the place-value chart on page 440. What would happen if the decimal points were not lined up?

CA Standards
NS 2.2 Round two-place decimals to one decimal or to the nearest whole number and judge the reasonableness of the rounded answer.

MR 2.5 Indicate the relative advantages of exact and approximate solutions to problems and give answers to a specified degree of accuracy.

Also KEY NS 1.1, KEY NS 1.9, MR 1.0, MR 1.1, MR 2.0, MR 2.2, MR 2.3, MR 2.4, MR 3.1

Vocabulary

round

Round Decimals

Objective Round decimals by using a number line or rounding rules.

Learn by Example

Ami sells nuts and fruit at an outdoor market. He has 1.35 pounds of kola nuts to sell. What is the weight of the kola nuts to the nearest whole pound? To the nearest tenth?

When you **round** a number you tell *about* how many or *about* how much.

Use rules for rounding to round 1.35.

Example 1

1 Find the place you want to round to.

1.35
↑
ones place

2 Look at the digit to the right.

1.35
↑
digit to the right

3 Round as you do with whole numbers.

1.35
↑
3 < 5, so 1.35 rounds down to 1.

1.35 is closer to 1, so round 1.35 to 1.

Solution: To the nearest whole pound, the weight of the kola nuts is 1 pound.

Example 2

1.35
↑
tenths place

1.35
↑
digit to the right

1.35
↑
5 = 5, so 1.35 rounds up to 1.4

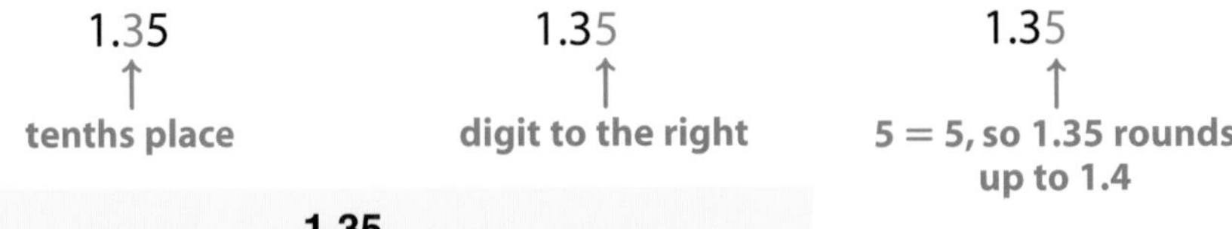

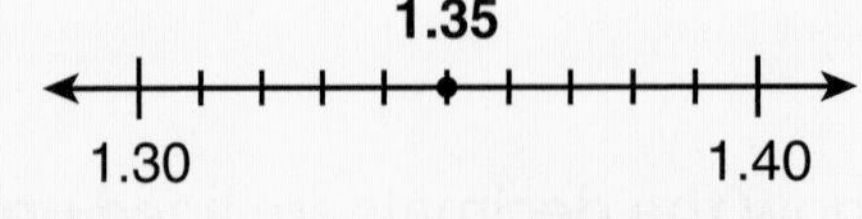
1.35 is halfway between 1.3 and 1.4, so round 1.35 to 1.4.

Solution: To the nearest tenth, the kola nuts weigh 1.4 pounds.

Guided Practice

Use the number line to round the decimals to the nearest tenth.

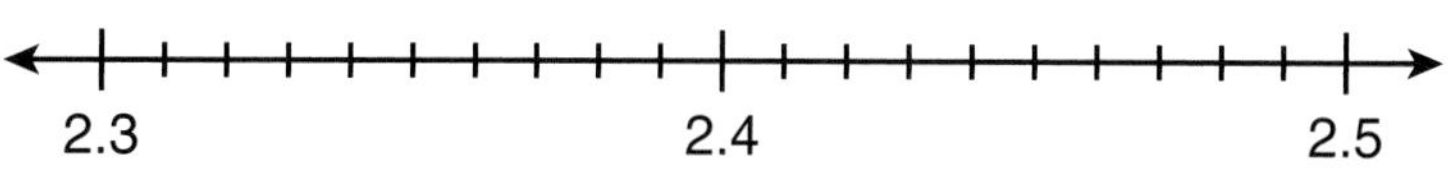

1. 2.31 **2.** 2.38 **3.** 2.46 **4.** 2.43

Round the decimals to the place of the underlined digit.

5. $3\underline{8}.6$ **6.** $9\underline{5}.05$ **7.** $7.\underline{3}7$ **8.** $153.\underline{9}6$ **9.** $45\underline{6}.5$

Ask Yourself

- Which digit do I need to look at in order to round the decimal?
- Should the rounding-place digit change or stay the same?

Guided Problem Solving

Use the questions to solve this problem.

10. Ami also sells rice at the outdoor market. What is the weight of the rice to the nearest pound? What is the weight to the nearest tenth of a pound?

a. **Understand** What do you need to do?

b. **Plan** What rounding rule can you use to decide whether to round up or round down?

c. **Solve** Round 3.47 to the nearest whole number.

Since 4 tenths < 5 tenths, 3.47 rounds down to ◯.

Now round 3.47 to the nearest tenth.

Since 7 hundredths > 5 hundredths, 3.47 rounds up to ◯.

d. **Look Back** Which rounded number is more exact? If Ami charges \$1 a pound, would he make more money if he charged for 3 pounds or 3.5 pounds of rice?

Math Talk Mori rounds 29.5 to 3. Is that reasonable? Why or why not?

Practice and Problem Solving

Use the number line to round the decimals to the nearest tenth.

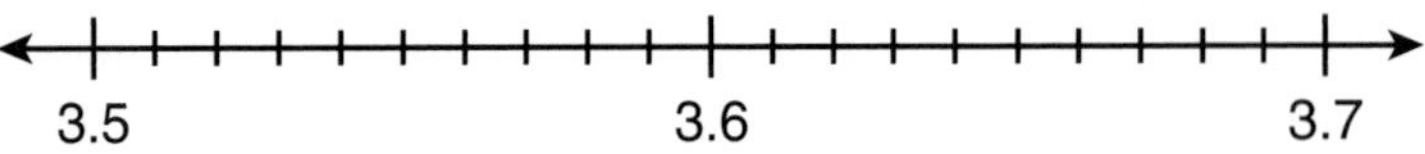

11. 3.57 **12.** 3.61 **13.** 3.69 **14.** 3.65 **15.** 3.52

Round the decimal to the place of the underlined digit.

16. $\underline{2}.8$ **17.** $11\underline{8}.16$ **18.** $7.\underline{8}6$ **19.** $73.\underline{5}7$ **20.** $6.\underline{5}1$

History-Social Science Link

Use the Fun Facts to solve.

21. Explain California produced about 998 million pounds of almonds in 2004–2005. Do you think that number is rounded or exact? Explain your thinking.

22. Estimate Suppose you buy three pounds of shelled almonds at $4.25 a pound. Will the total price be closer to $12 or $15?

California Almonds

- California is the only state that produces almonds. California produces $\frac{4}{5}$ of the world's almonds. California exports almonds to more than 35 countries.
- In 2004–2005, California exported about 984,100,000 pounds of almonds.

History-Social Science 4.4.6

Spiral Review and Test Practice

Copy and complete. KEY AF 1.5 page 196

	Rule: $b = 2a - 4$	
	Input (a)	Output (b)
23.	5	
24.	8	

	Rule: $y = x + 10$	
	Input (x)	Output (y)
25.	48	
26.	32	

27.

Rule: ________	
Input (x)	Output (y)
12	14
20	22

Write the letter of the correct answer. NS 2.2

28. The length of a field is 410.83 meters. What is its length rounded to the nearest whole number?

A 400 meters **B** 410 meters **C** 410.8 meters **D** 411 meters

Extra Practice See page 455, Set A.

Key Standards Review

Need Help?
See Key Standards Handbook.

Order the numbers from least to greatest. KEY NS 1.2

1. 1.3 1.1 1.31
2. 2.08 2.1 2.09
3. 4.6 4.06 4.05
4. 0.01 0.1 0.02

Compare. Use >, <, or = for each ●. KEY NS 1.2

5. 1.8 ● 1.81
6. 4.2 ● 4.02
7. 3.1 ● 3.10
8. 5.3 ● 5.03

Use the number line to solve. KEY NS 1.8

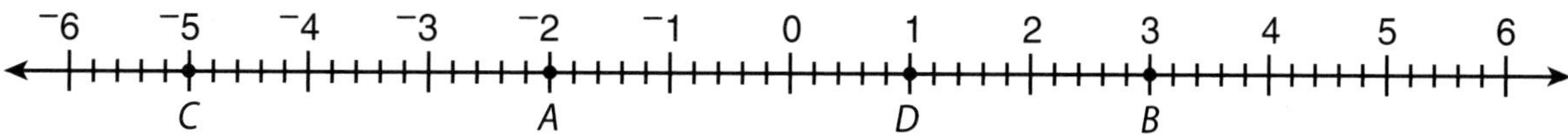

9. What numbers do points *A*, *B*, *C*, and *D* represent on the number line?
10. What point is 2 more than ⁻4?
11. What point is 4 fewer than ⁻1?
12. What point is 3 more than 0?
13. What point is 3 more than point *A*?

Math Reasoning

Reasonable Rounding

Use what you know about rounding to answer the question. NS 2.1

When 3.9 and another decimal in tenths are rounded to the nearest whole number, their sum is 9. What could the other decimal be?

CA Standards
NS 2.1 Estimate and compute the sum or difference of whole numbers and positive decimals to two places.
NS 2.2 Round two-place decimals to one decimal or to the nearest whole number and judge the reasonableness of the rounded answer.
Also KEY NS 1.1, KEY NS 1.3, KEY NS 1.4, NS 2.0, MR 1.0, MR 1.1, MR 1.2, MR 2.0, MR 2.2, MR 2.3, MR 2.4, MR 2.5, MR 3.1

Vocabulary

estimate

Estimate Decimal Sums and Differences

Objective Use rounding to estimate decimal sums and differences.

Learn by Example

Jacob and his grandfather want to ride on the shorter trail. Should they pick Mountain View Trail or Timber Trail?

You may not need an exact answer. So try to solve the problem with an **estimate**.

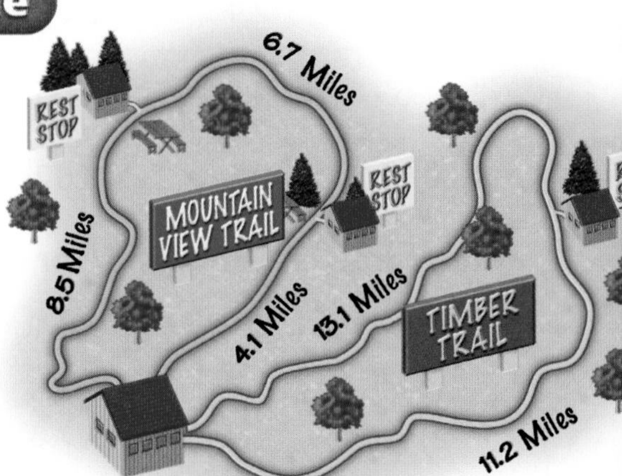

1 Estimate the length of each trail.

- Round each decimal to the nearest whole number.
- Then add the rounded numbers.

Mountain View Trail

8.5	rounds to	9
6.7	rounds to	7
+ 4.1	rounds to	+ 4
		20 miles

Timber Trail

11.2	rounds to	11
+ 13.1	rounds to	+ 13
		24 miles

2 Compare the two estimates: 20 miles < 24 miles

Solution: Based on this estimate, Jacob and his grandfather should pick Mountain View Trail.

Other Examples

A. Estimate Differences

18.5	rounds to	19
− 16.9	rounds to	− 17
		2

B. Estimate Money

$308.17	rounds to	$308
− 163.82	rounds to	− 164
		$144

Guided Practice

Estimate the sum or difference by rounding each decimal to the nearest whole number.

1. $4.7 + 2.5 + 3.1$

2. $5.1 - 1.7$

3. $\$44.63 + 14.35$

4. $73.78 - 32.15$

Ask Yourself

- How do I round each decimal to the nearest whole number?
- Should I add or subtract?

Math Talk Look back at the example on page 446. Are the estimates that Jacob made reasonable? Why or why not? Why is an exact answer not needed?

Practice and Problem Solving

Estimate the sum or difference by rounding each decimal to the nearest whole number.

5. $8.6 + 5.2$

6. $13.5 + 15.9$

7. $198.1 + 238.5$

8. $\$349.29 + 34.51$

9. $8.2 - 3.9$

10. $\$23.82 - 20.49$

11. $527.49 - 248.21$

12. $\$600.46 - 64.92$

13. $4.37 + 8.40 + 2.53$

14. $\$67.17 + 31.25 + 8.24$

Solve.

15. **Multistep** Judy has 15 meters of silk. She uses 7.15 meters for one kite and 5.76 meters for another kite. About how much silk does she have left?

16. **Explain** Give a reasonable estimate for the sum of \$4,109,384.75 and \$9,834,523.78. What place did you round to?

Spiral Review and Test Practice

Add or subtract. NS 1.5 page 380

17. $\frac{7}{8} - \frac{4}{8}$

18. $\frac{1}{5} + \frac{4}{5}$

19. $\frac{6}{10} - \frac{2}{10}$

20. $\frac{5}{6} - \frac{1}{6}$

21. $\frac{7}{10} + \frac{2}{10}$

Write the letter of the correct answer. NS 2.1

22. Kumar ran 1.15 miles on Friday and 3.7 miles on Saturday. Approximately how many miles did Kumar run in the two days?

A 5 miles **B** 3 miles **C** 152 miles **D** 78 miles

Extra Practice See page 455, Set B.

Add and Subtract Decimals

Objective Add and subtract decimals.

CA Standards
NS 2.1 Estimate and compute the sum or difference of whole numbers and positive decimals to two places.
NS 2.2 Round two-place decimals to one decimal or to the nearest whole number and judge the reasonableness of the rounded answer.
Also KEY NS 1.4, NS 2.0, KEY AF 2.1, KEY AF 2.0, MR 1.0, MR 2.0, MR 2.1, MR 2.2, MR 2.3, MR 2.4, MR 2.5, MR 2.6

Vocabulary

decimal point

Learn by Example

Sharon is making a dessert. She has one 8.25-ounce can of peaches and one 8.8-ounce can of pears. How much fruit does she have?

Add. $8.25 + 8.8 = n$

Example 1

1 Line up the **decimal points**. Add.

$$\begin{array}{r} \overset{1}{8}.25 \\ +\ 8.80 \\ \hline 17\ 05 \end{array}$$

Place a zero in the hundredths place.

2 Place the decimal point in the answer.

$$\begin{array}{r} \overset{1}{8}.25 \\ +\ 8.80 \\ \hline 17.05 \end{array}$$

decimal point

3 Estimate to check the answer. Round and add.

8.25 rounds to 8
8.80 rounds to + 9
17

17.05 is close to 17, so the answer is reasonable.

Solution: Sharon has 17.05 ounces of fruit.

Sharon uses 14.5 ounces of the fruit. How much fruit is left?
Subtract. $17.05 - 14.5 = n$

Example 2

1 Line up the decimal points. Subtract.

$$\begin{array}{r} 1\overset{6}{\not7}.\overset{10}{\not0}5 \\ -\ 14.50 \\ \hline 2\ 55 \end{array}$$

Place a zero in the hundredths place.

2 Place the decimal point in the answer.

$$\begin{array}{r} 1\overset{6}{\not7}.\overset{10}{\not0}5 \\ -\ 14.50 \\ \hline 2.55 \end{array}$$

decimal point

3 Estimate to check the answer. Round and subtract.

17.05 rounds to 17
14.5 rounds to − 15
2

2.55 is close to 2, so the answer is reasonable.

Solution: There will be 2.55 ounces of fruit left.

Think
Remember, after you line up the decimal points, you add or subtract as you would with whole numbers.

Guided Practice

Add or subtract. Use estimation to check.

1. $8.2 + 2.5$

2. $2.32 + 1.71$

3. $83.35 - 20.6$

4. $24.3 + 2.5$

5. $14.8 - 6.43$

6. $\$9.31 - 3.45$

Ask Yourself

- Should I add or subtract?
- Where do I put the decimal point?

Math Talk If you round to estimate the sum of 7.8 and 6.5, how would the estimate compare to the actual sum?

Practice and Problem Solving

Add or subtract. Use estimation to check.

7. $2.4 + 7.1$

8. $3.25 + 3.49$

9. $\$91.42 - \$35.21$

10. $13.3 - 3.85$

11. $71 + 31.6$

12. $45.36 - 23$

13. $\$35.92 + 63.29$

Algebra Equations

Find the value of *n*.

14. $n - 1.3 = 3.1$

15. $n - 6.9 = 12.54$

16. $n - 7.07 = 35$

17. $n + 5.1 = 9.3$

18. $n + 1.98 = 12.23$

19. $0.32 + n = 4.07$

Rewrite and place the decimal points in the addends to make the sentences correct.

20. $14 + 32 = 4.6$

21. $47 + 189 = 23.6$

22. $12 + 295 + 41 = 45.15$

Solve.

23. Emilio and his family drove 80.25 km to visit his uncle and 78.4 km to visit his grandmother. How far did they drive altogether?

24. **Explain** Suppose Problem 23 asked whether Emilio and his family drove more than 175 km. Would you need to find an exact sum? Why or why not?

Solve.

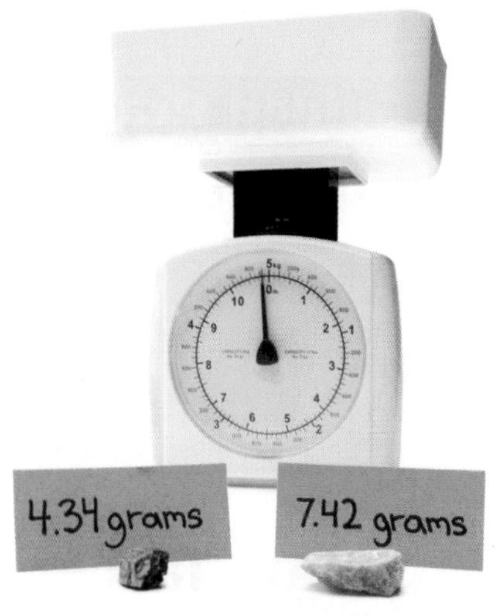

25. Analyze Evan wants to find the combined mass of these two rocks to the nearest tenth of a gram. However, the scale cannot measure masses greater than 11 grams. He decides to round the numbers first and add.

a. Will 7.4 + 4.3 give him a reasonable estimate?

b. Will his estimate be the same as the actual combined mass to the nearest tenth of a gram?

Science Link

Students in Ms. Kuan's class are growing bean plants. They measure the height of the plants each school day.

Height (in inches)					
Plant	**Day 1**	**Day 2**	**Day 3**	**Day 4**	**Day 5**
A	0	0.63	1.3	2.07	4.42
B	0	0.51	1.27	1.88	3.76
C	0	0.7	1.39	2.4	4.29

Use the table to solve Problems 26–29.

Science LS 3.b

26. After the third day, how much taller is the tallest plant than the shortest?

27. What day does Plant A grow the most? How much does it grow?

28. On Day 5, what is the height of each plant rounded to the nearest tenth?

29. If each plant grows another 1.4 inches after Day 5, how tall will each plant be?

Spiral Review and Test Practice

Write each as a decimal. NS 1.6 pages 420, 424

30. one and seven tenths **31.** $5\frac{4}{100}$ **32.** $\frac{1}{2}$

Write the letter of the correct answer. NS 2.1

33. 85.7 − 8.25 =

A 0.32 **B** 77.45 **C** 93.95 **D** 7745

Extra Practice See page 455, Set C.

Every Second Counts

The job of a pit crew is to make sure that a racecar is always going as fast as it can. They need to fix parts of a racecar during a race very quickly. Changing tires, giving the racecar gas, and other quick repairs are all a part of working in a pit crew. Every second counts when cars are traveling at almost 200 miles per hour.

Crew chief Robert "Bootie" Barker at Phoenix International Raceway, Phoenix, AZ

Solve.

1. It takes the Johnson Pit Crew 15.43 seconds to change all 4 tires on their car during a race. If the Wilson Pit Crew can change all 4 tires in 12.37 seconds, how much faster are they?

2. The jackman lifts the car so the tires can be changed. If it takes him 2.71 seconds to lift the car, and the tires can be changed in 8.33 seconds, how long will the pit stop take?

3. The Rodriguez Pit Crew needs to change all 4 tires in 19.88 seconds to keep the lead. It takes them 18.98 seconds. Do they still have the lead? If so, how much time are they ahead?

4. Garrett's racecar is in the lead! He is winning the race by 25.42 seconds. If he makes a pit stop that takes 25.65 seconds, will he still have the lead? How far ahead or behind is he?

CA Standards
NS 2.0, NS 2.1

LESSON 5

Problem Solving Strategy
Work Backward

Objective Work backward to solve a problem.

CA Standards
MR 2.6 Make precise calculations and check the validity of the results from the context of the problem.
NS 2.0 Students extend their use and understanding of whole numbers to the addition and subtraction of simple decimals.
Also KEY NS 4.2, NS 2.1, NS 2.2, KEY NS 3.0, MR 1.0, MR 1.1, MR 1.2, MR 2.0, MR 2.3, MR 2.4, MR 3.0, MR 3.1, MR 3.2, MR 3.3

Learn by Example

The Millers bought pet food for their 4 pets. Cat food costs twice as much as dog food. Fish food costs $14.75 less than cat food. Ferret food costs $11.21 more than fish food. Ferret food costs $14.46. How much does dog food cost?

UNDERSTAND

You want to find the cost of the dog food.

PLAN

You can use what you know. You know how much the ferret food cost. Work backward and use inverse operations.

SOLVE

Start with the cost of the ferret foot. Use inverse operations.

Ferret food		Fish food		Cat food		Dog food
$14.46	− $11.21	$3.25	+ $14.75	$18.00	÷ 2	$9.00
This is $11.21 more than the fish food.		This is $14.75 less than the cat food.		This is twice as much as the dog food.		

The dog food cost $9.00.

LOOK BACK

Check your answer by reading through the word problem again. Start with the cost of the dog food and do the operations as they are written in the problem. Did you get $14.46 for the ferret food?

Think

- Addition and subtraction are inverse operations.
- Multiplication and division are inverse operations.

Guided Problem Solving

Solve using the Ask Yourself questions.

1. Gwen, Lauren, Tanya, and Marta are part of a running club. One weekend, Gwen ran 9.3 fewer miles than Lauren. Tanya ran 4.5 more miles than Gwen. Marta ran twice as many miles as Tanya. Marta ran 22 miles. How many miles did Lauren run?

Ask Yourself

- What facts do I know?
- What number do I know?
- Did I use inverse operations?

Math Talk Explain how you decided which number to start with when you solved Problem 1.

Independent Problem Solving

Solve. Explain why your answer makes sense.

2. Sagar bought some bottled water for a bike trip. He drank 3 bottles. Then he bought 5 more. After drinking another 2 bottles, he had 4 bottles left. How many bottles of water did Sagar start with?

3. On Thursday, Mr. Riccio's bicycle shop received its first shipment of bicycle helmets. That day, he sold 8 helmets. On Friday, he sold 9 helmets. On Saturday, after 10 more helmets were delivered, he had 18 helmets in his shop. How many helmets were delivered on Thursday?

4. Twice as many people went on the first bicycle tour as the second tour. Three times as many went on the third tour as the second tour. If 90 people went on the third tour, how many went on the first tour?

5. Martin is thinking of a decimal number. He adds 16.22 and then subtracts 4.91. The result is 102.53. What was Martin's original number, rounded to the nearest tenth?

6. **Challenge** Victoria is thinking of a prime number. She adds 3, divides by 5, subtracts 2, and multiplies by 5. The result is 40. What was Victoria's original number?

Hint
Check that your answer is prime. Remember, a prime number has only 2 factors, itself and 1.

7. **Create and Solve** Write a number puzzle like the one in Problem 6. Then solve your puzzle.

Reading & Writing 

Vocabulary

Addition and subtraction of **decimals** is similar to addition and subtraction of **whole numbers**.

Two of Theo's homework problems look very much alike.

A	B
8 12	8 12
4~~9~~~~2~~	4.~~9~~~~2~~
− 167	− 1.67

Answer these questions about Theo's homework problems.

1. Do you think the problems have the same answer? Explain.
2. What is the value of the small 8 above the 9 in each problem?
3. What is the value of the small 12 above the 2 in each problem?

Here are two more of Theo's homework problems.

C	D
395	3.95
− 276	− 2.76
119	1.29

4. Are Theo's answers to Problems C and D correct?
5. Copy both problems and solve them correctly.

Writing Explain how to line up the numbers in a subtraction problem. Explain why it is important to line them up correctly.

Reading Look for this book in your library. *Once Upon a Dime: A Math Adventure*, by Nancy Kelly Allen

CA Standards
MR 2.3 Use a variety of methods, such as words, numbers, symbols, charts, graphs, tables, diagrams, and models, to explain mathematical reasoning.

Also NS 2.0

Standards-Based Extra Practice

Set A

NS 2.2 page 442

Round the decimal to the nearest tenth.

1. 1.12 **2.** 2.67 **3.** 5.62 **4.** 9.45

5. 3.76 **6.** 8.51 **7.** 7.84 **8.** 5.26

9. **Justify** Emilio poured 4.75 cups of sugar into a large bucket of lemonade. What is the amount of sugar to the nearest tenth of a cup? Justify your answer.

Set B

NS 2.1 page 446

Estimate the sum or difference by rounding each decimal to the nearest whole number.

1. 4.75 + 5.61 **2.** 2.45 + 3.68 **3.** 5.65 − 4.37 **4.** 9.36 − 4.78

5. 2.59 − 1.78 **6.** 8.42 + 3.71 **7.** 5.68 − 3.22 **8.** 3.45 + 5.23

9. 5.91 + 4.91 **10.** 2.23 − 1.79 **11.** 10.67 + 5.22 **12.** 9.63 − 6.54

13. **Connect** Benito poured 5.68 cups of plaster into a bucket. He added 7.97 cups of plaster to the bucket. About how much plaster is in the bucket?

Set C

NS 2.1 page 448

Add or subtract. Use estimation to check.

1. 3.70 + 6.82 **2.** 5.67 − 4.32 **3.** 4.76 + 5.31 **4.** 10.76 − 5.81

5. 3.4 − 2.5 **6.** 4.7 + 5.8 **7.** 6.7 − 5.1 **8.** 7.6 + 5.4

9. 2.64 + 5.66 **10.** 16.78 − 6.95 **11.** 7.45 + 3.23 **12.** 32.45 − 16.71

13. 8.76 − 6.21 **14.** 13.49 + 5.31 **15.** 17.82 − 12.35 **16.** 34.71 + 13.38

17. 23.56 + 67.21 **18.** 21.39 − 6.45 **19.** 34.46 + 16.32 **20.** 13.92 − 5.82

21. **Analyze** Ramon connected two hoses end-to-end so he could water his garden. One hose was 2.25 meters long and the other was 3.37 meters long. How long were the two hoses together?

Education Place
Visit www.eduplace.com/camap/ for more **Extra Practice**.

Chapter Review/Test

Vocabulary and Concepts — MR 2.3, MR 2.6, NS 1.0, NS 1.6

Write the best word to complete the sentence.

1. The first digit to the right of a decimal point is in the ______ place.

2. When you round a decimal, you look at the place value to the ______ of the rounding digit.

Skills — NS 2.0, NS 2.1, NS 2.2

Round the decimal to the place of the underlined digit.

3. $41.\underline{7}6$ **4.** $106.\underline{3}29$ **5.** $4.\underline{1}59$ **6.** $3\underline{5}.71$

Estimate each sum or difference by rounding each decimal to the nearest whole number.

7. 17.89 − 4.57 **8.** \$5.45 + \$3.62 **9.** $\begin{array}{r} \$380.30 \\ -\ 79.41 \\ \hline \end{array}$ **10.** $\begin{array}{r} 12.12 \\ +\ 25.49 \\ \hline \end{array}$

Add or subtract. Use estimation to check.

11. 5.63 + 4.88 **12.** 4.23 − 3.37 **13.** 16.92 + 5.26 **14.** 14.52 − 6.81

15. 7.89 − 4.57 **16.** 5.7 − 3.3 **17.** 89.63 + 7.4 **18.** 2.9 + 1.8

Problem Solving and Reasoning — MR 2.3, MR 2.6, MR 1.0, NS 2.0, NS 2.1

Solve.

19. Sandra ran 75.6 fewer yards than Laura. Michael ran 86.5 more yards than Sandra. Nancy ran twice as many yards as Michael. Nancy ran 440 yards. How many yards did Laura run?

20. Vanessa writes a decimal number. She adds 14.78 and then subtracts 5.63. The result is 112.63. What was the original number Vanessa wrote, to the nearest tenth?

Writing Math How do you round a decimal number to the nearest tenth?

Spiral Review and Test Practice

1. There are 4 sections in a concert hall. Each section has 2,500 seats. How many seats is this in all?

A 1,000 seats

B 10,000 seats

C 12,000 seats

D 100,000 seats

KEY NS 3.0 page 224

---

2. Neil divides 618 photographs equally into 3 albums. How many photographs are in each album?

A 26 photographs

B 203 photographs

C 206 photographs

D 1,854 photographs

KEY NS 3.4 page 290

---

3. At noon the temperature was $^{-}4$°F. By 4:00 P.M. the temperature was 3 degrees lower. What was the temperature at 4:00 P.M.?

A $^{-}7$°F

B $^{-}1$°F

C 1°F

D 7°F

KEY NS 1.8 page 352

---

4. Which number is best represented by point *M* on this number line?

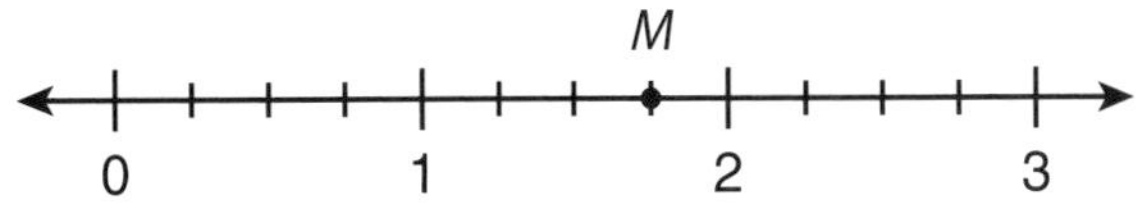

A $\frac{3}{4}$

B $1\frac{3}{5}$

C $\frac{7}{4}$

D $2\frac{1}{4}$

Test Tip
Locate each number on the number line.

KEY NS 1.9 page 400

---

5. Which fraction or mixed number means the same as 3.25?

A $\frac{3}{25}$

B $3\frac{2}{5}$

C $3\frac{1}{4}$

D $3\frac{3}{4}$

Test Tip
Write each fraction as a decimal to check your answer.

NS 1.6 page 424

---

6. The total length of a driveway is 330.79 meters. What is the length of the driveway rounded to the nearest meter?

A 300 meters

B 330 meters

C 330.8 meters

D 331 meters

NS 2.2 page 442

Education Place
Visit www.eduplace.com/camap/ for **Test-Taking Tips** and **Extra Practice**.

Unit 9 Test

Vocabulary and Concepts

MR 2.3 Chapters 19–20

Complete each sentence with a vocabulary word from this unit.

1. A _______ number has one or more digits to the right of the _______ point.

2. You can _______ 4.39 to 4.4.

Skills

KEY NS 1.2, NS 1.6, KEY NS 1.9, NS 2.0, NS 2.1, NS 2.2

Write each number as a decimal, fraction, or mixed number.

3. $2\frac{3}{10} =$ ▢ **4.** $8\frac{2}{8} =$ ▢ **5.** $1.75 =$ ▢ **6.** $0.03 =$ ▢

Compare. Write >, <, or = for the ⬭.

7. $\frac{1}{2}$ ⬭ 0.51 **8.** $\frac{6}{8}$ ⬭ 0.64 **9.** $3\frac{4}{5}$ ⬭ 3.8

Order these numbers from greatest to least.

10. $1\frac{2}{8}$ $\frac{75}{100}$ $\frac{6}{4}$ 1.2 **11.** 2.73 $\frac{10}{4}$ $2\frac{75}{100}$ $\frac{65}{25}$ **12.** 3.23 $\frac{27}{9}$ $\frac{31}{10}$ $\frac{332}{100}$

Round to the nearest tenth and the nearest whole number.

13. 2.57 **14.** 4.83 **15.** 8.16

Estimate the sum or difference to the nearest tenth.

16. $4.38 + 5.69$ **17.** $7.23 - 3.89$ **18.** $3.21 + 4.93$

Add or subtract.

19. $6.79 + 4.23 = n$ **20.** $9.33 - 5.67 = n$ **21.** $14.96 + 3.25 = n$

Problem Solving and Reasoning

KEY NS 1.2, NS 1.6, NS 2.1, NS 2.2, MR 2.2, MR 2.3

Solve.

22. The three yo-yos on the shelf are $3\frac{2}{5}$, $\frac{7}{2}$, and 2.5 inches wide. Order the widths from least to greatest.

23. Kea saw a yo-yo that had a diameter of $\frac{19}{4}$ inches. What decimal is equivalent to this number?

Solve.

24. Trinh added three decimal numbers, and the sum rounded to 152. Could these be the numbers he added?
96.68 21.23 34.62
Explain your answer.

25. A bracelet cost twice as much as a necklace. A pair of shoes cost $11.86 less than the bracelet. A jacket cost $12.23 more than the shoes. The jacket cost $45.65. How much did the other items cost?

Writing Math Why do decimal place values get smaller as you move to the right? Include an example with your answer.

Performance Assessment

School Supplies

NS 2.1

Paola has $20 to buy her school supplies.

Task	Information You Need
How should Paola spend her $20.00 to get everything she needs and still have money left over? Explain your thinking.	She needs twelve pencils.
	A notebook and two red pens are required for her science class.
	Paola loves crayons, and she also needs them for art class.
	She needs a new backpack.
	She wants to buy either a box of markers or a calculator but not both.

Greg Tang's **Go Fast, Go Far**

Unit 9 Mental Math Strategies

Multiply by 12

A group of 12 is fast to do, start with 10 and then add 2!

I have a fast way to multiply 12 × 6. To find 12 groups of 6, I add 10 groups of 6 to 2 groups of 6 and get 60 + 12 = 72. The secret to big numbers is breaking them into easier, smaller numbers!

1. 12 × 6 = [60] + [12] = [72] (10 × 6, 2 × 6)
2. 12 × 7 = ▢ + [14] = ▢ (10 × 7, 2 × 7)
3. 12 × 8 = ▢ + ▢ = ▢ (10 × 8, 2 × 8)
4. 12 × 9 = ▢ + ▢ = ▢ (10 × 9, 2 × 9)

Very nice work! Keep it up!

5. 12 × 12 = ▢ + ▢ = ▢
6. 12 × 21 = ▢ + ▢ = ▢
7. 12 × 14 = ▢ + ▢ = ▢
8. 12 × 24 = ▢ + ▢ = ▢
9. 12 × 15 = ▢ + ▢ = ▢
10. 12 × 25 = ▢ + ▢ = ▢

Good For You!

Take It Further!

Now try doing all the steps in your head!

11. 12 × 16
12. 12 × 35
13. 12 × 39
14. 12 × 55

Unit

Graphs and Algebra

BIG IDEAS!

- The location of every point on a coordinate grid can be shown by an ordered pair.
- You can graph ordered pairs and connect the points to draw lines or line segments.
- The coordinate plane is formed by two intersecting perpendicular lines called axes.

Chapter 21
Graphs and Ordered Pairs

Chapter 22
Integers on a Coordinate Grid

Songs and Games

Math Music Track 10:
A Coordinate Grid
eGames at
www.eduplace.com/camap/

Math Readers

Get Ready **Game**

Find Your Way

Object of the Game Be the first player to go to all 4 places on the grid map and get back Home.

Materials
- Learning Tool 32 (*Find Your Way* Game Board) (1 per player)
- ones blocks to use as counters (1 per player)
- number cube labeled 1–6

Number of Players 2

How to Play

1. Each player puts his or her counter at the point for Home. Players must travel from Home to School to the Library to Soccer Practice to the Pizzeria and back to Home, in that order.
2. Player 1 rolls the number cube and moves that number of spaces up, down, left, or right toward the next point. Players may not move diagonally.
3. Players continue to take turns rolling the number cube and moving their counters around the map.
4. The first player to get back Home wins.

CA Standards
KEY MG 2.0 Students use two-dimensional coordinate grids to represent points and graph lines and simple figures.

Education Place
Visit www.eduplace.com/camap/ for **Brain Teasers** and **eGames** to play.

Reading You can use a graphic organizer to help you organize information and understand a reading selection. You can also use a graphic organizer, such as a table, to help you organize information and solve a word problem.

Read the word problem. Study the table.

Problem 1

A construction crew is at work on a new 12-story community center. At the end of a month, 2 stories are up. At the end of 2 months, 4 stories are up. At the end of 3 months, 6 stories are up. If the pattern continues, how long will it take the crew to build the community center?

Month	Stories
1	2
2	4
3	6

It will take 6 months.

Writing Read Problem 2. Then use a table to organize the information and solve the problem.

I can use the table to continue the pattern.

Problem 2

Mimi joins a walk-a-thon to raise money for the community center. Her sponsors volunteer to contribute $7 if she walks 1 mile, $14 if she walks 2 miles, $21 if she walks 3 miles, and so on. What will they contribute if she walks 7 miles?

Graphs and Ordered Pairs

Brightly colored apartments in northern California's Silicon Valley

Check What You Know

Vocabulary and Concepts KEY AF 1.5, KEY NS 1.8, MR 2.3

Word Bank
- positive
- negative
- ordered pair
- function table

Choose the best term to complete the sentence. pages 190, 350

1. A table of pairs that follows a rule is a _____.
2. A number that is greater than zero is a _____ number.

Skills KEY AF 1.5

Copy and complete the function table. page 196

	Rule: $y = 7 + x$	
	Input (x)	Output (y)
3.	4	
4.	19	
5.	33	

	Rule: $y = 3x$	
	Input (x)	Output (y)
6.	2	
7.	5	
8.		24

Problem Solving and Reasoning KEY NS 3.0

9. George read for 2 hours a day. How much does he read in 2 weeks?
10. Patricia earns $2 for walking her neighbor's dog. How many times does she need to walk to the dog to earn $56?

Vocabulary

Visualize It!

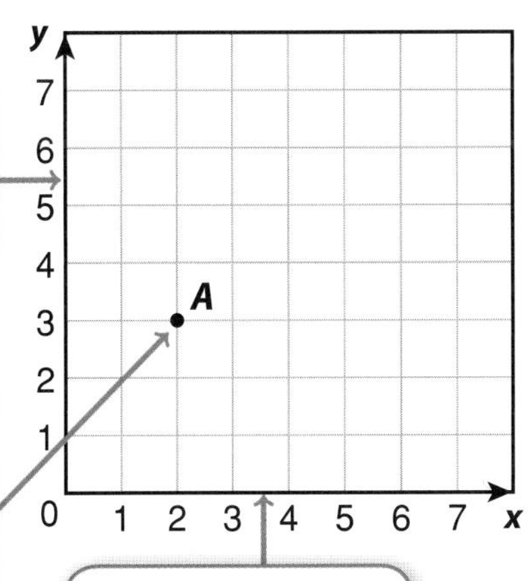

y-axis
the vertical number line

Point *A* is named by the **ordered pair** (2, 3). This point is across 2 on the *x*-axis and up 3 on the *y*-axis.

***x*-axis**
the horizontal number line

Language Tip

Math words that look similar in English and Spanish often have the same meaning.

English	Spanish
coordinate	**coordenada**
horizontal line	**línea horizontal**
vertical line	**línea vertical**

See **English-Spanish Glossary** pages 644–666.

Education Place Visit www.eduplace.com/camap/ for the **eGlossary** and **eGames**.

CA Standards MR 2.3 Use a variety of methods, such as words, numbers, symbols, charts, graphs, tables, diagrams, and models, to explain mathematical reasoning. **Also KEY MG 2.0**

Hands On
Plot Points

Objective Plot and connect points on a grid to draw line segments.

CA Standards
KEY MG 2.0 Students use two-dimensional coordinate grids to represent points and graph lines and simple figures.
MR 2.3 Use a variety of methods, such as words, numbers, symbols, charts, graphs, tables, diagrams, and models, to explain mathematical reasoning.
Prepares for
KEY MG 2.1, KEY MG 2.2, KEY MG 2.3
Also MR 1.0, MR 1.1, MR 2.4, MR 3.0, MR 3.3

Vocabulary

plot
ordered pair
coordinates

Materials
- Workmat 6
- straightedge

Explore

In this lesson, you will **plot**, or place, points on a grid using two numbers called an **ordered pair**. An example of an ordered pair is (4, 6). The **coordinates**, or numbers, in an ordered pair represent a location on the grid.

vertical line segment

horizontal line segment

neither horizontal nor vertical

Question How can you use two ordered pairs to draw a line segment on a grid?

Use Points *A* and *B* to draw a line segment. Tell if the line segment is *horizontal*, *vertical*, or *neither*.

Point *A* (4, 6) Point *B* (6, 2)

1 Use Workmat 6. Use the ordered pair (4, 6) to plot Point *A*.
- Start at 0 on the grid.
- The first number tells how far to move to the right. Move 4 units to the right.
- The second number tells how far to move up. Move 6 units up.
- Make a dot at this point.
- Label the point *A*.

2 Now use the ordered pair (6, 2) to plot Point *B*.
- Start at 0 on the grid.
- Move 6 units to the right.
- Next, move 2 units up.
- Make a dot at this point.
- Label the point *B*.

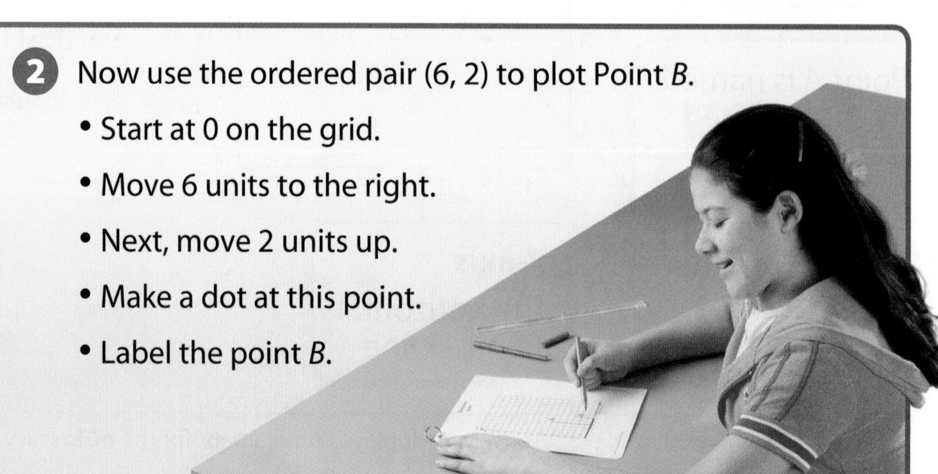

3 Use a straightedge to connect Point *A* and Point *B*. Label the line segment as *horizontal*, *vertical*, or *neither*.

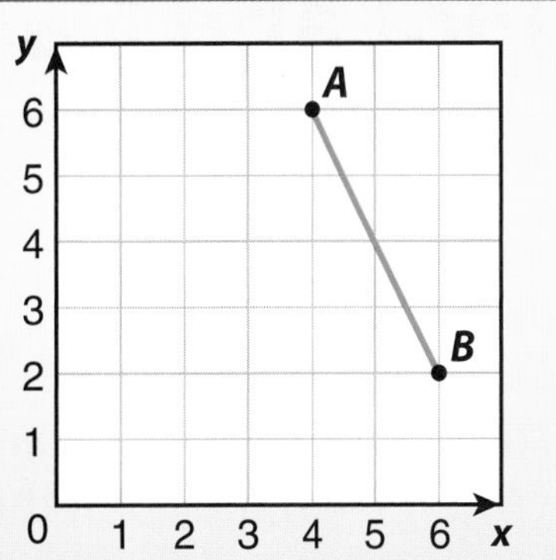

Other Examples

A. Do Point *C* (10, 1) and Point *D* (10, 8) make a horizontal or vertical line segment?

Plot and connect the points. The line segment is vertical.

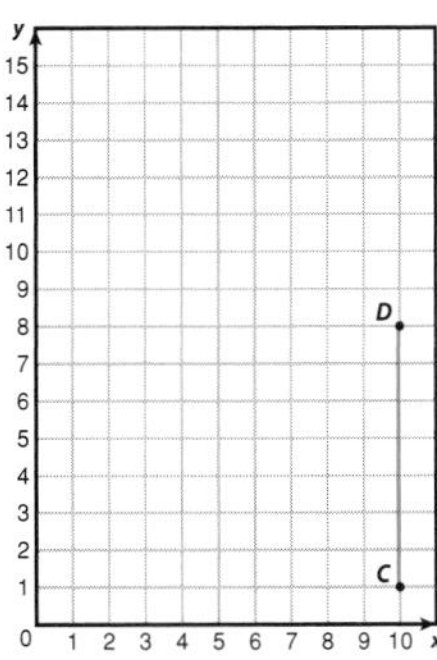

B. Do Point *E* (1, 12) and Point *F* (8, 12) make a horizontal or vertical line segment?

Plot and connect the points. The line segment is horizontal.

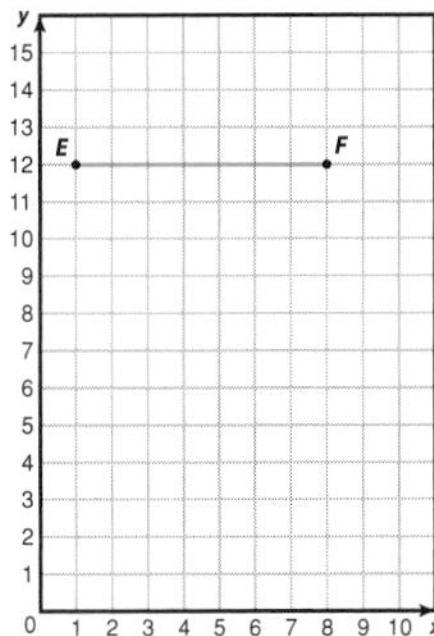

Extend

Use Workmat 6. Plot and connect the points. Tell if the line segment is *horizontal*, *vertical*, or *neither*.

1. *A* (4, 7) *B* (4, 9)
2. *C* (1, 5) *D* (6, 5)
3. *E* (8, 4) *F* (6, 6)
4. *G* (7, 0) *H* (2, 9)

Solve.

5. What do you notice about the first number in each ordered pair of a vertical line segment? What about the second number in each ordered pair of a horizontal line segment?
6. Do (3, 5) and (5, 3) name the same point? Why or why not?
7. **Generalize** What happens if you connect points that have the same first coordinate? What happens if you connect points that have the same second coordinate?

Writing Math

Explain Why does knowing both numbers in an ordered pair help you locate a point?

CA Standards
KEY MG 2.0 Students use two-dimensional coordinate grids to represent points and graph lines and simple figures.

MR 2.3 Use a variety of methods, such as words, numbers, symbols, charts, graphs, tables, diagrams, and models, to explain mathematical reasoning.

Prepares for KEY MG 2.1
Also MR 1.0, MR 1.1, MR 2.0, MR 2.4

Vocabulary

coordinate grid

Materials
- Learning Tool 33 (Grids)
- straightedge

Plot and Name Points on a Grid

Objective Use ordered pairs to plot and name points on a grid.

Learn by Example

Li and Maria are playing *Hit the Target*. They take turns naming the coordinates of a point that they think will be inside the target. Then they plot the point on the **coordinate grid**.

The first coordinate tells the distance to the right.
The second coordinate tells the distance up.

Maria names (5, 7). Is she inside the target?

Plot the point named by (5, 7).

- Start at 0.
- Move 5 units to the right.
- Move 7 units up.
- Make a dot on the point.
- Label the point (5, 7).

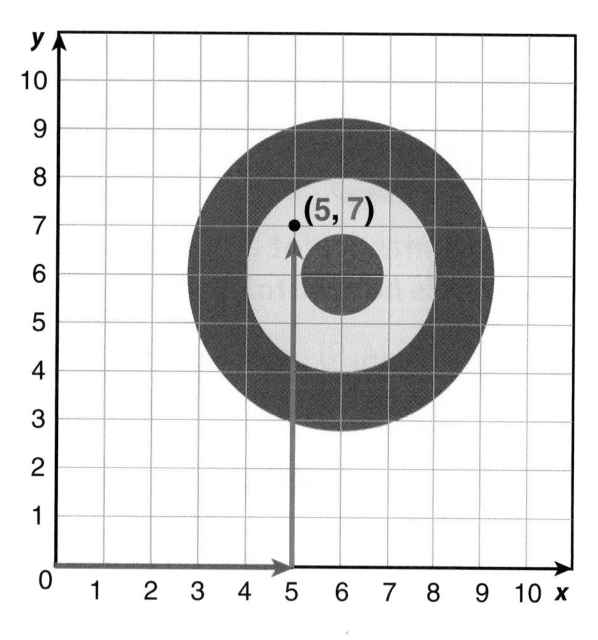

Solution: The point named by (5, 7) is in the target.

Guided Practice

Tell whether the point named by the ordered pair is in the target.

1. (5, 2) **2.** (8, 4) **3.** (3, 6) **4.** (8, 2)

5. (9, 9) **6.** (3, 4) **7.** (6, 9) **8.** (4, 4)

Ask Yourself
- Did I move to the right the correct number of units?
- Did I move up the correct number of units?

Guided Problem Solving

Use the questions to solve this problem.

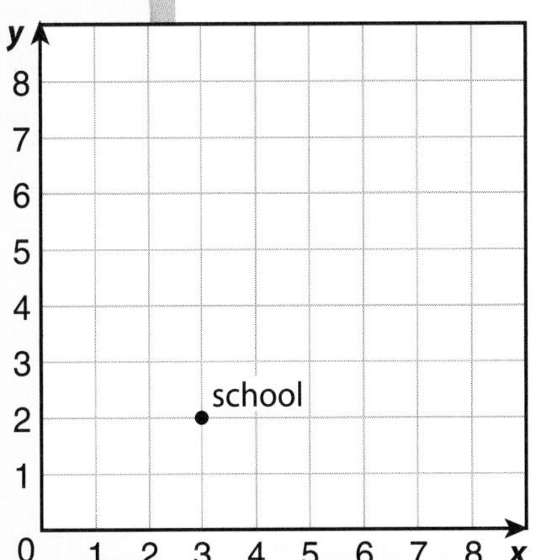

9. The coordinate grid represents a map of Greenville, CA. The hospital is located 1 unit to the right and 5 units up from the school. What is the ordered pair for the hospital?

a. Understand What can you tell by looking at the grid? What do you want to find out?

b. Plan What is the ordered pair of the school? How do you get to the hospital from there?

c. Solve Follow your plan. Where did you end up on the grid?

d. Look Back Check your answer. Is the point you named 1 unit to the right and 5 units up from the school?

Math Talk If the coordinates of a point are (0, 0), where is the point on the coordinate grid?

Practice and Problem Solving

Use Learning Tool 33 or copy the coordinate grid. Plot the point and label it with the correct letter.

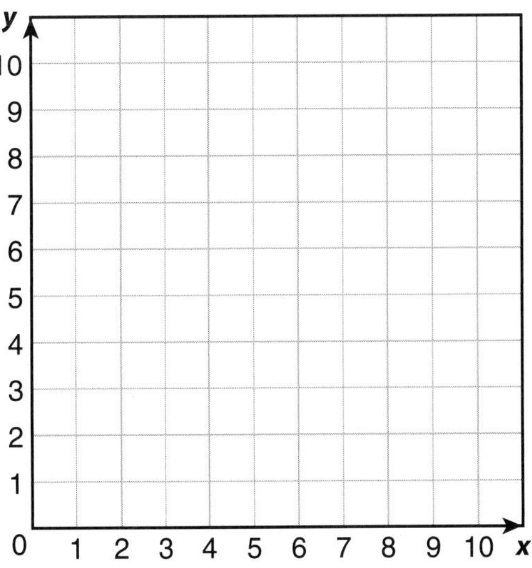

10. *E* (1, 5)

11. *R* (3, 5)

12. *W* (0, 2)

13. *L* (4, 4)

14. *T* (0, 5)

15. *M* (7, 8)

16. *X* (4, 1)

17. *S* (4, 7)

18. *Z* (5, 3)

19. *P* (8, 7)

Solve.

20. Plot the points *A* (2, 2), *B* (2, 5), *C* (8, 5), and *D* (8, 2) on a grid like the one on page 469. Connect the points to form a rectangle.

21. Maria thinks the center of the target on page 468 is at (5, 6). Caroline thinks the center is at (6, 7). Which point is closer to the center? Explain.

Real World Data

Use the data to solve.

22. Toshiro collected rainfall data for a science experiment. He wants to make a line graph of his data, which is shown at the right.

a. Rewrite the data as ordered pairs. Use the day as the first coordinate and the inches of rainfall as the second coordinate.

b. Use Learning Tool 33. Then plot and connect the points to make a line graph.

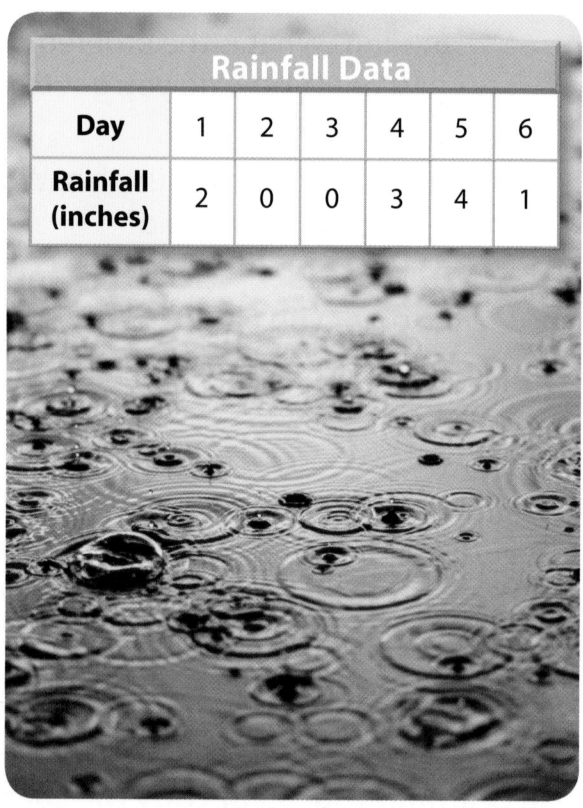

Rainfall Data

Day	1	2	3	4	5	6
Rainfall (inches)	2	0	0	3	4	1

23. How much rain fell on the second and third days combined?

24. What is the difference between the wettest day and the driest day?

25. Toshiro recorded the amount of rain that fell for the next two days as 0 inches and 1 inch. Plot and connect the new points on your graph.

Spiral Review and Test Practice

Use divisibility rules to tell if 2, 3, 5, 9, or 10 are factors of the given numbers. NS 4.1 page 302

26. 30 **27.** 130 **28.** 45 **29.** 202

Write the letter of the correct answer. KEY MG 2.0

30. Which letter shows the ordered pair (0, 4)?

A *A* **B** *B* **C** *C* **D** *D*

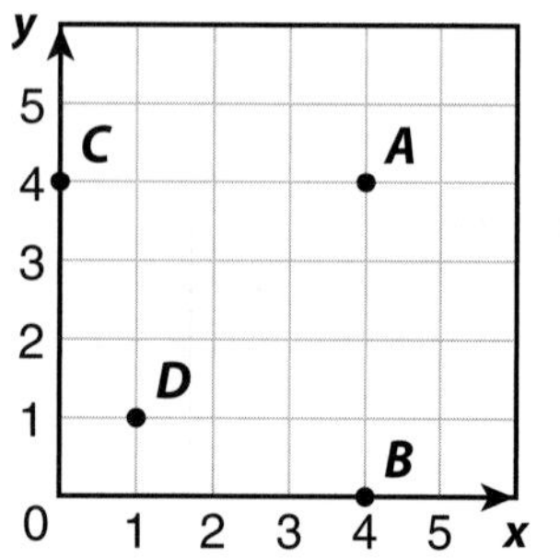

Extra Practice See page 481, Set A.

Practice Game

Graph Tick-Tack-Toe

Object of the Game Try to be the first to get four in a row.

Materials
Workmat 6

Set Up
Decide which player will use X and which player will use O.

Number of Players 2

How to Play

1. Players take turns choosing a point by naming its coordinates and marking the point with *X* or *O*.

2. If the point has already been marked, the player loses a turn.

3. The winner is the first player to get four *X*'s or four *O*'s together in a line—horizontally, vertically, or diagonally.

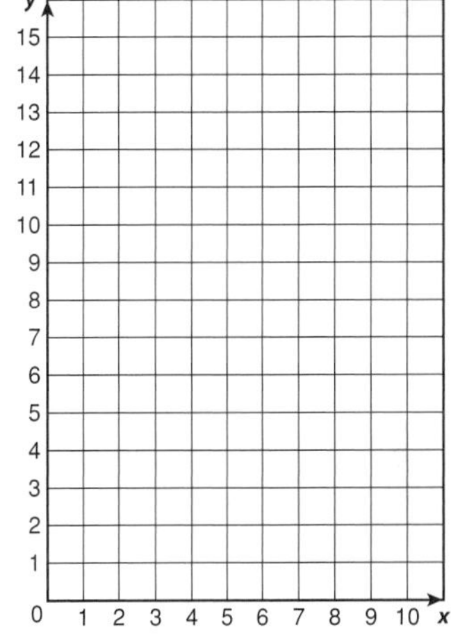

CA Standards
KEY MG 2.0 Students use two-dimensional coordinate grids to represent points and graph lines and simple figures.

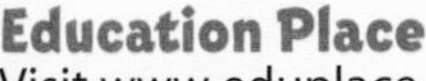

Education Place
Visit www.eduplace.com/camap/ for **Brain Teasers** and **eGames** to play.

Graphs of Functions

Objective Plot ordered pairs from a function table and draw the corresponding line.

CA Standards
KEY MG 2.0 Students use two-dimensional coordinate grids to represent points and graph lines and simple figures.
KEY MG 2.1 Draw the points corresponding to linear relationships on graph paper (e.g., draw 10 points on the graph of the equation $y = 3x$ and connect them by using a straight line).
Also KEY AF 1.5, SDAP 1.3, MR 1.0, MR 1.1, MR 2.0, MR 2.2, MR 2.3, MR 2.4

Vocabulary

origin
x-axis
y-axis
axes

Materials
- Learning Tool 48 (Centimeter Grid Paper)
- straightedge

Vocabulary Tip

A **function** pairs each input with one and only one output. A function table shows these pairs of numbers.

Learn by Example

Anan is buying flags for the party. Each package has 2 flags. He wants to know how many flags are in 5 packages.

Packages of Flags $y = 2x$	
Number of Packages (x)	**Number of Flags (y)**
1	2
2	4
3	6

Anan could find the answer by extending the function table on the right or by solving the equation $y = 2x$ when $x = 5$. He could also see the answer by graphing points.

1 Write the numbers in the table as ordered pairs. Use the number of packages as the first coordinate and the number of flags as the second coordinate.

2 Plot and connect the points on the grid. The vertical number line is the **y-axis**. The horizontal number line is the **x-axis**. The point where the number lines, or **axes**, cross is the **origin**. The coordinates of the origin are (0, 0).

3 Observe that the points appear to lie on a straight line. Extend the line. Find the point on the line for 5 packages.

- Start at 0.
- Move right 5 units.
- Then move up until you meet the line at (5, 10).

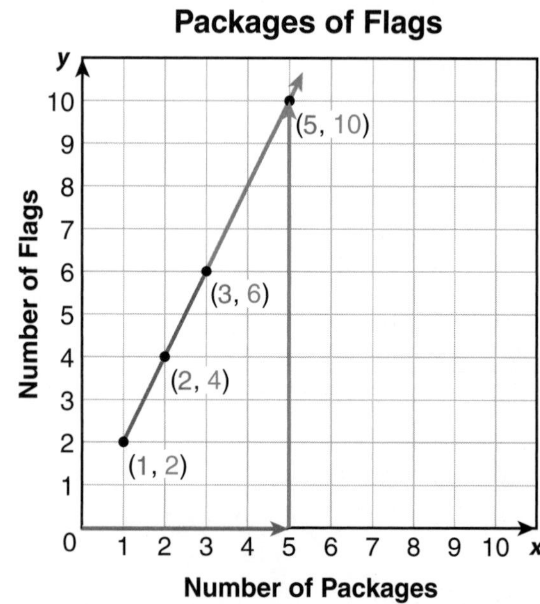

Solution: There are 10 flags in 5 packages.

Guided Practice

Use the grid and the table below for Problems 1–3.

Packages of Streamers $y = 3x$	
Number of Packages (x)	**Number of Rolls (y)**
1	3
2	6
3	9

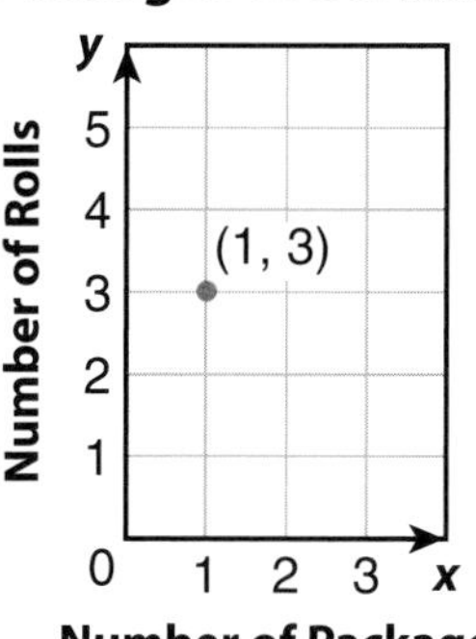

Ask Yourself

- Did I record ordered pairs in the correct order?
- Are all points on a line?

1. Write the data in the function table as ordered pairs. Use the number of packages as the first coordinate. Use the number of rolls as the second coordinate.

2. Use Learning Tool 48 to copy the grid. Plot and connect the points. Extend the line. Check that the points lie on a line.

3. How many rolls are in 4 packages?

Math Talk Is the point named by (6, 16) on the line? Explain.

Practice and Problem Solving

Use the function table for Problems 4–6.

4. Copy the function table at the right and extend it to 6 packages. Then write the data as ordered pairs.

5. Make a grid. Label the x-axis to 10 and the y-axis to 34. Plot and connect the points named by the ordered pairs. Check that the points lie on a line.

6. Extend the line. Find the number of balloons in 8 packages.

Packages of Balloons $y = 4x$	
Number of Packages (x)	**Number of Balloons (y)**
1	4
2	8
3	12

Science Link

The table shows the rate of erosion in one area over five years. Use the table to solve Problems 7–10.

7. Write ordered pairs from the table. Use the year as the first coordinate. Use the number of inches of erosion as the second coordinate.

8. Make a grid. Label the *x*-axis and the *y*-axis to 8. Then plot and connect the points named by the ordered pairs.

9. **Analyze** Do the points on your grid lie on a straight line?

10. **Challenge** Look at the table and your graph. What is the approximate erosion at $1\frac{1}{2}$ years? $2\frac{1}{2}$ years? How did you get your answer?

Erosion

- Erosion by water can create fantastic natural bridges.
- Water erosion can also be very destructive.
- Ocean waves erode beach cliffs.

Sea Cliff Erosion

Year	1	2	3	4	5	6
Erosion (inches)	4	5	7	3	6	7

Natural Bridges State Beach, Santa Cruz, CA

Science ES 5.c

Spiral Review and Test Practice

Think about a number line. Use >, <, or = for each ◯. KEY NS 1.8, NS 1.0 page 350

11. 10 ◯ $^{-}10$ **12.** $^{-}9$ ◯ $^{-}1$ **13.** 25 ◯ 25 **14.** $^{-}14$ ◯ 2

Write the letter of the correct answer. KEY MG 2.0

15. Blanca plotted 3 points on a grid. The 3 points were all on the same straight line. If she plots another point on the line, what could be its coordinates?

A (3, 6) **C** (8, 1)

B (5, 2) **D** (1, 7)

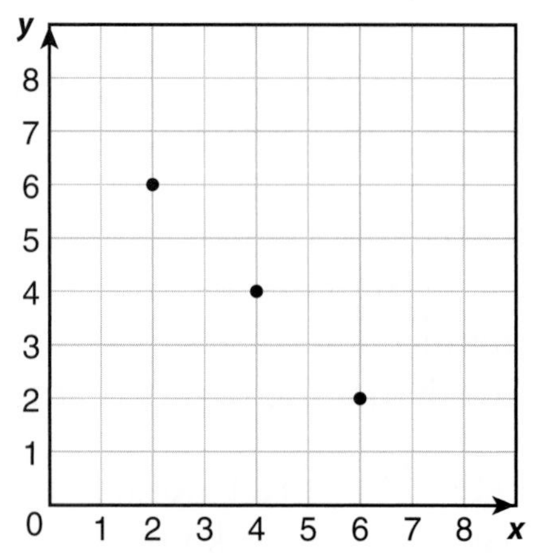

Extra Practice See page 481, Set B.

Key Standards Review

Need Help?
See Key Standards Handbook.

Use the number line to solve. KEY NS 1.9

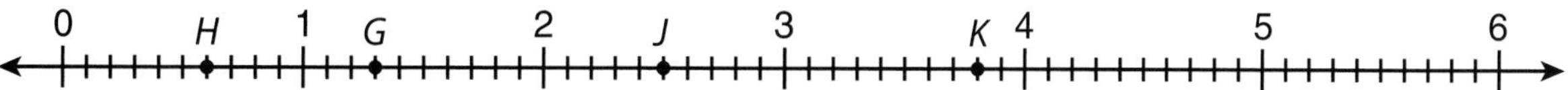

1. Write the fraction for *H*.
2. Write the mixed number for *G*.
3. Write the decimal for *J*.
4. Write the improper fraction for *K*

Divide. Use multiplication and addition to check. KEY NS 3.4

5. $952 \div 6$
6. $478 \div 7$
7. $863 \div 5$
8. Galyn has 136 sock puppets. She wants to display them in 4 large baskets. How many sock puppets will be in each basket? Will there be any left over?

Algebraic Thinking

What's My Rule?

Choose the equation that shows the rule for each graph. KEY AF 1.5

1. 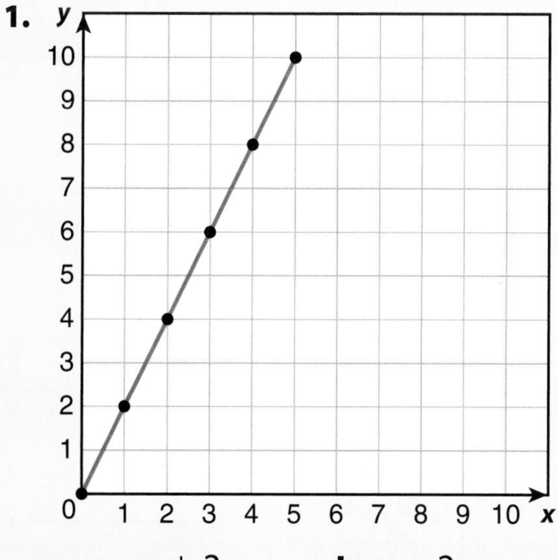

a. $y = x + 2$ **b.** $y = 2x$ 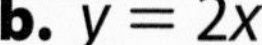

2. 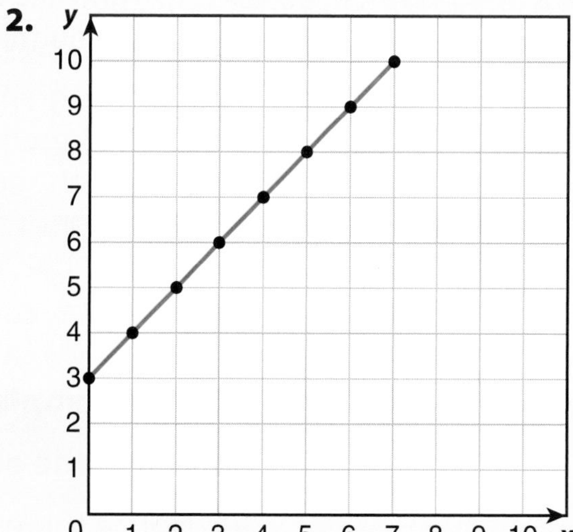

a. $y = x + 3$ **b.** $y = 3x$

CA Standards

KEY MG 2.0 Students use two-dimensional coordinate grids to represent points and graph lines and simple figures.

KEY MG 2.1 Draw the points corresponding to linear relationships on graph paper (e.g., draw 10 points on the graph of the equation $y = 3x$ and connect them by using a straight line).

Prepares for KEY MG 2.2, KEY MG 2.3

Also KEY AF 1.5, MR 1.1, MR 2.0, MR 2.2, MR 2.3, MR 2.4

Vocabulary

horizontal line

vertical line

Materials

- Learning Tool 33 (Grids)
- straightedge

Graph Equations

Objective Graph equations on a coordinate grid.

Learn by Example

In this lesson, you will learn how to graph equations. You can think of an equation as a rule for a function. So, you can use an equation to make a function table of input and output values.

Draw a graph to represent the equation $y = 2x + 1$.

1 Use the equation to make a function table. Choose x-values that make the values of y easy to find, such as 1, 2, 3, and 4.

Use the equation to find the values for y.

For $x = 1 \longrightarrow y = 2 \cdot 1 + 1$
$= 2 + 1 = 3$

Rule: $y = 2x + 1$	
Input (x)	**Output (y)**
1	3
2	5
3	7
4	9

2 Use the function table to write ordered pairs.

(1, 3), (2, 5), (3, 7)

3 Plot the ordered pairs on a coordinate grid like the one shown. Draw a line through the points.

The graph is a straight line that represents all the values of x and y for the equation $y = 2x + 1$.

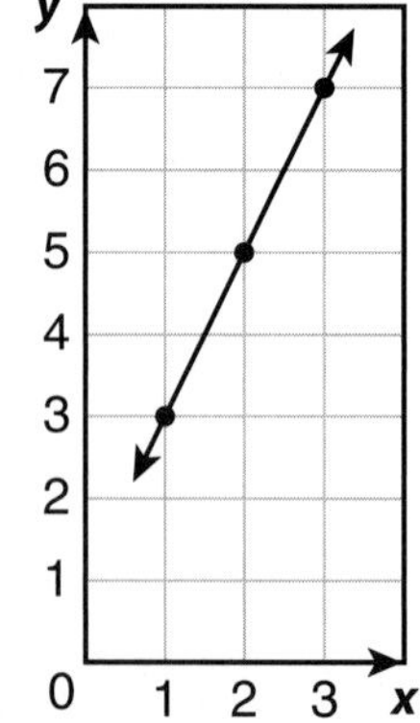

Other Examples

A. Graph the equation $y = 3$.

Notice there is no x in the equation. So for any x you choose, y is always 3.

So $y = 3$ is a **horizontal line**.

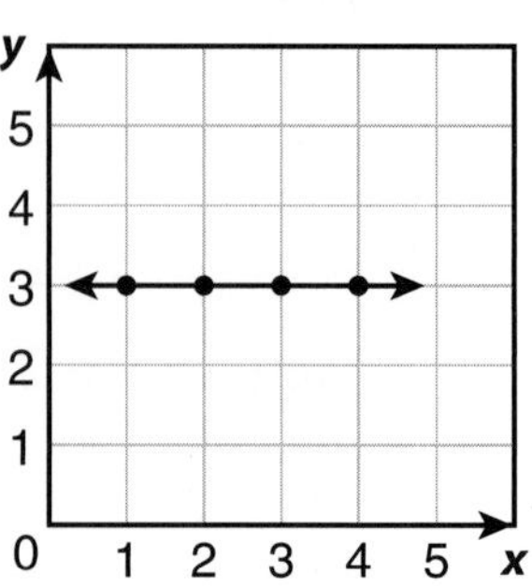

B. Graph the equation $x = 4$.

Notice there is no y in the equation. So for any y you choose, x is always 4.

So $x = 4$ is a **vertical line**.

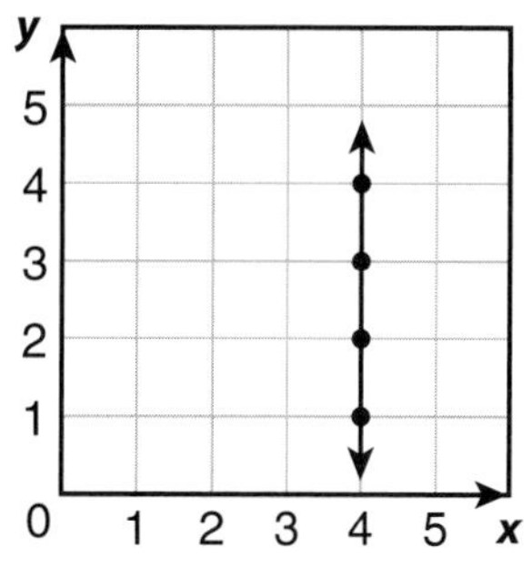

Guided Practice

Use the equation to make a function table with 10 values. Then graph the equation on a coordinate grid.

1. $x = 10$ **2.** $y = 2x + 3$ **3.** $y = 5$

Math Talk Is the graph of the equation $x = 6$ a horizontal or vertical line? How can you tell without plotting any points?

Ask Yourself

- Did I use the horizontal axis for the x values and the vertical axis for the y values?
- Do the points lie in a line?

Practice and Problem Solving

Use the equation to make a function table with 10 values. Then graph the equation on a coordinate grid.

4. $x = 15$ **5.** $y = 4x$ **6.** $y = 9$ **7.** $y = 3x + 4$

Solve.

8. Look back at the graphs that you made for Exercises 4–7. Which graph is a horizontal line? Which is a vertical line?

9. Think about the graphs for $x = 6$ and $y = 3$. At what point would the lines cross?

Spiral Review and Test Practice

Round the decimal to the place of the underlined digit. NS 2.2 page 442

10. $1\underline{0}.11$ **11.** $527.\underline{2}7$ **12.** $0.\underline{4}4$ **13.** $13\underline{7}.55$ **14.** $29.\underline{9}5$

Write the letter of the correct answer. KEY MG 2.1

15. Which point would be on the graph of the equation $y = 4x - 2$?

A (1, 4) **B** (1, 6) **C** (2, 8) **D** (3, 10)

Extra Practice See page 481, Set C.

Problem Solving Strategy
Use a Graph

Objective Use graphs to solve problems.

CA Standards
MR 2.3 Use a variety of methods, such as words, numbers, symbols, charts, graphs, tables, diagrams, and models, to explain mathematical reasoning.

KEY MG 2.1 Draw the points corresponding to linear relationships on graph paper (e.g., draw 10 points on the graph of the equation $y = 3x$ and connect them by using a straight line).

Also KEY MG 2.0, KEY AF 1.5, SDAP 1.3, MR 1.1, MR 1.2, MR 2.0, MR 2.4, MR 3.0, MR 3.1, MR 3.2, MR 3.3

Learn Through Reasoning

When you see a line graph, think about what the points on the line mean.

Students are planning for family night at school. They are using graphs to help them plan. They need to know how much snacks will cost.

Example 1

Sometimes only some of the points on a line have meaning.

You can use this graph to find the cost of 1 box of crackers, 2 boxes, 3 boxes and so on.

For example, the cost of 3 boxes of crackers is $9.

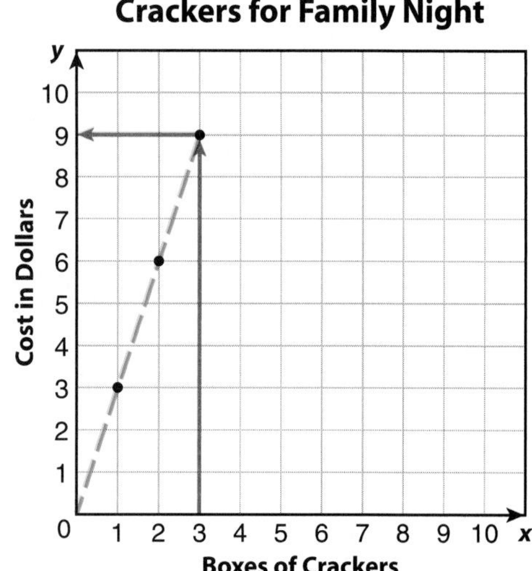

Think

It doesn't make sense to use the graph in Example 1 to find the cost of $2\frac{1}{2}$ boxes of crackers. Crackers are not sold in fractions of boxes.

Example 2

Sometimes every point on a line has meaning.

You can use this graph to find the cost of any amount of cheese.

For example, the cost of $2\frac{1}{2}$ pounds of cheese is $7.50.

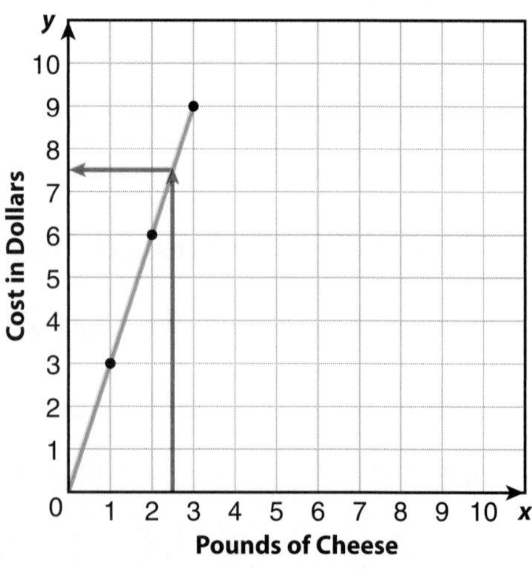

Guided Problem Solving

Solve using the Ask Yourself question.

1. Students want to find the cost of tortilla chips. The graph gives the cost of 1 bag, 2 bags, 3 bags, and so on. What is the cost of 4 bags of tortilla chips?

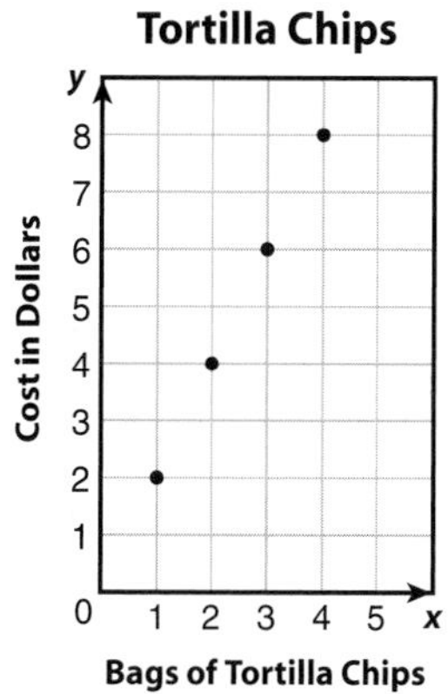

Ask Yourself

What is the cost of 1 bag of tortilla chips?

Math Talk Why does the graph consist of individual points instead of a line?

Independent Problem Solving

Solve. Explain why your answer makes sense.

2. Some parents offer to bring salsa. How much will it cost to make $3\frac{1}{2}$ quarts of salsa?

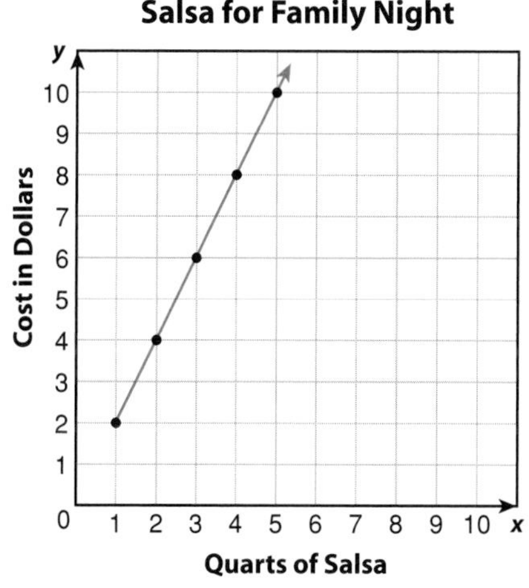

3. A restaurant offers a breakfast special of all the orange juice you can drink for one price. Use the graph to find the cost of all amounts of orange juice.

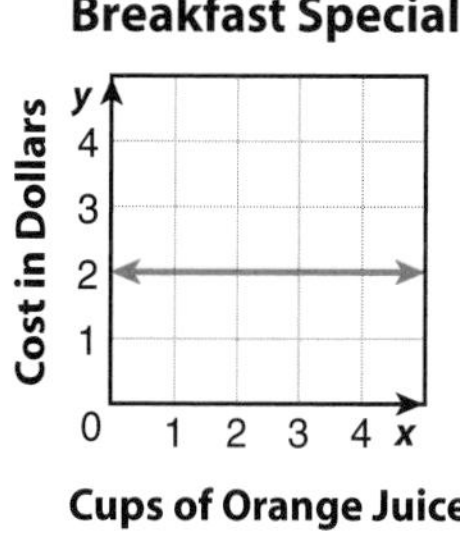

Use the graph to solve Problems 4–5.

4. Multistep Claudio sold 8 tickets. Hector sold 6 tickets. How much more money did Claudio make than Hector?

5. Challenge Sarah sold 24 tickets. How much money did she make?

6. Create and Solve Draw 5 points on the graph of the equation $y = 2x + 1$. Write a word problem that can be solved using your graph.

Band Concert Ticket Sales

Sales in Dollars

Number of Tickets Sold

Vocabulary

A **coordinate grid** is made up of horizontal and vertical lines that cross one another. You can **plot** a point on a **coordinate grid** using **ordered pairs**.

Word Bank
x-axis
y-axis
origin
ordered pair

Complete each sentence with a term from the word bank.

1. An ________ is a pair of numbers that gives a location on a grid.
2. The number line at the bottom of a coordinate grid is called the ________.
3. The number line on the side of a coordinate grid is called the ________.
4. The point where the *x*-axis and the *y*-axis meet is called the ________.

The coordinate grid represents the locations of the animals in the Alaskan Habitat of the Central Park Zoo. Study the grid.

5. Give the coordinates where each animal can be found.

Seals	Puffins
Moose	Grizzly Bears
Wolves	Reindeer
Musk Oxen	

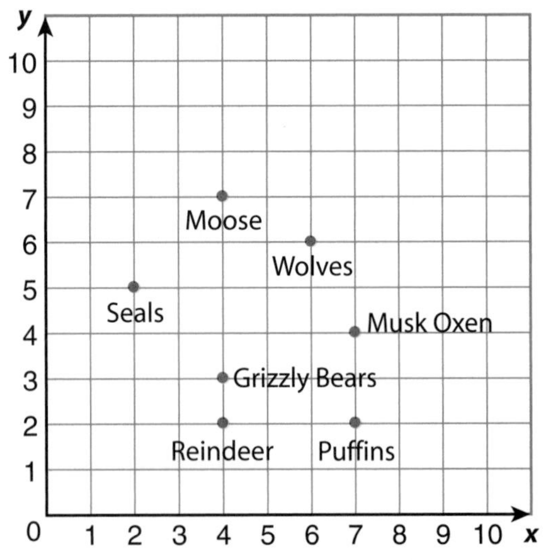

Writing The graph of a function is a line that contains the points (3, 0), (5, 0), and (7, 0). How would you describe the graph?

Reading Check out this book in your library.
Graph-X, by Dorothy Linville

CA Standards
MR 2.3 Use a variety of methods, such as words, numbers, symbols, charts, graphs, tables, diagrams, and models, to explain mathematical reasoning.
Also KEY MG 2.0

Standards-Based Extra Practice

Set A

KEY MG 2.0 page 468

Determine if the points named by each ordered pair are inside the circle.

1. (2, 2)
2. (1, 4)
3. (3, 1)
4. (2, 4)
5. (0, 0)
6. (4, 3)
7. (3, 2)
8. (0, 1)
9. (2, 1)

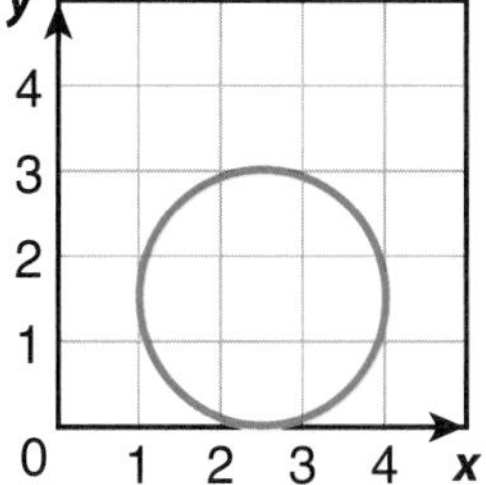

10. **Explain** What do the numbers in an ordered pair tell you?

Set B

KEY MG 2.1 page 472

Use the function table for Problems 1 and 2.

Snail Movement y x					
Hour (x)	1	2	3	4	5
Inches (y)	1	2	3	4	5

1. Write the data from the function table as ordered pairs.
2. Make a grid. Label the x-axis and the y-axis to 5. Plot and connect the points named by the ordered pairs.

Set C

KEY MG 2.1, KEY AF 1.5 page 476

For each equation, make a function table with 10 values. Then graph the equation on a coordinate grid.

1. $y = 3x + 1$
2. $y = 2x + 4$
3. $y = 5x - 1$
4. **Analyze** Michael is using the function $y = 6x + 4$ to model plant growth. What is y when x is 4 in Michael's model?

Education Place
Visit www.eduplace.com/camap/ for more **Extra Practice.**

Chapter Review/Test

Vocabulary and Concepts

KEY MG 2.0, MR 2.3

Write the best term to complete the sentence.

1. Using a(n) ______ ______ such as (2, 3), you can plot a point on a grid.

2. When you draw a coordinate grid, the horizontal number line is called the ______.

Skills

KEY MG 2.0, KEY MG 2.1, KEY AF 1.5

Make a grid. Plot the point and label it with the correct letter.

3. K (5, 4)
4. N (1, 4)
5. M (4, 7)
6. Q (8, 6)
7. S (0, 9)
8. T (10, 2)

Use the equation to make a function table with 10 values. Then graph on a coordinate grid.

9. $x = 3$
10. $y = 4$
11. $y = x + 1$

Problem Solving and Reasoning

MR 2.3, KEY NS 3.0

Solve.

12. Melissa is making key chains for the school craft fair. The cost to make them can be written as the points (1, \$8), (2, \$6), (3, \$4), (4, \$2). How much does it cost to produce 2 key chains?

13. Miguel is making lemonade for the school carnival. The cups of sugar needed per quart can be written as the points (1, 1), (2, 2), (3, 3). How much sugar is needed to make 4 quarts?

14. A Mexican restaurant is making salsa. The pints of tomato puree needed to make quarts of salsa is given by (1, 2), (2, 4), (3, 6). How many pints of tomato puree are needed to make 8 quarts of salsa?

15. Carmen is keeping track of her babysitting earnings. She makes \$5 per hour. How much money did Carmen earn for babysitting 10 hours?

Writing Math Is the location on a grid the same for the ordered pairs (2, 5) and (5, 2)? Explain your answer.

Spiral Review and Test Practice

1. Kate solved the problem below. Which expression could she use to check her answer?

$17 \div 3 \rightarrow 5$ R2

A $(17 - 2) + 5$ **C** $(5 \times 3) \times 2$

B 5×3 **D** $(5 \times 3) + 2$

KEY NS 3.2 page 130

2. Which of these is another way to write 16×3?

A $9 \times 7 \times 3$

B $8 \times 2 \times 3$

C $8 \times 8 \times 3$

D $6 \times 10 \times 3$

Test Tip
Find each product to see which one equals 16×3.

NS 4.0 page 308

3. Which equation below represents the perimeter (P) of the rectangle in centimeters?

8 cm

22 cm

A $22 = (2 \times 8) + (2 \times P)$

B $P = (2 \times 8) + (2 \times 22)$

C $22 = P \times 8$

D $P = 22 \times 8$

MG 1.0, AF 1.4 page 328

4. Which of the following has the greatest value?

A 39.03

B 0.93

C 8.77

D 41.01

Test Tip
Remember to line up the decimal points before comparing.

KEY NS 1.2 page 426

5. Shawn swam 1.21 miles on Monday and 2.8 miles on Saturday. Approximately how many miles did Shawn swim in the two days?

A 2 miles

B 4 miles

C 56 miles

D 149 miles

NS 2.1 page 446

6. Which letter shows the ordered pair (0, 2)?

A 

B 

C 

D 

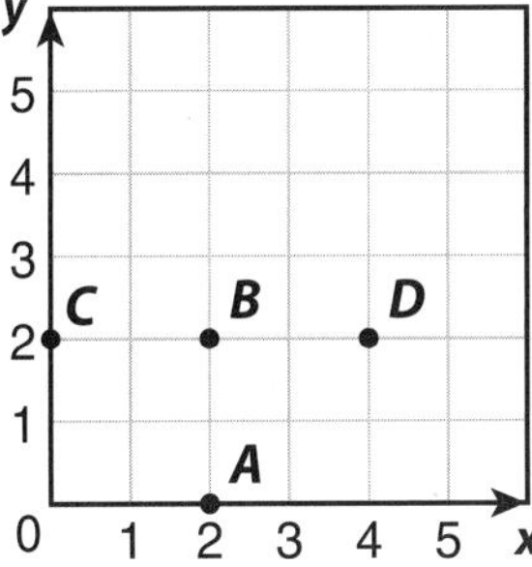

KEY MG 2.0 page 468

Education Place
Visit www.eduplace.com/camap/ for **Test-Taking Tips** and **Extra Practice**.

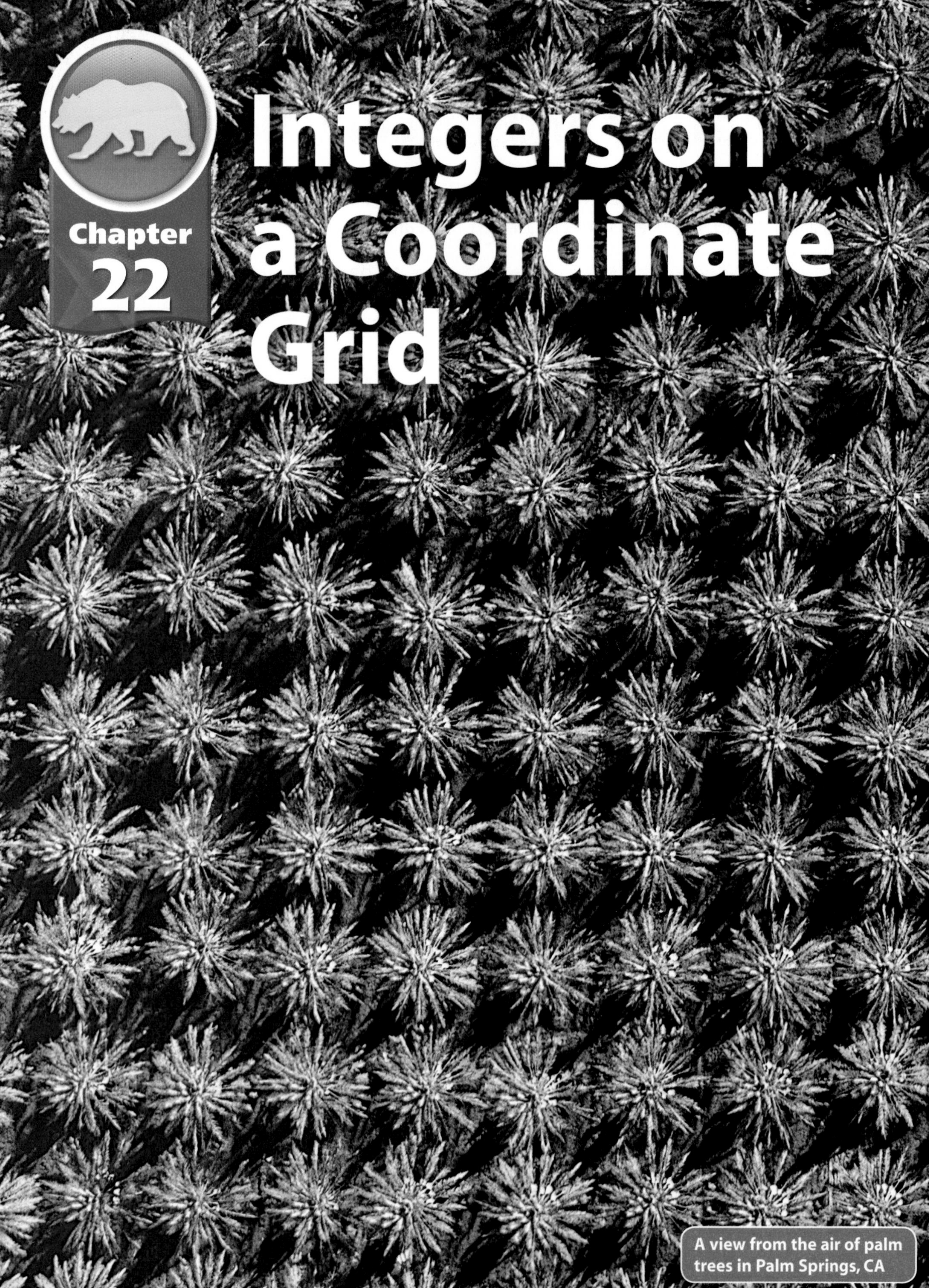

Chapter 22

Integers on a Coordinate Grid

A view from the air of palm trees in Palm Springs, CA

Check What You Know

Word Bank
- opposite
- negative
- ordered pair
- function

Vocabulary and Concepts KEY NS 1.8, MR 2.3

Choose the best word to complete each sentence. pages 350, 468

1. The numbers 7 and $^-7$ are _____ numbers.
2. The numbers (3, 4) form an _____.

Skills KEY NS 1.8

Write >, <, or = to compare. Use the number line. pages 348, 350

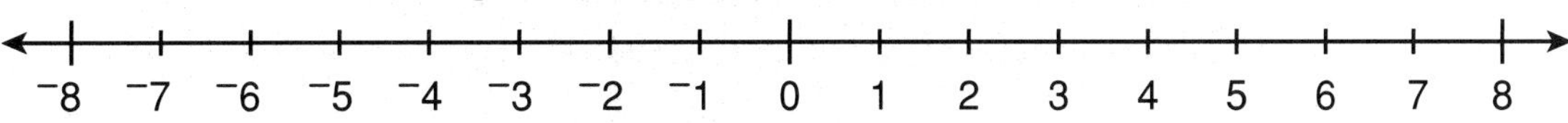

3. $^-8$ ◯ $^-6$
4. 0 ◯ $^-5$
5. 3 ◯ $^-7$
6. 4 ◯ $^-4$
7. 2 ◯ 2
8. $^-7$ ◯ 0

Problem Solving and Reasoning KEY NS 3.0

9. An elevator starts on the eighth floor of a building. It goes up 3 floors, then down 5 floors, and then up 9 floors. On what floor of the building is the elevator now?

Vocabulary

Visualize It!

coordinate plane
A plane with two perpendicular number lines in which every point is associated with an ordered pair of numbers.

ordered pair
A pair of numbers in which one number is identified as the first and the other number as the second.

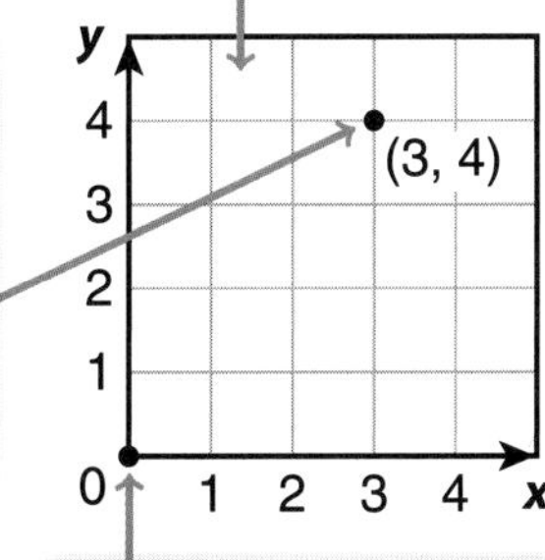

origin
The point where the *x*- and *y*-axes intersect in a coordinate system.

Language Tip

Math words that look similar in English and Spanish often have the same meaning.

English	Spanish
coordinate	coordenada
origin	origen

See **English-Spanish Glossary** pages 644–666.

Education Place Visit www.eduplace.com/camap/ for the **eGlossary** and **eGames**.

CA Standards MR 2.3 Use a variety of methods, such as words, numbers, symbols, charts, graphs, tables, diagrams, and models, to explain mathematical reasoning. **Also KEY MG 2.0**

LESSON 1

Hands On
Graph Ordered Pairs of Integers

Objective Use ordered pairs with integer coordinates to locate and name points on a coordinate plane.

CA Standards
KEY MG 2.0 Students use two-dimensional coordinate grids to represent points and graph lines and simple figures.
KEY NS 1.8 Use concepts of negative numbers (e.g., on a number line, in counting, in temperature, in "owing").
PREPARES FOR
KEY MG 2.1, KEY MG 2.2, KEY MG 2.3
Also MR 2.2, MR 2.3, MR 1.1, MR 3.3, MR 3.0

Vocabulary

coordinate plane

***x*-coordinate**

***y*-coordinate**

Materials
- Workmat 7
- Learning Tool 34 (Coordinate Plane)
- straightedge

Explore

You already know how to plot points on a coordinate grid when both coordinates are positive. Now you will plot points on a **coordinate plane** when one or both coordinates may be negative.

A coordinate grid that shows both positive and negative numbers is sometimes called a coordinate plane.

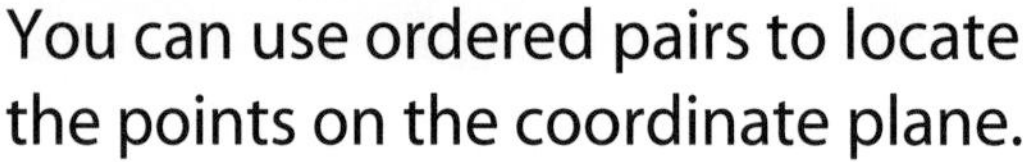

You can use ordered pairs to locate the points on the coordinate plane.

The first coordinate of an ordered pair is called the ***x*-coordinate** because it describes the distance on the *x*-axis.

- If the *x*-coordinate is positive, move to the right.
- If the *x*-coordinate is negative, move to the left.

The second coordinate of an ordered pair is called the ***y*-coordinate** because it describes the distance on the *y*-axis.

- If the *y*-coordinate is positive, move up.
- If the *y*-coordinate is negative, move down.

Question How can you find and label a point on the coordinate plane?

Look at the coordinate plane of the treasure map. The Treasure Trunk is at ($^{-}4$, 1).

Find and label the point on Workmat 7.

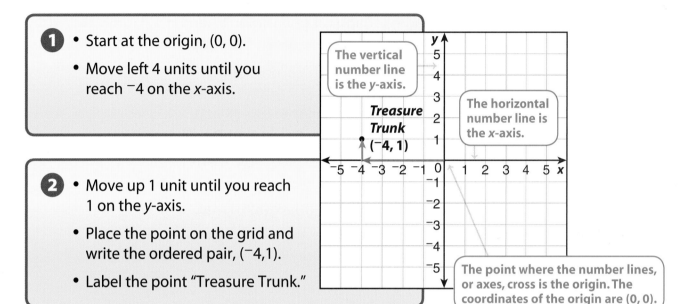

1
- Start at the origin, (0, 0).
- Move left 4 units until you reach $^{-}4$ on the *x*-axis.

2
- Move up 1 unit until you reach 1 on the *y*-axis.
- Place the point on the grid and write the ordered pair, ($^{-}4$,1).
- Label the point "Treasure Trunk."

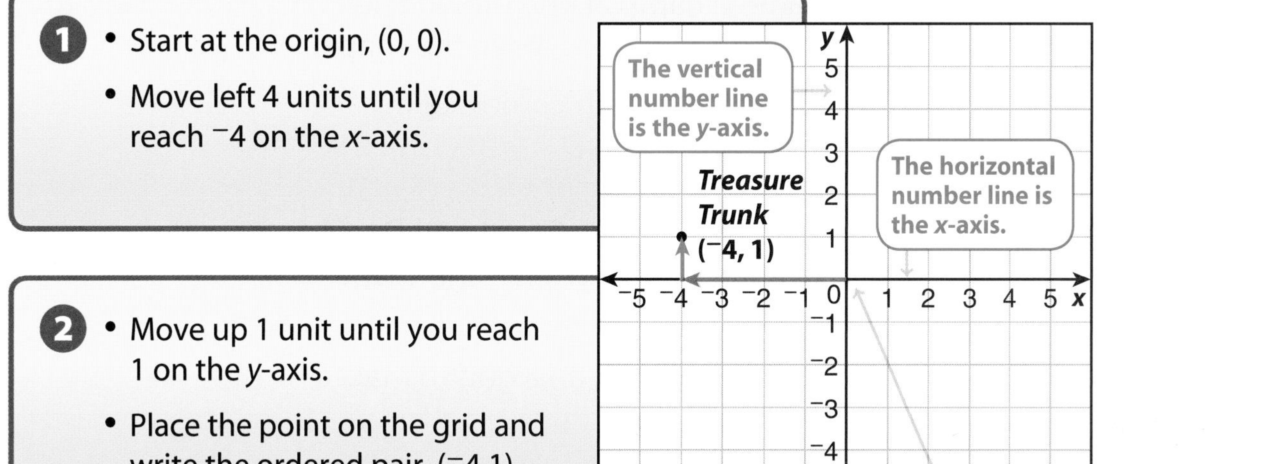
The vertical number line is the *y*-axis.
The horizontal number line is the *x*-axis.
Treasure Trunk ($^{-}4$, 1)
The point where the number lines, or axes, cross is the origin. The coordinates of the origin are (0, 0).
y
x

Extend

Look at the treasure map on page 486. Find and label these locations on Workmat 7.

1. Eagle Tree ($^{-}2$, $^{-}3$) **2.** Bear Rock (3, 4) **3.** Bat Haven (4, $^{-}2$)

Use Learning Tool 34. Plot and connect the set of points to make a rectangle.

4. ($^{-}5$, 1) ($^{-}5$, 4) ($^{-}2$, 1) ($^{-}2$, 4)

5. (0, 2) (0, 4) (5, 2) (5, 4)

6. (0, 0) (0, $^{-}4$) ($^{-}3$, 0) ($^{-}3$, $^{-}4$)

7. (2, $^{-}3$) (2, 4) (5, 4) (5, $^{-}3$)

8. **Generalize** What patterns do you notice in the ordered pairs that make up each rectangle?

Math Journal

Writing Math

What's Wrong? Juan says ($^{-}2$, 2) and (2, $^{-}2$) name the same point. Why is he wrong?

CA Standards
KEY (MG 2.0) Students use two-dimensional coordinate grids to represent points and graph lines and simple figures.

KEY (NS 1.8) Use concepts of negative numbers (e.g., on a number line, in counting, in temperature, in "owing").

Also MR 3.2, MR 3.3, MR 3.0, MR 1.1, MR 1.0, MR 2.3, MR 2.4, MR 2.0

Materials
- Learning Tool 48 (Centimeter Grid)
- straightedge

Graph Ordered Pairs of Integers

Objective Graph ordered pairs with integer coordinates on a coordinate plane.

Learn by Example

Harriet made a shape on grid paper. She told her friend Karl how to make the shape.

Harriet said, "The four corners of my shape are *A, B, C,* and *D*. *A* is at (5, 4). *B* is at (⁻4, 4). *C* is at (⁻4, ⁻3). *D* is at (5, ⁻3). Connect *A* to *B*, *B* to *C*, *C* to *D*, and *D* to *A* to make the shape." What is the shape Harriet made?

Plot and connect points on a grid to make the shape Harriet made.

1 Plot *A* (5, 4).
- Start at the origin.
- Move 5 units to the right.
- Then move 4 units up.
- Make a dot on the point.
- Label the point *A* (5, 4).

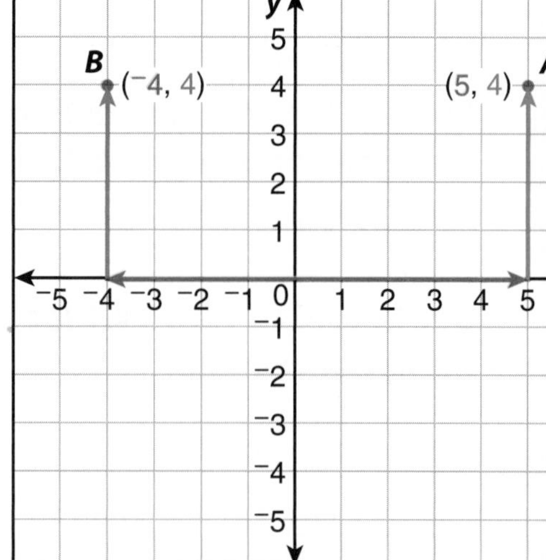

2 Plot *B* (⁻4, 4).
- Start at the origin.
- Move 4 units to the left.
- Then move 4 units up.
- Make a dot on the point.
- Label the point *B* (⁻4, 4).

3 Plot *C* (−4, −3).

- Start at the origin.
- Move 4 units to the left.
- Then move 3 units down.
- Make a dot on the point.
- Label the point *C* (−4, −3).

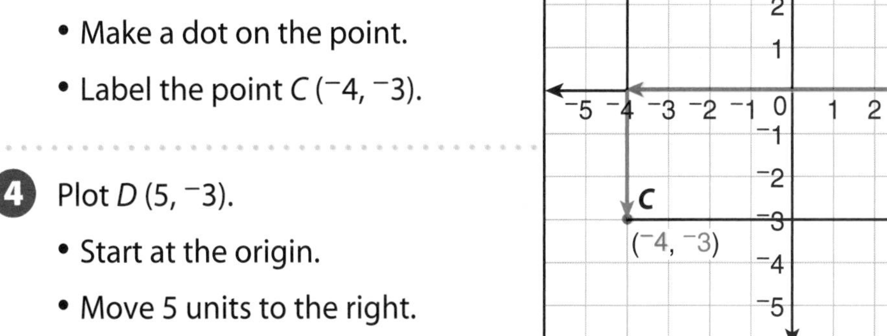

4 Plot *D* (5, −3).

- Start at the origin.
- Move 5 units to the right.
- Then move 3 units down.
- Make a dot on the point.
- Label the point *D* (5, −3)
- Connect *A* to *B*, *B* to *C*, *C* to *D*, and *D* to *A*.

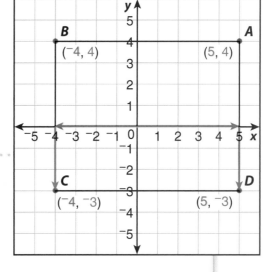

Solution: The shape Harriet made is a rectangle.

Guided Practice

Draw an *x*-axis and a *y*-axis on Learning Tool 48. Number each axis −7 to 7. Find, mark, and label the following points.

1. *M* (−3, 4) **2.** *N* (0, −1) **3.** *O* (−2, −7) **4.** *P* (−6, 3)

Ask Yourself

- Did I start at the origin?
- Do I move left or right first?
- Do I move up or down second?

Math Talk If both numbers in an ordered pair are positive, in what part of the coordinate plane will the point be? What if both numbers are negative?

Practice and Problem Solving

Draw an *x*-axis and a *y*-axis on Learning Tool 48. Number each axis −7 to 7. Find, mark, and label the following points.

5. *R* (2, −4) **6.** *U* (−4, 2) **7.** *S* (−1, −3) **8.** *W* (3, 6) **9.** *T* (4, 5) **10.** *Y* (−7, 2)

Use your graph to solve.

11. List the points that are above the *x*-axis. List the points that are below the *x*-axis.

12. Generalize How can you tell from an ordered pair whether a point will be above or below the *x*-axis?

History-Social Science Link

Use the map to solve.

13. Which town is at 0 on the *x*-axis?

14. What ordered pair describes the location of Rough and Ready?

15. What ordered pair describes the location of Rail Road Flat?

16. Which towns are above the *x*-axis and to the right of the *y*-axis?

17. Name two towns that have the same *x*-coordinate.

18. Challenge Name two pairs of towns that have the same *y*-coordinate.

Boomtowns

During the California Gold Rush, boomtowns developed along what is Highway 49 today. Many of these towns still exist, although their populations are much smaller than they once were. The map shows the location of eight of these towns.

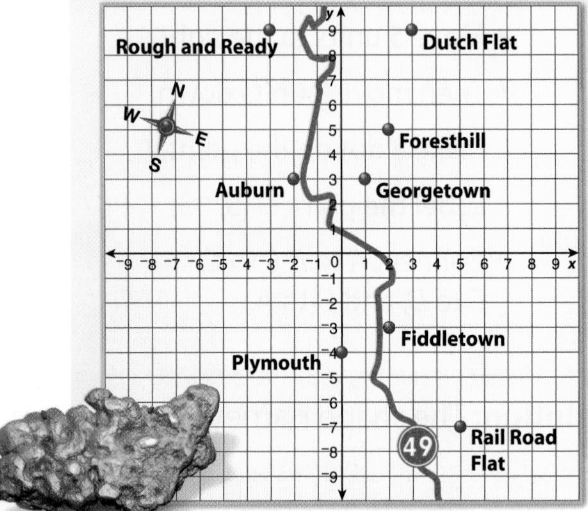

History-Social Science 4.3.2

Spiral Review and Test Practice

Find the perimeter, in feet, of the rectangle. MG 1.0 page 328

19. 14 ft, 13 ft

20.

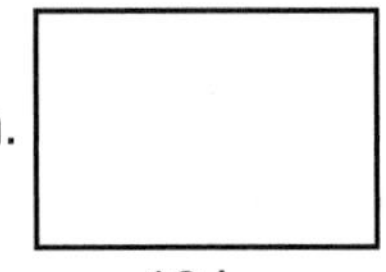

21.

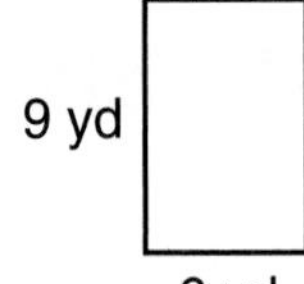

Write the letter of the correct answer. KEY MG 2.0

22. Tao wants to plot 4 points to represent the corners of a rectangle. She plotted the 3 points shown. What should the coordinates of the fourth point be?

A (⁻3, ⁻3)　　**C** (3, 4)

B (⁻4, ⁻3)　　**D** (4, 2)

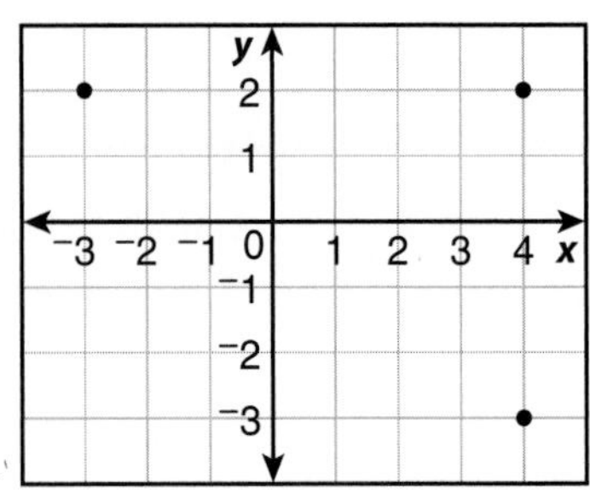

Extra Practice See page 501, Set A.

Key Standards Review

Need Help?
See Key Standards Handbook.

Locate the points on the coordinate grid. KEY MG 2.0, KEY MG 2.1

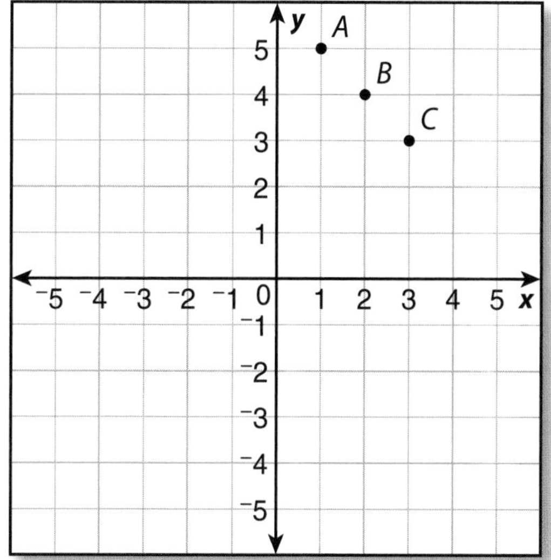

1. Name the ordered pair for *A*.
2. Name the ordered pair for *B*.
3. Name the ordered pair for *C*.
4. Name coordinates that would mark ten other points on the same line as points *A*, *B*, and *C*.

Ordered Pairs

Research at Sea

A group of scientists are working at a research station. Use ordered pairs to describe the location of each of the following. SDAP 1.1

1. Research station
2. Sea lions
3. Research boat
4. Killer whales
5. Bottle-nosed dolphins
6. The shortest distance between two points on a flat surface is a straight line. Suppose you drew a straight line between the research boat and the research station. Name 4 ordered pairs that would be on the line.

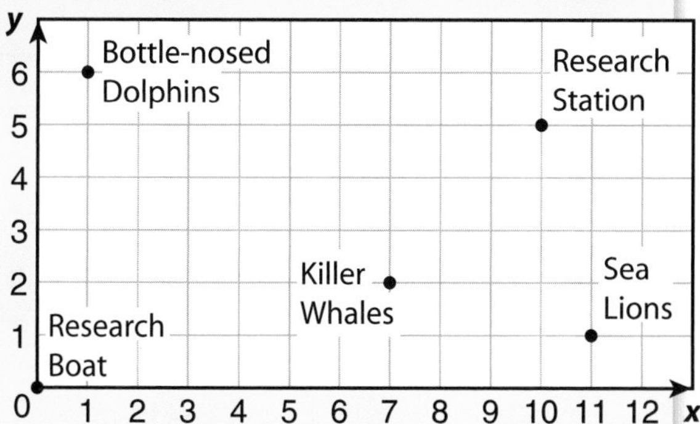

Lengths of Horizontal and Vertical Line Segments

Objective Use coordinates to find lengths of horizontal and vertical line segments.

CA Standards
KEY MG 2.2 Understand that the length of a horizontal line segment equals the difference of the x-coordinates.

KEY MG 2.3 Understand that the length of a vertical line segment equals the difference of the y-coordinates.

Also MG 2.0, MR 1.0, MR 1.1, MR 1.2, MR 2.0, MR 2.2, MR 2.3, MR 2.4

Vocabulary

horizontal line segment

vertical line segment

Materials
- Learning Tool 34 (Coordinate Plane)
- straightedge

Learn by Example

In this lesson, you will learn how to find the lengths of horizontal and vertical line segments using coordinates.

Diane plotted the points *A* (1, 2) and *B* (7, 2). Then she drew a **horizontal line segment** to connect the points. Carmen plotted the points *C* (5, 3) and *D* (5, 8). She connected these points with a **vertical line segment**. How many units long is each line segment?

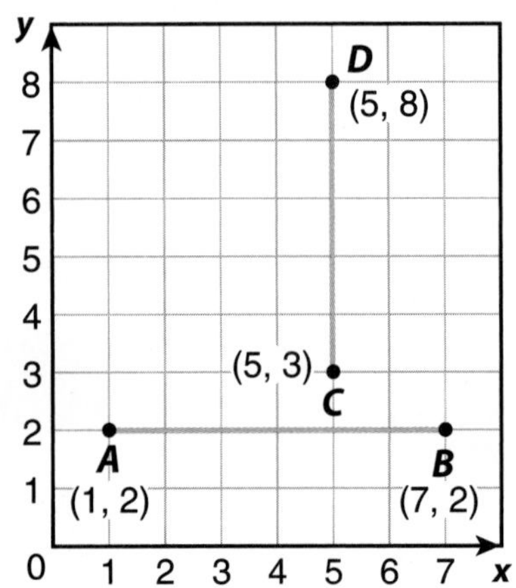

To find the length, you can count units. Another way is to find the difference between coordinates.

Find Lengths of Horizontal Segments

Find the difference between the x-coordinates. Subtract the smaller from the larger.

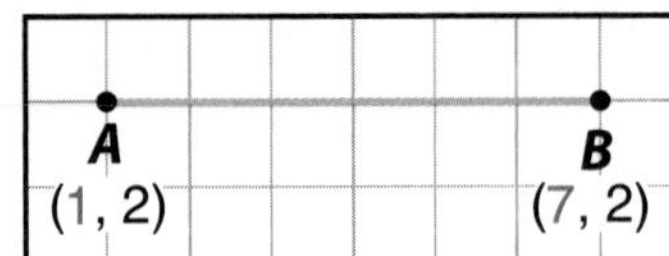

$7 - 1 = 6$

Find Lengths of Vertical Segments

Find the difference between the y-coordinates. Subtract the smaller from the larger.

$8 - 3 = 5$

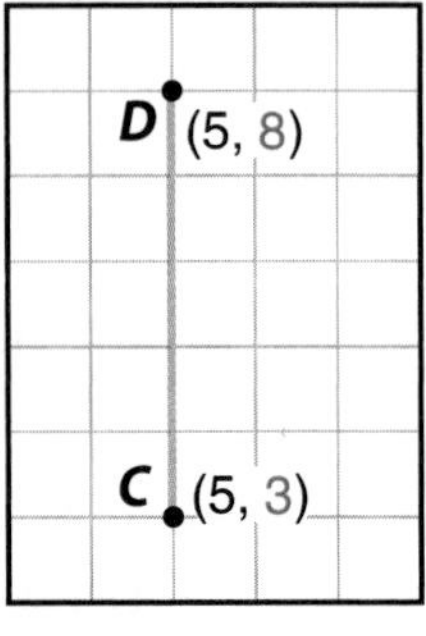

Check by counting the units on the grid.

Solution: The line segment connecting *A* and *B* is 6 units long. The line segment connecting *C* and *D* is 5 units long.

Guided Practice

Subtract to find the length of the line segment that connects the pair of points. Graph the points to check your answer.

1. (6, 2) (6, 10) **2.** (5, 3) (9, 3) **3.** (1, 8) (1, 6) **4.** (2, 4) (2, 7)

- Is the line segment horizontal or vertical?
- Should I subtract *x*-coordinates or *y*-coordinates?

Math Talk If you connect the points named by (2, 3) and (2, 8) with a line segment, will the line segment be horizontal or vertical? How can you tell without plotting the points?

Practice and Problem Solving

Subtract to find the length of the line segment that connects the pair of points. Graph the points to check your answer.

5. (2, 4) (2, 9) **6.** (3, 5) (10, 5) **7.** (4, 0) (4, 2) **8.** (4, 6) (8, 6)

9. (6, 0) (9, 0) **10.** (2, 1) (2, 7) **11.** (6, 1) (1, 1) **12.** (8, 4) (8, 13)

Solve.

13. Represent Point *Q* is at (10, 2). Point *R* is at (10, 8). Write a number sentence to find the length of the line segment connecting *Q* and *R*.

14. Analyze The length of the line segment connecting *X* and *Y* is 5 units. If *X* is named by (3, 6), and *Y* is named by (3, ■), then what are the possible values for ■?

Spiral Review and Test Practice

Make a coordinate grid. Plot the point and label it. KEY MG 2.0 page 468

15. Tree (0, 4) **16.** Swings (1, 2) **17.** Slide (4, 3) **18.** Bench (5, 0)

Write the letter of the correct answer. KEY MG 2.2

19. Look at the graph. Point *A* is at (3, 2). Point *B* is at (7, 2). How can you find the number of units from Point *A* to Point *B*?

A Add: $3 + 2$ **C** Subtract: $7 - 3$

B Add: $7 + 3$ **D** Subtract: $7 - 2$

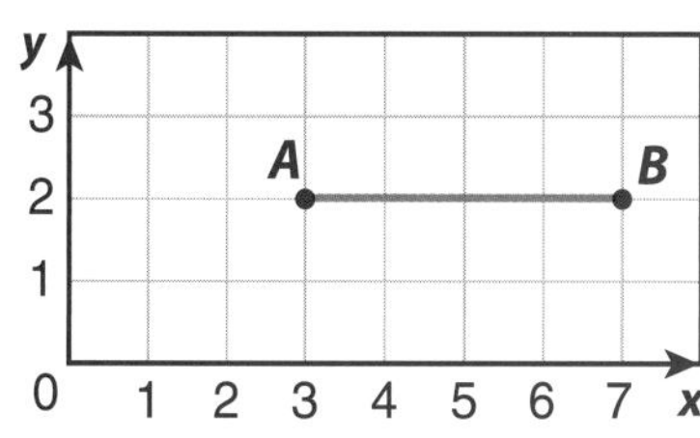

Extra Practice See page 501, Set B.

CA Standards

KEY MG 2.2 Understand that the length of a horizontal line segment equals the difference of the *x*-coordinates.

KEY MG 2.3 Understand that the length of a vertical line segment equals the difference of the *y*-coordinates.

Also MG 3.8, KEY NS 1.8, KEY MG 2.0, MR 3.2, MR 3.0, MR 1.2, MR 1.1, MR 2.2, MR 2.3, MR 2.4, MR 2.0, MR 1.0

Materials

- Learning Tool 34 (Coordinate Plane)
- straightedge

Line Segments in the Coordinate Grid

Objective Find lengths of horizontal and vertical line segments when one or more of the coordinates is a negative number.

Learn by Example

In this lesson, you will find the lengths of horizontal and vertical line segments when one or more of the coordinates is a negative number.

Percy plotted and connected the points *A* (1, ⁻3) and *B* (5, ⁻3) to make a horizontal line segment. Hoy plotted and connected the points *C* (⁻2, 1) and *D* (⁻2, 4) to make a vertical line segment. How many units long is each line segment?

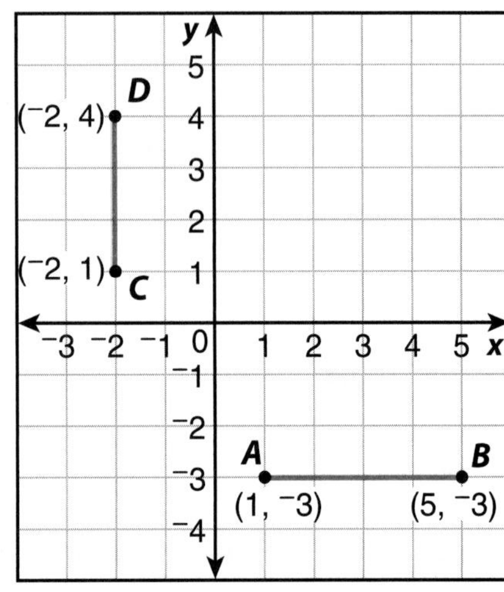

To find the length, you can count the units or you can find the difference between coordinates.

1 Find the length of the horizontal line segment connecting *A* and *B*.

Subtract the *x*-coordinates. Subtract the smaller from the larger.

$5 - 1 = 4$

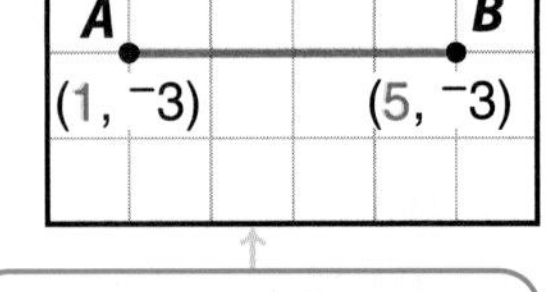

To check, count the units between *A* and *B*.

2 Find the length of the vertical line segment connecting *C* and *D*.

To check, count the units between *C* and *D*.

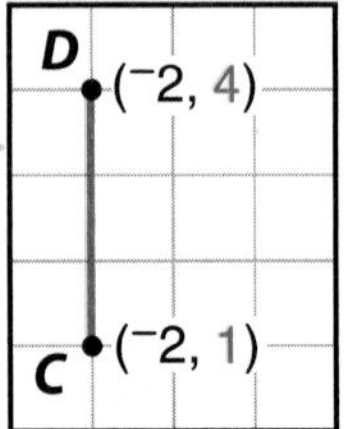

Subtract the *y*-coordinates.
Subtract the smaller from the larger.

$4 - 1 = 3$

Solution: The horizontal line segment connecting *A* and *B* is 4 units long. The vertical line segment connecting *C* and *D* is 3 units long.

Guided Practice

Subtract to find the length of the line segment that connects the pair of points. Graph the points to check your answer.

1. (⁻3, 5) (⁻3, 9) **2.** (2, ⁻2) (8, ⁻2) **3.** (⁻4, 2) (⁻4, 5)

4. (3, ⁻5) (6, ⁻5) **5.** (⁻2, 4) (⁻2, 9) **6.** (8, ⁻3) (6, ⁻3)

Ask Yourself

- Should I subtract *x*-coordinates or *y*-coordinates?
- Can I count the units to check my answer?

Guided Problem Solving

Use the questions to solve this problem.

7. Multistep Plot and connect the points *A* (⁻4, 2), *B* (2, 2), *C* (2, ⁻3), and *D* (⁻4, ⁻3) to form a rectangle. Then find the perimeter of the rectangle.

a. **Understand** How do you find the perimeter of a rectangle?

b. **Plan** What should you do first? Do you need to find the lengths of all four sides? Explain.

c. **Solve** Follow your plan. Then find the perimeter of the rectangle.

d. **Look Back** Count the units in the perimeter. Does your answer match?

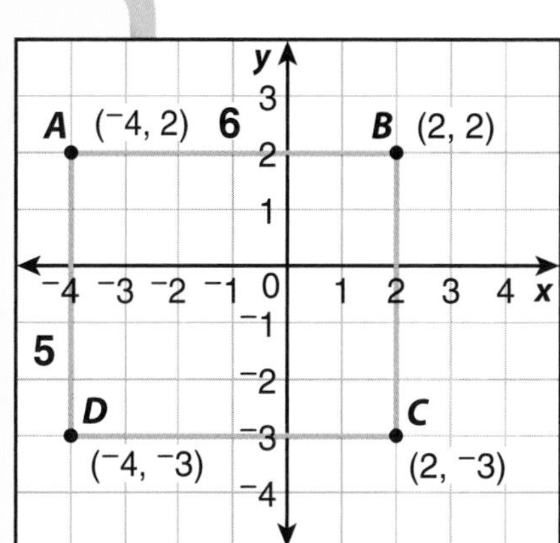

8. Analyze You can use a graph to help you subtract negative numbers. How could you use your graph from Problem 7 to find 2 − (⁻4)?

Think

2 − (⁻4) is the distance between 2 and ⁻4 on the number line.

Math Talk Describe two ways you could find the length of the line segment between (⁻3, 5) and (⁻3, 7).

Practice and Problem Solving

Subtract to find the length of the line segment that connects the pair of points. Graph the points to check your answer.

9. (2, ⁻7) (5, ⁻7) **10.** (⁻3, 9) (⁻3, 4) **11.** (0, 8) (0, 6) **12.** (10, ⁻7) (3, ⁻7)

13. (3, ⁻9) (8, ⁻9) **14.** (2, ⁻7) (9, ⁻7) **15.** (⁻6, 7) (⁻6, 1) **16.** (5, ⁻4) (9, ⁻4)

Solve.

17. **Challenge** The length of a line segment connecting X and Y is 3 units. Point X is $(^{-}4, 5)$. What are 4 possible ordered pairs for Y?

Use the graph to solve.

18. Mr. Lieber's class recorded the growth of wheatgrass in inches.
    a. What do the numbers on the x-axis represent?
    b. Why are there no line segments to the left of the y-axis?

19. What does the point (5, 4) mean?

20. What point names the length of the roots on Day 5?

21. What was the total length of the sprout, including its roots, measured on Day 5?

Grass

- Grasses and other plants are a primary source of energy in the food chain.
- Some people use wheatgrass juice in drinks!

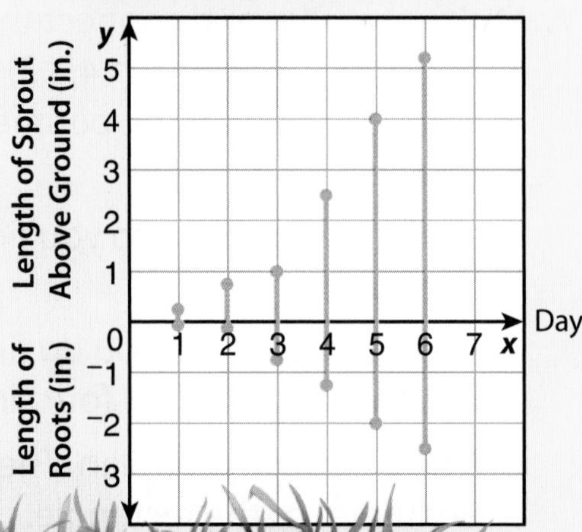

Science LS 2.a

Spiral Review and Test Practice

Compare. Use <, >, or = for the ⬭. You may use a number line to help. KEY NS 1.9 pages 394, 398, 400

22. $\frac{2}{3}$ ⬭ $\frac{5}{6}$

23. $\frac{1}{5}$ ⬭ $\frac{2}{10}$

24. $1\frac{3}{4}$ ⬭ $1\frac{2}{12}$

25. $4\frac{5}{8}$ ⬭ $4\frac{3}{4}$

Write the letter of the correct answer. KEY MG 2.3

26. What is the length of the line segment?

A 5 units **C** 4 units

B 2 units **D** 6 units

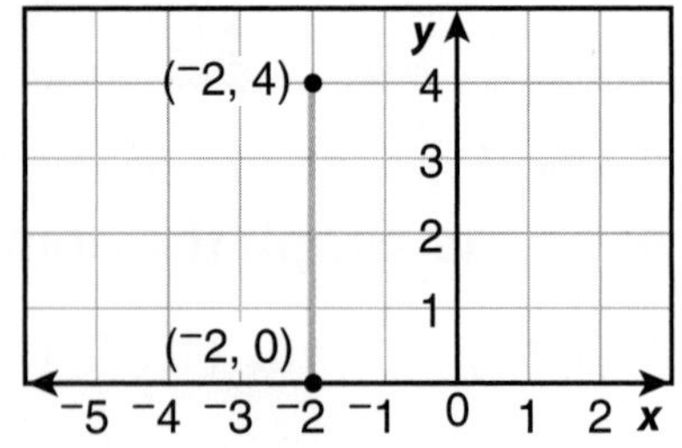

Extra Practice See page 501, Set C.

Math Works! Archaeologist

Search for Artifacts

Saria is an archaeologist. She studies the people and cultures of the past by examining artifacts found in the ground. Before Saria moves the artifacts, she uses stakes and string to build a coordinate grid over the ground. This helps her to identify and record the location of each artifact she finds.

Below is a coordinate grid that shows where some artifacts were found on the surface of an excavation site.

Solve. Use the grid for Problems 1–5.

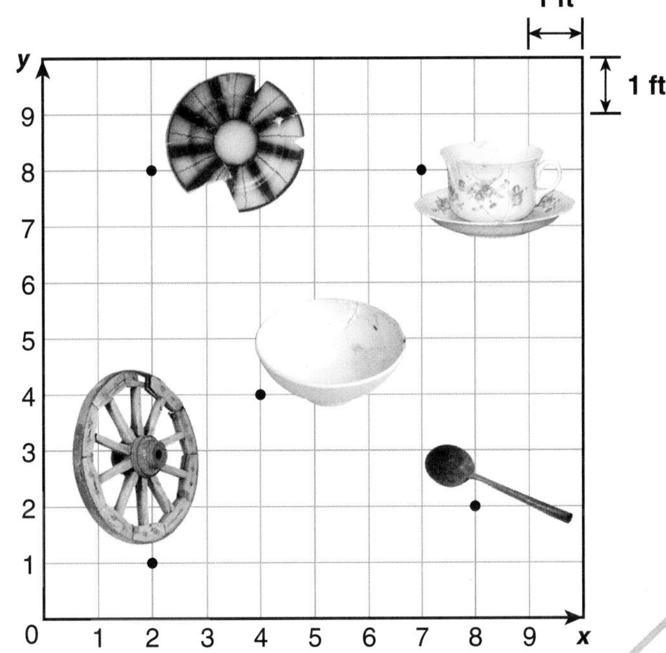

1. What artifact did she find at (8, 2)?
2. What artifact did she find at (4, 4)?
3. Write the coordinates where she found the wheel.
4. Which two artifacts lie on the same horizontal line? What is the length of the line segment if the two artifacts are the endpoints?
5. Which two artifacts lie on the same vertical line? What is the length of the line segment if the two artifacts are the endpoints?

CA Standards
KEY MG 2.0, KEY MG 2.2, KEY MG 2.3

LESSON 5
Field Trip...
Sonoma County, CA
CA Standards
MR 1.0, MR 1.1,
MR 2.0, KEY NS 1.2,
KEY MG 2.0, KEY MG 2.1,
KEY AF 1.5

Problem Solving

Objective Use skills and strategies to solve word problems.

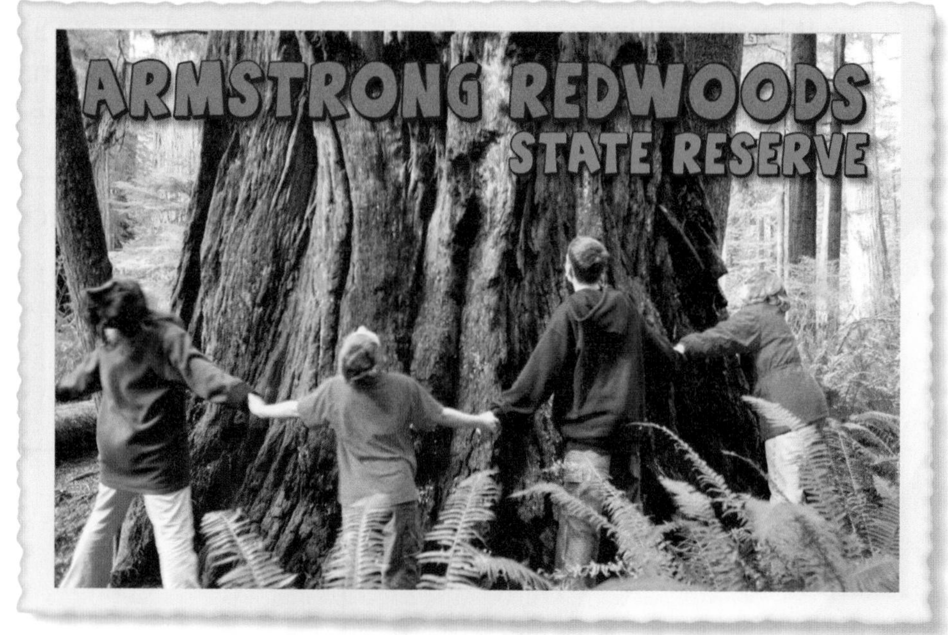

In the reserve, you can walk among the tallest living things on our planet.

The Armstrong Redwoods State Reserve is a grove of majestic coast redwoods. The tallest redwood in the reserve is 310 feet tall, longer than a football field. The oldest, the Colonel Armstrong tree, is 1,400 years old.

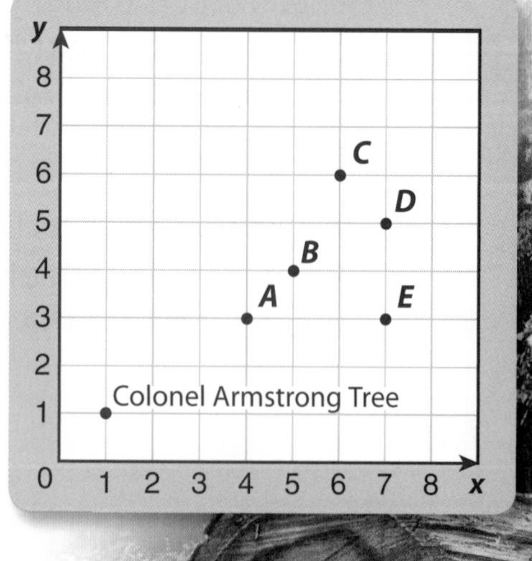

Solve. Use the map to solve Problems 1 and 2. Tell which strategy or method you used.

1. Trinh is standing at the Colonel Armstrong Tree. What ordered pair names this location?

2. Trinh is looking for Icicle Tree. If he walks in a straight line that passes through a point at (3, 3) he will reach this tree. Which point on the grid must be Icicle Tree? Use a function table and rule to support your answer.

3. The oldest known living tree is the Methuselah tree, a bristlecone pine estimated to be 4,838 years old. The oldest tree ever known was the Prometheus tree, a bristlecone pine 5,100 years old. Use comparison symbols to order the ages of the Prometheus, Methuselah, and Colonel Armstrong trees.

Problem Solving on Tests

Select a Strategy
- Write an Equation
- Make an Organized List
- Choose the Operation
- Draw a Picture
- Estimate

1. Caitlin drew this line segment on a grid. What is the length of the line segment?

A 0 units

B 2 units

C 4 units

D 8 units

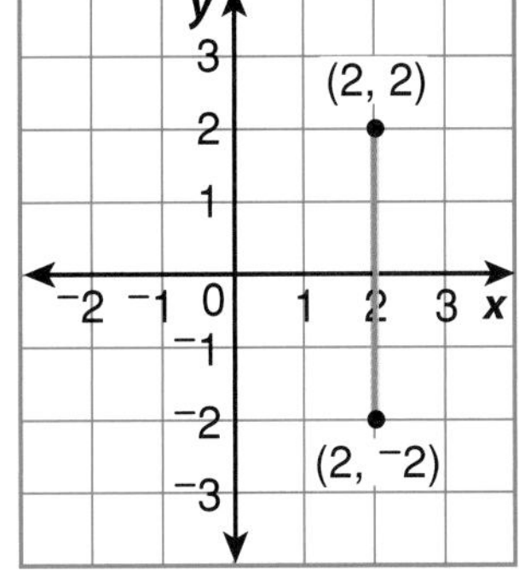

KEY MG 2.3 page 494

2. Kelly and James are playing a number game. James asks Kelly to name the next prime number greater than 47. Which number is the correct answer?

A 49 **C** 53

B 51 **D** 55

KEY NS 4.2 page 306

3. Lucy went on a 10-kilometer hike. There are 1,000 meters in 1 kilometer. What is the distance of Lucy's hike in meters?

A 100 m

B 900 m

C 1,010 m

D 10,000 m

KEY NS 3.0 page 334

4. Fourth grade students are having a long-jump contest. The *M* on the number line shows the number of yards Michelle jumped. What number is best represented by point *M* on this number line?

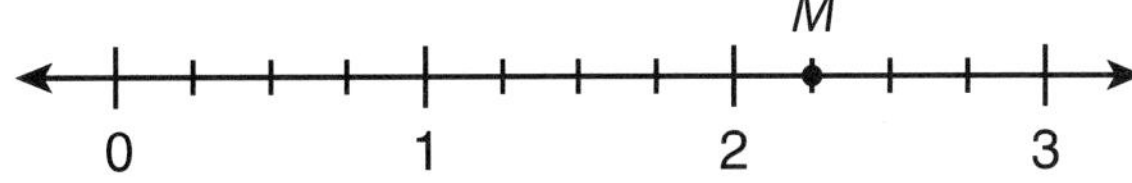

A $1\frac{1}{4}$ **B** $1\frac{3}{4}$ **C** $2\frac{1}{4}$ **D** $2\frac{1}{5}$

KEY NS 1.9 page 400

5. Paul drove 8.5 miles to the beach. What mixed number means the same as 8.5?

A $8\frac{5}{100}$ **C** $8\frac{1}{2}$

B $8\frac{1}{4}$ **D** $8\frac{3}{4}$

Test Tip
Write each mixed number as a decimal and compare.

NS 1.6 page 420

6. Tickets to a theme park cost $5. If 4,878 people visit the theme park, what is the total amount spent on tickets?

A $4,390 **C** $24,040

B $20,390 **D** $24,390

KEY NS 3.0 page 220

Education Place
Visit www.eduplace.com/camap/ for **Test-Taking Tips** and **Extra Practice.**

Reading & Writing Math

Vocabulary

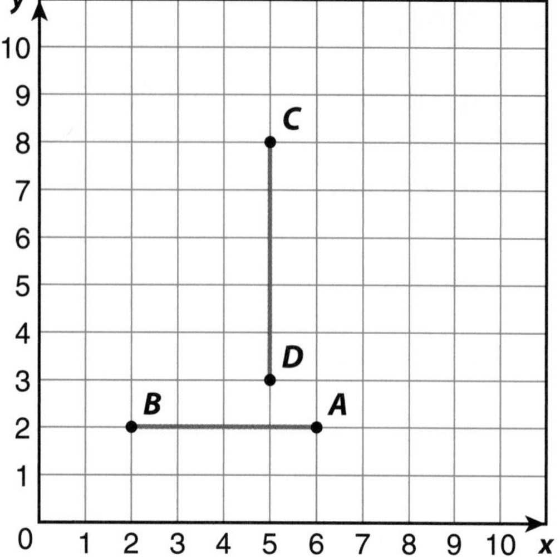

To find the length of a **horizontal line segment** on a **coordinate grid**, find the difference between the ***x*-coordinates**. To find the length of a **vertical line segment**, find the difference between the ***y*-coordinates**.

Use the coordinate grid to answer the questions.

1. What is the length of the line segment connecting *A* and *B*?
2. What is the length of the line segment connecting *C* and *D*?

Graph each pair of points. Then find the length of the line segment that connects the points.

3. (2, 5) (10, 5)
4. (⁻7, 8) (⁻7, 6)
5. (10, 3) (6, 3)
6. (1, ⁻4) (1, ⁻7)
7. Which line segments are vertical?
8. Which line segments are horizontal?

Writing If you connect the points (2, 3) and (2, 8) with a line segment, will the line segment be vertical or horizontal? How do you know?

Reading Look for this book in your library.
A Fly on the Ceiling, by Julie Glass

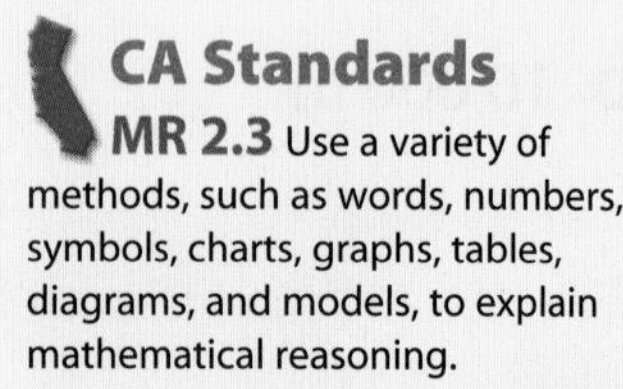

CA Standards
MR 2.3 Use a variety of methods, such as words, numbers, symbols, charts, graphs, tables, diagrams, and models, to explain mathematical reasoning.

Also KEY MG 2.2, KEY MG 2.3

Standards-Based Extra Practice

Set A

KEY MG 2.0, KEY NS 1.8 page 488

Write the coordinates of the points indicated.

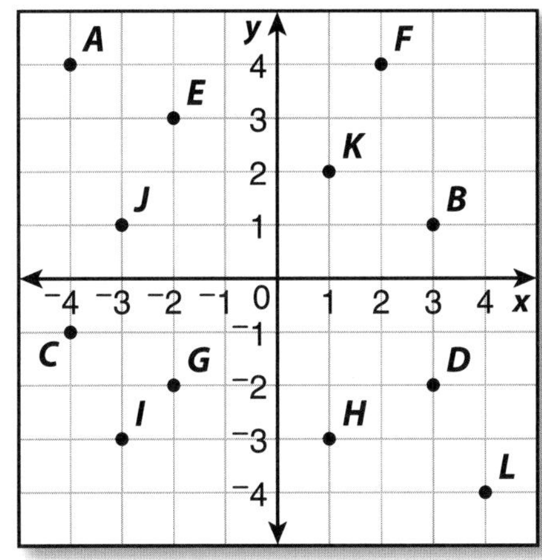

1. *A*
2. *B*
3. *C*
4. *D*
5. *E*
6. *F*
7. *G*
8. *H*
9. *I*
10. *J*
11. *K*
12. *L*

13. **Explain** Maya says a point is in the bottom left section of the coordinate plane if the numbers in an ordered pair are both negative. Is she correct? Explain.

Set B

KEY MG 2.2, KEY MG 2.3 page 492

Subtract to find the length of the line segment that connects the pair of points. Graph the points to check your answer.

1. (5, 2) (5, 10)
2. (6, 3) (10, 3)
3. (1, 8) (1, 1)
4. **Represent** Point *H* is at (9, 5). Point *L* is at (3, 5). Write a number sentence to find the length of the line segment connecting *H* and *L*.

Set C

KEY MG 2.2, KEY MG 2.3, MG 1.0 page 494

The corners of a rectangle are given as ordered pairs. Find the perimeter of the rectangle.

1. (⁻2, 2), (2, 2), (⁻2, ⁻1), (2, ⁻1)
2. (⁻4, ⁻4), (⁻4, ⁻2), (3, ⁻4), (3, ⁻2)
3. **Analyze** Ricardo is planting a garden. The coordinates of his garden are (⁻3, 3), (4, 3), (⁻3, 0), and (4, 0). What are the length and width of Ricardo's garden?

Education Place
Visit www.eduplace.com/camap/ for more **Extra Practice.**

Chapter Review/Test

Vocabulary and Concepts

KEY MG 2.0, KEY MG 2.2, KEY MG 2.3, MR 2.3

Write the best term to complete the sentence.

1. A coordinate grid that shows both positive and negative numbers is sometimes called a ______.

2. The ______-coordinate in a coordinate pair tells you how far up or down from the *x*-axis you move.

3. To find the length of a horizontal line segment between two points, you can subtract the ______-coordinates.

Skills

KEY MG 2.1, KEY MG 2.2, KEY MG 2.3, KEY NS 1.8

Make a grid. Number each axis $^{-}7$ to 7. Find, mark, and label the following points.

4. *A* (2, 1)
5. *K* ($^{-}1$, $^{-}1$)
6. *F* (3, $^{-}2$)
7. *L* (2, $^{-}6$)
8. *D* (4, 3)
9. *G* ($^{-}4$, 1)
10. *H* ($^{-}3$, 2)
11. *I* (7, $^{-}3$)

Subtract to find the length of the line segment that connects the pair of points.

12. (2, 4) (2, 10)
13. (1, 1) (7, 1)
14. ($^{-}2$, 4) ($^{-}2$, 8)
15. (10, $^{-}2$) (0, $^{-}2$)
16. ($^{-}3$, 2) ($^{-}3$, $^{-}4$)
17. ($^{-}4$, 4) ($^{-}4$, $^{-}1$)
18. (1, $^{-}2$) (3, $^{-}2$)

Problem Solving and Reasoning

KEY MG 2.0, MG 1.0, MR 2.3

Solve.

19. Plot and connect the points *A* ($^{-}5$, $^{-}4$), *B* ($^{-}5$, $^{-}2$), *C* (2, $^{-}4$), and *D* (2, $^{-}2$) to form a rectangle. Find the perimeter of the rectangle.

20. Plot and connect the points *E* (5, 3), *F* (5, 6), *G* (9, 6), and *H* (9, 3) to form a rectangle. Count squares to find the area of the rectangle.

Writing Math How do you find the length of a rectangle if you are given the coordinates of the four corners?

Spiral Review and Test Practice

1. Which number is represented by n?

$9 \bullet n = 126$

A 135

B 12

C 14

D 117

Test Tip
Check your answer by substituting the number for the variable n.

KEY AF 2.0 page 176

2. Rhonda walked two kilometers. There are 1,000 meters in 1 kilometer. How many meters did she walk?

A 500 meters

B 1,000 meters

C 1,100 meters

D 2,000 meters

KEY NS 3.0 page 334

3. On the number line below, what number does Point M represent?

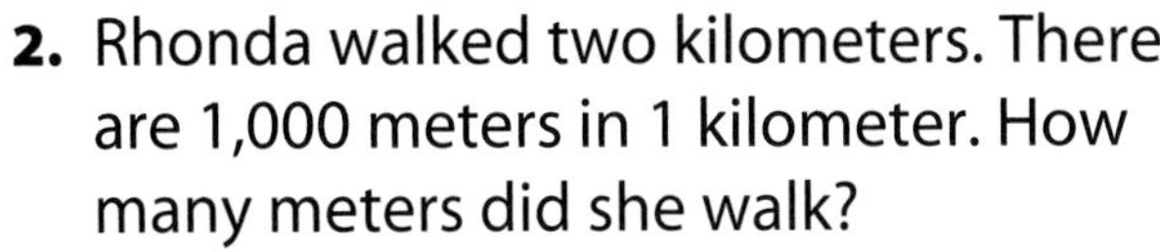

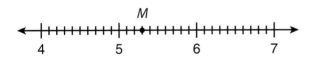

A 5.03

B 5.3

C 6.3

D 6.03

KEY NS 1.9 page 428

4. $63.6 - 4.15 =$

A 2.21

B 59.45

C 67.75

D 5,945

Test Tip
Align decimal points before subtracting.

NS 2.1 page 448

5. Rachel plotted 3 points on a grid. The 3 points were all on the same straight line. If she plots another point on the line, what could be its coordinates?

A (2, 6)

B (5, 2)

C (4, 8)

D (4, 10)

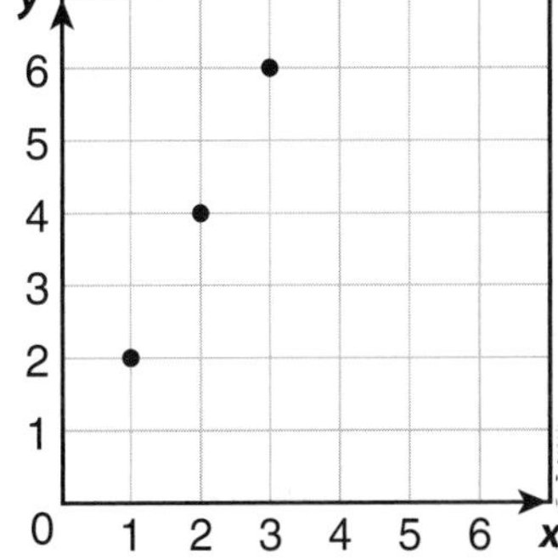

KEY MG 2.1 page 472

6. Tim wants to plot 4 points to represent the corners of a rectangle. He plotted the 3 points shown. What should the coordinates of the fourth point be?

A $(^-3, ^-2)$

B $(^-2, ^-3)$

C (3, 2)

D $(^-3, 1)$

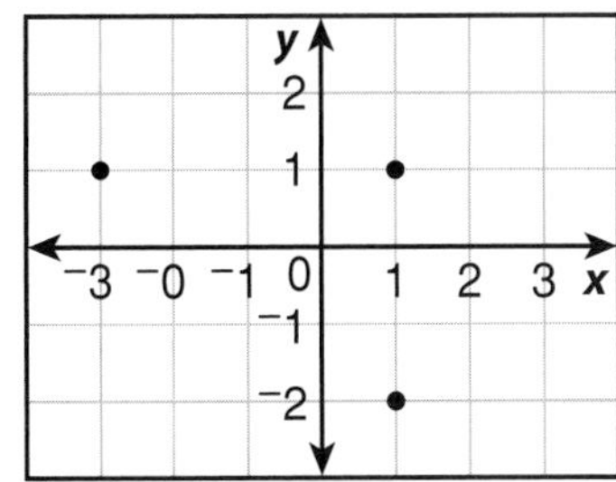

KEY MG 2.0 page 488

Education Place
Visit www.eduplace.com/camap/ for **Test-Taking Tips** and **Extra Practice.**

Unit 10 Test

Vocabulary and Concepts

KEY MG 2.0 Chapters 21–22

Complete each sentence with a vocabulary word from this unit.

1. Two numbers in the form (x, y) are called a(n) ______ pair.

2. In the equation of a ______ line, there is no value for y.

3. For the point named by (3, 4), the 3 represents the distance to the right along the ______-axis.

4. The vertical axis on a coordinate grid is the ______-axis.

Computation

KEY MG 2.0, KEY MG 2.2, KEY MG 2.3 Chapter 21, Lessons 1–2

Does the point named by each ordered pair score 1 point, 2 points, or no points?

5. (2, 5)

6. (2, 2)

7. (1, 3)

8. (3, 3)

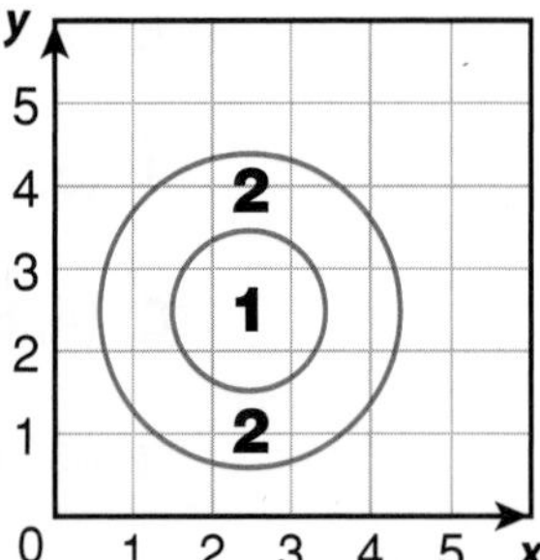

Find the length of the line segment that connects each pair of points. Is it horizontal or vertical? Chapter 22, Lessons 3–4

9. (3, 5) (5, 5)

10. (3, 4) (7, 4)

11. (0, 1), (0, 6)

12. (2, 4), (2, 9)

Problem Solving and Reasoning

KEY AF 1.5, KEY MG 2.0, KEY MG 2.1, KEY MG 2.2, KEY MG 2.3 Chapters 21–22

Solve.

13. The paints Lauren uses come 6 jars to a box. She wants to show this in a function table. Write the data for 1–6 boxes of paint as ordered pairs. What is the rule for this function?

14. John is drawing a rectangle that measures 5 units by 3 units. The first point he makes is at (2, 2). What could be the coordinates for the other three points?

15. Use grid paper to graph the points in the function table at the right. Then extend the graph to find the number of pencils in 6 packages.

Packages of Pencils $y = 6x$	
Number of Packages (x)	Number of Pencils (y)
1	6
2	12
3	18

Writing Math Is the point (3, 5) on a graph of the line $y = 2x + 2$? Explain your answer. (Hint: start with 3 as the x-value.)

Performance Assessment

The Scavenger Hunt

KEY NS 1.8, KEY MG 2.2, KEY MG 2.3, MR 2.2

Four friends are playing a scavenger hunt game. The person who finds the last item, a ketchup bottle located at the point E (4, 3), wins.

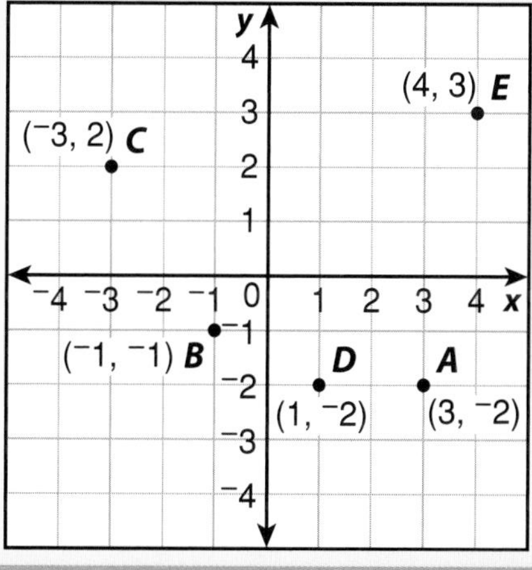

Task	Information You Need
Use the information above and to the right. Camilla needs to move 6 units to win. $(3, ^-2)$ to $(4, ^-2) = 1$ unit $(4, ^-2)$ to $(4, 3) = 5$ units How far do the other players need to move to win? Support your answer by listing the coordinates for each vertical and horizontal direction moved.	The players can move in horizontal or vertical directions only. Camilla is at $(3, ^-2)$. Yuki is at point B. Juan is at point C. Freddie is at $(1, ^-2)$

Greg Tang's **Go Fast, Go Far**

Unit 10 Mental Math Strategies

Divide by 4

Divide by 4? This way's shorter. Half of half, it's called a quarter!

I have a fast way to do 24 ÷ 4. Since dividing by 4 is the same as dividing by 2 twice, first I divide 24 by 2 to get 12, then I divide 12 by 2 to get 6. Dividing in two steps is easier than dividing in one!

1. 24 ÷ 4 → [12] → [6]
Divide 24 by 2. Divide by 2.

2. 64 ÷ 4 → ■ → ■
Divide 64 by 2. Divide by 2.

3. 48 ÷ 4 → ■ → ■
Divide 48 by 2. Divide by 2.

4. 32 ÷ 4 → ■ → ■
Divide 32 by 2. Divide by 2.

Way to go! Nice job!

5. 56 ÷ 4 → ■ → ■

6. 36 ÷ 4 → ■ → ■

7. 28 ÷ 4 → ■ → ■

8. 76 ÷ 4 → ■ → ■

Go Faster!

Take It Further!

Now try doing all the steps in your head!

9. 40 ÷ 4

10. 88 ÷ 4

11. 96 ÷ 4

12. 60 ÷ 4

Unit

Statistics and Probability

BIG IDEAS!

- You can use line plots, coordinate graphs, tables, and charts to display and organize data.
- *Mode* and *median* are two ways to describe what is typical in a set of data.
- You can describe the probability of each outcome of a situation.

Chapter 23
Data

Chapter 24
Probability

Songs and Games

Math Music Track 11: *Mean, Median, and Mode*
eGames at
www.eduplace.com/camap/

Math Readers

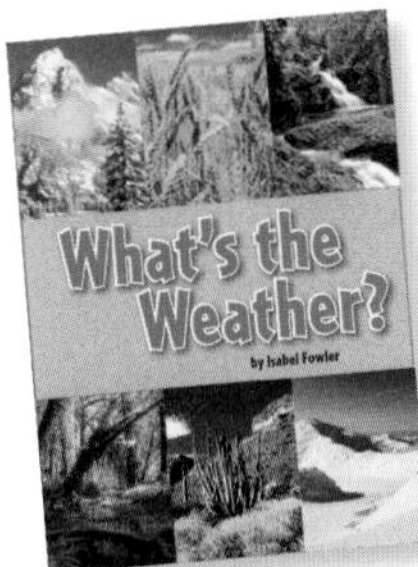

Get Ready **Game**

Igba-ita

Object of the Game Toss pennies and observe outcomes.

Materials
40 pennies

Number of Players 2

This game is based on an African game played with small shells called *cowries*.

How to Play

1. Each player receives 20 pennies—a substitute for cowries. Player 1 and Player 2 each toss four pennies.

2. Each player counts the number of heads he or she tossed. The player with the greater number of heads tossed takes all eight pennies. If both players tossed the same number of heads, they toss again.

3. Players continue until one of them has less than four pennies. The player with more pennies wins the game.

CA Standards
SDAP 2.2 Express outcomes of experimental probability situations verbally and numerically (e.g., 3 out of 4; $\frac{3}{4}$).

Education Place
Visit www.eduplace.com/camap/ for **Brain Teasers** and **eGames** to play.

Reading & Writing 

Reading When you read a story, you start at the top of the page, and you read to the bottom. When you read graphs or tables, you often have to look in more than one place and in more than one direction.

Sara surveyed fourth-graders about their favorite color. The results are shown in the bar graph below. Use the checklist on the right to preview the bar graph. How many students chose green?

Find:

- ✓ the title
- ✓ the headings
- ✓ the labels
- ✓ the number scale
- ✓ the bars

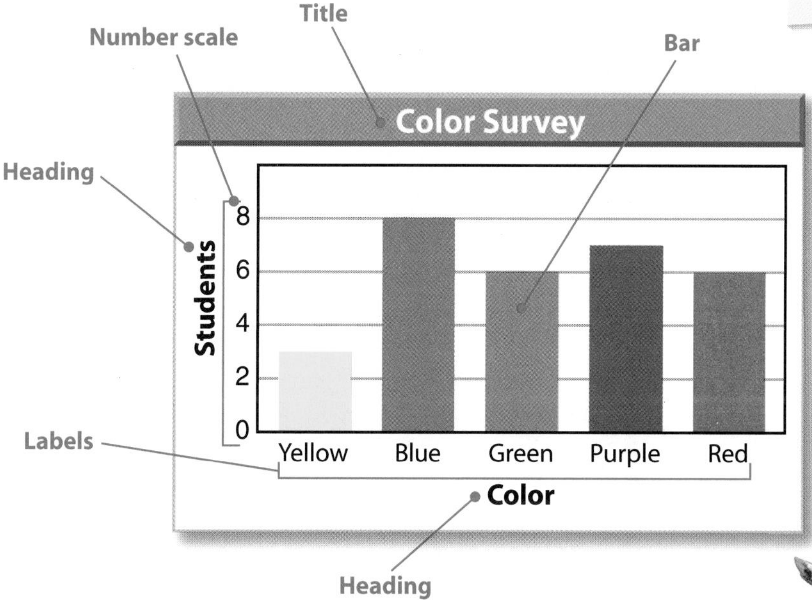

The green bar goes up to the 6 on the number scale. That means that 6 students chose green.

Writing Write four questions about the bar graph. Exchange questions with a classmate and answer them.

Chapter 23 Data

The Los Angeles, CA skyline during a thunderstorm

Check What You Know

Word Bank
- tally mark
- pattern
- bar graph

Vocabulary and Concepts GRADE 3 KEY SDAP 1.3, MR 2.3

Choose the best term to complete the sentence.

1. A mark on a tally chart that stands for 1 of something is a _____.
2. Identify the _____ to figure out the next number.

Skills KEY NS 3.2

Multiply or divide. pages 220, 266

3. 5 × 92
4. 6 × 92
5. 7 × 92
6. 208 ÷ 8
7. 182 ÷ 7
8. 156 ÷ 6

Problem Solving and Reasoning MR 1.1

Write the next two numbers in the pattern.

9. 1, 4, 7, 10, ___ , ___
10. 2, 8, 5, 11, 8, 14, ___ , ___

Vocabulary

Visualize It!

median
the middle number
The median of these data is 10.

5 6 7 7 9 10 11 13 14 15 19

mode
the number that occurs most often
The mode of these data is 7.

Language Tip

Math words that look similar in English and Spanish often have the same meaning.

English	Spanish
median	mediana

See **English-Spanish Glossary** pages 644–666.

Education Place Visit www.eduplace.com/camap/ for the **eGlossary** and **eGames**.

CA Standards MR 2.3 Use a variety of methods, such as words, numbers, symbols, charts, graphs, tables, diagrams, and models, to explain mathematical reasoning. **Also SDAP 1.2**

LESSON 1

Hands On
Collect and Organize Data

Objective Conduct a survey and organize and represent data.

CA Standards
SDAP 1.1 Formulate survey questions; systematically collect and represent data on a number line; and coordinate graphs, tables, and charts.

SDAP 1.0 Students organize, represent, and interpret numerical and categorical data and clearly communicate their findings.

Also MR 1.0, MR 1.1, MR 2.0, MR 2.3, MR 2.4

Vocabulary

survey

data

Explore

A **survey** is a way to collect information. The name for this kind of information is **data**. When you conduct a survey, you ask a question and record the responses.

Analyze the survey results in the tally chart.

- 30 people answered the survey question.
  $2 + 8 + 13 + 7 = 30$
- The answer *summer* was given most often. Thirteen students liked summer best.

What is Your Favorite Season?

Season	Tally	Number
Winter	||	2
Spring	卌 |||	8
Summer	卌 卌 |||	13
Fall	卌 ||	7

Question How can you conduct a survey and organize and represent the data collected?

Work with a partner. Conduct a survey and organize your data.

1 Write a question that has 3 or 4 possible answers. List the possible answers in a tally chart like the one shown.

Question:____________

Answer	Tally	Number

2 Survey 20 classmates. Allow each person to give only one answer. Make a tally mark for each answer. Then count the tally marks and write the number.

3 Analyze your data.

- Which answer was given most often? Least often?
- What did you learn about your classmates?

Extend

Use the tally chart for Problems 1–5.

What Is Your Favorite Summer Activity?		
Activity	**Tally**	**Number**
Bicycling	𝍸 𝍸 ||	12
Going to camp	|||	3
Playing video games	𝍸 |	6
Swimming	𝍸 𝍸 𝍸 |	16
Visiting grandparents	||||	4

1. What is the survey question?
2. Which answer was given the most often? Least often?
3. How many students answered the survey question?
4. What is the order of the activities from most to least popular?
5. **Right or Wrong?** Dora says that more than half the class likes swimming or visiting grandparents best. Is she right? Explain.

Use the list at the right to make a tally chart. Then solve Problems 6–9.

6. What are the possible answers on your tally chart?
7. How many students never bring their lunch to school?
8. How many students sometimes bring their lunch to school?
9. How many students sometimes or always bring their lunch to school?
10. Suppose a principal wants to know what color people prefer for the walls of the cafeteria. Does it make sense for the principal to survey only the fourth graders? Why or why not?

How Often Do You Bring Your Lunch to School?

Sandy	always
Lourdas	sometimes
Wilson	never
Paco	sometimes
Joy	sometimes
Rosalie	always
Bob	sometimes
Joanna	sometimes
José	always

Writing Math

Explain Would the question "What kind of food do you bring to school for lunch?" be a good survey question? Why or why not?

CA Standards
SDAP 1.1 Formulate survey questions; systematically collect and represent data on a number line; and coordinate graphs, tables, and charts.

SDAP 1.2 Identify the mode(s) for sets of categorical data and the mode(s), median, and any apparent outliers for numerical data sets.

Also SDAP 1.0, SDAP 1.3, MR 1.0, MR 1.1, MR 2.0, MR 2.3, MR 2.4, MR 2.6, MR 3.0, MR 3.2, MR 3.3

Vocabulary

line plot
median
mode
outlier

Median and Mode

Objective Find the median and mode of a set of data.

rain gauge

Learn by Example

Mr. Cooper recorded the total inches of rain his town received each month for seven months. The **line plot** shows the data he collected.

Monthly Rainfall (in inches) for 7 Months

0	1	2	3	4	5	6	7	8	9
X	X X		X	X X					X

There are different ways to describe the data presented in the line plot.

Different Ways to Describe Data

Way 1 When a set of numbers is ordered from least to greatest, the middle number is called the **median**.

0 1 1 3 4 4 9

The median is 3 inches.

If there are 2 middle numbers, the number halfway in between them is the median.

Way 2 The **mode** is the number that occurs most often in a data set. Some data sets do not have a mode. Others have one or more modes.

In the line plot, there are more Xs above both 1 and 4 than any other. The modes are 1 and 4 inches.

Way 3 An **outlier** is a number that is much larger or much smaller than the other data. Some data sets do not have outliers. Other data sets have one or more outliers.

For most months, the rainfall is 4 inches or less, so 9 inches is an outlier.

Guided Practice

Samuel recorded the total yearly snowfall in his city for seven years. Use the line plot for Problems 1–3.

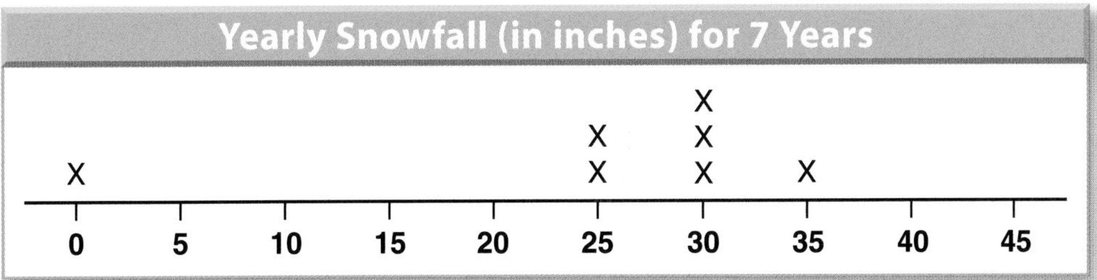

Ask Yourself

- Have I ordered the numbers?
- Is there any number that is much larger or much smaller than the other numbers?

1. Which number or numbers are the outliers? Explain.

2. Find the median and mode.

3. How would the median and mode change if the next 3 years each had snowfalls of 25 inches?

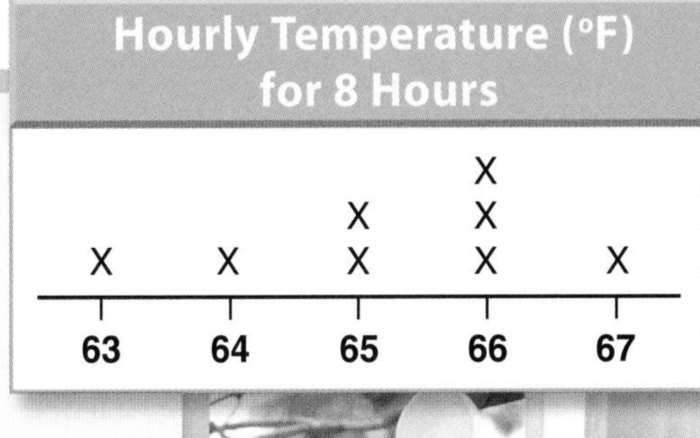

Guided Problem Solving

Use the questions to solve this problem.

4. Tracy measures the outdoor temperature every hour for eight hours and records her data in a line plot. What is the median temperature?
   a. **Understand** What do you need to find?
   b. **Plan** Order the numbers from least to greatest. Is there more than one middle number?
   c. **Solve** Write the two middle numbers. Tell what number is halfway between.
   d. **Look Back** Explain why the median is a number other than a number in the data set.

5. Look back at the line plot in Problem 4. How would the median change if there were another X above the 67?

Math Talk Look at the line plot you used in Problems 1–3. What does the outlier mean?

Practice and Problem Solving

Use the line plot for Problems 6–7.

6. Which number is an outlier?

7. Find the median and mode.

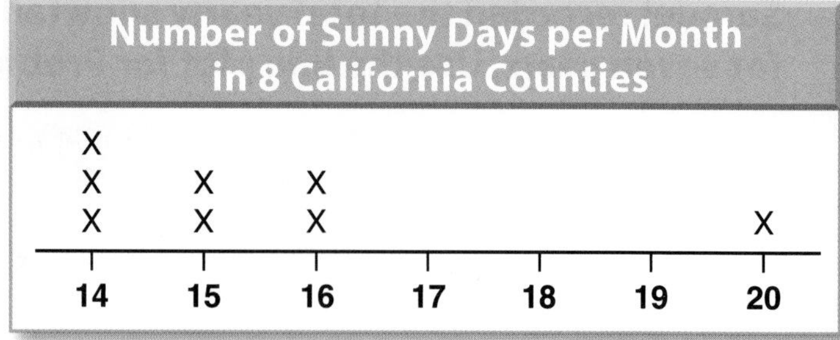

Order the data from least to greatest. Find the mode, median, and any outliers.

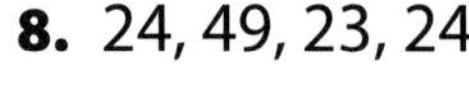

8. 24, 49, 23, 24

9. 5, 8, 18, 6, 9, 8

10. 17, 4, 19, 17, 18

Real World Data

Sometimes a mode is not a number. These dog tags are grouped by size. The size that occurs the most number of times is *medium*. So the mode for size is *medium*.

Solve. Use the data from the picture for Problems 11–12.

11. What is the mode for the dog tag shape—octagon, rectangle, or circle?

12. What is another way to group the tags? What is the mode for that grouping?

13. **Take a Survey** Think of a question that can be answered with a number. Ask 10 or more people. Record the data on a line plot. Tell the median and mode of your data.

Spiral Review and Test Practice

Order from least to greatest. KEY NS 1.2 pages 426, 428

14. 0.75 0.63 0.7

15. $1\frac{1}{2}$ $2\frac{1}{4}$ $2\frac{3}{4}$

16. $\frac{3}{4}$ 0.53 $1\frac{1}{2}$

Write the letter of the correct answer. SDAP 1.2

17. What is the mode of this set of numbers?

{2, 2, 2, 3, 5, 6, 6}

A 2 **B** 3 **C** 4 **D** 6

Extra Practice See page 527, Set A.

Practice **Game**

Middle and Most

Object of the Game Find the median and mode.

Materials
Learning Tool 35 (*Middle and Most* Game Cards)

Set Up
Use one set of game cards for each pair of students. Place the cards face down in a pile.

Number of Players 2

How to Play

1. Player 1 picks a card and finds the median of the data set.
2. Player 2 finds the mode of the data on the same card.
3. Players check each other's answers. Players earn one point for each correct answer.
4. The players take turns until all the cards are used. The player with the greater number of points wins.

CA Standards
SDAP 1.2 Identify the mode(s) for sets of categorical data and the mode(s), median, and any apparent outliers for numerical data sets.

Education Place
Visit www.eduplace.com/camap/ for **Brain Teasers** and **eGames** to play.

CA Standards
SDAP 1.3 Interpret one- and two-variable data graphs to answer questions about a situation.

SDAP 1.0 Students organize, represent, and interpret numerical and categorical data and clearly communicate their findings.

Also SDAP 1.1, MR 1.1, MR 2.0, MR 2.3, MR 2.4, MR 3.0, MR 3.1

Vocabulary

double bar graph

key

interval

Materials
- grid paper
- colored pencils

Hands On
Double Bar Graphs

Objective Make a double bar graph to compare two sets of data.

Explore

A **double bar graph** can be used to compare two sets of data.

The table shows the number of rainy days during May, June, and July in Cleveland, Ohio, and Raleigh, North Carolina.

Number of Rainy Days

	May	June	July
Cleveland, OH	13	11	10
Raleigh, NC	10	9	11

Question How can a double bar graph make it easy to compare data?

Work with a partner to make a double bar graph to compare the data.

1 Choose a title and labels for the graph. Then choose colors for the key. The **key** shows what each bar stands for.

Next, choose an interval. The difference between two numbers on the scale is the **interval**.

The interval is 2. Each bar can end on a line or halfway between lines.

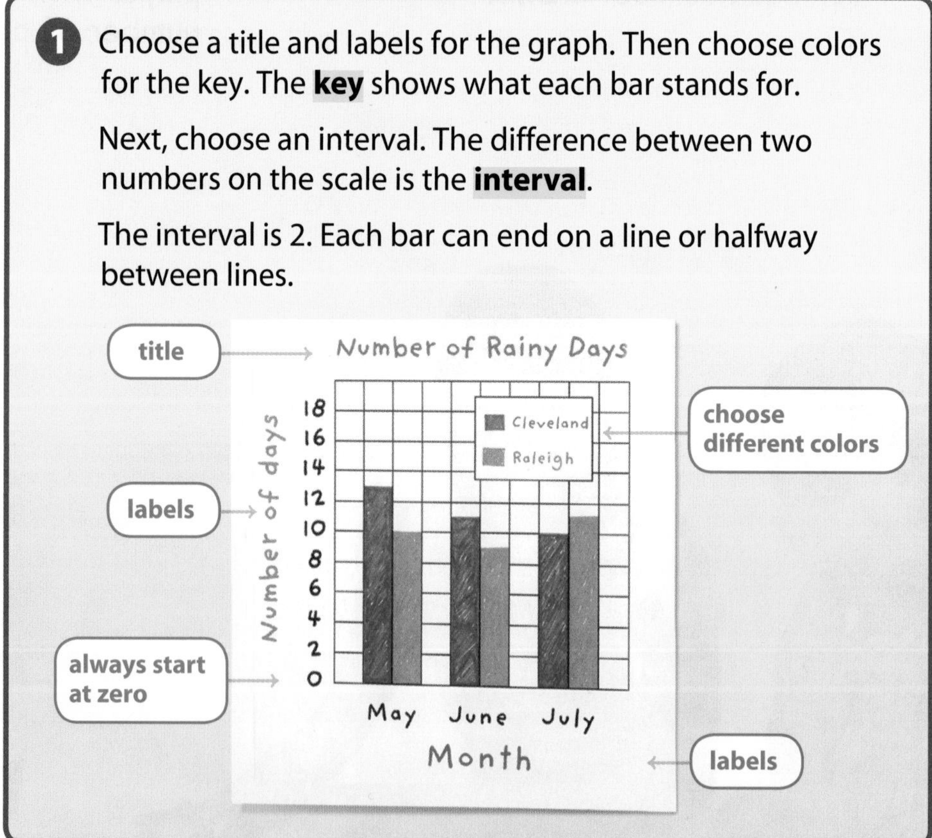

2 Use the data from the table to make the graph.

3 You can use the completed graph to compare data.

For example, the graph shows that in May, there were more rainy days in Cleveland than in Raleigh.

Extend

Solve. Use the table to make a double bar graph. Then use your graph for Problems 1–3.

Number of Rainy Days			
	August	**September**	**October**
Hilo, HI	26	23	24
Syracuse, NY	11	11	12

1. What interval did you choose for your graph? Explain.
2. In which month were there twice as many rainy days in Hilo as in Syracuse?
3. In which city was the number of rainy days the same in August as in September?
4. **Take a Survey** Choose four rainy-day activities. Ask the girls and boys in your class which activity they like best. Record the data in a table. Use the table to make a double bar graph.
5. How would the length of the bars change if a graph's interval changed from 2 to 4? Explain why.

A rainy day in San Francisco

Writing Math

Explain Is a double bar graph a good way to show how much a puppy grew from birth to age 6? Why or why not?

Read and Understand Line Graphs

CA Standards
SDAP 1.0 Students organize, represent, and interpret numerical and categorical data and clearly communicate their findings.

SDAP 1.3 Interpret one- and two-variable data graphs to answer questions about a situation.

Also MR 1.0, MR 1.1, MR 2.0, MR 2.3, MR 2.4, MR 3.0, MR 3.1, MR 3.2, MR 3.3

Vocabulary

line graph

Objective Use a line graph to solve problems.

Learn by Example

You can use a **line graph** to show how data change over time.

This line graph shows how much snow fell in 4 hours. How deep was the snow after 2 hours?

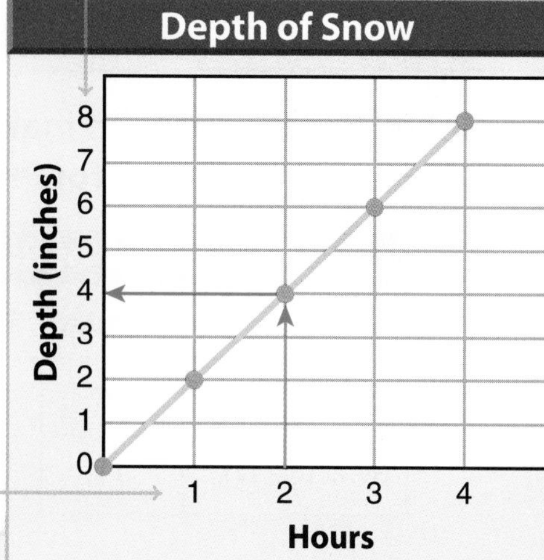

The horizontal axis represents time in hours.

Example 1

1. Find 2 on the horizontal axis labeled *Hours*.
2. Move up to the line.
3. Move left to the vertical axis labeled *Depth*. Read the depth in inches.

Solution: After 2 hours, the snow was 4 inches deep.

How deep was the snow after 3 hours?

Example 2

1. Find 3 on the horizontal axis labeled *Hours*.
2. Move up to the line.
3. Move left to the vertical axis labeled *Depth*. Read the depth in inches.

Solution: After 3 hours, the snow was 6 inches deep.

Guided Practice

The line graph shows how high a cottonwood tree has grown. Use the graph for Problems 1–3.

> **Ask Yourself**
> What do the numbers on the side and the bottom of the graph stand for?

1. What was the height of the cottonwood tree after 2 years? After 3 years?
2. According to the graph, how much does the tree grow each year?
3. From left to right the graph is going up. Could its direction ever change? Explain your reasoning.

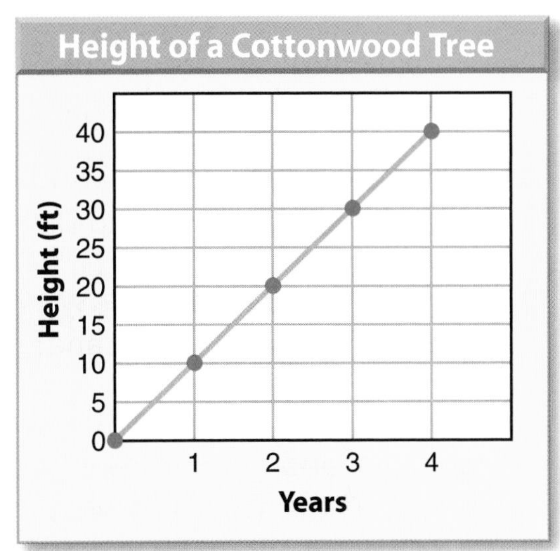

Math Talk Predict the height of the cottonwood tree after 5 years. Explain your prediction.

Practice and Problem Solving

The line graph shows the highest temperature for each day of the week. Use the graph for Problems 4–8.

4. What was the high temperature on Thursday?
5. Between which two days did the temperature drop the most?
6. What is the difference between the highest and lowest temperatures shown?
7. What day was the coldest? What was the high temperature that day?
8. **Predict** Based on the graph, would you expect the high temperature on the day after Sunday to be 0°F, 20°F, 50°F, or 90°F? Explain your answer.

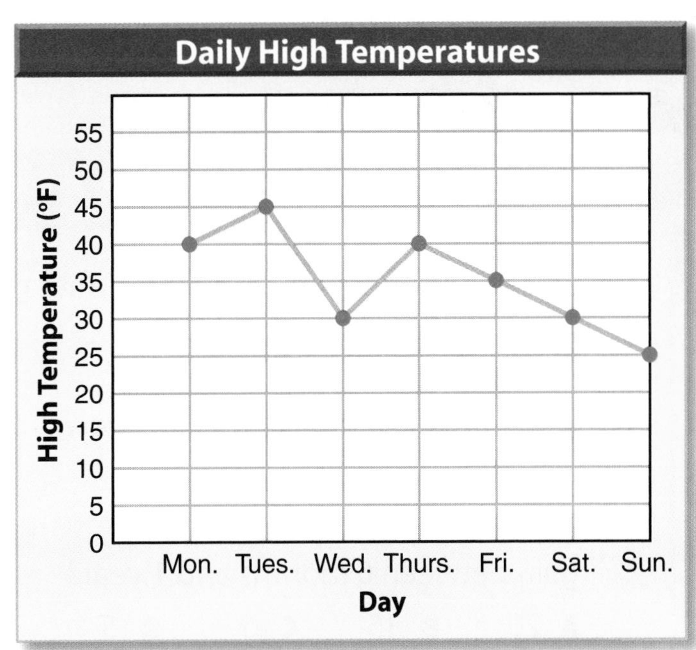

Science Link

Use the Fun Facts and line graph to solve Problems 9–13.

9. Around what day does the storm become a Category 1 hurricane?

10. What is Hurricane Betsy's highest wind speed? On what day does it occur?

11. What is the difference in wind speed between Day 5 and Day 7?

12. **Justify** Did Hurricane Betsy ever reach a Category 5 hurricane? Explain.

13. **Analyze** If you graphed the wind speed of another hurricane, what might be the same and what might be different about the two graphs?

Hurricane Betsy

- Meteorologists can use line graphs to track hurricane wind speeds.
- Hurricane winds can blow over trees and cause strong waves and flooding.
- Hurricanes are rated on a scale from 1–5. A Category 1 hurricane has winds 74–95 miles per hour. A Category 5 hurricane has winds greater than 155 miles per hour.

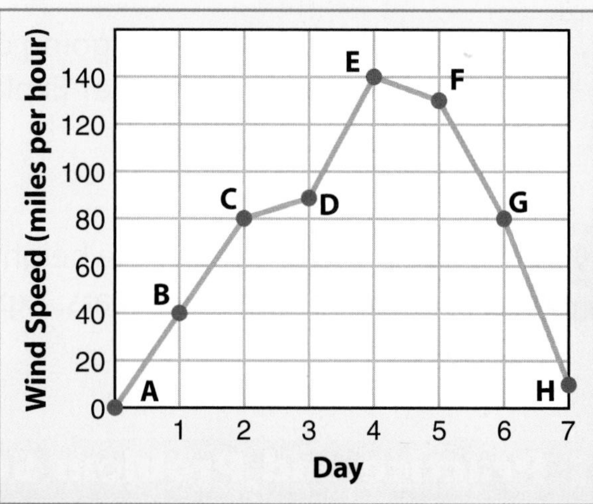

Science LS 5.a

Spiral Review and Test Practice

Graph the ordered pair on a coordinate grid. KEY MG 2.0 page 488

14. (3, 5) **15.** (⁻2, 1) **16.** (⁻4, 3) **17.** (⁻3, 4)

Write the letter of the correct answer.

SDAP 1.3

18. How many pounds did the puppy gain between 6 months and 1 year?

A 20 **B** 15 **C** 6 **D** 5

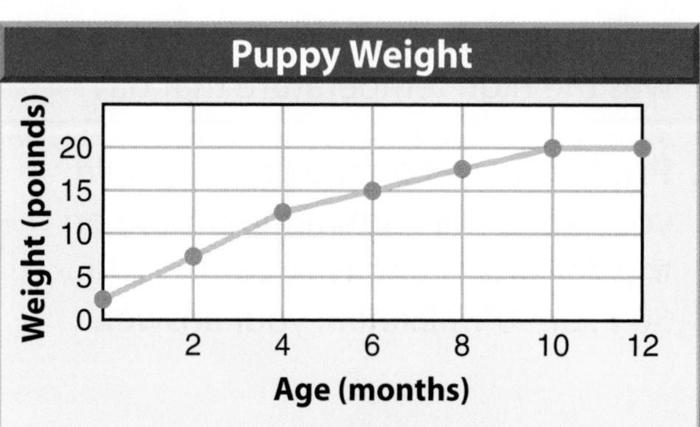

Extra Practice See page 527, Set B.

Key Standards Review

Need Help?
See Key Standards Handbook.

Subtract to find the length of the line segment that connects each pair of points. KEY MG 2.2

1. (5, $^-8$) (17, $^-8$)
2. (34, $^-3$) (6, $^-3$)
3. (1, $^-16$) (93, $^-16$)
4. (15, $^-12$) (23, $^-12$)
5. (41, $^-3$) (47, $^-3$)
6. (13, $^-26$) (21, $^-26$)

Challenge — Data

Rock Climb

Sometimes you can get information from a graph even though it does not have numbers or labels.

Last spring, Bill, Hannah, and their father visited Joshua Tree National Park in California. Bill kept a log of his rock climb and then graphed the data.

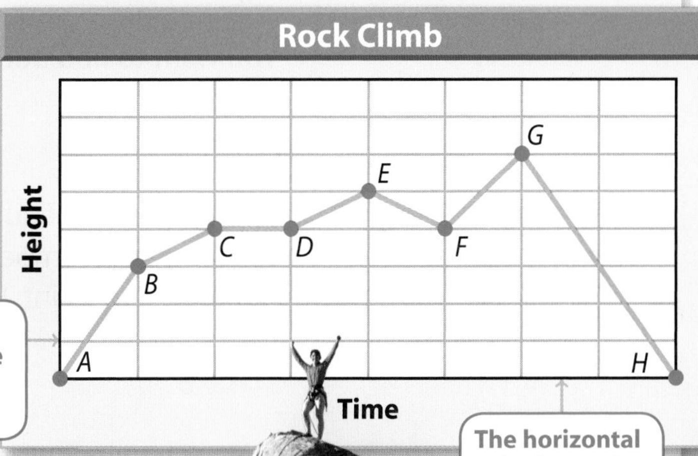

The vertical axis shows the height of the rock climb.

The horizontal axis shows the time spent climbing.

Use the graph to answer the questions. SDAP 1.3

1. Which points show when Bill stopped for lunch?
2. Did more time elapse between points A and C or between points C and F?
3. Explain what happened between points A and B. Tell how you know.
4. Between which two points did Bill climb the least distance?

Problem Solving Plan
Show Data in Different Ways

Objective Show data in different ways to solve problems.

CA Standards
MR 2.3 Use a variety of methods, such as words, numbers, symbols, charts, tables, graphs, diagrams, and models, to explain mathematical reasoning.

SDAP 1.0 Students organize, represent, and interpret numerical and categorical data and clearly communicate their findings.

Also SDAP 1.1, SDAP 1.2, SDAP 1.3, MR 1.0, MR 1.1, MR 2.0, MR 2.4, MR 3.0, MR 3.1, MR 3.2, MR 3.3

Learn by Example

You can show data in tables and graphs to solve problems.

The table shows the temperature at the same time at 8 different places on a mountain. How does the temperature change as you go up the mountain?

Height (ft)	700	3500	2900	3300	1800	3700	2100	2250
Temperature (°F)	44	26	32	29	39	23	38	38

A scatter plot can help you see the information and solve the problem.

UNDERSTAND

You want to find out how the temperature changes.

PLAN

Show the pairs of numbers in a scatter plot. Put height on the *x*-axis and temperature on the *y*-axis. Plot each pair of numbers as a point. Do not connect the points.

SOLVE

Plot each pair of numbers on the coordinate grid. For example, to plot 44°F at 700 feet, move horizontally to 700 and then vertically to 44.

The points look like a line sloping down from left to right. This tells you it is cooler as you go up the mountain.

Height and Temperature

LOOK BACK

What would the scatter plot look like if it got warmer as you went up the mountain?

Guided Problem Solving

Solve using the Ask Yourself questions.

1. New York had 18 tornadoes in 2003, 8 tornadoes in 2004, and 4 tornadoes in 2005. Idaho had 4 tornadoes in 2003, 5 tornadoes in 2004, and 6 tornadoes in 2005. Make a double bar graph to represent this information.

Ask Yourself

- What should the bars in my graph represent?
- What will my *x*-axis be? What will my *y*-axis be?

Math Talk Why wouldn't you use a scatter plot to represent the data in Problem 1?

Independent Problem Solving

Solve. Explain why your answer makes sense. Use the scatter plot for Problems 5 and 6.

2. Did New York always have more tornadoes than Idaho? Did you look back at the words in Problem 1 or at your double bar graph to answer the question?

3. In what year was the number of tornadoes in New York more than 4 times that of the number of tornadoes in Idaho?

4. What is the median of the number of tornadoes in Idaho from 2003 to 2005?

Temperature and Pool Attendance

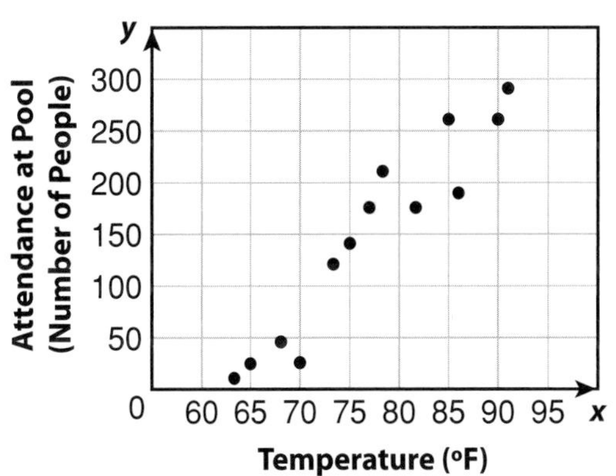

5. Pam recorded the temperature and number of people at a community pool every day for two weeks. She showed the data in the scatter plot at the right. What does the graph show about temperature and number of people at the pool?

6. **Challenge** If you drew a line through the points on the scatter plot, would the point (90, 50) be on your line?

7. **Create and Solve** Collect data from 5 of your classmates. Measure their heights and arm spans to the nearest inch. Make a graph to show the data you collected. What does your graph show?

Vocabulary

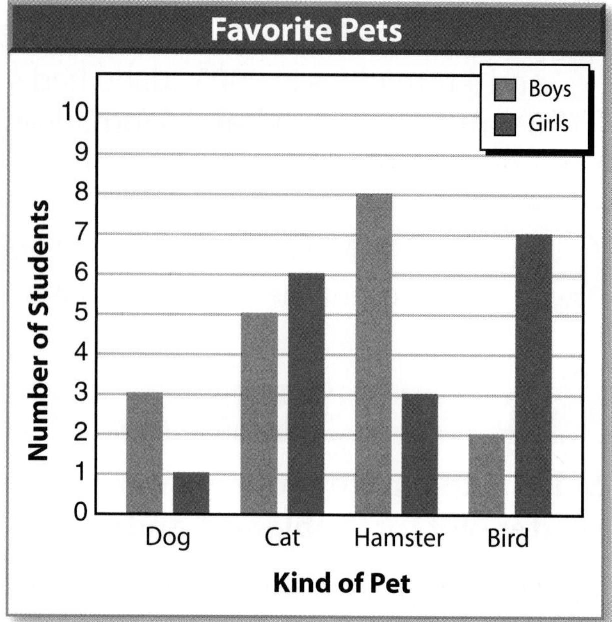

You can represent **data** in different ways. You can use tables, graphs, and charts.

When you collect information from two sets of data, a good way to show it is with a **double bar graph**.

Use the double bar graph to answer Questions 1–4.

1. Which pet is most popular with the boys?
2. Which pet is least popular with the girls?
3. How many more boys than girls chose hamsters?
4. How many girls chose a dog or a cat?

There are different ways to describe numbers in a data set.

For Questions 5–8, use the word box to help you find each value.

> The **median** is the number that is in the middle when the data is arranged in order from least to greatest.
>
> The **mode** is the number that occurs most often.
>
> An **outlier** is a number that is distant from the rest of the data.

5. 10, 0, 4, 2, 0
   The **mode** is ______.
6. 3, 6, 1, 18, 7
   The **median** is ______.
7. 10, 2, 19, 7, 5, 9, 7, 8, 9
   The **outlier** is ______.

Writing Create a data set in which the median and the mode of the data are the same number. What must be true about your data set?

Reading Look for this book in your library. *Tiger Math: Learning to Graph from a Baby Tiger,* by Ann Whitehead Nagda and Cindy Bickel

CA Standards
MR 2.3 Use a variety of methods, such as words, numbers, symbols, charts, graphs, tables, diagrams, and models, to explain mathematical reasoning.
Also SDAP 1.2, SDAP 1.3

Standards-Based Extra Practice

Set A
SDAP 1.2 page 514

Order the data from least to greatest. Find the mode, median and any outliers.

1. 40, 8, 12, 9, 8
2. 21, 29, 27, 25, 18, 3, 27
3. 2, 1, 3, 3, 5, 2, 1, 1
4. 16, 12, 18, 17, 19, 14
5. 1, 5, 4, 1, 5, 14, 2, 1
6. 8, 4, 9, 6
7. 11, 7, 88, 6, 3, 2
8. 50, 50, 50, 50
9. 20, 18, 23, 19
10. 164, 101, 111, 109, 109, 115
11. 8, 4, 2, 6
12. 11, 65, 23, 19, 23, 8
13. 400, 800, 600, 600
14. 800, 800, 800
15. 99, 77, 88, 99, 2, 77, 99
16. 78, 87, 78, 82, 788
17. **Explain** Why can an outlier never be equal to the median of a set of numbers?

Set B
SDAP 1.0, SDAP 1.3 page 520

The line graph shows the lowest temperature for each day of the week. Use the graph for Problems 1–4.

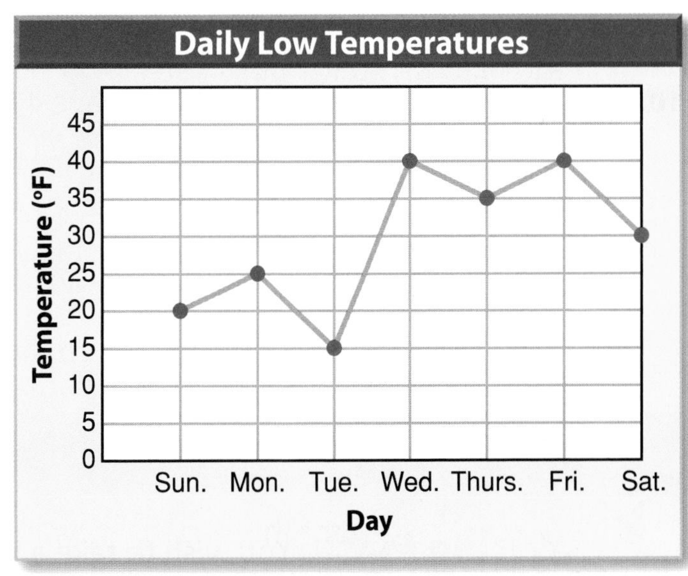

1. Which day was the coldest?
2. Between which two days did the temperature rise the most?
3. Which day had the same low temperature as Wednesday?
4. What was the low temperature on Thursday?

Education Place
Visit www.eduplace.com/camap/ for more **Extra Practice.**

Chapter Review/Test

Vocabulary and Concepts — SDAP 1.1, MR 2.3

Write the best term to complete the sentence.

1. A _______ can be used to compare two sets of data.

2. You can use a _______ to show how data change over time.

Skills — SDAP 1.2

Order the data from least to greatest. Find the mode and median and any outliers.

3. 2, 8, 6, 6
4. 14, 15, 14, 15, 15
5. 90, 32, 88, 87, 91, 87
6. 50, 45, 50
7. 49, 11, 39, 42, 49

Problem Solving and Reasoning — SDAP 1.0, SDAP 1.3, MR 2.3

Solve. Use the double bar graph.

8. Which city and which month had the fewest number of days of rain?

9. In what month was the number of rainy days in Lake Spaulding 4 times that of the number of rainy days in Anaheim?

10. In what month did Lake Spaulding have 4 more rainy days than Anaheim?

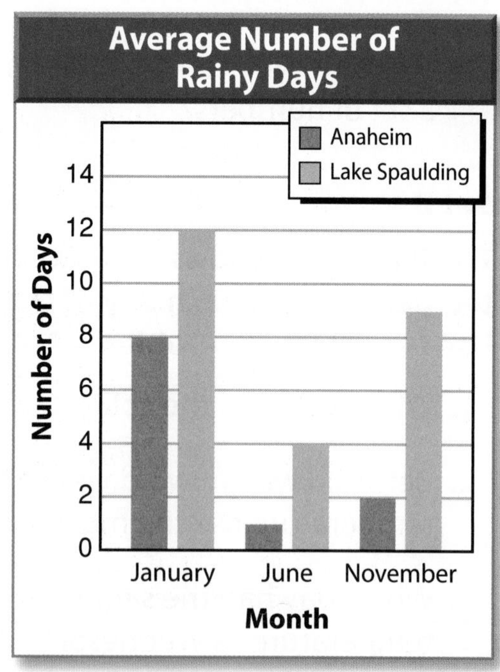

Writing Math You wish to take a survey to determine the favorite subject of students in your school. Would taking a survey in science club after school be a good choice? Explain.

Spiral Review and Test Practice

1. $27 + 8 = 27 + \square$

   A $4 + 2$

   B $4 \cdot 2$

   C $5 + 2$

   D $6 \cdot 2$

> **Test Tip**
> Substitute each expression into the equation to find which one makes the equation true.

KEY AF 2.1 page 102

2. Vicky rode a train 90 kilometers. There are 1,000 meters in 1 kilometer. How many meters did she ride the train?

   A 90 m

   B 9,000 m

   C 90,000 m

   D 900,000 m

KEY NS 3.3 page 334

3. What is the value of the expression $(15 \div 3) \times (9 - 4)$?

   A 0

   B 10

   C 25

   D 41

> **Test Tip**
> Remember to evaluate expressions inside parentheses first.

KEY AF 1.2 page 144

4. Which of the points below would be on the graph of the equation $y = 3x - 1$?

   A (1, 3)

   B (1, 4)

   C (2, 6)

   D (3, 8)

KEY MG 2.1 page 476

5. Look at the graph. Point *A* is at (2, 3). Point *B* is at (6, 3). How can you find the number of units from Point *A* to Point *B*?

   A Add: $2 + 3$

   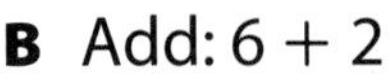
   B Add: $6 + 2$

   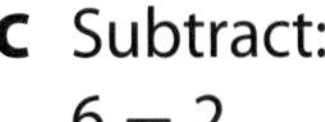
   C Subtract: $6 - 2$

   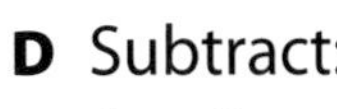
   D Subtract: $6 - 3$

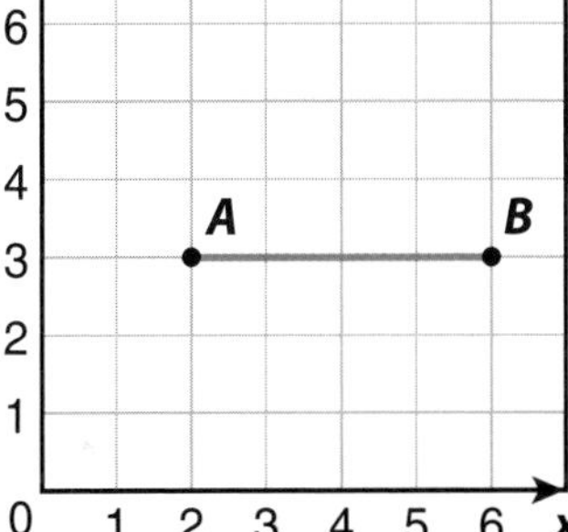

KEY MG 2.2 page 492

6. What is the mode of this set of data?

   {3, 3, 4, 5, 5, 5, 6}

   A 3

   B 4

   C 5

   D 6

SDAP 1.2 page 514

Education Place
Visit www.eduplace.com/camap/ for **Test-Taking Tips** and **Extra Practice.**

Probability

Check What You Know

Word Bank
equally likely
probability
predict

Vocabulary and Concepts GRADE 3 SDAP 1.0, MR 2.3

Choose the best term to complete the sentence.

1. The chance that an event will occur is its ______.
2. You can sometimes _____ outcomes of events.

Skills GRADE 3 NS 2.0

List all the pairs of positive whole numbers with the given sum.

3. 8
4. 10
5. 12
6. 7

Multiply.

7. $5 \times 3 \times 8$
8. $2 \times 6 \times 5$
9. $7 \times 2 \times 6$

Problem Solving and Reasoning GRADE 3 KEY SDAP 1.2

10. How many times would you predict a coin would land on *heads* if you tossed it 100 times? How many times would you predict it would land on tails?

Vocabulary

Visualize It!

You can use a **tree diagram** to show all the possible combinations of coats and shoes that Jackie can wear.

Jackie's Clothes	
Coats	**Shoes**
red coat	black boots
blue jacket	blue sneakers

red coat: black boots, blue sneakers

blue jacket: black boots, blue sneakers

There are 4 possible **combinations** that Jackie can wear.

Language Tip

Math words that look similar in English and Spanish often have the same meaning.

English	Spanish
combinations	**combinaciones**
diagram	**diagrama**

See **English-Spanish Glossary** pages 644–666.

Education Place Visit www.eduplace.com/camap/ for the **eGlossary** and **eGames**.

CA Standards MR 2.3 Use a variety of methods, such as words, numbers, symbols, charts, graphs, tables, diagrams, and models, to explain mathematical reasoning. **Also SDAP 2.1**

Hands On
Probability and Outcomes

Objective Explore probability and outcomes.

CA Standards
SDAP 2.0 Students make predictions for simple probability situations.
SDAP 2.2 Express outcomes of experimental probability situations verbally and numerically (e.g., 3 out of 4; $\frac{3}{4}$)
Also MR 1.1, MR 2.0, MR 2.3, MR 2.4

Vocabulary
- probability
- outcome
- certain
- likely
- unlikely
- impossible
- equally likely

Materials
- Learning Tool 36 (Spinners)
- markers or colored pencils

Explore

Probability is a mathematical way of measuring how likely it is that something will happen. An **outcome** is a result of a probability experiment.

Question How can you make spinners so that the outcomes of landing on red are different?

1. Use Learning Tool 36. Color Spinner 1 so that you are **certain** to land on red.

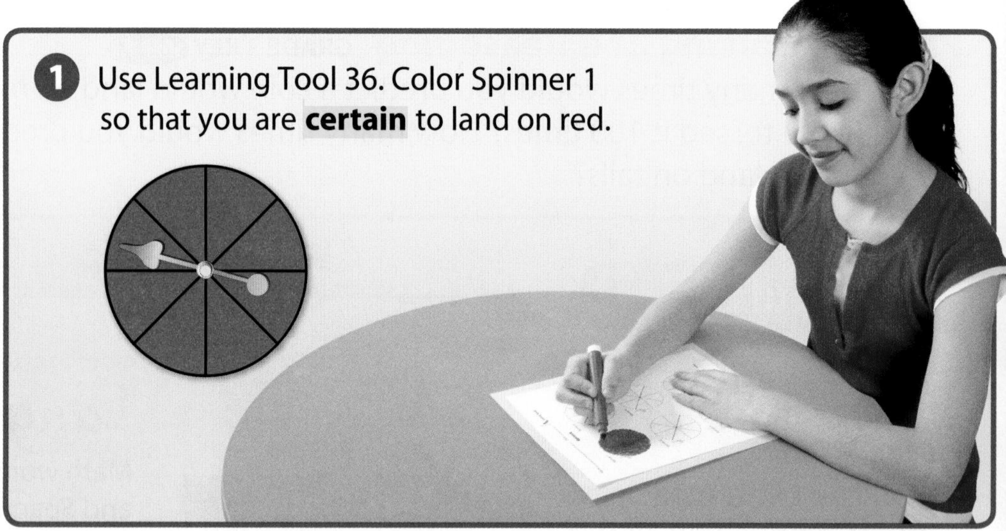

2. Color Spinner 2 so that landing on red is **likely**.

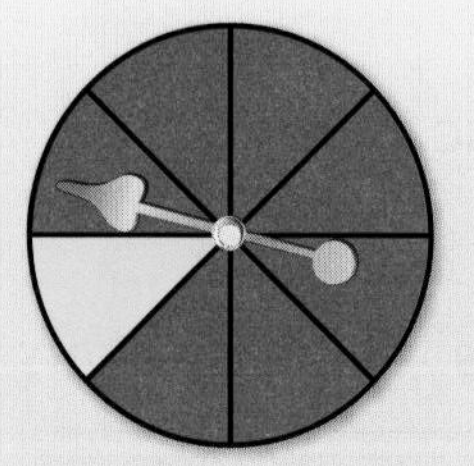

3. Color Spinner 3 so that landing on red is **unlikely**.

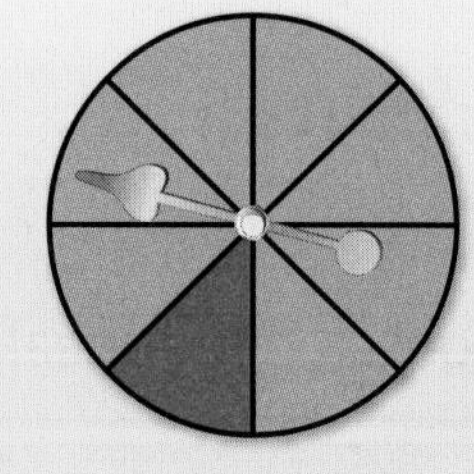

4. Color Spinner 4 so that landing on red is **impossible**.

5. Color Spinner 5 so that landing on red is as **equally likely** as landing on another color.

Extend

Look at the bag of marbles. Write *certain, likely, equally likely, unlikely,* or *impossible* to describe the outcomes of picking each color without looking.

1. blue

2. yellow

3. red

4. blue or red

Write *certain, likely, equally likely, unlikely,* or *impossible* to describe the outcome of landing on blue.

5. 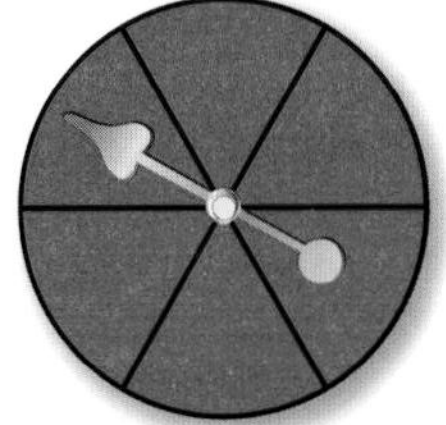

6. 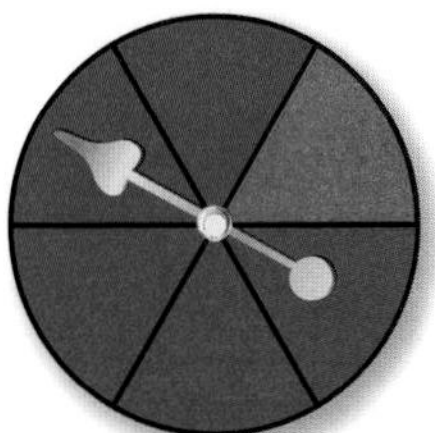

7. 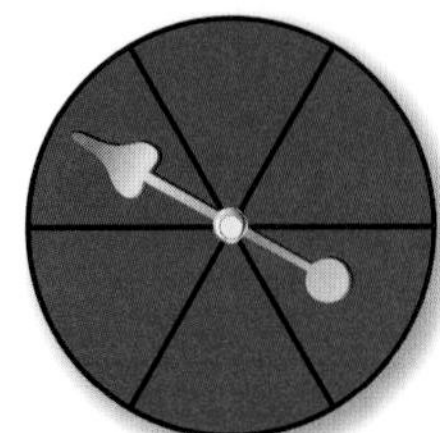

8. 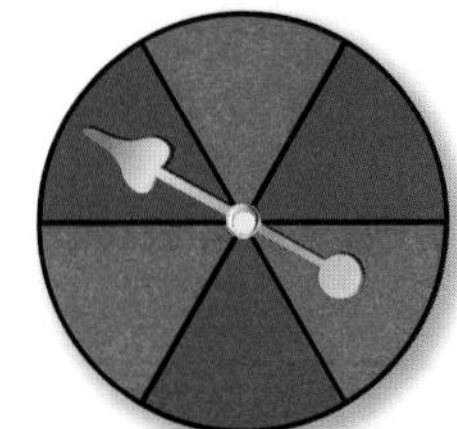

9. Use Spinner 6 on Learning Tool 36. Color the spinner so that

- the outcome of landing on yellow is most likely.
- the outcome of landing on red is possible but least likely.
- the outcomes of landing on orange or purple are equally likely.
- the outcome of landing on pink is impossible.

10. Describe a spinner for which the outcomes of spinning yellow and blue are equally likely.

Writing Math

Predict Look at your Spinner 2. If you spin it 8 times, how many times do you think it will land on red? Can you be sure? Explain your thinking.

CA Standards
SDAP 2.0 Students make predictions for simple probability situations.

SDAP 2.2 Express outcomes of experimental probability situations verbally and numerically (e.g., 3 out of 4; $\frac{3}{4}$).

Also SDAP 2.1, MR 1.0, MR 2.0, MR 2.3, MR 2.4, MR 3.0, MR 3.2

Vocabulary

favorable outcome

Find Probability

Objective Find and write the probability of an event in words and as a fraction.

Learn by Example

The spinner shown has eight equally likely outcomes: 1, 2, 3, 4, 5, 6, 7, and 8.

A **favorable outcome** is one result you are looking to find.

You can use words or fractions when you describe the probability of an event.

$$\frac{\text{number of favorable outcomes}}{\text{total number of outcomes}}$$

Event 1 Landing on 3

Probability $= \frac{1}{8}$ ⟵ favorable outcome (3) / ⟵ total outcomes (1, 2, 3, 4, 5, 6, 7, 8)

Event 2 Landing on a Number Greater than 3

Probability $= \frac{5}{8}$ ⟵ favorable outcomes (4, 5, 6, 7, 8) / ⟵ total outcomes (1, 2, 3, 4, 5, 6, 7, 8)

Event 3 Landing on 9

Probability $= \frac{0}{8}$ ⟵ favorable outcome (none, 9 is not possible) / ⟵ total outcomes (1, 2, 3, 4, 5, 6, 7, 8)

Event 4 Landing on 1 or Greater

Probability $= \frac{8}{8}$ ⟵ favorable outcomes (1, 2, 3, 4, 5, 6, 7, 8) / ⟵ total outcomes (1, 2, 3, 4, 5, 6, 7, 8)

Think

You can say "one out of eight" for the fraction $\frac{1}{8}$.

The probability of an event ranges from 0 (impossible) to 1 (certain). The closer a probability is to 1, the more likely an event is to occur.

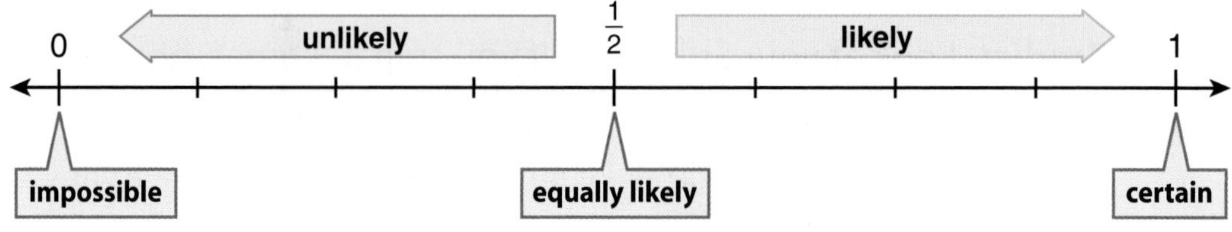

Guided Practice

Suppose you pick a tile without looking. Write the probability of each event in fraction form and in words.

M A T H E M A T I C S

1. T **2.** C **3.** H or A **4.** a vowel **5.** a consonant

6. Which letter is least likely to be picked, M, A, T, or H?

7. Which vowel is most likely to be picked, A, E, or I?

Ask Yourself

- How many tiles are there altogether?
- How many tiles have the letter or letters I am looking for?

Guided Problem Solving

Use the questions to solve this problem.

8. There are 9 socks in Hana's drawer: 3 blue, 2 red, and 4 white. What is the probability that the sock she pulls out is blue? Write the probability in fraction form and in words.

a. **Understand** What is the question?

b. **Plan** How many socks are in the drawer? How many blue socks are in the drawer?

c. **Solve** How do you express probability as a fraction?

The probability that Hana pulls out a blue sock is ◯ out of ◯, or $\frac{◯}{◯}$.

d. **Look Back** How can you check that you answered the original question completely?

9. Look back at Problem 8. Suppose there were 7 blue socks and 4 white socks in the drawer. What would the probability be that the sock Hana pulls out is blue?

Math Talk Shin-Yi says you are equally likely to land on red as you are to land on blue on her spinner. What do you know about the probabilities of landing on red or blue? Explain.

Practice and Problem Solving

Suppose you pick one tile from this bag without looking. Write the probability of each event in words and in fraction form.

10. picking 1

11. picking a multiple of 3

12. picking 3 or 5

13. picking a number greater than 4

14. Explain Is the probability of picking an even number greater or less than the probability of picking an odd number?

Hint
Even numbers are divisible by 2.

Real World Data

Use the tally chart to solve Problems 15–18.

15. The six faces of the number cube are numbered 1, 2, 3, 4, 5, and 6. Lexi and Sara each rolled the number cube 25 times. Write a fraction that tells the probability of rolling a number greater than 4.

16. Write a fraction to show the number of times Lexi actually rolled a number greater than 4.

17. Look at Sara's data. What is the mode and the median?

18. Make a double bar graph to show the data in the table.

Number Cube Experiment

Outcomes	Lexi	Sara
1	𝍷𝍷𝍷	𝍷𝍷𝍷𝍷
2	𝍷𝍷𝍷𝍷	𝍸 𝍷
3	𝍸	𝍷𝍷𝍷
4	𝍷𝍷𝍷𝍷	𝍷𝍷𝍷𝍷
5	𝍸 𝍷	𝍷𝍷𝍷
6	𝍷𝍷𝍷	𝍸

Spiral Review and Test Practice

Find the fractional part of the number. NS 1.5 page 372

19. $\frac{3}{5}$ of 20

20. $\frac{1}{4}$ of 16

21. $\frac{1}{3}$ of 33

22. $\frac{3}{8}$ of 16

Write the letter of the correct answer. SDAP 2.2

23. What is the probability that the spinner will land on red?

A 3 out of 10

B 4 out of 6

C 4 out of 10

D 6 out of 10

Extra Practice See page 547, Set A.

What Are the Chances?

Nick is a video game programmer. When he programs the "brains" or artificial intelligence of creatures that live in a video game, he uses probability to figure out how likely they are to have certain behaviors.

One of the creatures Nick is programming is a lion. The spinner shows the probability the lion might take a nap, eat, play, or attack.

Solve. Use fractions for Problems 1–4.

1. What is the probability of the lion taking a nap?
2. What is the probability of the lion eating?
3. What is the probability of the lion playing?
4. What is the probability of the lion attacking?
5. Is the probability of the lion napping more or less likely than the probability of the lion attacking?
6. How does the probability of the lion playing compare with the probability of the lion eating?

CA Standards
SDAP 2.0, SDAP 2.2

CA Standards
SDAP 2.0 Students make predictions for simple probability situations.

SDAP 2.2 Express outcomes of experimental probability situations verbally and numerically (e.g., 3 out of 4; $\frac{3}{4}$).

Also SDAP 1.0, SDAP 1.1, SDAP 1.3, SDAP 2.1, MR 1.1, MR 2.0, MR 2.3, MR 2.4

Vocabulary

prediction

Materials
- paper bag
- Learning Tool 37 (Probability Cards)
- number cube labeled 1, 2, 2, 3, 4, 4

Hands On
Make Predictions

Objective Predict outcomes in a probability experiment.

Explore

Sometimes you will want to make a **prediction** or a guess about the outcome in a probability experiment.

Question How can you use what you know about probability to make a prediction?

1 Work with a partner. Make 12 cards like the ones shown and put them in a bag.

2 Predict what may happen if you pick one card from the bag without looking.

- What is the probability of picking each kind of card?
- Suppose you pick from the bag 48 times and put the card back each time. Predict how many times you will pick each shape. Record your predictions in a chart like the one below.

Card Experiment

Outcome	Probability	Prediction	Tally
Circle			
Square			
Triangle			

3 Pick a card without looking. Make a tally mark to record the result in your chart. Put the card back in the bag. Do this 47 more times.

How did your predictions compare to your actual results?

Follow these steps to conduct another probability experiment.

1 Label the faces of a cube with the numbers 1, 2, 2, 3, 4, and 4.

2 Predict how many times the cube will land on each number if you toss the cube 30 times.

3 Toss the same cube. Record the result on a line plot like the one to the right. Do this 29 more times.

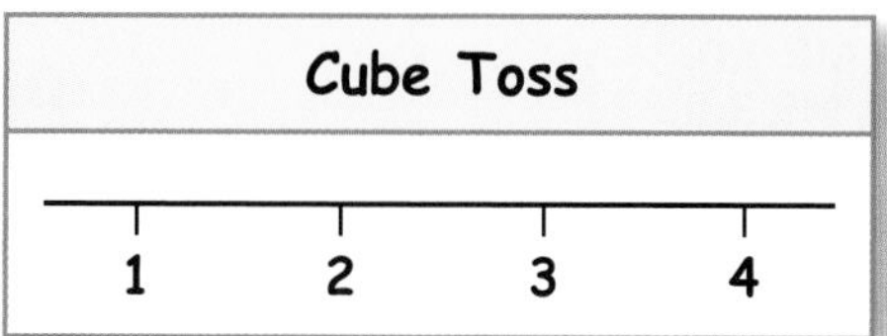

Extend

1. Compare your predictions for the cube toss with your results. Were your predictions accurate? Explain your thinking.
2. **Explain** Look at your line plot. Which other number was rolled about as many times as the number 4? Explain why.
3. What is the probability of rolling a 2 with the number cube you used in the experiment?
4. If you rolled the number cube 600 times, about how many times do you think you would roll the number 2? Explain.
5. **Generalize** How is the probability of rolling a 2 related to the fraction of times a 2 is actually rolled?

Writing Math

Predict Suppose you toss a cube with the numbers 1, 2, 3, 4, 5, and 6. Why would you predict that you would toss a number less than 4 more often than a number greater than 4?

Represent Outcomes

Objective Show all possible outcomes of a probability experiment using a grid or tree diagram.

CA Standards
SDAP 2.1 Represent all possible outcomes for a simple probability situation in an organized way (e.g., tables, grids, tree diagrams).
SDAP 2.2 Express outcomes of experimental probability situations verbally and numerically (e.g., 3 out of 4; $\frac{3}{4}$).
Also SDAP 2.0, MR 2.0, MR 2.3, MR 2.4, MR 3.0, MR 3.3

Vocabulary

tree diagram

Learn by Example

A quarter is tossed twice. What is the probability that it will land heads-up once and tails-up once?

To answer the question, represent all outcomes. Then circle those that match 1 heads, 1 tails.

Different Ways to Represent Outcomes

Way 1 Use a grid.

- Write the possible outcomes for the first toss at the left.
- Write the possible outcomes for the second toss at the top.
- Put the possible outcomes for both tosses in the grid.

		Second Toss	
		heads	**tails**
First Toss	**heads**	heads, heads	heads, tails
	tails	tails, heads	tails, tails

Way 2 Use a tree diagram.

- Show the possible outcomes for the first toss. Use H for heads and T for tails.
- Draw branches and show the possible outcomes for the second toss.
- List the possible outcomes for both tosses.

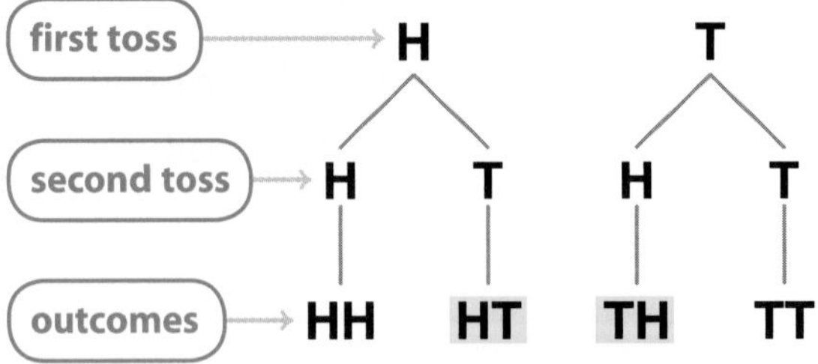

Way 3 Use a table.

Possible Outcomes			
HH	**HT**	**TH**	TT

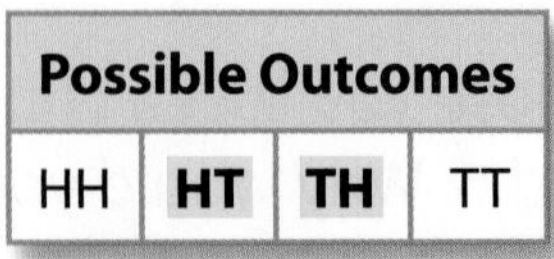

Solution: The probability is 2 out of 4, or $\frac{2}{4}$.

Guided Practice

A bag holds two cards, one with the letter T and one with the letter Y. A card is picked twice and put back each time.

1. Make a tree diagram or a grid to show all possible outcomes. How many outcomes are there?

2. What is the probability of spelling the name TY?

Ask Yourself

- What are all the possible outcomes?
- How many ways can the outcome I want occur?

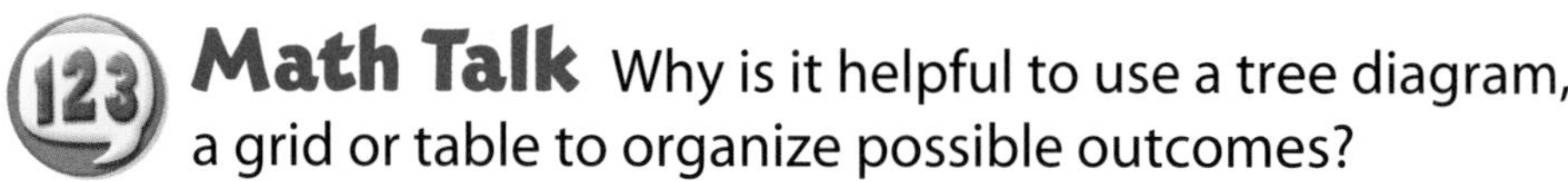

Math Talk Why is it helpful to use a tree diagram, a grid or table to organize possible outcomes?

Practice and Problem Solving

The tree diagram shows the possible outcomes when a coin is tossed and a four-part spinner is spun. Use the tree diagram for Problems 3–5.

3. Make a grid to show the same outcomes.

4. How many possible outcomes show heads and red or blue?

5. What is the probability of heads and yellow or heads and green?

Coin	Spinner	Outcome
heads	blue	heads, blue
	red	heads, red
	yellow	heads, yellow
	green	heads, green
tails	blue	tails, blue
	red	tails, red
	yellow	tails, yellow
	green	tails, green

Use the spinners for Problems 6–7.

6. Draw a grid to show all the possible outcomes of spins on both spinners.

7. Find the probability of spins of both spinners landing on yellow.

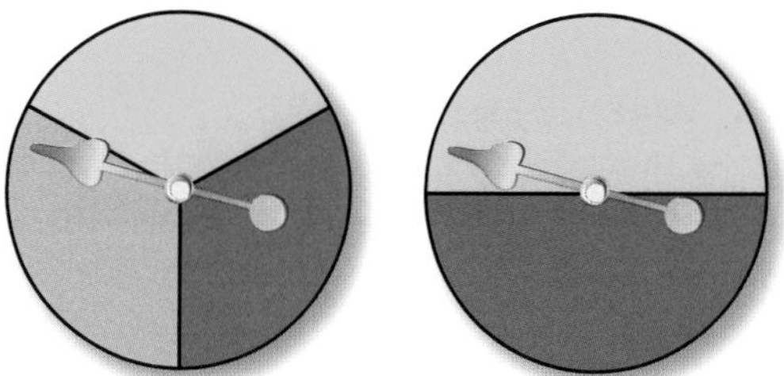

For Problems 8–9, make a grid or tree diagram to show the possible outcomes when one of each is chosen.

8. **Sandwiches**
   Bread: white, wheat, rye
   Filling: cheese, peanut butter, tuna, ham

9. **Outfits**
   Shirts: white, red, blue
   Pants: black, green, brown

10. **Generalize** Look back at Problems 1–9. Can you predict the number of possible outcomes without making a grid or tree diagram?

Science Link

Use the picture to solve.

11. Copy and complete the tree diagram to show the possible outcomes for the parallel circuit.

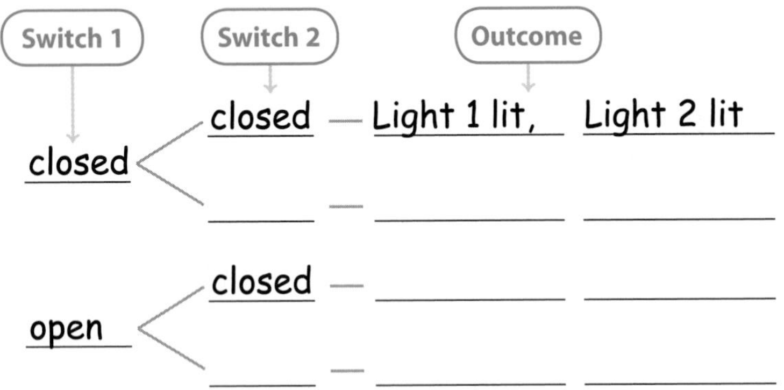

12. How many different possible outcomes are there?

13. **Challenge** If a third switch and bulb are added to the circuit, how many possible outcomes are there?

Circuits

- An electric current travels through a closed path called a circuit.
- Each switch is either closed or open.
- When a switch is open, electricity cannot travel through the circuit.
- The switch controls the outcome of either a lit or unlit light bulb next to it.

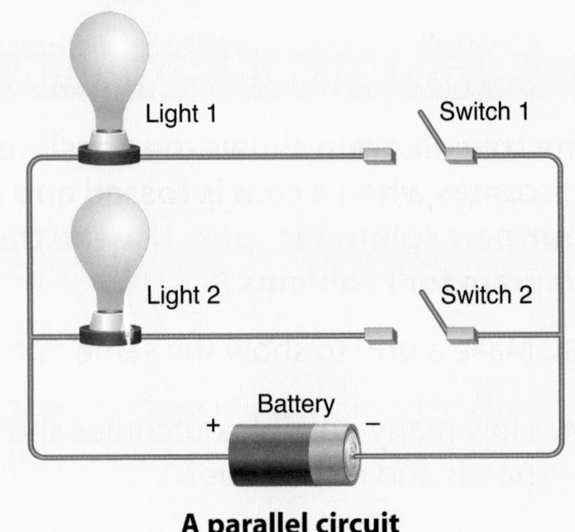

A parallel circuit

Science PS 1.a

Spiral Review and Test Practice

Solve. SDAP 1.2 page 514

14. What is the mode of these spelling scores?

89, 75, 88, 89

Write the letter of the correct answer. SDAP 2.2

15. A bag holds 1 red marble and 1 blue marble. A marble is picked twice and put back each time. What is the probability of picking 2 red marbles?

A $\frac{1}{4}$ **B** $\frac{1}{2}$ **C** $\frac{2}{4}$ **D** $\frac{4}{4}$

Extra Practice See page 547, Set B.

Key Standards Review

Need Help?
See Key Standards Handbook.

Use the number line. KEY NS 1.9

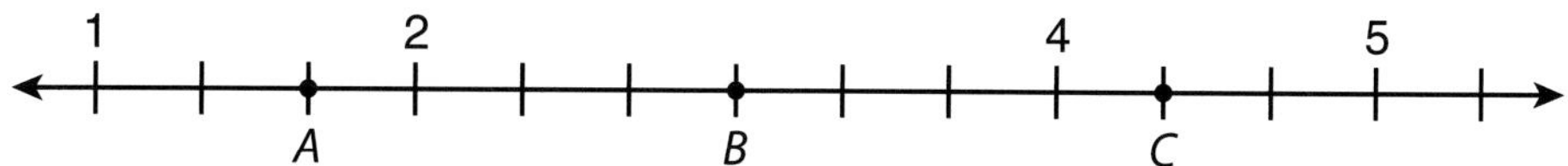

1. Write a number for *A*.
2. Write a decimal for *B*.
3. Write a number for *C*.

Subtract to find the length of the line segment that connects each pair of points. KEY MG 2.3

4. What is the length of the line segment joining the points (130, 16) and (130, 32)?
5. What is the length of the line segment joining the points ($^-11$, 4) and ($^-11$, 27)?
6. What is the length of the line segment joining the points (23, 15) and (23, 42)?
7. What is the length of the line segment joining the points ($^-2$, 67) and ($^-2$, 81)?
8. What is the length of the line segment joining the points (37, 12) and (37, 38)?

Probability

Toss Sums SDAP 2.1

You have two number cubes labeled 1 through 6. Suppose you roll both number cubes. Make a list to show all the possible sums. Are all the sums equally likely? Explain.

Problem Solving

Objective Use skills and strategies to solve word problems.

CA Standards
MR 1.0, MR 1.1, MR 2.0, MR 2.3, MR 2.4, MR 3.1, KEY NS 1.8, SDAP 1.3, SDAP 2.2
History-Social Science 4.4.2

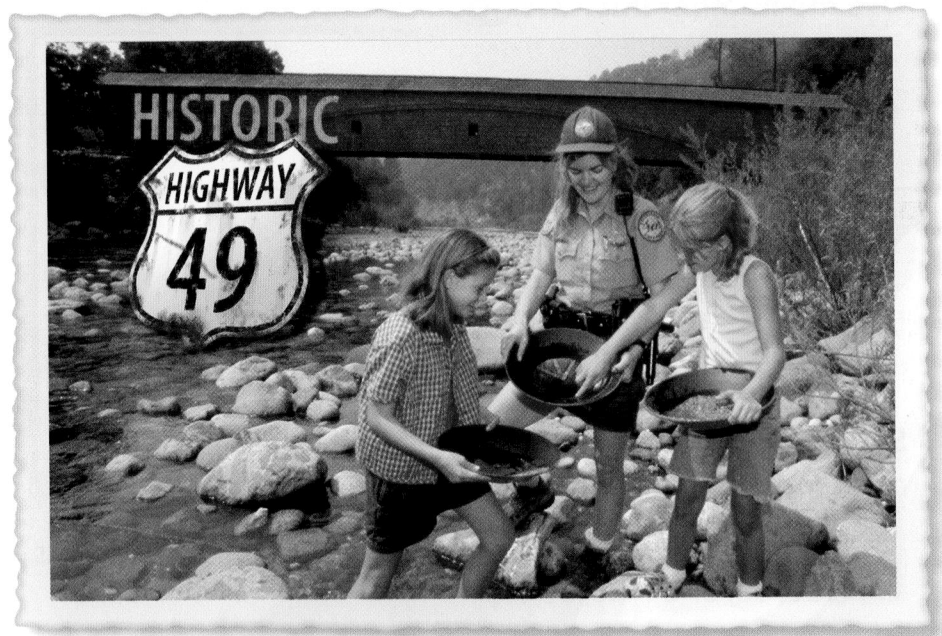

Panning for gold in Feather River along Highway 49 is still a popular activity.

State Highway 49 is named for the "49ers" who came to California searching for gold in 1849.

Use the graph to solve.

1. During which 2-year period did the price decrease by $13 an ounce?

2. What was the change in the price of gold between 1868 and 1870? Express the change using a positive or negative integer.

3. Suppose an 1864 poster advertising for people to come to California says that there is a 1.5 probability of finding gold on any day. Do you think this statement could be true? Why or why not?

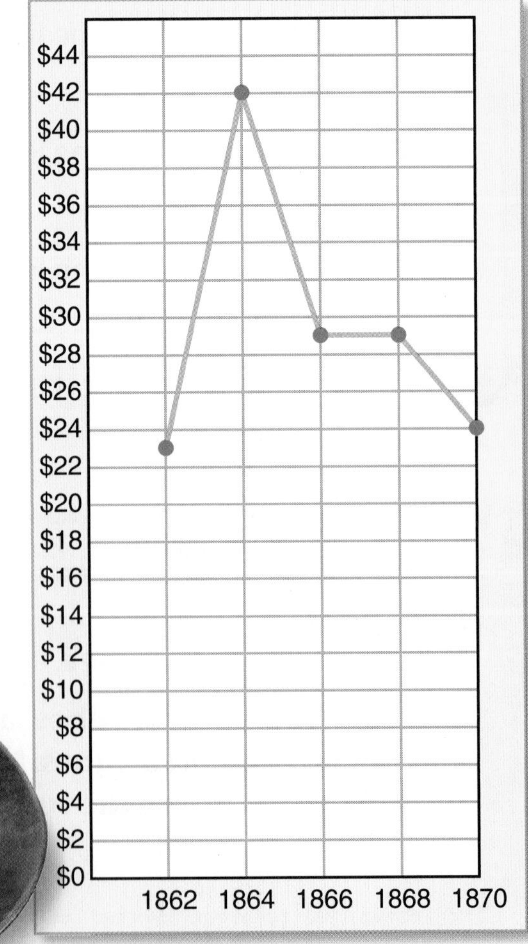

Problem Solving on Tests

Select a Strategy
- Choose the Operation
- Write an Equation
- Draw a Picture
- Guess and Check
- Estimate

1. Candace pulls 1 marble out of a bag of 9 red marbles, 2 blue marbles, 6 green marbles, and 6 yellow marbles. Which color is she least likely to choose?

A red **B** blue **C** green **D** yellow

SDAP 2.0 page 532

2. Mary's age is 3 years greater than twice Albert's age. If Mary is 17 years old, how old is Albert?

A 3 **B** 7 **C** 14 **D** 20

KEY AF 1.2 page 170

3. There are 7 buses taking students on a field trip. Each bus has the same number of seats. If there is a total of 259 seats, how many seats are in each bus?

A 37 **C** 263

B 252 **D** 1,813

Test Tip
Estimate a solution to check the reasonableness of your answer.

KEY NS 3.4 page 286

4. Karen is building a rectangular pen for her horse. The pen will be 20 feet long and 10 feet wide. Which equation represents the perimeter (P) of the pen in feet?

20 ft
10 ft

A $P = 20 + 10$

B $P = 20 \times 10$

C $P = 20 \times 10 \times 20 \times 10$

D $P = 20 + 10 + 20 + 10$

MG 1.0, AF 1.4 page 328

5. A camp counselor wants to divide a large group of campers into smaller groups. Each group will have the same number of campers and no campers will be left over. The counselor finds that it is impossible to divide the campers into groups this way. Which of the following could be the total number of campers in the large group?

A 33 **B** 39 **C** 167 **D** 75

KEY NS 4.2 page 306

6. Look at the line segment. It represents the distance between the school and the library. What is the length of the line segment?

A 3 units **C** 5 units

B 4 units **D** 10 units

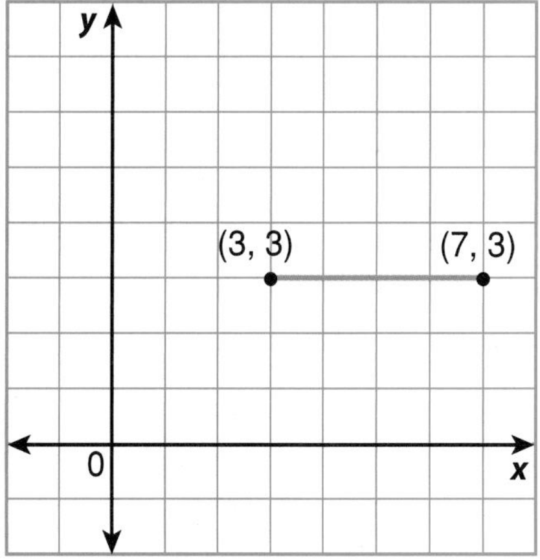

KEY MG 2.2 page 492

Education Place
Visit www.eduplace.com/camap/ for **Test-Taking Tips** and **Extra Practice.**

Reading & Writing Math

Vocabulary

Probability is a way to describe how **likely** it is that something will happen. A **prediction** is a guess about the **outcome** of an experiment. You can show all the possible outcomes of a probability experiment using a **grid** or a **tree diagram**.

For Problem 1, make a grid or a tree diagram to show the possible combinations when one of each is chosen.

1. Shoes and Socks
Shoes: black, brown, blue
Socks: white, striped, polka dot

Answer these questions based on the spinner. Write the probability in words and as a fraction.

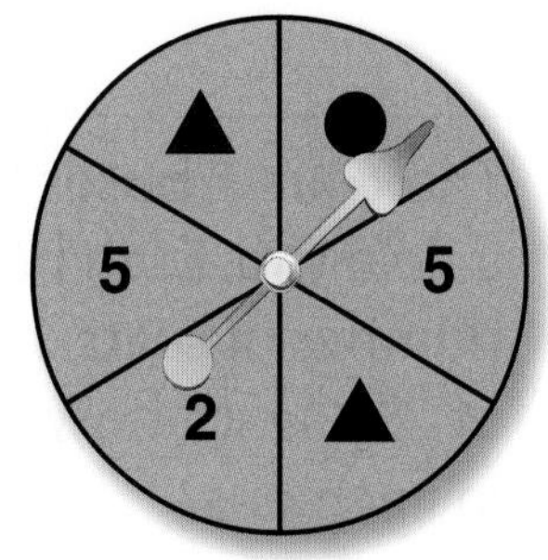

2. What is the probability the arrow will land on

a. a 5?

b. an even number?

c. a triangle?

d. a square?

e. a shape?

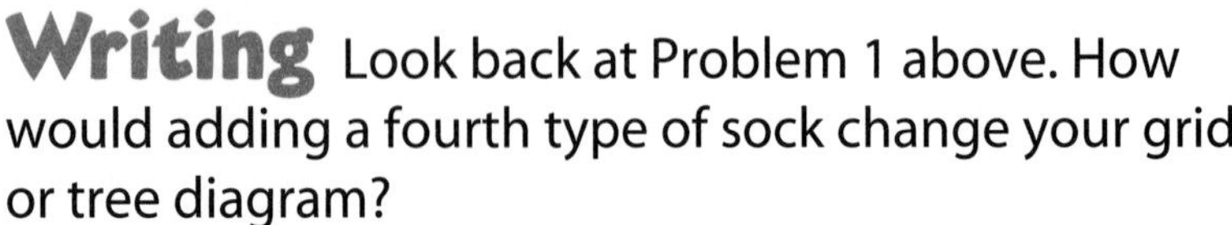

Writing Look back at Problem 1 above. How would adding a fourth type of sock change your grid or tree diagram?

Reading Check out this book in your library. *Do You Wanna Bet? Your Chance to Find Out About Probability*, by Jean Cushman

CA Standards
MR 2.3 Use a variety of methods, such as words, numbers, symbols, charts, graphs, tables, diagrams, and models, to explain mathematical reasoning.

Also SDAP 2.0, SDAP 2.1, SDAP 2.2

Standards-Based Extra Practice

Set A

SDAP 2.0, SDAP 2.2 page 534

The six faces of a number cube are numbered 1, 2, 3, 4, 5, and 6. Suppose you toss the number cube one time. Write the probability of each event in words and in fraction form.

1. Rolling a 2
2. Rolling an even number
3. Rolling a number less than 5
4. Rolling a number greater than or equal to 2
5. Rolling an odd number
6. Rolling a number greater than 6
7. **Compare** On which spinner is the probability of landing on red greater? Explain your answer.

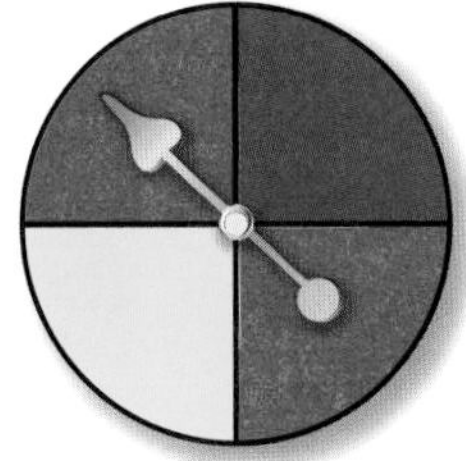

Spinner A

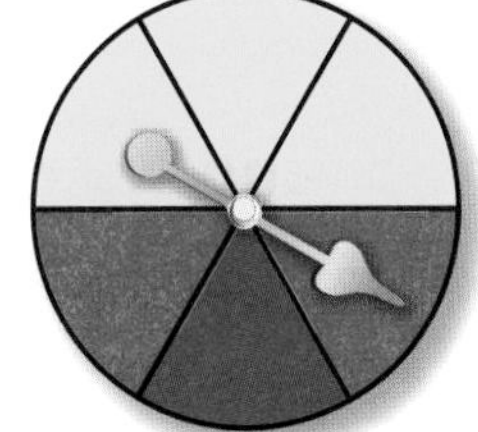

Spinner B

Set B

SDAP 2.1, SDAP 2.2 page 540

Copy and complete the grid to show the total number of possible outcomes when one of each is chosen.

Sandwich \ Soup	Chicken Noodle	Tomato
Cheese	1.	2.
Ham	3.	4.
Tuna	5.	6.

7. **Explain** What is the probability of receiving a ham sandwich and tomato soup for lunch? Explain how this probability relates to the other possible outcomes.

Education Place
Visit www.eduplace.com/camap/ for more **Extra Practice**.

Chapter Review/Test

Vocabulary and Concepts

SDAP 2.0, MR 2.3

Write the best term to complete each sentence.

1. If you spin a spinner that has 3 sections, and all sections are red, it is _______ that you will spin red.
2. To use a fraction to express probability, write the number of _______ _______ in the numerator and the total number of outcomes in the denominator.
3. _______ is a mathematical way of measuring how likely it is that something will happen.

Skills

SDAP 2.2, SDAP 2.0

Write the probability in fraction form and in words.

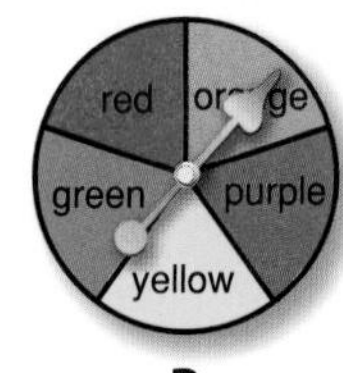

4. Spinner A landing on red.
5. Spinner B landing on red.
6. Spinner A landing on yellow.
7. Spinner B landing on orange.
8. If all 6 sections of a spinner are blue, what is the probability it will land on blue, when spun?

Problem Solving and Reasoning

SDAP 2.2, MR 2.3

Solve.

9. A bag contains 5 marbles: 1 yellow, 3 blue, and 1 red. If one marble is chosen from the bag, which marble colors are equally likely to be chosen?
10. Cards with 3 shapes are in a bag. One card was chosen, then replaced 10 times. Look at the table. What shape do you predict will be picked next?

Shape	square	circle	triangle
Number of times chosen	2	7	1

Writing Math Explain how you would use a grid to find the probability of tossing heads on a coin and a number less than 5 on a number cube numbered 1–6.

Spiral Review and Test Practice

1. $231 \div 4 =$

A 56

B 56 R3

C 57

D 57 R3

KEY NS 3.2 page 262

2. Which fraction represents the largest part of a whole?

A $\frac{1}{3}$

B $\frac{1}{6}$

C $\frac{1}{9}$

D $\frac{1}{12}$

NS 1.5 page 394

3. Luis biked 3.8 miles on Friday, 4.25 miles on Saturday, and 1.1 miles on Sunday. Approximately how many miles did Luis bike in the three days?

A 8 miles

B 9 miles

C 10 miles

D 11 miles

Test Tip
Add the numbers without rounding them to check the reasonableness of your answer.

NS 2.1 page 446

4. What is the length of the line segment shown on the grid?

A 6 units

B 5 units

C 4 units

D 6 units

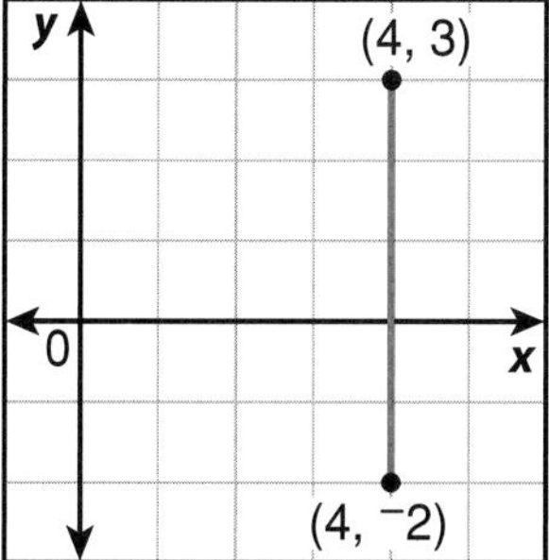

KEY MG 2.3 page 494

5. The letters *M* and *N* stand for numbers. If $M - 25 = N - 25$, which statement is true?

A $M = N$

B $M = N + 25$

C $M > N$

D $M > N + 25$

Test Tip
Substitute actual numbers for the variables *M* and *N* to check your answer.

KEY AF 2.1 page 102

6. What is the probability that the spinner will land on yellow?

A 2 out of 10

B 3 out of 6

C 3 out of 10

D 5 out of 10

SDAP 2.2 page 534

Education Place
Visit www.eduplace.com/camap/ for **Test-Taking Tips** and **Extra Practice.**

Unit 11 Test

Vocabulary and Concepts

SDAP 1.2 Chapters 23–24

Write *true* or *false* for the statements.

1. The mode in a set of numbers is the number that occurs most often.

2. The following set of numbers does not have an outlier: 18, 14, 78, 16, 16.

3. In a fair coin, the probability of tossing a head is certain.

4. Outcomes that are equally likely mean they have an equal chance of occurring.

5. A tree diagram lists all of the possible outcomes.

Skills

SDAP 1.1, SDAP 1.2, SDAP 1.3, SDAP 2.2 Chapter 23, Lesson 2

Order the data from least to greatest. Find the mode and median. Look for any outliers.

6. 10, 9, 15, 56, 9

7. 95, 89, 27, 91, 100, 89, 89

8. 17, 19, 13, 15

9. 11, 7, 16, 51,17, 7

Write each probability as a fraction in simplest terms. Chapter 24, Lesson 2

10. 7 out of 21

11. $\frac{100}{200}$

12. 15 out of 15

13. 9 out of 10

Use the line graph for Problems 14–18. Chapter 23, Lesson 4

14. Robert has 7 days to finish his book. How many pages does he have left?

15. How many pages did Robert read the first day?

16. On what day(s) did he read 10 pages?

17. Did Robert read every day? Explain.

18. Did Robert complete his book in 7 days? Explain.

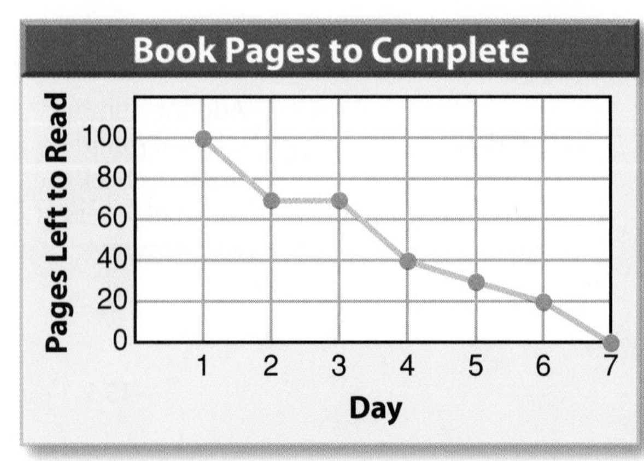

Problem Solving and Reasoning

SDAP 2.2, MR 1.1, MR 2.4 Chapter 24, Lessons 2–4

Solve.

19. A box contains 20 colored pencils. The probability of picking a red pencil is 5 out of 10. The probability of picking a blue pencil is 5 out of 20. Which pencil color has a better chance of being picked? Explain.

20. Josh has two choices: guess heads or tails and then flip a fair coin, OR guess a number between 1 and 6 and then toss a number cube. Which does he have the best chance of winning? Explain.

BIG IDEA!

Writing Math A bag contains 2 blue marbles, 1 red marble, and 3 yellow marbles. Write the probabilities of picking each marble color. What do you observe about the sum of the probabilities?

Performance Assessment

What's for Lunch?

KEY NS 3.0, SDAP 1.0, SDAP 1.3, MR 1.0

Mr. Reed's class did a survey of 4th and 5th grades to see what their favorite lunch is. They will display the results on a double bar graph. Tim started his graph at school. His homework assignment is to complete it by adding the bars for the grade 4 data.

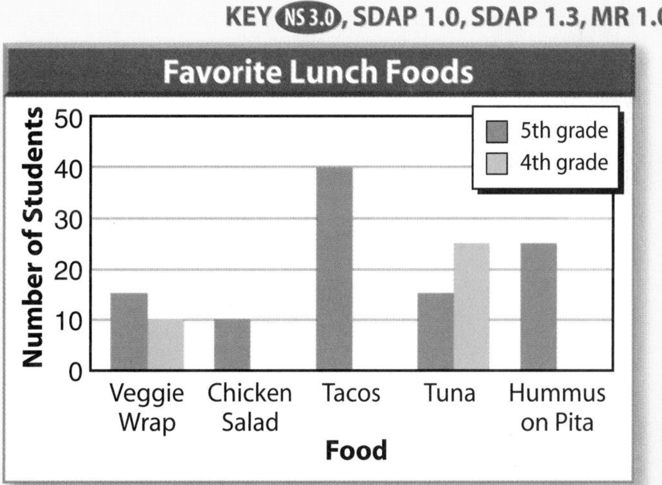

Task	Information You Need
Use the information above and to the right. Tim left the data at school. Use the clues on the right to help Tim complete his graph. List the 4th grade's favorite lunch foods from most to least favorite.	The number of 4th graders who picked chicken salad is twice the number of those who prefer veggie wraps.
	The number of 4th graders who like hummus on pita bread is 10 less than the number of students who prefer tuna.
	The number of 4th graders who like tacos is five more than those who prefer tuna.

Greg Tang's **Go Fast, Go Far**

Unit 11 Mental Math Strategies

Divide by 8

It's easy to divide by 8.
Half three times will work just great!

I have a fast way to do 24 ÷ 8. I take half of 24 which is 12, then half of 12 which is 6, and finally half of 6 which is 3. Dividing by 2 three times is the same as dividing by 8 all at once!

1. 24 ÷ 8 → [12] → [6] → [3]
Divide 24 by 2. Divide by 2. Divide by 2.

2. 48 ÷ 8 → [24] → [12] → ▢
Divide 48 by 2. Divide by 2. Divide by 2.

3. 128 ÷ 8 → ▢ → ▢ → ▢
Divide 128 by 2. Divide by 2. Divide by 2.

4. 144 ÷ 8 → ▢ → ▢ → ▢
Divide 144 by 2. Divide by 2. Divide by 2.

Nice work! Now try these!

5. 32 ÷ 8 → ▢ → ▢ → ▢

6. 88 ÷ 8 → ▢ → ▢ → ▢

7. 96 ÷ 8 → ▢ → ▢ → ▢

8. 120 ÷ 8 → ▢ → ▢ → ▢

9. 280 ÷ 8 → ▢ → ▢ → ▢

10. 560 ÷ 8 → ▢ → ▢ → ▢

Doing Great!

Take It Further!

Now try doing all the steps in your head!

11. 64 ÷ 8

12. 256 ÷ 8

13. 72 ÷ 8

14. 360 ÷ 8

Unit

Geometry and Measurement

BIG IDEAS!

- You can define and classify plane figures. You can describe and model solid figures by relating them to plane figures.
- You can make drawings, measure, and use formulas to show how perimeter and area relate.

Songs and Games

Math Music Track 12: *Kitchen Squares*
eGames at **www.eduplace.com/camap/**

Math Readers

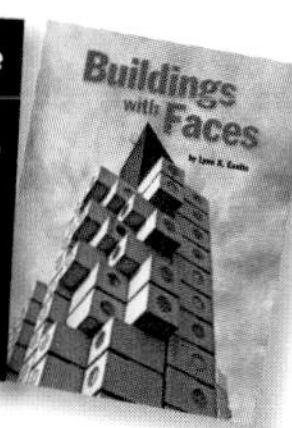

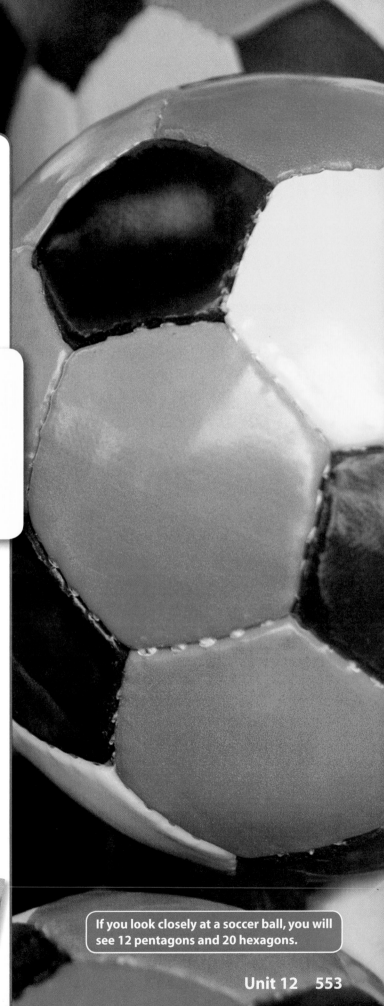

If you look closely at a soccer ball, you will see 12 pentagons and 20 hexagons.

Get Ready **Game**

What's the Measure?

Object of the Game Compare angles to right angles to earn more points than the other player.

Materials
Learning Tool 38 (Angle Cards)

Number of Players 2

Set Up
Cut out the angle cards and place them face down in a stack.

How to Play

1. Player 1 picks a card from the stack and decides if the angle shown is a right angle, is less than a right angle, or is greater than a right angle.
   - If the angle is less than a right angle, Player 1 gets one point.
   - If the angle is a right angle, Player 1 gets two points.
   - If the angle is greater than a right angle, Player 1 gets three points.

2. Player 2 repeats Step 1. If a player incorrectly classifies an angle, the points go to the other player.

3. When all cards have been used, players add up their points.

4. The player with more points wins.

CA Standards
GRADE 3 MG 2.4 Identify right angles in geometric figures or in appropriate objects and determine whether other angles are greater or less than a right angle.

Education Place
Visit www.eduplace.com/camap/ for **Brain Teasers** and **eGames** to play.

Reading Vocabulary is important in everyday language. Mathematics also has its own set of words that you need to learn.

1. **Math words have precise meanings.** The figures shown below are all quadrilaterals. As the word *quadrilateral* suggests, each has 4 *(quadri-)* sides *(lateral)*. Which three of the figures are also parallelograms? How can you tell?

2. **You need to know the language of math in order to keep learning.** In mathematics, you learn something new in every grade. You learn something new in every chapter and lesson. In mathematics, you always build on what you know.

I keep a log of all the math words I learn.

Writing Preview Chapter 25. Make a list of words that are highlighted or in boldface type. Write "Yes" next to each word you know. Write "No" next to those that are new. Keep the list handy as you work on the lessons. Turn every "No" into a "Yes"!

WORD LOG—Chapter 25

	Word	Already Know?	Meaning
Lesson 1	point	No	
	line	Yes	
	line segment		

Plane Figures

Check What You Know

Word Bank
line
circle
triangle
rectangle

Vocabulary and Concepts GRADE 3 MG 2.0, MR 2.3

Choose the best word to complete the sentence.

1. A straight, continuous path that goes on without end in both directions is a _____.
2. A polygon with exactly three sides is a _____.
3. A _____ is a polygon with four right angles and opposite sides that are parallel.

Skills GRADE 3 MG 2.0

Tell whether the figure is a line, a line segment, or an angle.

4. •———•
5. ←———→
6. 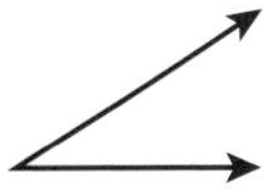 (angle)

Draw a polygon for the description. Name the polygon.

7. a figure with four equal sides
8. a figure with five sides

Problem Solving and Reasoning GRADE 3 KEY MG 2.1

9. I have 4 sides and 3 angles. All of my angles are obtuse. Am I a polygon? Explain your answer.

Vocabulary

Visualize It!

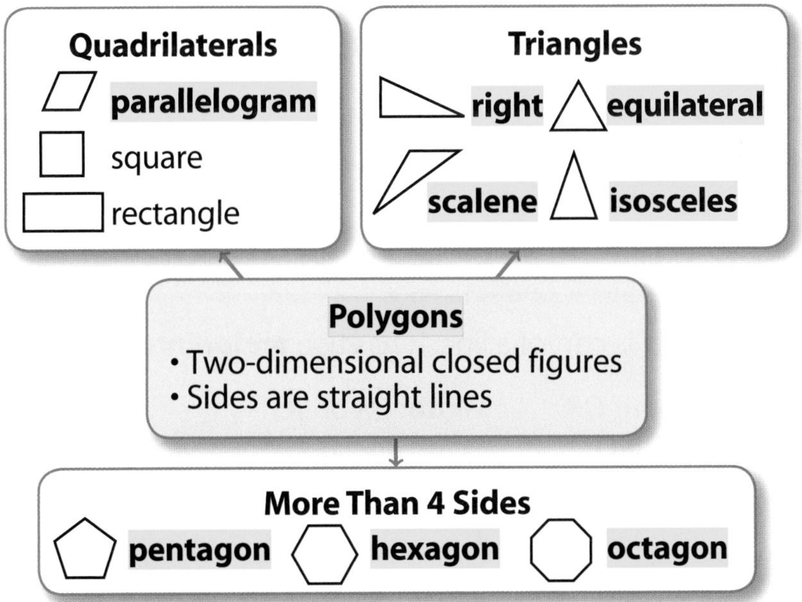

Quadrilaterals
- parallelogram
- square
- rectangle

Triangles
- right
- equilateral
- scalene
- isosceles

Polygons
- Two-dimensional closed figures
- Sides are straight lines

More Than 4 Sides
- pentagon
- hexagon
- octagon

Language Tip

Some words are similar in English and Spanish.

English	Spanish
quadrilateral	cuadrilátero
triangle	triángulo
hexagon	hexágono
pentagon	pentágono

See **English-Spanish Glossary** pages 644–666.

Education Place Visit www.eduplace.com/camap/ for the **eGlossary** and **eGames**.

CA Standards MR 2.3 Use a variety of methods, such as words, numbers, symbols, charts, graphs, tables, diagrams, and models, to explain mathematical reasoning. **Also MG 3.0**

LESSON 1

CA Standards

MG 3.1 Identify lines that are parallel and perpendicular.

MG 3.0 Students demonstrate an understanding of plane and solid geometric objects and use this knowledge to show relationships and solve problems.

Also MR 2.3, MR 2.4

Vocabulary

point
line
line segment
endpoint
parallel lines
intersecting lines
right angle
perpendicular lines

Materials
- yarn
- construction or unlined paper
- glue
- scissors

Hands On
Points, Lines, and Line Segments

Objective Identify geometric figures.

Explore

Many everyday things can model geometric figures. The period at the end of this sentence is a model of a point. A solid stripe painted in the middle of a road is a model of a line. The sides of the letter H in the Hollywood sign model parallel line segments.

Question How can you model and label geometric figures?

Glue yarn onto paper to make models of these geometric figures. Name an everyday object that can also be a model.

1 A **point** is a location in space.

Say: point *B* **Write:** *B*

Model and label a point. • *B*

2 You can draw a **line** through any two points.

A line goes on without end in both directions.

Say: line *CD* or line *DC* **Write:** $\overleftrightarrow{CD}$ or $\overleftrightarrow{DC}$

Model and label a line. (line through *C* and *D*)

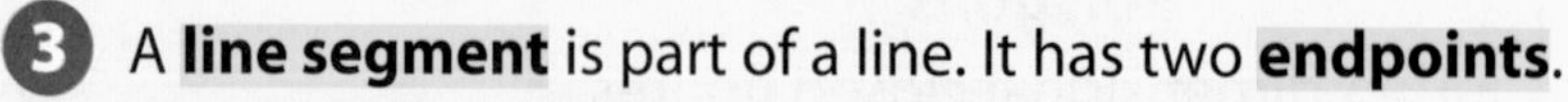

3 A **line segment** is part of a line. It has two **endpoints**.

Say: line segment *QR* or line segment *RQ* **Write:** $\overline{QR}$ or $\overline{RQ}$

Model and label a line segment. (segment from *Q* to *R*)

4 Lines that are always the same distance apart are **parallel**.

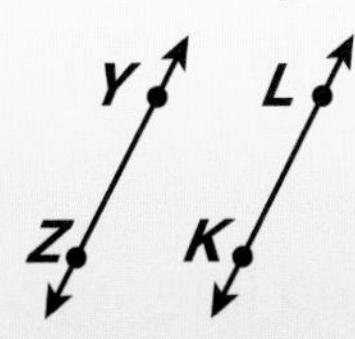

Say: Line *ZY* is parallel to line *KL*.

Write: $\overleftrightarrow{ZY} \parallel \overleftrightarrow{KL}$

The symbol || means "is parallel to."

Model and label parallel lines.

5 Lines that cross each other are **intersecting**.

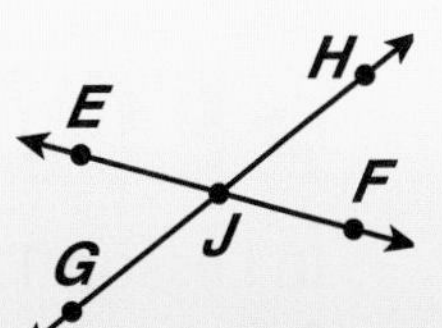

Say: Line *EF* and line *GH* intersect at point *J*.

Model and label intersecting lines.

6 Two lines that form **right angles** are **perpendicular**.

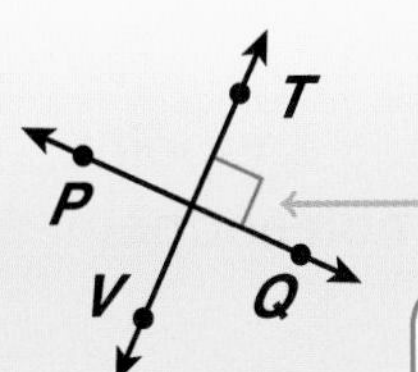

The symbol is used to show a right angle.

Say: Line *PQ* is perpendicular to line *TV*.

Write: $\overleftrightarrow{PQ} \perp \overleftrightarrow{TV}$

The symbol ⊥ means "is perpendicular to."

Model and label parallel lines.

Extend

Use words and symbols to name the figure.

1. 

2. S

3. 

4. T V

Write *parallel, intersecting,* or *perpendicular* to describe the relationship between the pair of lines.

5. 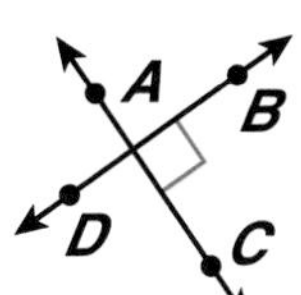

6. 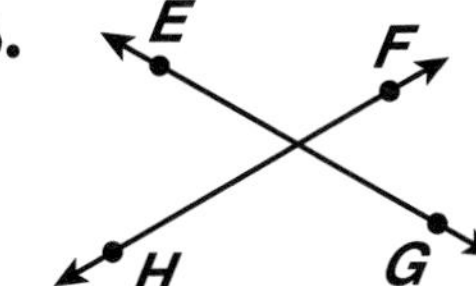

7. 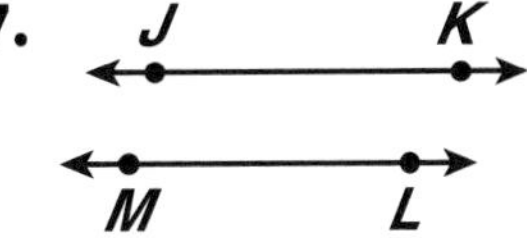

8. 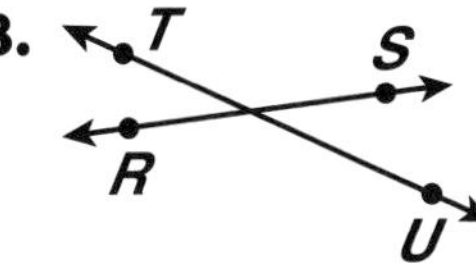

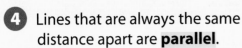

Writing Math

Explain Can two lines be both intersecting and perpendicular? Can two lines be both intersecting and parallel? Explain your thinking.

CA Standards
MG 3.5 Know the definitions of a right angle, an acute angle, and an obtuse angle. Understand that 90°, 180°, 270°, and 360° are associated, respectively, with $\frac{1}{4}$, $\frac{1}{2}$, $\frac{3}{4}$, and full turns.

MG 3.0 Students demonstrate an understanding of plane and solid geometric objects and use this knowledge to show relationships and solve problems.

Also MG 3.1, MR 2.3, MR 2.4

Vocabulary

ray
angle
sides
vertex
right angle
obtuse angle
acute angle

Rays and Angles

Objective Name and describe rays and angles.

Learn by Example

In Lesson 1, you learned about points, lines, and line segments. Rays and angles are also geometric figures.

Rays and Angles

A **ray** is a part of a line. It has one endpoint and goes on without end in one direction.

Say: ray *BA* **Write:** $\overrightarrow{BA}$

An **angle** is formed by two rays with a common endpoint. The rays are the **sides** of the angle. The common endpoint is the **vertex** of the angle.

Say:	Write:
angle *C*	$\angle C$
angle *BCD*	$\angle BCD$
angle *DCB*	$\angle DCB$

Angles are named by the vertex or by three points—a point on each side and the vertex. The vertex is always the middle letter.

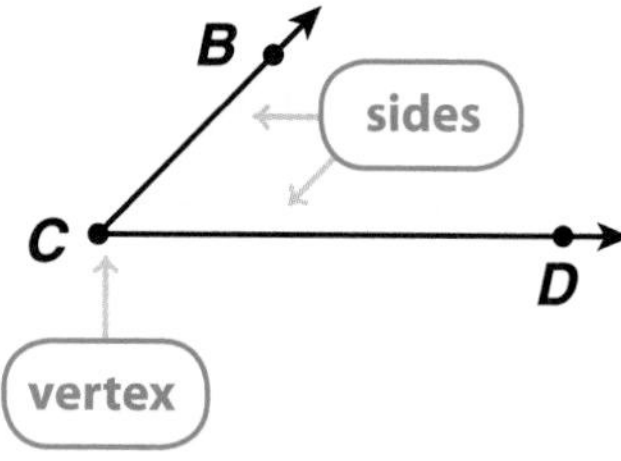

Angles are classified by the size of the opening between the rays.

$\angle MNP$ is a **right angle.**

A right angle forms a square corner. The rays are perpendicular.

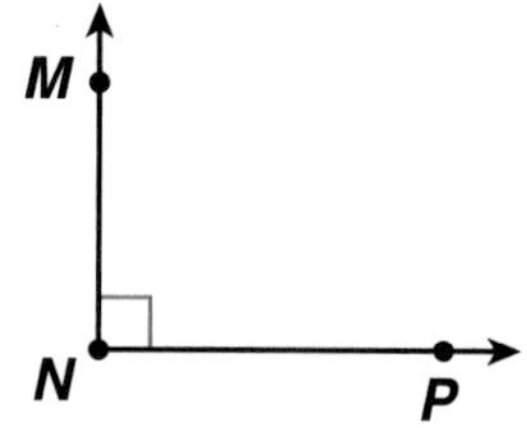

$\angle RJW$ is an **obtuse angle**.

An obtuse angle has a larger opening than a right angle.

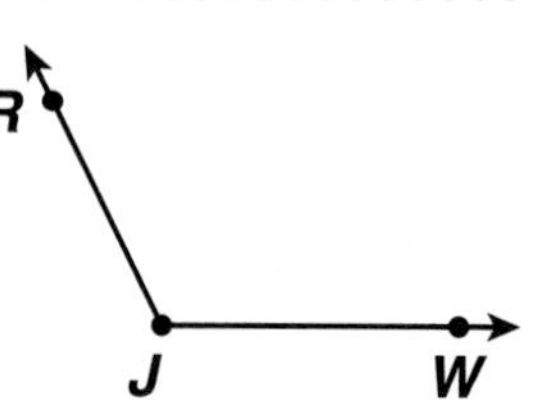

$\angle XYS$ is an **acute angle**.

An acute angle has a smaller opening than a right angle.

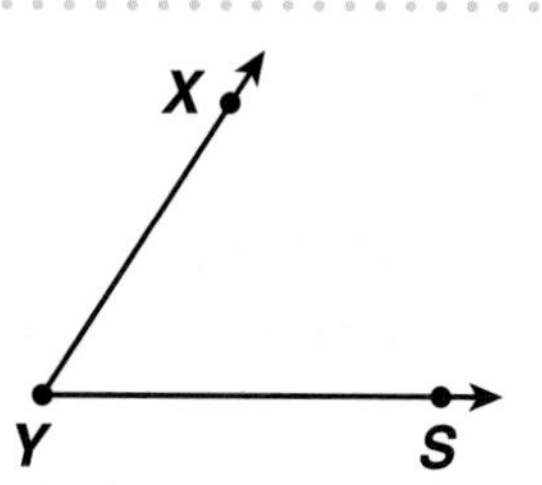

Guided Practice

Name the angle in three ways. Then classify the angle as *acute*, *obtuse*, or *right*.

1. 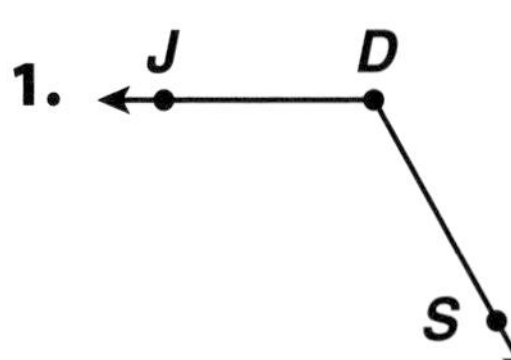

2. 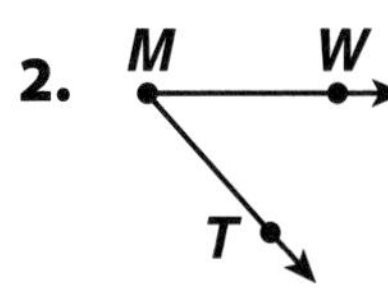

3. 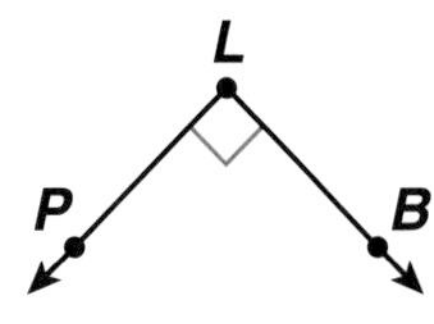

Ask Yourself

- What point will be the middle letter in the name of the angle?
- How does the size of the angle compare to the size of a right angle?

Guided Problem Solving

Use the questions to solve this problem.

4. What angle do the hands of the clock form when it is 3:00?

a. **Understand** What are you asked to find?

b. **Plan** Make a model of a clock. Show 3:00.

c. **Solve** Write the angle the hands of your clock form.

d. **Look Back** Read the problem again. Does your clock show the time asked for?

Clock at Los Angeles Union Station

5. Draw a clock that shows an acute angle. What time does your clock show?

Math Talk Draw 2 lines that are perpendicular. How many right angles are there?

Practice and Problem Solving

Name the angle in three ways. Then classify the angle as *acute*, *obtuse*, or *right*.

6. 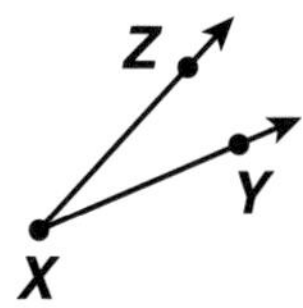

7. 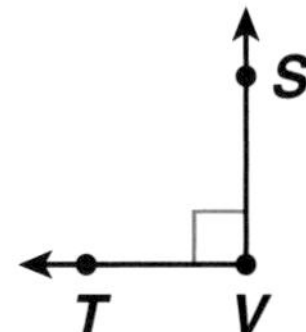

8. 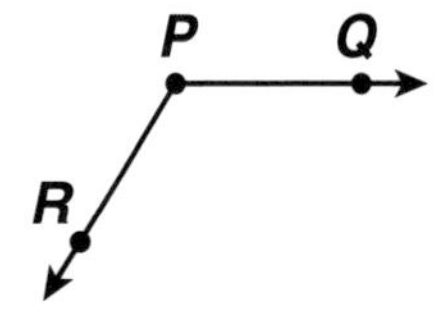

9. K J H

Solve.

10. **Analyze** Copy the word shown below. Put a 1 in the angles that appear to be acute, a 2 in the obtuse angles, and a 3 in the right angles.

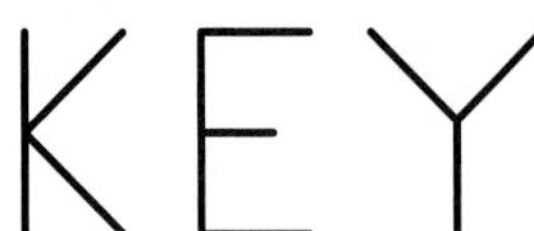

11. What kind of angle is formed when a clock shows 4:00?

12. Draw angles *MHP* and *TWZ*. Describe each angle using the words *vertex* and *sides*. Classify the angles you drew.

13. **Challenge** Draw obtuse angle *ABC*. Is it possible to draw ray *BD* to form two right angles? two acute angles? Explain.

Real World Data

Use the picture to solve Problems 14–18.

14. Name 3 right angles.

15. Name an obtuse angle.

16. Name an acute angle.

17. Name 2 line segments that are parallel.

18. Name 2 line segments that are perpendicular.

Spiral Review and Test Practice

Add or subtract. KEY NS 3.1 page 448

19. $18.7 + 2.61$

20. $35.09 - 12.2$

21. $9.38 - 1.99$

22. $\$4.10 + 6.25 + 3.30$

23. $2.08 + 3.5 + 0.65$

Write the letter of the correct answer. MG 3.5

24. Look at angle *PQR*. Angle *PQR* appears to be

A an acute angle. **C** an obtuse angle.

B a right angle. **D** a line segment.

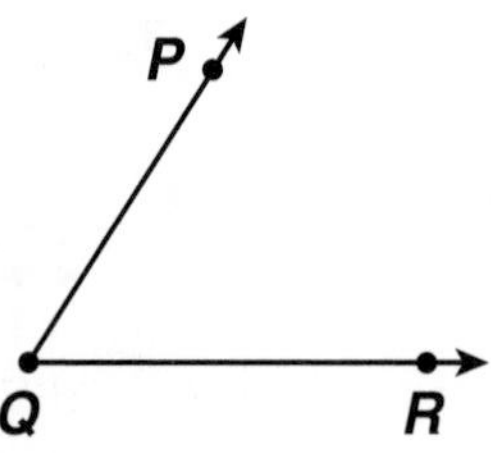

Extra Practice See page 575, Set A.

Key Standards Review

Need Help?
See Key Standards Handbook.

Write the rule for the function table. KEY AF 1.5

1.

Rule: ?	
x	*y*
3	12
5	20
7	28
9	36

2.

Rule: ?	
x	*y*
5	9
6	10
7	11
8	12

3.

Rule: ?	
x	*y*
10	4
14	8
18	12
22	16

Copy and complete the function table. KEY AF 1.5

	Rule: $y = 5x - 8$	
	x	*y*
4.	2	
5.	3	
6.	4	
7.	5	

	Rule: $y = 2 + 4x$	
	x	*y*
8.	1	
9.	2	
10.		14
11.	4	

	Rule: $y = 1 + (x \div 4)$	
	x	*y*
12.	8	
13.	12	
14.	16	
15.	20	

Challenge — Visual Thinking

Where's the Angle? MG 3.5

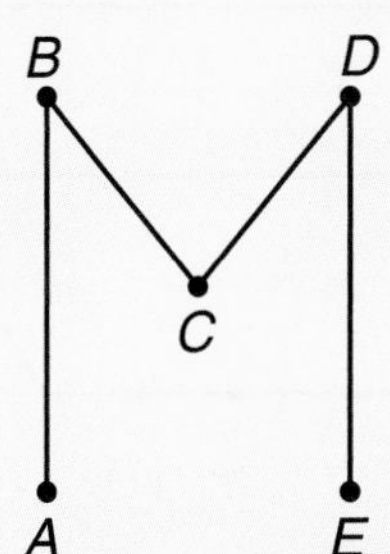

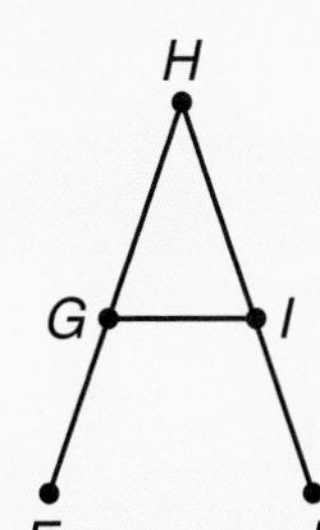

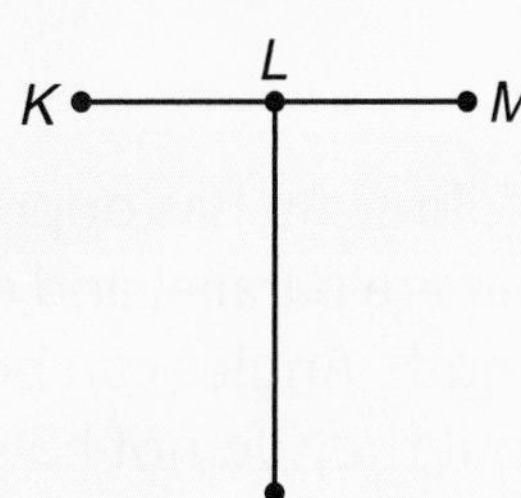

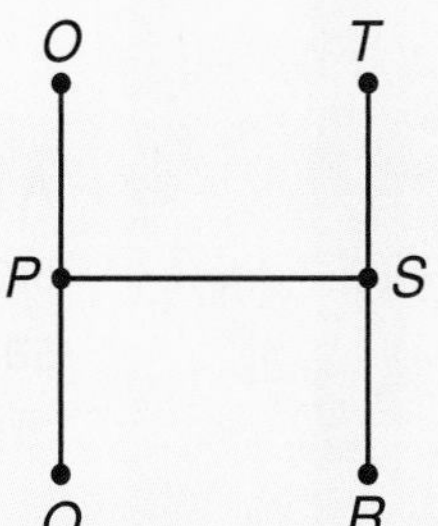

1. Are there right angles? If so, where?
2. Are there acute angles? If so, where?
3. Are there obtuse angles? If so, where?

CA Standards
MG 3.8 Know the definition of different quadrilaterals (e.g., rhombus, square, rectangle, parallelogram, trapezoid).

MG 3.0 Students demonstrate an understanding of plane and solid geometric objects and use this knowledge to show relationships and solve problems.

Also KEY MG 2.0, KEY MG 2.2, KEY MG 2.3, MG 3.1, MR 2.3, MR 2.4

Vocabulary

polygon
sides
rectangle
square
trapezoid
parallelogram
rhombus

Materials
Learning Tool 7 (Grid 2)

Polygons and Quadrilaterals

Objective Name and classify polygons.

Learn by Example

A **polygon** is a flat, closed plane figure made up of three or more line segments called **sides**.

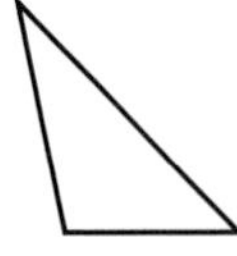
triangle
3 sides

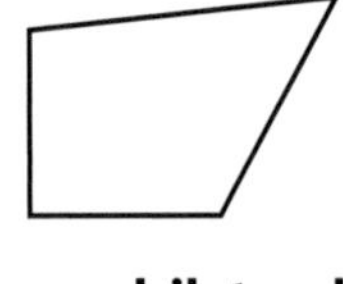
quadrilateral
4 sides

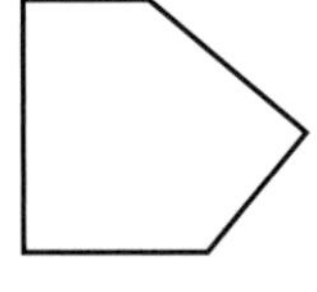
pentagon
5 sides

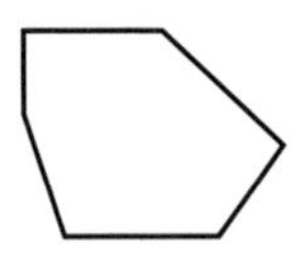
hexagon
6 sides

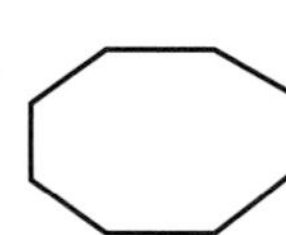
octagon
8 sides

Some quadrilaterals have special names.

Quadrilaterals

A **rectangle** has opposite sides that are of equal length and parallel, and four right angles.

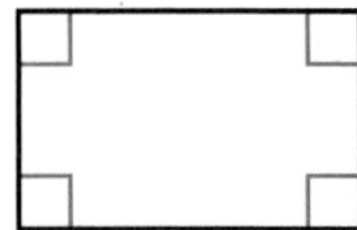

A **square** has opposite sides that are parallel, four equal sides, and four right angles.

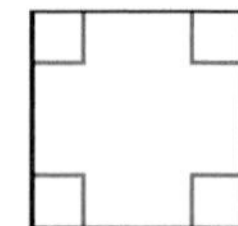

A **trapezoid** has only one pair of parallel sides.

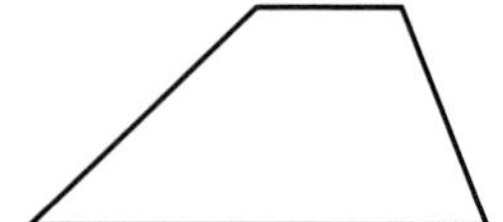

A **parallelogram** has opposite sides that are parallel and of the same length. Angles can be right angles but they do not have to be.

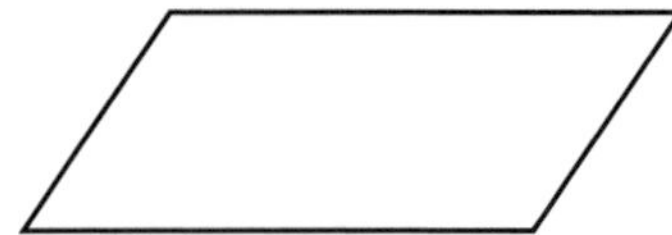

A **rhombus** has opposite sides that are parallel, and four sides of equal length. Angles can be right angles but they do not have to be.

Guided Practice

Name the polygon. If the polygon is a quadrilateral, write all names that apply.

1. 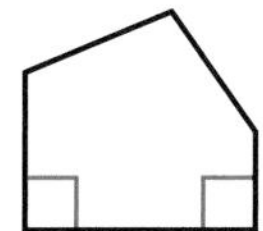

2. 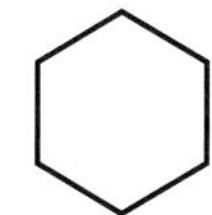

3. 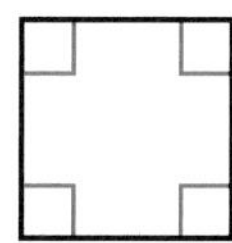

Ask Yourself

- How many sides does the polygon have?
- If there are 4 sides, are there any parallel sides or right angles?

Math Talk Why are rectangles, squares, and rhombuses all parallelograms?

Practice and Problem Solving

Name the polygon. If the polygon is a quadrilateral, write all names that apply.

4. 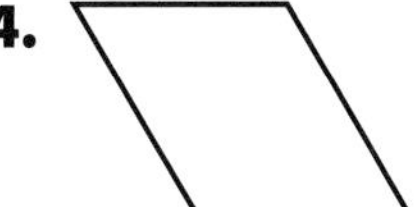

5. 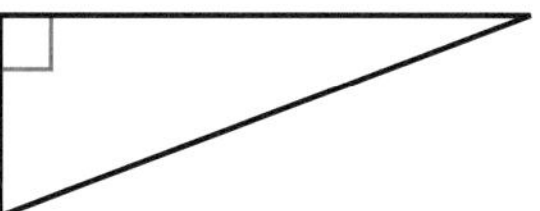

6. 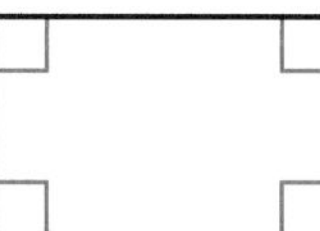

7. 

Use Learning Tool 7 to answer Exercises 8–9.

8. Plot and connect ($^-2$, 2), (2, 2), ($^-2$, 3), (2, 3), and (0, 5). What polygon did you make?

9. Plot and connect (2, 0), (4, 0), and (4, 2). What ordered pair could you plot to make a square?

10. **Challenge** These points can form a rectangle 5 units long: ($^-2$, $^-1$), (3, $^-1$), ($^-2$, 2), (3, 2). Without drawing the rectangle, find its width. Explain your thinking. Then use Learning Tool 7 to check your work.

Spiral Review and Test Practice

Find the length of the line segment that connects the pair of points. KEY MG 2.2, KEY MG 2.3 page 492

11. (1, $^-2$), (5, $^-2$)

12. (3, 3), (3, 5)

13. (0, 5), (4, 5)

Write the letter of the correct answer. MG 3.8

14. Which statement is true?

A All rectangles are squares.

B All parallelograms are rhombuses.

C All trapezoids are rectangles.

D All squares are rectangles.

Extra Practice See page 575, Set B.

CA Standards
MG 3.7 Know the definitions of different triangles (e.g., equilateral, isosceles, scalene) and identify their attributes.
MG 3.0 Students demonstrate an understanding of plane and solid geometric objects and use this knowledge to show relationships and solve problems.
Also MR 2.3, MR 2.4

Vocabulary

equilateral triangle
isosceles triangle
scalene triangle
right triangle
obtuse triangle
acute triangle

Classify Triangles

Objective Name and classify triangles.

Learn by Example

In Lesson 3, you learned that quadrilaterals can be classified by their characteristics. Triangles are also classified by their characteristics.

Triangles are used to build many things. Triangles help make structures rigid and strong.

Different Ways to Classify Triangles

Way 1 **You can classify triangles by the lengths of their sides.**

Equilateral Triangle

All sides are the same length.

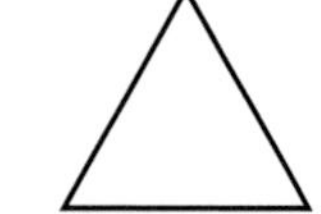

Isosceles Triangle

At least two sides are the same length.

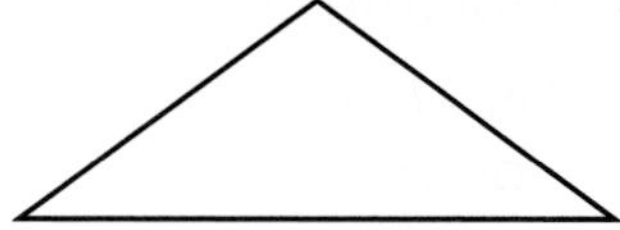

Scalene Triangle

No sides are the same length.

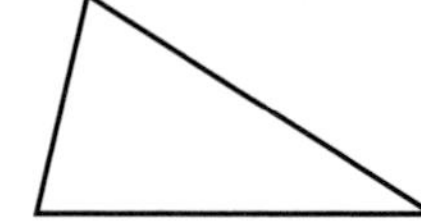

Way 2 **You can classify triangles by the measure of their angles.**

Right Triangle

One angle is a right angle.

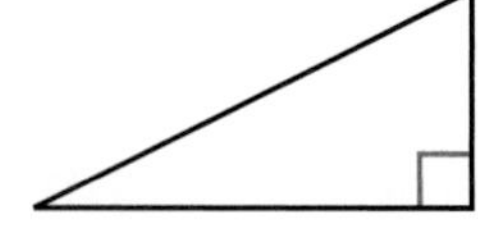

Obtuse Triangle

One angle is an obtuse angle.

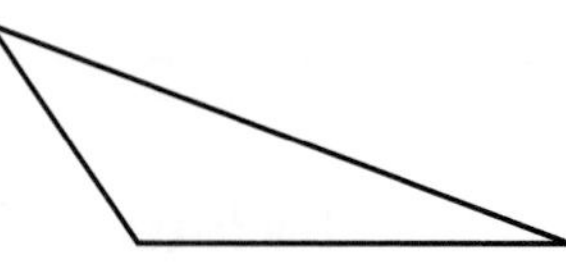

Acute Triangle

All angles are acute angles.

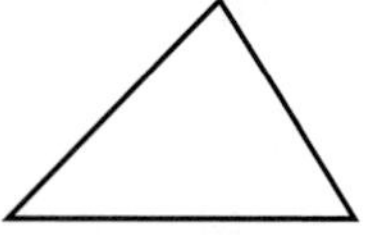

Guided Practice

Tell whether the triangle appears to be *equilateral, isosceles,* or *scalene.* Then tell whether the triangle appears to be *right, obtuse,* or *acute.*

1. 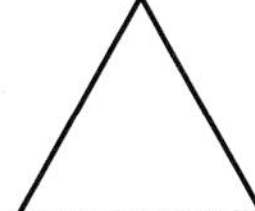

2. 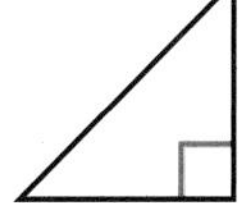

3. 

Ask Yourself

- Are any sides the same length?
- What kinds of angles does the triangle have?

Math Talk Can a triangle be both isosceles and obtuse? Explain why or why not.

Practice and Problem Solving

Tell whether the triangle appears to be *equilateral, isosceles,* or *scalene.* Then tell whether the triangle appears to be *right, obtuse,* or *acute.*

4. 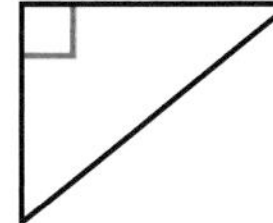

5. 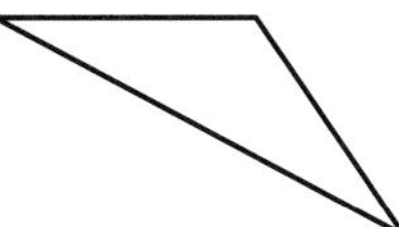

6. 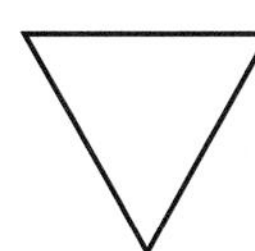

Tell whether the triangle is *equilateral, isosceles,* or *scalene.* Explain.

7. **Analyze** A triangle measures 3 cm on one side. The other sides are twice as long as the first side.

8. Alex built a model bridge. For one section, he built a triangle with sides of 4 cm, 3 cm, and 5 cm.

Spiral Review and Test Practice

Plot each point. Name another point on the line. KEY MG 2.0 page 494

9. (3, 3), (4, 4), (2, 2)

10. (0, 0), (1, 2), (2, 4)

Write the letter of the correct answer. MG 3.7

11. Which kind of triangle always has 1 right angle and 2 acute angles?

A right **B** obtuse **C** acute **D** equilateral

Extra Practice See page 575, Set C.

LESSON 5

CA Standards
MG 3.2 Identify the radius and diameter of a circle.
MG 3.5 Know the definitions of a right angle, an acute angle, and an obtuse angle. Understand that 90°, 180°, 270°, and 360° are associated, respectively, with $\frac{1}{4}$, $\frac{1}{2}$, $\frac{3}{4}$, and full turns.
Also MG 3.0, MR 2.3, MR 3.0, MR 3.3

Vocabulary

circle
center
radius (radii)

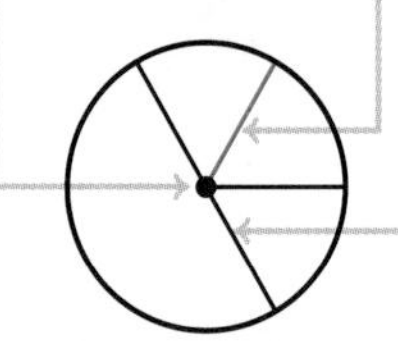

diameter

Circles

Objective Identify parts of a circle.

Learn by Example

A **circle** is made up of all points in a plane that are the same distance from a given point called the **center**. Point *D* is the center of the circle below.

A **radius** is any line segment that joins a point on the circle to the center. $\overline{DE}$, $\overline{DG}$, and $\overline{DF}$ are **radii** of this circle.

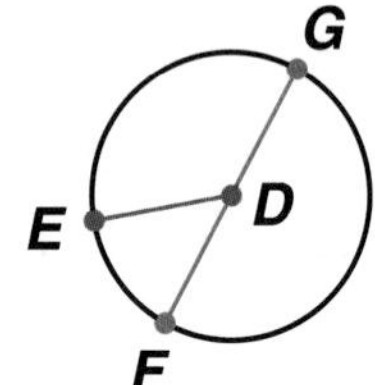
G
E
D
F

A **diameter** is any line segment that passes through the center of a circle and has its endpoints on the circle.

$\overline{GF}$ or $\overline{FG}$ is a diameter of the circle above.

The number of degrees (°) in a full circle is 360. You can turn an object around the point that is the center of a circle. Each turn is measured from the start position. The start position is at the mark for 0°.

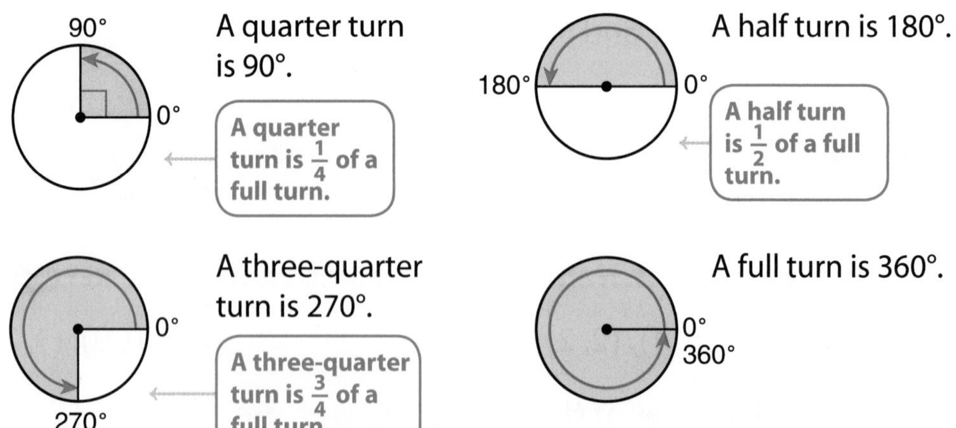
90°
0°
A quarter turn is 90°.
A quarter turn is $\frac{1}{4}$ of a full turn.
180°
0°
A half turn is 180°.
A half turn is $\frac{1}{2}$ of a full turn.
0°
270°
A three-quarter turn is 270°.
A three-quarter turn is $\frac{3}{4}$ of a full turn.
0°
360°
A full turn is 360°.

Guided Practice

Name the parts of the circle.

1. $\overline{FH}$
2. $\overline{FG}$
3. G

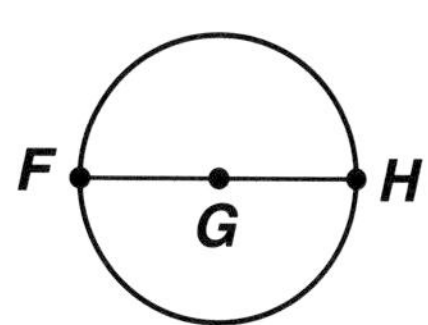

4. If the minute hand of this clock moves from 12 to 6, will it have made a quarter turn, a half turn, or a three-quarter turn? What time will it be when the minute hand has made a full turn?

Ask Yourself

Does the line segment connect a point on the circle to the center?

Math Talk How does the length of a diameter of a circle compare to the length of a radius of that same circle?

Practice and Problem Solving

Name the part of the circle that is shown in red.

5. 

6. 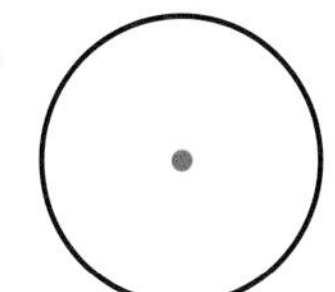

7. 

Marvin and Lisa are riding the wheel on the right. Use the picture for Problems 8–10.

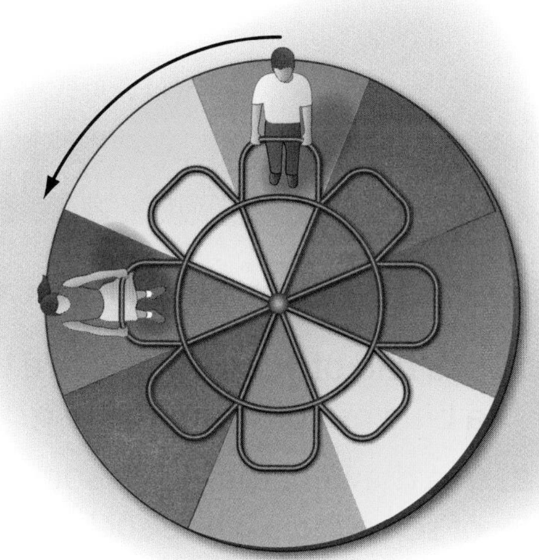

8. The arrow shows the direction the wheel is turning. Which best describes the turn needed to move Marvin to Lisa's current location—half turn, quarter turn, or full turn?

9. From the starting position, which best describes the turn needed to move Lisa to Marvin's current position—quarter turn, half turn, or three-quarter turn?

10. How many degrees has the wheel turned each time Lisa arrives back in the same place she started?

11. **Generalize** One radius of a circle is 4 meters long. How long would a different radius of the same circle be? Explain.

12. **Challenge** Trace around a circular object. Draw 2 radii that do not form a diameter.

Vocabulary Tip

Radii is the plural of **radius**.

Science Link

Use the Fun Facts to solve.

13. The compass needle is pointing north. A magnet pulls the needle 90° to the right. What direction is the needle then pointing?

14. Raymond is holding a compass and he is facing north. He turns to face south. How many degrees did Raymond turn?

15. Raymond is facing south, and Lisa is facing east. There are two ways that Raymond can turn so that he is facing the same direction as Lisa. What are they? Use *clockwise* and *counter-clockwise* in your description.

16. Raymond and Lisa are facing north. Raymond turns 90° clockwise, and Lisa turns 270° counter-clockwise. In which direction is each person facing? Explain.

Magnetic Compasses

- A compass shows north, south, east, and west.
- The magnetic end of the compass needle points toward Earth's magnetic north pole.

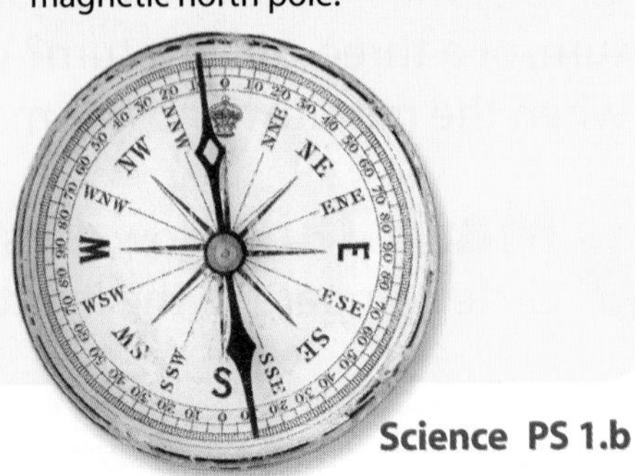

Science PS 1.b

Spiral Review and Test Practice

Solve. Write the probability as a fraction. SDAP 2.2 pages 534, 538, 540

17. In a bag of 10 marbles, 4 are blue. What is the probability of choosing a blue marble from the bag?

18. In a drawer are 6 white socks and 3 colored socks. What is the probability of selecting a white sock from the drawer?

19. What is the probability of rolling a 6 on a number cube labeled 1–6?

Write the letter of the correct answer. MG 3.2

20. Look at the circle with center *O*. The line segment *AB* appears to be

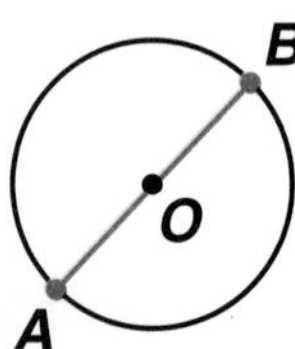

A a diameter. **C** a radius.
B a perimeter. **D** a center.

Extra Practice See page 575, Set D.

Practice **Game**

Concentration

Object of the Game Match geometric pictures with their names.

Materials
Learning Tool 39 (*Concentration* Game Cards)

Set Up
Use one set of game cards for each pair of students.

Number of Players 2

How to Play

1. Shuffle the cards. Place them face down in a 3 × 6 array.

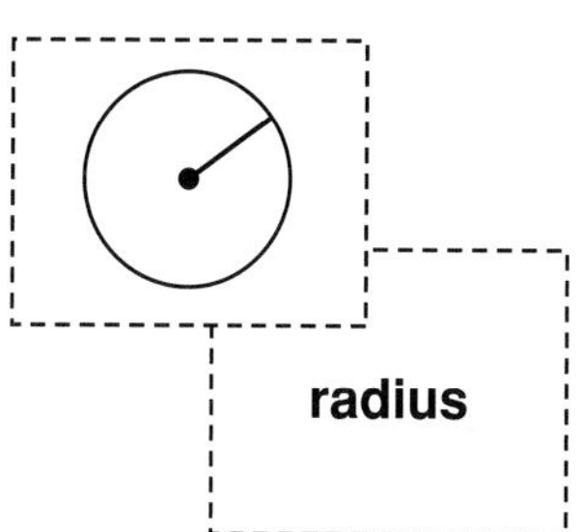

2. Player 1 turns up two cards.
   - If the cards match (picture and name), Player 1 collects those cards.
   - If the cards do not match, Player 1 turns the cards face down.

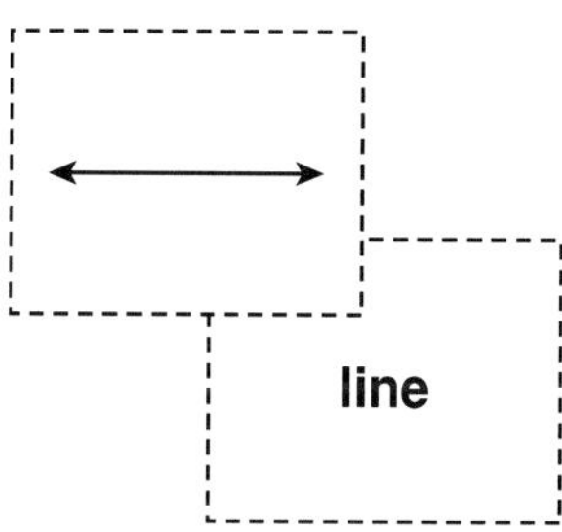

3. Player 2 repeats Step 2. Players take turns until all matches have been made. The player with more cards wins.

CA Standards
MG 3.0 Students demonstrate an understanding of plane and solid geometric objects and use this knowledge to show relationships and solve problems.

MG 3.2 Identify the radius and diameter of a circle.

Education Place
Visit www.eduplace.com/camap/ for **Brain Teasers** and **eGames** to play.

Problem Solving

Objective Use skills and strategies to solve word problems.

CA Standards
MR 1.0, MR 2.0, MR 2.4, NS 1.6, AF 1.4, MG 1.0, MG 3.0, MG 3.2, MG 3.7, MG 3.8

Many of the unique structures in the playground were kid-designed.

The Adventure Playground is not an ordinary playground. You can hammer, saw, and paint things as well as ride the zip line. Working with the staff, you might build a fire, cook pancakes, or build a birdhouse to take home.

Solve. Tell which strategy or method you used.

1. One June, the playground staff offered 4 fishing, 4 building, 4 crafts, and 4 special courses. What part of the programs were fishing courses? Express your answer as a fraction and a decimal.

2. Trent wants to build a fort. He wants the floor of the fort to be a rectangle 7 feet long and 8 feet wide. What will the perimeter of the floor be?

3. The roof of Trent's fort will have a triangular panel like the one shown. Name this triangle in two ways.

4. Trent will have windows in the fort that are circles like the one shown. What is the diameter of the window? What is the radius?

Problem Solving on Tests

Select a Strategy

- Write an Equation
- Make a Table
- Draw a Picture
- Guess and Check

1. Juan made a graph of the equation $y = 5x - 4$. Which of the following points could be on the graph?

A (4, 16)

B (4, 20)

C (5, 29)

D (11, 3)

Test Tip
Test each ordered pair to see if it makes the equation true.

KEY AF 1.5 page 476

2. Ricky is making a blueprint of his house on a coordinate grid. He wants to plot 4 points to represent the corners of a rectangular room. He plotted 3 points on the grid. What will be the coordinates of the fourth point?

A (4, 3) **C** (3, ⁻4)

B (3, 4) **D** (1, 4)

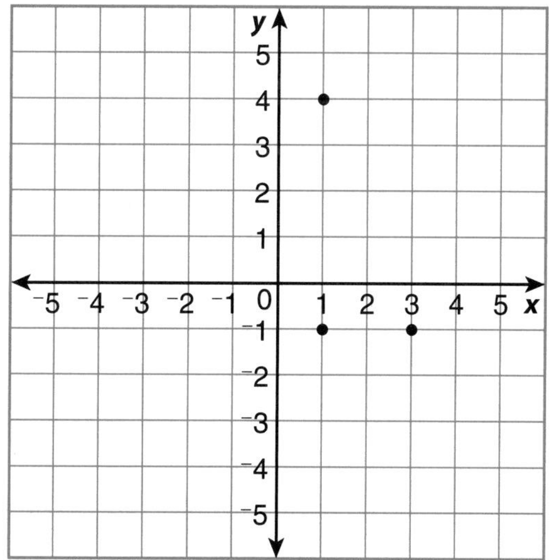

KEY MG 2.0 page 488

3. Chairs were arranged in rows for the talent show. Each row has the same number of chairs, and there are no chairs left over. There is more than one row of chairs. How many chairs could have been arranged?

A 47 **B** 51 **C** 59 **D** 67

NS 4.1 page 302

4. Janice uses the equation $d = 8 \times h$ to calculate the dollars d she earns for working h hours. How many hours must Janice work to earn \$336?

A 8 **B** 42 **C** 328 **D** 2688

KEY AF 2.2 page 176

5. Brooke wants to measure the distance from one side to the other side of her swimming pool. The figure below represents Brooke's swimming pool.

She measures the length of the line segment that passes through the center of the pool. Which of the following did she measure?

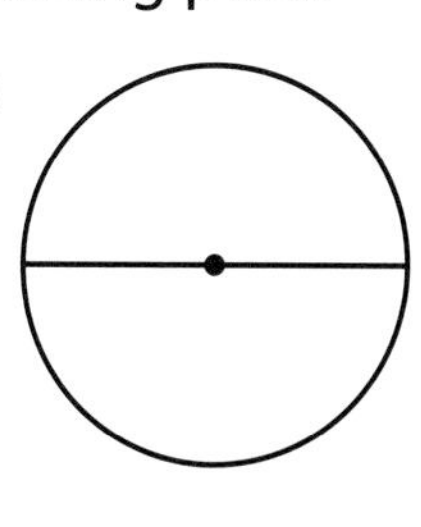

A the perimeter **C** the radius

B the diameter **D** the center

MG 3.2 page 568

Education Place
Visit www.eduplace.com/camap/ for **Test-Taking Tips** and **Extra Practice.**

Vocabulary

A **polygon** is a **closed plane figure** whose sides are all **line segments**. There are many kinds of polygons.

Read each description. Write *yes* if the figure described is a polygon, and *no* if it is not.

1. I have two sides and two endpoints.
2. I am a circle.
3. I have three angles and three sides.
4. I am a pyramid.
5. I am a rhombus.

For Questions 6–8, fill in the missing labels on the word map.

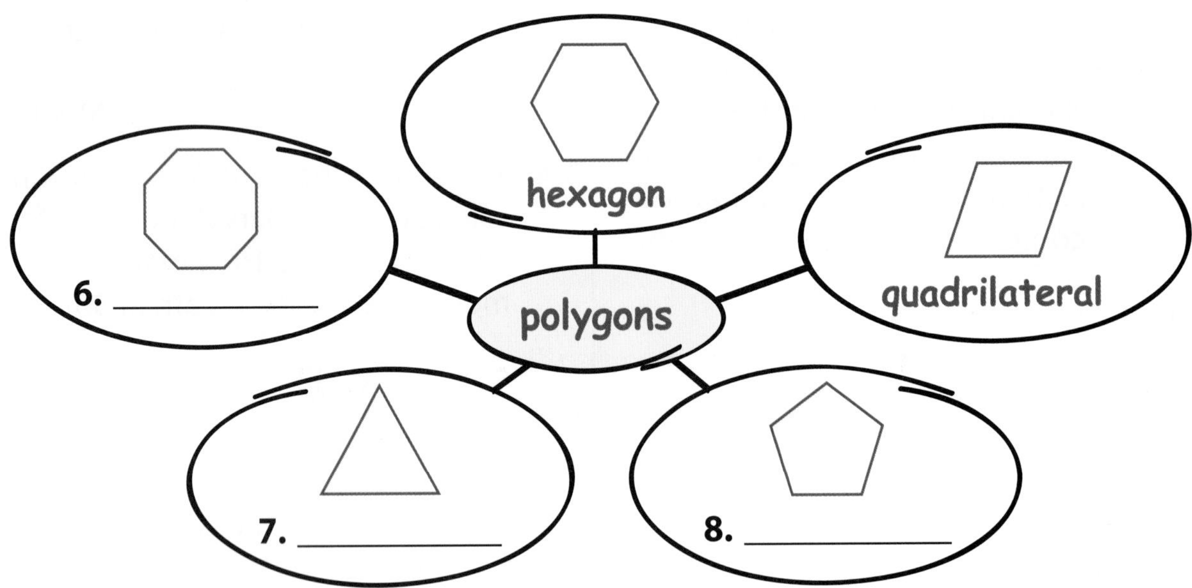

9. Which of the following shapes belong in the quadrilateral circle on the word map? Explain.

a square	a scalene triangle	a circle
a rectangle	a parallelogram	a trapezoid

Writing Describe the differences between equilateral, isoceles, and scalene triangles.

Reading Look for this book in your library. *Grandfather Tang's Story: A Tale Told with Tangrams,* by Ann Tompert

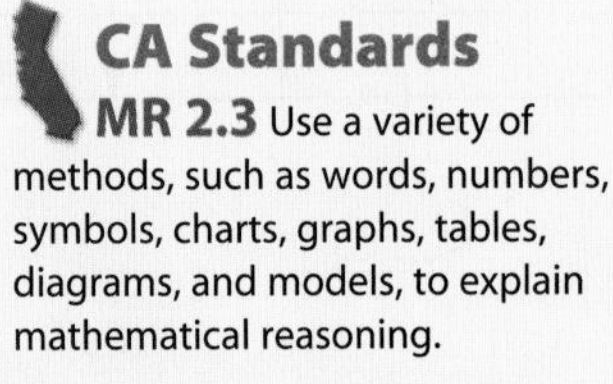
CA Standards
MR 2.3 Use a variety of methods, such as words, numbers, symbols, charts, graphs, tables, diagrams, and models, to explain mathematical reasoning.

Also MG 3.8, MG 3.0

Standards-Based Extra Practice

Set A

MG 3.5 page 560

Classify the angle as *acute*, *obtuse*, or *right*.

1. 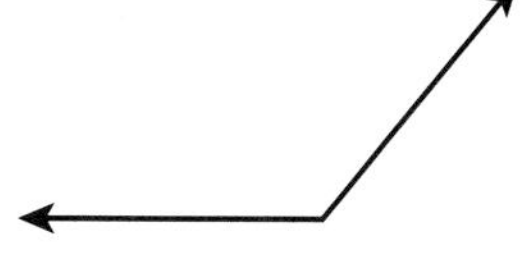
2. 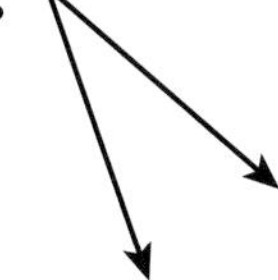
3. 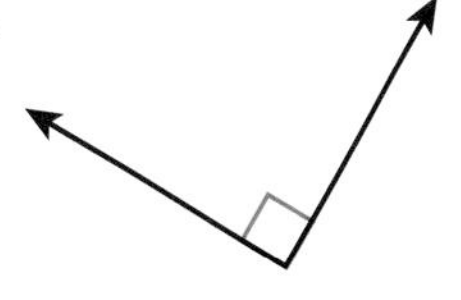
4. 

Set B

MG 3.8 page 564

Name the polygon. If the polygon is a quadrilateral, write all names that apply.

1. 
2. 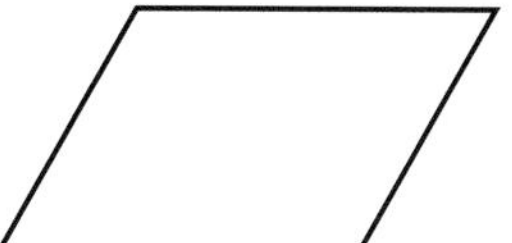
3. 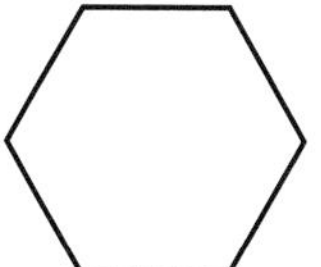
4. 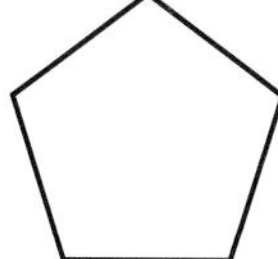

Set C

MG 3.7 page 566

Tell whether each triangle appears to be *equilateral*, *isosceles*, or *scalene*. Then tell whether each triangle appears to be *right*, *obtuse*, or *acute*.

1. 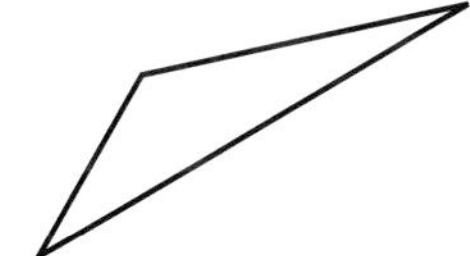
2. 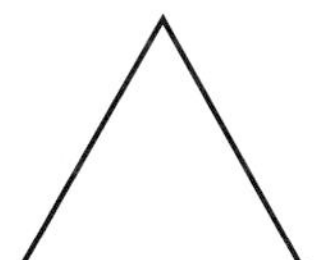
3. 
4. 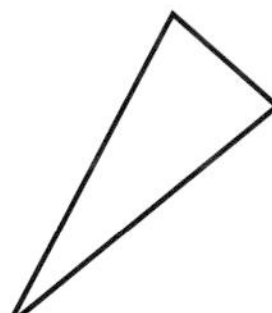

Set D

MG 3.2 page 568

Name the part of the circle that is shown in red. Write *center*, *radius*, or *diameter*.

1. 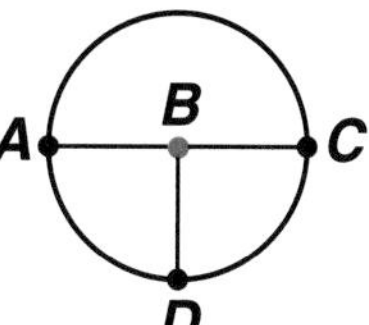

2. 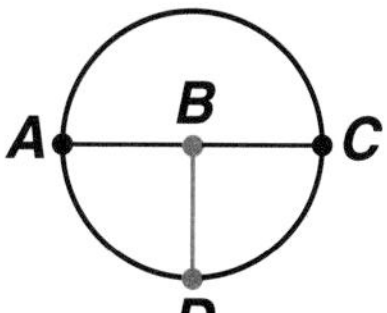

3. 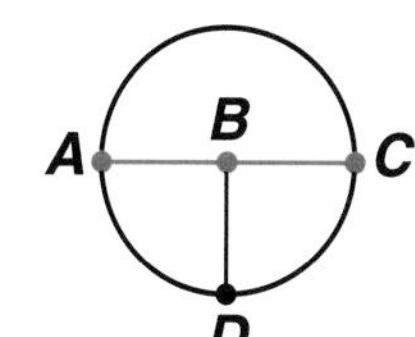

Education Place
Visit www.eduplace.com/camap/ for more **Extra Practice**.

Chapter Review/Test

Vocabulary and Concepts

MG 3.0, MG 3.1, MR 2.3

Write the best word to complete the sentence.

1. Lines that intersect at a right angle are ______.
2. A ______ has one endpoint and goes on without end in one direction.
3. Lines that are always the same distance apart are called ______ lines.

Skills

MG 3.0, MG 3.7

Tell whether the triangle appears to be *equilateral*, *isosceles*, or *scalene*. Then tell whether the triangle appears to be *right*, *obtuse*, or *acute*.

4.

5.

6.

Problem Solving and Reasoning

MG 3.0, MG 3.5, MG 3.7, MR 2.3

Solve.

7. A bicycle wheel moves forward a half turn. How many degrees has the wheel moved?
8. Carol cut out a triangle for her scrapbook. All sides were 4 inches long. What kind of triangle was it?
9. Diane's quilt has repeated figures that are 6-sided polygons. What figures are in the quilt?
10. What kind of angle is formed when a clock shows 10 minutes after 12?

Writing Math What kind of triangle will you make if you draw a line from one vertex to the opposite vertex of a rectangle? Explain.

Spiral Review and Test Practice

1. What is the value of the expression below if $n = 8$?

$20 - n \div 2$

A 4 **C** 12

B 6 **D** 16

Test Tip
Substitute each choice for the variable *n* to see which number makes the equation true.

AF 1.1 page 170

2. There are 7 equal rows of parking spaces in a parking lot. If there are 252 spaces in all, how many are in each row?

A 30 spaces **C** 259 spaces

B 36 spaces **D** 1,764 spaces

KEY NS 3.4 page 282

3. Song-Yi plotted 3 points on a grid. All 3 points were on the same straight line. If she plots another point on the line, what could be its coordinates?

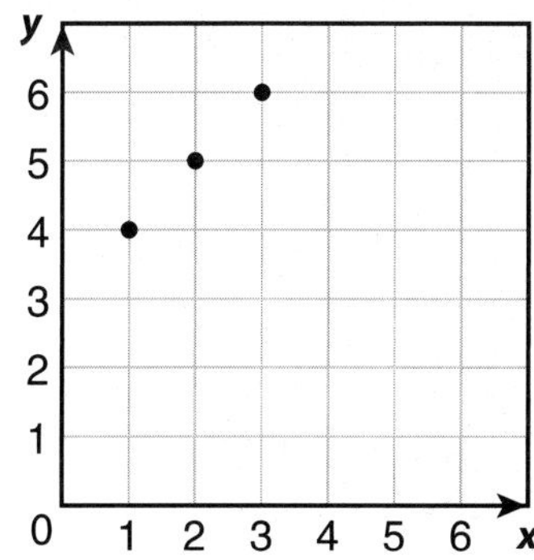

A (3, 4) **C** (4, 8)

B (4, 7) **D** (7, 4)

KEY MG 2.1 page 472

4. How many inches did the bean plant grow between 6 weeks and 8 weeks?

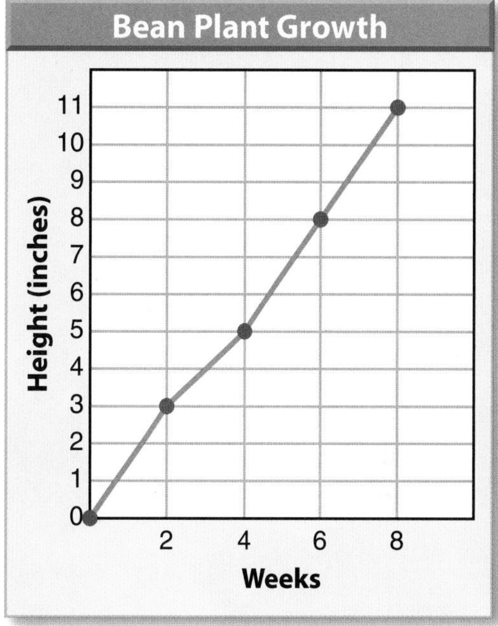

A 11 inches **C** 3 inches

B 8 inches **D** 2 inches

SDAP 1.3 page 520

5. Look at angle *PQR*.
Angle *PQR* appears to be

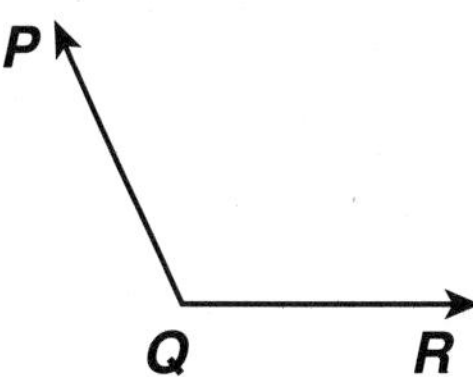

A an acute angle.

B a right angle.

C an obtuse angle.

D a line segment.

MG 3.5 page 560

Education Place
Visit www.eduplace.com/camap/ for **Test-Taking Tips** and **Extra Practice.**

Congruence and Symmetry

The California dogface butterfly is the official state insect of California.

Check What You Know

Vocabulary and Concepts MG 3.0, MR 2.3

Choose the best word to complete the sentence. pages 558, 560

Word Bank
- angle
- line
- point

1. A figure that is formed by two rays with a single endpoint is called an _____.

2. A location in space is called a _____.

Skills GRADE 3 MG 2.0

3. Are the figures the same size and shape?

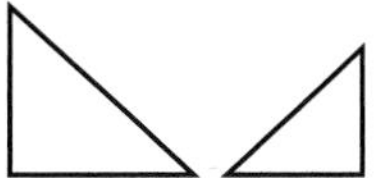

4. Which figures can be folded exactly in half?

A. **B.** **C.** **D.**

Problem Solving and Reasoning GRADE 3 MG 2.5

5. I am a solid figure. I have two round faces. I am the same shape as a drum or a can. What am I?

Vocabulary

Visualize It!

Figures that have **line symmetry** can be folded in half so that the two sides match exactly.

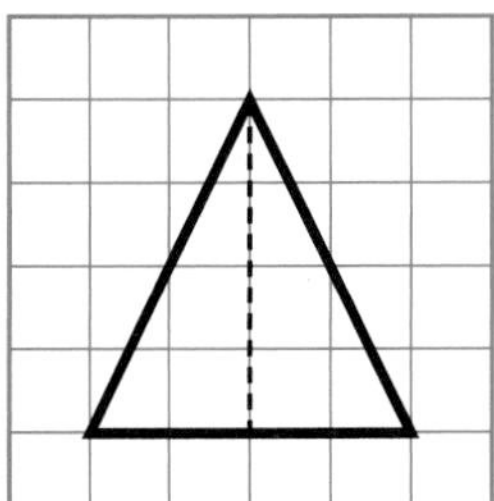

This figure has line symmetry.

Congruent figures have exactly the same size and shape.

These squares are congruent.

Language Tips

Some words have roots that help you know what they mean.

con- means "together with"

Some words are similar in English and Spanish.

English	Spanish
symmetry	**simetría**

See **English-Spanish Glossary** pages 644–666.

Education Place Visit www.eduplace.com/camap/ for the **eGlossary** and **eGames**.

CA Standards MR 2.3 Use a variety of methods, such as words, numbers, symbols, charts, graphs, tables, diagrams, and models, to explain mathematical reasoning. **Also MG 3.3, MG 3.4**

Hands On
Line Symmetry

Objective Model concepts of line symmetry.

CA Standards
MG 3.4 Identify figures that have bilateral and rotational symmetry.
MG 3.0 Students demonstrate an understanding of plane and solid geometric objects and use this knowledge to show relationships and solve problems.
Also MR 1.1, MR 2.0, MR 2.2, MR 2.3, MR 2.4

Vocabulary

line symmetry

line of symmetry

Materials
- Learning Tool 40 (Symmetrical Heart)
- tracing paper
- scissors

Explore

If a figure is folded in half and the two parts match exactly, the figure has **line symmetry**. The fold line is a **line of symmetry**.

Question How can you use models to identify figures that have line symmetry?

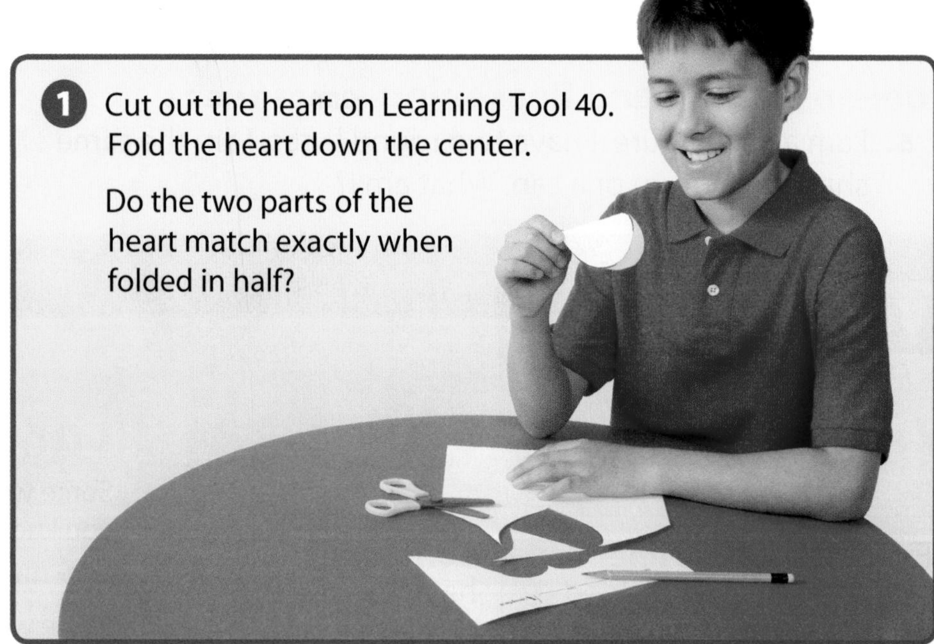

1 Cut out the heart on Learning Tool 40. Fold the heart down the center.

Do the two parts of the heart match exactly when folded in half?

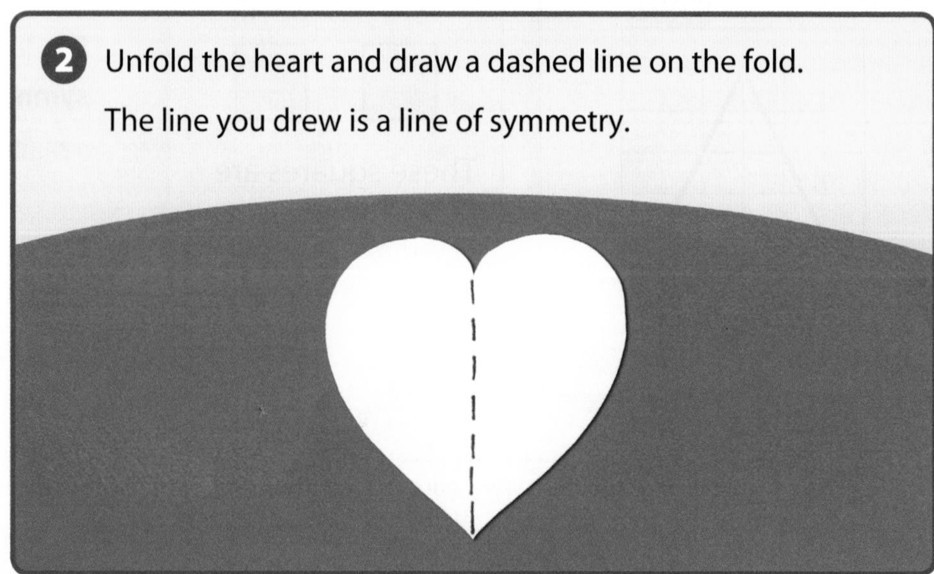

2 Unfold the heart and draw a dashed line on the fold.

The line you drew is a line of symmetry.

Figures can have more than one line of symmetry.

Look at the shapes below. Trace the shapes, cut them out, and fold them. Draw dashed lines to show all the lines of symmetry.

Figure A

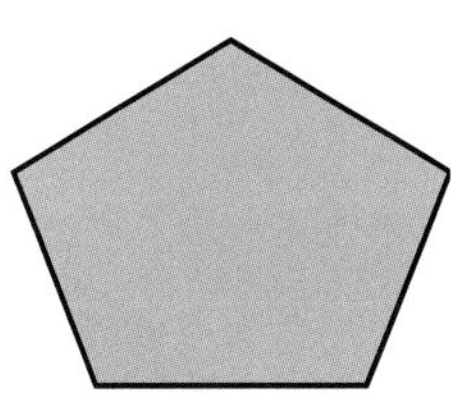

Figure B

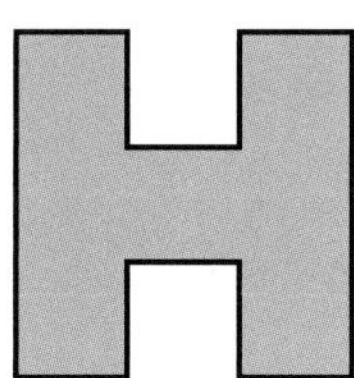

Figure C

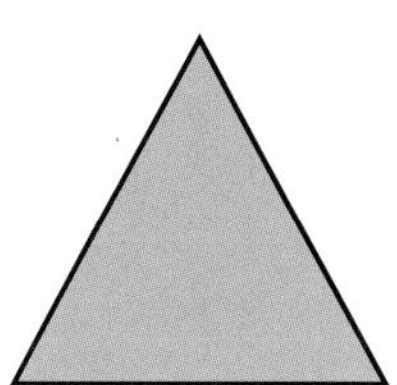

Figure D

Figure E

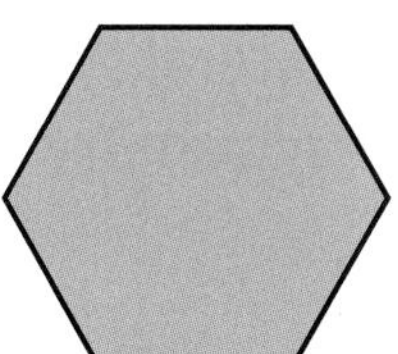

Figure F

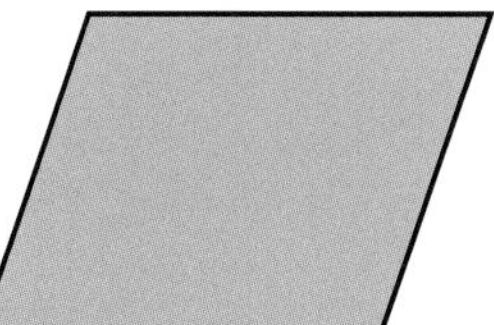

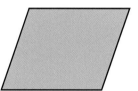

Copy and complete the table.

	Figure	Does It Have Line Symmetry?	How Many Lines of Symmetry?
1.	Figure A		
2.	Figure B		
3.	Figure C		
4.	Figure D		
5.	Figure E		
6.	Figure F		

Writing Math

Analyze Is the dashed line in the rectangle a line of symmetry? Explain why or why not.

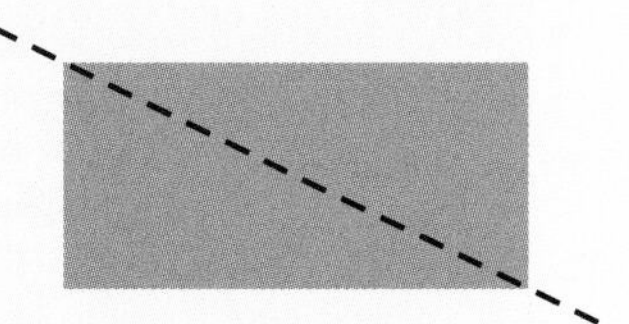

Extra Practice See page 595, Set A.

Line or Bilateral Symmetry

Objective Identify figures that have line or bilateral symmetry.

CA Standards
MG 3.4 Identify figures that have bilateral and rotational symmetry.
MG 3.0 Students demonstrate an understanding of plane and solid geometric objects and use this knowledge to show relationships and solve problems.
Also MR 2.0, MR 2.2, MR 2.3, MR 2.4

Vocabulary

bilateral symmetry

Materials
Learning Tool 48 (Centimeter Grid Paper)

Learn by Example

In Lesson 1, you explored figures that had lines of symmetry. You learned that a figure has a line of symmetry if you can fold it so that both parts match. If both parts match, the fold line is a line of symmetry.

Line symmetry can also be called **bilateral symmetry**. This butterfly has bilateral symmetry. There is one line of symmetry.

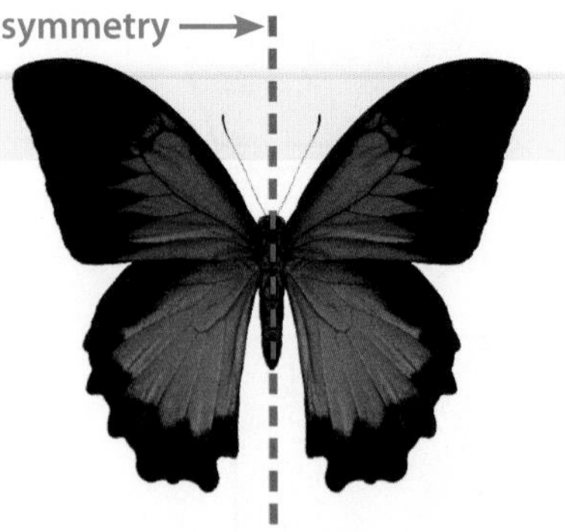

Ask Yourself
If you fold on the dashed line, would the two parts match exactly?

Guided Practice

Is the dashed line a line of symmetry?

1. 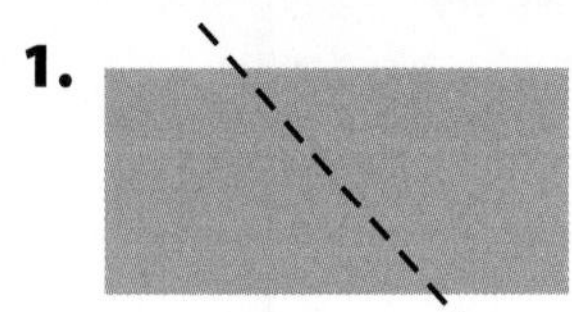

2. 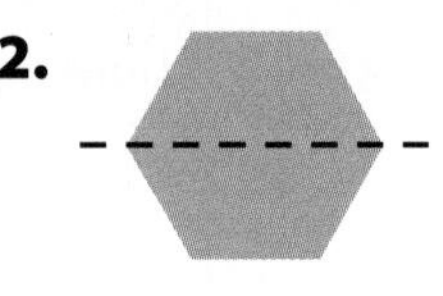

Draw each figure on grid paper. Draw the line of symmetry. Draw the other half of the figure on your grid paper.

3. 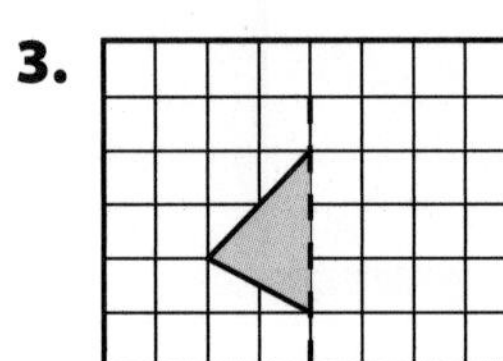

4. 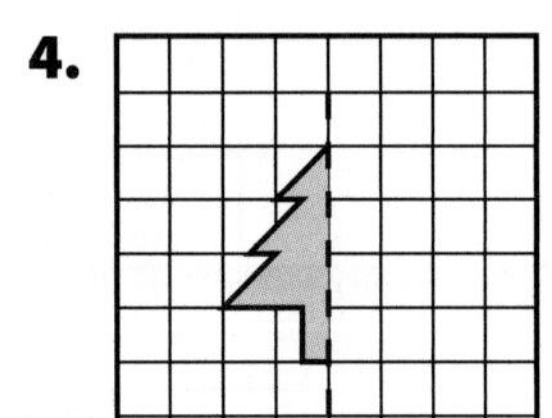

5. 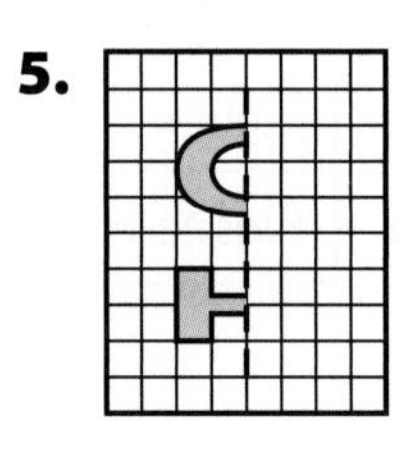

Math Talk How can you prove or disprove that the figure in Exercise 1 shows a line of symmetry?

Practice and Problem Solving

Is the dashed line a line of symmetry?

6. 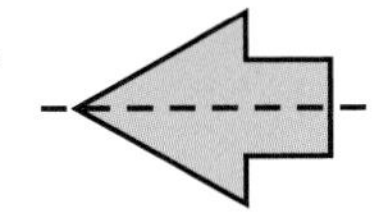

7. 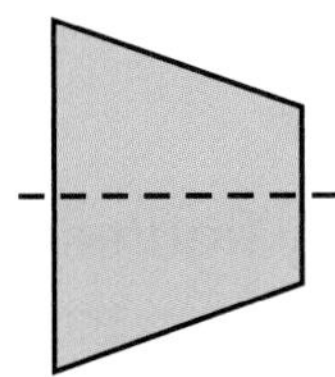

8. 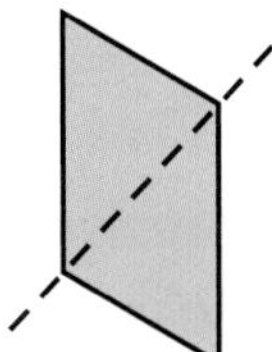

9. 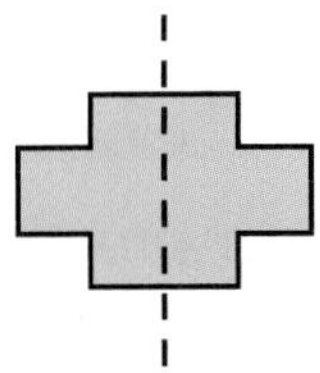

Draw each figure on grid paper. Draw the line of symmetry. Draw the other half of the figure on your grid paper.

10. 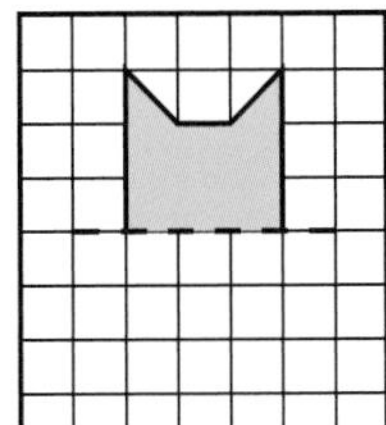

11. 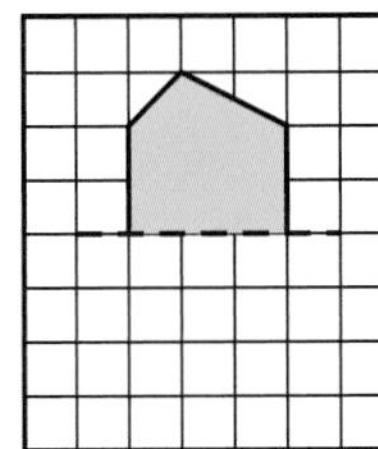

12. 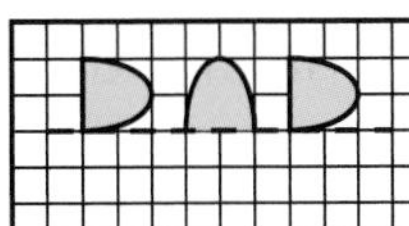

Solve.

13. Trace the circle at the right. Cut it out. Fold it on the line segment *NP*. What happens to the points *M* and *O*? How many lines of symmetry does a circle have? Explain your thinking.

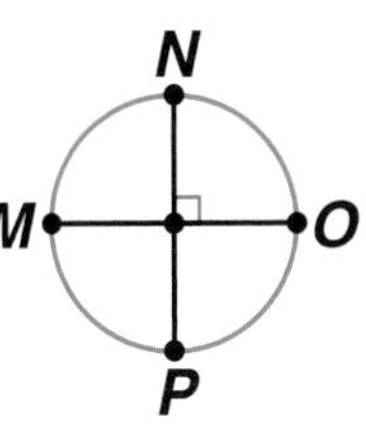

14. Which of the letters have line symmetry? Use a drawing to help you explain.

Spiral Review and Test Practice

Name each angle in three ways and classify it as *acute, obtuse, right,* or *straight*. MG 3.5 page 560

15. 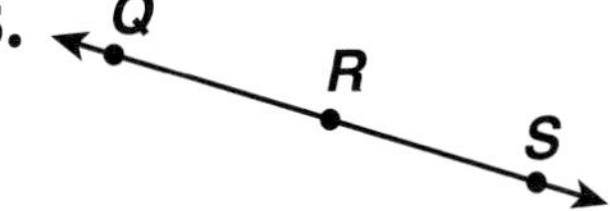

16. 

17. 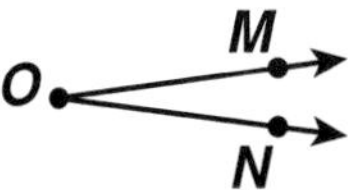

Write the letter of the correct answer. MG 3.4

18. Which picture appears to show a line of symmetry?

A 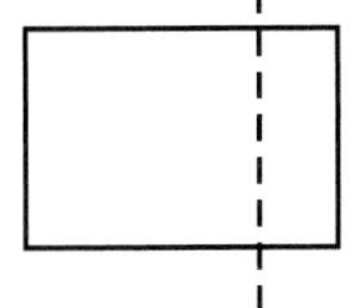

B 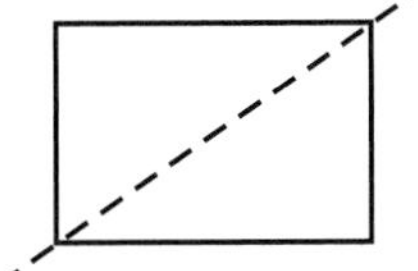

C 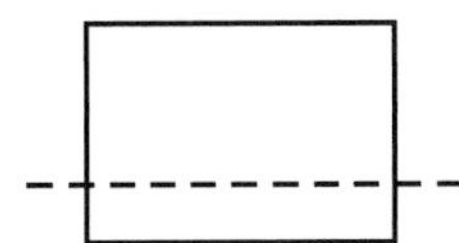

D 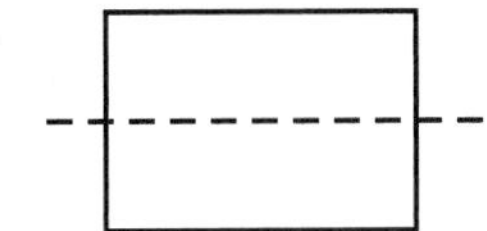

Rotational Symmetry

Objective Identify figures that have rotational symmetry.

CA Standards
MG 3.4 Identify figures that have bilateral and rotational symmetry.

MG 3.5 Know the definitions of a right angle, an acute angle, and an obtuse angle. Understand that 90°, 180°, 270°, and 360° are associated, respectively, with $\frac{1}{4}$, $\frac{1}{2}$, $\frac{3}{4}$, and full turns.

Also MG 3.0, MG 3.7, MR 1.0, MR 1.1, MR 2.0, MR 2.3, MR 2.4, MR 3.0, MR 3.2, MR 3.3

Vocabulary

rotational symmetry

Materials
tracing paper

Learn by Example

You already know how to identify figures with line symmetry. In this lesson, you will learn to identify figures with rotational symmetry.

A figure has **rotational symmetry** about a point if you can rotate it less than a full turn (360°) about that point, and the figure looks the same as it did before the rotation.

Example 1

quarter turn
90°

half turn
180°

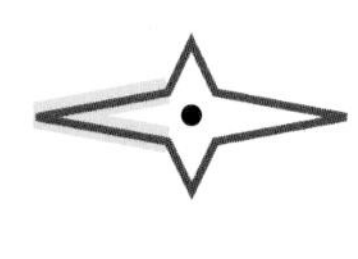
three-quarter turn
270°

full turn
360°

This figure looks the same after a half turn as it did before the rotation, so the figure has rotational symmetry.

Example 2

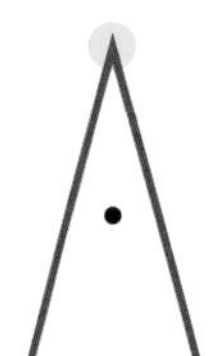

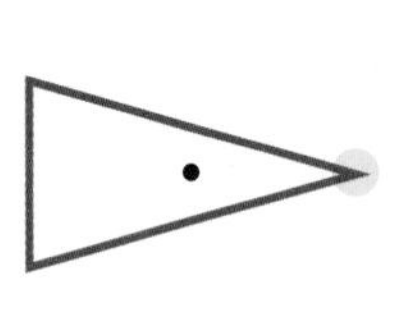
quarter turn
90°

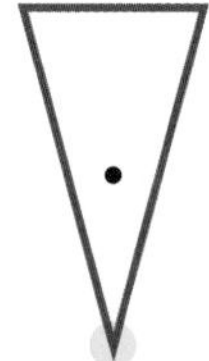
half turn
180°

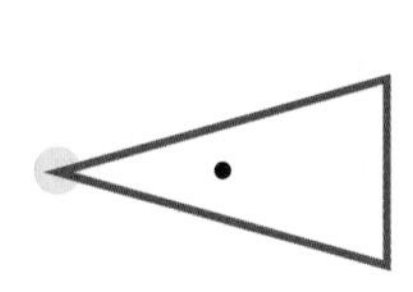
three-quarter turn
270°

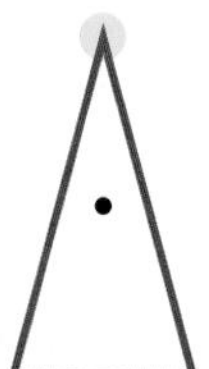
full turn
360°

This figure does not look the same until it has been rotated through a full turn, so the figure does not have rotational symmetry.

Guided Practice

Trace each figure. Does the figure have rotational symmetry?

1. 

2. 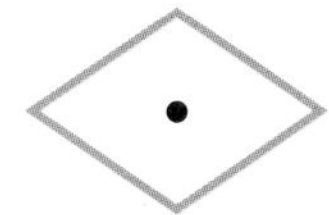

3. 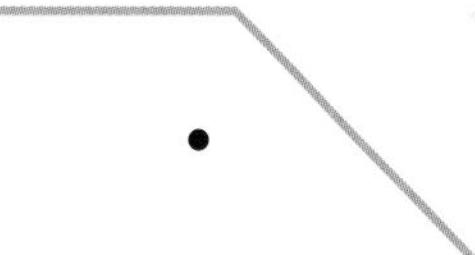

Ask Yourself

Can I turn the figure less than a full turn and make it look like it did before I turned it?

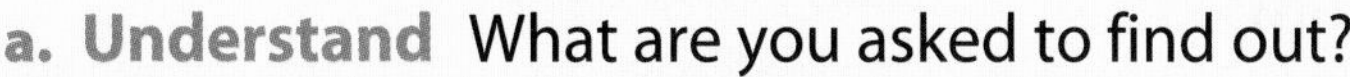

Guided Problem Solving

Use the questions to solve this problem.

4. Does this equilateral triangle have rotational symmetry?

a. **Understand** What are you asked to find out?

b. **Plan** How can you use a tracing of the figure to find out if it has rotational symmetry?

c. **Solve** Use tracing paper to solve the problem.

d. **Look Back** Did the figure look the same before a half turn?

5. Generalize Do all equilateral triangles have rotational symmetry?

Math Talk Can a figure have line symmetry but not rotational symmetry? Give an example.

Practice and Problem Solving

Trace each figure. Does the figure have rotational symmetry?

6. 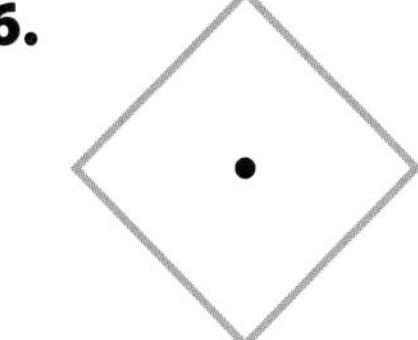

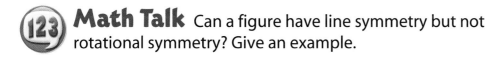

7. 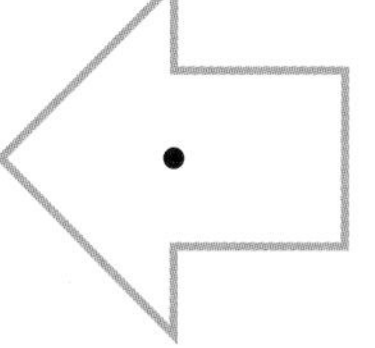

8. 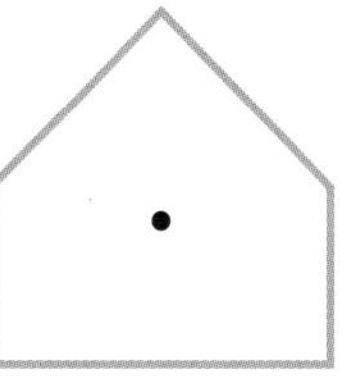

9. 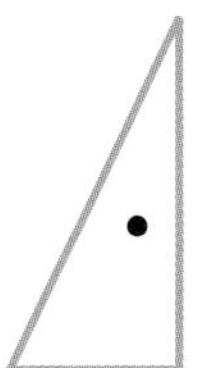

10. 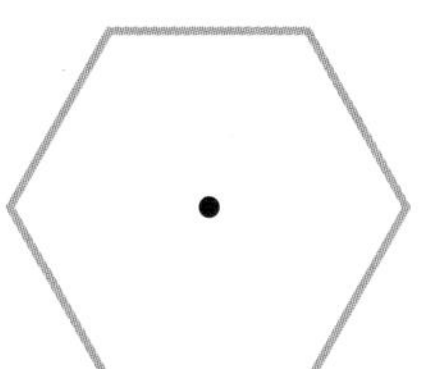

11. 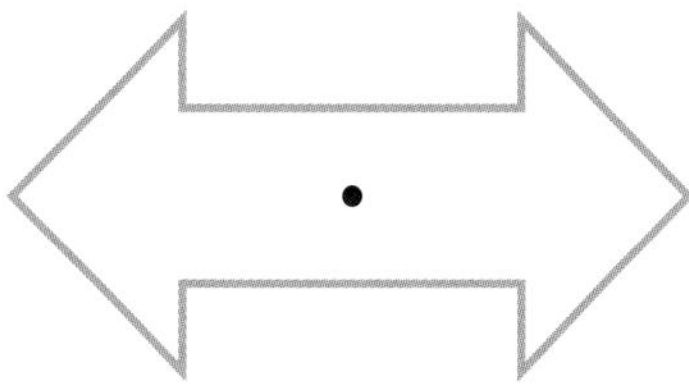

Solve.

12. Sora made the figure at the right in art class. Trace the figure. Turn it. Does the figure have rotational symmetry around the point? Explain how you got your answer.

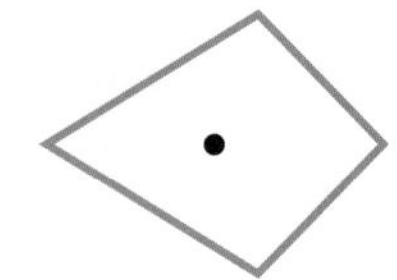

13. Draw 2 figures, one that has rotational symmetry and one that does not. Explain your thinking.

Science Link

Use the pictures to solve.

14. Would the California poppy look about the same after a quarter turn, a half turn, and a three-quarter turn?

15. **Challenge** Does the tulip have rotational symmetry? Explain.

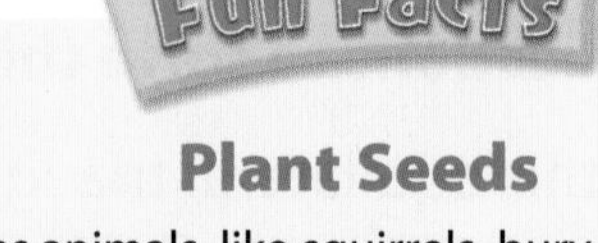

Plant Seeds

- Sometimes animals, like squirrels, bury seeds in the ground to store them.
- Some seeds have hooks that catch onto an animal's fur as it walks by.
- Many animals eat fruit with seeds in them. When the seed passes out of the animal, the seed can be a long way from where it started!

California poppy

Tulip

Star anise

Science LS 3.c

Spiral Review and Test Practice

Name each polygon with all names that apply. MG 3.7, MG 3.8 pages 564, 566

16. 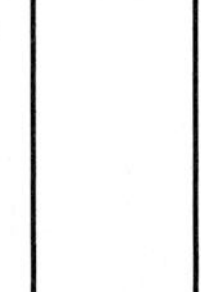

17. 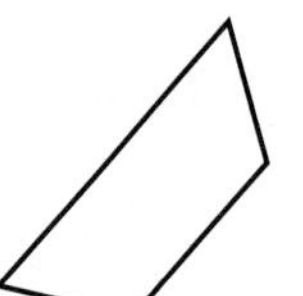

18. 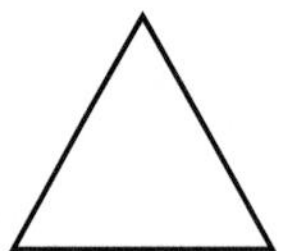

19. 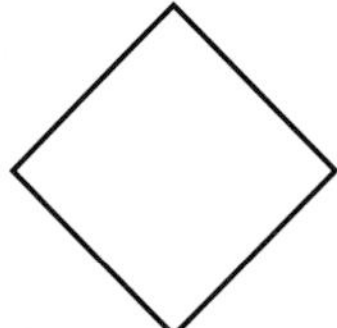

Write the letter of the correct answer. MG 3.4

20. Which letter appears to have rotational symmetry?

A 

B 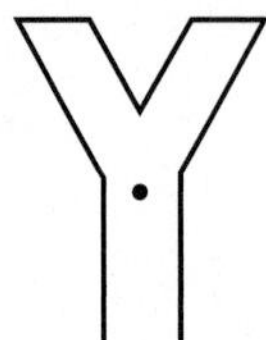

C 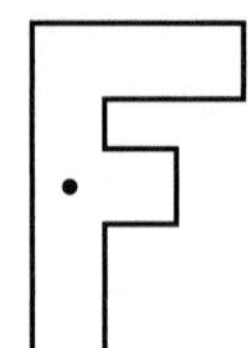

D 

Extra Practice See page 595, Set B.

Key Standards Review

Need Help?
See Key Standards Handbook.

Write the number in standard form. KEY NS 1.1

1. six hundred, eighty-seven million
2. two million, nine hundred seven thousand, two hundred thirteen
3. seventy four million, six hundred thousand
4. three million, eight hundred thousand, five hundred seven
5. two hundred forty-six million, nine hundred thousand

Write the number in word form. KEY NS 1.1

6. 12,341,792
7. 103,783,009

Compare. Use >, <, or = for each ⬭. KEY NS 1.2

8. 3.5 ⬭ 3.05
9. 2.14 ⬭ 2.13
10. 5.0 ⬭ 4.9

Order the decimals from least to greatest. KEY NS 1.2

11. 1.02 1.12 1.20
12. 1.34 1.43 1.4
13. 3.33 3.03 3.30
14. 2.10 2.22 2.32

Challenge Visual Thinking

Draw Symmetry MG 3.4

1. Draw a figure with line symmetry.
2. Draw a figure with no rotational symmetry.
3. Draw a figure with two lines of symmetry that is not a rectangle.

CA Standards

MG 3.3 Identify congruent figures.

MG 3.0 Students demonstrate an understanding of plane and solid geometric objects and use this knowledge to show relationships and solve problems.

Also MG 3.8, MR 1.0, MR 1.1, MR 2.0, MR 2.3, MR 2.4, MR 3.0, MR 3.3

Vocabulary

congruent

Materials

centimeter ruler

Congruent Figures

Objective Identify congruent figures.

Learn by Example

You can tell that the puzzle piece belongs in the puzzle because it is the same size and shape as the empty space in the puzzle.

Plane figures that have the same size and shape are **congruent** figures. Congruent figures do not have to be in the same position.

One way to tell whether two figures are congruent is to trace one figure and then check if it matches the other figure.

These figures are congruent.

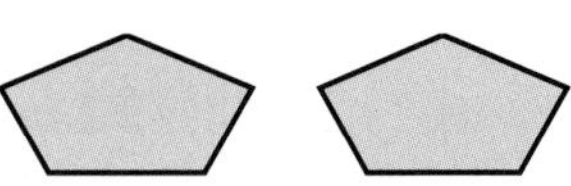

These figures are not congruent.

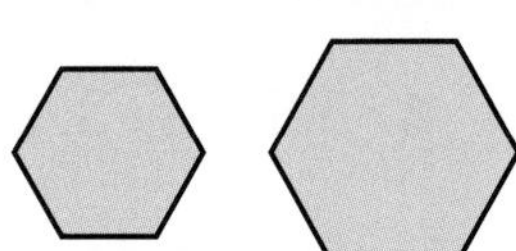

These figures are congruent.

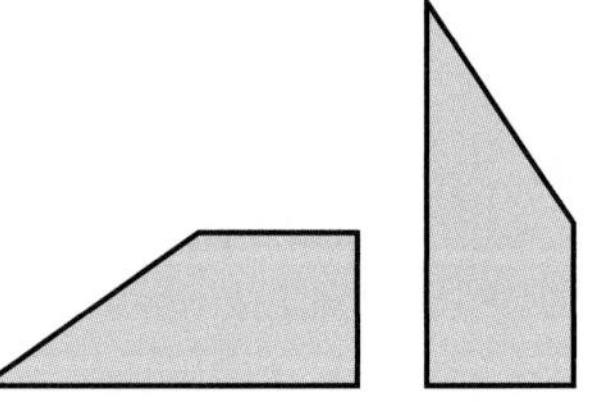

Another Example

Sometimes different parts of the same figure are congruent. Look at figure *ABCD*.

$\overleftrightarrow{BC}$ is congruent to $\overleftrightarrow{CD}$.

$\overleftrightarrow{AB}$ is congruent to $\overleftrightarrow{AD}$.

$\angle B$ is congruent to $\angle D$.

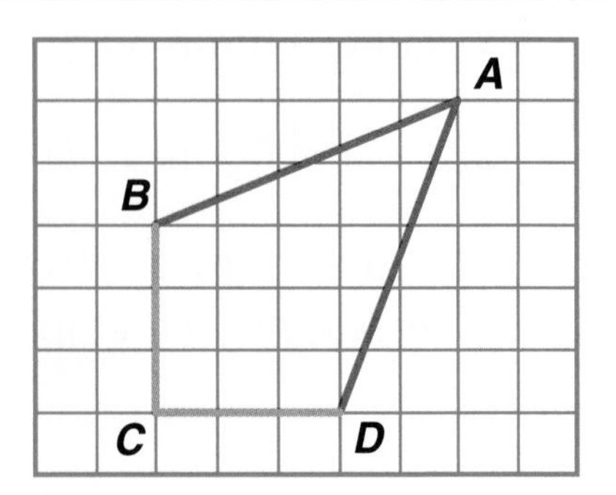

Guided Practice

Do the figures in each pair appear to be congruent?

1. 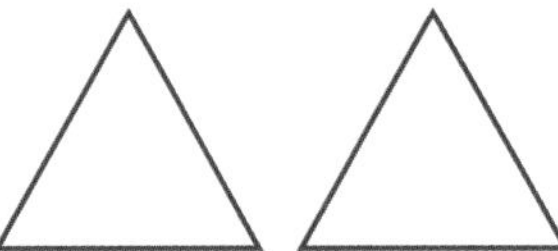

2. 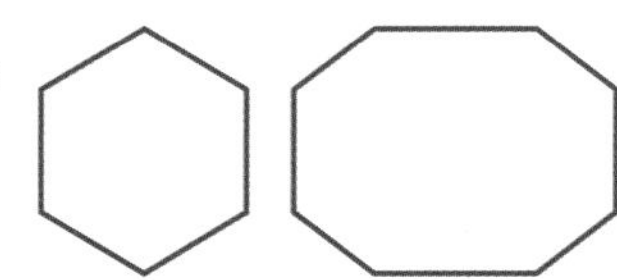

3. 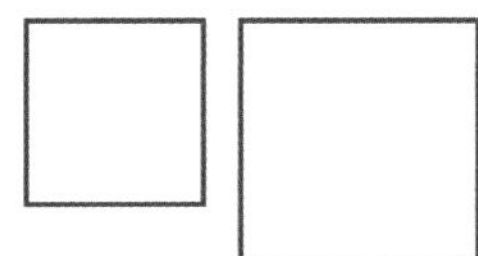

4. 

> **Ask Yourself**
> - Are the figures the same shape?
> - Are the figures the same size?

Math Talk Are all hexagons congruent? Explain why or why not.

Practice and Problem Solving

Do the figures in each pair appear to be congruent?

5. 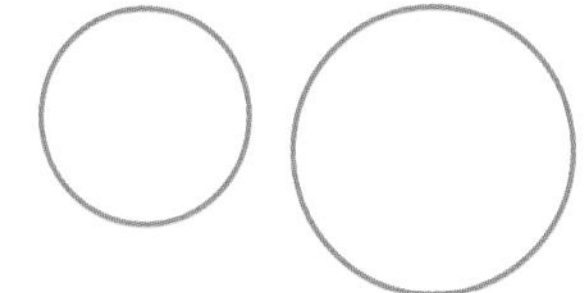

6. 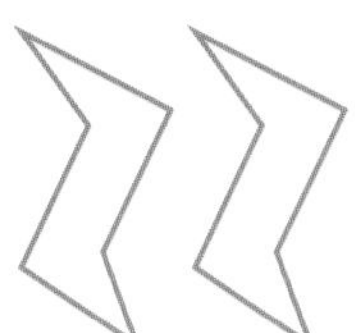

7. 

8. 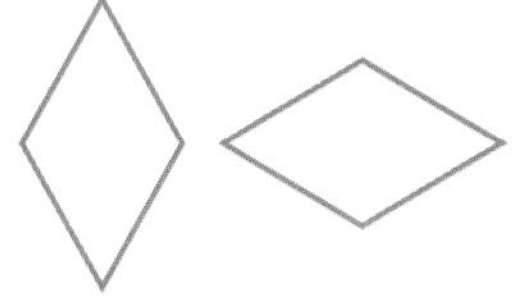

9. 

10. 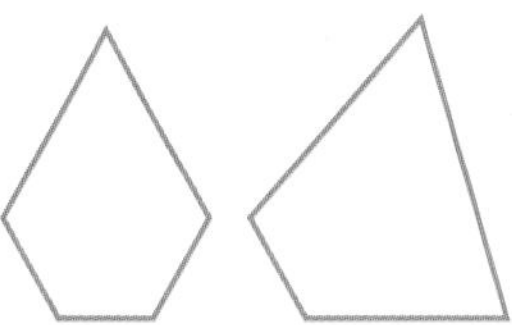

Choose the figure that appears to be congruent to the first figure. Write *A*, *B*, or *C*.

11. 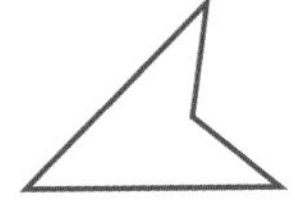 **A.** 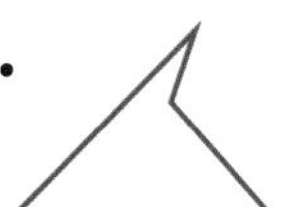 **B.** 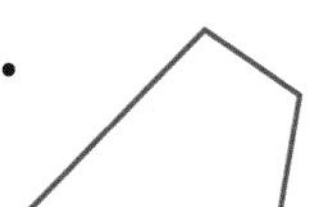 **C.** 

12. 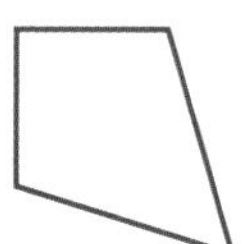 **A.** 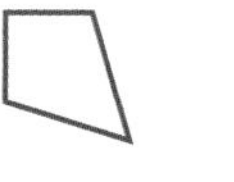 **B.** 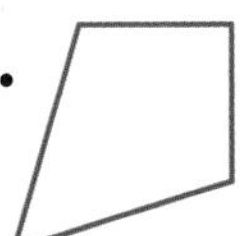 **C.** 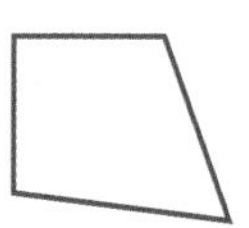

13.  **A.**  **B.**  **C.** 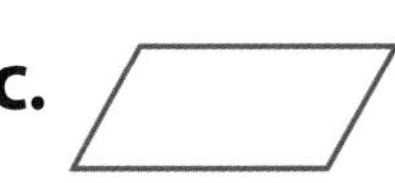

Use the figures at the right for Problems 14–16.

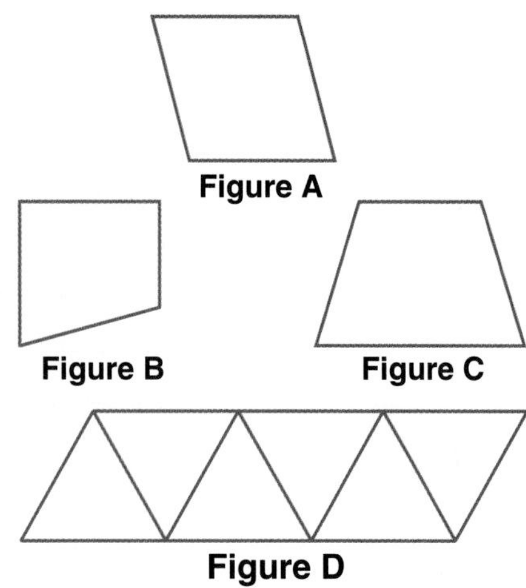

14. A rhombus has 4 sides that are congruent. Use a centimeter ruler. Which of the 4 figures is a rhombus?

15. Which figure has right angles? Is it a rectangle? A square? Explain your answer.

16. **Challenge** Six congruent triangles form Figure D. What geometric figure is it? Draw a picture of another way to combine the triangles to make a different geometric figure.

Real World Data

Solve.

17. An architect needed to design a window. She drew a rhombus with a perimeter of 24 feet. What was the length of one of the sides of the window?

18. **Create and Solve** Draw a picture of one side of a house. Include windows, doors, and a roof. Include a pair of congruent figures. Exchange problems with a partner and identify the congruent shapes in each other's drawings.

Plane Figures in Architecture

- Floors, ceilings, walls, windows, and doors are often quadrilaterals.
- Triangles are often used in support structures because their 3-sided shape makes them especially strong. Steel bridges often include triangular forms.

Spiral Review and Test Practice

Use the bar graph for Problems 19–20. SDAP 1.3 page 518

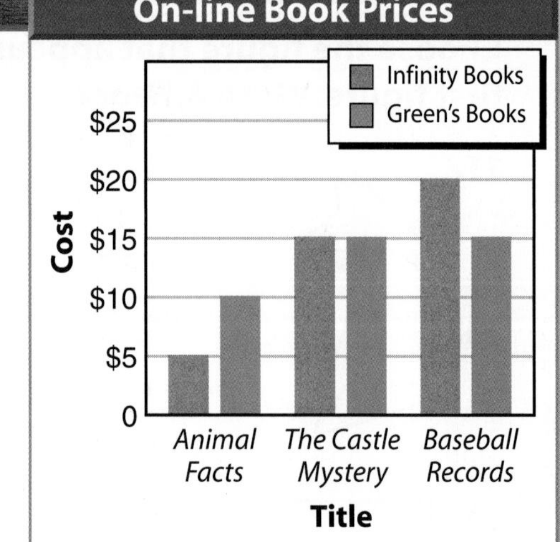

19. How much does the book *Animal Facts* cost at Green's Books?

20. Which book costs the same at both sites?

Write the letter of the correct answer. MG 3.3

21. Which best describes congruent figures?

A same size and shape **C** same shape

B same size **D** same size or shape

Tiling Floors

Many of the floors you walk down every day are tiled, from kitchens to bathrooms to school hallways. Tiles can come in all shapes, sizes, and colors. Contractors work with home and building owners to choose the right tiles and patterns for floors.

The size and shape of a room can help determine the size and shape of the tiles used. Some floors can even have tiles of different shapes that create interlocking patterns.

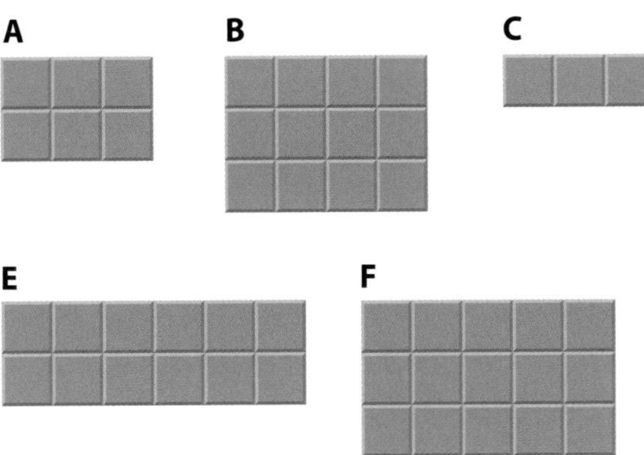

Use what you know about perimeter, geometric shapes, and symmetry to solve Problems 1–4.

1. Which of the groups of tiles have the same perimeter? Do they also have the same number of tiles?
2. Which of the groups of tiles have the same number of tiles? Do they also have the same perimeter?
3. Look at the tile pattern to the right. Are the red tiles congruent to the yellow tiles? How do you know?

4. How many lines of symmetry do the red tiles have? Do they also have rotational symmetry? How do you know?

CA Standards
MG 1.2, MG 1.3, MG 3.3, MG 3.4

Problem Solving Strategy
Patterns in the Coordinate Grid

Objective Identify patterns in the coordinate grid to solve a problem.

CA Standards
MR 1.1 Analyze problems by identifying relationships, distinguishing relevant from irrelevant information, sequencing and prioritizing information, and observing patterns.
MG 3.0 Students demonstrate an understanding of plane and solid geometric objects and use this knowledge to show relationships and solve problems.
Also MG 3.3, KEY MG 2.0, MR 1.2, MR 2.0, MR 2.2, MR 2.3, MR 2.4, MR 3.0, MR 3.1, MR 3.2

Think
Remember, ***vertices*** is the plural of *vertex*.
Coordinates is another word for the numbers in an ordered pair.

Learn by Example

The congruent triangles form a pattern in the coordinate grid. The ordered pairs that name the vertices form a pattern as well. If the pattern continues, what are the ordered pairs for the vertices of the fifth triangle?

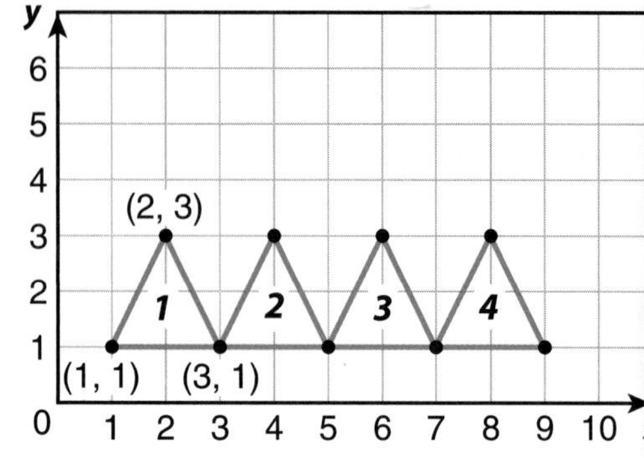

UNDERSTAND

You want to find the ordered pairs for the vertices of the next triangle in the pattern.

PLAN

Write the ordered pairs for each vertex of the first four triangles. Look for a pattern to find the coordinates for the fifth triangle.

How do the *x* values change? How do the *y* values change?

SOLVE

Left Vertex

△	*x*	*y*
1	1	1
2	3	1
3	5	1
4	7	1
5		

Top Vertex

△	*x*	*y*
1	2	3
2	4	3
3	6	3
4	8	3
5		

Right Vertex

△	*x*	*y*
1	3	1
2	5	1
3	7	1
4	9	1
5		

The three vertices of the fifth triangle are (9, 1), (10, 3), and (11, 1).

LOOK BACK

Why do the *x*-coordinates change while the *y*-coordinates do not?

Solve using the Ask Yourself questions.

1. The congruent triangles form a pattern in the coordinate grid. If the pattern continues, what are the coordinates for the vertices of the fourth triangle?

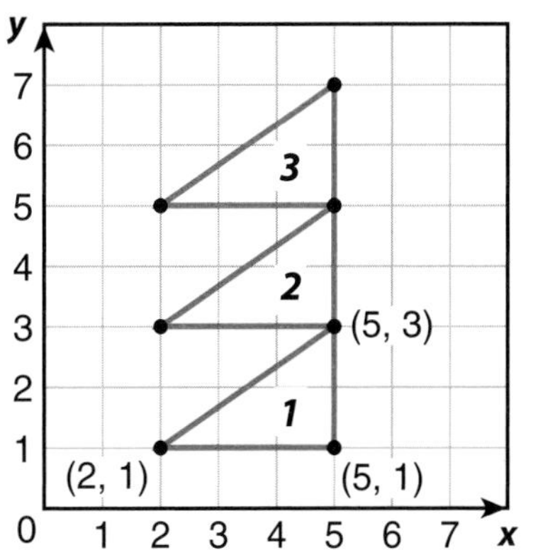

Ask Yourself

- What are the coordinates for the second and third triangles?
- What patterns do I see?

Math Talk How is the pattern of these coordinates different from the pattern on page 592?

Independent Problem Solving

Solve. Explain why your answer makes sense.

2. The triangles shown are congruent. Find the coordinates for the vertices of the fourth triangle if the pattern continues.

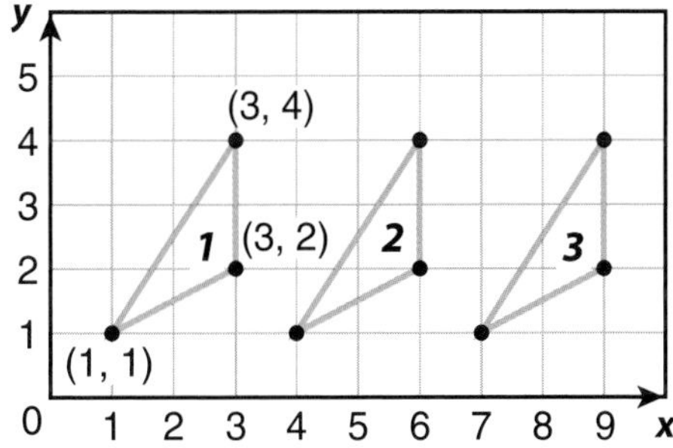

3. The congruent squares form a pattern in the coordinate grid. If the pattern continues, what are the ordered pairs of the vertices of the fourth square?

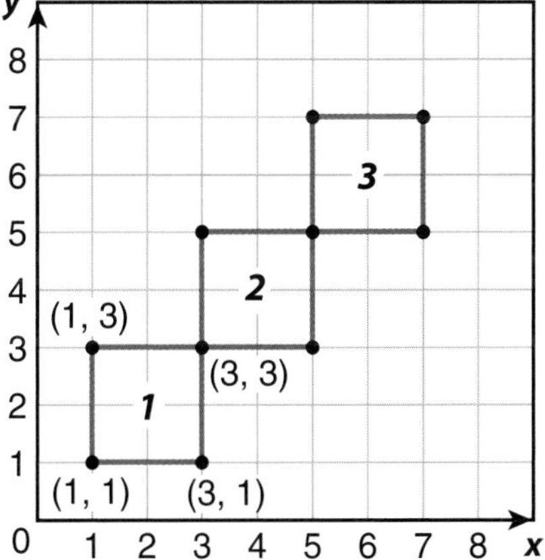

4. Challenge What are the coordinates of the vertices of the quadrilateral after a 90° clockwise rotation around the given point? A 180° rotation? A 270° rotation? A 360° rotation?

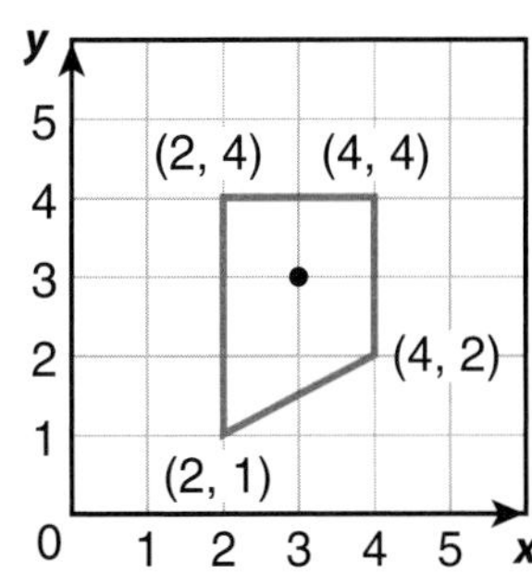

5. Create and Solve On a coordinate grid, use five congruent triangles to create a pattern. Find the coordinates of the sixth, seventh, and eighth triangles if your pattern continues.

Reading & Writing Math

Vocabulary

A **line of symmetry** is a line along which a figure can be folded so that the two halves match exactly. Two figures that match exactly are called **congruent**.

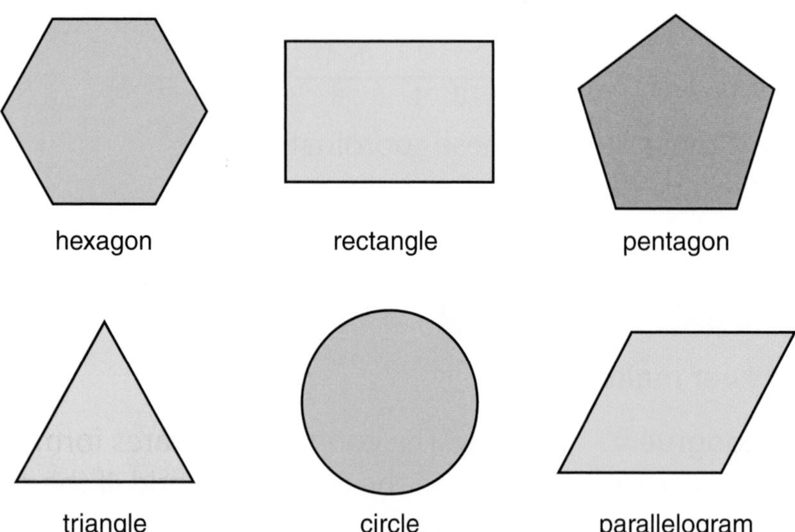

Complete the chart by naming the figures in the appropriate column.

Two Lines of Symmetry	Three Lines of Symmetry	More Than Three Lines of Symmetry

Writing What kind of figure or figures would you use to tile a floor? Explain why and make a sketch of your pattern.

Reading Look for this book in your library. *Sam Johnson and the Blue Ribbon Quilt*, by Lisa Campbell Ernst

CA Standards
MR 2.3 Use a variety of methods, such as words, numbers, symbols, charts, graphs, tables, diagrams, and models, to explain mathematical reasoning.

Also MG 3.3, MG 3.4, MG 3.0

 Standards-Based Extra Practice

Set A

MG 3.4 page 580

How many lines of symmetry does the figure or letter have?

1. 

2.

3.

4. 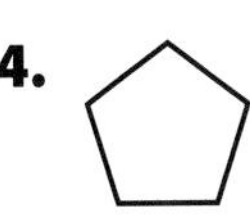

5. 

6. 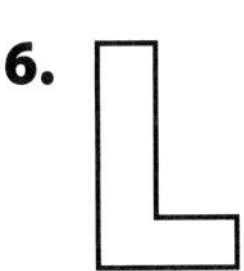

7. 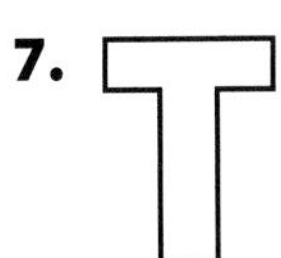

8. 

9. 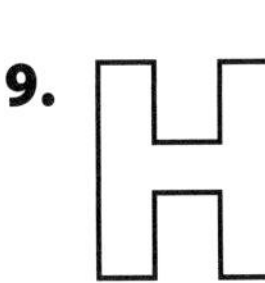

10. Explain If an equilateral triangle has lines of symmetry, do all triangles have lines of symmetry? Why or why not?

Set B

MG 3.4 page 584

Does the figure or letter have rotational symmetry? Write *yes* or *no*.

1. 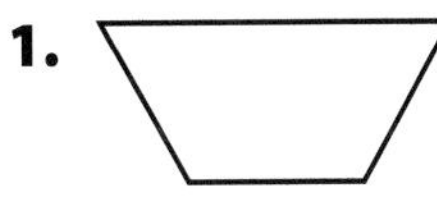

2. 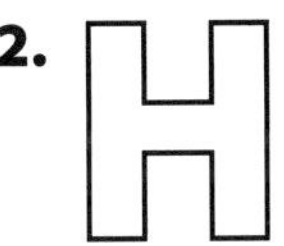

3. 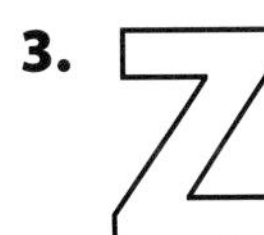

4. 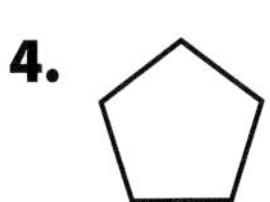

5.

6. 

7.

8.

9.

10. Compare What is the relationship between rotational symmetry and the number of lines of symmetry for an equilateral triangle?

Education Place
Visit www.eduplace.com/camap/ for more **Extra Practice.**

Chapter Review/Test

Vocabulary and Concepts — MG 3.0, MG 3.4, MR 2.3

Write the best word to complete the sentence.

1. A circle has line symmetry and ______ symmetry.
2. Another name for line symmetry is ______.

Skills — MG 3.3, MG 3.4

Is the dashed line a line of symmetry?

3. 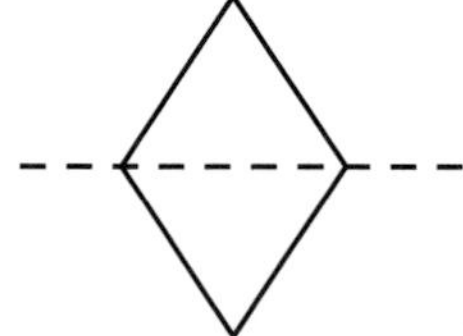

4. 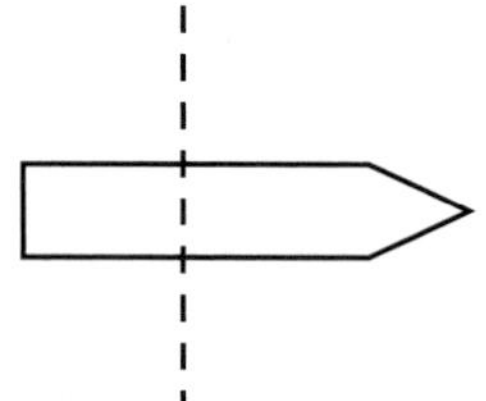

5. 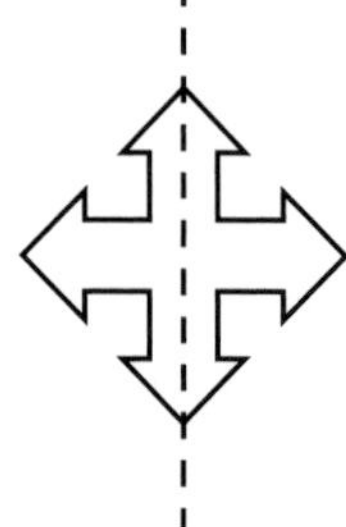

Do the figures in each pair appear to be congruent? Write *yes* or *no*.

6. 

7. 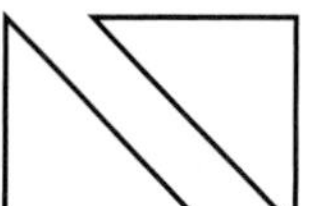

8. 

Problem Solving and Reasoning — MG 3.0, MG 3.4, MR 2.3

Solve.

9. A sticker is shaped like an equilateral triangle. Does it have rotational symmetry?

10. A new postage stamp is a square. How many lines of symmetry does it have?

Writing Math Explain why a square has more lines of symmetry than a rectangle.

Spiral Review and Test Practice

1. A store has 495 boxes of pens. If there are 36 pens in each box, what is the total number of pens in all the boxes?

A 459 pens

B 531 pens

C 4,455 pens

D 17,820 pens

Test Tip
Use estimation to check if your answer is reasonable.

MR 2.1, KEY NS 3.3 page 242

2. The total length of a fence is 287.39 meters. What is the length of the fence rounded to the nearest whole number?

A 287 meters **C** 288 meters

B 287.4 meters **D** 300 meters

NS 2.2 page 442

3. What is the length of the line segment shown on the grid?

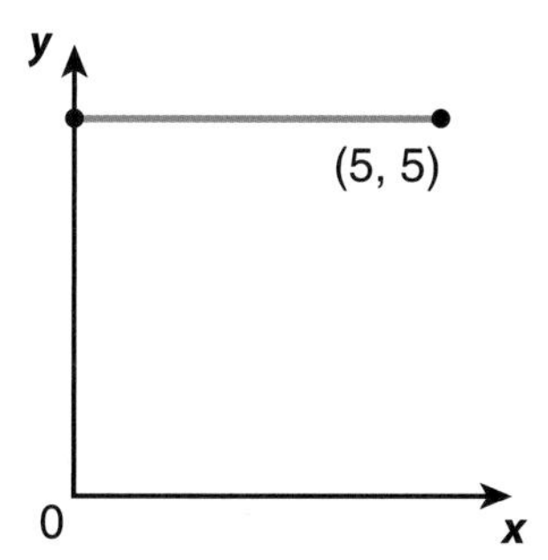

A 1 unit **C** 5 units

B 4 units **D** 6 units

KEY MG 2.2 page 492

4. A bag holds 1 red marble and 1 blue marble. A marble is picked and put back twice. What is the probability of picking 2 red marbles?

A $\frac{1}{4}$ **C** $\frac{2}{4}$

B $\frac{1}{2}$ **D** $\frac{4}{4}$

SDAP 2.1 page 540

5. Which statement is true?

A All rectangles are squares.

B All squares are rectangles.

C All parallelograms are rectangles.

D All trapezoids are rectangles.

MG 3.8 page 564

6. Which picture appears to show a line of symmetry?

Test Tip
Remember that a line of symmetry divides a figure in identical halves.

A
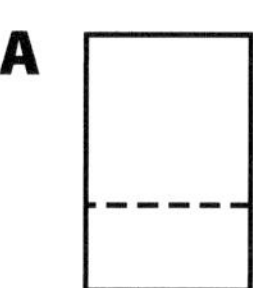

C
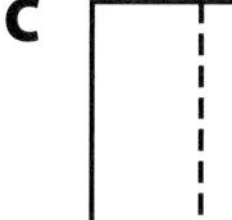

B
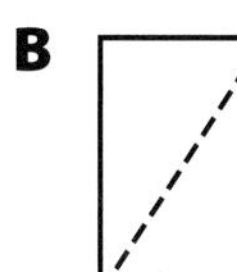

D
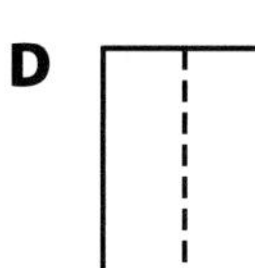

MG 3.4 page 582

Education Place
Visit www.eduplace.com/camap/ for **Test-Taking Tips** and **Extra Practice.**

Perimeter and Area

Check What You Know

Word Bank
- perimeter
- square units
- congruent
- area
- length

Vocabulary and Concepts GRADE 3 KEY MG 1.2, KEY MG 1.3, MR 2.3

Choose the best word to complete the sentence.

1. Area is measured in ____.
2. The measure of the distance around a figure is its ____.
3. Figures that are ____ have the same size and shape.

Skills GRADE 3 KEY MG 1.2, KEY MG 1.3

Find the perimeter of the figure in units.

4.
5.
6.

Find the area of the figure in square units.

7.
8.
9.

Problem Solving and Reasoning GRADE 3 KEY MG 1.2

10. A square has a perimeter of 12 units. What is its area? Draw a diagram to solve.

Vocabulary

Visualize It!

Perimeter is the sum of the lengths of the sides of a polygon.

1 unit

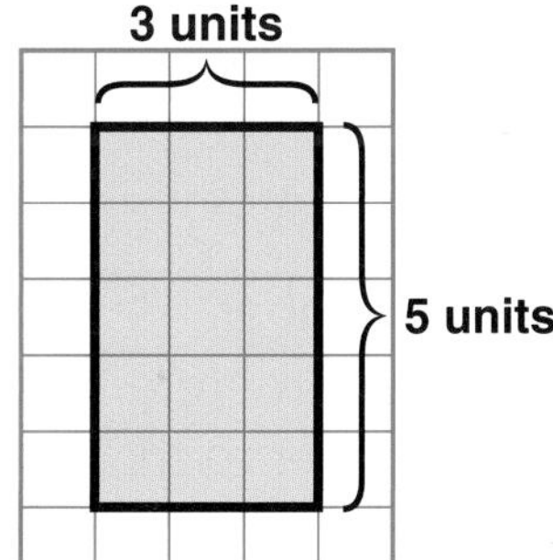

Perimeter = 16 units
Area = 15 square units

Area is the number of square units that cover a surface.

1 square unit 1 unit 1 unit

Language Tip

Some words are similar in English and Spanish.

English	Spanish
perimeter	perímetro
area	área
unit	unidad

See **English-Spanish Glossary** pages 644–666.

Education Place Visit www.eduplace.com/camap/ for the **eGlossary** and **eGames**.

CA Standards MR 2.3 Use a variety of methods, such as words, numbers, symbols, charts, graphs, tables, diagrams, and models, to explain mathematical reasoning. **Also MG 1.0**

Hands On
Model Perimeter and Area

Objective Use models to explore how perimeter and area can vary.

CA Standards
MG 1.2 Recognize that rectangles that have the same area can have different perimeters.
MG 1.3 Understand that rectangles that have the same perimeter can have different areas.
Also MG 1.0, MG 1.1, MR 1.1, MR 2.0, MR 2.3, MR 2.4, MR 3.0, MR 3.3

Vocabulary
- perimeter
- area
- square unit

Materials
Workmat 5

Explore

The **perimeter** is the distance around a figure.
The **area** is the size of a plane figure measured in **square units**.

Question Does the perimeter determine the area?

Work with a partner to compare perimeter and area.

1 Draw each figure on Workmat 5. Each box in Workmat 5 is 1 centimeter long and 1 centimeter wide. Find the perimeter of each figure.

- Count the number of centimeters around the outside of the figure.
- Record your answers in a table like the one below.

Square A (3 cm by 3 cm) **Rectangle B** (4 cm by 2 cm)

Figure	Perimeter	Area
Square A	12 centimeters	
Rectangle B		

2 Find the area.

- Count the number of square centimeters needed to cover each figure.
- Record. Use square units.

3 Compare perimeter and area.

The figures have the same perimeter, but different areas.

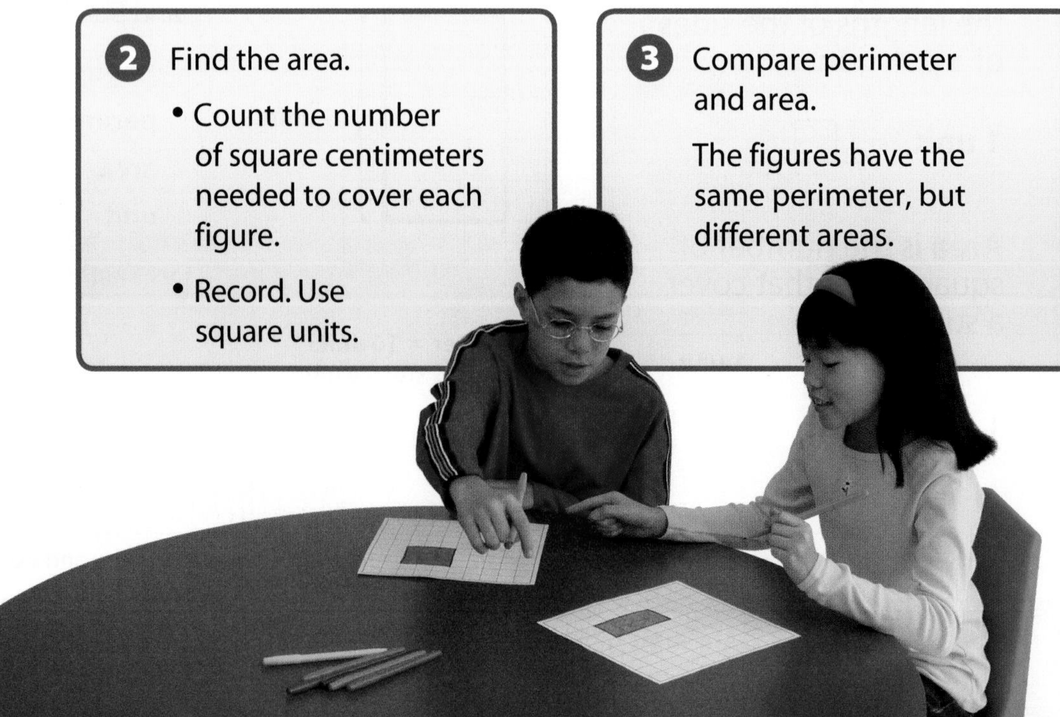

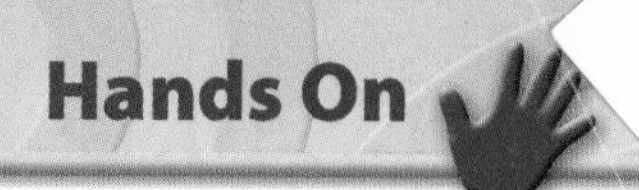

Draw the figures on Workmat 5.
Then copy and complete the table.

	Figure	Perimeter	Area
1.	Rectangle C	▒ cm	▒ cm^2
2.	Square D	▒ cm	▒ cm^2
3.	Rectangle E	▒ cm	▒ cm^2

Rectangle C

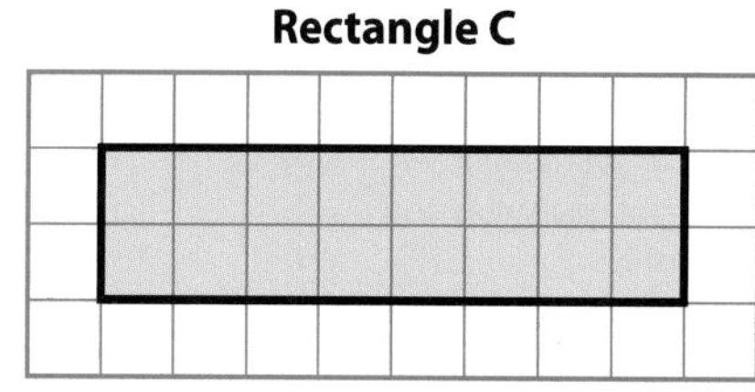

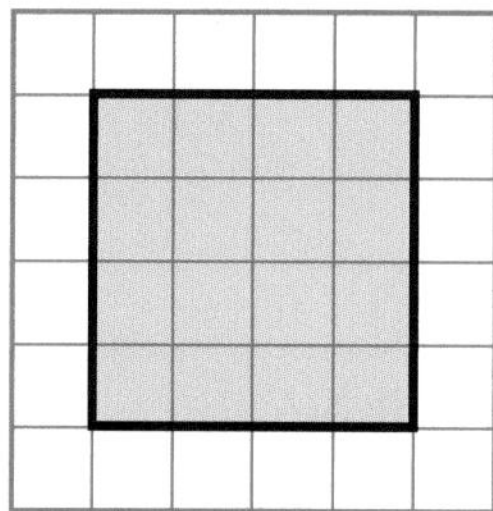

Rectangle E

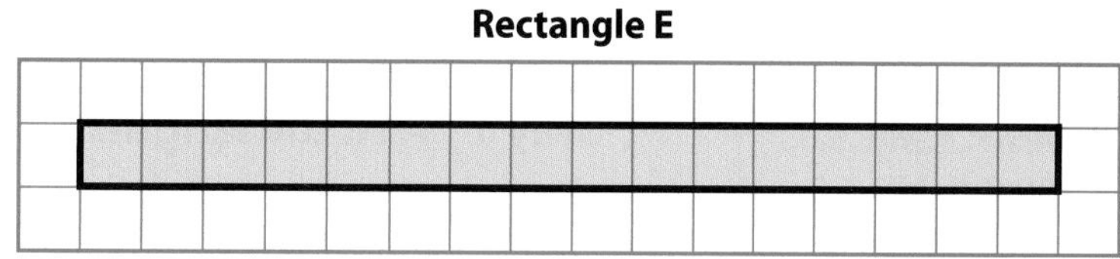

Use your table to answer Questions 4 and 5.

4. Can a square have the same area as a rectangle?

5. Can a rectangle and a square with the same area have different perimeters?

Use Workmat 5 to solve Problems 6–10.

6. Draw a rectangle with an area of 20 square centimeters and a perimeter that is greater than 20 centimeters.

7. Draw a rectangle with an area of 18 square centimeters and a perimeter that is greater than 18 centimeters.

8. If you double the length and width of a figure, does the area double? Double the length and width of Rectangle C. What happens to the area?

9. If you triple the length and width of a figure, does the area triple? Triple the length and width of Rectangle E. What happens to the area?

10. How are perimeter and area different?

Writing Math

Generalize Can two squares with the same area have different perimeters? Use examples to explain.

CA Standards

AF 1.4 Use and interpret formulas (e.g., area = length × width or $A = lw$) to answer questions about quantities and their relationships.

MG 1.4 Understand and use formulas to solve problems involving perimeters and areas of rectangles and squares. Use those formulas to find the areas of more complex figures by dividing the figures into basic shapes.

Also AF 1.1, KEY AF 1.2, MG 1.0, MG 3.7, MR 2.0, MR 2.3, MR 3.0, MR 3.3

Vocabulary

formula

perimeter

Use Formulas for Perimeter

Objective Use a formula to find the perimeter of a polygon.

Learn by Example

In this lesson, you will use **formulas** to find the perimeter.

Paul is building a diorama. He plans to glue a strip of leather around the edge. The diorama is 12 inches long and 8 inches wide. How many inches of leather will he need?

Find the **perimeter**, or distance, around the diorama.

Different Ways to Find Perimeter

Way 1 **Add the lengths of the sides.**

Perimeter = $l + w + l + w$

P = 12 in. + 8 in. + 12 in. + 8 in.

P = 40 in.

Way 2 **Use a formula.**

Perimeter = $(2 \times l) + (2 \times w)$

P = (2 × 12 in.) + (2 × 8 in.)

P = 24 in. + 16 in.

P = 40 in.

Hint

An equilateral triangle has 3 equal sides.

Solution: Paul needs 40 inches of leather edging.

Another Example

Find the perimeter of an equilateral triangle.

Way 1 **Add the lengths of the sides.**

Perimeter = $s + s + s$

P = 1 in. + 1 in. + 1 in.

P = 3 in.

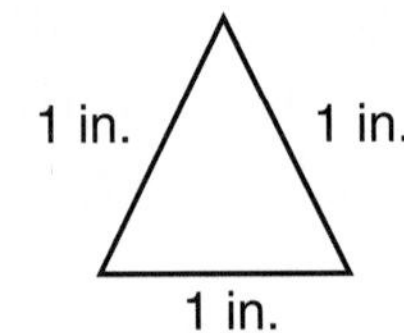

Way 2 **Use a formula.**

Perimeter = $3 \times s$

P = 3 × 1 in.

P = 3 in.

Guided Practice

Find the perimeter of the polygon. If you used a formula, write it.

1.

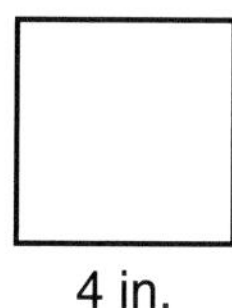

2.

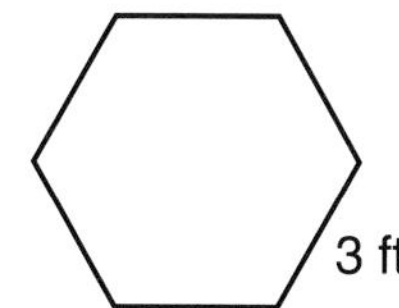

3.

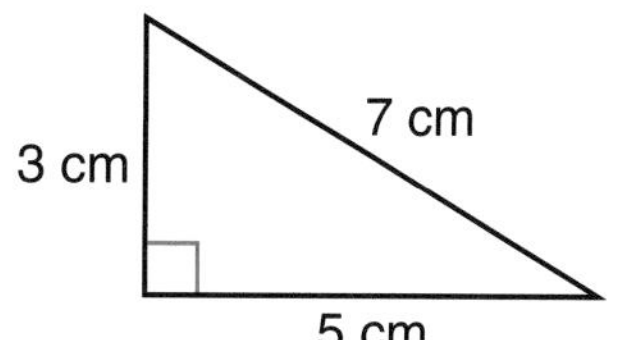

Ask Yourself

- Do all sides have the same length?
- Can I use a formula?

Math Talk How is finding the perimeter of a square different from finding the perimeter of a rectangle? Write a formula for finding the perimeter of a square.

Practice and Problem Solving

Find the perimeter of the polygon. Write the formula.

4.

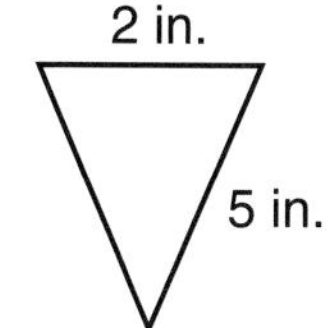

5.

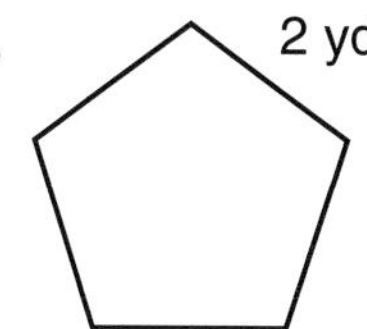

6.

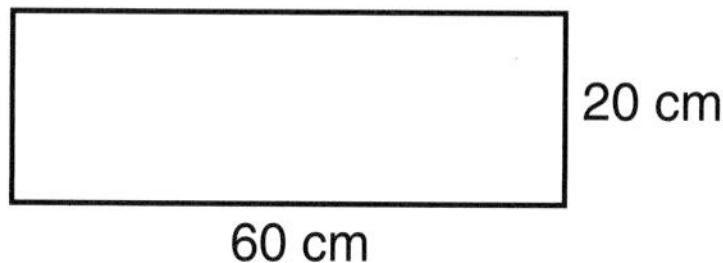

Write a formula to find the perimeter. Then solve.

7. a pentagon with all sides 8 cm long

8. a hexagon with all sides 8 cm long

9. an octagon with all sides 8 cm long

Spiral Review and Test Practice

Use the line graph to solve. **SDAP 1.0, SDAP 1.3** page 520

10. How long did Ken run before he reached his greatest speed?

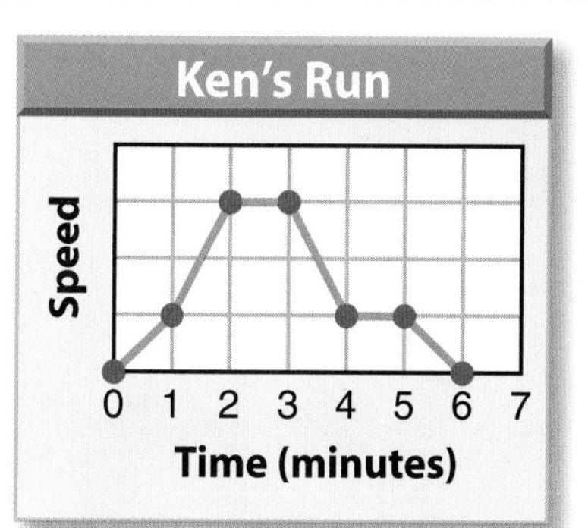

Write the letter of the correct answer. **AF 1.4**

11. Which formula below best represents the perimeter (P) of the figure in centimeters?

A $P = 3 \times 12$

B $12 = P \times 3$

C $P = (2 \times 3) + (2 \times 12)$

D $P = (1 \times 3) + (2 \times 12)$

12 cm

3 cm

CA Standards
MG 1.4 Understand and use formulas to solve problems involving perimeters and areas of rectangles and squares. Use those formulas to find the areas of more complex figures by dividing the figures into basic shapes.

AF 1.4 Use and interpret formulas (e.g., area = length × width or $A = lw$) to answer questions about quantities and their relationships.

Also AF 1.1, MG 1.0, MG 1.1, MG 1.2, MG 1.3, MG 3.8, MR 1.0, MR 1.1, MR 1.2, MR 2.0, MR 2.2, MR 2.3, MR 3.0

Vocabulary

area

Use Formulas for Area

Objective Find the area of a rectangle.

Learn by Example

In this lesson, you will use a formula to find the **area** of a rectangle.

Jake's grandfather is tiling his front walk. He needs to know how many square feet of slate he should order.

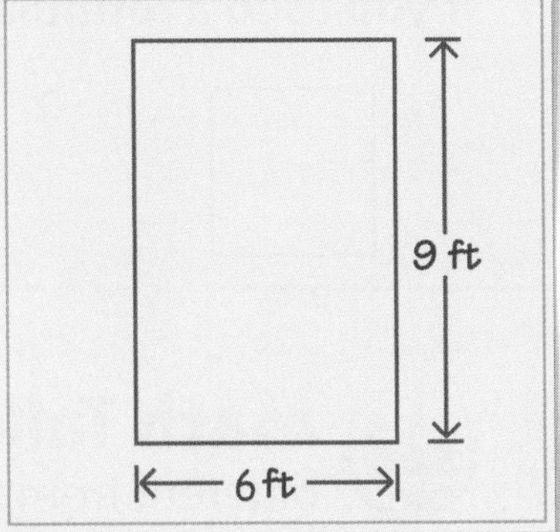

To find out how much slate is needed, you need to find the area, or square units, of the patio. You can find area in two ways.

Different Ways to Find Area

Way 1 **Draw a model and count the squares.**

1	2	3	4	5	6
7	8	9	10	11	12
13	14	15	16	17	18
19	20	21	22	23	24
25	26	27	28	29	30
31	32	33	34	35	36
37	38	39	40	41	42
43	44	45	46	47	48
49	50	51	52	53	54

Way 2 **Use a formula.**

Area = length × width

$A = l \times w$

$A = 9 \text{ ft} \times 6 \text{ ft}$

$A = 54 \text{ ft}^2$ or 54 square feet

Solution: Jake's grandfather will need 54 square feet of slate.

Area of a Square

$A = s \times s$

$A = 11 \text{ m} \times 11 \text{ m}$

$A = 121 \text{ m}^2$ or 121 square meters

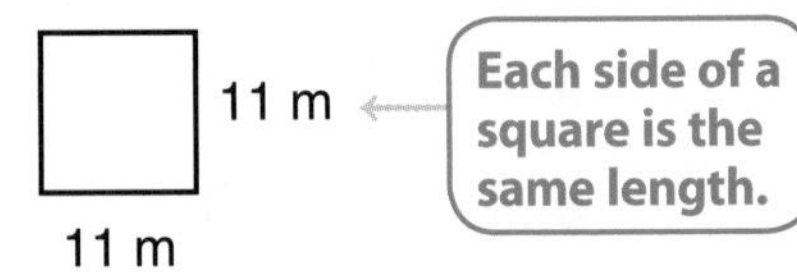

Guided Practice

Write and use a formula to find the area of the figure.

1. 3 mi by 2 mi rectangle

2. 16 ft by 16 ft square

3. 24 m by 6 m rectangle

Ask Yourself

- What formula can I use?
- What unit do I need?

Guided Problem Solving

Use the questions to solve this problem.

4. In Mr. Lee's town, a house cannot be more than half the area of the lot on which it is built. Mr. Lee's lot is 50 feet long and 40 feet wide. What is the largest area his house can have?

a. Understand What are the length and width of Mr. Lee's lot? What fraction of the lot is the largest possible house?

b. Plan What formula can you use to find the area of the lot?

c. Solve Find the area of the lot and the largest possible house.

Mr. Lee's house must be ◯ square feet or less.

d. Look Back Does your answer make sense? How do you know?

Math Talk How could you find the perimeter of a square that has an area of 25 square inches?

Practice and Problem Solving

Write and use a formula to find the area of the figure.

5. 14 in. by 14 in. square

6. 9 yd by 12 yd rectangle

7. 20 cm by 16 cm rectangle

Use a formula to find the perimeter and area of the rectangle.

8. 14 m long, 6 m wide

9. 3 yd long, 7 yd wide

10. 15 cm long, 4 cm wide

Real World Data

Use the blueprint to solve.

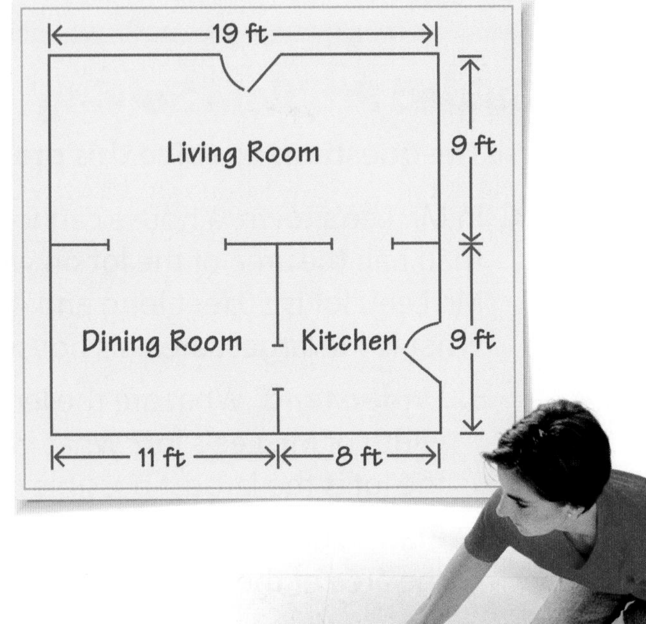

11. Find the perimeter and area of the dining room.

a. Name a rectangle that has the same perimeter as the dining room, but a different area.

b. Name a rectangle that has the same area as the dining room, but a different perimeter.

12. Multistep Miguel wants to tile the kitchen floor. Each tile is 1 square foot and costs $2. How much will Miguel spend on the tiles? Show the equations you used to solve the problem.

Spiral Review and Test Practice

Choose the figure that appears to be congruent to the first figure. **MG 3.3** page 588

13. 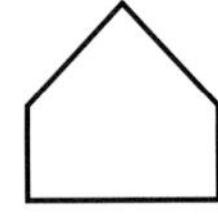

A 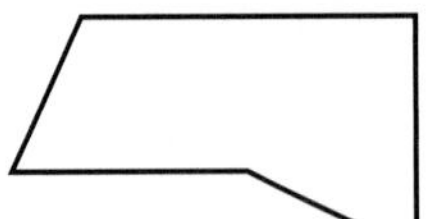

B 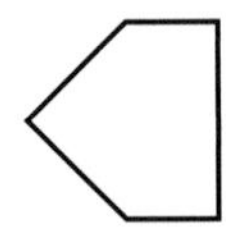

C 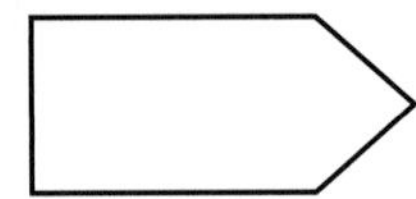

Write the letter of the correct answer. **AF 1.4**

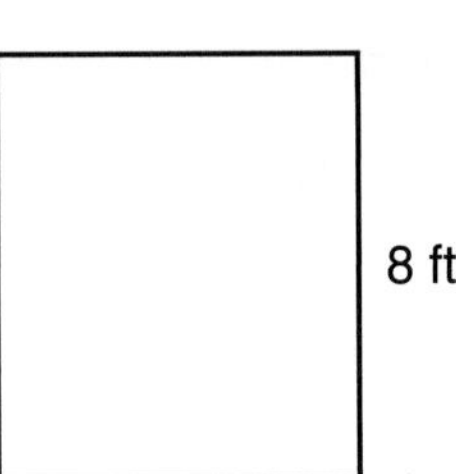

14. Which formula represents the area, *A*, of the rectangle in square feet?

A $56 = A \times 8$

B $A = 8 \times 7$

C $A = (2 \times 8) + (2 \times 7)$

D $A = 7 \div 8$

Extra Practice See page 615, Set B.

Key Standards Review

Need Help?
See Key Standards Handbook.

Use the grid to solve. KEY MG 2.0, KEY MG 2.1

1. Name the ordered pair for *H*.
2. Name an ordered pair that would be on the same horizontal line as *H*.
3. Name 10 ordered pairs on the graph of the equation $y = 7$.
4. Name 10 ordered pairs on the graph of the equation $y = 2x + 1$.

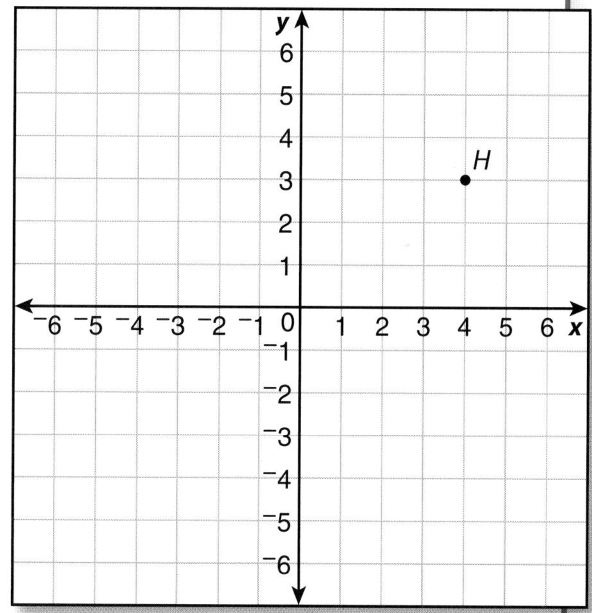

Challenge Math Reasoning

Area Finder

Find the area of the isosceles right triangle. Explain your answer. MG 1.4

1.

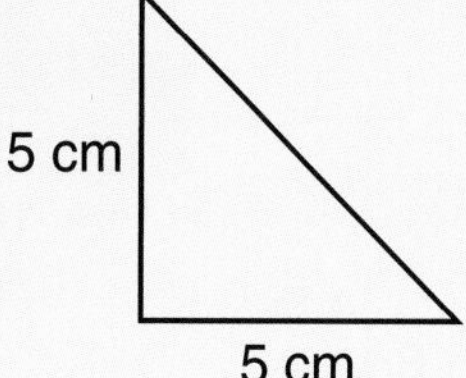

5 cm

5 cm

2.

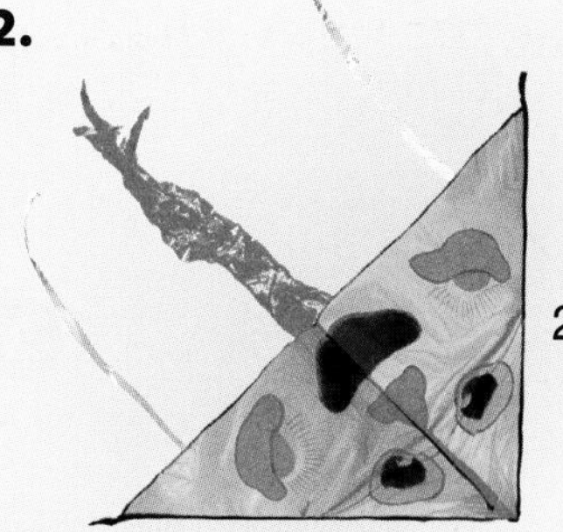

3.

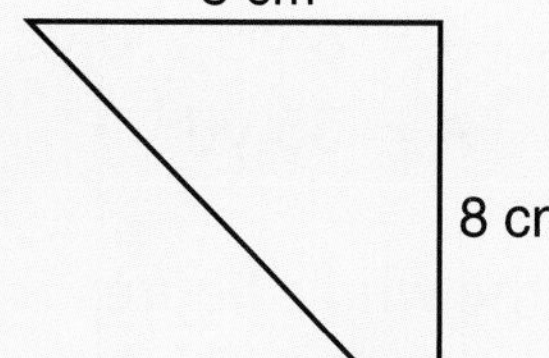

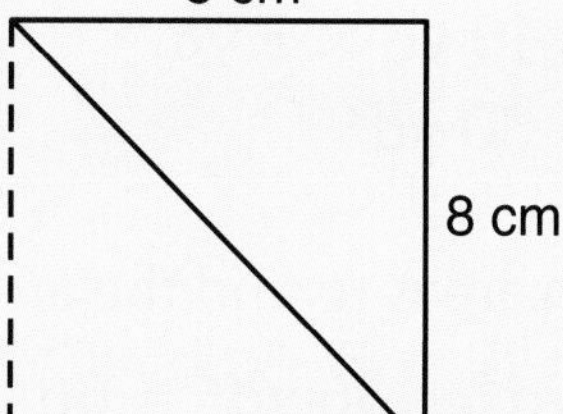

CA Standards

MG 1.4 Understand and use formulas to solve problems involving perimeters and areas of rectangles and squares. Use those formulas to find the areas of more complex figures by dividing the figures into basic shapes.

AF 1.4 Use and interpret formulas (e.g., area = length × width or $A = lw$) to answer questions about quantities and their relationships.

Also MG 1.0, MG 1.1, MG 3.3, MG 3.8, AF 1.1, MR 1.0, MR 1.1, MR 1.2, MR 2.0, MR 2.2, MR 2.3, MR 2.4, MR 2.6, MR 3.0, MR 3.2

Perimeter and Area of Complex Figures

Objective Find the perimeter and area of figures that are not rectangles.

Learn by Example

Andy wants to build a fence around this garden. How much fencing material should he buy? What is the area of the garden?

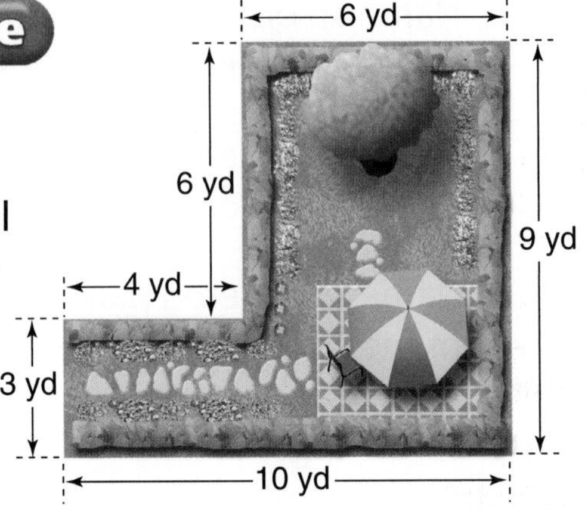

Perimeter

Perimeter = 10 yd + 3 yd + 4 yd + 6 yd + 6 yd + 9 yd

P = 38 yd

Solution: Andy should buy 38 yards of fence.

Area

1 Separate the figure into a rectangle and a square.

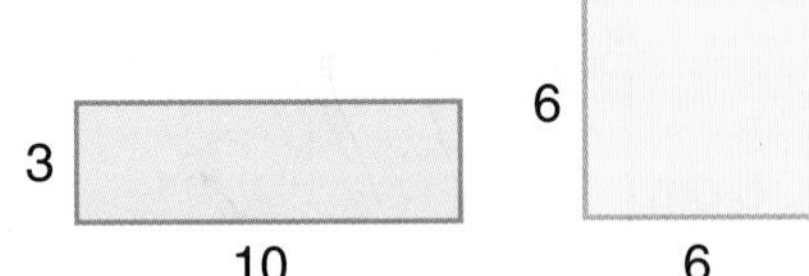

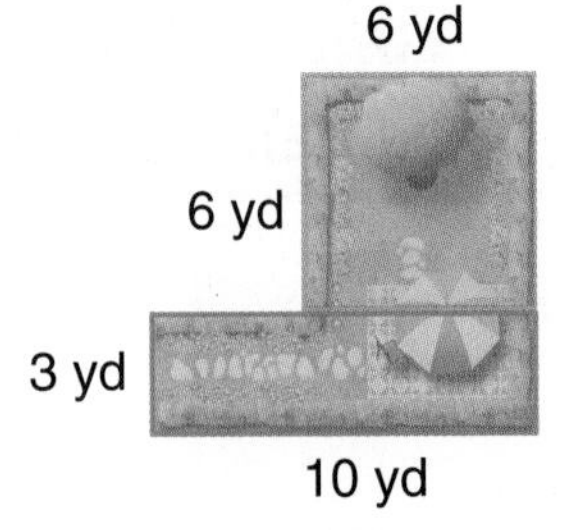

2 Use a formula to find the area of each figure.

Area of a Rectangle = $l \times w$

$A = 10 \text{ yd} \times 3 \text{ yd}$

$A = 30 \text{ yd}^2$

Area of a Square = $s \times s$

$A = 6 \text{ yd} \times 6 \text{ yd}$

$A = 36 \text{ yd}^2$

3 Add both areas to find the area of the whole figure.

$30 \text{ yd}^2 + 36 \text{ yd}^2 = 66 \text{ yd}^2$

Solution: The area of Andy's garden is 66 square yards.

Guided Practice

Draw the complex figure. Show how you separated the figure. Find the perimeter and area.

1.

15 ft
5 ft
10 ft
5 ft
10 ft

2.

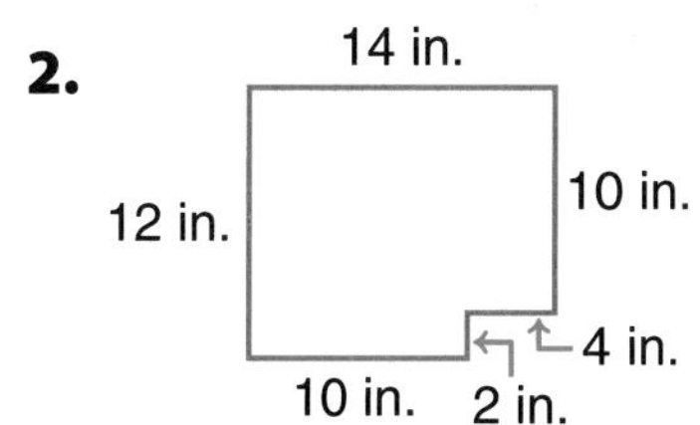

Ask Yourself

- How can I separate the figure into two rectangles?
- What units do I use?

Guided Problem Solving

Use the questions to solve this problem.

3. Multistep A rectangular garage is 18 feet long, with a perimeter of 56 feet. What is the area of the garage?

a. **Understand** What parts of the formula for perimeter do you know? What part is missing?

b. **Plan** How can you use the formula for perimeter to find the missing information?

c. **Solve** Find the missing information. Use it to find the area of the garage.

d. **Look Back** Did you use the correct units?

Math Talk How could you find the area of your classroom? What tools would you need? What formula would you use?

Practice and Problem Solving

Draw the complex figure. Show how you separated the figure. Find the perimeter and area.

4.

28 m
7 m
21 m
21 m
14 m
7 m

5.

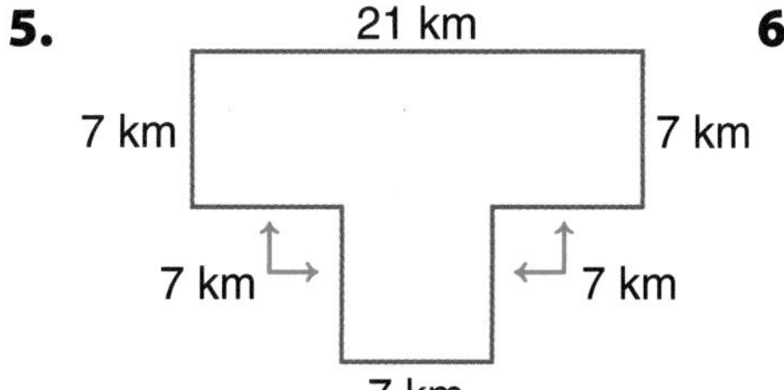

6.

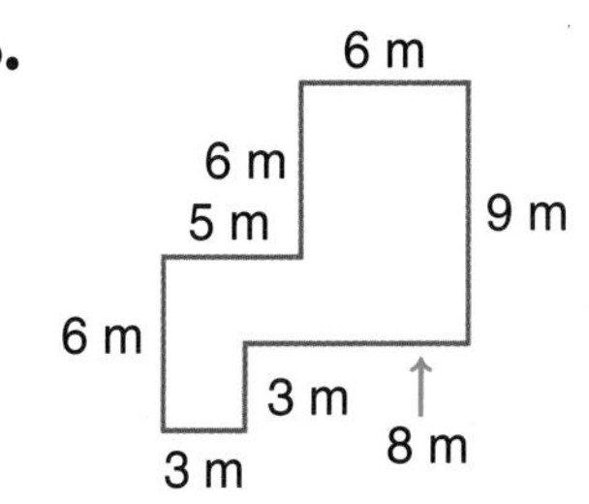

Find the length of the missing side.

7. Perimeter = 24 inches

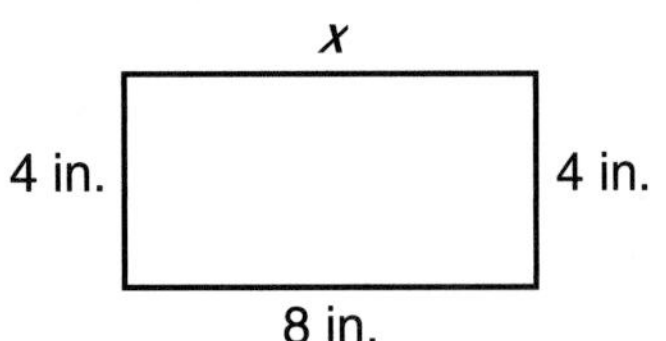

8. Perimeter = 40 meters

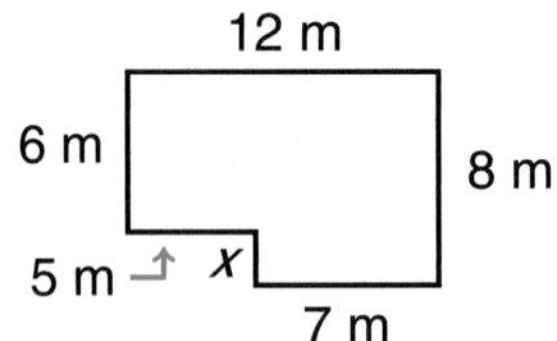

9. Perimeter = 24 yards

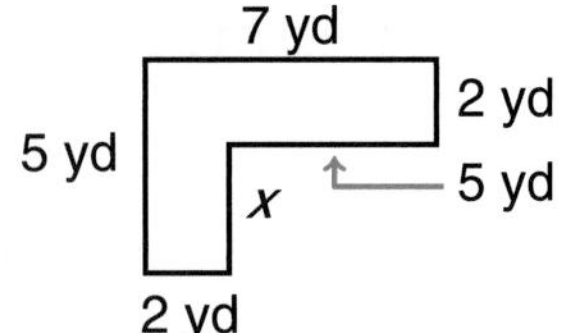

Science Link

Use the Fun Facts to solve.

10. **a.** What are the perimeter and area of the cover for the compost bin?

  b. Are the cover and the bottom of the bin congruent figures? Without doing any calculations, give the perimeter and area of the bottom of the bin.

11. Copy and complete the table below to show how many worms are needed to process the food scraps.

Pounds of Food Scraps	Pounds of Worms	Number of Worms
1		
2		
5		

Fun Facts

How to Make a Compost Bin

Compost is a mixture of decaying organic matter used to improve soil quality and provide nutrients for plants.

- Fill a bin with wet, shredded newspapers and leaves.
- Put in 1,000 red worms (1 lb) for every $\frac{1}{2}$ pound of daily food scraps.
- Bury food scraps like fruit peels under the shredded newspaper.
- Keep the compost warm and moist.

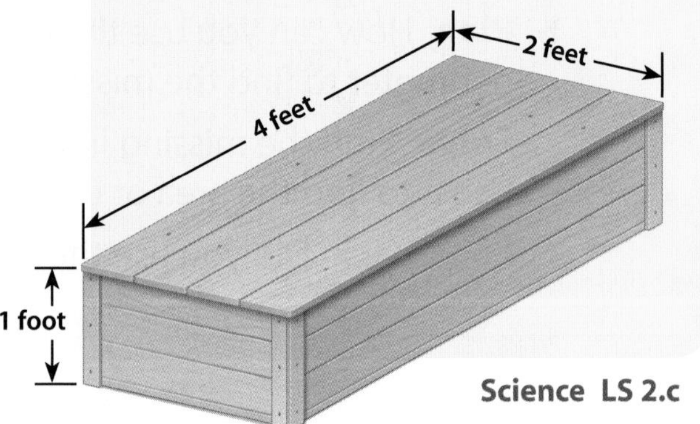

Science LS 2.c

Spiral Review and Test Practice

Trace the figure. Then answer the question. Explain how you decided. MG 3.4 pages 582, 584

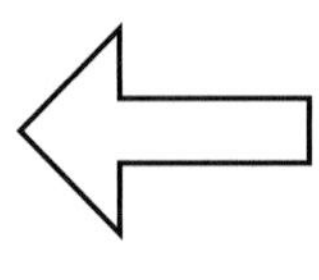

12. Does the figure have a line of symmetry?

13. Does the figure have rotational symmetry?

Write the letter of the correct answer. MG 1.4

14. What is the area of the complex figure?

A 30 yd^2 **B** 56 yd^2 **C** 16 yd^2 **D** 26 yd^2

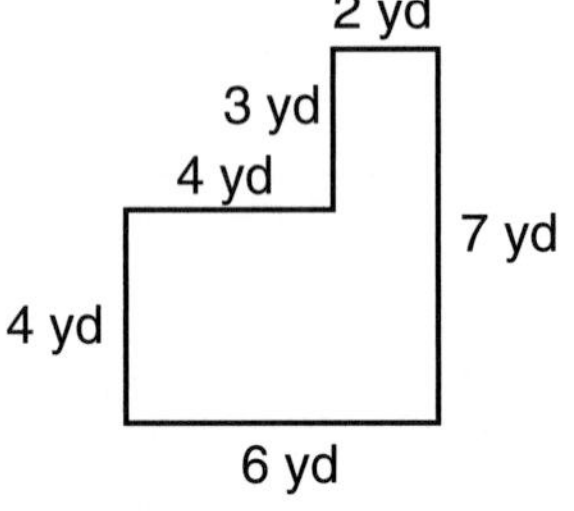

Extra Practice See page 615, Set C.

Practice **Game**

Pick a Figure

Object of the Game Use formulas to find the perimeter and area of shapes and earn the most points.

Materials

- Learning Tool 41 (*Pick a Figure* Game Cards)
- cube labeled with the letter *A* on 3 sides and the letter *P* on the other 3 sides

Set Up

Place the game cards in a pile face down.

Number of Players 2

How to Play

1. Player 1 draws a card from the pile and rolls the letter cube.
2. If Player 1 rolls an *A*, he or she uses a formula to find the area of the shape on the card picked. If Player 1 rolls a *P*, he or she uses a formula to find the perimeter of the shape on the card.
3. Player 2 checks that Player 1's answer is correct by counting the units. If correct, Player 1 scores 1 point. If Player 1 did not find the correct area or perimeter, Player 2 gets 1 point.
4. Player 2 repeats Steps 1–3.
5. Play continues until all of the cards in the pile have been drawn. The player with the greater number of points wins.

CA Standards

MG 1.4 Understand and use formulas to solve problems involving perimeters and areas of rectangles and squares. Use those formulas to find the areas of more complex figures by dividing the figures into basic shapes.

MG 1.0 Students understand perimeter and area.

Education Place

Visit www.eduplace.com/camap/ for **Brain Teasers** and **eGames** to play.

Problem Solving Strategy
Use Formulas

Objective Use formulas to solve problems.

CA Standards
MR 2.3 Use a variety of methods, such as words, numbers, symbols, charts, graphs, tables, diagrams, and models, to explain mathematical reasoning.

AF 1.4 Use and interpret formulas (e.g., area = length × width or $A = lw$) to answer questions about quantities and their relationships.

Also MG 1.2, MG 1.3, MG 1.4, MG 1.0, MG 3.0, MG 3.8, KEY NS 3.2, KEY NS 3.3, MR 1.0, MR 1.1, MR 1.2, MR 2.0, MR 2.1, MR 2.4, MR 2.6, MR 3.0, MR 3.1, MR 3.2

Learn by Example

You can use formulas for perimeter and area to solve problems.

Jana has a terrarium that is 24 inches long and 18 inches wide. She wants to cover one third of the bottom with tiles. Each tile is 1 square inch and costs \$2. How much will the tiles cost?

UNDERSTAND

You want to find out how much the tiles will cost.

This is what you know:

- The terrarium is 24 inches long and 18 inches wide.
- The tiles will cover one third of the bottom of the terrarium.
- One tile is 1 square inch and costs \$2.

PLAN

To find the area of the bottom of the tank, use this formula: Area $(A) = l \times w$

Put the known values in the formula and solve. To find the number of tiles needed, find one third of that area. Then multiply to find the total cost of the tiles.

SOLVE

1. Area $= l \times w$ — $A = 24 \times 18$; $A = 432$ square inches
2. Find how many tiles are needed to cover one third of the bottom of the terrarium. — $432 \div 3 = 144$ tiles
3. Multiply the number of tiles by the cost of each tile. — $144 \times \$2 = \$288$

The tiles will cost \$288.

LOOK BACK

Use estimates to check each calculation. Is your answer reasonable?

Guided Problem Solving

Solve using the Ask Yourself questions.

1. **Multistep** The borders of a town form a rectangle 18 miles long and 12 miles wide. A town worker used 5 gallons of gas to drive around the perimeter of the town in a truck. Explain how you can use formulas to calculate the truck's mileage in miles/gallon.

Ask Yourself

- What is the question?
- What formula can I use to solve the problem?

Math Talk How did you know whether to use the formula for perimeter or area?

Independent Problem Solving

Solve using the formula for perimeter or area. Explain why your answer makes sense.

2. Walter's backyard measures 12 feet long and 10 feet wide. Walter made a garden to cover one sixth of the yard. What is the size of the garden in square feet?

3. **Guess and Check** Rena used 26 feet of fencing to completely enclose a rectangular pen for her puppy. One side of the pen is 7 feet long. What are the lengths of the other three sides?

4. **Multistep** A rectangular floor is 12 feet long and 11 feet wide. A rug that is 9 feet long and 7 feet wide covers part of the floor. How many square feet of the floor are *not* covered by the rug?

5. **Challenge** The diagram shows the floor plan of a stage that can be separated into a rectangle that has an area of 42 square feet and a square that has an area of 16 square feet. The lengths of two sides of the stage are shown. Use formulas to find the missing side lengths *e*, *f*, *g*, and *h*.

6. **Create and Solve** Draw and label 2 rectangles that have the same perimeter but different areas. Then draw and label 2 rectangles that have the same area but different perimeters. Use formulas to check your work.

Vocabulary

The **perimeter** is the distance around a figure. The **area** is the number of square units needed to cover the figure. You can find perimeter and area in two ways.

9 ft

6 ft

Ways to Find Perimeter

Way 1 **Add the lengths of the sides.**

Perimeter $= l + w + l + w$

$P = 9\text{ ft} + 6\text{ ft} + 9\text{ ft} + 6\text{ ft}$

$P =$ ______

Way 2 **Use a formula.**

Perimeter $= (2 \times l) + (2 \times w)$

$P = (2 \times 9\text{ ft}) + (2 \times 6\text{ ft})$

$P =$ ______

The perimeter is ______ feet.

Ways to Find Area

Way 1 **Draw a model and count the squares.**

9 ft

6 ft

There are ______ squares.

The area is ______ square feet.

Way 2 **Use a formula.**

Area = length × width

Area $= l \times w$

$A = 9\text{ ft} \times 6\text{ ft}$

$A =$ ______ ft^2 or ______ square feet

The area is ______ square feet.

Writing Suppose you want to cover the floor of your room with carpet squares. Explain what measurements you need and why.

Reading Check out this book in your library. *Sir Cumference and the Isle of Immeter*, by Cindy Neuschwander and Wayne Geehan

CA Standards

MR 2.3 Use a variety of methods, such as words, numbers, symbols, charts, graphs, tables, diagrams, and models, to explain mathematical reasoning.

Also MG 1.0, AF 1.4

Standards-Based Extra Practice

Set A

AF 1.4, MG 1.4 page 602

Find the perimeter of the polygon. If you used a formula, write it.

1. 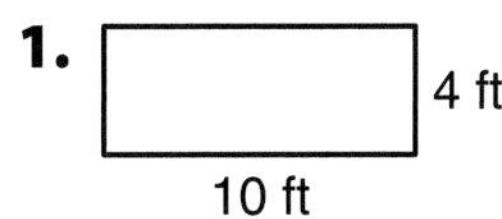

2. 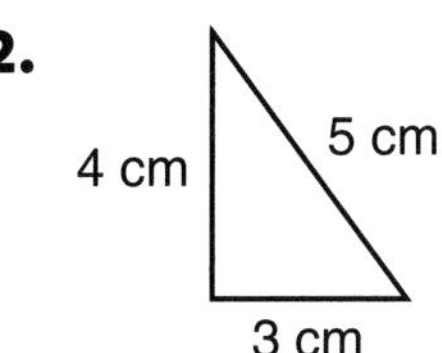

3. 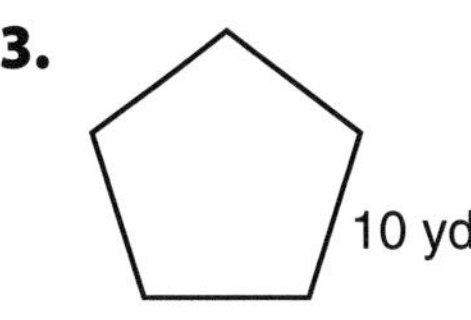

4. **Explain** What is the side length of a square if the perimeter of the square is 36 feet? Does this method apply to a rectangle? Why or why not?

Set B

AF 1.4, MG 1.4 page 604

Use a formula to find the perimeter and the area of the rectangle.

1. 20 ft long, 10 ft wide
2. 7 in. long, 10 in. wide
3. 17 cm long, 1 cm wide
4. 16 yd long, 16 yd wide
5. **Explain** Why is perimeter written in units while area is written in square units?

Set C

KEY MG 1.4 page 608

Find the length of the missing side.

1. Square, Perimeter = 48 in.
2. Rectangle, Area = 60 cm^2, Length = 10 cm
3. Square, Area = 49 ft^2
4. Rectangle, Perimeter = 36 yd, Length = 16 yd
5. **Explain** What is the area of the polygon? Explain your answer.

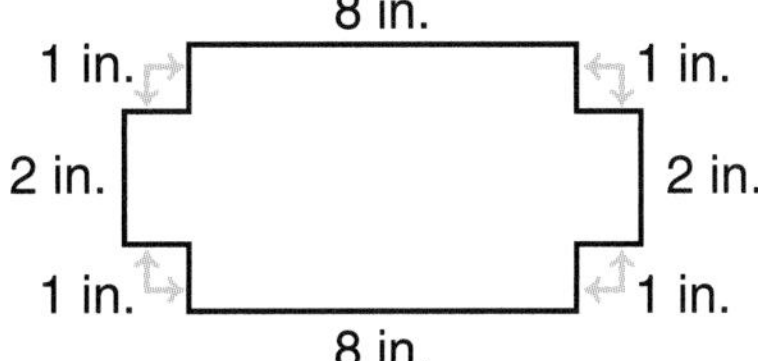

Education Place
Visit www.eduplace.com/camap/ for more **Extra Practice**.

Chapter Review/Test

Vocabulary and Concepts — MG 1.0, MR 2.3

Write the best word to complete each sentence.

1. When you find the area of a figure, the answer is in ______ units.

2. To find the ______ of a complex figure, separate the figure into simpler figures.

Skills — AF 1.4, KEY AF 1.2, MG 1.4, MG 1.0

Find the perimeter of the polygon. Write the formula.

3. 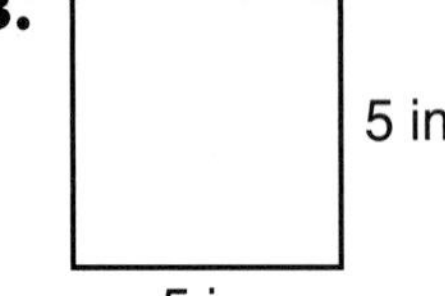

4. 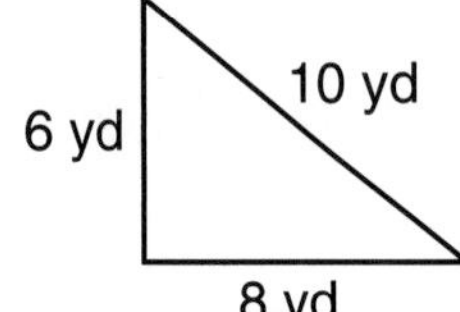

5. 10 cm, 10 cm, 10 cm, 10 cm, 10 cm

Use a formula to find the perimeter and area of the rectangle.

6. 10 m long, 4 m wide
7. 2.5 in. long, 2 in. wide
8. 7 cm long, 7 cm wide

Problem Solving and Reasoning — MG 1.4, MG 1.0, MR 1.0, MR 2.3

Solve.

9. Heather is making a pillow with her initial H on it. The H is made of 3 rectangles, each 6 inches by 2 inches. How many square inches of fabric will she need to make the H?

10. A rectangular hallway floor is 10 feet long and 5 feet wide. A rug that is 8 feet long and 3 feet wide covers part of the floor. How many square feet of the floor are not covered by the rug?

Writing Math Explain why rectangles with different dimensions can have the same area. Give an example.

Spiral Review and Test Practice

1. Ron divides his 77 baseball cards into 5 boxes. If each of the boxes has the same number of cards, how many cards are left over?

A 0 cards

B 1 card

C 2 cards

D 3 cards

page 262

2. John walks his dog 4 kilometers. There are 1,000 meters in 1 kilometer. How many meters did he walk his dog?

A 4 m

B 250 m

C 2,500 m

D 4,000 m

Test Tip
Make sure that your answer has the correct number of zeroes.

page 334

3. Which kind of triangle has 3 sides that are the same length?

A right

B obtuse

C acute

D equilateral

MG 3.7 page 566

4. Which letter appears to have rotational symmetry?

A 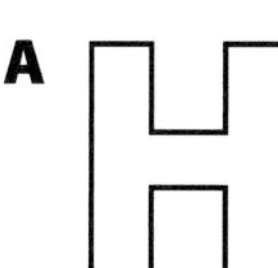

C 

B 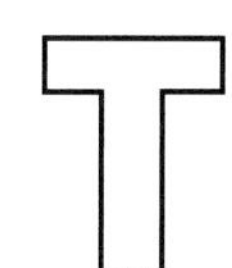

D 

MG 3.4 page 584

5. Which formula below best represents the perimeter, P, of the figure in centimeters?

A $P = 7 \times 16$

B $16 = P \times 7$

C $P = (2 \times 7) + (2 \times 16)$

D $P = (1 \times 7) + (2 \times 16)$

7 cm
16 cm

AF 1.4 page 602

6. Which formula shows the area of the rectangle in square feet?

A $72 = A \times 8$

B $A = 9 \times 8$

C $A = 9 + 8$

D $A = 9 \div 8$

8 ft
9 ft

AF 1.4 page 604

Education Place
Visit www.eduplace.com/camap/ for **Test-Taking Tips** and **Extra Practice.**

Chapter 28
Solid Figures

Native American Paiute beaded baskets at the End of the Trail Museum in Klamath, CA

Check What You Know

Word Bank
face
edge
vertex
cube
volume

Vocabulary and Concepts GRADE 3 MG 2.0, MR 2.3

Choose the best word to complete the sentence.

1. A point where three or more edges meet on a three-dimensional figure is called a ____.
2. The word ____ describes the line segment where two faces of a three-dimensional figure meet.
3. The faces of a ____ are congruent.

Skills GRADE 3 MG 2.0

Write the number of faces and the number of vertices for the three-dimensional figure.

4. 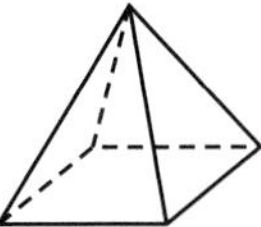
5. 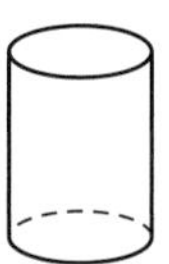
6. 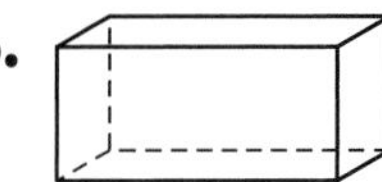

Find the volume of the figure in cubic units.

7. 
8. 
9. 

Problem Solving and Reasoning GRADE 3 MG 2.0

10. Jordan has a box of small cubes. He builds a large cube using 8 of the small cubes. What is the least number of small cubes Jordan can use to make an even larger cube?

Vocabulary

Visualize It!

A **rectangular prism** has six faces that are rectangles.

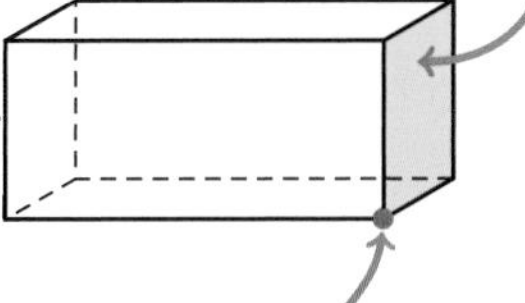

face
a flat surface

edge
the line segment where two faces meet

vertex
the point where 3 edges meet

Language Tip

Some words are similar in English and Spanish.

English	Spanish
rectangular prism	prisma rectangular
vertex	vértice

See **English-Spanish Glossary** pages 644–666.

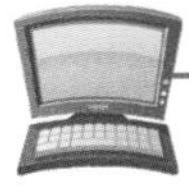

Education Place Visit www.eduplace.com/camap/ for the **eGlossary** and **eGames**.

CA Standards MR 2.3 Use a variety of methods, such as words, numbers, symbols, charts, graphs, tables, diagrams, and models, to explain mathematical reasoning. **Also MG 3.0**

LESSON 1

CA Standards

MG 3.6 Visualize, describe, and make models of geometric solids (e.g., prisms, pyramids) in terms of the number and shape of faces, edges, and vertices; interpret two-dimensional representations of three-dimensional objects; and draw patterns (of faces) for a solid that, when cut and folded, will make a model out of a solid.

MR 2.3 Use a variety of methods, such as words, numbers, symbols, charts, graphs, tables, diagrams, and models to explain mathematical reasoning.

Also MG 3.0, MR 1.1, MR 2.0

Vocabulary

net

face

edge

vertex (vertices)

Materials

- Learning Tool 42 (Cube Net)
- Learning Tool 43 (Rectangular Prism Net)
- Learning Tool 44 (Square Pyramid Net)
- Learning Tool 46 (Triangular Prism Net)
- Learning Tool 47 (Triangular Pyramid Net)
- scissors
- tape

Hands On
Use Nets to Build Solid Figures

Objective Use nets to build solid figures.

Explore

In Chapter 27, you used formulas to find the perimeter or area of two-dimensional figures. Now you will learn how to use **nets** to form solid figures.

A solid figure has length, width, and depth. A cube is one type of solid figure. A plane figure has only length and width. A square is one type of plane figure. It has no volume.

A **face** is a flat surface. An **edge** is a line segment that is formed where two faces of a solid meet. A **vertex** is the point where three or more edges meet.

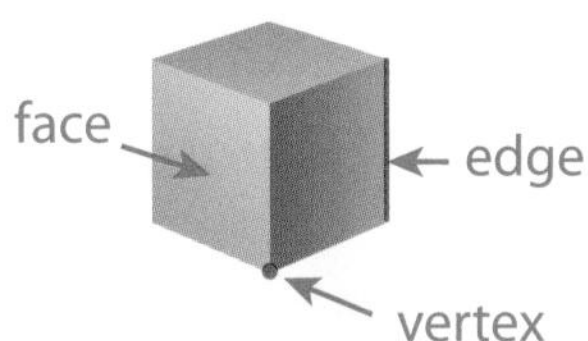

Question How can you see a solid figure in two dimensions?

1 Use Learning Tool 42. Cut along the dotted line to make one cutout.

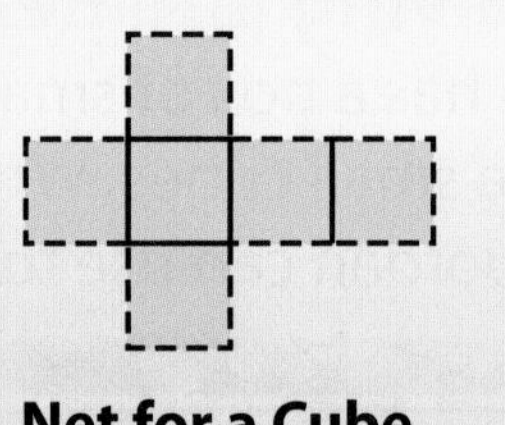

Net for a Cube

2 Fold along the solid lines to make a solid figure.

3 Tape the flaps to the sides.

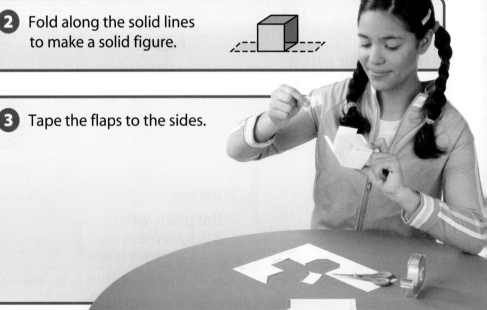

Extend

Use Learning Tools to make the solid figures below.

1. 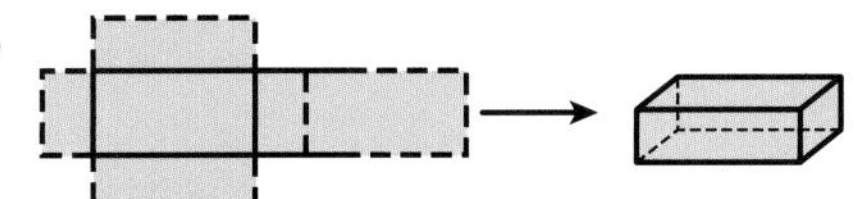

Net for a Rectangular Prism

2. 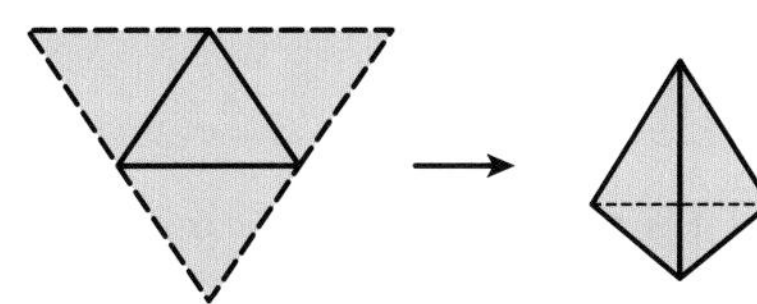

Net for a Triangular Pyramid

3. 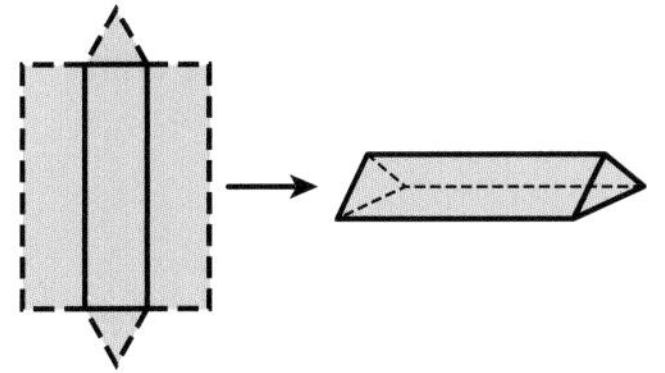

Net for a Triangular Prism

4. 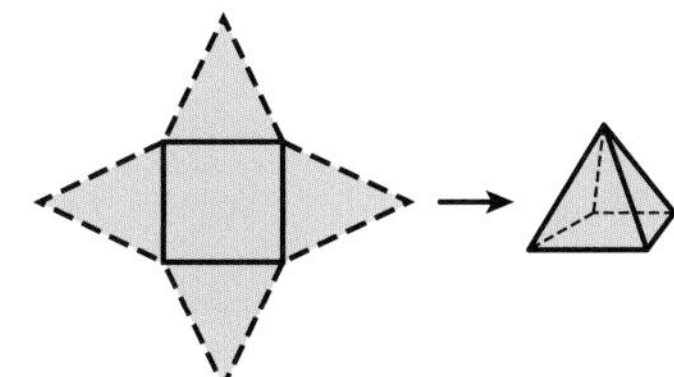

Net for a Square Pyramid

5. Make a table like the one below to record the name of each figure you constructed. Then complete the table.

Solid Figure	Number of Faces	Number of Edges	Number of Vertices
Cube			
Rectangular Prism			
Triangular Pyramid			
Triangular Prism			
Square Pyramid			

Name the solid figure that can be made with the net.

6. 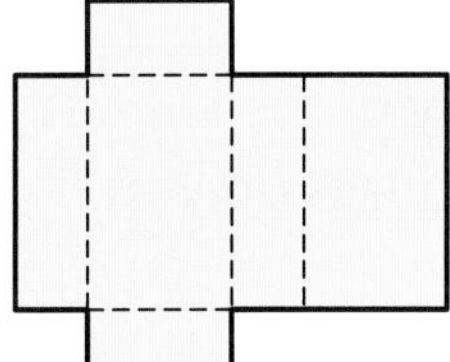

7. 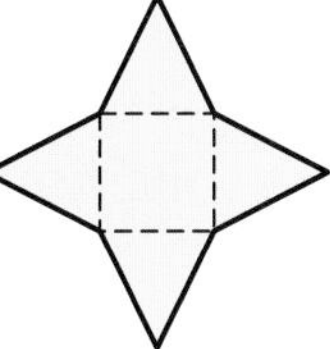

8. 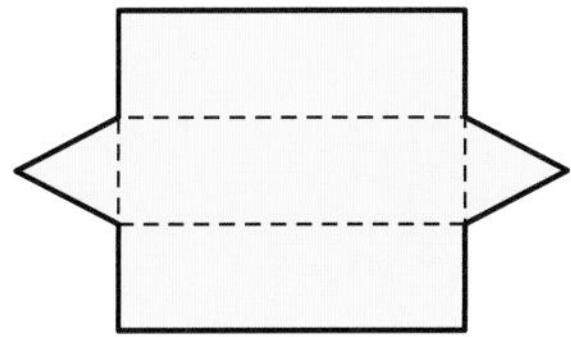

Writing Math

Connect How are solid figures and plane figures alike? How are they different?

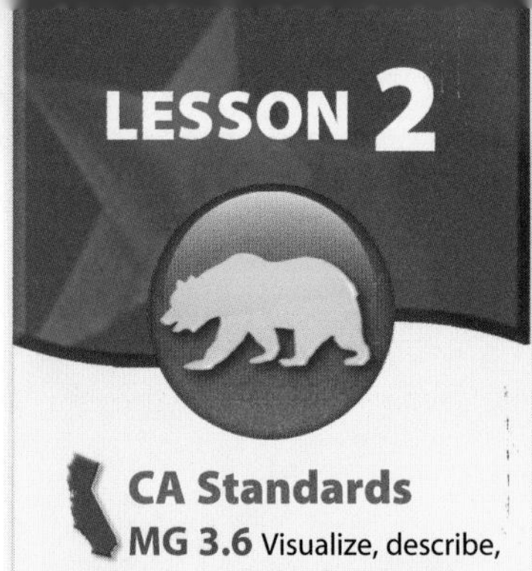

LESSON 2

CA Standards

MG 3.6 Visualize, describe, and make models of geometric solids (e.g., prisms, pyramids) in terms of the number and shape of faces, edges, and vertices; interpret two-dimensional representations of three-dimensional objects; and draw patterns (of faces) for a solid that, when cut and folded, will make a model out of a solid.

MG 3.0 Students demonstrate an understanding of plane and solid geometric objects and use this knowledge to show relationships and solve problems.

Also MR 1.0, MR 1.1, MR 2.0, MR 2.3, MR 2.4

Vocabulary

face

Solid Figures

Objective Identify and describe solid figures.

Learn by Example

The **faces** of these solid figures are polygons.

Cube

Rectangular Prism

Triangular Prism

Square Pyramid

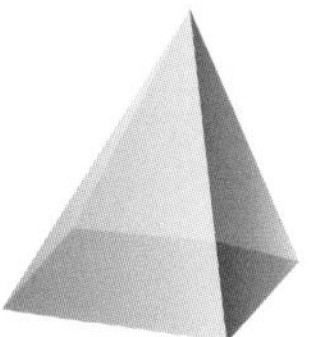

Rectangular Pyramid

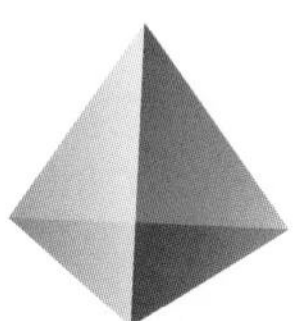

Triangular Pryamid

The faces of these solid figures are not polygons. They are circles.

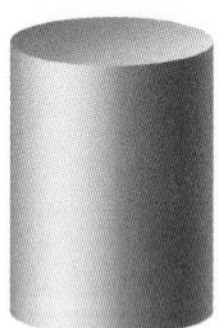

Cylinder

Cone

You can find solid figures all around you. Many of the shapes in a sand castle are solid figures. What solid figures do you see in the sand castle to the left?

1. Find the solid figures with faces that are polygons. There are 5 cubes. There are 2 rectangular prisms. There is 1 square pyramid.

2. Find the solid figures with faces that are circles. There are 4 cylinders. There are 2 cones.

Guided Practice

Name the solid figure.

1. 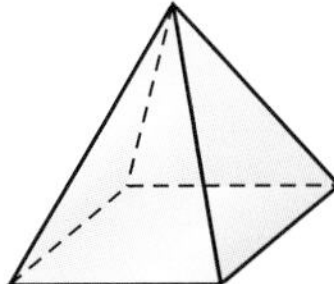

2. 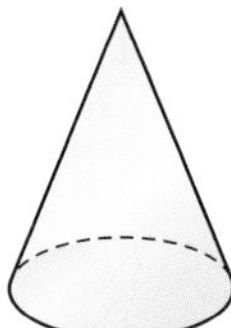

3. 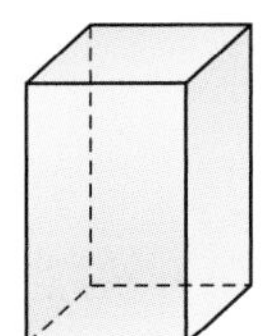

Ask Yourself

Are the faces of the solid figure polygons?

Name a solid figure that could have the face shown.

4. 

5. 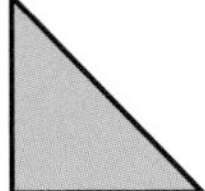

6. 

Math Talk Which solid figure has faces that are all triangles?

Practice and Problem Solving

Name the solid figure.

7. 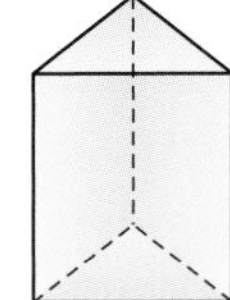

8. 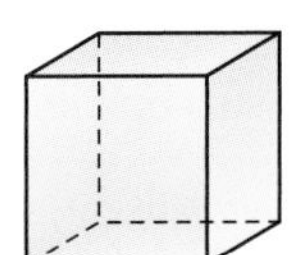

9. 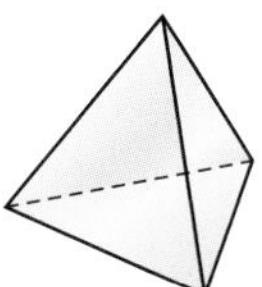

10. 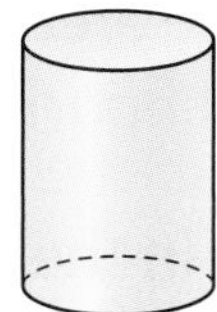

Name a solid figure that could have the face shown.

11. 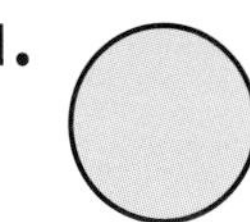

12. 

13. 

14. 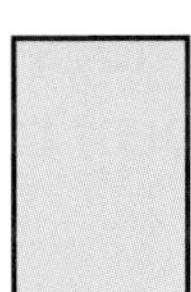

15. 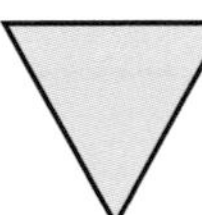

16. 

17. 

18. 

Name the solid figure that the object looks like.

19. 

20. 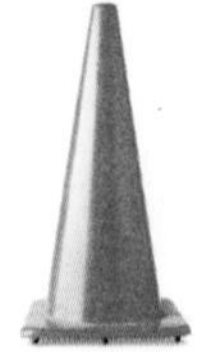

21. 

22. 

23. 

24. 

25. 

26. 

History-Social Science Link

Solve.

27. All of the floors in the Transamerica Building are square. The largest floor is 145 feet on each side, and the smallest floor is 45 feet on each side. How much greater is the area of largest floor than the smallest floor? Show your work.

28. **Challenge** In the Transamerica Building, what is the area of the smallest floor in square yards?

29. What shape does the Transamerica Building appear to be?

Transamerica Building

California has different styles of architecture. The city of San Francisco is known for its Victorian row houses and its tall, modern skyscrapers.

The Transamerica Building is San Francisco's tallest and most unusual building.

History-Social Science 4.1.5

Spiral Review and Test Practice

Solve. MG 3.2 page 568

30. The radius of a circle is 4 inches. What is the diameter?

31. The diameter of a circle is 12 feet. What is the radius?

Write the letter of the correct answer. MG 3.6

32. Which solid figure does the net make?

A triangular pyramid **C** square pyramid
B rectangular prism **D** triangular prism

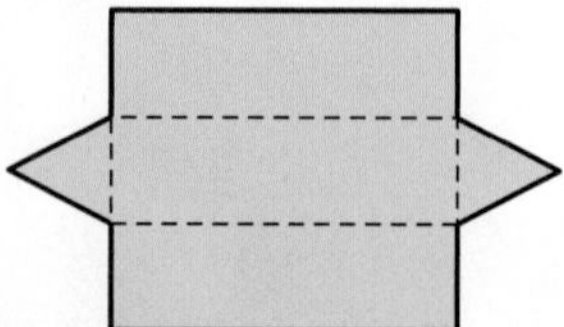

Extra Practice See page 635, Set A.

Visual Thinking

Make Solid Figures

Below are three incomplete nets for solid figures.

- Draw each pattern on grid paper or dot paper.
- Draw lines to complete the net for each figure.
- Then cut out and fold to make each solid figure.
- Finally, write the name of the solid figure and tell how many faces, edges, and vertices each has.

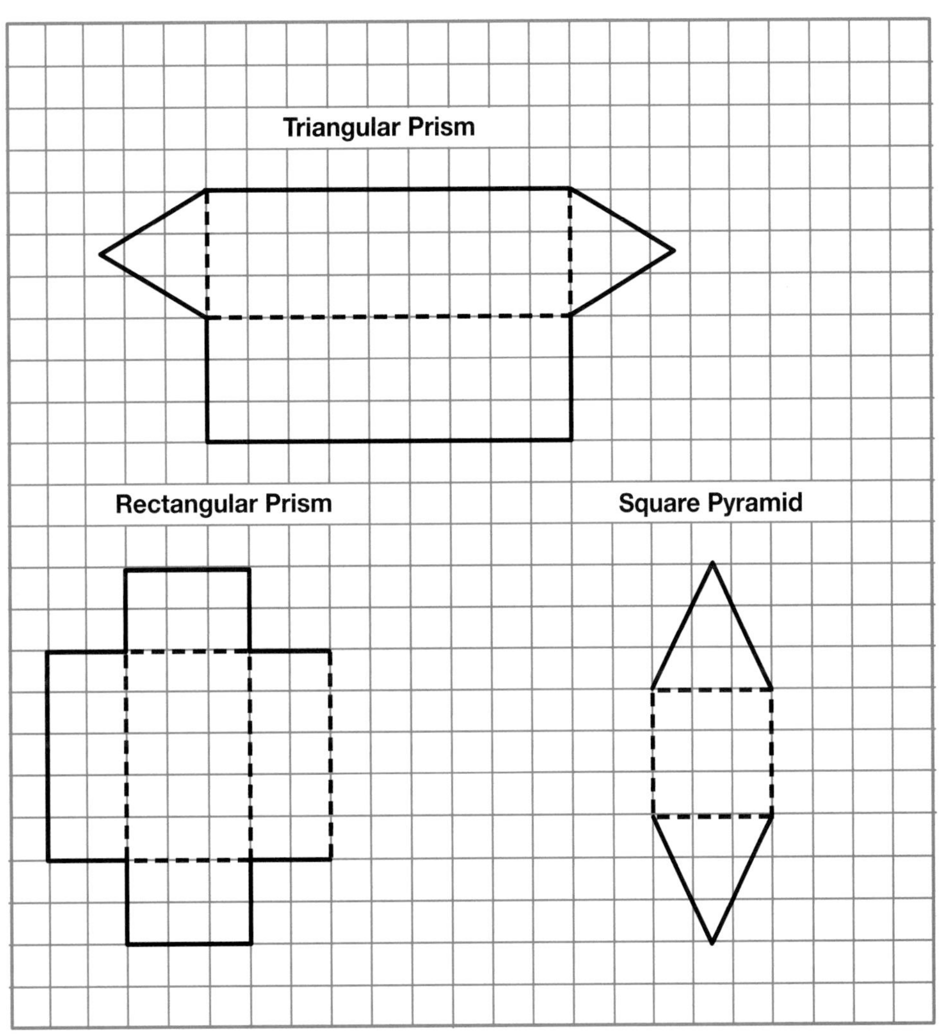

CA Standards

MG 1.1 Measure the area of rectangular shapes by using appropriate units, such as square centimeter (cm^2), square meter (m^2), square kilometer (km^2), square inch ($in.^2$), square yard (yd^2), or square mile (mi^2).

MG 1.4 Understand and use formulas to solve problems involving perimeters and areas of rectangles and squares. Use those formulas to find the areas of more complex figures by dividing the figures into basic shapes.

Also MG 1.0, MG 3.0, MG 3.3, MG 3.6, MR 1.1, MR 2.0, MR 2.2, MR 2.3, MR 2.4, MR 3.0, MR 3.3

Vocabulary

surface area

Materials

Learning Tool 48 (Centimeter Grid Paper)

Surface Area

Objective Find the surface area of a solid figure.

Learn by Example

The **surface area** of a solid figure is the sum of the areas of all the faces of the figure.

Find the surface area of this rectangular prism.

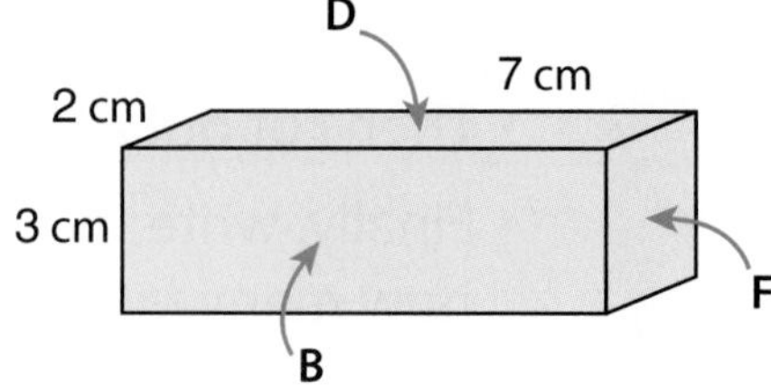

1 Draw the net for the rectangular prism. Label it with the dimensions of each face.

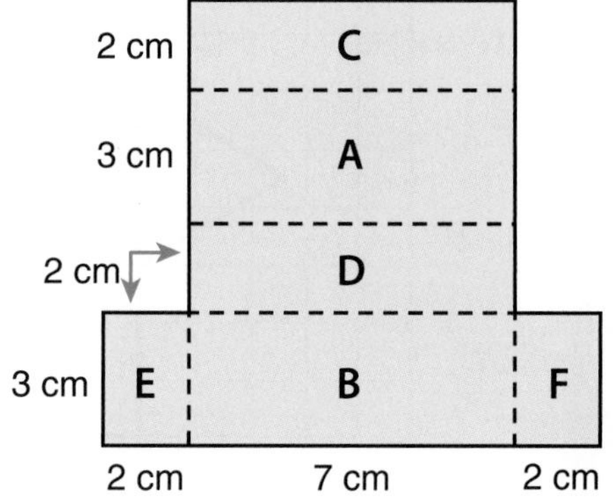

2 Find the area of each face of the net using the formula $A = l \times w$.

Face	Length (l)	Width (w)	Area (A)
A	7 cm	3 cm	21 cm^2
B	7 cm	3 cm	21 cm^2
C	7 cm	2 cm	14 cm^2
D	7 cm	2 cm	14 cm^2
E	3 cm	2 cm	6 cm^2
F	3 cm	2 cm	6 cm^2

3 Add the areas of all the faces.

$21\ cm^2 + 21\ cm^2 + 14\ cm^2 + 14\ cm^2 + 6\ cm^2 + 6\ cm^2 = 82\ cm^2$

Solution: The surface area of the rectangular prism is 82 square centimeters, or 82 cm^2.

Guided Practice

Use the net to find the surface area of the solid figure.

1.

> **Ask Yourself**
> - What are the dimensions of the face?
> - What formula will I use to find the area of the face?

Math Talk What can you conclude about the area of faces that are on opposite sides of a rectangular prism?

Practice and Problem Solving

Use the net to find the surface area of the solid figure.

2.

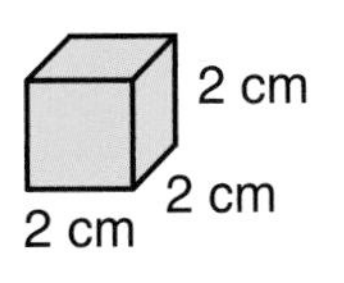

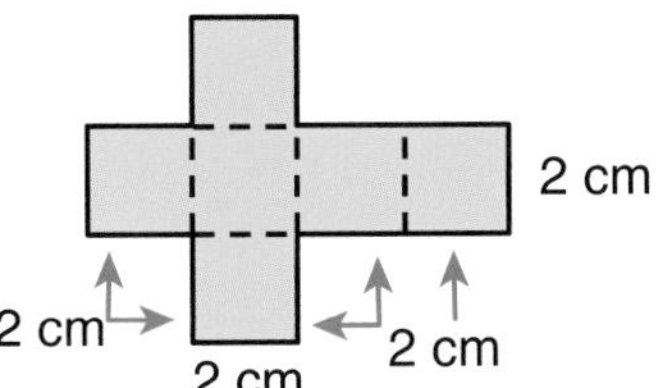

3.

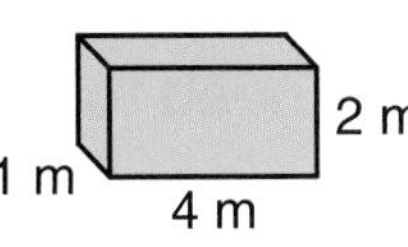

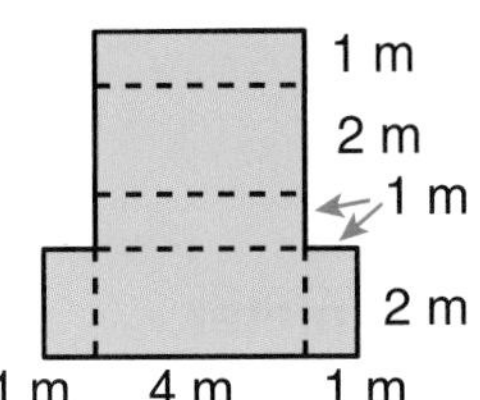

Solve.

4. The edges of a cube all measure 10 inches. What is the surface area of the cube?

5. **Challenge** A square pyramid has a base with an area of 16 in.^{2}. Each of the triangular faces has an area of 6 in.^{2}. Write the expression to show the surface area of the pyramid.

Spiral Review and Test Practice

Use a formula to solve. Show your work. **MG 1.4** pages 602, 604

6. A rectangular garden is 6.5 meters wide and 10 meters long. What is the perimeter of the garden?

7. Find the area of a garden that is 5.25 m long and 3 m wide.

Write the letter of the correct answer. **MG 1.4**

8. Find the surface area of the figure.

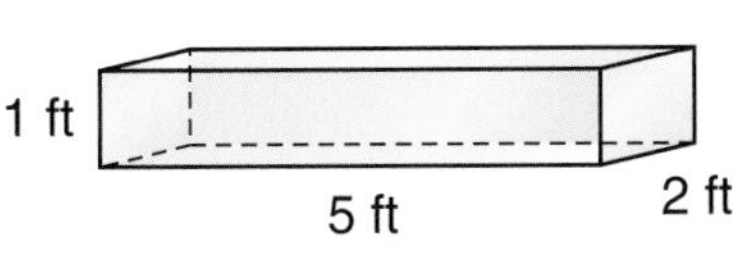

A 24 ft^2 **B** 30 ft^2 **C** 34 ft^2 **D** 10 ft^2

Extra Practice See page 635, Set B.

Volume

Objective Find the volume of a solid figure.

CA Standards
AF 1.4 Use and interpret formulas (e.g., area = length × width or $A = lw$) to answer questions about quantities and their relationships.

MG 3.0 Students demonstrate an understanding of plane and solid geometric objects and use this knowledge to show relationships and solve problems.

Also MG 3.6, MR 1.0, MR 1.2, MR 2.0, MR 2.3, MR 3.0, MR 3.3

Vocabulary

volume

cubic units

cubic centimeter

Learn by Example

Volume is the amount of space inside a solid figure. Volume is measured in **cubic units**.

One standard unit for describing volume is a cube where each edge measures 1 centimeter. This unit is called a **cubic centimeter**.

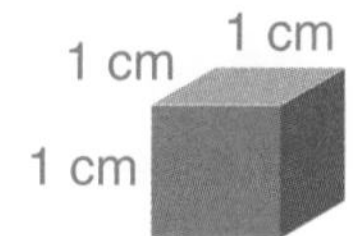

Suppose you want to ship books across the country. Before you can decide how many boxes you need, you must find out how much a box can hold. You need to find the volume of the box.

Different Ways to Find Volume

Way 1 Use cubes.

- Fill the box with unit cubes.
- Count the cubes.

There are 24 cubes in this box.

Way 2 Use a formula.

A rectangular prism has three dimensions: length (l), width (w), and height (h).

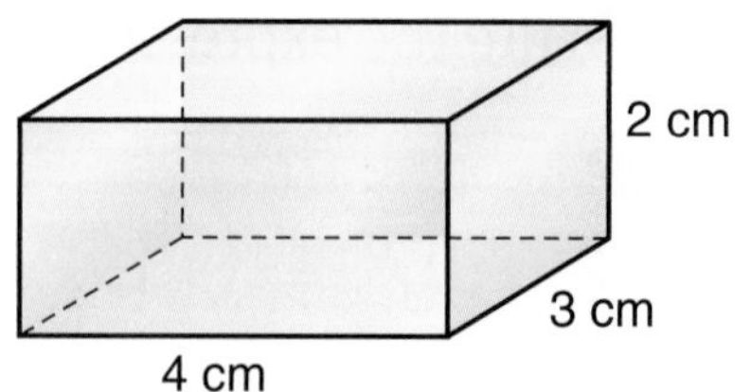

You can find its volume (V) by multiplying these dimensions.

Volume = length × width × height
$V = l \times w \times h$
$V = 4 \text{ cm} \times 3 \text{ cm} \times 2 \text{ cm}$
$V = 24 \text{ cm}^3$ or 24 cubic centimeters

Solution: The volume of the box is 24 cubic centimeters or 24 cm^3.

Guided Practice

Find the volume of the figure.

1. 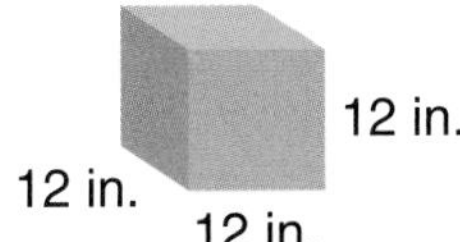

2. 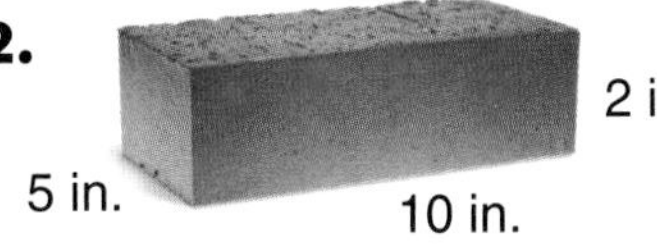

Ask Yourself

- What formula can I use to find the volume?
- What units do I use to label the answer?

Guided Problem Solving

Use the questions to solve this problem.

3. Peli fills a planter that is 9 inches by 13 inches by 8 inches with soil. How many cubic inches of soil does he use?

a. **Understand** What do you need to find?

b. **Plan** What formula can you use?

c. **Solve** What measurements should you use in the formula?
What is the volume of the planter?

d. **Look Back** Did you use the right units to label the answer? How do you know?

 **Math Talk** Why is volume always written in cubic units?

Practice and Problem Solving

Find the volume of the figure.

4. 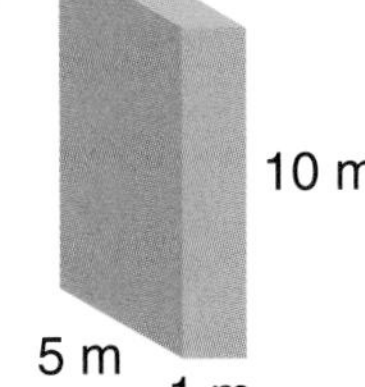

5. 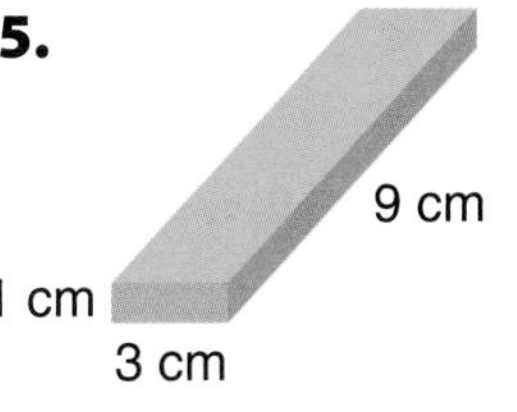

6. 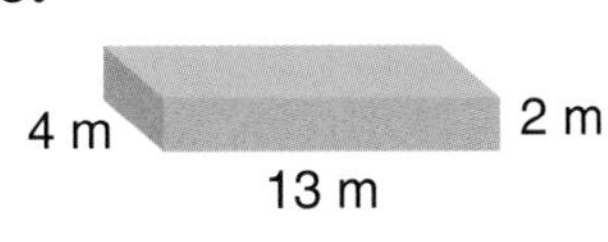

7. 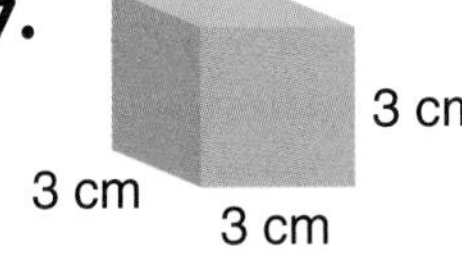

8. 

9. 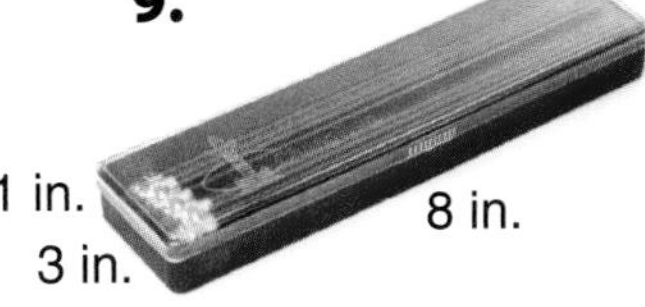

10. 

11. 

Science Link

Solve.

12. Ronnie packed a box full of small pieces of sedimentary rock. The box measures 27 cm by 14 cm by 9 cm. What volume of rock filled the box?

13. **Right or Wrong?** Tiles made from basalt, an igneous rock, cover the floor in Myrna's front hall. The tiles are 2 cm thick. The hall measures 200 cm by 200 cm. Myrna says the volume of the basalt tiles is 40,000 cm^3. Is she right or wrong? Explain.

14. **Challenge** Nancy wants to carve a statue of a bison from marble, a metamorphic rock. Bison are six feet long and five feet tall and have horns nearly two feet wide. The marble measures 70 inches by 26 inches by 80 inches. Does Nancy have enough marble to carve a bison? Explain.

The Rock Cycle

- Igneous rock forms when molten rock cools and solidifies.
- Sedimentary rock forms when rock breaks into tiny pieces that form layers, which get cemented together.
- Metamorphic rock forms when rock is subjected to very high pressure and heat.
- During the rock formation cycle, each type of rock can change into another type.

Vesicular basalt (igneous)

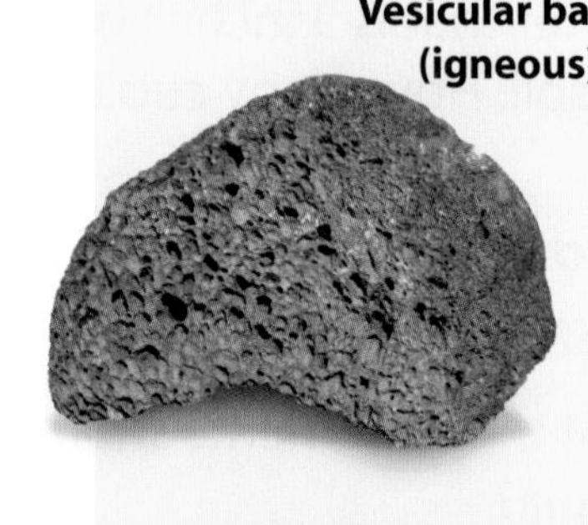

Banded sandstone (sedimentary)

Slate (metamorphic)

Science ES 4.a

Spiral Review and Test Practice

Use a formula to solve. Show your work. MG 1.4 page 626

15. Find the surface area of a cube whose edges are 3 feet in length.

Write the letter of the correct answer. AF 1.4

16. Janette receives a package that is 5 inches long, 4 inches wide, and 3 inches thick. What is the volume of Janette's package?

A 94 in.^{2} **B** 60 in.^{3} **C** 12 in.^{3} **D** 60 in.^{2}

Extra Practice See page 635, Set C.

Key Standards Review

Need Help?
See Key Standards Handbook.

Use the number line to solve. KEY NS 1.9

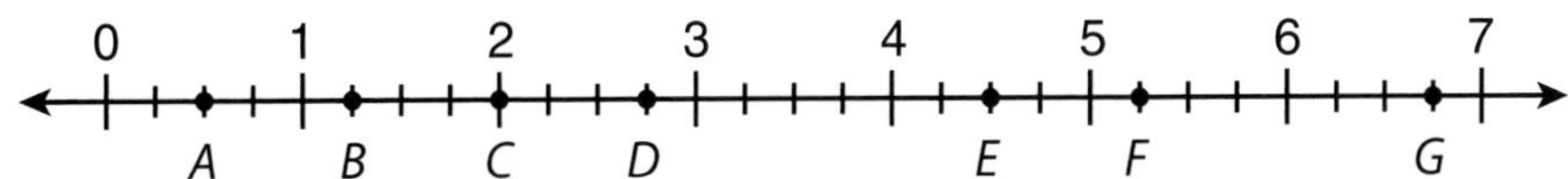

1. Write the decimal and fraction equivalents for *A*, *B*, *C*, *D*, *E*, *F*, and *G* on the number line.
2. $E + D =$ ▭ (decimal form)
3. $G - C =$ ▭ (decimal form)
4. Name a fraction greater than *D* but less than *E*, not using fourths.
5. $B + D =$ ▭ (decimal form)

Challenge Geometry

Volume Search AF 1.4

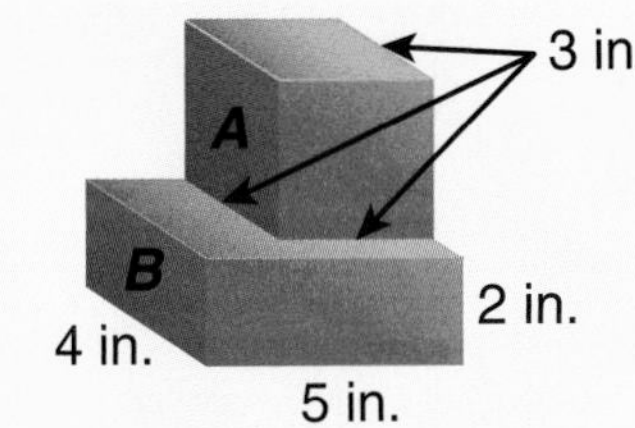

1. Find the volume of Solid *A*.
2. Find the volume of Solid *B*.
3. Find the volume of Solids *A* and *B* combined.
4. Find the volume of Solids *C* and *D* combined.
5. Find the volume of Solid *D*.
6. Find the volume of Solid *C*.
7. Could you find the volume of Solid *C* without finding the volume of Solid *D* first? Explain.

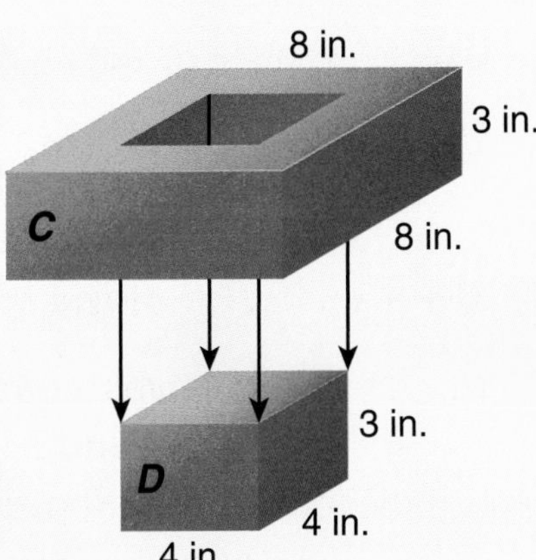

Problem Solving Plan
Surface Area or Volume

Objective Solve problems involving surface area and volume.

CA Standards
MR 1.0 Students make decisions about how to approach problems.
MG 3.0 Students demonstrate an understanding of plane and solid geometric objects and use this knowledge to show relationships and solve problems.
Also MG 1.0, MG 1.1, MG 1.4, MG 3.6, NS 1.5, MR 1.1, MR 1.2, MR 2.0, MR 2.3, MR 2.4, MR 3.0, MR 3.1, MR 3.2, MR 3.3

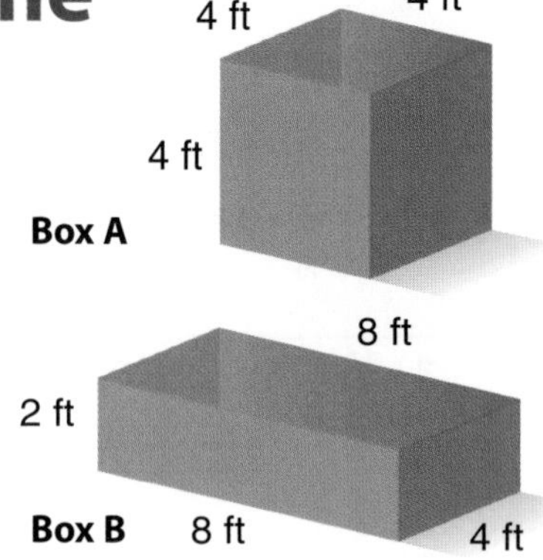

Learn by Example

Antonio knows that both boxes have a volume of 64 ft^3 so he thinks they must also have the same surface area. Is he correct?

UNDERSTAND

You want to find out if Box A and Box B have the same surface area. You know the dimensions and volume of each box.

PLAN

Find the surface area of each box and compare.

SOLVE

Look for surfaces that have the same dimensions. Find the areas and add.

Box A

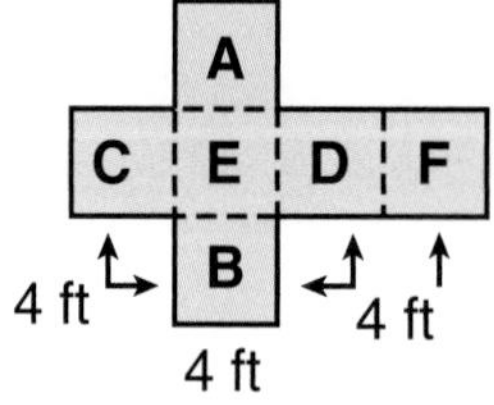

Box B

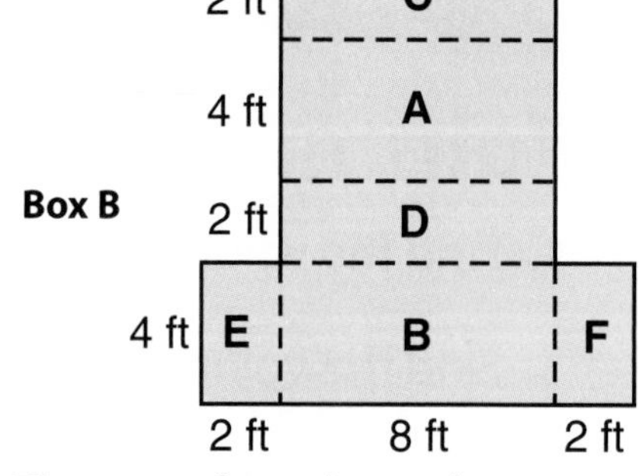

All surfaces have the same area.

$4 \times 4 = 16 \text{ ft}^2$

$16 + 16 + 16 + 16 + 16 + 16 = 96 \text{ ft}^2$

These surfaces have the same area:

A and B $\quad 8 \times 4 = 32 \text{ ft}^2$

C and D $\quad 8 \times 2 = 16 \text{ ft}^2$

E and F $\quad 4 \times 2 = 8 \text{ ft}^2$

$32 + 32 + 16 + 16 + 8 + 8 = 112 \text{ ft}^2$

$112 \text{ ft}^2 > 96 \text{ ft}^2$, so Antonio is not correct.

LOOK BACK

Did you answer the question that was asked?

Guided Problem Solving

Solve using the Ask Yourself questions.

1. Karsten wants to gift-wrap the present at the right. How much wrapping paper does he need?

Ask Yourself

- What do I need to find?
- What formula should I use?

Math Talk Do you think Karsten will actually need more wrapping paper than your answer to Problem 1?

Independent Problem Solving

Solve. Explain why your answer makes sense.

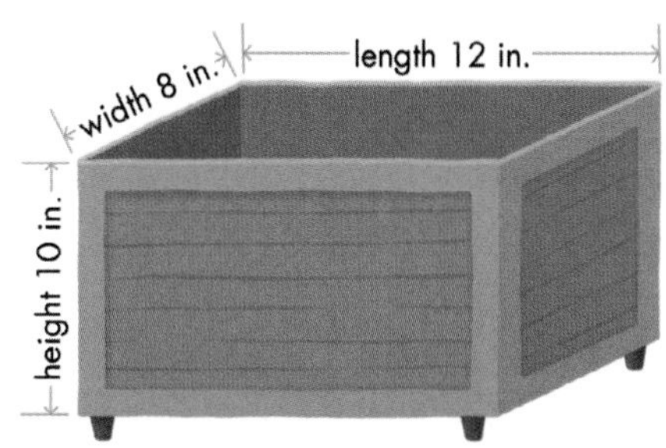

2. Carrie wants to know how much the planter at the right can hold. Should she find the surface area or the volume of the planter?

3. **Multistep** Carrie decides to fill one fourth of the planter with soil. How much soil will she use?

4. **Justify** Noyes says that the rectangular prism shown by this net has the same volume and surface area as a cube with a length of 2 inches. Is he correct? Explain your thinking.

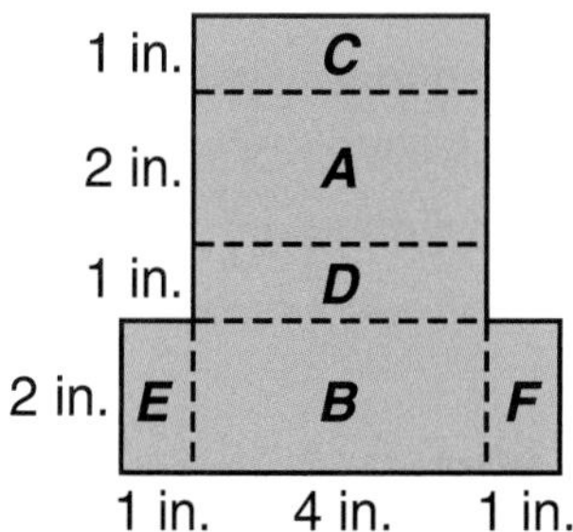

5. **Challenge** Natasha has a cube with a volume of 27 cubic feet. What is the surface area of her cube? Explain how you solved the problem.

6. **Create and Solve** Write two word problems, one that can be solved by finding the volume of a figure and another that can be solved by finding the surface area of a figure.

Vocabulary

Think about how the parts of an object can be used to name the object.

Label each part of the prism shown below.

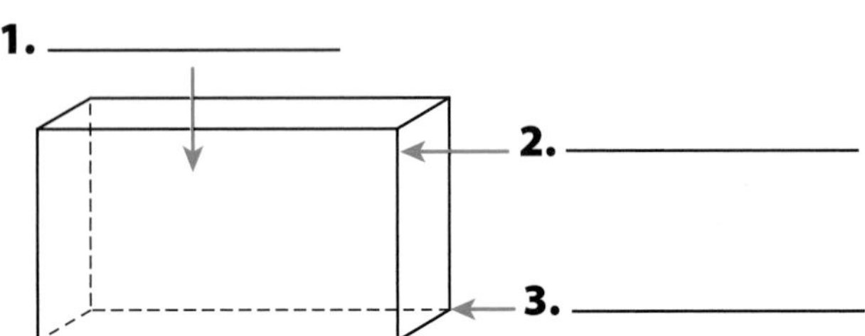

Complete the table with one real-life object that belongs to each group.

	Group	Object
4.	rectangular prism	
5.	triangular prism	
6.	cube	
7.	cylinder	
8.	square pyramid	
9.	triangular pyramid	

Writing Sort the solid figures shown in the table above into two or more categories. Explain your categories.

Reading Look for this book in your library. *Build It With Boxes*, by Joan Irvine

CA Standards
MR 2.3 Use a variety of methods, such as words, numbers, symbols, charts, graphs, tables, diagrams, and models, to explain mathematical reasoning.

Also MG 3.6, MG 3.0

Standards-Based Extra Practice

Set A

MG 3.0, MG 3.6 page 622

Name the solid figure.

1. 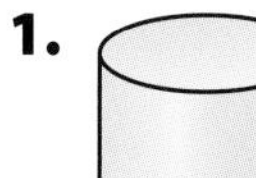

2. 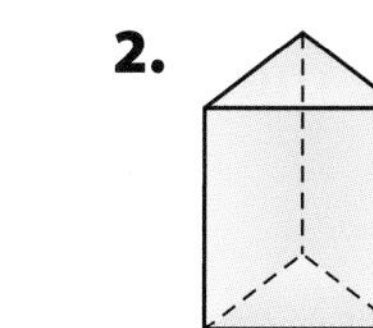

3. 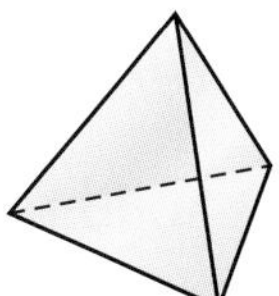

4. **Explain** What is the difference between a triangular prism and a triangular pyramid? Discuss the faces and number of vertices for each solid figure.

Set B

MG 1.1, MG 1.4 page 626

Use the net to find the surface area of the solid figure.

1. 4 in. 4 in. 4 in.

2. **Explain** How is the surface area related to the faces of a solid figure? Explain your reasoning.

3. **Justify** A cube has edges that each measure 5 in. What is the area of one side of the cube? Why can you multiply this area by 6 to find the surface area of the cube?

Set C

MG 3.0, AF 1.4 page 628

Find the volume of the figure.

1. 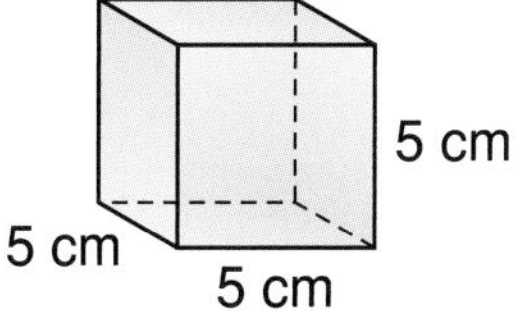

2. 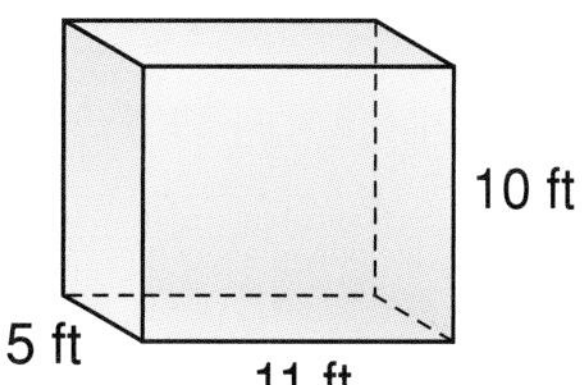

3. **Analyze** A box of rice is 5 in. long, 2 in. wide, and 8 in. tall. What is the volume of the box?

Education Place
Visit www.eduplace.com/camap/
for more **Extra Practice.**

Chapter Review/Test

Vocabulary and Concepts — MG 3.0, MR 2.3

Write the best word to complete each sentence.

1. A(n) ______ is where two faces of a solid figure meet.
2. A flat part of a solid figure is called a ______.
3. The point where three edges of a solid figure meet is called a ______.
4. You can use a pattern called a ______ to build a three-dimensional solid figure.

Skills — AF 1.4, MG 3.6, MG 3.0, MG 2.3

Find the volume of the figure.

5. 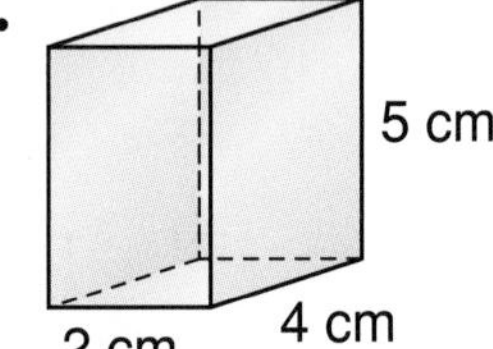

6. 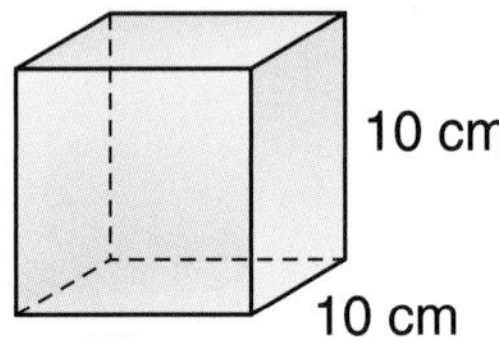

7. 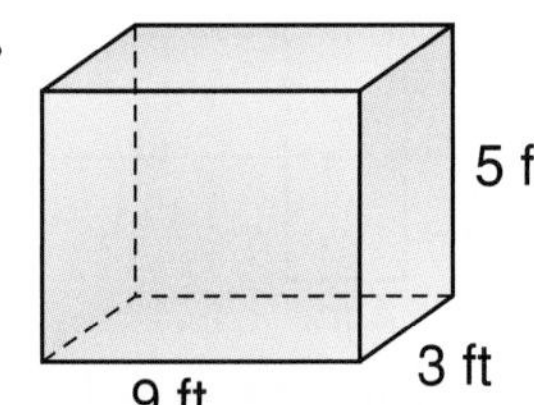

8. 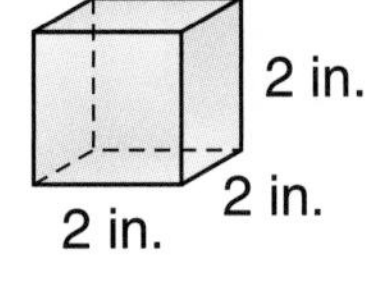

Problem Solving and Reasoning — MG 1.4, MG 3.0, MG 3.6, MR 2.2, MR 1.0

Solve.

9. An unusual box has 3 rectangular faces and 2 triangular faces. What type of solid figure would fit perfectly in this box?

10. Kristi collected sand at the beach. She filled half of the box with sand. What is the volume of the sand in the box?

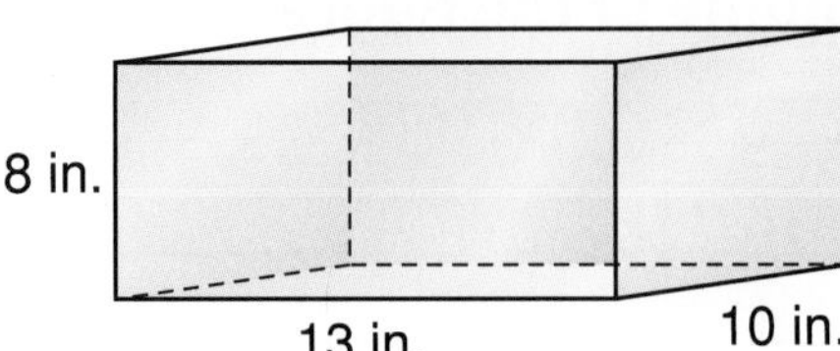

Writing Math Explain why more than one net can be created for a cube.

Spiral Review and Test Practice

1. Look at the circle with center *O*.

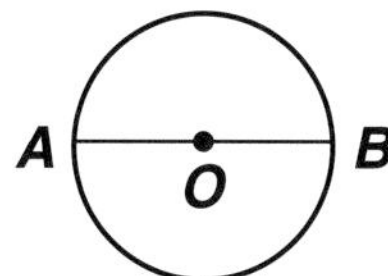

The line segment *AB* appears to be

A a center.
B a radius.
C a diameter.
D a perimeter.

MG 3.2 page 568

2. Which figure appears to be congruent to the figure below?

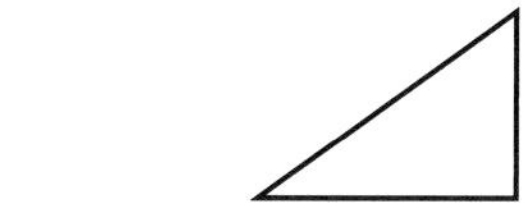

A
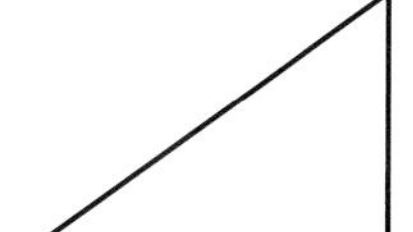

C
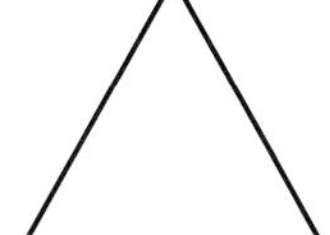

B
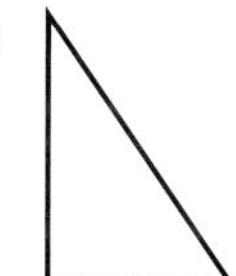

D

MG 3.3 page 588

3. A farmer collected 60 cartons of eggs. Each carton contains 12 eggs. How many eggs did the farmer collect?

A 50 eggs
B 120 eggs
C 360 eggs
D 720 eggs

KEY NS 3.3 page 238

4. Which solid figure does the net make?

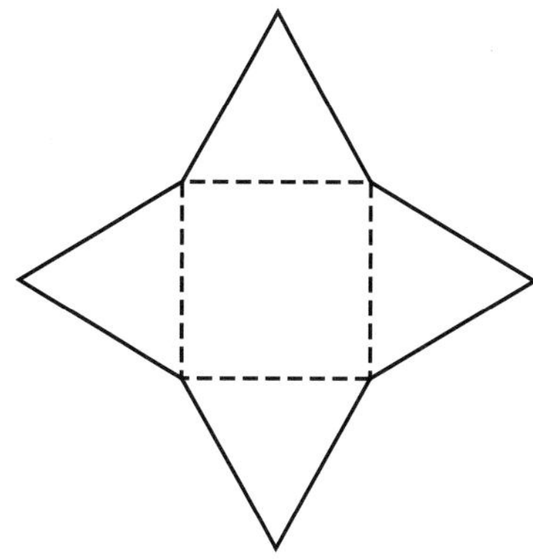

A triangular pyramid
B rectangular prism
C square pyramid
D triangular prism

MG 3.6 page 622

5. Find the surface area of the figure.

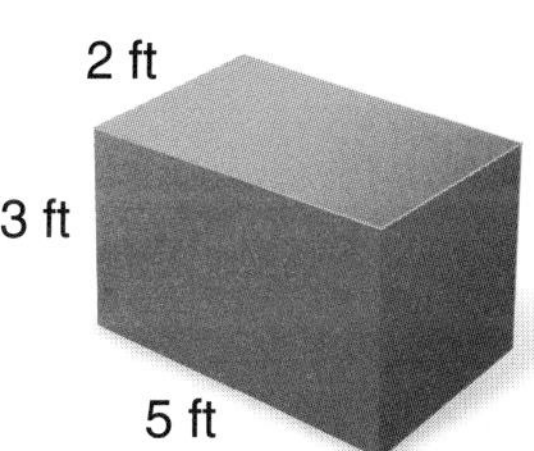

A 31 ft^2
B 50 ft^2
C 62 ft^2
D 30 ft^3

MG 1.4 page 626

Education Place
Visit www.eduplace.com/camap/ for **Test-Taking Tips** and **Extra Practice.**

Unit 12 Test

Vocabulary and Concepts — MG 3.1, MG 3.2, MG 3.5, MG 3.7. MR 2.3 Chapter 25, Lessons 2–4

Complete each sentence with a vocabulary word from this unit.

1. _______ lines do not intersect.
2. An angle that forms a square corner is a _______ angle.
3. The _______ of a circle is a line segment that joins the center and any point on the circle.

Computation — MG 3.3, MG 3.4, MG 3.7

Use the given side lengths to classify the triangles as *isosceles*, *scalene*, or *equilateral*. Chapter 25, Lesson 4

4. 10 yd, 10 yd, 10 yd
5. 3 ft, 5 ft, 10 ft
6. 8 cm, 14 cm, 8 cm

Do the figures in each pair appear to be congruent? Write *yes* or *no*. Chapter 26, Lesson 4

7.
8.
9.

Use the figures above for Questions 10 and 11. Chapter 26, Lessons 2 and 3

10. Do the triangles in Problem 7 have bilateral symmetry? Explain.
11. Do the figures in Problem 9 have rotational symmetry? Explain.

Problem Solving and Reasoning — MG 1.3, MG 1.4, MG 3.2, MG 3.5, MR 2.4 Chapters 25–28

Solve. Show your work, including any formulas used.

12. Carla drew the rectangular prism on the right. Find the surface area and volume of the figure.

10 ft

4 ft

6 ft

13. Bob created two questions to go with this figure. Answer Bob's questions.

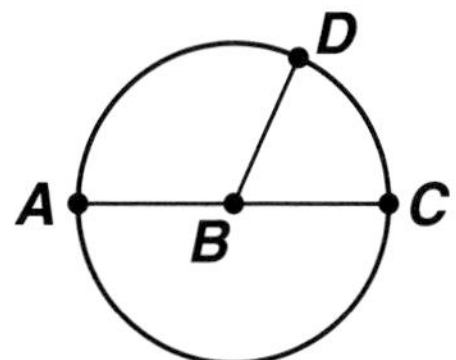

- Name the line segment that forms the diameter.
- What type of angle is angle *ABD*?

14. When the minute hand on a clock moves from 12 to 3, how many degrees has it turned?

15. Eddie has a pentagon and a square. Every side of the two figures measures 3 inches. Eddie pushes the shapes together to make one figure. How many sides does the new figure have? What is its perimeter?

Writing Math Do all rectangles with the same perimeter have the same area? Support your answer with examples.

Performance Assessment

Net It!

MG 3.6

For math class, Paul and Robin both made a net for a box of breakfast cereal.

Task	Information You Need
Use the information above and to the right. Will both the nets fold to make a box like the cereal box? Explain. Draw a third net that will fold to make a box like the cereal box.	Paul's net looks like this. 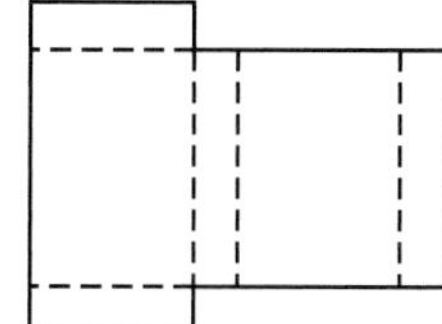 Robin's net looks like this. 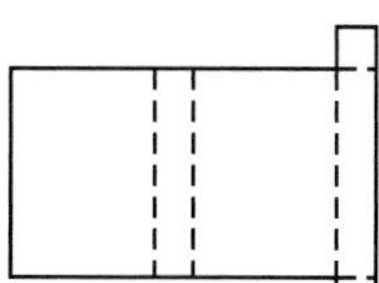

Greg Tang's

Go Fast, Go Far

Unit 12 Mental Math Strategies

Multiply by 11

Eleven can be fast and fun, simply just insert the sum!

I have a fast way to do 11 × 45. I split 45 by putting the 4 in the hundreds place and the 5 in the ones place. Then I insert their sum in the middle, the tens place, and get 495. If the sum is greater than 9, I just regroup!

	100s	10s	1s	
1. 11 × 45 =	4	9	5	= ▢
2. 11 × 66 =	6	12	6	= ▢
3. 11 × 24 =	2	▢	4	= ▢
4. 11 × 88 =	8	▢	8	= ▢

Great work! Keep on going!

5. 11 × 23 = ▢ ▢ ▢ = ▢

6. 11 × 77 = ▢ ▢ ▢ = ▢

7. 11 × 31 = ▢ ▢ ▢ = ▢

8. 11 × 49 = ▢ ▢ ▢ = ▢

9. 11 × 52 = ▢ ▢ ▢ = ▢

10. 11 × 84 = ▢ ▢ ▢ = ▢

Good For You!

Take It Further!

Now try doing all the steps in your head!

11. 11 × 63 **12.** 11 × 75 **13.** 11 × 57 **14.** 11 × 99

Looking Ahead

THIS YEAR I learned to ...

Number Sense

- use place value to compare, order, and round large whole numbers;
- decide when an estimated solution is called for and explain why;
- use negative numbers;
- factor small whole numbers;
- add, subtract, multiply, and divide with large numbers; and
- identify the position of fractions, mixed numbers, and decimals on a number line.

Which letter best represents where the number would go on the number line? KEY NS 1.9

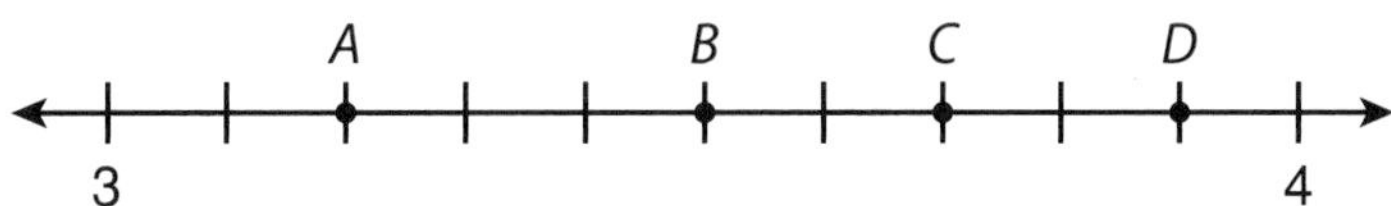

1. 3.90 **2.** $3\frac{7}{10}$ **3.** 3.2 **4.** $3\frac{1}{2}$

Algebra and Functions

- interpret and evaluate mathematical expressions that use parentheses;
- use parentheses to indicate which operation to perform first;
- understand and solve equations containing variables; and
- manipulate an equation using "equals."

Evaluate the expression. KEY AF 1.2

5. $36 - (15 - 5)$ **6.** $(3 + 7) - (2 \times 4)$ **7.** $(27 - 5) + 3$

Measurement and Geometry

- use coordinate grids to represent points and to graph lines and simple figures;
- draw the points corresponding to an equation on a coordinate grid and connect the points using a straight line; and
- understand how to find the length of a horizontal and a vertical line segment on the coordinate grid.

Solve. KEY MG 2.1

8. Complete the function table for the equation $y = 2x$.

x	0	1	2	3	4
y	0	2	4		

9. Make a graph like the one shown at the right on grid paper. Draw the points from Exercise 8 on your graph. Draw 3 more points for the equation $y = 2x$.

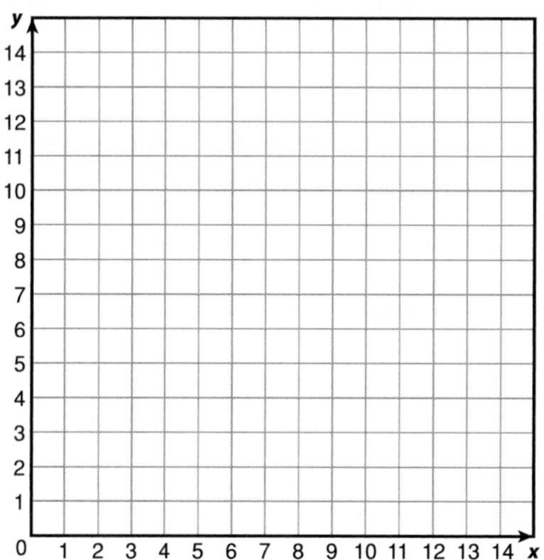

NEXT YEAR I will learn more about...

- computing with fractions, decimals, and positive and negative numbers;
- using units of measurement to find length and area;
- using formulas to find the volume of simple geometric figures;
- measuring angles; and
- using a protractor and compass to solve problems.

I can use the Review/Preview worksheets to get ready for next year.

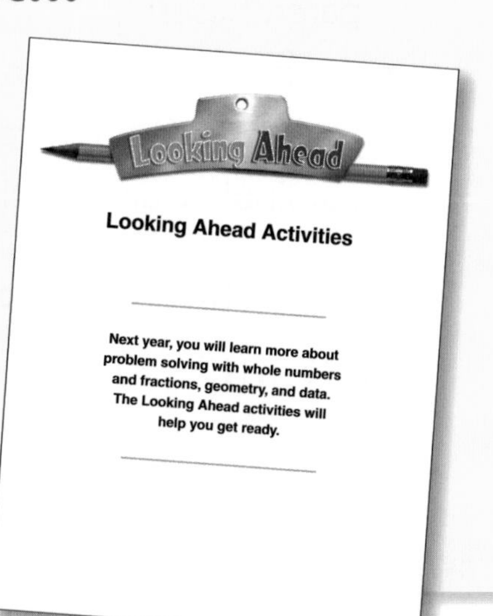

Looking Ahead
Looking Ahead Activities
Next year, you will learn more about problem solving with whole numbers and fractions, geometry, and data. The Looking Ahead activities will help you get ready.

Table of Measures

Length

Customary Units of Measure		Metric Units of Measure	
1 foot (ft)	= 12 inches (in.)	1 centimeter (cm)	= 10 millimeters (mm)
1 yard (yd)	= 36 inches	1 decimeter (dm)	= 10 centimeters
1 yard	= 3 feet	1 meter (m)	= 100 centimeters
1 mile (mi)	= 5,280 feet	1 meter	= 10 decimeters
1 mile	= 1,760 yard	1 kilometer (km)	= 1,000 meters

Capacity

Customary Units of Measure		Metric Units of Measure	
1 pint (pt)	= 2 cups (c)	1 liter (L)	= 1,000 milliliters (mL)
1 quart (qt)	= 4 cups	1 gallon	= 128 ounces
1 quart	= 2 pints	1 quart	= 2 pints
1 gallon (gal)	= 16 cups	1 pint	= 2 cups
1 gallon	= 4 quarts	1 cup	= 8 ounces

Weight/Mass

Customary Units of Measure		Metric Units of Measure	
1 pound (lb)	= 16 ounces (oz)	1 gram (g)	= 1,000 milligrams (mg)
1 ton (T)	= 2,000 pounds	1 kilogram (kg)	= 1,000 grams

Units of Time

1 minute (min)	= 60 seconds (s)	1 year	= 52 weeks
1 hour (hr)	= 60 minutes	1 year	= 365 days
1 day (d)	= 24 hours	1 leap year	= 366 days
1 week (wk)	= 7 days	1 decade	= 10 years
1 year (yr)	= 12 months (mo)	1 century	= 100 years
		1 millennium	= 1,000 years

Money

1 penny	= 1 cent (¢)	1 quarter	= 25 cents
1 nickel	= 5 cents	1 half-dollar	= 50 cents
1 dime	= 10 cents	1 dollar ($)	= 100 cents

California English-Spanish

Glossary

acute angle An angle with a measure less than that of a right angle.

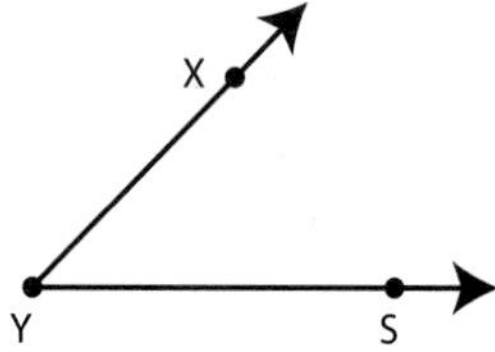

ángulo agudo Ángulo menor que un ángulo recto.

acute triangle A triangle in which each of the three angles is acute.

triángulo acutángulo Triángulo en el que los tres ángulos son agudos.

addend A number to be added in an addition expression. In 7 + 4 + 8, the numbers 7, 4, and 8 are addends.

sumando Número que se suma en una expression de suma. En 7 + 4 + 8, los números 7, 4 y 8 son los sumandos.

algebraic expression An expression that includes one or more variables.
Example: $2x + 3y + 6$

expresión algebraica Expresión que tiene una o más variables.
Ejemplo: $2x + 3y + 6$

angle An angle is formed by two rays with the same endpoint.

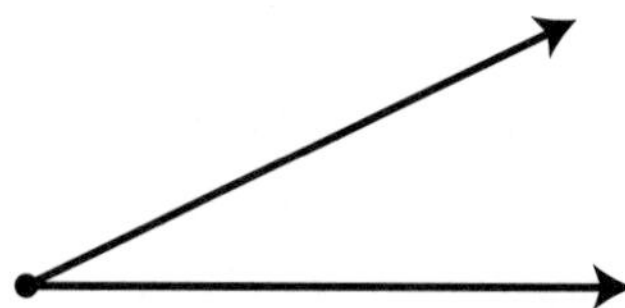

ángulo Un ángulo está formado por dos semirrectas que tienen un mismo extremo.

area The number of square units in a region.

área Número de unidades cuadradas en una región.

array An arrangement of numbers, objects, or pictures in columns and rows.

matriz Agrupación de números, objetos o dibujos en columnas y filas.

Associative Property of Addition (Also called **Grouping Property of Addition**) The property that states that the way in which addends are grouped does not change the sum.
Example: (3 + 4) + 5 = 3 + (4 + 5)

Propiedad asociativa de la suma (También llamada **Propiedad de agrupación en la suma**) Propiedad que establece que la forma en que se agrupan los sumandos no altera la suma.
Ejemplo: (3 + 4) + 5 = 3 + (4 + 5)

Associative Property of Multiplication (Also called **Grouping Property of Multiplication**) The property that states that the way in which factors are grouped does not change the product.
Example: (6 × 7) × 9 = 6 × (7 × 9)

Propiedad asociativa de la multiplicación (También llamada **Propiedad de agrupación en la multiplicación**) Propiedad que establece que la forma en que se agrupan los factores no altera el producto.
Ejemplo: (6 × 7) × 9 = 6 × (7 × 9)

average The number found by dividing the sum of a group of numbers by the number of addends.

promedio Número que se obtiene al dividir la suma de un grupo de números entre el número de sumandos.

axes In a coordinate plane, the horizontal and vertical lines along which the coordinates are measured.

ejes En un plano de coordenadas, la línea horizontal y la línea vertical en las que se miden las coordenadas.

bilateral symmetry (see **line symmetry**)

simetría bilateral (ver **eje de simetría**)

capacity The amount a container can hold.

capacidad Cantidad que puede contener un recipiente.

Celsius The metric temperature scale. The freezing point of water is 0 degrees Celsius, and the boiling point is 100 degrees Celsius.

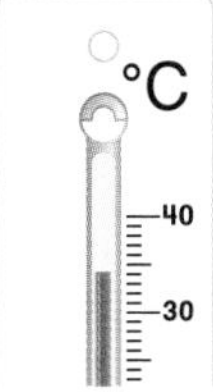

Celsio Escala métrica de temperatura. El punto de congelación del agua es 0 grados Celsios y el punto de ebullición es 100 grados Celsios.

center (of a circle) A point that is the same distance from all points on a circle.

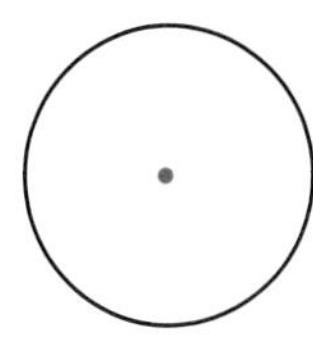

centro (de un círculo) Punto que está a la misma distancia de todos los puntos que forman un círculo.

centimeter (cm) A metric unit used to measure length.
100 centimeters = 1 meter

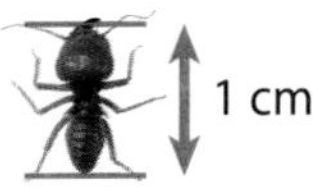

centímetro (cm) Unidad métrica que se usa para medir la longitud.
100 centímetros = 1 metro

certain A prediction that a particular event of a probability experiment will absolutely happen.

seguro Predicción de que un suceso ocurrirá con toda certeza, como resultado de un experimento de probabilidad.

circle A closed plane figure in which every point is the same distance from a given point, called the center of the circle.

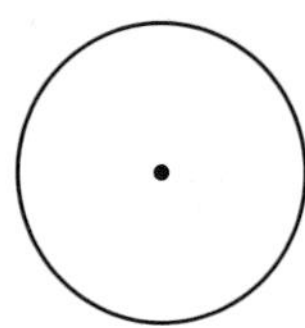

círculo Figura plana cerrada en la que todos los puntos están a la misma distancia de un punto dado, llamado centro del círculo.

Commutative Property of Addition (Also called **Order Property of Addition**) The property that states that the order of addends does not change the sum. Example: $2 + 4 = 4 + 2$

Propiedad conmutativa de la suma (También llamada **Propiedad del orden de la suma**) Propiedad que establece que el orden de los sumandos no cambia la suma. Ejemplo: $2 + 4 = 4 + 2$

Commutative Property of Multiplication (Also called **Order Property of Multiplication**) The property that states that the order of factors does not change the product. Example: $3 \times 5 = 5 \times 3$

Propiedad conmutativa de la multiplicación (También llamada **Propiedad del orden de la multiplicación**) Propiedad que establece que el orden de los factores no altera el producto. Ejemplo: $3 \times 5 = 5 \times 3$

compare To examine numbers to find if they are greater than, less than, or equal to one another.

comparar Examinar números para hallar si son mayores, menores o iguales a otro.

composite number A whole number that has more than two factors. For example, 6 is a composite number. Its factors are 2, 3, 1, and 6.

número compuesto Número entero que tiene más de dos factores. Por ejemplo, el 6 es un número compuesto. Sus factores son 2, 3, 1 y 6.

cone A three-dimensional figure that has a circular base and a curved surface that comes to a point called the vertex.

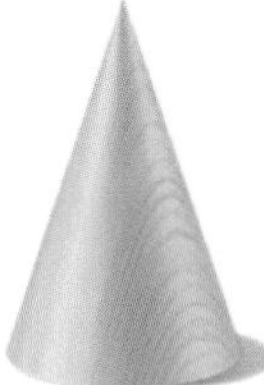

cono Figura tridimensional que tiene una base circular y una superficie curva que termina en un punto llamado vértice.

congruent Figures that have the same size and the same shape are congruent.

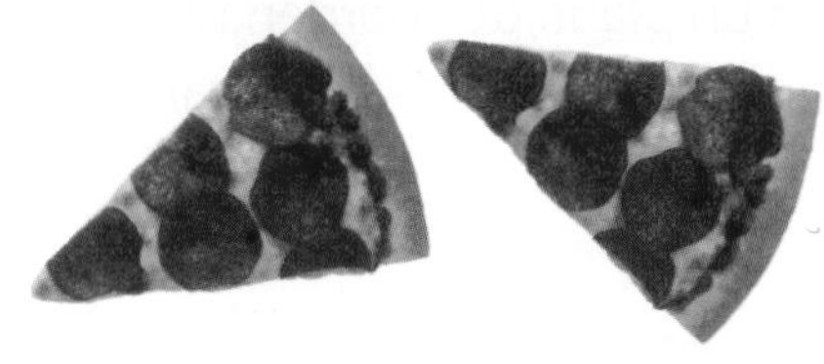

congruentes Las figuras que tienen la misma forma y el mismo tamaño son congruentes.

coordinate grid (see **coordinate plane**)

cuadrícula de coordenadas (ver **plano de coordenadas**)

coordinate plane A grid with two perpendicular number lines in which every point is associated with an ordered pair of numbers.

plano de coordenadas Cuadrícula con dos rectas numéricas perpendiculares en la que cada punto está asociado con un par ordenado de números.

coordinates An ordered pair of numbers that locates a point in the coordinate plane with reference to the *x*- and *y*-axes.

coordenadas Par ordenado de números que representa un punto en el plano de coordenadas con respecto a los ejes *x* e *y*.

cube A three-dimensional figure that has six congruent square faces.

cubo Figura tridimensional que tiene seis caras cuadradas congruentes.

cubic centimeter A metric unit for measuring volume. It is the volume of a cube with each edge 1 centimeter long.

centímetro cúbico Unidad métrica para medir volumen. Es el volumen de un cubo con lados de 1 centímetro de largo.

cubic unit A unit for measuring volume.

unidad cúbica Unidad que se usa para medir el volumen.

cup (c) A customary unit used to measure liquid capacity.
2 cups = 1 pint

taza (tz) Unidad del sistema usual para medir capacidad líquida.
2 tazas = 1 pinta

customary system A system of measurement that uses inches and feet to measure length, cups and gallons to measure capacity, and ounces and pounds to measure weight.

sistema usual Sistema de medidas que usa pulgadas y pies para medir longitud, tazas y galones para medir capacidad, y onzas y libras para medir peso.

cylinder A three-dimensional figure that has parallel, congruent circular faces joined by a curved surface.

cilindro Figura tridimensional que tiene caras circulares paralelas congruentes unidas por una superficie curva.

data A set of numbers or other pieces of information.

datos Conjunto de números u otra información.

decimal number A number with one or more digits to the right of a decimal point. For example, 3.5 is a decimal.

número decimal Número con uno o más dígitos a la derecha de un punto decimal. Por ejemplo, 3.5 es un número decimal.

decimal equivalent A decimal that is equal to a number expressed as a fraction. $0.10 = \frac{1}{10}$

decimal equivalente Decimal que es igual a un número expresado como una fracción. $0.10 = \frac{1}{10}$

decimal point A symbol used to separate the ones and tenths places in a decimal number.

punto decimal Símbolo usado para separar las unidades y las décimas en un número decimal.

decimeter (dm) A metric unit used to measure length.
10 decimeters = 1 meter

decímetro (dm) Unidad métrica que se usa para medir longitud.
10 decímetros = 1 metro

degree A unit used to measure angles or temperature. The symbol is °.

grado Unidad que se usa para medir ángulos o temperatura. El símbolo es °.

denominator The number below the bar in a fraction.

denominador Número que está abajo de la barra en una fracción.

diameter A line segment that connects two points on a circle and passes through the center.

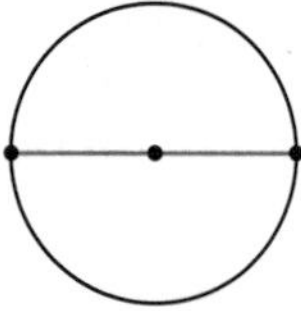

diámetro Segmento de recta que conecta dos puntos en un círculo y pasa a través del centro.

difference The answer in a subtraction problem.

diferencia Respuesta de un problema de resta.

digit Any of the symbols 0, 1, 2, 3, 4, 5, 6, 7, 8, and 9.

dígito Cualquiera de los símbolos 0, 1, 2, 3, 4, 5, 6, 7, 8 y 9.

Distributive Property When two addends are multiplied by a factor, the products are the same as if each addend were multiplied by the factor and those products were added.
Example: $a \times (b + c) = (a \times b) + (a \times c)$

Propiedad distributiva Cuando se multiplican dos sumandos por un factor, los productos son los mismos que al multiplicar cada sumando por el factor y sumar esos productos.
Ejemplo: $a \times (b + c) = (a \times b) + (a \times c)$

dividend The number that is divided in a division problem. In $10 \div 2 = 5$, the dividend is 10.

dividendo Número que se divide en un problema de división. En $10 \div 2 = 5$, el dividendo es 10.

divisible One number is divisible by another if the quotient is a whole number and the remainder is 0. For example, 10 is divisible by 2, since $10 \div 2 = 5$.

divisible Un número es divisible entre otro si el cociente es un número entero y el residuo es 0. Por ejemplo, 10 es divisible entre 2, dado que $10 \div 2 = 5$.

divisor The number by which a number is divided. In $6 \div 3 = 2$, the divisor is 3.

divisor Número entre el cual se divide un número. En $6 \div 3 = 2$, el divisor es 3.

double bar graph A graph in which data are compared by pairs of rectangular bars drawn next to each other.

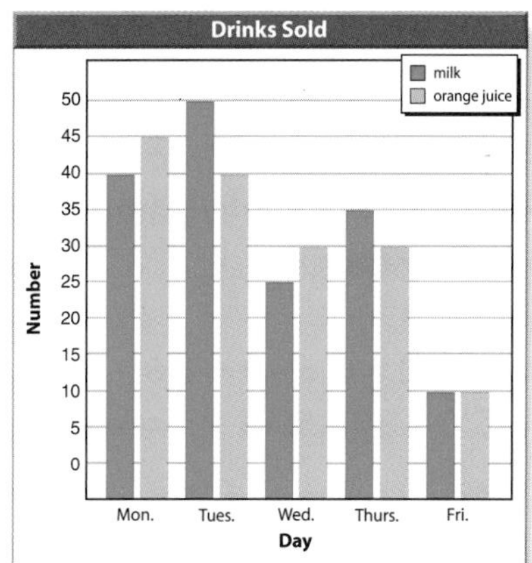

gráfica de doble barra Gráfica en la que los datos se comparan a través de pares de barras rectangulares dibujadas una al lado de otra.

edge The segment where two faces of a solid figure meet.

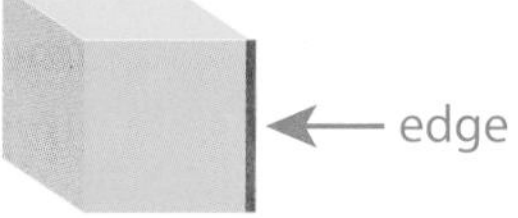

arista Segmento donde se encuentran dos caras de un cuerpo geométrico.

endpoint The point at either end of a line segment, or at the end of a ray.

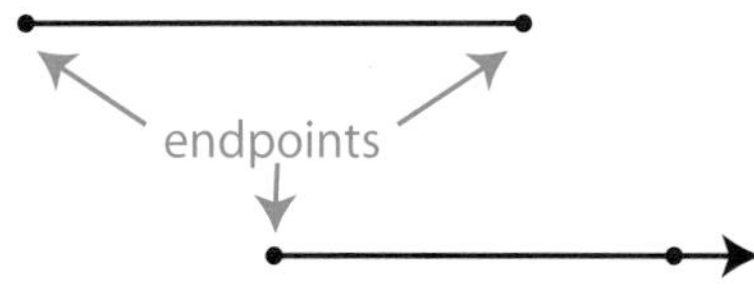

extremo Punto ubicado en el punto inicial o final de un segmento de recta o al final de una semirrecta.

equally likely Having the same probability of happening.

igualmente probable Que tiene la misma posibilidad de ocurrir.

equation A mathematical sentence with an equal sign. For example, $3 + 1 = 4$ and $2x + 5 = 9$ are equations.

ecuación Enunciado matemático que tiene un signo de igual. Por ejemplo: $3 + 1 = 4$ y $2x + 5 = 9$ son ecuaciones.

equilateral triangle A triangle that has three congruent sides.

triángulo equilátero Triángulo que tiene tres lados congruentes.

equivalent fractions Different fractions that represent the same number. For example, $\frac{1}{2}$ and $\frac{4}{8}$ are equivalent fractions.

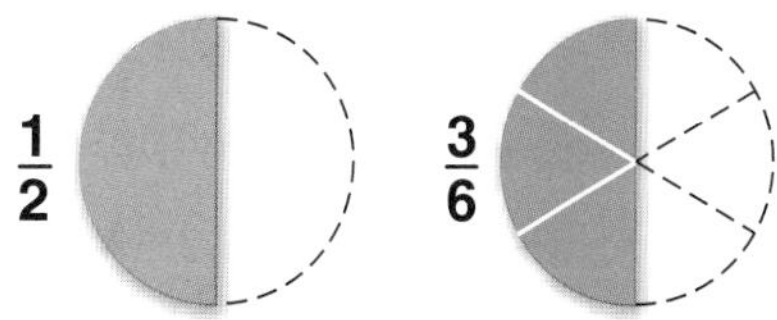

fracciones equivalentes Fracciones diferentes que representan el mismo número. Por ejemplo, $\frac{1}{2}$ y $\frac{4}{8}$ son fracciones equivalentes.

estimate A number close to an exact amount. An estimate tells *about* how much or *about* how many.

estimación Número cercano a una cantidad exacta. Una estimación dice *aproximadamente* cuánto o *aproximadamente* cuántos.

Glossary

evaluate To substitute the values given for the variables and to perform the operations to find the value of an expression.

hallar el valor Sustituir los valores dados para las variables y realizar las operaciones para resolver una expresión.

even number A whole number that is a multiple of 2. The ones digit in an even number is 0, 2, 4, 6, or 8. The numbers 56 and 48 are examples of even numbers.

número par Número entero que es múltiplo de 2. El dígito de las unidades en un número par es 0, 2, 4, 6 u 8. Los números 56 y 48 son ejemplos de números pares.

expanded notation A way of writing a number as the sum of the values of its digits. The number 583 written in expanded notation is 500 + 80 + 3.

notación extendida Manera de escribir un número como la suma de los valores de sus dígitos. El número 583 escrito en notación extendida es 500 + 80 + 3.

expression A number, variable, or any combination of numbers, variables, and operation signs. For example, $2x$, 4, and $3x + 4$ are expressions.

expresión Número, variable o cualquier combinación de números, variables y signos de operación. Por ejemplo, $2x$, 4 y $3x + 4$ son expresiones.

face A flat surface of a solid figure.

cara Superficie plana de un cuerpo geométrico.

fact family Facts that are related, using the same numbers.
Examples:
$2 + 4 = 6; 4 + 2 = 6; 6 - 4 = 2; 6 - 2 = 4;$
$3 \times 5 = 15; 5 \times 3 = 15; 15 \div 3 = 5; 15 \div 5 = 3$

familia de operaciones Operaciones relacionadas que usan los mismos números.
Ejemplos:
$2 + 4 = 6; 4 + 2 = 6; 6 - 4 = 2; 6 - 2 = 4;$
$3 \times 5 = 15; 5 \times 3 = 15; 15 \div 3 = 5; 15 \div 5 = 3$

factor One of two or more numbers that are multiplied to give a product.

$$4 \times 5 = 20$$

factor factor

factor Uno de dos o más números que se multiplican para obtener un producto.

factor tree A diagram that is used to determine the prime factors of a number.

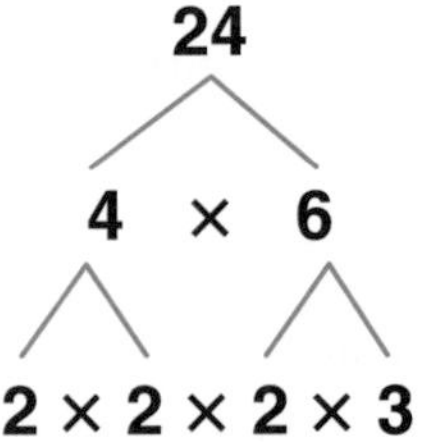

árbol de factores Diagrama usado para determinar los factores primos de un número.

Fahrenheit The customary temperature scale. The freezing point of water is 32 degrees Fahrenheit, and the boiling point is 212 degrees Fahrenheit.

Fahrenheit Escala de temperatura del sistema usual. El punto de congelación del agua es 32 grados Fahrenheit y el punto de ebullición es 212 grados Fahrenheit.

favorable outcome A desired result in a probability experiment.

resultado favorable Resultado deseable en un experimento de probabilidad.

foot (ft) A customary unit used to measure length.
1 foot = 12 inches

pie Unidad del sistema usual para medir longitud.
1 pie = 12 pulgadas

formula An equation that shows a mathematical relationship.

fórmula Ecuación que muestra una relación matemática.

fraction A way of writing a number to show a part of a whole, a part of a set, or division of whole numbers by whole numbers.
Examples: $\frac{1}{2}, \frac{3}{4}, \frac{2}{3}$

fracción Manera de escribir un número para mostrar una parte de un entero, de un conjunto, o división de números enteros entre números enteros.
Ejemplos: $\frac{1}{2}, \frac{3}{4}, \frac{2}{3}$

full turn A 360° rotation of a figure about a point.

giro completo Rotación de 360° de una figura sobre un punto.

function rule A rule that gives exactly one output value for each input value.

regla de función Regla en la que hay exactamente un valor de salida para cada valor de entrada.

function table A table that matches each input value with a unique output value.

Rule: $t = p \times 2$	
Input (x)	Output (y)
4	8
6	12
10	20

tabla de función Tabla en la que cada valor de entrada corresponde a un único valor de salida.

gallon (gal) A customary unit used to measure liquid capacity.
1 gallon = 16 cups

galón (gal) Unidad del sistema usual para medir capacidad líquida.
1 galón = 16 tazas

gram (g) A metric unit used to measure mass.
1,000 grams = 1 kilogram

gramo (g) Unidad métrica para medir masa.
1,000 gramos = 1 kilogramo

half-turn A 180° rotation of a figure about a point.

medio giro Rotación de 180° de una figura sobre un punto.

hexagon A six-sided polygon.

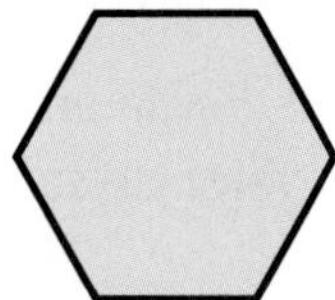

hexágono Polígono de seis lados.

horizontal axis The x-axis in a coordinate plane. It is a number line that locates points to the left or to the right of the vertical axis.

eje horizontal Eje de las x en un plano de coordenadas. Es una recta numérica que representa puntos a la izquierda o a la derecha del eje vertical.

horizontal line A line that lies straight across.

recta horizontal Línea que se extiende paralela al horizonte.

horizontal line segment A line segment that lies straight across, parallel to the horizon.

segmento de recta horizontal Segmento de recta que se extiende paralelo al horizonte.

hundredths One or more of one hundred equal parts of a whole.

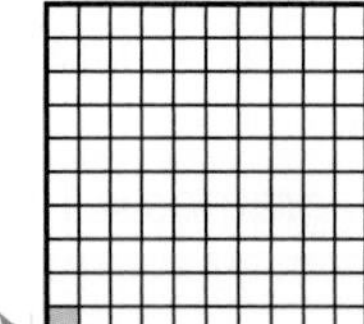

centésimas Una o más de las cien partes iguales de un entero.

Identity Property of Multiplication The property that states that the product of 1 and any number is that number.
Example: $2 \times 1 = 2$

Propiedad de identidad en la multiplicación Propiedad que establece que el producto de 1 y cualquier número es ese mismo número.
Ejemplo: $2 \times 1 = 2$

improper fraction A fraction that is greater than or equal to 1. The numerator in an improper fraction is greater than or equal to the denominator. For example, $\frac{3}{2}$ and $\frac{15}{11}$ are improper fractions.

fracción impropia Fracción mayor o igual a 1. El numerador de una fracción impropia es mayor o igual al denominador. Por ejemplo, $\frac{3}{2}$ y $\frac{15}{11}$ son fracciones impropias.

impossible A prediction that a particular event of a probability experiment cannot happen.

imposible Predicción de que un suceso particular de un experimento de probabilidad no puede ocurrir.

inch (in.) A customary unit used to measure length.
12 inches = 1 foot

pulgada (pulg) Unidad del sistema usual para medir longitud.
12 pulgadas = 1 pie

inequality A sentence that contains > (*is greater than*) or < (*is less than*).
Examples: $8 > 2$, $5 < 6$

desigualdad Enunciado que contiene > (*mayor que*) o < (*menor que*).
Ejemplos: $8 > 2$, $5 < 6$

integers The set of whole numbers, their opposite negative numbers, and 0.
. . ., -3, -2, -1, 0, 1, 2, 3, . . .

números enteros positivos y negativos Conjunto de números enteros, sus números negativos opuestos y el 0.
. . ., -3, -2, -1, 0, 1, 2, 3, . . .

intersecting lines Lines that meet or cross at a common point.

rectas secantes Líneas que se encuentran o cruzan en un punto en común.

interval The difference between two numbers on a scale.

intervalo Diferencia entre dos números en una escala.

inverse operations Opposite operations. Addition and subtraction are inverse operations. Multiplication and division are inverse operations.

operaciones inversas Operaciones opuestas. La suma y la resta son operaciones inversas. La multiplicación y la división son operaciones inversas.

is greater than (>) An inequality relation such as 7 > 2. Read: 7 is greater than 2.

mayor que (>) Relación de desigualdad como 7 > 2. Se lee así: 7 es mayor que 2.

is less than (<) An inequality relation such as 3 < 8. Read: 3 is less than 8.

menor que (<) Relación de desigualdad como 3 < 8. Se lee así: 3 es menor que 8.

isosceles triangle A triangle that has two congruent sides.

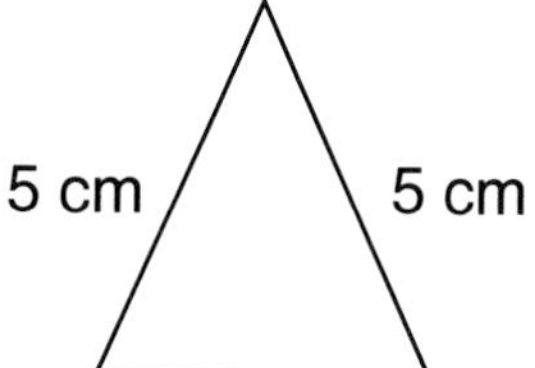

triángulo isósceles Triángulo que tiene dos lados congruentes.

key A part of a map, graph, or chart that explains what symbols mean.

clave Parte de un mapa, gráfica o tabla que explica lo que significan los símbolos.

kilogram (kg) A metric unit used to measure mass.
1 kilogram = 1,000 grams

kilogramo (kg) Unidad métrica para medir masa.
1 kilogramo = 1,000 gramos

kilometer (km) A metric unit used to measure length or distance.
1 kilometer = 1,000 meters

kilómetro (km) Unidad métrica para medir longitud o distancia.
1 kilómetro = 1,000 metros

likely A prediction that a particular event of a probability experiment has a greater chance of happening than not happening.

probable Predicción de que un suceso particular de un experimento de probabilidad tiene más probabilidad de suceder que de no suceder

like denominators Denominators that are equal in two or more fractions.

denominadores comunes Denominadores que son iguales en dos ó más fracciones.

line A continuous straight path that goes on without end in opposite directions.

recta Línea recta y continua que se extiende sin fin en direcciones opuestas.

line graph A graph that uses a broken line to show changes in data.

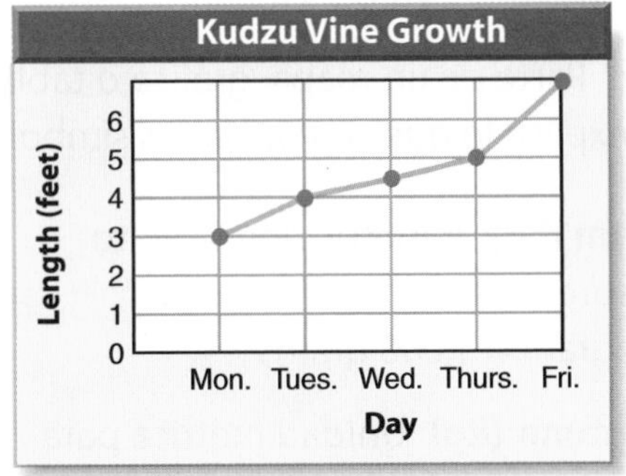

gráfica lineal Gráfica que usa una línea quebrada para mostrar cambios en los datos.

line of symmetry The line along which a figure can be folded so that the two parts match exactly.

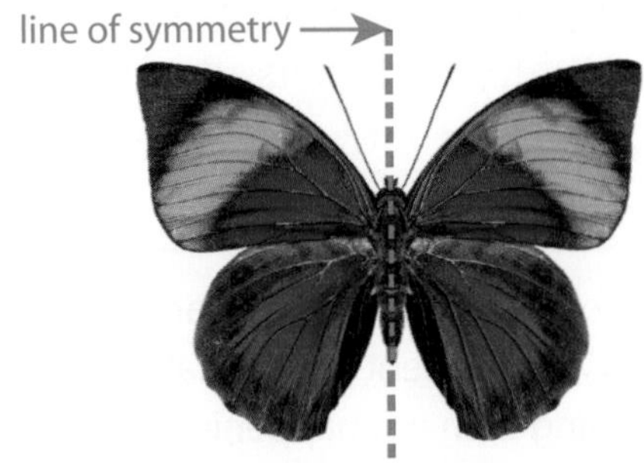

eje de simetría Línea por la cual se puede doblar una figura, de forma que las dos partes se correspondan exactamente.

line plot A diagram that organizes data along a number line.

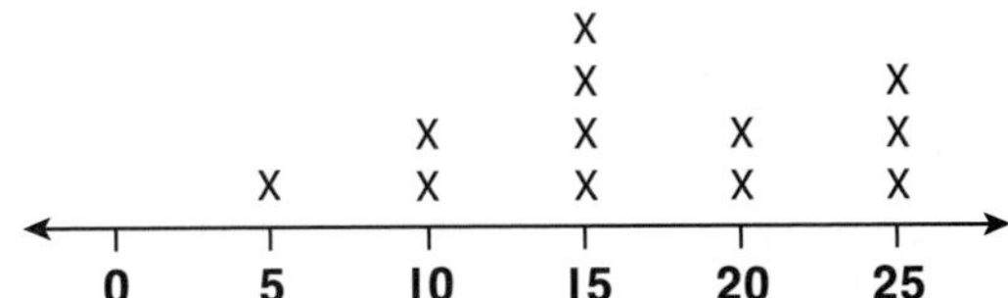

diagrama de puntos Diagrama que organiza los datos sobre una recta numérica.

line segment Part of a line. A line segment has two endpoints.

segmento de recta Parte de una recta. Un segmento de recta tiene dos extremos.

line symmetry (Also called **bilateral symmetry**) A plane figure has line symmetry if it can be folded along a line so that the two parts match exactly.

simetría lineal (También **llamada simetría bilateral**) Una figura plana tiene simetría lineal si puede ser doblada sobre una línea de forma que las dos partes se correspondan exactamente.

liter (L) A metric unit used to measure capacity.
1 liter = 1,000 milliliters

litro (L) Unidad métrica para medir capacidad.
1 litro = 1,000 mililitros

mass The amount of matter in an object. Mass is often measured using grams or kilograms.

masa Cantidad de materia que hay en un objeto. Frecuentemente es medida usando gramos o kilogramos.

median The middle number when a set of numbers is arranged in order from least to greatest.
Examples: The median of 2, 5, 7, 9, and 10 is 7. For an even number of numbers, it is the number halfway between the two middle numbers. The median of 2, 5, 7, and 12 is 6.

mediana Número del medio en un conjunto de números ordenado de menor a mayor.
Ejemplos: La mediana de 2, 5, 7, 9 y 10 es 7. Para un número par de números, es el número que está en la mitad entre los dos números del medio. La mediana de 2, 5, 7 y 12 es 6.

meter (m) A metric unit used to measure length.
1 meter = 100 centimeters

metro (m) Unidad métrica para medir longitud.
1 metro = 100 centímetros

metric system A system of measurement that uses meters to measure length, liters to measure capacity, and kilograms to measure mass.

sistema métrico Sistema de medida que usa metros para medir longitud, litros para medir capacidad y kilogramos para medir masa.

mile (mi) A customary unit used to measure length or distance.
1 mile = 5,280 feet

milla (mi) Unidad del sistema usual para medir longitud o distancia.
1 milla = 5,280 pies

milliliter (mL) A metric unit used to measure capacity.
1,000 milliliters = 1 liter

mililitro (mL) Unidad métrica para medir capacidad.
1,000 mililitros = 1 litro

millimeter (mm) A metric unit used to measure length.
1,000 millimeters = 1 meter

milímetro (mm) Unidad métrica para medir longitud.
1,000 milímetros = 1 metro

million One thousand thousands, or 1,000,000 (one million).

millón Mil millares ó 1,000,000 (un millón).

mixed number A number containing a whole number part and a fraction part. For example, $3\frac{1}{2}$ is a mixed number.

número mixto Número que contiene una parte entera y una parte fraccionaria. Por ejemplo, $3\frac{1}{2}$ es un número mixto.

Glossary

mode The number or numbers that occur most often in a set of data.
Example: 2, 4, 3, 4, 5, 4, 3
In this set of data, 4 is the mode.

moda Número o números que se presentan con más frecuencia en un conjunto de datos.
Ejemplo: 2, 4, 3, 4, 5, 4, 3
En este conjunto de datos, 4 es la moda.

multiple A number that is the product of the given number and another number. For example, 12 is a multiple of 4, because $4 \times 3 = 12$.

múltiplo Número que es producto de un número dado y otro número. Por ejemplo, 12 es un múltiplo de 4, porque $4 \times 3 = 12$.

negative (number) A number that is less than zero.

Examples: $^{-}2$, $^{-}5$, $^{-}26$, $-\frac{3}{4}$, and $^{-}2\frac{1}{3}$ are negative numbers.

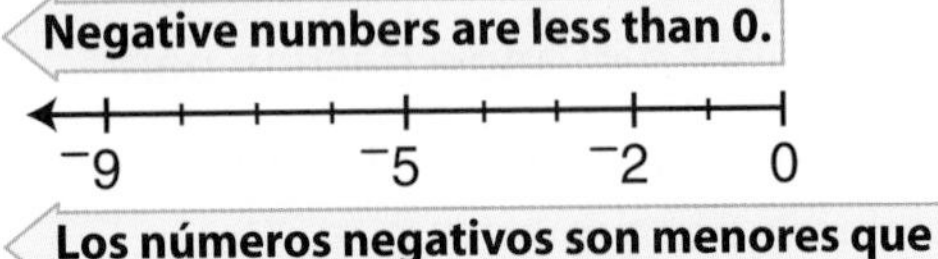

(número) negativo Número que es menor que cero.
Ejemplos: $^{-}2$, $^{-}5$, $^{-}26$, $-\frac{3}{4}$ y $^{-}2\frac{1}{3}$ son números negativos.

net A flat pattern that can be folded to make a solid.

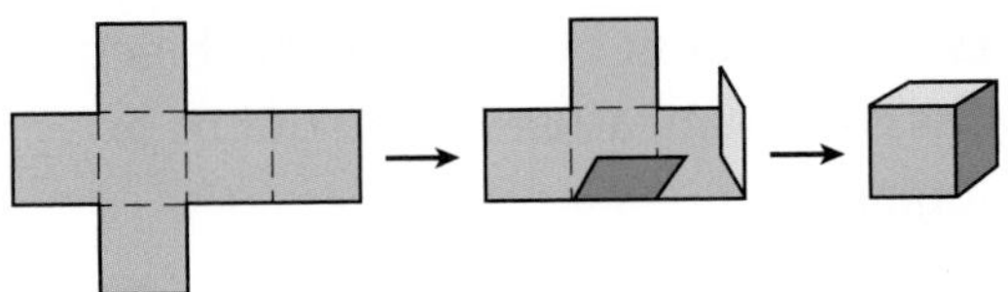

red Patrón plano que puede doblarse para formar un cuerpo geométrico.

number line A line on which numbers are assigned points.

recta numérica Recta en la que hay números que son puntos asignados.

numerator The number above the bar in a fraction.

$\frac{1}{3}$ ⟵ numerator

numerador Número sobre la barra de una fracción.

obtuse angle An angle with a measure greater than that of a right angle (90°) and less than 180°.

ángulo obtuso Ángulo mayor que un ángulo recto (90°) y menor que 180°.

obtuse triangle A triangle that has one obtuse angle.

triángulo obtusángulo Triángulo que tiene un ángulo obtuso.

octagon An eight-sided polygon.

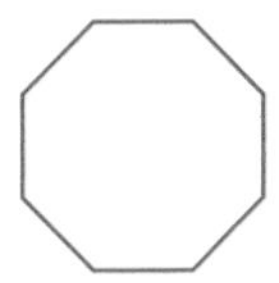

octágono Polígono de ocho lados.

odd number A whole number that is not a multiple of 2. The ones digit in an odd number is 1, 3, 5, 7, or 9. The numbers 67 and 493 are examples of odd numbers.

número impar Número entero que no es múltiplo de 2. El dígito de las unidades en un número impar es 1, 3, 5, 7 ó 9. Los números 67 y 493 son ejemplos de números impares.

opposite (of a number) One number is the opposite of a second number if their sum is 0. Examples of opposite numbers are 2 and −2, and −7 and 7.

opuesto (de un número) Un número es el opuesto de un segundo número si su suma es 0. Ejemplos de números opuestos son 2 y −2, y -7 y 7.

order To arrange numbers from greatest to least or least to greatest.

ordenar Agrupar números de mayor a menor o de menor a mayor.

ordered pair A pair of numbers in which one number is identified as the first coordinate and the other number as the second coordinate.

par ordenado Par de números en el que un número es identificado como la primera coordenada y el otro número como la segunda coordenada.

order of operations Rules for performing operations when simplifying expressions.

orden de las operaciones Reglas para realizar operaciones cuando se simplifican expresiones.

origin A point assigned to zero on the number line or the point where the x- and y-axes intersect in a coordinate plane.

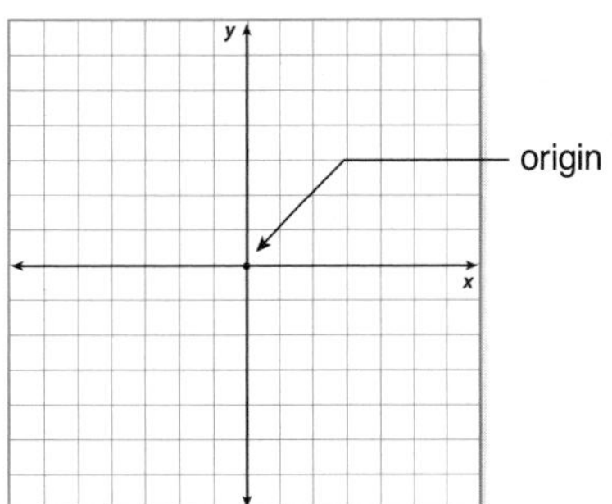

origen Punto asignado a cero en una recta numérica, o el punto donde los ejes x e y se intersecan en un plano de coordenadas.

ounce (oz) A customary unit used to measure weight.
16 ounces = 1 pound

onza (oz) Unidad del sistema usual para medir peso.
16 onzas = 1 libra

outcome A result in a probability experiment.

resultado Respuesta en un experimento de probabilidad.

outlier When data are arranged in order, an outlier lies before or beyond most of the other data.

valor extremo Cuando los datos están ordenados, un valor extremo aparece antes o después de la mayoría de los datos.

P

parallel lines Lines that are in the same plane and do not intersect. Parallel lines are the same distance apart at all points.

rectas paralelas Líneas que están en el mismo plano y que no se intersecan. La distancia entre líneas paralelas es la misma en cualquier punto.

parallelogram A quadrilateral in which both pairs of opposite sides are parallel.

paralelogramo Cuadrilátero en el que ambos pares de lados opuestos son paralelos.

parentheses Grouping symbols that indicate what operations in an expression should be performed first.
Example: $(3 + 6) \times 8$

paréntesis Símbolos de agrupación que indican qué operaciones en una expresión deben realizarse primero.
Ejemplo: $(3 + 6) \times 8$

pentagon A five-sided polygon.

pentágono Polígono de cinco lados.

perimeter The sum of the lengths of the sides of a polygon.

perímetro Suma de las longitudes de los lados polígono.

period Each group of three digits in a number that usually are separated by a comma.

período Cada grupo de tres dígitos en un número, que generalmente está separado por una coma.

perpendicular lines Lines that intersect to form right angles.

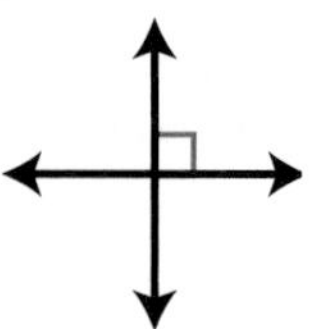

rectas perpendiculares Líneas que se intersecan y forman ángulos rectos.

pint (pt) A customary unit used to measure liquid capacity.
2 pints = 1 quart.

pinta (pt) Unidad del sistema usual para medir capacidad líquida.
2 pintas = 1 cuarto de galón.

place value The value assigned to each place in a number written in standard form. In 346, the digit 3 is in the hundreds place. The value of the 3 is 3×100 or 300.

valor de posición Valor asignado a cada lugar en un número escrito en forma normal. En 346, el dígito 3 está en el lugar de las centenas. El valor del 3 es 3×100 o 300.

plane figure A geometric figure that has two dimensions.

figura plana Figura geométrica que tiene dos dimensiones.

plot (points) To locate and mark points in a coordinate grid given the points' coordinates. To plot (-3, 2) in a coordinate grid, go 3 units to the left from the origin and up 2.

trazar (puntos) Ubicar y marcar puntos en una cuadrícula de coordenadas, según las coordenadas de los puntos. Para trazar (-3, 2) en una cuadrícula de coordenadas, avanza 3 unidades hacia la izquierda desde el origen y 2 hacia arriba.

point An exact location in space, represented by a dot.

punto Ubicación exacta en el espacio representada por un punto.

polygon A closed two-dimensional figure made up of three or more line segments.

polígono Figura plana cerrada formada por tres ó más segmentos de recta.

positive (number) A number that is greater than zero.

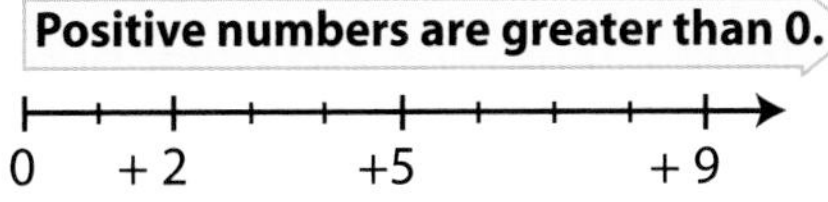

(número) positivo Número que es mayor que cero.

pound (lb) A customary unit used to measure weight.
1 pound = 16 ounces

libra (lb) Unidad del sistema usual que se usa para medir peso.
1 libra = 16 onzas

prediction In probability, a guess describing what the outcome of an experiment will be.

predicción En probabilidad, suposición que describe cuál será el resultado de un experimento.

prime factors Factors of a number that are prime.

factores primos Factores de un número que son primos.

prime number A whole number that has exactly two factors, itself and 1. For example, 3 is a prime number because its only factors are 3 and 1.

número primo Número entero que tiene exactamente dos factores: el mismo número y 1. Por ejemplo, el 3 es un número primo porque sus únicos factores son 3 y 1.

prism A three-dimensional figure that has two parallel congruent bases and parallelograms for faces.

prisma Figura tridimensional que tiene dos bases paralelas congruentes y cuyas caras son paralelogramos.

probability A measure of the chance that an event will occur in an experiment. A probability can be any number from 0 through 1.

probabilidad Medida de la posibilidad de que un suceso ocurra en un experimento. La probabilidad puede ser cualquier número de 0 a 1.

product The answer in a multiplication problem.

$4 \times 5 = 20$

↑ product

producto Respuesta a un problema de multiplicación.

pyramid A three-dimensional figure whose base can be any polygon and whose faces are triangles that intersect at a point called the vertex.

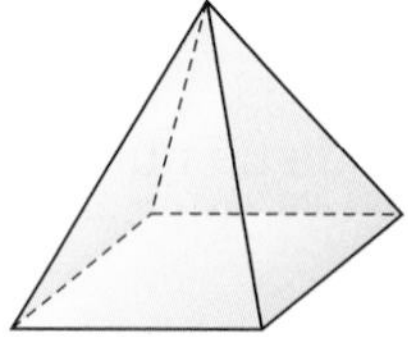

pirámide Figura tridimensional cuya base puede ser cualquier polígono y cuyas caras son triángulos que se intersecan en un punto llamado el vértice.

quadrilateral A four-sided polygon.

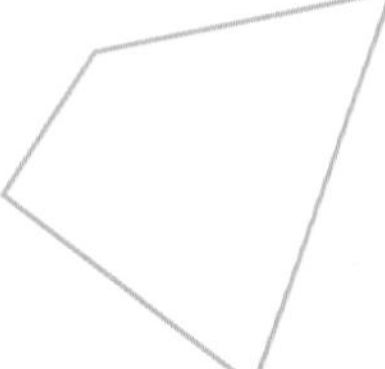

cuadrilátero Polígono de cuatro lados.

quart (qt) A customary unit used to measure liquid capacity. 1 quart = 4 cups

cuarto de galón (ct) Unidad del sistema usual para medir capacidad líquida. 1 cuarto de galón = 4 tazas

quarter turn A 90° rotation of a figure about a point.

cuarto de giro Rotación de 90° de una figura sobre un punto.

quotient The answer in a division problem.

$35 \div 7 = 5$

↑ quotient

cociente Respuesta a un problema de división.

radius A line segment that connects the center of a circle to any point on the circle.

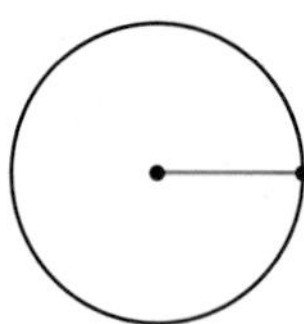

radio Segmento de recta que conecta el centro de un círculo con cualquier punto en el círculo.

ray Part of a line that starts at an endpoint and goes on forever in one direction.

semirrecta Parte de una recta que empieza en un extremo y se extiende de manera infinita en una dirección.

rectangle A polygon with opposite sides parallel and four right angles.

rectángulo Polígono que tiene lados opuestos paralelos y cuatro ángulos rectos.

rectangular prism A three-dimensional figure whose bases and faces are rectangles.

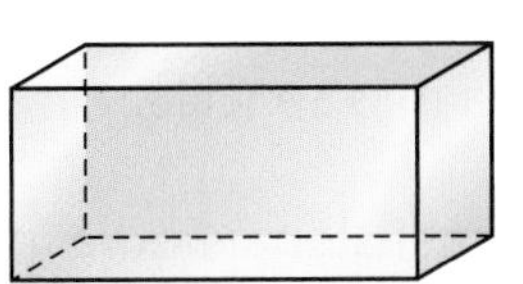

prisma rectangular Figura tridimensional cuyas bases y caras son rectángulos.

rectangular pyramid A pyramid whose base is a rectangle.

pirámide rectangular Pirámide cuya base es un rectángulo.

reflection A transformation that flips a figure over a line.

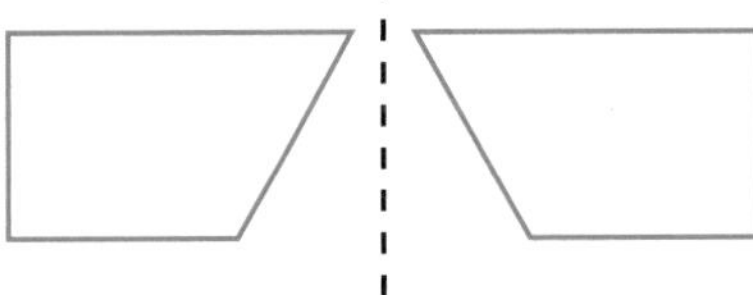

reflexión Transformación en la que se invierte una figura sobre una línea.

regroup To use place value to exchange equal amounts when renaming a number.

reagrupar Nombrar de forma diferente un número al intercambiar cantidades iguales entre valores de posición.

remainder The number less than the divisor that is left over after a whole number is divided by a divisor that is not one of its factors.

residuo Número menor que el divisor que sobra luego de dividir un número entero entre un divisor que no es uno de sus factores.

rhombus A parallelogram with all four sides the same length.

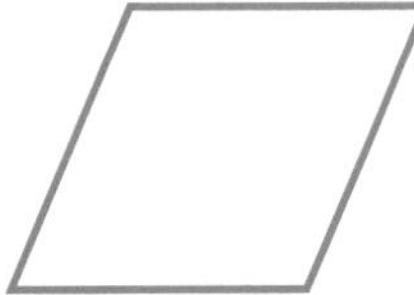

rombo Paralelogramo cuyos cuatro lados tienen la misma longitud.

right angle An angle that measures 90°.

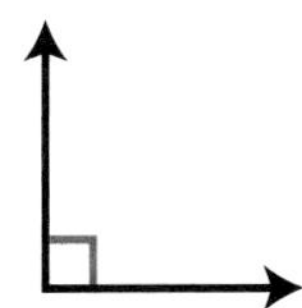

ángulo recto Ángulo que mide 90°.

right triangle A triangle that has one right angle.

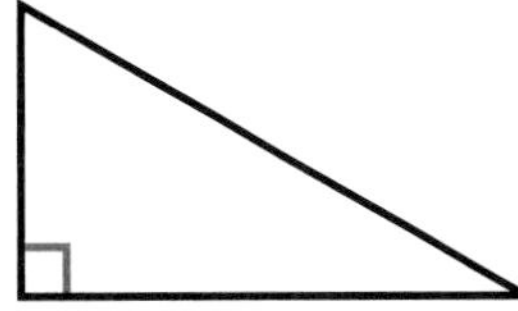

triángulo rectángulo Triángulo que tiene un ángulo recto.

rotation To turn a figure about a point.

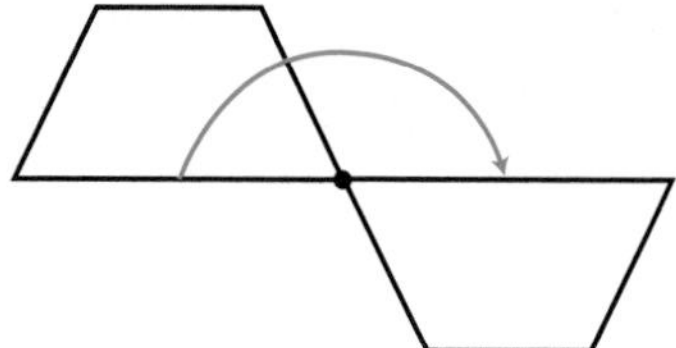

rotación Girar una figura sobre un punto.

rotational symmetry A figure has rotational symmetry if, after the figure is rotated less than a full turn, the rotated figure lands exactly on itself.

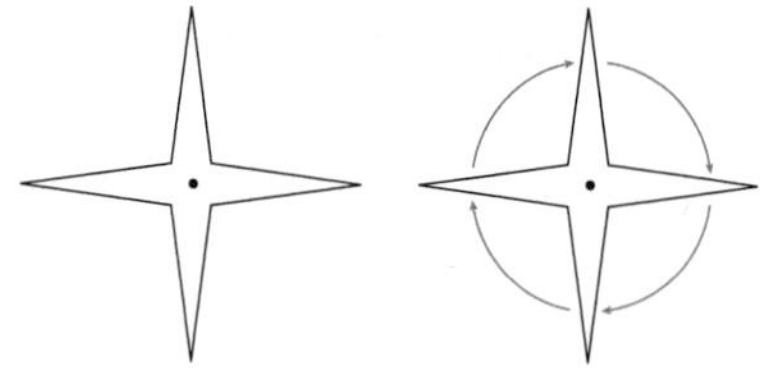

simetría rotacional Una figura tiene simetría rotacional si, después de ser rotada en menos de un giro completo, la figura rotada cae exactamente en ella misma.

round To express a number to the nearest ten, hundred, thousand, or other place value.

redondear Aproximar un número a la decena, centena, millar u otro valor de posición más cercano.

S

scalene triangle A triangle with all sides of different lengths.

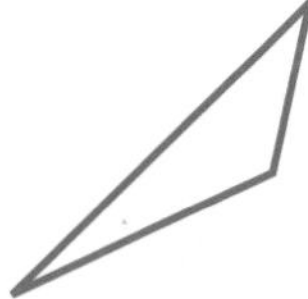

triángulo escaleno Triángulo con todos los lados de longitudes diferentes.

side (of a polygon) One of the line segments that make up a polygon.

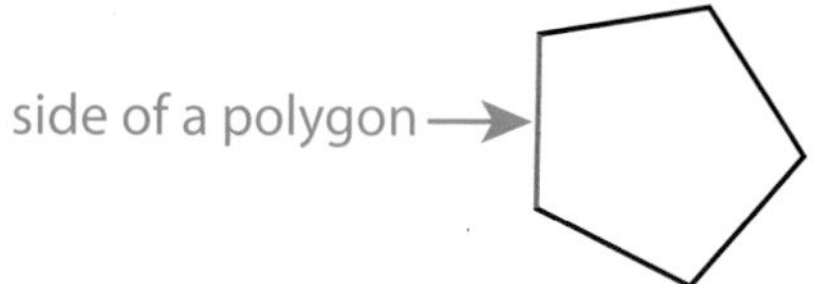

lado (de un polígono) Segmento de línea que es parte de un polígono.

simplify (an expression) To reduce an expression to a simpler form.

simplificar (una expresión) Reducir una expresión a una forma más sencilla.

solid figure A three-dimensional figure in space. A cube and a sphere are examples of solid figures.

cuerpo geométrico Figura de tres dimensiones en el espacio. El cubo y la esfera son ejemplos de cuerpos geométricos.

solve To find the value of the variable that makes an equation true.

resolver Hallar el valor de la variable, de modo que una ecuación sea verdadera.

sphere A three-dimensional figure that is shaped like a round ball. Every point on the surface is the same distance from the center of the sphere.

esfera Figura tridimensional con forma de pelota. Cada punto de la superficie es equidistante del centro de la esfera.

square A polygon with four right angles and four congruent sides.

cuadrado Polígono que tiene cuatro ángulos rectos y cuatro lados congruentes.

square number The product of two factors that are the same.

número al cuadrado El producto de dos factores que son el mismo número.

square pyramid A pyramid whose base is a square.

pirámide cuadrada Pirámide cuya base es un cuadrado.

square unit A unit for measuring area.

unidad cuadrada Unidad para medir área.

standard form A way of writing a number using only digits. Fifty-two written in standard form is 52.

forma normal Manera de escribir un número usando sólo dígitos. Cincuenta y dos escrito en forma normal es 52.

sum The answer in an addition problem.

suma Respuesta en un problema de suma.

surface area The total area of the surface of a solid.

área de la superficie Área total de la superficie de un cuerpo geométrico.

survey One method of collecting information.

encuesta Método de reunir información.

tally chart A way to organize data, in which each tally mark stands for one piece of information.

tabla de conteo Manera de organizar datos, en la que cada marca de conteo representa una parte de la información.

temperature A measure of how hot or cold something is.

temperatura Medida de cuán caliente o frío es algo.

tenths One or more of ten equal parts of a whole.

décimas Una o más de las diez partes iguales de un entero.

three-quarter turn A 270° rotation of a figure about a point.

giro de tres cuartos Rotación de 270° de una figura sobre un punto.

ton (T) A customary unit used to measure weight.
1 ton = 2,000 pounds

tonelada (T) Unidad del sistema usual para medir peso.
1 tonelada = 2,000 libras

trapezoid A quadrilateral with exactly one pair of parallel sides.

trapecio Cuadrilátero que tiene exactamente un par de lados paralelos.

tree diagram In probability, a diagram that shows combinations of outcomes of an experiment.

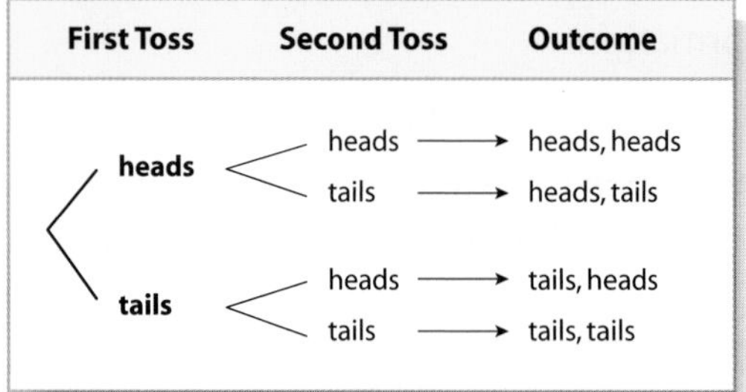

diagrama de árbol En probabilidad, diagrama que muestra combinaciones de resultados de un experimento.

triangle A three-sided polygon.

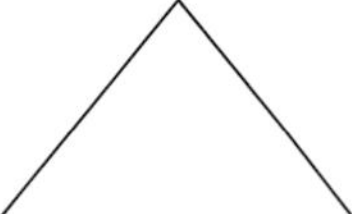

triángulo Polígono de tres lados.

triangular prism A prism whose bases are triangles.

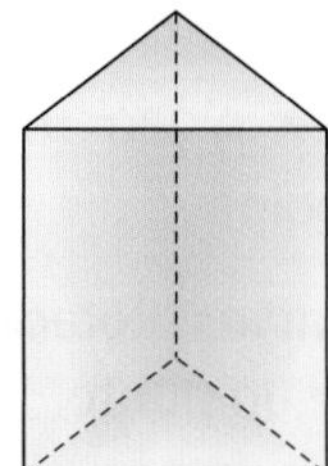

prisma triangular Prisma cuyas bases son triángulos.

triangular pyramid A pyramid whose base is a triangle.

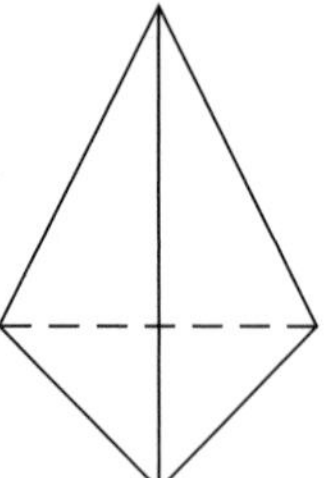

pirámide triangular Pirámide cuya base es un triángulo.

two-variable equation An equation that has two different variables. For example, $y = 10 - 3x$ is a two-variable equation.

ecuación de dos variables Ecuación que tiene dos variables diferentes. Por ejemplo, $y = 10 - 3x$ es una ecuación de dos variables.

unlike denominators Denominators that are not equal in two or more fractions.

denominadores no comunes Denominadores que no son iguales en dos o más fracciones.

unlikely A prediction that a particular event of a probability experiment has a greater chance of not happening than it does of happening.

poco probable Predicción de que un suceso particular de un experimento tiene más probabilidad de no ocurrir que de ocurrir.

variable A letter or a symbol that represents a number in an algebraic expression.

variable Letra o símbolo que representa un número en una expresión algebraica.

vertex A point common to the two sides of an angle or two sides of a polygon.

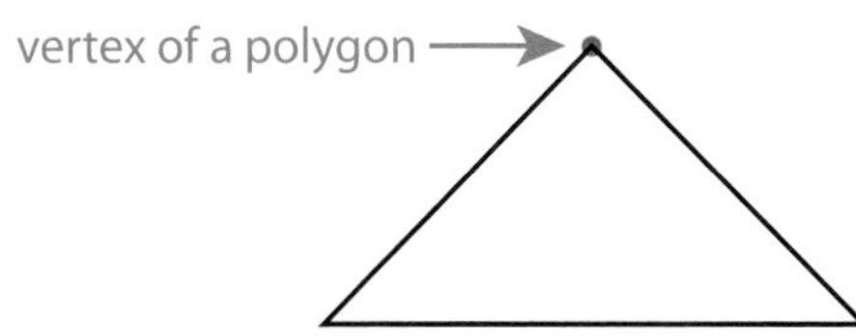

vértice Punto común de los dos lados de un ángulo o de dos lados de un polígono.

vertical axis The *y*-axis in a coordinate plane. It is a number line that locates points above or below the horizontal axis.

eje vertical El eje de las *y* en un plano de coordenadas. Es una recta numérica que representa puntos hacia arriba o hacia abajo del eje horizontal.

vertical line A line that lies straight up and down.

recta vertical Línea recta que se extiende hacia arriba y hacia abajo.

vertical line segment A line segment that lies straight up and down, perpendicular to the horizon.

segmento de recta vertical Segmento de recta que se extiende hacia arriba y hacia abajo, perpendicular al horizonte.

volume The number of cubic units in a three-dimensional figure.

volumen Número de unidades cúbicas en una figura tridimensional.

weight The measure of how heavy something is.

peso Medida de cuán pesado algo es.

word form A way of writing a number using only words. The number 56 written in word form is fifty-six.

forma verbal Manera de escribir un número usando solamente palabras. El número 56 escrito en forma verbal es cincuenta y seis.

***x*-axis** The horizontal number line in a coordinate plane.

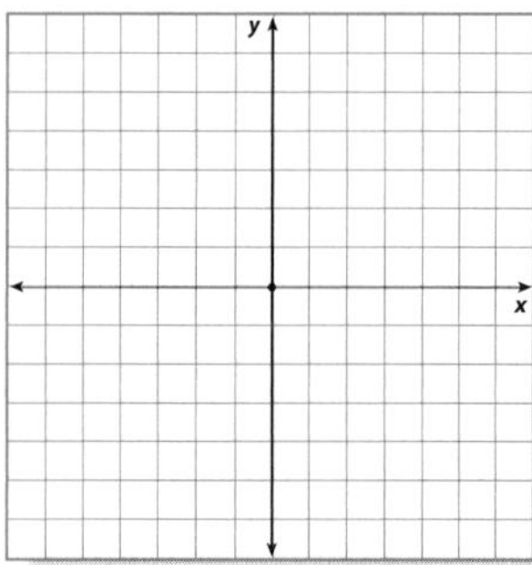

eje de las *x* Recta numérica horizontal en un plano de coordenadas.

***x*-coordinate** The first number of an ordered pair of numbers that locates a point in a coordinate plane.

coordenada *x* Primer número de un par ordenado de números que representa un punto en un plano de coordenadas.

yard (yd) A customary unit used to measure length or distance.
1 yard = 3 feet

yarda (yd) Unidad del sistema usual para medir longitud o distancia.
1 yarda = 3 pies

***y*-axis** The vertical number line in a coordinate plane.

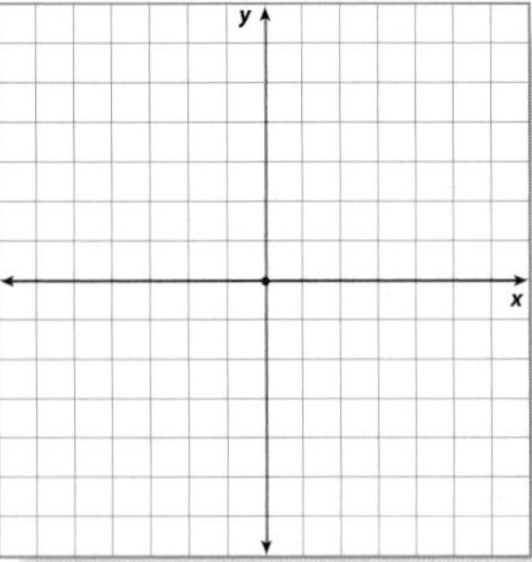

eje de las *y* Recta numérica vertical en un plano de coordenadas.

***y*-coordinate** The second number of an ordered pair of numbers that locates a point in a coordinate plane.

coordenada *y* Segundo número de un par ordenado de números que representa un punto en un plano de coordenadas.

Zero Property of Addition The property that states that if 0 is added to a number, the sum equals that number.
Example: $2 + 0 = 2$

Propiedad del cero en la suma Propiedad que establece que si 0 se suma a un número, la suma es igual a ese número.
Ejemplo: $2 + 0 = 2$

Zero Property of Multiplication The property that states that if a number is multiplied by 0, the product is 0.
Example: $2 \times 0 = 0$

Propiedad del cero en la multiplicación Propiedad que establece que si un número es multiplicado por 0, el producto es 0.
Ejemplo: $2 \times 0 = 0$

Index

Index

E

Index

N

Index

Credits

COV ©HMCo./Bruton-Stroube Studios cover

COV ©Image Source/Corbis Cover

PHOTOGRAPHY

1 ©Dinodia Images/Alamy bckgd **4-5** ©Fran Lanting/Minden Pictures spread **8** ©Stock Connection / Alamy bl **10** ©Roger Ressmeyer/CORBIS cr **12** ©Stock Connection / Alamy bl **14** ©Coinery / Alamy cr **15** ©Bernd Vogel/Veer/Corbis bckgd **15** ©Catherine Karnow/CORBIS b **16** ©Elsa/Getty Sport Images/Getty Images b **18** ©MICHAEL QUINTON/Minden Pictures t **24-5** ©Dennis Hallinan/ Alamy spread **28** ©Sascha Burkard/Shutterstock bl **30** ©Michael Melford/The Image Bank/Getty Images cr **32** © Reed Kaestner/ Corbis bl **33** Peter Chadwick (c) Dorling Kindersley br **34** ©Gibson Stock Photography bl **35** ©Claire Hayden/Stone/Getty Images cr **36** ©Joyce Photographics/Photo Researchers, Inc. inset **36** ©Jim Sugar/ CORBIS cr **39** ©Randy Faris/Corbis cr **47** ©Brand X Pictures/age fotostock bckgd **50-1** ©INSADCO Photography/Alamy spread **53** ©David Young-Wolff / Photo Edit cr **58** ©BananaStock / Alamy cl **59** ©MM Productions/Corbis cr **60** ©Phil Schermeister/CORBIS cr **62** ©Kevin Fleming/CORBIS cl **63** ©Hugh Threlfall / Alamy cr **64** ©Michael Newman/PhotoEdit t **64** ©Kelly-Mooney Photography/ Corbis br **70-1** ©Nick Pope/Dorling Kindersley/Getty Images spread **72** ©Stockdisc/Corbis tr **74** ©Jose Fuste Raga/CORBIS bl **75** ©Ariel Skelley/CORBIS cr **76** ©Alexander Gitlits/Shutterstock cr **78** ©Elnur/ Shutterstock tr **82** ©AP Images/U.S. Postal Service t **82** ©AP Images/ USPS b **83** ©Dinodia Images / Alamy cr **84** ©Galen Rowell/CORBIS tr **84** ©Gerald French/CORBIS bl **85** ©Gerald C. Kelley / Photo Researchers, Inc. br **90-1** ©Visual&Written SL/Alamy spread **96** ©David Osborn / Alamy c **100** ©AP Images/Damian Dovarganes cr **104** ©John Conrad/CORBIS bl **105** ©Kennan Ward/CORBIS cr **113** ©Visions of America, LLC/Alamy cr **115** ©Huw Jones/Alamy bckgd **118-9** ©Pat Behnke/Alamy spread **126** ©Joseph Sohm; ChromoSohm Inc./CORBIS cr **130** ©Dave Bartruff/Stock Boston tr **131** ©www.nowitz.com tr **132** ©Pictorial Press Ltd / Alamy cr **134** ©credit to come t **134** ©Chinese Historical and Cultural Project t **134** ©David Young Wolff/Photo Edit Inc. br **140-1** ©Glen Allison/ Stone/Getty Images spread **146** ©Royalty-free/Tom Hoenig/ Westend61 /Getty Images cr **147** ©Royalty Free/David Buffington/ Photodisc Blue/Getty Images tr **148** ©News Ltd. bl **150** ©FRANS LANTING/Minden Pictures tr **151** ©David Ashley/Corbis inset **151** ©David Ashley/Corbis b **155** ©Rough Guides / Alamy br **163** ©Sharon Hudson/Corbis bckgd **166-7** ©John Lund/The Image Bank/ Getty Images **170** ©Jeff Foot/Discovery Images/PictureQuest bl **171** ©Frank Krahmer/Pictor International. Ltd/Picture Quest br **172** ©GRAHAM ROBERTSON/AUSCAPE/Minden Pictures cr **174** ©BananaStock / Alamy bl **176** ©Georgette Douwma/Photographer's Choice/Getty Images bl **177** ©Blasius Erlinger/Stone/Getty Images cr **178** ©Charles O'Rear/CORBIS cr **180** ©James L. Amos/CORBIS bl **181** ©John cancalosi / Alamy cr **188-9** ©Pixtal/age fotostock spread **193** ©Mike Watson Images/Corbis cr **194** ©Tim de Waele/Corbis br **195** ©Phil Degginger/Alamy bc **196** ©Elena Elisseeva, 2007 used under license from Shutterstock, Inc. bl **198** ©Photo Researchers, Inc. 2002 c **198** ©Ariel Skelley/CORBIS t **199** © Jose Luis Pelaez, Inc./ CORBIS b **199** © Darrin Jenkins / Alamy bckgd **200** ©Gibson Stock Photography t **207** © Mary Evans Picture Library / Alamy br **207** ©Juniors Bildarchiv/Alamy bl **209** ©Steve Hamblin/Alamy bckgd **212-3** ©B&Y Photography/Alamy spread **216** ©Inger Hogstrom / DanitaDelimont.com tr **217** ©Jenny Horne, 2007 Used under license from Shutterstock, Inc. r **218** ©Jim Craigmyle/Corbis cr **220** ©Picture Partners /Alamy tr **222** ©Blend Images / Alamy cr **223** ©Susanne Blavarg/StockFood Creative/Getty Images t **223** ©TongRo Image Stock / Alamy bckgd **223** ©William Tangorra b **224** ©Frances L Fruit/ Shutterstock cl **226** ©Eyal Nahmias/Alamy t **226** ©David Young-Wolff / Alamy br **232-3** ©Ken Fisher/Stone/Getty Images spread **236** ©D. Hurst/Alamy tr **238** ©Thinkstock/Corbis bl **239** The Natural History Museum / Alamy r **240** © Craig Aurness/CORBIS cr **242** © Cathrine Wessel/CORBIS bl **243** © FAN travelstock / Alamy cr **244** ©Corbis cr **246** ©Vince Streano/CORBIS bl **247** © George D. Lepp/ CORBIS cr **253** ©Royalty Free/John A Rizzo/Photodisc Green/Getty Images cr **255** ©Gary Gay/Alamy bckgd **258-9** ©Kelly-Moony Photography/Corbis spread **260** ©John T. Unger tr **263** ©Neo Edmund/Shutterstock tr **265** ©Yellow Dog Productions/The Image Bank/Getty Images cr **267** ©Lake County Museum/CORBIS tr **267** ©Lake County Museum/CORBIS br **268** ©Lake County Museum/ CORBIS tr **268** ©Anthony Redpath/Corbis cr **271** HMCO cr **272** ©Lake County Museum/CORBIS bl **273** ©Ariel Skelley/CORBIS br **273** ©Lake Country Museum/CORBIS cr **273** ©Lake Country Museum/ CORBIS tr **278-9** ©Visual&Written SL/Alamy spread **282** ©Brand X Pictures / Alamy bl **283** ©Doug Norman / Alamy r **284** ©Eyal Nahmias / Alamy r **286** ©DLILLC/Corbis bc **286** ©George Grall/ National Geographic/Getty Images br **286** HMCO tl **286** HMCO **286** HMCO **286** HMCO bl **287** ©DLILLC/Corbis bc **287** ©George Grall/ National Geographic/Getty Images br **288** ©Art Wolfe / Photo Researchers, Inc. r **289** ©Davis Barber/Photo Edit inset **290** © fstop2 / Alamy l **291** © Michael S. Nolan/age fotostock r **291** © Michael S. Nolan/age fotostock cr **292** ©FRANS LANTING/Minden Pictures bl **293** ©MERVYN REES / Alamy br **298-9** ©Larry Brownstein/California Stock Photo spread **303** ©Nik Wheeler/CORBIS br **303** ©Stephen Saks Photography / Alamy tr **304** ©Keren Su/CORBIS r **305** ©Jozsef Szasz-Fabian/Shutterstock Inc. t **305** ©Ken Welsh/Alamy b **310** © Philip James Corwin/CORBIS r **312** ©Sandy Huffaker/Stringer/Getty Images News/Getty Images t **312** ©Wyland/San Diego County Fair b **321** ©SCPhotos/Alamy bckgd **324-5** ©Panoramic Images/Getty Images spread **326** ©PhotoDesc/Getty Images tc **327** ©PhotoDesc/ Getty Images t **327** ©PhotoDesc/Getty Images cl **327** ©Artville cr **327** ©Artville bl **327** ©Photodisc Green/Getty Images br **329** ©Blend Images / Alamy r **330** ©Richard Thornton/Shutterstock r **332** HMCO br **334** ©Jim Parkin/Shutterstock l **334** ©Image Source / Alamy cl **334** ©Clayton Thacker/Shutterstock cr **334** ©Stephanie Dankof/ Shutterstock r **336** © Royalty-Free/Corbis tr **338** ©Brian Hagiwara/ Brand X/Corbis r **340** ©David Frazier/Corbis bl **341** ©Douglas Peebles Photography/Alamy br **342** ©Robert Whitworth/Alamy bc **342** ©Ronnie Kaufman/CORBIS br **342** ©Emilia Stasiak/Shutterstock tc **342** ©Peter Baxter/Shutterstock tr **342** ©Robert Whitworth/Alamy **342** ©Ronnie Kaufman/CORBIS **346-7** ©Comstock Images/Alamy spread **351** ©Richard Broadwell / Alamy r **352** ©Agence Images / Alamy bl **356** © Paul Chesley/National Geographic/Getty Images b **356** ©Catherine Karnow/CORBIS t **365** ©Chris Luneski/Alamy bckgd

368-9 ©Laszio Selly/FoodPix/Jupiterimages spread **371** ©Envision/ Corbis tr **372** ©George Disario/CORBIS bl **373** ©Thinkstock/Corbis tr **376** ©Royalty Free/George Doyle/Stockbyte Platinum/Getty Images bl **377** ©Mika/zefa/Corbis r **382** ©David Brimm/Shutterstock b **382** © Maurice Nimmo; Frank Lane Picture Agency/CORBIS cl **382** ©Mark Schneider/Visuals Unlimited/Getty Images cr **384** ©Brian Hagiwara/ FoodPix/Jupiterimages l **385** ©Mika/zefa/Corbis br **390-1** ©Oleg Moiseyenko/Alamy spread **393** ©Radius Images / Alamy cr **394** ©Brand X Pictures / Alamy bl **396** ©Topical Press Agency/Stringer/ Hulton Archive/Getty Images cr **397** ©Artiga Photo/Corbis b **397** ©charles taylor/Shutterstock bckgd **398** ©Gabe Palmer / Alamy bl **399** ©Westend61 / Alamy br **401** ©BananaStock / Alamy r **402** ©Lloyd Cluff/CORBIS r **403** ©Sergey Shcherbakov / Alamy tr **404** ©Corbis Premium Collection/Alamy t **404** ©Lee Cohen/CORBIS b **413** ©Jon Arnold Images/Alamy bckgd **416-7** ©SCphotos/Alamy spread **419** ©Jakub Semeniuk/Shutterstock Inc. br **420** ©Myrleen Cate/Index Stock Imagery l **422** ©Brandon Cole/Alamy r **426** ©Grace/zefa/Corbis bl **428** ©David Young-Wolff / Photo Edit bl **429** ©Richard Hutchings / Photo Edit r **430** ©Cindy Charles / Photo Edit c **432** ©National Yo-Yo Museum t **432** ©National Yo-Yo Museum b **438-9** ©Nik Wheeler/Corbis spread **443** ©AGB Photo/Alamy r **444** ©Emilio Ereza / Alamy r **446** ©Gabe Palmer/CORBIS bl **450** ©White Packert/Photographer's Choice/Getty Images cr **451** ©Worth Canoy/ Icon SMI/Corbis bckgd **451** ©John Pyle/Icon SMI/Newscom.com tr **452** ©Robert Whitworth / Alamy tr **453** ©Corbis Premium Collection / Alamy r **461** ©Muriel de Seze/Digital Vision/Getty Images bckgd **464-5** ©Timothy Bell/zefa/Corbis spread **469** ©Dave Nagel/Taxi/ Getty Images r **470** ©Anthony Redpath/Corbis r **473** ©Steve Hamblin / Alamy bl **474** ©Charles Schafer / SuperStock r **478** ©Gideon Mendel/Corbis b **484-5** ©Sunset Avenue Productions/ Digital Vision/Getty Images spread **490** ©Steffen Foerster Photography/Shutterstock c **496** ©Brand X Pictures/Alamy c **497** ©San Diego Archaeological Center tl **497** ©San Diego Archaeological Center tr **497** ©San Diego Archaeological Center c **497** ©Hemera Technologies/Jupiter Images br **497** ©Wallenrock/ Shutterstock bl **497** ©Jonathan Blair/CORBIS b **498** ©Grant Faint/ Photographer's Choice/Getty Images t **498** ©Comstock Select/ Corbis b **507** ©Corbis Collection/Alamy bckgd **508** ©Robert Wróblewski/Shutterstock tc **508** ©Robert Wróblewski/Shutterstock tc **510-1** ©Scott Stulberg/Corbis spread **514** ©Tony Freeman / Photo Edit tr **519** ©David R. Frazier Photolibrary, Inc./Alamy r **520** © SuperStock / Alamy bl **522** © Brand X Pictures / Alamy c **523** © Brand X Pictures / Alamy br **525** © Michele Westmorland/CORBIS br **530-1** ©S.T. Yiap/age fotostock spread **535** © Estelle Klawitter/zefa/Corbis cr **537** © Bernd Vogel/Veer/Corbis b **537** ©Royalty-free/Jason Reed/ Photodisc Green/Getty Images bckgd **544** ©Lawrence Migdale/PIX t **544** © Comstock Images / Alamy b **553** ©Rachel Royse/Corbis bckgd **556-7** ©Charmayne Carava/Alamy spread **558** © Rolf Richardson / Alamy t **561** © PCL / Alamy r **564** © Felipe Rodriguez / Alamy bl **566** © B.S.P.I./Corbis tr **567** ©Vecchio/Hulton Archive/Getty Images cl **570** © Masterfile (Royalty-Free Div.) tr **572** ©Lia Sutton; July 2006; http://adventureplaygrounds.hampshire.edu t **572** ©Nick Hardy/The Daily Californian t **578-9** ©Kjell B. Sanved/Photo Researchers, Inc spread **586** © Jack Sullivan / Alamy l **586** ©joSon/Stone/Getty Images c **586** © Westend61 / Alamy r **587** ©The Metropolitan Museum of Art/Art Resource, NY br **588** ©Royalty Free/ Cartesia/ Photodisc Green/Getty Images l **590** Carsten Medom Madsen / Shutterstock cr **591** ©Randy McKown/Shutterstock bckgd **591** ©Lawrence Manning/Corbis **598-9** ©Wally Bauman/Alamy spread **604** © Tim Street-Porter/Beateworks/Corbis bl **605** © David Sailors/CORBIS cr **606** © mediacolor's / Alamy cr **607** ©Lior Filshteiner/Shutterstock, Inc. br **609** © Kim Kulish/Corbis cr **612** ©DK Limited/CORBIS bl **613** ©Philip James Corwin/CORBIS b **618-9** ©Mark Gibson Photography spread **622** © Mark M. Lawrence/ CORBIS bl **623** ©Corbis b **624** ©HMCo. Film Archive tl **624** ©PhotoDisc/Getty Images tcr **624** © Goodshoot/Corbis r **624** © Spencer Jones/PictureArts/CORBIS tr **624** ©1995 PhotoDisc, Inc. All rights reserved. Images provided by © 1995 CMCD **624** ©bluestocking/Shutterstock bl **624** ©Slobodan Babic/Shutterstock bcl **624** ©Julia Chernikova/Shutterstock bcr **624** ©J. Helgason/ Shutterstock br **626** © Goodshoot/Corbis bl **628** © Radius Images / Alamy bl **629** © Eric Chen / Alamy bl **629** © Eric Chen / Alamy bcl **629** ©Rob Byron/Shutterstock bcr **629** © D. Hurst / Alamy br **629** ©jeff gynane/Shutterstock tc **630** ©Joyce Photographics / Photo Researchers, Inc. tc **630** ©A. B. Joyce / Photo Researchers, Inc. r **630** ©Scientifica/Visuals Unlimited bc **633** © OnRequest Images, Inc. / Alamy tc

ASSIGNMENT PHOTOGRAPHY

i, vi, 4-5 HMCo./ Sharon Hoogstraten Photography. **KSH1** (t) HMCo.(r) Sharon Hoogstraten Photography.

538 ©HMCo. ./Michael Indresano l

624 ©HMCo. Film Archive tl

379 ©HMCo./Allan Landau b

266 tr **602** ©HMCo./Angela Coppola bl

179 bl **269** b **270** tr **600** ©HMCo./Carol Kaplan b

129 ©HMCo./Grey Anthony br

571 ©HMCo./Ken Karp b

3 br **37** b **116** b **133** b **190** bl **210** b **234** bl **245** b **260** cl **260** bl **260** cr **301** br **339** b **366** b **392** bl **414** b **418** b **441** tr **463** br **471** b **532** cr **580** tc **580** bc **611** Ed-Imaging b

2 br **6** cr **26** bl **45** br **47** br **48** b **52** cr **72** cl **72** cr **72** bl **72** br **72** b **73** tl **73** tr **73** cl **73** cr **92** c **117** br **120** t **120** b **142** c **145** cr **164** b **165** br **168** cl **168** cr **168** br **211** br **214** bl **221** br **234** bc **241** tr **257** br **300** c **300** b **322** b **323** br **326** b **339** cr **339** t **348** br **348** bl **349** t **353** cr **367** br **370** br **380** b **415** br **431** b **440** bl **450** tr **462** b **466** br **508** b **509** br **512** bl **515** bl **517** b **540** l **554** b **555** br **558** bl **620** Ray Boudreau Photography br

STOCK PHOTOGRAPHY

KSH1(b) SuperStock.

ILLUSTRATION

18 Joe LeMonnier **56** Ken Batelman **80** Ken Batelman **95** Dave Klug **144** Scott Burroughs **154** Marek Jagucki **161** Ken Batelman **200** Dorian Melton **247** Marek Jagucki **300** Ken Hansen **319** Andy Levine **328** Ken Batelman **363** Ken Hansen **370** Nathan Jarvis **378** Ken Hansen **383** William Brinkley **400** Scott Burroughs **411** ©Steve Attoe. **442** Ken Batelman **446** Rob Schuster **491** Patrice Rossi **542** Ken Batelman **562** Bart Vallecoccia **569** Ken Batelman **608** Joel Dubin **610** Ken Batelman **633** Nathan Jarvis

Credits